THE PAPERS
OF
JOHN MARSHALL

Sponsored by
The College of William and Mary
and
The Omohundro Institute of Early American History and Culture
under the auspices of
The National Historical Publications and Records
Commission

JOHN MARSHALL
Oil on canvas by Chester Harding, 1829.
Courtesy of the Boston Athenæum.

THE PAPERS
OF
JOHN MARSHALL

Volume XI

Correspondence, Papers, and Selected Judicial Opinions
April 1827–December 1830

CHARLES F. HOBSON, *Editor*

SUSAN HOLBROOK PERDUE   JOAN S. LOVELACE

The University of North Carolina Press, Chapel Hill
in association with the
Omohundro Institute of Early American History and Culture
Williamsburg, Virginia

*The Omohundro Institute of Early American History and Culture
is sponsored jointly by
The College of William and Mary in Virginia
and The Colonial Williamsburg Foundation.
On November 15, 1996, The Institute adopted the present
name in honor of a bequest from Malvern H. Omohundro, Jr.*

♾ *The paper in this book meets the guidelines for permanence and durability of the Committee on
Production Guidelines for Book Longevity of the Council on Library Resources.
The ornament on the title page is based upon John Marshall's personal seal, as it appears on a gold
watch fob that also bears the seal of his wife, Mary Willis Marshall. It was drawn by Richard J.
Stinely of Williamsburg, Virginia, from the original, now owned by the Association for the
Preservation of Virginia Antiquities, Richmond, Virginia, and is published with the
owner's permission.*

The Library of Congress has cataloged Vols. 1 and 2 as follows:

Marshall, John, 1755–1835.
   *The papers of John Marshall / Herbert A. Johnson, editor; Charles T. Cullen, associate editor;
Nancy G. Harris . . . [et al.], assistant editors.*
   *"Sponsored by the College of William and Mary and the Institute of Early American History and
Culture under the auspices of the National Historical Publications Commission."*
   Includes bibliographical references and indexes.

   *1. Marshall, John, 1755–1835 — Manuscripts.   2. United States — Politics and government —
1775–1783 — Sources.   3.   United   States — Politics   and   government — 1783–1865 —
Sources.   4.   Statesmen — United   States — Manuscripts.   5.   Judges — United   States — Manuscripts.   6. Manuscripts, American.   7. Judicial opinions.   I. Johnson, Herbert Alan.
II. Cullen, Charles T., 1940–   .   III. Hobson, Charles F., 1943–   .   IV. Institute of Early American History and Culture (Williamsburg, Va.)   V. Title.*
E302.M365   347.73'2634 — dc19   [347.3073534]   74-9575 CIP r986
                     ISBN 0-8078-1233-1 (v. 1)
                     ISBN 0-8078-1302-8 (v. 2)
                     ISBN 0-8078-1337-0 (v. 3)
                     ISBN 0-8078-1586-1 (v. 4)
                     ISBN 0-8078-1746-5 (v. 5)
                     ISBN 0-8078-1903-4 (v. 6)
                     ISBN 0-8078-2074-1 (v. 7)
                     ISBN 0-8078-2221-3 (v. 8)
                     ISBN 0-8078-2404-6 (v. 9)
                     ISBN 0-8078-2520-4 (v. 10)
                     ISBN 0-8078-2748-7 (v. 11)

To the memory of

ROBERT ALLEN RUTLAND

*Publication of this volume has been assisted by grants from the
National Endowment for the Humanities, the National Historical Publications
and Records Commission, and the William Nelson Cromwell Foundation.*

CONTENTS

APRIL 1827–DECEMBER 1830

1827

1828

1829

1830

ILLUSTRATIONS

Preface

At the close of 1830 John Marshall had passed his seventy-fifth year and completed his third decade as chief justice of the United States. The preceding four years had been among the busiest of his long and active life. His travels on judicial business took him from his Richmond home to Washington each winter and to Raleigh each spring and fall. He also made twice-yearly trips to Fauquier County to visit his sons and to attend to his business affairs in the upper country. In July 1828 Marshall attended a convention on internal improvements in Charlottesville. From October 1829 to mid-January 1830 he served as a delegate to the Virginia Constitutional Convention in Richmond, which, though it did not require him to travel, imposed arduous mental and physical demands on the aging jurist. Even without the additional responsibilities of these years, the regimen he followed would have tested the endurance of a much younger man.

During the period chronicled in this volume (April 1827–December 1830), Chief Justice Marshall delivered six Supreme Court opinions that raised issues of constitutional law. None of these cases was of landmark significance. *American Insurance Company* v. *Canter,* a marine insurance case heard at the 1828 term, elicited commentary on Congress's power to acquire and govern territories and on the jurisdiction of the federal courts. *Foster and Elam* v. *Neilson,* a land title case decided in 1829, implicitly recognized the constitutionality of the Louisiana Purchase while acknowledging the judiciary's duty to adhere to the political departments' understanding of national rights and interests acquired under treaties. Two other cases at the 1829 term were appeals from state courts under section 25 of the Judiciary Act and brought into question the constitutionality of local and state laws. In *Weston* v. *City Council of Charleston,* Marshall for the Court held that a city tax on stock of the United States unconstitutionally interfered with Congress's power to borrow money, a decision that produced two dissents. In *Willson* v. *Blackbird Creek Marsh Company,* Marshall for a unanimous Court upheld a state law as a valid exercise of the police power and not an interference with Congress's power to regulate commerce "in its dormant state." At the 1830 term the Court again considered the constitutionality of state laws in two cases under section 25. Again for a unanimous Court, the chief justice in *Providence Bank* v. *Billlings and Pitman* refused to accept the bank's contention that a state law imposing a tax upon corporations was repugnant to the contract clause. If the decisions in *Willson* and *Providence Bank* indicated a more accommodating attitude toward states' rights, *Craig* v. *Missouri* showed that the chief could still muster a majority (though a bare one of four to three) to strike down a state law — in this instance holding that state loan office certificates were "bills of credit" prohibited by the Constitution.

Two appointments to the Supreme Court occurred during these years. Following the death of Justice Robert Trimble in September 1828, Henry Clay urged Marshall to support John J. Crittenden as Trimble's replacement. This the chief justice was willing to do, though "delicacy" prevented him from writing directly to President Adams on the matter. "I cannot venture, unasked," he wrote to Clay, "to recommend an associate justice to the President, especially a gentleman who is not personally known to me. It has the appearance of assuming more than I am willing to assume" (to Henry Clay, 28 November 1828). Adams, to whom Clay showed Marshall's letter, did nominate Crittenden, but the nomination foundered on the politics of transition to a new administration. Andrew Jackson subsequently nominated John McLean, who took his seat as associate justice at the 1830 term. In November 1829 the death of Bushrod Washington, the Court's longest serving justice, created another vacancy. His seat was filled by Henry Baldwin, who also joined that Court at the 1830 term. Marshall left no record of his reaction to these judicial appointments, though he undoubtedly was relieved that Jackson had passed over candidates favored by the states' rights wing of his party. One other personnel change that took place was the appointment of Richard Peters as Supreme Court reporter in place of Henry Wheaton, who resigned in 1827 to accept a diplomatic post. Marshall supported the candidacy of Peters, son and namesake of his good friend the late Pennsylvania jurist.

The chief justice continued to be concerned that Congress would curb the powers of the Supreme Court, possibly by reducing or eliminating its appellate jurisdiction over the state courts and its authority to pronounce state laws unconstitutional. He also became increasingly apprehensive about a breakdown in the Court's internal unity and cohesiveness. The 1830 term witnessed the first breach in the justices' communal living arrangements, which for many years had served to promote collegiality and consensus as well as efficiency. "Judges Johnson and McClain do not live with us," he complained, "in consequence of which we cannot carry on our business as fast as usual" (to Mary W. Marshall, 31 January 1830). A more ominous indication of institutional disunity was the three dissenting opinions in *Craig* v. *Missouri*. Referring to this case, he gloomily predicted that the Supreme Court would divest itself of its appellate jurisdiction over the state courts: "I . . . think it requires no prophet to predict that the 25th. section [of the Judiciary Act] is to be repealed, or to use a more fashionable phrase, to be nullified by the Supreme court of The United States. I hope the case in which this is to be accomplished will not occur during my time, but, accomplished it will be, at no very distant period" (to Joseph Story, 15 October 1830).

On circuit, Marshall delivered eleven opinions for which a text survives — all given in the U. S. Circuit Court for Virginia. The cases generating them were preponderantly equity suits for the distribution of decedents' estates, actions against federal officials on performance bonds, and suits brought by the Bank of the United States. He also heard a patent case concerning ploughs that transformed his Richmond courtroom into a scene resembling an agricultural fair. In addition to the surviving opinion in that case, the chief justice delivered an unreported opinion that was said to exhibit great technical learning in the science of ploughs (Davis v. Palmer; Davis v. McCormick, Opinion, 2 June 1827). Still another circuit case, this one brought by a New York mercantile firm against a Petersburg merchant, raised perplexing questions about the law of principal and agent. Before deciding it, Marshall consulted the superior commercial knowledge of Joseph Story: "You commercial men are familiar with these questions — to us agriculturists they are at least novel" (to Joseph Story, 11 December 1827; Hamilton v. Cunningham, Opinion, 12 June 1828). Besides civil cases, Marshall heard two criminal cases on the Richmond circuit, one at a special session in July 1827 for the trial of three Spanish subjects accused of murder and piracy. The trial drew such a crowd of spectators that it was held in the House of Delegates chamber in the Virginia Capitol, where Aaron Burr had been tried for treason twenty years earlier (United States v. Casares and Others, Opinion, 12 July 1827). By contrast, the North Carolina circuit in Raleigh was uneventful, the term rarely extending beyond one or two days and sometimes lasting only a few hours. At the May 1827 term the chief justice delivered "a very lucid and elaborate opinion" (not reported) in a libel case held over from the previous term (*The Papers of John Marshall*, X, 291, 292 n. 2). He missed the November 1829 term because of his attendance at the Virginia Convention.

Apart from his judicial employment, Marshall twice answered a call to public service on behalf of the commonwealth. As a delegate to the Charlottesville convention on internal improvements in July 1828, he prepared the working draft of a memorial and resolutions that were subsequently laid before the General Assembly. In contrast to his well-known authorship of an 1812 report on the James River waterway, Marshall has not generally been recognized as the penman of this 1828 document (The Charlottesville Convention, Memorial and Resolutions, 16–17 July 1828). As it happened, the recommendations of the Charlottesville convention had little effect in producing legislative appropriations. The subject of internal improvements was soon subsumed in the broader contest for political power that occurred the following year at a convention in Richmond to draft a new constitution for Virginia.

Marshall at first refused to be nominated as a candidate for the constitutional convention, pleading that he could no longer perform effectively in a popular assembly. He relented, however, and easily won election as a delegate. Although chiding himself for allowing the flattery of friends and his own vanity to overcome his initial resolution, the chief justice soon turned his full attention to the questions of suffrage and representation that would agitate the convention — "I cannot apply my mind to anything else," he remarked shortly before the meeting (to Joseph Story, 30 September 1829). In private correspondence and at the convention, Marshall revealed his continuing attachment to the principles of Revolutionary republicanism in which he had been bred. He was partial to freehold suffrage and believed that representation in legislative assemblies should accord ample protection to property. He invariably aligned himself with the conservative eastern bloc of delegates who resisted westerners' demands for a more democratic suffrage and greater representation in the legislature. Yet on these issues Marshall preferred accommodation and compromise, realistically recognizing that the commonwealth's ancient political and constitutional order had to undergo some reform. The chief justice devoted his primary attention to the constitution of the judiciary, preparing a draft report as chairman of the judiciary committee and speaking on this subject in a series of set speeches and shorter remarks in debate. Here he proved to be a tenacious defender of judicial independence, showing no disposition to compromise when he perceived a threat to this vital principle. He could not accept a constitution that did not explicitly preserve life tenure for judges — which in his view meant that a judge could not be deprived of his office by abolition of his court. To secure this principle on his terms required all his legislative skill and eloquence. The issue remained in doubt until near the close of the convention, forcing him to postpone his attendance at the 1830 term of the Supreme Court (The Virginia Convention, Editorial Note, at 9 October 1829).

The presidential campaign of 1828 and the ensuing election of Andrew Jackson to the presidency provoked more political commentary than usual from Marshall. Privately, he wished for the reelection of Adams while trying carefully to maintain a public posture of neutrality and indifference to party politics. For more than twenty years he had not even voted in a presidential election. He was inclined to do so on this occasion, however, because of his "strong sense . . . of the injustice" of the "corrupt bargain" charge against Adams and Henry Clay that the Jackson forces constantly brought up. Much to his irritation and disgust, the chief justice found himself drawn into the campaign when a Baltimore newspaper quoted him as declaring that if Jackson were elected "I SHALL LOOK UPON THE GOVERNMENT AS VIRTUALLY DISSOLVED." The quotation was a complete fabrication, but Marshall was forced to make a public disavowal that in itself violated his sense of propriety (to John H. Pleasants, 29 March 1828). Although he did not mind being known as privately supporting Adams's reelection, he greatly objected to being "represented in the character of a furious partisan. Intemperate language does not become my age or office and is foreign from my disposition and habits. I was therefore not a little vexed at a publication which represented me as using language which could be uttered only by an angry party man" (to Joseph Story, 1 May 1828).

This incident caused only momentary embarrassment, but it was symptomatic of a profound change in the American political order that Marshall, a republican of the old school, viewed with anxious foreboding. From Marshall's perspective, a new kind of mass democratic politics had come to characterize presidential elections—a politics that was inherently turbulent and unstable and that threatened the existence of the constitutional system. Contests for the presidency, he observed, had become more or less permanent campaigns, constantly agitating party passions, promoting bitter recriminations, and undermining the tranquillity essential for wise and orderly government. They posed "the most serious danger to the public happiness. The passions of men are enflamed to so fearful an extent, large masses are so embittered against each other, that I dread the consequences. The election agitates every section of The United States, and the ferment is never to subside. . . . The angriest, I might say the worst passions are roused and put into full activity" (to James Hillhouse, 26 May 1830). Politics, he despaired, had become all-encompassing, all-consuming, spilling into the private realm and poisoning personal relations. It even stirred up family feuds, as happened in the Kentucky branch of his own family (to Martin P. Marshall, 2 September 1828; to Mary W. Marshall, 7 March 1830).

Marshall's anxiety about the future of the federal republic was further aggravated by the emergence of the doctrine of nullification during a notable debate in the Senate in the winter and spring of 1830. The chief justice warmly approved the pamphlets and speeches he received denouncing the doctrine and was particularly gratified by the publication of James Madison's letter refuting this constitutional heresy. That a state could nullify an act of Congress was an idea "so extravagant in itself, and so repugnant to the existence of Union between the States," wrote Marshall, that he could scarcely "believe it was serious[ly] entertained by any person" (to Josiah S. Johnston, 22 May 1830; to Joseph Story, 15 October 1830; to Edward Everett, 3 November 1830). In the course of the debate the Supreme Court was arraigned with unusual vehemence—further evidence in his mind that the institutional health of the national judiciary was in jeopardy. He expressed his fear that within his lifetime he would "see, though not as a Judge, the independence and consequently the usefulness of that department prostrated before opinions which are becoming every day more popular—at least in the south" (to Joseph Hopkinson, 17 December 1830).

Marshall wrote numerous letters to persons who sent him pamphlets, speeches, or other publications. More often than not he went beyond a polite acknowledgment and offered extended reflections on the subject at hand. In addition to the presidential election and the nullification controversy, he commented on a variety of topics: the relation between pauperism and population density and the role of education in alleviating poverty; scientific agriculture; legal codification; the union of law and equity; special pleading; religious establishments; and temperance (to Charles F. Mercer, 7 April 1827; to Thomas S. Grimké, 7 August 1827; to Henry B. Bascom, 19 November 1827; to Horace Binney, 19 November 1827; to Hugh D. Evans, 27 December 1827; to Peter S. Du Ponceau, 16 March 1828; to William B. Sprague, 22 July 1828). In another letter he expressed his agreement with the view that the "general welfare" clause of the Constitution did not amount to "a substantive grant of power" to Congress and that Congress did not have "a general power to make internal improvements" (to Timothy Pickering, 18 March 1828). To Lafayette, Marshall ruminated on the subject of slavery, observing pessimistically that "the disposition to expel slavery from our bosom, or even to diminish the evil if practicable, does not I think gain strength in the south." At the same time he was guardedly optimistic that "voluntary emigration" to Liberia would "releive us from our free coloured people" (to Marquis de Lafayette, 2 May 1827). In other letters he voiced his sympathy for the plight of the Native Americans and deplored the passage of the bill for removing the Indians to west of the Mississippi (to Joseph Story, 29 October 1828; to Edward Everett, 5 June 1830; to Dabney Carr, 26 June 1830). A few months before the Virginia Convention of 1829, Marshall set down his thoughts about suffrage in a letter that has recently come to light. In arguing that suffrage was a "social," not a "natural," right and that a property qualification should attach to voting, he presented his fullest statement of the orthodox republicanism that had shaped his political thinking since the Revolution (to James M. Garnett, 20 May 1829).

In 1829 Marshall read "with astonishment and deep felt disgust" the first published edition of the correspondence of Thomas Jefferson, prompting him to animadvert at some length about his late Monticello kinsman. He was particularly irritated to discover that Jefferson, "in his quiet retirement," adhered to the "fallacious" opinion that the Federalists in the 1790s were bent on overthrowing republicanism and installing a monarchy on the British model. Marshall also expressed skepticism about Jefferson's political philosophy, singling out for scornful mention the ideas "that all obligations and contracts civil and political expire of themselves at intervals of about (as well as I recollect) seventeen years" and "that a rebellion once in ten or twelve years, is a wholesome medicine for the body politic." From his earliest acquaintance with Jefferson, Marshall had "never beleived firmly in his infallibility" and "never thought him a particularly wise sound and practical statesman" (to Henry Lee, 25 October 1830).

With the death of Bushrod Washington, Joseph Story stood alone as Marshall's closest friend. Never in all the years they sat together on the

Supreme Court was the warm affection between these two jurists more fully in evidence. The New Englander was the recipient of eleven letters from the chief justice, including one written in July 1827 that covered sixteen folio pages of manuscript. Except for the first and last paragraphs, this letter consisted entirely of an autobiographical account of the writer's life and career to his judicial appointment in 1801 — a document that remains the single most important source of information about his early years. Story had requested this information after undertaking an assignment to write a review of Marshall's *History of the Colonies* for the *North American Review*. He made extensive use of it in composing his article, which in fact was mostly a biographical memoir of the chief justice rather than a review of his book. On receiving an advance copy of this "flattering Biography," Marshall gracefully accepted it as a mark of fond partiality: "The belief that the writer of this sketch views me through a medium which magnifies whatever may deserve commendation, and diminishes those failings which others may deem serious faults, is dearer to my heart than any impression which eulogy, were it even deserved, might make on others. Mutual esteem and friendship confer reciprocally on those who feel the sentiment, one of the most exalted pleasures of which the human mind is susceptible" (to Joseph Story, ca. 25 July 1827, 30 December 1827).

At a time when political developments made him despair for the future of the federal union, Marshall took refuge in his private pursuits, in the society of friends and family. Farming was a principal topic of discussion in letters to his sons, who were farmers in Fauquier County. He reported on conditions at his Chickahominy farm outside Richmond — the effects of weather that was either too hot or too cold, too wet or too dry, on his corn, wheat, rye, oats, and clover — and the prospect of good prices at market for his wheat and flour. On one occasion he tried to sell twenty-five hogs for his son, who had sent them down to Richmond in hopes of a good price. The son's large Parkinsons attracted few buyers, however, and his father advised him to change breeds if he intended to raise hogs as a business, adding: "The opinion is that the bacon is not so sweet as the common wood hog" (to James K. Marshall, 3 July 1827, 25 September 1828, 14 December 1828, ca. 21 December 1828). Marshall also dispensed savvy advice about prospective land purchases in Fauquier.

As a landlord (mostly an absentee one), Marshall dealt with the usual vexations of collecting rents from dilatory tenants and incurring excessive charges for repairs and purchases. These matters required occasional visits to distant Hampshire County on the Potomac River. He once received the "bad news" that one Hampshire tenant failed to pay his rent, that another "seems to expect to bring me in debt," and that an adjacent landowner claimed "a valuable part" of his land. "Thus it fares," he lamented "with those who do not look after their own affairs" (to Joseph Sprigg, 25 May 1829; to Mary W. Marshall, 31 January 1830).

The chief justice continued to work on revising his *Life of George Washington*. The original edition "was hurried into the world with too much precipitation," but having "given it a careful examination & correction," he hoped that the new edition would "be less fatiguing, & more worthy of the character which the Biographer of Washington ought to sustain." By the end of 1829 he was ready to offer the revised work to Cary & Lea, the Philadelphia firm that eventually published the second edition in 1832. As late as December 1830, he was seeking further information about Washington's ancestry to include in the biography (to Archibald D. Murphey, 6 October 1827; to Robert H. Small, 3 December 1829; to George C. Washington, 20 December 1830).

Marshall experienced the joys and sorrows of family life. In February 1829 he received news of the birth of a grandson and of the marriage of Edward, his youngest son, to a young woman of Fauquier (an event that brought his son the happiness thwarted three years earlier by a prospective father-in-law). But casting a pall over this happy news was word that Margaret Marshall, wife of the chief justice's oldest son Thomas, had died in childbirth. Marshall "made a feeble attempt to console" his son and was gratified to hear that he struggled with his "heavy affliction" by invoking "the only aids which Heaven holds out to us — Religion and Reason" (to Mary W. Marshall, 19 February 1829, 28 February 1829; to Thomas Marshall, 20 March 1829).

Family pain of a lesser order also visited Marshall. His sons, notably John (who had been dismissed from Harvard in 1815), had a distressing habit of incurring large debts. In 1827 John's financial indiscretions involved the chief justice "in debts which require all my resources and from which I shall be several years in extricating myself." The father's displeasure with his son was registered in a will he drew up in that year (here published for the first time) in which he placed "the property I intended for him in the hands of trustees for the benefit of his family." Annoyed as he was, Marshall accepted the trials of parenthood with philosophic calm. Those "who have several children cannot expect that all will be prudent, and I have a portion of happiness with which I ought to be content" (to Martin P. Marshall, 7 April 1828, Appendix II, Calendar; Revoked Will and Codicils, 12 April 1827–17 August 1830; to Philip Slaughter, 22 September 1827, Appendix II, Calendar).

When travels took him away from home, Marshall wrote affectionate letters to his "dearest Polly." He kept her informed about the Washington social scene — dinners with the president, the British minister (who "always gives most excellent dinners & very superior wine"), and secretary of state. The decidedly convivial chief justice enjoyed the company of "agreeable as well as handsome" ladies. At one such "splendid dinner party," he was introduced to "three young Ladies who professed a great desire to be acquainted with the Judges . . . and you would have been quite surprized to see how gay sprightly and gallant the wine made me."

As if feeling guilty about taking too much pleasure in society, he quickly added that he hoped "very sincerely" not to "be invited out again, as I greatly prefer remaining at home and attending to our business" (to Mary W. Marshall, 1 February 1829, 14 February 1830). Rather than "witness all the pomp and parade" of Jackson's inauguration, he wished he "could leave it all and come to you" (to Mary W. Marshall, 1 February 1829, 5 March 1829).

An abiding concern expressed in his letters to Polly was the precarious state of her health. Perhaps because of her extreme nervous condition, she herself did not write letters, leaving her husband dependent on others for news of her. "I have looked eagerly through this week for a letter from some one of our friends giving me some information respecting you," he wrote in February 1829, "but have been disappointed. In spite of my firm resolution always to hope for the best, I cannot suppress my uneasiness about you. Your general health is so delicate, your spirits so liable to depression that I cannot controul my uneasiness." On another occasion the receipt of a letter from a granddaughter relieved the "fears" that had gotten "the better of me" on not hearing from her sooner (to Mary W. Marshall, 28 February 1829, 28 February 1830). In her fragile condition Polly could not endure noise of any kind. In the summer of 1829 the "incessant barking" of a neighbor's dog caused her such distress that Marshall feared for her life. This incident drew forth a remarkable letter that communicated his wife's desperate situation while regretting in the most polite terms the necessity of imposing on a neighbor. The fate of the dog is unknown, but Polly Marshall survived the crisis and lived on for more than two years (to James Rawlings, 25 July 1829).

Acknowledgments

We owe our primary debt of gratitude to the staffs of the Earl Gregg Swem Library and the Marshall-Wythe Law Library at the College of William and Mary. We recognize in particular Margaret C. Cook, curator of manuscripts and rare books, and James S. Heller, law librarian, for their kindly services extending over many years. The following persons also supplied information or documents used in the preparation of this volume: Norma Aubertin-Potter, Codrington Library, All Souls College, Oxford University; Tom Ford, Houghton Library, Harvard University; John K. Gott, Fauquier Heritage Society; Dane Hartgrove, National Historical Publications and Records Commission; Margaret Hrabe, Special Collections, University of Virginia Library; Martha King, Papers of James Madison; Edward G. Lengel, Papers of George Washington; Harold Moser, Papers of Andrew Jackson; Kathy Stewart, Library of Virginia; Celeste Walker, Adams Papers; Melanie Wisner, Houghton Library, Harvard University.

Associate Editor Susan Holbrook Perdue resigned in August 2000 to accept an appointment as associate editor of the Papers of Thomas Jefferson (Retirement Series) at Monticello. Her exemplary skills as a documentary editor contributed importantly to the preparation of this volume.

The College of William and Mary provides generous monetary and in-kind support for this edition. The Omohundro Institute of Early American History and Culture contributes the services of its highly esteemed book publishing program. Special thanks are due to Fredrika J. Teute and Gilbert Kelly for their editorial advice. Preparation of this volume was assisted by a major grant from the National Endowment for the Humanities and by grants from the from the National Historical Publications and Records Commission and the William Nelson Cromwell Foundation.

The Plan of the Volume
and
Editorial Policy

Volume XI is composed of 172 documents published in full and another 91 that are either calendared or listed. Most of the documents fall into two broad categories, correspondence and judicial papers. Documents that do not belong to either of these classifications include a draft of Marshall's will; a memorial and resolutions drawn for the Charlottesville convention on internal improvements; reports, speeches, and debates at the Virginia Convention of 1829; a conversation as reported in a diary; and a poem. Together, these documents chronicle Marshall's public and private activities from April 1827 through December 1830.

CORRESPONDENCE

Large portions of Marshall's correspondence have been lost or destroyed. What survives does not form a continuous record and consists overwhelmingly of letters Marshall wrote to others. Of a total of 144 letters published in full in Volume XI, 121 are from Marshall to various recipients. Eleven are to Joseph Story, who takes the place of Bushrod Washington (who died in 1829) as Marshall's most frequent correspondent. Other multiple correspondents include Timothy Pickering, John Randolph, and Henry Clay. Twenty-three letters are addressed to family members, including nine to Mary W. Marshall ("Polly") and eleven to Marshall's sons.

JUDICIAL PAPERS

Over the course of his long judicial tenure, Marshall delivered nearly 700 reported opinions in the Supreme Court and in the U.S. Circuit Courts for Virginia and North Carolina. From 1801 on, judicial opinions constitute an ever-increasing proportion of the documentary record of his career. The editors have adopted the following policy with respect to this voluminous material.

This edition is not a documentary history of the Supreme Court from 1801 to 1835. Nor does its scope entail reproducing all 550 opinions Marshall delivered on the Supreme Court, the full texts of which are accessible in the official *United States Reports*. The original drafts of the great majority of his opinions have not survived, and their loss precludes rendering more accurately the texts that we now have. Only 88 of Marshall's manuscript opinions (16 percent of the total) are extant, most of them dating from his last years in office. Before 1828, the reporter either destroyed or made no special effort to preserve the original opinion after it was published. Richard Peters, Jr., who became reporter in 1828, saved a number of Marshall's manuscripts and eventually turned them over to the clerk of the Supreme Court. (For a fuller description of the sources documenting Marshall's Supreme Court career, see the *Papers of John Marshall*, VI, 69–73.) Yet an edition of Marshall's papers cannot omit altogether such a large and important group of documents. As a workable compromise between total inclusion and total exclusion, this edition is publishing in full most of the constitutional opinions (about 30) and a small but representative selection of nonconstitutional opinions. It also presents calendar entries for all the opinions given by the chief justice during the years covered by a volume. (See Appendix I for a list of the opinions from 1828 through 1830.)

Selecting from the huge mass of nonconstitutional opinions presents an editorial problem that admits of no fully satisfactory solution. Even eliminating many relatively insignificant cases that were disposed of in a brief opinion still leaves a sizable body of judicial literature. From this corpus the editors have attempted to provide a sampling of Marshall's jurisprudence in the several fields that occupied the major share of the Court's attention, including procedure, real property, contracts and commercial law, admiralty, and international law. With this general purpose in mind, they have flexibly applied several other criteria to shorten the list of potential choices. Priority is given to opinions that illuminate Marshall's broader views on politics, society, and economy; that reflect an important public issue or policy of the time; and that can be amply documented from the official case file and other sources, especially if the supplementary materials provide new information about the case not found in the printed report. Another consideration is the availability of the original manuscript opinion. There is an unavoidable element of arbitrariness in the selection process. For every opinion chosen for inclusion, many others could equally suffice as examples of the chief justice's style, mode of reasoning, and learning in a particular field of law.

Although publishing in full only a small fraction of the Supreme Court opinions, this edition presents complete texts of all extant opinions given in the U.S. Circuit Courts for Virginia and North Carolina. Marshall spent much the greater part of his judicial life on circuit, yet this side of his career is relatively unknown, and the documents are less accessible. His circuit court papers include more than 60 autograph opinions delivered in the Virginia court. The one previous edition of Marshall's circuit opinions, prepared by John W. Brockenbrough in 1837, is extremely rare. Although Brockenbrough's reports have been reprinted in *Federal Cases*, the alphabetical arrangement of that work scatters Marshall's opinions over many volumes. Brockenbrough also took certain liberties with Marshall's drafts, regularizing his spelling and punctuation, for example, and occasionally improving what he regarded as infelicitous phrasing. He misdated certain opinions and in one instance misidentified an opinion as issuing from the circuit court that in fact was prepared for a Supreme Court case. The editors believe that bringing these opinions together and presenting texts that more faithfully adhere to the original drafts serve a sound documentary purpose. By comparison with the Virginia materials, judicial papers from the North Carolina court are scanty—no manuscript opinions and only a handful of published reports of cases. (Marshall's circuit court papers are described at greater length in the *Papers of John Marshall*, VI, 126–29, 142–44.)

Six Supreme Court opinions are published in the main body of Volume XI, all of which belong to the category of constitutional law. Thanks to Peters's preservation habit, Marshall's autograph draft survives as the source text for four of the opinions. For one of these cases his notes on arguments have survived and are included along with the opinion. All of the circuit court documents in this volume pertain to cases in the U.S. Circuit Court for Virginia. These include eleven opinions given in civil cases, for nine of which Marshall's autograph draft is the source text. In addition, the volume presents reports of Marshall's sentences and opinions in two criminal cases.

OMITTED PAPERS

As a general editorial policy, dinner invitations and routine documents arising from Marshall's financial transactions—bills of exchange, promissory notes, bank drafts, and the like—are omitted entirely, though they may be referred to in the annotation. The same holds true for land deeds, even though in previous volumes these have been calendared and sometimes printed in full. Also omitted are routine annual reports to Congress that Marshall signed as a commissioner of the sinking fund.

Editorial Apparatus

Editorial Method

The editors have applied modern historical editing standards in rendering the texts of documents. Transcriptions are as accurate as possible and reflect format and usage as nearly as is feasible, with the following exceptions. The first letter of a sentence is capitalized, and redundant or confusing punctuation has been eliminated. Superscript letters have been brought down to the line. Words abbreviated by a tilde ($\sim$) have not been expanded, but the tilde has been omitted and a period added. Layout and typography attempt to replicate the appearance of the originals. The location of the dateline in letters, however, has been standardized, placed on the first line of the letter, flush to the right margin. The salutation has been set flush to the left margin. The complimentary closing has been run into the last paragraph of letters. Signatures, regardless of whether they are autograph, have been set in large and small capital letters and indented one space from the right margin. Other names at the foot of a document (for example, those of witnesses, sureties, and pledges) are rendered in the same distinctive type as signatures and are placed approximately where they appear in the originals.

Obvious slips of the pen, usually repeated words, have been silently corrected, as have typographical errors in printed sources. Words or parts of words illegible or missing because of mutilation are enclosed in angle brackets; letters or punctuation added by the editors for clarity's sake are set off by square brackets. If the editors are uncertain about their rendition, the words are enclosed within brackets followed by a question mark. If a portion of the manuscript is missing, the lacuna is shown by ellipsis points within angle brackets. Undecipherable words or phrases are indicated by the word "illegible" set in italics within angle brackets.

This volume follows the format first adopted in Volume V. Footnotes follow immediately at the end of the document, and identification of the source occurs in an unnumbered provenance note (referred to as "n." in cross-references) preceding the first numbered footnote. This note also supplies information on other copies, endorsements, dating, description, or peculiarities of the original. The provenance contains a full citation for the source of each document, except that the symbols listed in the Library of Congress's *Symbols of American Libraries* (14th ed.; Washington, D.C., 1992) are used throughout. Elsewhere the editors have employed abbreviated titles for the most frequently cited public collections of manuscripts and secondary sources. These appear below in the lists of symbols and short titles. For other publications, a full citation is given the first time a source is cited in a document.

For books, periodicals, and articles, the editors follow the style of citation used in standard academic history. Reports of cases, however, are given in legal citation form. The name of the case is followed by the volume number and abbreviated title (usually the reporter's last name); the page number on which the case begins; and, if needed, the court and year within parentheses. For the old English cases, the volume number and page of the reprint of the case in the *English Reports* (abbreviated "Eng. Rep.") are also given. Full titles of all reports cited in this volume are provided in the short-title list. References to statutes also follow the historical style. In citing English statutes, the editors use the standard abbreviated form giving the regnal year, chapter and section (if appropriate), and year of enactment (if not otherwise indicated), e.g., 13 Edw. I, c. 31 (1285); 4 and 5 Anne, c. 3, sec. 12 (1705).

This edition increasingly uses electronic sources and databases in conducting research. Prominent among these are *A Century of Lawmaking for a New Nation, U.S. Congressional Documents, 1774–1873* (http://memory.loc.gov/ammem/amlaw/lawhome.html), which is part of the Library of Congress's American Memory Historical Collections for the National Digital Library; and the Library of Virginia, Digital Library Program (http://www.lva.lib.va.us/dlp/index.htm). For documents examined as digital images in these collections (such as the debates of Congress or a land office bounty certificate), the editors do not cite the online source but only the printed source or manuscript depository where the document is found. If the information used in annotation has been taken from an online source, the citation includes the name and address of the site and the date visited (e. g., History of the Federal Judiciary [http://www.fjc.gov], Federal Judicial Center, Washington, D.C., Nov. 2000).

Annotation consists of footnotes to documents, occasional editorial notes preceding a document or group of documents, and short contextual notes preceding Marshall's court opinions. The guiding principle is to supply enough information and explanation to make the document intelligible to the general reader. The editors prefer to let the documents speak for themselves as much as possible. This laissez-faire policy is more easily followed in the case of personal correspondence. Legal materials by nature require denser annotation. Without presuming any knowledge of law on the reader's part, the editors attempt to strike a balance between too little and too much commentary.

The provenance note is followed, if needed, by one or more numbered footnotes that address matters arising immediately from the document: identifications of persons, places, technical words and phrases, statutes, authorities, cases, pamphlets, newspaper articles, and the like. If the information is available in a standard reference or secondary work, the note is brief, often no more than a citation to that source. Three standard reference works are not cited: *Dictionary of American Biography, Dictionary of National Biography,* and *Biographical Directory of Congress* (also online). In a few instances dates of persons identified have been taken from the OCLC FirstSearch bibliographic database, an online resource available through the Swem Library. If the source is a manuscript collection or archival record group that is relatively inaccessible, the information derived from it is reported in greater detail. Cross-references to other documents or notes in the same volume are kept to a minimum, relying on the index to bring them all together. Editorial notes provide more extensive information or interpretation than can be conveniently included in footnotes. They serve to introduce documents of unusual significance or important subjects or episodes that are reflected in a number of documents. In Volume VII the editors adopted the practice of supplying brief contextual notes to introduce court opinions. Unlike editorial notes, these notes are concerned only with setting the immediate context of the opinion to follow. They typically provide the full names of the parties, the essential facts of the dispute (including, in the case of Supreme Court appellate opinions, the history of the case in the lower federal court or in the state court), and the particular point or motion addressed by the opinion.

Textual Notes

Marshall's manuscript drafts of judicial opinions receive special editorial treatment. With these documents, Marshall's intent as author takes on additional importance, for he meant them to be officially promulgated. In his opinions, Marshall made many deletions and insertions, which reveal his thought process at work; his choice of words and redrafting of phrases show a careful consideration of meaning. The final result was what he intended the public to hear, and, in keeping with that object, the editors have followed their standard rules of transcription and editorial method in presenting nearly clear texts of these documents as the main entries. In order to provide an inclusive list of Marshall's alterations in the manuscript, however, they have appended a set of textual notes, following the annotation, to each of these autograph opinions and drafts. By this means, a genetic text can be reconstructed, and a complete record of Marshall's revisions is preserved. In this volume textual notes also accompany Marshall's autobiographical sketch, which the author knew was to be used as the basis of a published account of his life and career.

Marshall made changes in his text in a variety of ways: he struck through words, erased them, wrote over them, added words above the line, or indicated by means of a superscript symbol an addition to be inserted from the margin or a separate sheet. In recording Marshall's alterations, the editors have not distinguished among his various modes of deleting words, or between words inserted above the line as opposed to altered on the line. Marshall made many of his changes on the line, indicating that he amended as he was writing. The editors believe that the alterations were part of his process of refining his opinions and that he incorporated them into his final statement from the bench. He apparently did not go back later and revise his opinion as delivered orally in court.

Deletions are indicated by canceled type (~~ease~~), and insertions are surrounded by up and down arrows (↑court↓). Deleted punctuation will appear below the strike-through rule (~~,appeal~~), or above ("~~word~~). Illegible erasures or deletions are denoted by *"erasure"* within square brackets. Uncertain renderings are followed by a question mark within square brackets. Insertions within insertions are not indicated, but deletions within insertions are. Insertions within a deletion appear in canceled type and are set off by arrows.

Characteristically, in changing a preposition, article, indefinite pronoun, or verb ending, Marshall wrote over the end of the existing word to alter it to a new form. For instance, he transformed "that" to "this" by writing "is" over "at" and "on" to "in" by writing "i" over "o." Rather than placing internal marks within words to replicate Marshall's process of altering them, the editors have represented the change in substance by entering complete words. Canceled type shows his first version; up and down arrows indicate his substitution. Thus, a change from "that" to "this" will appear in the text notes as ~~that~~ ↑this↓, rather than tha↑t↑is↓. Although this method sacrifices the exact recording of how Marshall entered a change, it does make clear the alteration of the content of what he wished to say. Marshall's intentions are not always self-evident; irregularities in pen, ink, and manuscript preclude certainty in some instances. Sometimes it is not possible to know whether he added or erased a word, or whether he had crowded words on a line or blotted a drop of ink. Where Marshall inadvertently repeated a word or words, the repetition is left out in the main text but is recorded verbatim in the textual notes.

All deletions and insertions, as the editors have been best able to determine from appearance and context of the manuscript, are listed by paragraph and line numbers of the printed document. (Paragraph numbers appear in the margin of the main text to facilitate use.) A word or two before and after the alteration is included to aid the reader in finding the phrase and following the change. The succeeding designations indicate alterations made in places other than in the middle of the text: "Title," in the title of an opinion; "mar.," in a marginal note; "footnote," in a note at the bottom of the manuscript page; "beg.," at the beginning of a paragraph before the first word of the main text. To avoid confusion, footnote numbers in the document have been dropped from words appearing in the textual note.

Descriptive Symbols

AD	Autograph Document
ADf	Autograph Draft
ADS	Autograph Document Signed
ALS	Autograph Letter Signed
Df	Draft
DS	Document Signed
JM	John Marshall
LS	Letter Signed
MS	Manuscript
Tr	Transcript

All documents in an author's hand are designated as autograph items (e.g., ALS). If the attribution of autograph is conjectural, a question mark within parentheses follows the designation. Documents can be in the hand of someone else but signed by persons under whose names they are written (e.g., DS). If the signature has been cropped or obliterated, the "S" appears within square brackets (e.g., AL[S]). Copies are contemporary replications of documents; if they are made by the author, the type of document will be indicated by one of the above symbols followed by "copy" or "letterbook copy" within parentheses. For instance, an unsigned copy of a letter retained by the writer will be described as AL (copy). Transcripts are transcribed versions of documents made at a later time by someone other than the author.

Location Symbols

CoCCC	Colorado College, Colorado Springs, Colo.
CsmH	Huntington Library, San Marino, Calif.
Ct	Connecticut State Library, Hartford, Conn.
DLC	Library of Congress, Washington, D.C.
DNA	National Archives, Washington, D.C.
MB	Boston Public Library, Boston, Mass.
MH	Harvard University, Cambridge, Mass.
MH-H	Harvard University, Houghton Library, Cambridge, Mass.
MHi	Massachusetts Historical Society, Boston, Mass.
MdHi	Maryland Historical Society, Baltimore, Md.
MiU-C	University of Michigan, Clements Library, Ann Arbor, Mich.
Nc-Ar	North Carolina State Department of Archives and History
NcD	Duke University, Durham, N.C.
NhHi	New Hampshire State Historical Society, Concord, N.H.

NHi	New York Historical Society, New York, N.Y.
NIC	Cornell University, Ithaca, N.Y.
NjP	Princeton University, Princeton, N.J.
NjMoHiP	Morristown National Historical Park, Morristown, N.J.
NjR	Rutgers University, New Brunswick, N.J.
NN	New York Public Library, New York, N.Y.
NNPM	Pierpont Morgan Library, New York, N.Y.
PHC	Haverford College, Haverford, Pa.
PHarH	Pennsylvania Historical and Museum Commission, Harrisburg, Pa.
PHi	Historical Society of Pennsylvania, Philadelphia, Pa.
PPAmP	American Philosophical Society, Philadelphia, Pa.
PPAN	Academy of Natural Sciences of Philadelphia, Pa.
PPiU	University of Pittsburgh, Pittsburgh, Pa.
RPB	Brown University, Providence, R.I.
ScU	University of South Carolina, Columbia, S.C.
TxU	University of Texas, Austin, Tex.
Vi	Library of Virginia, Richmond, Va.
ViHi	Virginia Historical Society, Richmond, Va.
ViR	Richmond Public Library, Richmond, Va.
ViU	University of Virginia, Charlottesville, Va.
ViW	College of William and Mary, Williamsburg, Va.

Record Groups in the National Archives

RG 15	Records of the Veterans Administration
RG 21	Records of the District Courts of the United States
RG 59	General Records of the Department of State
RG 267	Records of the Supreme Court of the United States

Abbreviations for Court and Other Records

App. Cas.	Appellate Case RG 267, National Archives
U.S. Circ. Ct., N.C. Min. Bk.	U.S. Circuit Court, N.C. Minute Book RG 21, National Archives
U.S. Circ. Ct., Va. Ord. Bk. Rec. Bk.	U.S. Circuit Court, Va. Order Book Record Book Library of Virginia

U.S. Dist. Ct., Va.	U.S. District Court, Va.
Ord. Bk.	Order Book
	Library of Virginia

U.S. Sup. Ct.	U.S. Supreme Court
Minutes	Minutes
Dockets	Dockets
	RG 267, National Archives

| Va. Ct. App. Ord. Bk. | Virginia Court of Appeals Order Books |
| | Library of Virginia |

After the first citation of legal papers in a case, the court reference is omitted, and the suit record is designated simply by the names of plaintiff v. defendant. The exception is the provenance note, where complete depository information will be given for the document printed.

Abbreviations for English Courts

Ch.	Chancery
C.P.	Common Pleas
Crown	Crown Cases
Ex.	Exchequer
K.B.	King's Bench
N.P.	Nisi Prius
P.C.	Privy Council

Short Titles

ASP

American State Papers. Documents, Legislative and Executive, of the Congress of the United States . . . (38 vols.; Washington, D.C., 1832–61).

Atk.

John Tracy Atkyns, *Reports of Cases Argued and Determined in the High Court of Chancery, in the Time of Lord Chancellor Hardwicke* (3d ed.; London, 1794).

Black. W.

William Blackstone, *Reports of Cases Determined in the Several Courts of Westminster Hall, from 1746 to 1779* (2 vols.; London, 1780).

Brock.

John W. Brockenbrough, *Reports of Cases Decided by the Honorable John Marshall . . . in the Circuit Court of the United States for the District of Virginia and North Carolina, from 1802 to 1833 [1836] Inclusive* (2 vols.; Philadelphia, 1837).

Bro. C.C.

>William Brown, *Reports of Cases Argued and Determined in the High Court of Chancery* (4 vols.; London, 1785–94).

Call

>Daniel Call, *Reports of Cases Argued and Adjudged in the Court of Appeals of Virginia* (6 vols.; Richmond, Va., 1801–33). Beginning with vol. IV, the title reads: *Reports of Cases Argued and Decided.* . . .

Camp.

>John Campbell, Baron Campbell, *Reports of Cases Determined at Nisi Prius: In the Courts of Kings's Bench and Common Pleas* (4 vols.; London, 1811).

Cranch

>William Cranch, *Reports of Cases Argued and Adjudged in the Supreme Court of the United States (1801–15)* (9 vols.; New York and Washington, D.C., 1804–17).

Cro. Car.

>George Croke, Sir, *Reports of Sir George Croke, Knight, Formerly One of the Justices of the Courts of King's Bench and Common Pleas of Such Select Cases as Were Adjudged in the Said Courts During the Reign of Charles the First* (4th ed.; Dublin, 1793).

Dall.

>Alexander J. Dallas, *Reports of Cases Ruled and Adjudged in the Several Courts of the United States, and of Pennsylvania* . . . (4 vols.; Philadelphia, 1790–1807).

East

>Edward Hyde East, *Reports of Cases Argued and Determined in the Court of King's Bench* (16 vols.; London, 1801–14).

Eng. Rep.

>*The English Reports* (176 vols; reprint of all the early English reporters).

H. & M.

>William W. Hening and William Munford, *Reports of Cases Argued and Determined in the Supreme Court of Appeals of Virginia* . . . (4 vols.; Philadelphia, 1808–11).

Harp.

>William Harper, *Reports of Cases Determined in the Constitutional Court of South-Carolina* (Columbia, S.C., 1824).

Hening, *Statutes*

>William Waller Hening, ed., *The Statutes at Large; Being a Collection of All the Laws of Virginia, from the First Session of the Legislature* . . . (13 vols.; 1819–23; Charlottesville, Va., 1969 reprint: vols. I–IV from 2d ed.; vols. V–XIII from 1st ed.).

Johns.

>William Johnson, *Reports of Cases Argued and Determined in the Supreme Court of Judicature and in the Court for the Trial of Impeachments and the*

Correction of Errors in the State of New-York (20 vols.; Albany, N.Y., 1793–1823).

Mass.

Massachusetts, *Reports of Cases Argued and Determined in the Supreme Judicial Court of the Commonwealth of Massachusetts* (100 vols.; Boston, 1837–78).

Mau. & Sel.

George Maule and William Selwyn, *Reports of Cases Argued and Determined in the Court of King's Bench, [1813–1817]* (6 vols.; London, 1814–29).

Mer.

John Herman Merivale, *Reports of Cases Argued and Determined in the High Court of Chancery* (3 vols.; London, 1818).

Mo.

Reports of Cases Argued and Determined in the Supreme Court of the State of Missouri (101 vols.; St. Louis, Mo., 1856–91).

Mod.

Thomas Leach, *Modern Reports; or, Select Cases Adjudged in the Courts of King's Bench, Chancery, Common Pleas, and Exchequer* (5th ed.; 12 vols.; London, 1793–96).

Munf.

William Munford, *Reports of Cases Argued and Determined in the Supreme Court of Appeals of Virginia* (6 vols.; New York, Philadelphia, Fredericksburg, Richmond, 1812–21).

Paxton, *Marshall Family*

W. M. Paxton, *The Marshall Family*... (1885; Baltimore, 1970 reprint).

Pet.

Richard Peters, Jr., *Reports of Cases Argued in the Supreme Court of the United States (1828–42)* (16 vols.; Philadelphia, 1828–[45]).

PJM

Herbert A. Johnson et al., eds., *The Papers of John Marshall* (11 vols. to date; Chapel Hill, N.C., 1974–).

Proceedings and Debates

Proceedings and Debates of the Virginia State Convention of 1829–30 (Richmond, Va., 1830).

P. Wms.

William Peere Williams, *Reports of Cases Argued and Determined in the High Court of Chancery, and of Some Special Cases Adjudged in the Court of King's Bench* (2 vols.; London, 1740–49).

Rand.

Peyton Randolph, *Reports of Cases Argued and Determined in the Supreme Court of Appeals of Virginia* (6 vols.; Richmond, Va., 1823–29).

Raym. Ld.

Robert Raymond, *Reports of Cases Argued and Adjudged in the Courts of King's Bench and Common Pleas*... (3 vols.; London, 1743–90).

Revised Code of Va.
>   *The Revised Code of the Laws of Virginia* . . . (2 vols.; Richmond, Va., 1819).

Richmond Portraits
>   *Richmond Portraits in an Exhibition of Makers of Richmond, 1737–1860* (Richmond, Va., 1949).

Str.
>   John Strange, *Reports of Adjudged Cases in the Courts of Chancery, King's Bench, Common Pleas and Exchequer* (2 vols.; London, 1755).

Taunt.
>   William Pyle Taunton, *Reports of Cases Argued and Determined in the Court of Common Pleas* (8 vols.; London, 1814–23).

U.S. Statutes at Large
>   *The Public Statutes at Large of the United States of America, 1789–1873* (17 vols.; Boston, 1845–73).

Ves. jun. or Ves. (after vol. II)
>   Francis Vesey, Jr., *Reports of Cases Argued and Determined in the High Court of Chancery* . . . (20 vols.; London, 1795–1822).

Warren, *Supreme Court*
>   Charles Warren, *The Supreme Court in United States History* (2 vols.; Cambridge, Mass., 1926).

Wheat.
>   Henry Wheaton, *Reports of Cases Argued and Adjudged in the Supreme Court (1816–27)* (12 vols.; Philadelphia, 1816–27).

Wils. K.B.
>   George Wilson, *Reports of Cases Argued and Adjudged in the King's Courts at Westminster* (2 vols.; London, 1770–75).

Wms. Saund.
>   Edmund Saunders, *The Reports of the Most Learned Sir Edmund Saunders, . . . of Several Pleadings and Cases in the Court of King's Bench* (1st Am. ed., with notes and references to the pleadings and cases by John Williams; 2 vols.; London, 1807).

MARSHALL CHRONOLOGY

3 April 1827–31 December 1830

1827

1 April	At Richmond
27 April	Returns to Richmond after visit to Fauquier County
12 May	At Raleigh, attends U.S. Circuit Court, North Carolina
22 May–29 June	At Richmond, attends U.S. Circuit Court, Virginia
9 July–19 July	At Richmond, attends special court of U.S. Circuit Court, Virginia
10 August	At Warrenton, Fauquier County
19 August	At Winchester
12 November	At Raleigh, attends U.S. Circuit Court, North Carolina
18 November	Returns to Richmond
22 November–15 December	At Richmond, attends U.S. Circuit Court, Virginia

1828

14 January–17 March	At Washington, attends Supreme Court
28 February, 12 March	Sits for sculptor Horatio Greenough
21 March	Returns to Richmond
Ca. 9–27 April	Visits Fauquier County
30 April	Returns to Richmond
12–14 May	At Raleigh, attends U.S. Circuit Court, North Carolina
22 May–30 June	At Richmond, attends U.S. Circuit Court, Virginia
14–18 July	At Charlottesville, attends convention on internal improvements
21 July	Returns to Richmond
Ca. 12–27 August	Visits Fauquier County
Ca. 29 August	Returns to Richmond
12–17 November	At Raleigh, attends U.S. Circuit Court, North Carolina
22 November–3 December	At Richmond, attends U.S. Circuit Court, Virginia

1829

13 January–20 March	At Washington, attends Supreme Court
Ca. 23 March	Returns to Richmond
Ca. 5 May	Returns to Richmond after visit to Fauquier County
12 May	At Raleigh, attends U.S. Circuit Court, North Carolina
22 May–9 June	At Richmond, attends U.S. Circuit Court, Virginia
22 August	In Fauquier County
5 October–13 January 1830	At Richmond, attends Virginia Convention
23 November–3 December	At Richmond, attends U.S. Circuit Court, Virginia

1830

15 January	Elected to American Philosophical Society
18 January–22 March	At Washington, attends Supreme Court
Ca. 26 March	Returns to Richmond
Ca. 6 May	Returns to Richmond after visit to Fauquier County
12–14 May	At Raleigh, attends U.S. Circuit Court, North Carolina
22 May–16 June	At Richmond, attends U.S. Circuit Court, Virginia
1 September 1830	In Fauquier County
12–15 November	At Raleigh, attends U.S. Circuit Court, North Carolina
22 November–11 December	At Richmond, attends U.S. Circuit Court, Virginia

CORRESPONDENCE, PAPERS,

AND

SELECTED JUDICIAL OPINIONS

April 1827–December 1830

From Jared Sparks

Dear Sir,   Mount Vernon, April 3d, 1827.

Your kind favor is just received, and I shall apply to Mr. Cazenove for the papers, as you direct.[1] Some of the papers seem still to be missing, especially the third volume of Orders. You doubtless recollect, that there were seven volumes. The third was not in the box with the others, nor has it yet come in my way.

For three weeks I have been very closely employed in a general examination of the papers here, and I assure you they go far beyond my expectation both as to quantity and value. I shall be exceedingly disappointed if a selection cannot be made, which will add much to the historical literature of the country, and be highly acceptable to the public. The labor before me is prodigious, but I engage in it with a hearty zeal and good will, and despair not of seeing the end in due time.

Enclosed I have the pleasure of transmitting to you a copy of the order which you requested. It seems to me rather an exhortation, or harangue to the soldiers than an order, but it is all that is recorded of this nature on the day preceding the Battle of Germantown.[2] As the expedition was to be kept as secret as possible, I suppose no other intimation of it was given to the soldiers. Among the miscellaneous papers here I find a private letter from Gen. Washington to his brother John A. Washington, written shortly after the battle, which is more minute, than his public report. He says expressly that the American army came upon the enemy's guards by surprise.[3] I am, Sir, with the highest respect &c

JARED SPARKS

Letterbook copy, Sparks Collection, MH-H.

1. See JM to Sparks, 28 Mar. 1827, *PJM*, X, 420.

2. See JM to Sparks, ca. 13 Mar. 1827, *PJM*, X, 410. The document JM requested was General Orders for Attacking Germantown, [3 Oct. 1777]. Sparks sent a different document, evidently a portion of the General Orders for 3 Oct. 1777. Both documents are published in Philander D. Chase and Edward G. Lengel, eds., *The Papers of George Washington: Revolutionary War Series*, XI, *August–October 1777* (Charlottesville, Va., 2001), 372–75, 375–80.

3. Washington to John A. Washington, 18 Oct. 1777 (ibid., 551–53).

To Charles F. Mercer

My dear Sir   Richmond April 7th. 1827

I had the pleasure of receiving while in Washington your "discourse on popular education" delivered at Princeton in September 1826; but was then too much pressed with official duties to afford time for its perusal, and therefore deferred my acknowledgements for the favor.[1] Since my return to this place I have read it with the interest to which the subject is entitled; and surely none is entitled to greater. It is more indispensable in governments entirely popular than in any other, that the mass of the people should receive that degree of instruction which will enable them to perform with some intelligence the duties which devolve on them; and you have certainly placed the subject on its proper ground.

I was peculiarly struck with the melancholy future you draw of English pauperism, a picture which I fear is as just as it is somb⟨r⟩e.[2] Is this gloomy state of things to be ascribed entirely to an overflowing population, or does it proceed from the policy of the laws? The accumulation of landed property in the hands of a few individuals, and its continuance in those hands by the law of entails and of descent may contribute to this effect, but cannot produce it entirely. The extremes of wealth and poverty in personal estate have perhaps more influence on the mass of the people, than the extremes in real estate. The doctrines of entails and primogeniture do not reach this part of the subject. When population becomes very dense, agriculture alone will not afford employment for all the inhabitants of the country. The surplus hands must find employment in some other manner. As the supply exceeds the demand the price of labour will cheapen until it affords a bare subsistence to the labourer. The super added demands of a family can scarcely be satisfied, and a slight indisposition, one which suspends labour and compensation for a few days produces famine and pauperism. How is this to be prevented? What is the state of the poor on the continent of Europe? — especially in Holland and Flanders? I believe with you that education — that degree of education which is adapted to the wants of the labouring class, and which prevails generally in the United States — especially in those of the north — is the surest preservation of the morals, and of the comforts of human life. In the present state of our population, and for a long time to come it may be relied on with some confidence. But as our country fills up how shall we escape the evils which have followed a dense population?

The systems of education which have been adopted in the different states form a subject for useful reflection and will I hope attract the attention of our legislature. I have always thought and I still think, whatever importance may be attached to our university and colleges, and I admit their importance, the primary schools are objects of still deeper interest.[3]

Accept my thanks for this flattering mark of your attention, and believe me to be with sincere & respectful esteem, Your Obedt.

J MARSHALL

ALS, MB. Addressed to Mercer at Loudoun and franked; postmarked Richmond, 7 Apr. Endorsed by Mercer.

1. Charles Fenton Mercer, *A Discourse on Popular Education; Delivered in the Church at Princeton* . . . (Princeton, N.J., 1826). Mercer delivered his address at the College of New

Jersey's annual commencement, where he received an honorary degree (James Mercer Garnett, *Biographical Sketch of Hon. Charles Fenton Mercer* [Richmond, Va., 1911], 42–43.)

2. Mercer noted the paradox of Great Britain's accumulation of great national wealth accompanied by a multiplying incidence of poverty. He attributed the prevalence of pauperism and crime at least in part to the circumstance that "not one cent" of the nation's annual expenditure was "bestowed on public education" (*Discourse on Popular Education*, 24–29).

3. Mercer appended to the published address a copy of his 1817 bill on public education that he presented to the Virginia legislature. His bill called for funding primary schools as the top priority rather than the state university, the plan favored by Thomas Jefferson (Garnett, *Biographical Sketch*, 42–43; Douglas R. Egerton, *Charles Fenton Mercer and the Trial of National Conservatism* [Jackson, Miss., 1989], 116–31).

Revoked Will and Codicils
12 April 1827–17 August 1830

Apl. 12th. 1827

I John Marshall do make this my last will and testament.[1]

I give to my much loved wife instead of her dower and distributive share of my estate my negroes Celia, Becky the daughter of Daniel, & Mary daughter of Hannah, Sally and her children born and to be born, Knelly the daughter of Lucy, Roger, Robin and his two sons Jack and Robin, Moses, Henry and Oby, during her natural life and after her death to my children and Grandchildren in such proportions as she may direct. I give her all the bank and turnpike stock of which I may die possessed whether the same stand in her name or mine own, for her life, and desire that one hundred and fifty five shares including those in her own name, which are in truth her own property, should be disposed of as she may think proper. I also give to my beloved wife during her natural life my estates in Hampshire commonly called The Swan ponds, and Andersons bottom,[2] also the house I now live in with the two eastern lotts in the square and the lott opposite to my house, which is now occupied by Mr. Crouch, and my interest in the stable lott, and my tract of land on chiccahominy. I give her all my household and kitchen furniture, all the spirits, wine, and provision which may be in my house at my death, and my carriage and horses. I also give her the interest on the debts due me.

I owe nothing so far as I recollect on my own account except five hundred pounds Virginia money to Mrs. Robinson which were bequeathed to her by Mrs. Jaquelin and placed in my hands by Mr. Ambler the exr. of Mrs. Jaquelin.[3] I should long since have paid it could I consult my own wishes, but do not think my self at liberty to do so as the interest is given to her for life, and the principal is distributable among her children at her death, and I know of no friend of hers on whom I could impose the trouble of lending it out for her and taking the trouble of collecting the interest regularly. I have lent it to Mr. Philip Slaughter of Culpeper and have made a memorandum on the bond which is taken to the exrs. of Mr. Ambler, that it is her money.[4] But I shall during my life hold myself responsible for the interest. I have however become surety either alone or jointly with others for my friend and son in law Mr. Jaquelin B Harvie in considerable sums of money which I hope my estate will never be required to pay. Should adverse circumstances compel me to pay any part of the money for which I am bound on his account, I charge the same on the property given to his family.

I have given to my son Thomas the estate called Oak hill together with all my adjoining land to the top of the little cobler or north Cobler eastward of a line drawn along its top and extending northward to the outside manor line and Southward to the high point of the little or north cobler which is in a northwestern direction from the house lately occupied by Mrs. Holmes decd. thence to a pile of rocks near the road in front of the house of the late Mrs. Holmes and thence with Dixons line, and the line of the land formerly Rixy's now Baily's, and the line of Harrison to the Oakhill tract. I also give him the two western lotts of the square I now live on. These lands and lotts are I believe conveyed to him, but I mention them lest there should be any mistake in the conveyance. This devise includes the manor lotts held by Mr. Smith and Mr. Adams.

I give to my son Jaquelin Ambler the land on which he now resides called Prospect Hill, together with all my land lying west of the road between Prospect Hill and Hume, East of the Rappahannock, South of Thumb run, and North of Bee branch. I also give him one thousand acres of land lying south and adjoining the tract of Mr. Ambler and west of the manor road adjoining also the land of my brother James.

It was my intention to give my son John the reversion of all the land lying north of the line agreed on between him and my son James and south of Mallorys lease, and west of the fence which now divides him from my son James, and east of the land I have sold but I beleive not conveyed to Mr. Ambler together with all the negroes and stock in his possession. Some indiscretions on his part in the management of his pecuniary affairs extremely painful to me, have induced me to place the property I intended for him in the hands of trustees for the benefit of his family.[5] I therefore give to my son James K. Marshall and my Nephew Thomas M. Ambler, all my interest and all the interest which at the time of my death I may hold in the land adjoining my sons James Keith and Edward Carrington and my nephew Thomas M. Ambler, to them and to the survivor and to the heirs of the survivor for ever, also all the slaves and stock which I may place on the said land during my life on loan or hire to my son John or otherwise, and all the household furniture which I may lend to him, in trust that the profits shall be applied annually to the maintenance of his family and the education of his children. Should the trustees think proper to employ him as a manager they are not to be held accountable, for his disbursements of the money arising from the estate by way of annual profit.

I give to my son James Keith the tract of land on which he now resides called Moreland. I also give him all my interest in the land extending round the big cobler south and west as far as the dividing line which has been run between him and my son John. I also give him after the death of his mother one half of my tract of land in Hampshire county called the Swan ponds, for his own use, and I give him the other half also at the death of His mother in trust for the family of my son John in like trust as is described in the devise in trust to him & to my nephew Thomas M. Ambler for the benefit of the family of my son John.

Should I not dispose of a small tract of land I own on Pattesons creek I give that also to my son James Keith.[6]

I give to my son Edward Carrington Marshall the tract of land west of the Little Cobler on which he is now building a house with all my interest in the lands north of the lotts held by Mr. Chancellor running to the top of the Little cobler and adjoining my son Thomas. I also give him all my slaves and property of every description usually on the said land. I also give him my tract of land in Hampshire commonly called Andersons bottom, at the death of his mother.

I give to Thomas Marshall Ambler my tract of land on chiccahominy and all the stock and one moity of the slaves thereon in trust to apply the annual profits to the maintainance of my daughter Mary Harvie and her family, and to the education of her children. I also give to the said Thomas M. Ambler after the death of my wife and on the like trust the house in which I reside and the two eastern lotts in the square also the house and lott opposite to me in which Mr. Crouch now resides also my part of the stable lott. The property given in trust for my daughter and her family is for her separate use not to be subject to the controul of her husband or to his debts; but as it would be burdensome to the trustee to take upon himself the management of the property and the disbursement of the money arising annually therefrom I recommend that my son in law Jaquelin B. Harvie be an agent for that purpose, and my trustee is not to be responsible to the family for any disbursements he may make. Should my son in law Jaqueline B. Harvie survive my daughter it is my desire that one half of the annual profits of the property bequeathed in trust for my daughter and her family be paid to him for his own use. It is farther my will that a reasonable advancement may be made during the life of my daughter to any of her children with the consent and approbation of their Father, as they shall respectively arrive at the age of twenty one years or marry.

I give my interest in the tract of land called Canaan in Randolph county to be equally divided between my Grandsons John Marshall son of Thomas, John Marshall son of Jaquelin Ambler, John Marshall son of

John, John Marshall son of James Keith, John Marshall Harvie son of my daughter Mary and the eldest son of my son Edward C. Marshall.

The moiety of my slaves on Chiccahominy not yet bequeathed I desire may be divided into three parts. One I give to my son James Keith Marshall and my Nephew Thomas Marshall Ambler in trust for the separate use and benefit of the wife and children of my son John. One I give to my son James K. Marshall. The third I give to my son Edward C. Marshall.

It is my desire that a reasonable advancement may be made by the consent of my son John for any of his children as they shall respectively arrive at age or marry or afterwards.

The residue of my estate I give to my sons Thomas, Jaquelin Ambler, James Keith, and Edward Carrington to be divided between them in the following proportions. Supposing it to be divided into fifty parts I give to my son Thomas fourteen parts to my son Jaquelin Ambler thirteen parts to my son James Keith twelve parts, and to my son Edward Carrington eleven parts. I make this distribution because I suppose the estates given to my sons are not very unequal and I give the residuum so that the parts may in the natural course of things equalize themselves as each legatee attains the age of the oldest. I give no part to my daughter under the conviction that what I have given her family with what I know to be intended for her by her Mother will amount to at least one sixth of my estate. Revoking all former will I declare this to my last will and testament

J MARSHALL

I appoint my sons Thomas Jaquelin Ambler, James Keith exrs. of this my last will. No surety is to be required from them

J MARSHALL

A codicil to my will dated the 12th. of April 1827   May 5th. 1827

I have sold to my Nephew Thomas M. Ambler the reversion of the lott between his original land & Mr. Chancellor which is now in his possession together with some wood land on which there is no lease on his side the mountain. My sons know the line. Should I die before I make a conveyance, this codicil by which I devise it to him is instead for a conveyance.

J MARSHALL

Additional Codicil to my will,   Jany 5th. 1829

I have made several a[l]terations in my will by erasing some words and by inserting others. I have struck out the family of my son John from the residuary clause because I have since my will was written advanced sums of money for him which I beleive to be fully equivalent to his share of the residuum of my estate. I had intended to give my wife my estate on chiccahominy but I have on reflection altered my will so as to give that estate immediately in trust for my daughter and her family; but I reserve for my wife during her life the free use of the house and yard with their appurtenances, and desire that she may be supplied from the said estate with as much hay and wood as she may require for her use. At her request I give Henry on her death to my son Thomas. In lieu of my estate on chiccahominy which I had intended for my beloved wife during her life, it is my desire that the lands comprehended in the residuary clause of my will may be kept together during her life and that the rents may be regularly collected and paid to her.

J MARSHALL

Additional codicil to my will   Aug.17th. 1830

I direct my slaves at Chiccahominy to be divided into two moieties preserving families together as near as may be except young men and young women. One moity I give to my nephew Thomas M. Ambler in trust for the separate use of my daughter Mary Harvie and her children in like manner as the real estate has been bequeathed to the same trustees on the same trust. The remaining moity to be divided as was directed for the wh⟨?⟩

Upon reflection I have determined to reinstate in part the bequest to my son Johns family in my residuary estate. Instead of twelve parts I give six to my son James Keith and my Nephew Thomas M. Ambler in trust for the wife and children born & to be born of my son John.

J MARSHALL

ADS, Ambler v. Marshall, Ended Chancery File 1838–006, Clerk's Office, Fauquier County Circuit Court, Warrenton, Va. Vertical line through entire document and horizontal line through signatures indicating that will was revoked.

1. This is the first of three wills JM is known to have written. He wrote a second will in Sept.1831 on the eve of his departure for Philadelphia, where he underwent an operation for the removal of bladder stones. In Apr. 1832, several months after his wife's death, he drew up a third will, which was probated after his death in July 1835.

2. These two Hampshire County (now West Va.) tracts, Swan Ponds containing nine hundred acres and Andersons Bottom containing seven hundred acres, had been allotted to JM in a partition deed of June 1799 that divided up the residuary manor lands conveyed by Denny Fairfax to James M. Marshall in Aug. 1797 (*PJM*, VII, 186, 187 n. 5; VIII, 110; copy of partition deed [in JM's hand], 24 June 1799, Martin v. Moffet, U.S. Cir. Ct., Va., Ended Cases [Restored], 1824, Vi).

3. Mrs. Robinson was undoubtedly Mildred Smith Robinson (b. 1763), who was adopted by her great-aunt Martha Jaquelin (1711–1792). She married a son of John Robinson, the noted Speaker of the House of Burgesses, and later moved to Annapolis, Md. Although he speaks of "Mrs. Jaquelin," JM evidently meant Martha Jaquelin, who died unmarried. Martha Jaquelin's executor was Jaquelin Ambler, JM's father-in-law (Louise Pecquet Du Bellet, *Some Prominent Virginia Families* [4 vols.; 1907; Baltimore, 1976 reprint], I, 22; III, 10, 25).

4. In 1824 Slaughter executed a deed of trust to secure payment of a bond to JM and of a separate bond to JM, Daniel Call, and George Fisher as executors of Jaquelin Ambler in Ambler's capacity as Martha Jaquelin's executor. This deed was part of the case file (not found) of Long v. Slaughter, JM, et al., which was decided in the Fredericksburg Superior

Court of Chancery in 1829 (Irwin S. Rhodes, *The Papers of John Marshall: A Descriptive Calendar* [2 vols.; Norman, Okla, 1969], II, 233–34, 282). See also JM to Slaughter, 22 Sept. 1827 (App. II, Cal.).

5. On John's financial indiscretions, see also JM to Philip Slaughter, 22 Sept. 1827 and n. 1 (App. II, Cal.).

6. The Patterson Creek tract, in Hampshire County and containing 328 acres, was also allotted to JM by the 1799 partition deed (see n. 2).

From Jared Sparks

Dear Sir,   Mount Vernon, April 17th, 1827.

The copy of a letter to Judge Washington, which I have the honor to enclose, is so full on the point in question that I forbear to add more.[1] I can hardly think you will hesitate as to the expediency of removing the papers in the manner proposed, or that you will consider the risk incurred as affording a serious objection, especially as the papers are nearly all copies. I really do not see how it is possible for me to go through the whole of my labors at Mount Vernon; the obstacles are insuperable. I hope therefore that you will look upon my proposal in a favorable light, and represent your opinion accordingly to Judge Washington. As you are so perfectly acquainted with the papers in all their details, he will rely greatly on your judgment and views of the case.

With assurances of the highest respect, and perfect esteem, I am, Sir, Your most Obedt. humble Servt.

JARED SPARKS

Letterbook copy, Sparks Papers, MH.

1. Sparks to Bushrod Washington, 17 Apr. 1827, in which he made his case for the removal of the Mount Vernon papers to his Boston home to carry out his ambitious editorial task. Sparks offered to transport and return the papers at his own expense and to insure them against fire for ten thousand dollars. Sparks also noted that he was sending a copy of this letter to JM (Herbert B. Adams, *The Life and Writings of Jared Sparks, Comprising Selections from His Journals and Correspondence* [2 vols.; Boston and New York, 1893], II, 15–23).

To Jared Sparks

Dear Sir   Richmond Apl. 27th. 1827

On my return to this place from a visit to my friends in our mountain Country I received your letter inclosing one to Mr. Washington proposing a removal of the papers of General Washington from Mount Vernon.

The reasons you assign for the removal are in my opinion conclusive. From my first view of your plan I believed it to be impossible for you to execute it without a permanent residence under the same roof with the papers—or at any rate in their neighbourhood. I was confident that perpetual recurrence to them would be indispensable. The fuller details in your letter place the subject beyond the possibility of doubt. So much time has elapsed since you wrote to Judge Washington that I presume he has decided on the matter and that a letter from me will be useless. Indeed I do not consider myself as authorised to intrude my opinion and should not do so were it not that your direct reference to me may induce him to expect a letter from me and to wait for it. As this is possible I shall write to him immediately & shall express the opinion I have given to you.[1]

I have also received your letter enclosing the order of the 3d. of October 1777. I am much oblig⟨ed⟩ by the trouble you have taken. The order I wishe⟨d⟩ contained the arrangements for the battle. It was before me when I described the battle of Germantown & I suppose I had seen it in the order book. It may be a paper recorded elsewhere, or not recorded at all & preserved in its original form. Of course I must abandon the hope of seeing it again. With great respect I am, your obedt

J MARSHALL

ALS, Sparks Papers, MH. Addressed to Sparks "at Mount Vernon / near Alexandria." endorsed by Sparks, noted as received 30 Apr.

1. Bushrod Washington wrote to Sparks on 29 Apr. consenting to the removal plan unless JM objected. Sparks replied on 7 May that he was "gratified" by Washington's consent, noting that he had "also received an answer from Chief Justice Marshall, which accords so entirely with yours that I consider the arrangement as now settled" (Washington to Sparks, 29 Apr. 1827, Sparks Papers, MH; Sparks to Washington, 7 May 1827, Herbert B. Adams, *The Life and Writings of Jared Sparks, Comprising Selections from His Journals and Correspondence* [2 vols.; Boston and New York, 1893], II, 24).

To Marquis de Lafayette

My dear General   Richmond May 2d. 1827

I had the pleasure a day or two past of receiving your letter of the 25th. of February[1] accompanied by the valuable notes you had the goodness to send me, and the speech of the Duke de Broglie in the House of Peers on the subject of the slave trade.[2] I have read the notes with great attention and thank you for them, as well as for your permission to avail myself of them in the event of publishing a revised edition of The Life of Washington.[3] I perceive I was mistaken in supposing that the Court of France, while ostensibly discountenancing your engaging in the service of the United States, privately connived at that measure. The notes contain several other interesting details not previously understood.[3]

The applause of an unknown American citizen cannot flatter a Peer of France; but to you who allow me to beleive that you do not view my opinions with absolute indifference, I will say that I think the speech of the Duke de Broglie has great merit. I have read it with equal admiration of the justness of its sentiments and the solidity of its arguments. The subject deeply interests humanity. Should France engage seriously and earnestly in the great work of abolishing this flagitious traffic in human flesh, it must be accomplished; and one of the foulest stains on the character of Christendom will exist only in history. In the United States the trade itself is sufficiently execrated; but the disposition to expel slavery from our bosom, or even to diminish the evil if practicable, does not I think gain strength in the south. I am not sufficiently acquainted with the climate and situation of our more southern states to form any decided opinion on the practicability of carrying on the agriculture of the country with the labour of white men; but I say without hesitation that in Maryland, Virginia, Kentucky, and Missouri, and even in Tennessee, and North Carolina unless it be immediately on the sea board, white labour might be substituted for black with advantage. The positive prosperity and happiness of these states, as well as their relative power and weight in the union, would, I confidently believe, be promoted by this change. But it is impossible to impress this opinion on those who might contribute to the establishment of this beneficial policy. An excessive jealousy of the free states, and an extreme apprehension of the domestic evils which might grow out of any measure having even a remote tendency to effect the object, stifles any attempt towards it.

I do not know enough of the interior of Mexico to form any opinion on the possibility of giving our coloured population that direction; but I am persuaded that it cannot be safely located on any lands within the United States. The only secure asylum within our reach — beneficial for them and safe for us — is Africa. The colony of Liberia is rapidly advancing to a state of solidity and permanent prosperity which will make it so great an object to our people of colour to migrate thither as to justify the hope that the colonization society may soon be relieved from the expence of transporting those who wish to remove to that country. They receive rich lands which they can cultivate in safety; and the prospect of a profitable commerce is very flattering. Under these encouraging circumstances, the hope that voluntary emigration will releive us from our free coloured people may, I trust, be indulged without the charge of being over sanguine.

Measures are now taking by some of our extreme southern states which must have a material influence on the value of our slaves, and may produce effects not to be foreseen. They are prohibiting the introduction of slaves among them for sale under heavy penalties. The sales in the south have upheld the price in the middle states; and the withdrawal of this market will reduce the price so low as to bring it in the farming country to a level with the expence of raising them under the humane course which at present generally prevails. Should this policy become universal, we cannot predict its effects with certainty.

I persuade myself you will excuse my indulging in conjecture on this subject, because I know it is very near your heart.

I hear with regret your opinion that the English government does not take a sincere interest in the cause of gallant and suffering Greece. The information, or rather the speculations of the papers, had cherished the belief that a combined interference of the Christian powers of Europe to terminate the present desolating war, and guarantee the partial independence of Greece on the payment of a tribute which might compensate Turkey for her loss of territory was to be expected. I fear however that this hope, so consoling to humanity, will be disappointed.

Our papers have informed you that the debates of the last session of Congress have been scarcely less tempestuous than those of 1805–6. We dare not indulge the hope that those of the ensuing session will be more temperate. It is infinitely to be deplored that the contests concerning the election of the President, and the factions they generate; should mingle themselves with the legislation of the country. I fear however it is a disease for which no remedy is attainable.

While I hear with real sympathy the family loss you have sustained, I trust I may congratulate you on the health as well as happiness you enjoy at la Grange.[4] That charming seat has been described to me as having every claim to the preference you bestow upon it. The United States and her citizens still look with their accustomed and grateful affection to every thing which concerns you.

Allow me to charge you with my sincere compliments to Messieurs Lafayette[5] and le Vasseur,[6] and to assure you that I remain with great and respectful esteem and attachment, Your Obedt

J MARSHALL

ALS, Dean Lafayette Collection, Division of Rare and Manuscript Collections, NIC.

1. Letter not found.

2. Achille Charles Léonce Victor, duc de Broglie, *Discours Prononcé par M. le Duc de Broglie à la Chambre des Pairs le 28 mars 1822, sur la Traite des Nègres* (Paris, 1822).

3. For examples of JM's use of Lafayette's notes in second edition, see *The Life of George Washington* (2 vols.; 2d ed.; Philadelphia, 1838), I, 423–33 and n., 435 and n., 439, 447 and n., 448 and n., 450–51 and n., 453–55 and nn.

4. Lafayette's son-in-law, Louis de Lasteyrie, died in late Dec. 1826 from a "cerebral fever" (Lafayette to Richard Peters, 19 Jan. 1827, *Letters of the Marquis de Lafayette in the Collection of Stuart Wells Jackson*, American Friends of Lafayette, Publication No. 6 [Easton, Pa., 1954], 31, 34).

5. George Washington Lafayette (1779–1849), Lafayette's son.

6. Auguste Levasseur, Lafayette's secretary during his 1824–25 tour of the U.S. He subsequently wrote an account of the trip (*Lafayette in America in 1824 and 1825, or, Journal of a Voyage to the United States* [2 vols.; Philadelphia, 1829).

To Bushrod Washington

Dear Sir   Richmond May 2d. .27

On my return from Fauquier a few days past I received the copy of a letter addressed to you by Mr. Sparks respecting the removal of the papers of General Washington to Boston. As a decision on that proposition rests exclusively with yourself my first intention was not to intrude any opinion of mine upon you. But on looking over the letter again I find there is a reference in it to me, & I have supposed it possible that you might expect to hear from me on the subject. This induces me to say that from my knowledge of the papers I am convinced that the work he contemplates cannot be executed on the plan he proposes without a constant recurrence to the papers.

I hope your health continues to improve. You were so visibly better at the conclusion of our last term than you were at the commencement as to justify this hope. With the most sincere wish that it may be realized I am dear Sir Yours truely

J MARSHALL

I have just received a letter from Genl. Lafayette transmitting some notes he had promised me respecting himself, in which after mentioning in terms of affection and speaking of some original letters for which you had written he adds "tell him with my affectionate compliments, it will be for the next packet. Sickness prevented my availing myself of Captain Allyn's departure."[1]

ALS, NHi. Addressed to Washington in Philadelphia; postmarked Richmond, 2 May. Endorsed by Washington.

1. Capt. Francis Allyn of New London, Conn., was commander of the *Cadmus,* on which Lafayette sailed to America in 1824. On that voyage Allyn formed a close friendship with Lafayette and his son, George Washington Lafayette (Edward Everett Dale, ed., *Lafayette Letters* [Oklahoma City, Okla., 1925], 1–9).

United States v. Amedy
Sentence
U.S. Circuit Court, Virginia, 24 May 1827

You have been tried for the crime of destroying a vessel at sea, of which you were the commander, for the purpose of injuring the underwriters; and, after as skilful a defence as perhaps was ever made, have been found guilty by an intelligent and impartial jury.[1] Some doubt having arisen respecting the admissibility of testimony which was received at the trial, that question was referred to the Supreme Court of the United States, where it has been argued and deliberately considered. The opinion of that Court is, that the testimony was properly admitted; and with this direction, the case has been remanded to this Court.[2] Our duty requires, that, in obedience to this mandate, we pronounce the judgment of the law, on the verdict of the jury.[3] But before we perform that duty, let us exhort you most earnestly to avail yourself of the short portion of life which yet remains, to prepare for that still more awful judgment which will be passed upon you by that Being, who looks into the heart and penetrates its most secret recesses. We are assured that, with him, true repentance will obtain pardon for the blackest crimes. His mercy transcends even the sinfulness of man, if that mercy be sincerely implored by an humble and a contrite heart. We conjure you, then, to recommend yourself to him.

To this Court, nothing remains but to pronounce the sentence of the law, which is, that you, John B. Amedie, be taken to the place from which you were brought, and be there closely confined until Friday, the 29th of June next. On that day between the hours of nine in the morning and two in the afternoon, you are to be conveyed from the place of confinement to the place of execution, and there be hanged by the neck until you shall be dead. And may God have mercy on your soul.[4]

Printed, *Richmond Enquirer*, 29 May 1827.

1. John B. Amedy of Hingham, Mass., owner and master of the schooner *Pacific* of Boston, was convicted at the Nov. 1825 term of fraudulently scuttling and sinking his vessel to the prejudice of the company that insured the ship on a voyage from Boston to Amsterdam in the summer of 1824. After the destruction of the vessel, Amedy returned to Boston but fled under suspicion to Key West and changed his name. There he was apprehended in Mar. 1825 and brought into Norfolk by the commander of a U.S. navy ship and held for arraignment. After a trial lasting six hours on 30 Nov. 1825, a jury deliberated about an hour before returning a verdict of guilty. Nine of the jurors recommended mercy, including one who expressed his belief that Amedy had "been duped by other persons equally guilty with himself." This was a reference to testimony presented at the trial that John P. Froding, then Swedish consul at Boston, was the real mastermind of the plot to commit the insurance fraud and that his threats and persuasion had induced Amedy to become a party (*Richmond Enquirer*, 2 Dec. 1825; U.S. Cir. Ct., Va., Ord. Bk. XII, 47, 50–51, 57, 58, 59–60; U.S. v. Amedy, U.S. Cir. Ct., Va., Ended Cases [Unrestored], 1827, Vi).

2. On 14 Dec. 1825 Amedy's counsel moved for a new trial on the ground that illegal evidence had been admitted to the jury and that the court had given an erroneous opinion concerning this evidence. JM and U.S. District Court Judge Hay divided on the motion for a new trial in order to certify the question to the Supreme Court. At the Feb. 1826 term the Court certified that the circuit court had properly ruled on the points of law at the trial (U.S. Cir. Ct., Va., Ord. Bk. XII, 79–88, 149–50; *Richmond Enquirer*, 15 Dec. 1825; U.S. v. Amedy, 11 Wheat. 392–413).

3. Amedy was indicted under the 1804 act "in addition" to the act for the punishment of crimes against the U.S., which prescribed the death penalty for any person found guilty of "wilfully and corruptly" destroying his vessel on the high seas with an intent to prejudice the underwriters of an insurance policy on that vessel (*U.S. Statutes at Large*, II, 290).

4. President Adams suspended execution of the sentence on 28 May 1827 and gave Amedy a "full and free pardon" on 24 Feb. 1829 (*Richmond Enquirer*, 22 June 1827; Copies of Presidential Pardons and Remissions, IV [1822–1836], 166, 216–17, RG 59, DNA).

Davis v. Palmer; Davis v. McCormick
Opinion
U.S. Circuit Court, Virginia, 2 June 1827

In 1825 Gideon Davis of Georgetown, District of Columbia, obtained a patent for a plough with a new and improved moldboard. In the summer of 1826 Davis sued Stephen McCormick (1784–1876) of Auburn in Fauquier County and William Palmer (d. 1870) of Richmond for infringing his patent. McCormick (a cousin of Cyrus McCormick, inventor of the reaper) was himself a manufacturer and inventor of ploughs. Palmer owned an agricultural implements factory and had a contract to manufacture McCormick's ploughs. In addition to actions of trespass on the case against McCormick and Palmer for infractions of his patent rights, Davis also sought an injunction on the chancery side of the court to restrain Palmer from manufacturing and selling those ploughs that Davis claimed adopted the same principle of improvement secured by his patent. Marshall granted a temporary injunction in August 1826. After Palmer filed his answer in October, the court at the November 1826 term heard arguments on a motion to dissolve the injunction. Benjamin W. Leigh and Robert Stanard served as Davis's counsel, while John Wickham and Chapman Johnson represented Palmer. Arguments on the injunction consumed three weeks in a courtroom so "encumbered with ploughs of every variety of form and dimensions, works on agriculture, encyclopædias, &.c.," that a spectator might have imagined being "at an agricultural fair, rather than at the trial of a cause in a Court of Justice." On 23 December Marshall issued a provisional decree dissolving the injunction, accompanied by a memorable opinion for which no text survives. According to an eyewitness who participated as junior counsel in the cause, the chief justice demonstrated so great a technical mastery of the science of ploughs as to cause Davis to declare that if the jurist "had been himself the inventor of his improvement, he could not possibly have had more exact notions of the subject, than those embodied in his opinion." The trial of the actions at law took place at the May 1827 term. During the trial, on 1 June, the defendants presented a motion raising certain matters of law that Marshall discussed in the opinion below, given on 2 June (Davis v. McCormick; Davis v. Palmer, Ended Cases [Unrestored], 1827, Vi; Davis v. Palmer [chancery suit], Ended Cases [Unrestored], 1827, Vi; U.S. Cir. Ct., Va., Ord. Bk. XII, 148, 154–59; Eugene M. Scheel, *The Guide To Fauquier: A Survey of The Architecture and History of a Virginia County* [Warrenton, Va., 1976], 38; Mary Wingfield Scott, *Houses of Old Richmond* [1941; New York, 1971 reprint], 87; *Richmond Enquirer,* 24 Dec. 1825; Gustavus H. Schmidt, "Reminiscences of the Late Chief Justice Marshall," *Louisiana Law Journal,* I [1841], 92, 95).

OPINION

These suits are brought by the plaintiff, to recover damages for the alleged violation of his patent, for an improvement on the plough. His improvement is, in part, made on the face, throat, and hind part of the mould-board. The counsel for the defendants had moved the Court,[1]

1. To declare the patent void, because the specification, so far as it regards the improvements in the mould-board, does not describe this part of the improvement with the certainty required by the act of Congress.

Should the patent be submitted to the jury, they then move that it be accompanied with the following instructions;

1. That so much of the patent as respects the face of the mould-board is not violated, unless the defendants have adopted the same spheric lines as are described in the plaintiff's specification.

2. That the jury must be satisfied that the former mould-board is described with sufficient certainty, to distinguish between it and the improvement claimed.

3. If the jury shall be satisfied that M'Cormick has made and used mould-boards, worked out by transverse and concave circular lines, before the plaintiff obtained his patent, or made his alleged improvement, then the particular spheric lines described in his specification constitute only a change of form and proportion, and is not an invention capable of being patented.

In the course of the argument, the counsel have also contended that the same uncertainty exists in that part of the specification which describes the throat and hind part of the mould-board, as in that which describes its face.

1. We will first consider the proposition, that the patent is void for uncertainty.

It is, undoubtedly, the province of the Court to construe every written instrument offered in evidence; and it results from this duty, that if the instrument be so uncertain in its terms as to have no meaning; if it be insensible, or have no application to the case, it may be rejected. Is the patent, on which the present actions are founded, of this description?

The specification, No. 1, relates to the face of the mould-board. It consists, first, of a general, and then of a more particular description of this part of the improvement. The defendants contend that these descriptions are uncertain in themselves, and that there is also a fatal uncertainty which of them describes the improvement for which the plaintiff claims his patent.

The plaintiff, after a general description of the mould-board then in use, and the inconveniences arising from its form, proceeds thus: "In order to meet and remedy the inconveniences arising from this form of structure, I form my mould-board into a different shape, and, instead of working the moulding part, or face of the mould-board to straight lines, my improvement is to work it to circular or spheric lines."[2] The specification then proceeds to a more particular description of the lines used, and of the manner in which they are applied, in order to form the face of the mould-board.

The counsel for the plaintiff seem disposed to consider this general description, as constituting the essential part of the specification, and the subsequent more particular description, as merely an illustration of the general principle, as one mode of carrying it into execution.

If the specification will admit of this construction, then the subsequent and particular description may be expunged without affecting the patent. A principle remains the same, whether it be accompanied by any case put for illustration or not. It may be comprehended more easily, but is not varied by the illustration.

If we consider this general part of the specification as standing alone, and as describing this part of the improvement, it is not liable to the charge of uncertainty. It claims, as an improvement, "to work it (the mould-board) by circular or spheric lines." Every mould-board worked by circular or spheric lines, however those lines may cross each other, and whatever may be their relative proportions, is within the plaintiff's patent. If the face of no mould-board previously in use will fit this description, the plaintiff's patent may, perhaps, legally cover the broad ground it would occupy. But if any mould-board previously in use would fit this description, then the plaintiff would claim, as his invention, that which was previously known, and his patent would be void.

But we do not think the specification will admit of this construction. It proceeds to say, "By repeated experiments I have ascertained, that in one direction, viz: from *a*, fig. 4," (which is the point of the share) "inclining to the back part of the mould-board the circle or segment to which the mould-board is wrought, should have about three times the radius of the smaller segments represented by the letters *c, c*, &c., the former being about thirty-six inches, the latter twelve." This is intended for a plough which will turn a furrow slice of twelve inches. The specification then proceeds to detail minutely the mode of operation by which these lines are to be applied, in order to give the face of the mould-board the required shape, and says: "The plough may be made larger or smaller, suited to deep or shallow ploughing by enlarging or diminishing the radii of the segments which it is wrought by."[3]

"Believing," the specification adds, "that this mode of shaping the moulding part, or face of the mould-board, is an original invention of my own, not heretofore used or known, and that it is a most important improvement in the shape of the plough, I claim the exclusive privilege of making, using, and vending the same."[4]

This claim applies conclusively, we think, to the particular and laboured description of the mould-board which immediately precedes it. The language seems to us to require this construction; and the subject seems also require it. If the patent were to extend to all mould-boards worked out to circular lines, crossing each other in any direction, or in any proportion, it would be unnecessary to describe with so much labour and minuteness, the direction of the longitudinal and perpendicular circular lines, by which the face of the mould-board should be worked out, and the proportions those lines should bear to each other, and the size of the plough. It is obvious, then, that the person who makes his improvement to consist in the peculiar shape given to the face of his mould-board, and who describes the lines and their several proportions, which will give that peculiar shape, must mean to appropriate the shape produced by the application of those new lines. We are then decidedly of opinion, that a mould-board conforming to the particular description contained in the specification, is the invention which the plaintiff claims, and that instead of being a mere illustration of the principle stated in the introductory part of the specification, it is itself the essential improvement, of which only a general idea was given in the introductory part.

It is contended on the part of the plaintiff that, if the patent be limited to the more particular part of the specification, still the claim is not confined to mould-boards worked out by segments of circles of the exact form and proportions mentioned in the specification. To support this argument, counsel rely on the word "about," which is introduced into the description; he has found, Mr. Davis says, by repeated experiments, that the segment of the larger circle should have about three times the radius of the smaller segments, &c. The claim, therefore, is not for a mould-board of the precise shape described, but for one "about" the shape described.

It will at once be perceived, that unless the extent of this word "about," be limited, it introduces all the uncertainty which it was supposed would be fatal to the patent, according to the general description contained in the introductory part of the specification. If, instead of thirty-six inches and twelve, the proportions may be thirty-seven and eleven, thirty-eight and ten, why not forty and eight, or thirty-five and fifteen? The proportions may be enlarged or diminished, and with every change of proportion, the shape of the mould-board will be changed. If this be the construction of the patent, then it covers all the various forms of mould-boards which may be made under this latitudinous exposition of its terms; and if any mould-board has been previously used, whose face may be formed by transverse segments of circles, whose radii bear to each other "about" the proportion of thirty-six to twelve, the patent is void.

Will it be said that it may be left to the jury to determine, what is "about" the proportion particularly designated? This expedient will not remove the difficulty. We doubt how far it may consist with the principle that the Court is to construe every written instrument. But, waiving this doubt, if the word has any limits, they must be always the same. When applied to a mould-board, it cannot be endowed with an elastic principle, to expand or contract itself according to circumstances. It cannot admit of being varied to a certain extent, if no mould-board has been in use of the shape which that degree of variation would produce, and at the same time of being restricted, if a mould-board of such a shape has been in use. The word "about," cannot be equivalent to a general claim of the exclusive right to all concave mould-boards, varying in any degree from those previously in use. The definiteness of the shape, which the specification professes to give to the mould-board, cannot be sacrificed by this loose word. It is further observable, that where the specification describes the process of the workman, it drops the word "about."

It has been supposed that the precise proportion required between the radii of the larger and smaller segments of circles, may be relaxed under the concluding part of the description. After giving the mode of operation, the specification adds: "This being thus worked off, uniformly forms a section of a loxodromic or spiral curve, and when applied to practice, is found to fit or embrace every part of the furrow-slice, far more than any other shaped plough."[5]

The argument is, that it is a mould-board whose face forms a section of a loxodromic or spiral curve that is patented, and that any lines which will give such a surface, are within the specification, and consequently, within the patent.

Without noticing the difficulties growing out of this construction, it is sufficient to say, that the specification does not claim the loxodromic or spiral curve as the invention, but states it as the result of the prescribed application of the transverse circular lines, the application of which, in the relative proportions prescribed, is the invention. The language of this part of the specification, tends to confirm, we think, the opinion already indicated, that the plaintiff intended to claim a mould-board of the precise and definite shape prescribed, not one about that shape. He says his mould-board, "so worked off," "When applied to practice, is found to fit or embrace every part of the furrow-slice, far more than any other shaped plough."[6]

In construing this specification, we must keep in view the notice of the improvement which Mr. Davis claims to have invented and to describe. It is an improvement in the shape of a machine which has been in common use a great number of years, and in a great variety of shapes. The concave mould-board has been long considered as the most eligible shape that part of the plough can assume, and multiplied essays have been made to perfect it. Mr. Davis has recently added to their number; he professes to have discovered that precise concavity in the surface of the mould-board, which will better than any other fit every part of the furrow-slice, and, consequently, turn it over with less labour. For this discovery he claims a patent; we may reasonably expect, that a specification for such a patent, will give a precise and definite shape to the improvement to be patented.

We are then decidedly of opinion, that in construing this specification, the word "about" must be disregarded, and the patent be restricted to the mould-board as described, independent of that word.

If we consider the particular part of the specification as describing the object to be patented, the defendants insist that the description given in that part is not sufficiently clear to enable a skilful mechanic to construct the machine.

It may not, perhaps, be easy to draw a precise line of distinction between a specification so uncertain, as to claim no particular improvement, and a specification so uncertain as not to enable a skilful workman to understand the improvement, and to construct it. Yet, we think, the distinction exits. If it does, it is within the province of the jury to decide, whether a skilful workman can carry into execution the plan of the inventor. In deciding this question, the jury will give a liberal common sense construction to the directions contained in the specification.

If the patent be submitted to the jury, the defendants request the Court to give the several instructions which have been already mentioned.

1. The first is, that so much of the patent as relates to the face of the mould-board is not violated, unless the defendants have adopted the same circular lines as are described in the specification.

This instruction will be given. But it may perhaps be understood with some slight modification. The patent, undoubtedly, covers only the improvement precisely described. But if the imitation be so nearly exact as to satisfy the jury that the imitator attempted to copy the model, and to make some almost imperceptible variation, for the purpose of evading the right of the patentee, this may be considered as a fraud on the law, and such slight variation be disregarded.

2. The second instruction is, that the jury must be satisfied that the former mould-board is described with sufficient certainty, to distinguish between it and the improvement claimed.

We do not think a particular description of the former mould-board is necessary. A general reference to it, either in general terms which are not untrue, or by reference to a particular mould-board, commonly known, accompanied by such a description of the improvement as will enable a workman to distinguish what is new, will be sufficient.

3. The Court is also requested to instruct the jury that, if M'Cormick has made and used mould-boards, worked out by transverse circular lines, so as to produce a concave surface, before the plaintiff obtained his patent, or made his alleged improvement, then the particular lines described in his specification, constitute only a change of form and proportion, not an invention capable of being patented.

It is stated on both sides, that the clause in the statute, to which this instruction refers, is one of considerable doubt. It is in these words: "And it is hereby enacted and declared, that simply changing the form or the proportion of any machine, shall not be deemed a discovery."[7]

In construing this provision, the word "simply," has, we think, great influence. It is not every change of form and proportion which is declared to be no discovery, but that which is *simply* a change of form or proportion, and nothing more. If, by changing the form and proportion, a new effect is produced, there is not simply a change of form and proportion, but a change of principle also.

In every case, therefore, the question must be submitted to the jury, whether the change of form and proportion, has produced a different effect.

With respect to the throat and hind part of the mould-board, the Court need only say, that the description of the specification is general, not giving the particular shape of those parts of the mould-board. If either the throat or hind part of a mould-board, was in use before, which answers the description contained in this specification, then the plaintiff has patented what belonged to the public, and his patent is void.[8]

Printed, John W. Brockenbrough, *Reports of Cases Decided by the Honourable John Marshall...*, II (Philadelphia, 1837), 302–10.

1. The written motion of the defendant's counsel is in the case papers (Davis v. McCormick).

2. Gideon Davis, *The United States of America, to All to Whom These Letters Patent Shall Come...* (Washington, 1825), 4.

3. Ibid., 4–5.

4. Ibid., 5.

5. Ibid., 4–5.

6. Ibid.

7. *U.S. Statutes at Large*, I, 318, 321. This general law of 1793 was still in effect. It gave circuit courts jurisdiction in actions on the case for violation of patent. An 1819 law extended jurisdiction to equity in cases arising under patent law (ibid., III, 481–82).

8. Rather than proceed with the trial, Davis worked out a compromise with McCormick and Palmer by which both the cases at law and the chancery suit were dismissed on 6 June 1827. According to one of Davis's lawyers, patent law as it existed at this time provided little security for inventors. A patent could "be set aside for defects and ambiguities in the specification, or description of the invention. It might also be annulled, if it could be shown that the invention, patented, had been known in any other portion of the world prior to the patent, or if it had been in public use before that time, and in short; the difficulties which beset the path of the unfortunate inventor, at this period, were such, that it is probably not too much to assert, that no patent which ever was granted, could stand the test of the ordeal to which it might be subjected by skilful lawyers" (Gustavus H. Schmidt, "Reminiscences of the Late Chief Justice Marshall," *Louisiana Law Journal*, I [1841], 92).

Swann v. Bank of the United States
Opinion
U.S. Circuit Court, Virginia, 8 June 1827

In January 1825 John T. Swann (d. 1841), a physician who for many years served as cashier of the Bank of Virginia in Richmond, filed his bill praying an injunction on a judgment obtained by the Bank of the United States against him at the May 1824 term of the U.S. Circuit Court. In addition to the bank, defendants named in the bill were the executors of Samuel W. Venable (1754–1821) of "Springfield" in Prince Edward County. The executors were Venable's sons, Nathaniel E. Venable (1791–1846), a partner with his father in the firm of Venable & Company, and Abraham W. Venable (1799–1876), who later moved to North Carolina and represented that state in Congress. Swann had endorsed a promissory note given by Blake B. Woodson of Cumberland County to obtain a loan from the Bank of the United States. Heavily indebted, Woodson executed several deeds of trust on his extensive landholdings in Cumberland and Prince Edward to secure creditors, including Walthall Holcombe of Cumberland County, who with Swann was co-endorser of the note, and Samuel W. Venable. Venable's executors gave their answers in August 1825, and the depositions of various witnesses were taken in November 1825. Benjamin W. Leigh represented the plaintiff, while Robert Stanard served as attorney for the defendants. Marshall's opinion accompanied his decree of 8 June 1827 and fully states the facts of the case (U.S. Cir. Ct., Va., Rec. Bk. XVIII, 245–64; *Richmond Enquirer,* 14 Dec. 1841; S. Bassett French Biographical Sketches, Vi; Elizabeth Marshall Venable, *Venables of Virginia . . .* [New York, 1925], 41–50, 105–7, 149–51; Henry Morton Woodson, comp., *Historical Genealogy of the Woodsons and Their Connections* [2 vols.; 1915; Roanoke, Va., 1990 reprint], I, 125).

Swan

v

The Bank of the U.S.

Blake B Woodson had obtained a loan from the Bank of the United States on his note with John T Swan the plaintiff, as his indorser. After some time an additional indorser was required by the bank whereupon Walthal Holcombe agreed to add his name to that of Swan upon which this accomodation was continued.[1] In October 1818 Blake B Woodson executed a deed conveying a tract of land in the county of Cumberland to Benoni Overstreet in trust that "if the said Walthal Halcombe shall be likely to suffer on account of the undertaking of the said Walthall Holcombe for the said Blake B Woodson at the bank aforesaid in the opinion of the said Benoni Overstreet, or in the case the note in the said bank now or hereafter with the name of the said Walthall Holcombe as indorser thereon for the said Blake B Woodson shall be protested whereby the said Walthal Holcombe his heirs &c shall in the opinion of the said Benoni Overstreet be likely to suffer for the amount of any such protest cost & charges or any part thereof, the said Benoni Overstreet at the request of the said Walthall Holcombe, shall" on thirty days notice proceed to sell the trust premises.[2] ¶1

Blake B. Woodson executed other deeds of trust on the same land for the security of other creditors, and among others for the security of Samuel W Venable, under whose deed the land was sold and the said Venable became the purchaser thereof.[3] ¶2

The deed to Benoni Overstreet for the benefit of Holcombe was not recorded, but full notice of it was given to Samuel W Venable. At and before the sale it was shown to him by Benoni Overstreet the trustee. After he had read it, the said Overstreet observed that it was not recorded, on which Venable admitted its validity as to him.[4] Before the ¶3 deed to secure Venable was executed, he had a conversation with Edward Redford respecting the affairs of Blake B Woodson in which Redford informed him of the several liens on Woodsons land including that for the security of Holcombe, on which Venable made a calculation of their amount & said that the land would be sufficient to discharge those liens and pay the debts due to him.[5] The deed for his benefit was executed soon afterwards. When the conversation took place between Venable and Overstreet at the sale they again made a calculation of the liens which were found to amount, including the debt due to the Bank, to about $9000. The land was sold for payment of the debt due to Venable, subject to the prior liens, among which the debt due to the Bank was mentioned, and Venable bid the amount of his own debt, and, being the highest bidder, the land was struck out to him.

¶4   A higher price had been offered for the land, and rejected by Blake B Woodson. This offer was repeated during the bidding and again rejected, about which time the land was struck out to Samuel W Venable.

¶5   The accomodation to Blake B Woodson with John T Swan & Walthal Holcombe as his indorsers was continued by the Bank and before any change took place in the debt Samuel W Venable died leaving Nathaniel E Venable and Abraham W Venable his exrs. They proposed to the Bank to pay the debt provided the bank would put the note in suit against John T Swan for their benefit. This proposition was acceded to, and a judgement was obtained in the name of the bank against John T Swan. He filed his bill stating the foregoing circumstances, alleging his ignorance of these transactions until after the judgement was rendered, and praying an injunction.[6] The defendants, the exrs. of Samuel W Venable admit their liability to Walthall Holcombe, but insist that as he Holcombe has not been compelled to pay anything, and is now discharged from all responsibility, his lien cannot be set up by the plaintiff.[7]

¶6   It is perfectly clear that Holcombe, as a subsequent indorser, having made no arrangement whatever with Swan the previous indorser, which connected them in any manner with each other, would not have been responsible to Swan for any portion of the debt paid by that indorser, but would have had recourse against Swan to be indemnified for any sum he might be compelled to pay. It must also be admitted that the deed of trust was intended solely as an indemnity to Holcombe, and was not executed for the benefit of Swan. If Swan can now avail himself of it, his right to do so grows out of subsequent transactions.

¶7   In considering this case the first enquiry which presents itself to the mind is, could Swan, in the event of being compelled to pay the debt to the bank before the sale of the trust property, have resorted to that property for his indemnity? By force of the meer terms of the deed, he undoubtedly could not; but would a court of equity have given its aid?

¶8   The property after Holcombe was discharged from his indorsement would have reverted to Woodson, and the trustees would have been seized in trust for him. Consequently any creditor might have pursued it, and a court of equity would if necessary, at least have removed the trust out of the way. But when the land became charged with subsequent deeds of trust, the creditors for whose benefit those deeds were made would not be postponed to that made for Holcombe farther than was necessary to satisfy the terms of that deed. Consequently Swan, had he in that state of things been compelled to pay the debt to the Bank, could have had no pretext for claiming the aid of Holcombes deed against the holder of any subsequent deed or against any purchaser at a sale made in pursuance of such deed. If his case is mended, it is by the facts attending the sale and the discharge of the note in Bank as disclosed by the testimony.

It is proved that when Mr. Venable obtained the deed of trust he valued ¶9 the property at a sum sufficient for the discharge of the debt due to himself after discharging all prior incumbrances including that of Holcombe. It is also proved that this computation was again made at the sale, and that the land was at that time thought a good purchase supposing it to be charged not contingently, but positively with the debt to the bank. These facts show that, in the mind of Mr. Venable himself, the debt due to the Bank constituted a part of the purchase money; and would probably have afforded strong inducements to any creditor acting solely under the influence of his own feelings, and with the single desire of obtaining his debt, to press Mr. Holcombe who was secured, rather than Mr. Swan who could resort to no fund for reimbursement. Had the creditor pursued this course the land purchased by Mr. Venable would have been subjected to the debt, and it will not be alleged that he could have had any recourse in law or equity against Mr. Swan as the prior indorser. Had the land still retained the value at which it was estimated when sold, all would admit that this is the course which in right and justice the affair ought to take.

But, although the fact is not alleged in the record, the reduced price of ¶10 real as well as other property is a matter of general notoriety, and will certainly justify the defendants in avoiding the payment of this debt if the law will enable them to do so. Had the Bank, without their interposition, proceeded of itself, to coerce payment from Mr. Swan, he could not perhaps have obtained the aid of a court of equity. Had the representatives of Mr. Venable remained passive spectators of the procedure, it is probable that the circumstances attending the purchase made by their testator would not have affected the estate. But they have not remained passive spectators. The Bank has acted at their instigation and by their procurement. They have been the means of inducing the bank to proceed against a surety having no indemnity, rather than against one holding an indemnity from the original creditor. Although this might have been perfectly justifiable in a court of equity if disconnected from the circumstances attending the taking of the trust deed, and the sale of the property under that deed, it cannot be sustained when viewed in connexion with those circumstances.

¶11   A⟨n a⟩dditional argument which is entitled to great weight has been suggested by my brother Judge.[8] It is that if Mr Venable may coerce the payment of this money from Swan by using the name of the Bank he gives Swan an action against Woodson and thus renders Woodson liable for the money which his land was intended to secure.

¶12   The injunction is made perpetual.[9]

AD, Marshall Judicial Opinions, PPAmP; printed, John W. Brockenbrough, *Reports of Cases Decided by the Honourable John Marshall . . .*, II (Philadelphia, 1837), 294–98. For JM's deletions and interlineations, see Textual Notes below.

1. At the time of the chancery suit, Woodson was living in Clarksburg, Harrison County (now West Va.), where he moved after the death of his first wife. There he married Julia Neale Jackson, widowed mother of Thomas "Stonewall" Jackson, the Confederate general. He gave his deposition in Clarksburg on 1 Nov. 1825 (Woodson, comp., *Historical Genealogy of the Woodsons*, I, 125; U.S. Cir. Ct., Va., Rec. Bk. XVIII, 249–50).

2. Deed of trust, Oct. 1818, ibid., XVIII, 254–55.

3. The deed of trust for the benefit of Venable was executed on 23 Aug. 1819. Under this deed the land was sold to Venable on 12 Jan. 1821 (ibid., XVIII, 258–62).

4. Deposition of Benoni Overstreet, 15 Nov. 1825, ibid., XVIII, 252–54.

5. Deposition of Edward Redford, 15 Nov. 1825, ibid., XVIII, 250–52.

6. Bill in chancery, sworn 25 Jan. 1825, ibid., XVIII, 245–46.

7. Answer of Abraham W. Venable and Nathaniel E. Venable, sworn 18 and 19 Aug. 1825, ibid., XVIII, 247–48.

8. George Hay.

9. Venable's executors took an appeal to the Supreme Court, which at the 1830 term dismissed the case because the appellants failed to file a transcript of the record. At the same term, however, JM overruled a motion by Wirt, Swann's counsel, for an official certificate of dismissal. The appellants, he said, could still file a transcript at this term and move to reinstate the appeal (U.S. Sup. Ct. Minutes, 30 Jan., 1 Feb. 1830; 3 Pet. 68). The appellants evidently decided to drop the appeal.

Textual Notes

¶ 1	l. 1	Blake B ~~Watson~~ ↑Woodson↓ had obtained ~~an accomodation~~ ↑a loan↓ from the
	l. 3	some time ↑an↓ additional ~~sure~~ ↑indorser↓ was
	l. 6	a deed ~~of trust of a~~ ↑conveying a↓ ~~for a~~ tract of
	ll. 12–13	indorser thereon ~~shall~~ for the
¶ 3	l. 3	sale it was ~~mentioned~~ ↑shown↓ to him
	ll. 3–4	the trustee ~~on which he~~ ↑.↓ After he
	ll. 7–8	which Redford informed ↑him↓ of the
	l. 14	to the Bank, ~~which were found to amount~~ to about
¶ 5	l. 1	with John T ~~Wal~~ ↑Swan↓ & Walthal
	l. 4	Venable and ~~Sa~~ Abraham W
	ll. 11–12	insist that as he ↑Holcombe↓ has not ↑been↓ compelled to
¶ 6	l. 6	It ~~is~~ ↑must↓ also ~~to~~ be admitted
¶ 8	l. 5	the land ~~was~~ ↑became↓ charged with
	ll. 10–11	the holder of ~~the~~ ↑any↓ subsequent deed or ↑against↓ any purchaser
	l. 13	discharge of ~~ths~~ ↑the↓ note in

¶10 l. 8   attending the ~~transaction~~ purchase made
    ll. 13–14   Although this ~~would~~ ↑might↓ have been perfectly justifiable
              ↑in a court of equity↓ if disconnected
¶11 l. 2   It is that if ~~the Bank~~ ↑Mr Venable↓ may

To Henry Wheaton

Dear Sir   Richmond June 21st. 1827

I had the pleasure of receiving a few minutes past your letter of the 16th. informing me of your acceptance of the diplomatic appointment which has been offered, and of your purpose to embark for London on the first of July.[1]

I cannot repine at your changing your situation in the court of which I am a member for one more agreeable to yourself, but I can assure you of my real wish that the place you have resigned had been more eligible, and had possessed sufficient attractions to retain you in it. I part with you with regret, and can assure you that I have never in a single instance found reason to wish Your conduct different from what it was.

That you may be happy and successful in the department you have now entered is the sincere wish of him who is dear Sir, Yours truely

J MARSHALL

ALS, Wheaton Papers, NNPM.

1. Letter not found. Wheaton recently accepted President Adams's appointment as chargé d'affaires to Denmark

To James K. Marshall

My dear Son   Richmond July 3d. 1827

I have postponed answering your letter of the 28th. of May[1] til I should have it in my power to remit the additional sum which I promised to send Mr. Smith. I now enclose you a check on the bank of Winchester for $600 which you will indorse to Mr. Smith taking from him a receipt similar to that which he gave on a former occasion.[2]

I am very well satisfied with the business of the sale but am surprized at its being for 200$ less than it ought to have been. Alexander Marshall informed me that he had settled 200$ which he owed me with Mr. Smith in executions which were under his controul & I mentioned this in a letter to Mr. Smith.[3] I thought I had also mentioned it to you but suppose I must be mistaken. I wish you would enquire into this matter when you see Mr. Smith.

Your mother is very much gratified with the account you give from yourself and Claudia of all your affairs & especially of your children, and hopes for its continuance. She looks with some impatience for similar information from John. She desires me to send her love to all the family including Miss Maria[4] and to tell you that this hot weather distresses her very much. She wishes you also to give her love to John & Elizabeth & their children.

I finished cutting my wheat and rye last week. The grain is fine, but the crop not very abundant. The late wheat, where the land was indifferent, was much injured by the fly, and the low ground, which was Mexican, by the severity of the winter. This injury was confined to wet places. My corn has suffered a good deal first by the cold wet spring and now by the drought. It has not rained since about the 10th. of June, if I except one or two light scuds which broke up with a cold northwester. This sudden & sever[e] drought after our floods of rain has baked a part of my land so that the surface is as hard as cement and the corn is dying in the hill; though in the dry parts of the bottom it looks flourishing. I shall finish planting this week but am obliged to give over about twenty acres of rich land I had intended to plant.

The oats rye & grass are re⟨asonabl?⟩y fine. I never saw young clover more promising till lately. It begins to perish.

With my love to the family and to those of your brothers, I am your affectionate Father

J Marshall

ALS, ViW. Addressed to James at "Moreland / near Oak hill / Fauquier"; postmarked Richmond, 3 July. Endorsed by James "My Fathers letter enclosing a check on bank for $600 paid C B Smith Shff."

1. Letter not found.

2. Charles B. Smith was deputy sheriff of Fauquier County. The nature of this transaction is unknown, but according to a later receipt Smith distributed money received from JM in payment of various debts, perhaps to satisfy legal judgments. (Receipt, 11 Apr. 1828 [owned by Mrs. James R. Green, Markham, Va., 1971]).

3. Letter not found. Alexander Marshall was possibly Alexander J. Marshall (1803–82), son of JM's brother Charles Marshall. He studied law but ceased to practice after becoming clerk of Fauquier Court in 1832, a post he held for fourteen years (Paxton, *Marshall Family*, 148; *Fauquier County, Virginia* [Warrenton, Va., 1959], 74).

4. Maria Willis (1784–1835) was Claudia Marshall's aunt (Paxton, *Marshall Family*, 102).

United States v. Casares and Others
Opinion
U.S. Circuit Court, Virginia, 12 July 1827

The trial of Jose Hilario Casares, Felix Barbeito, and Jose Morando, Spanish subjects indicted for murder and piracy, took place at a special session of the U.S. Circuit Court held in the hall of the House of Delegates in the capitol at

Richmond from 9 to 19 July 1827. The alleged crimes occurred on board the American brig *Crawford* during a voyage from Matanzas, Cuba, to New York in late May and early June 1827. The Spaniards were accused of being the accomplices of Alexander Tardy, a Frenchman and notorious pirate, in murdering most of the crew and passengers of the *Crawford* and then seizing the vessel with the object of going to Hamburg, Germany. With Tardy in command the ship proceeded to the Chesapeake to obtain provisions at Norfolk, anchoring off Old Point Comfort on the evening of 12 June. Soon thereafter the mate of the *Crawford* (whose life had been spared in order to serve as a navigator on the transatlantic voyage) escaped and notified local authorities of the situation on board the vessel. Rather than be captured, Tardy committed suicide by cutting his throat. In the meantime, the three Spaniards managed to escape and commence a flight that took them to Hampton and then across the James River to Isle of Wight County, where they were captured on 14 June. Confined to the jail at Norfolk, the prisoners were eventually brought by steamboat to Richmond in early July. On 9 July a grand jury was sworn but adjourned until the arrival of witnesses on 11 July. After hearing testimony on five indictments (one for piracy and four for murder) drawn by U.S. Attorney Stanard, the grand jury on 11 and 12 July returned true bills. In a hall "filled to overflowing" on 12 July the prisoners heard the indictments read and interpreted to them by Adolphus Crozet, a professor of the French and Spanish languages. They requested Gustavus Schmidt (1795–1877), a native of Sweden who was then practicing law in Richmond, to defend them. The court assigned Benjamin W. Leigh to assist in the defense (*Richmond Enquirer,* 19, 22 June, 3, 6, 10, 13 July 1827; U.S. Cir. Ct., Va., Ord. Bk. XII, 198–204; Glenn R. Conrad, ed., *A Dictionary of Louisiana Biography* [2 vols.; New Orleans, La., 1988], II, 722–23).

OPINION

Monday, the 16th of July, having been appointed as the day of their trial, Mr. Schmidt, on behalf of the prisoners, prayed that the Court would award that a jury be summoned *de medietate linguæ,* which, after some discussion, was awarded, the Court declaring, that though not perfectly satisfied that the prisoners were entitled to claim it as a right, under the existing laws of the United States, still, from a desire to afford the prisoners an impartial trial, it felt disposed to grant their request, if left to the exercise of its discretion.[1]

The Court further said, that as in the State Courts, the practice of which was adopted by the Circuit Court, it was admitted that the Judges had at least a discretionary power to award a jury *de medietate linguæ* if desired by an alien,[2] and the Act of Congress which had been referred to, to prove that in all trials in the United States' Courts, the jurors ought to be citizens of the United States,[3] did not, in his opinion, prescribe a practice differing from that adopted by the State Courts, (here the Judge examined the provisions of that act) it thought that in deciding on the motion, it was left in the exercise of a sound discretion, and would accordingly order a jury to be summoned composed of an equal number of aliens and citizens, although the execution of such order might, in the present instance, be attended with some inconvenience; and thereupon, the Court adjourned.

Printed, *A Brief Sketch of the Occurrences on Board the Brig Crawford*, . . . *Together with an Account of the Trial of the Three Spaniards* . . . (Richmond, Va., 1827), 8.

1. A jury *de medietate linguæ* was a mixed jury of citizens and foreigners. JM had previously heard a request for such a jury at the trial of Manuel Catacho, also accused of piracy, in Oct. 1823 (*PJM,* IX, 344 and n. 1, 346).

2. Virginia's act concerning juries provided that mixed juries could be "directed by the courts respectively." See *Revised Code of Va.,* I, 266; Conway Robinson, *The Practice in the Courts of Law and Equity in Virginia* (3 vols.; Richmond, Va., 1832–39), III, 152.

3. The Judiciary Act of 1789, sec. 29, stated that jurors in capital cases "shall have the same qualifications as are requisite for jurors by the laws of the State of which they are citizens, to serve in the highest courts of law of such State" (*U.S. Statutes at Large,* I, 88).

United States v. Casares and Others
Opinion
U.S. Circuit Court, Virginia, 16 July 1827

On Monday, 16 July 1827, the prisoners were arraigned and pleaded not guilty. Schmidt then submitted an affidavit on their behalf and a motion asking for a postponement of the trial until November. The reasons urged for the postponement were the great excitement and prejudice generated by newspaper accounts of the crime and the need for time to collect evidence from Cuba. After Stanard and Schmidt argued the motion, Marshall delivered the following opinion (U.S. Cir. Ct., Va., Ord. Bk. XII, 204–5 ; *Richmond Enquirer,* 17 July 1827; *A Brief Sketch,* 10–16).

OPINION

The *Court* then examined the grounds on which the motion was made, and declared, that it was convinced that no such excitement existed, as would prevent the prisoners from having an impartial trial; that if it prevailed, it must have been produced by the accounts circulated in the news-papers, and not by the sight of the transactions. It was true, that our feelings might be strongly affected by the mere narration of some horrid outrage; but not probable that such narration would so sway the understanding, as to prevent it long afterwards from exercising the judgment. The sight, indeed, of some frightful object or some bloody catastrophe, may affect the mind so strongly, as for sometime to deprive it of the coolness and equipoise necessary to deliberation; but, as in this particular instance, the crimes were committed on the high-sea; it was impossible that any person, who would be called upon to act as a juror, could have any knowledge of the transactions, derived from actual observation. It was the duty of the Court, impartially to administer the laws; and in the discharge of this duty, it was as much bound to prevent the guilty from escaping punishment, as it was to protect the accused in their right to an impartial trial. It felt desirous to do both, and as it was admitted, that if the witnesses were discharged it would be difficult again to collect them, the Court would feel constrained to order them into close confinement until November next, should it grant a continuance. This would be a positive evil, to which it would not resort unless it was absolutely necessary. The Court could not see any reason why the accused could not now have an impartial trial. The evidence which they wished to procure, might not be obtained, but admitting that it could, would it have any bearing on the charge? The offence was committed on the high-sea, and was expected to be proved by persons, who were eye-witnesses. In this aspect, neither the character of the accused, nor occurrences in the Island of Cuba, could have much influence on a jury, who would have to determine whether the facts proved, left no reasonable doubt of the guilt of the prisoners. The Court further declared, that it was certain that it felt no prepossessions unfavorable to the prisoners, and that as it possessed the power to protect them, *it would* certainly exercise that power, and grant a new trial, should it have the least reason to believe, that prejudice had influenced the verdict of guilty.

The motion was over-ruled.[1]

Printed, *A Brief Sketch of the Occurrences on Board the Brig Crawford, . . . Together with an Account of the Trial of the Three Spaniards . . .* (Richmond, Va., 1827), 16–17.

1. Leigh, who compiled and published a report of the trial, inserted the following passage after his report of JM's opinion: "[The above is but a slight sketch of the opinion of the Chief Justice, as the low tone of voice in which it was delivered, and the motions of the spectators, pressing forward to hear what was said, prevented many parts of it from being distinctly understood.]" (*A Brief Sketch,* 17).

United States v. Casares and Others
Sentence
U.S. Circuit Court, Virginia, 19 July 1827

At their request the prisoners were tried separately, in each case only on the indictment for piracy. The remainder of 16 July was taken up with the trial of Jose Hilario Casares, most of which was taken up with the testimony of the two principal witnesses, Edmund Dobson, the mate of the *Crawford,* and Ferdinand Ginoulhiac, a Frenchman who had been a passenger on the brig. After the presentation of evidence, the case was submitted without argument to the jury, which took only a few minutes to return a verdict of guilty. The trials of Felix Barbeito and Jose Morando took place on 17 and 18 July, the juries in each case quickly returning guilty verdicts. On 19 July the prisoners returned to court to hear the sentence pronounced

RICHMOND, AUGUST 21.

Execution of the Pirates.—In pursuance of the sentence of the Federal Court, the three Spaniards, Pepe, Couro and Felix were executed on Friday last. The history of the crimes for which these men had been sentenced, has been already published, as developed on their trials. Since they were convicted, they had, at times, evinced much contrition, and acknowledged the atrocity of their guilt. We have not been able to learn the extent of their communications to those who visited them in prison, and were enabled to converse with them in the Spanish language; but understand that some details have been collected, that will probably be given to the public.

They were taken from the jail of Henrico county about 11 o'clock. Several thousand persons had assembled about the jail. The Governor had ordered . . .

RICHMOND ENQUIRER REPORTS EXECUTION OF PIRATES

Execution of Jose Casares and others, convicted of piracy in the U.S. Circuit Court, reported in newspaper of 21 August 1827.

Courtesy of the Library of Virginia

(U.S. Cir. Ct., Va. Ord Bk. XII, 204–8; *Richmond Enquirer,* 20 July 1827; *A Brief Sketch,* 18–40).

SENTENCE

The Judge replied,[1] that it was his duty to execute the laws; and that they did not permit him to comply with the request made to him — that it would be happy for the prisoners, if their consciences were as much at peace as they professed — but that all, that was left to him, was to discharge the duty imposed upon him.

He then enquired of the Prisoners, whether they had any thing to say, why the sentence of the law should not be pronounced upon them. Through Dr. Lemosy (the Interpreter)[2] they requested time to hear from their friends in Havana, in order to obtain evidences of their character, &c — The Judge replied, that it was out of his power to suspend the course of the law — But, that every indulgence should be extended to them, which it was possible to grant; that they might communicate with their friends, and that facilities would be granted to them for this purpose: — he recommended to them to think of the awful situation in which they were placed; and assured them, that every means should be afforded them of communicating with the ministers of their own religion, (the Catholic.)

He then pronounced their sentence, and fixed the day of their execution to Friday the 17th of August.[3]

Printed, *Richmond Enquirer,* 20 July 1827.

1. Prior to sentencing, Leigh submitted affidavits signed by Casares and Barbeito protesting their innocence and requesting a delay (*Richmond Enquirer,* 20 July 1827; *A Brief Sketch,* 40–41).

2. Dr. Lemosy, who served as interpreter during the trial of Morando, was probably Frederick A. Lemosy (d. 1847), a Richmond resident (*A Brief Sketch,* 37; *Richmond Semi-Weekly Whig,* 9 Apr. 1847).

3. The prisoners were executed by hanging in Richmond on the appointed day, an event witnessed by a multitude of spectators "estimated at not less than 7000." Two of the prisoners suffered the ordeal twice, the rope having broken the first time (*Richmond Enquirer,* 21 Aug. 1827).

Autobiographical Sketch

EDITORIAL NOTE

In the summer of 1827 Joseph Story accepted an assignment to write a review of Marshall's *History of the Colonies* for the *North American Review.* Intending to supplement the review with a biographical notice of the author, Story wrote Marshall for information and received the letter below in reply. On 1 August 1827 Story wrote Jared Sparks, editor of the *North American Review:* "I have begun the article on Marshall's History, and shall complete it by the 1st of September. It has been hitherto delayed in expectation of a letter from the Chief Justice himself, to whom I sent a request for *facts*. I received a letter from him the day before yesterday. It is long and full of interesting matter, and will enable me to be very accurate as to his public character. I think the article may be made quite valuable from the materials so furnished. I shall use them in an ample manner."[1] Story's article, which appeared in the January 1828 issue of the *Review,* in fact devoted only a few of its forty printed pages to the *History,* focusing instead on the life and character of the chief justice.

Marshall's autobiographical letter remained in the possession of the Story family until the 1930s, when it was acquired by the William L. Clements Library at the University of Michigan. In 1937 the Clements Library published the letter for the first time, along with the draft and fair copy of Marshall's letter to Story of 30 December 1827 acknowledging receipt of an advance copy of the article.[2] Marshall did not date his autobiographical reminiscences, though at some later time Story wrote in the dateline at the top of the first page: "(Written in 1827) / JS." The editor of the 1937 edition made no attempt to assign a more precise date, but Story's letter to Sparks shows that the Massachusetts jurist received Marshall's letter on 30 July. As he noted in the first paragraph of his letter, the chief justice was prompted to set down the narrative of his life on receiving Story's "favour of the 14th inst." Marshall must have received this letter about the time he was finishing up the trial of Jose Casares and others, which ended on 19 July. He probably drafted his reply over several days, posting it around 25 July.

The letter to Story was the second autobiography composed by Marshall. The first, a highly compressed narrative from his birth to his appointment as chief justice, was embodied in a letter to Joseph Delaplaine in March 1818. Delaplaine intended to use it in a volume of his *Repository of the Lives and Portraits of Distinguished Americans* that was never published. The letter was subsequently published in a pamphlet in 1848 and in facsimile in 1852.[3] Although apparently not based on autobiographical material from Marshall, the earliest known biographical sketch of the chief justice appeared anonymously in the January 1815 number of the *Port Folio,* a Philadelphia magazine. The author has recently been identified as John Wickham, Marshall's close friend and Richmond neighbor. As suggested by the imprecise dating of his subject's birth as "about the year 1756," Wickham wrote this piece with little or no assistance from Marshall. He relied on what was generally known about Marshall's public life to that time, supplemented by his own direct knowledge of the chief justice's character.[4]

As he confided to Sparks, Story did make "ample" use of Marshall's letter. Indeed, he artfully wove practically every sentence into his own narrative, incorporating passages verbatim or in close paraphrase. At various points, where Marshall was laconic or overly modest, Story amplified by quoting other sources or by interspersing his own commentary. For example, he supplemented Marshall's terse recital of his military service by inserting a recently published eyewitness account of Marshall at Valley Forge as a brave young officer of "superior intelligence." When the chief justice attributed his prosperous law practice to his "numerous military friends," who "took great interest in my favour," Story added: "And it is not improbable, that his success may have been somewhat aided by their commendation and support. But in our judgment his success was mainly owing to his own great talents and exertions." He fleshed out Marshall's role in the Virginia ratifying convention of 1788 by quoting extensively from his speeches as recorded in the published debates. Where Marshall wrote only a few offhand sentences about his service in Congress in 1799 and 1800, Story devoted two pages to the Virginian's celebrated speech defending the administration's conduct in the case of Jonathan Robbins.[5] Contemporary readers of the *North American Review* article might have suspected that the author obtained much of his information from the chief justice himself. Indeed, in recounting the meeting at which General Washington urged Marshall and Bushrod Washington to become candidates for Congress, Story came close to identifying his informant: "What took place upon that occasion, we happen to have the good fortune to know from an authentic source."[6] Justice Story relied on this "authentic source" on two other occasions, a sketch published in 1834 for the *National Portrait Gallery of Distinguished Americans,* and in his 1835 eulogy of the chief justice.[7]

Marshall composed this letter with great care and deliberation. The editors have accordingly treated it like his judicial opinions (and other documents intended for publication), assigning paragraph numbers and appending textual notes that show the changes he made while writing.

1. Herbert B. Adams, *The Life and Writings of Jared Sparks, Comprising Selections from His Journals and Correspondence* (2 vols.; Boston and New York, 1893), I, 341–42.

2. John Stokes Adams, ed., *An Autobiographical Sketch by John Marshall* (Ann Arbor, Mich., 1937).

3. JM to Joseph Delaplaine, 22 Mar. 1818, *PJM,* VIII, 186–88 and nn.; Adams, ed., *Autobiographical Sketch,* xii–xiii.

4. *Port Folio,* 3d. ser., V (1815), 1–6. Wickham's identity is established by a letter from Bushrod Washington to Wickham, 25 May 1814 (filed with Wickham's autograph draft of the sketch), ViHi.

5. *North American Review,* XXVI (1828), 8, 9, 12–16, 29–31.

6. Ibid., 28.

7. "John Marshall, LL.D., Chief Justice of the United States," in James Herring and James B. Longacre, *National Portrait Gallery of Distinguished Americans* (4 vols.; New York, 1834–39), I, 103–20; *A Discourse Upon the Life, Character, and Services of the Honorable John Marshall . . .* (Boston, 1835).

To Joseph Story

My Dear Sir   [Richmond, ca. 25 July 1827]

The events of my life are too unimportant, and have too little interest ¶1 for any person not of my immediate family, to render them worth communicating or preserving. I felt therefore some difficulty in commencing their detail, since the meer act of detailing, exhibits the appearance of attaching consequence to them; — a difficulty which was not overcome till the receipt of your favour of the 14th. inst.[1] If I conquer it now, it is because the request is made by a partial and highly valued friend.

I was born on the 24th. of Septr. 1755 in the county of Fauquier, at ¶2 that time one of the frontier counties of Virginia.[2] My Father possessed scarcely any fortune, and had received a very limited education; but was a man to whom nature had been bountiful, and who had assiduously improved her gifts. He superintended my education, and gave me an early taste for history and for poetry.[3] At the age of twelve I had transcribed Pope's essay on man, with some of his moral essays.

¶3   There being at that time no grammar school in the part of the country in which my Father resided I was sent, at fourteen, about one hundred miles from home, to be placed undr. the tuition of Mr. Campbell a clergy-man of great respectability. I remained with him one year, after which I was brought home and placed under the care of a Scotch gentleman who was just introduced into the parish as Pastor, and who resided in my Fathers family.[4] He remained in the family one year, at the expiration of which time I had commencd. reading Horace and Livy. I continued my studies with no other aid than my Dictionary. My Father superintended the English part of my education, and to his care I am indebted for anything valuable which I may have acquired in my youth. He was my only intelligent companion; and was both a watchfull parent and an affection-ate instructive friend. The young men within my reach were entirely uncultivated; and the time I passed with them was devoted to hardy athletic exercises.

¶4   About the time I entered my eighteenth year, the controversy between Great Britain and her colonies had assumed so serious an aspect as al-most to monopolize the attention of the old and the young. I engaged in it with all the zeal and enthusiasm which belonged to my age; and de-voted more time to learning the first rudiments of military exercise in an Independent company of the gentlemen of the county, to training a militia company in the neighbourhood, and to the political essays of the day, than to the classics or to Blackstone.

¶5   In the summer of 1775 I was appointed a first lieutenant in a company of minute men designed for actual servic⟨e⟩, who were assembled in Battalion on the first of September. In a few days we were ordered to march into the lower country for the purpose of defending it against a small regular and predatory force commanded by Lord Dunmore. I was engaged in the action at the Great Bridge; and was in Norfolk when it was set on fire by a detachment from the British ships lying in the river, and afterwards when the remaining houses were burnt by orders from the Committee of safety.

¶6   In July 1776 I was appointed first Lieutenant in the 11th. Virginia regiment on continental establishment; and, in the course of the suc-ceeding winter marched to the north, where, in May 1777, I was pro-moted to the rank of Captain. I was in the skirmish at iron hill where the Light Infantry was engaged; and in the battles of Brandy Wine, German town, and Monmouth.

¶7   As that part of the Virginia line which had not marched to Charleston was dissolving by the expiration of the terms for which the men had enlisted, the officers were directed to return home in the winter of 1779–80, in order to take charge of such men as the legislature should raise for

them. I availed myself of this inactive interval for attending a course of
law lectures given by Mr. Wythe, and of lectures of Natural philosophy
given by Mr. Madison then President of William and Mary College. The
vacation commenced in july, when I left the University, and obtained a
license to practice law. In October I returned to the army, and continued
in service until the termination of Arnolds invasion after which, in February 1781, before the invasion of Phillips, there being a redundancy of
Officers, I resigned my commission. I had formed a strong attachment to
the young lady whom I afterwards married; and, as we had more officers
than soldiers, thought I might without violating the duty I owed my country, pay some attention to my future prospects in life.

It was my design to go immediately to the bar; but the invasion of   ¶8
Virginia soon took place, and the courts were closed till the capitulation
of Lord Cornwallis. After that event the courts were opened and I commenced practice.

In the spring of 1782 I was elected a member of the legislature; and,   ¶9
in the autumn of the same year was chosen a member of the Executive Council. In January 1783 I was married to Miss Ambler the second
daughter of our then Treasurer,⁵ and in april 1784 resigned my seat at
the Council board in order to return to the bar. In the same month I was
again elected a member of the legislature for the county of Fauquier of
which I was only a nominal resident having resided actually in Richmond
as a membe⟨r⟩ of the Council. Immediately after the election I established myself in Richmond for the purpose of practising law in the superior courts of Virginia.

My extensive acquaintance in the army was of great service to me. My   ¶10
numerous military friends, who were dispersed over the state, took great
interest in my favour, and I was more successful than I had reason to
expect. In April 1787, I was elected into the legislature for the county in
which Richmond stands; and though devoted to my profession, entered
with a good deal of spirit into the politics of the state. The topics of the
day were paper money, the collection of taxes, the preservation of public
faith, and the administration of justice. Parties were nearly equally divided on all these interesting subjects; and the contest concerning them
was continually renewed. The state of the Confederacy was also a subject
of deep solicitude to our statesmen. Mr. James Madison had been for two
or three years a leading member of the House of Delegates, and was the
parent of the resolution for appointing members to a general Convention to be held at Philadelphia for the purpose of revising the confederation. The question whether a continuance of the Union or a separation
of the states was most to be desired was sometimes discussed; and either
side of the question was supported without reproach. Mr. Madison was
the enlightened advocate of Union and of an efficient federal government; but was not a member of the legislature when the plan of the
constitution was proposed to the states by the general Convention. It was

at first favorably received; but Mr. P. Henry, Mr. G Mason, and several other gentlemen of great influence were much opposed to it, and permitted no opportunity to escape of inveighing against it and of communicating their prejudices to others. In addition to state jealousy and state pride, which operated powerfully in all the large states, there were some unacknowledged motive⟨s⟩ of no inconsiderable influence in Virginia. In the course of the session, the unceasing efforts of the enemies of the constitution made a deep impression; and before its close, a great majority showed a decided hostility to it. I took an activ⟨e⟩ part in the debates on this question and was uniform in support of the proposed constitution.

¶11   When I recollect the wild and enthusiastic democracy with which my political opinions of that day were tinctured, I am disposed to ascribe my devotion to the union, and to a government competent to its preservation, at least as much to casual circumstances as to judgement. I had grown up at a time when a love of union and resistance to the claims of Great Britain were the inseparable inmates of the same bosom; when patriotism and a strong fellow feeling with our suffering fellow citizens of Boston were identical; when the maxim "united we stand, divided we fall" was the maxim of every orthodox American; and I had imbibed these sentiments so thoughroughly that they constituted a part of my being. I carried them with me into the army where I found myself associated with brave men from different states who were risking life and every thing valuable in a common cause beleived by all to be most precious; and where I was confirmed in the habit of considering America as my country, and Congress as my government. I partook largely of the sufferings and feelings of the army, and brought with me into civil life an ardent devotion to its interests. My immediate entrance into the state legislature opened to my view the causes which had been chiefly instrumental in augmenting those sufferings, and the general tendency of state politics convinced me that no safe and permanent remedy could be found but in a more efficient and better organized general government. The questions too which were perpetually recurring in the state legislatures, and which brought annually into doubt principles which I thought most sacred, which proved that everything was afloat, and that we had no safe anchorage ground, gave a high value in my estimation to that article in the constitution which imposes restrictions on the states. I was consequently a determined advocate for its adoption, and became a candidate for the convention to which it was to be submitted.[6]

¶12   The county in which I resided was decidedly antifederal; but I was at that time popular, and parties had not yet become so bitter as to extinguish the private affections.

¶13   A great majority of the people of Virginia was antifederal; but in several of the counties most opposed to the adoption of the constitution, individuals of high character and great influence came forward as candidates and were elected from personal motives. After an ardent and eloquent discussion to which justice never has been and never can be done, during which the constitution was adopted by nine states, the question was carried in the affirmative by a majority of eight voices.

I felt that those great principles of public policy which I considered ¶14 as essential to the general happiness were secured by this measure & I willingly relinquished public life to devote myself to my profession. Indeed the county was so thoroughly antifederal, & parties had become so exasperated, that my election would have been doubtful. This however was not my motive for withdrawing from the legislature. My practice had become very considerable, and I could not spare from its claims on me so much time as would be necessary to maintain such a standing in the legislature as I was desirous of preserving. I was pressed to become a candidate for Congress, and, though the district was unequivocally antifederal I could have been elected because that party was almost equally divided between two candidates who were equally obstinate and much embittered against each other. The struggle between the ambition of being engaged in the organization of the government, and the conviction of the injury which would be sustained by my private affairs was at length terminated in the victory of prudence, after which the federalists set up and elected Colonel Griffin, who obtained rather more than one third of the votes in the district which constituted a plurality.

Colonel Griffin named me to General Washington as the attorney for ¶15 the district, an office which I had wished, but I declined accepting it because at that time the circuit courts of the United States were held at two distinct places far apart, and distant from the seat of government where the superiour courts of the state sat. Consequently I could not attend them regularly without some detriment to my state practice. Before this inconvenience was removed the office was conferred on another gentleman.[7]

In December 1788 the legislature passed an act allowing a representa- ¶16 tive to the city of Richmond, and I was almost unanimously invited to become a candidate. The city was federal. I yielded to the general wish partly because a man changes his inclination after retiring from public life, partly because I found the hostility to the government so strong in the legislature as to require from its friends all the support they could give it, and partly because the capitol was then completed, and the courts and the legislature sat in the same building, so that I could without much inconvenience ⟨leave?⟩ the bar to take part in any debate in which I felt a particular interest.

I continued in the assembly for the years 1789 & 1790 & 1791, during ¶17 which time almost every important measure of the government was discussed, and the whole funding system was censured; that part of it especially which assumes the state debts was pronounced unconstitutional.

After the session of 1791 I again withdrew from the assembly, determined to bid a final adieu to political life.

¶18   The arrival and conduct of Mr. Genet excited great sensation throughout the southern states. We were all strongly attached to France — scarcely any man more strongly than myself. I sincerely beleived human liberty to depend in a great measure on the success of the French revolution. My partiality to France however did not so entirely pervert my understanding as to render me insensible to the danger of permitting a foreign minister to mingle himself in the management of our affairs, and to intrude himself between our government and people. In a public meeting of the citizens of Richmond, some of the earliest if not the very first resolutions were passed expressing strong disapprobation of the irregular conduct of Mr. Genet, our decided sense of the danger of foreign influence, and our warm approbation of the proclamation of neutrality. These resolutions, and the address to the President which accompanied them, were drawn and supported by me.[8]

¶19   The resentments of the great political party which led Virginia had been directed towards me for some time, but this measure brought it into active operation. I was attacked with great virulence in the papers and was so far honoured in Virginia as to be associated with Alexander Hamilton, at least so far as to be termed his instrument. With equal vivacity, I defended myself and the measures of the government. My constant effort was to show that the conduct of our government respecting its foreign relations were such as a just self respect and a regard for our rights as a sovereign nation rendered indispensable, and that our independence was brought into real danger by the overgrown & inordinate influence of France.[9] The public & frequent altercations in which I was unavoidably engaged gradually weakened my decision never again to go into the legislature, & I was beginning to think of changing my determination on that subject, when the election in the spring of 1795 came on.

¶20   From the time of my withdrawing from the legislature two opposing candidates had divided the city, the one was my intimate friend whose sentiments were very much those which I had entertained, and the other was an infuriated politician who thought every resistance of the will of France subserviency to Britain, and an adhesion to the coalition of despots against liberty.[10] Each election between these gentlemen, who were both popular, had been decided by a small majority; & that which was approaching was entirely doubtful. I attended at the polls to give my vote early & return to the court which was then in session at the other end of the town. As soon as the election commenced a gentleman came forward and demanded that a poll should be taken for me. I was a good deal surprized at this entirely unexpected proposition & declared my decided dissent. I said that if my fellow citizens wished it I would become a candidate at the next succeeding election, but that I could not consent to serve this year because my wishes & my honour were engaged for one of the candidates. I then voted for my friend & left the polls for the court which was open and waiting for me. The gentleman said that he had a right to demand a poll for whom he pleased, & persisted in his demand that one should be opened for me — I might if elected refuse to obey the voice of my constituents if I chose to do so. He then gave his vote for me.

As this was entirely unexpected — not even known to my brother who ¶21 though of the same political opinions with myself, was the active & leading partisan of the candidate against whom I had voted, the election was almost suspended for ten or twelve minutes, and a consultation took place among the principal freeholders. They then came in and in the ⟨e⟩vening information was brought me that I was elected. I regretted this for the sake of my friend. In other respects I was well satisfied at being again in the assembly.

Throughout that part of the year which followed the advice of the ¶22 senate to ratify Mr. Jays treaty, the whole country was agitated with that question. The commotion began at Boston and seemed to rush through the Union with a rapidity and violence which set human reason and common sense at defiance. The first effort was to deter the President from ratifying the instrument — the next to induce Congress to refuse the necessary appropriations. On this occasion too a meeting of the citizens of Richmond was convened and I carried a series of resolutions approving the conduct of the President.[11]

As this subject was one in which every man who mingled with public ¶23 affairs was compelled to take part, I determined to make myself master of it, and for this purpose perused carefully all the resolutions which were passed throughout the United States condemning the treaty and compared them with the instrument itself.[12] Accustomed as I was to political misrepresentation, I could not view without some surprize the numerous gross misrepresentations which were made on this occasion; and the virulent asperity, with which the common terms of decency in which nations express their compacts with each other, was assailed. The constitutionality of the treaty was attacked with peculiar vehemence, and, strange as it may appear, there was scarcely a man in Virginia who did not beleive that a commercial treaty was an infringement of the power given to Congress to regulate commerce. Several other articles of the treaty were pronounced unconstitutional; but, on the particular ground of commerce, the objectors beleived themselves to be invulnerable.

As it was foreseen that an attempt would be made in the legislature to ¶24 prevent the necessary appropriations, one or two of my cautious friends advised me not to engage in the debate. They said that the part which it was anticipated I would take, would destroy me totally. It was so very unpopular that I should scarcely be permitted to deliver my sentiments, and would perhaps be treated rudely. I answered that the subject would not be introduced by me; but, if it should be brought before the house by others, I should undoubtedly take the part which became an independent member. The subject was introduced; and the constitutional objections were brought forward most triumphantly. There was perhaps never a political question on which any division of opinion took place which was susceptible of more complete demonstration; and I was fully prepared not only on the words of the constitution and the universal practice of nations, but to show on the commercial proposition especially, which was selected by our antagonists as their favorite ground, that Mr. Jefferson, and the whole delegation from Virginia in Congress, as well as all our leading men in the convention on both sides of the question, had manifested unequivocally the opinion that a commercial treaty was constitutional. I had reason to know that a politician even in times of violent party spirit maintains his respectability by showing his strength; and is most safe when he encounters prejudice most fearlessly. There was scarcely an intelligent man in the house who did not yield his opinion on the constitutional question. The resolution however was carried on the inexpediency of the treaty.

¶25   I do not know whether the account given of this debate, which was addressed to some members of Congress in letters from Richmond, and was published, was written by strangers in the gallery or by some of my partial friends.[13] Be this as it may my arguments were spoken of in such extravagant terms as to prepare the federalists of Congress to receive me w⟨ith⟩ marked attention and favour, the ensuing winter when I attended in Philadelphia to argue the cause respecting British debts before the Supreme court of the United States.[14] I then became acquainted with Mr. Cabot, Mr. Ames, & Mr. Dexter & Mr. Sedgewic, of Massachusetts, with Mr. Wadsworth of Connecticut, and with Mr. King of New York. I was delighted with these gentlemen. The particular subject which introduced me to their notice was at that time so interesting, and a Virginian who supported with any sort of reputation the measures of the government was such a *rara avis,* that I was received by them all with a degree of kindness which I had not anticipated. I was particularly intimate with Ames, & could scarcely gain credit with him when I assured him that the appropriations would be seriously opposed in Congress.

¶26   It was about or perhaps a little after this time that I was invited by General Washington to take the office of Attorney General of the United States. I was too deeply engaged in the practice in Virginia to accept this office, though I should certainly have preferred it to any other.[15]

¶27   I continued in the assembly though I took no part in the current business. It was I think in the session of 1796–97 that I was engaged in a debate which called forth all the strength and violence of party. Some Federalist moved a resolution expressing the high confidence of the house in the virtue, patriotism, and Wisdom of the President of the United States. A motion was made to strike out the work "wisdom." In the debate the whole course of the administration was reviewed, and the whole talent of each party was brought into action. Will it be believed that the word was retained by a very small majority. A very small majority in the legislature of Virginia acknowledged the Wisdom of General Washington.[16]

When the cabinet decided on recalling Mr. Monroe from France, the President invited me to succeed him. But I thought my determination to remain at the bar unalterable, and declined the office. My situation at the bar appeared to me to be more independent and not less honorable than any other, and my preference for it was decided.[17]   ¶28

In June 1797 I was placed by Mr. Adams, then President of the United States, in the commission for accomodating our differences with France,[18] and received a letter requesting my attendance in Philadelphia in order to receive the communications of the government respecting the mission previous to my embarcation. It was the first time in my life that I had ever hesitated concerning the acceptance of office. My resolution concerning my profession had sustained no change. Indeed my circumstances required urgently that I should adhere to this resolution because I had engaged with some others in the purchase of a large estate the arrangements concerning which were not yet made. On the other hand I felt a very deep interest in the state of our controversy with France. I was most anxious and believed the government to be most anxious for the adjustment of our differences with that republic. I felt some confidence in the good dispositions which I should carry with me into the negotiation, and in the temperate firmness with which I should aid in the investigations which would be made. The subject was familiar to me, and had occupied a large portion of my thoughts. I will confess that the *eclat* which would attend a successful termination of the differences between the two countries had no small influence over a mind in which ambition, though subjected to controul, was not absolutely extinguished. But the consideration which decided me was this. The mission was temporary, and could not be of long duration. I should return after a short absence, to my profession, with no diminution of character, & I trusted, with no diminution of practice. My clients would know immediately that I should soon return & I could make arrangements with the gentlemen of the bar which would prevent my business from suffering in the meantime. I accepted the appointment and repaired to Philadelphia where I embarked for Amsterdam. I found General Pinckney at the Hague, and we obtained passports from the Minister of France at that place to secure our passage in safety to Paris. While at the Hague intelligence was received of that revolution which was effected in the French government by the seizure of two of the Directory and of a majority of the legislature by a military force acting under the orders of three of the Directory combined with a minority of the councils. This revolution blasted every hope of an accomodation between the United States and France.   ¶29

On reaching Paris General Pinckney and myself communicated our arrival to Mr. Talleyrand & expressed a wish to suspend all negotiation till   ¶30 our colleague should be united to us. In a week or ten days Mr. Gerry joined us, and we immediately addressed ourselves to the minister. The failure of our attempts at negotiation is generally known. A journal which I kept exhibits a curious account of transactions at Paris.[19] As soon as I became perfectly convinced that our efforts at conciliation must prove abortive I proposed that we should address a memorial to Mr. Talleyrand in which we should review fully the reciprocal complaints of the two countries against each other, and bring the whole controversy, at least our view of it before the French government in like manner as if we had been actually accredited.[20] My motive for this was that if the memorial should fail to make its due impression on the government of France, it would show the sincerity with which we had laboured to effect the objects of our mission, and could not fail to bring the controversy fairly before the American People and convince them of the earnestness with which the American government sought a reconciliation with France. General Pinckney concurred with me in sentiment and we acted most cordially together. I found in him a sensible man, and one of high and even romantic honour. Mr. Gerry took a different view of the whole subject. He was unwilling to do anything, and it was with infinite difficulty we prevailed on him to join us in the letter to the minister of exterior relations. It was with the same difficulty we prevailed on him to sign the reply to this answer of the Minister.[21] We were impatient to hasten that reply from a fear that we should be ordered to leave France before it could be sent. We knew very well that this order would come and there was a trial of skill between the minister and ourselves, (Genl. Pinckney & myself) he endeavouring to force us to demand our passports, we endeavouring to impose on him the necessity of sending them. At length the passports came and I hastened to Bordeaux to embark for the United States. On my arrival in New York I found the whole country in a state of agitation on the subject of our mission. Our dispatches had been published and their effect on public opinion had fully equalled my anticipations.

¶31   I returned to Richmond with a full determination to devote myself entirely to my professional duties, and was not a little delighted to find that my prospects at the bar had sustained no material injury from my absence. My friends welcomed my return with the most flattering reception, and pressed me to become a candidate for Congress. My refusal was peremptory, and I did not believe it possible that my determination could be shaken. I was however mistaken.

¶32   General Washington gave a pressing invitation to his nephew, the present Judge, & myself, to pass a few days at Mount Vernon. He urged us both very earnestly to come into Congress & Mr. Washington assented to his wishes. I resisted, on the ground of my situation, & the necessity of attending to my pecuniary affairs. I can never forget the manner in which he treated this objection.

¶33   He said there were crises in national affairs which made it the duty of a

citizen to forego his private for the public interest. We were then in one of
them. He detailed his opinions freely on the nature of our controversy
with France and expressed his conviction that the best interests of our
country depended on the character of the ensuing Congress. He concluded a very earnest conversation, one of the most interesting I was ever
engaged in, by asking my attention to his situation. He had retired from
the Executive department with the firmest determination never again to
appear in a public capacity. He had communicated this determination to
the public, and his motives for adhering to it were too strong not to be
well understood. Yet I saw him pledged to appear once more at the head
of the American army. What must be his convictions of duty imposed by
the present state of American affairs?

I yielded to his representations & became a candidate. I soon after-   ¶34
wards received a letter from the secretary of state offering me the seat on
the bench of the supreme court which had become vacant by the death of
Judge Iredell; but my preference for the bar still continued & I declined
it.[22] Our brother Washington was intercepted in his way to Congress by
this appointment.

My election was contested with unusual warmth, but I succeeded, and   ¶35
took my seat in the House of Representatives in Decr. 1799. There was a
good deal of talent in that Congress both for and against the ad⟨m⟩in-
istration, and I contracted friendships with several gentlemen whom I
shall never cease to value. The greater number of them are no more.

In May 1800, as I was about to leave Philadelphia (though Congress   ¶36
was still in session) for the purpose of attending the courts in Richmond,
I stepped into the war office in order to make some enquiries respecting
patents for some of my military friends, and was a good deal struck with a
strange sort of mysterious coldness which I soon observed in the countenance of Mr. McHenry, the secretary of war, with whom I had long been
on terms of friendly intimacy. I however prosecuted my enquiries until
they brought me into conversation with Mr. Fitzsimmons the chief clerk,
who congratulated me on being placed at the head of that department,
and expressed the pleasure it gave all those who were engaged in it. I did
not understand him, and was really surprized at hearing that I had been
nominated to the senate as secretary of war. I did not believe myself to be
well qualified for this department, and was not yet willing to abandon my
hopes of reinstating myself at the bar. I therefore addressed a letter to
Mr. Adams making my acknowledgements for his notice of me, and requesting that he would withdraw my name from the senate, as I was not
willing openly to decline a place in an administration which I was disposed cordially to support.[23] After writing this letter I proceeded immediately to Virginia.

Mr. Adams did not withdraw my name, & I believe the nomination was   ¶37
approved. I had not been long in Virginia when the rupture between Mr.
Adams and Mr. Pickering took place, and I was nominated to the senate

as secretary of state. I never felt more doubt than on the question of accepting or declining this office. My decided preference was still for the bar. But on becoming a candidate for Congress I was given up as a lawyer, and considered generally as entirely a political man. I lost my business all together, and perceived very clearly that I could not recover any portion of it without retiring from Congress. Even then I could not hope to regain the ground I had lost. This experiment however I was willing to make, and would have made had my political enemies been quiet. But the press teemed with so much falsehood, with such continued and irritating abuse of me that I could not bring myself to yield to it. I could not conquer a stubbornness of temper which determines a man to make head against and struggle with injustice. I felt that I must continue a candidate for Congress, and consequently could not replace myself at the bar. On the other hand the office was precisely that which I wished, and for which I had vanity enough to think myself fitted. I should remain in it while the party remained in power; should a revolution take place it would at all events relieve me from the competition for Congress without yielding to my adversaries, and enable me to return once more to the bar in the character of a lawyer having no possible view to politics. I determined to accept the office.

¶38   I was very well received by the President, and was on very cordial terms with all the cabinet except Mr. Wolcot. He at first suspected that I was hostile to the two exsecretaries, & to himself, because they were all three supposed to be unfriendly to the President to whom I was truely attached. My conduct soon convinced him however that I had no feeling of that sort, after which I had the satisfaction of finding myself on the same cordial footing with him as with the rest of the cabinet.

¶39   On the resignation of Chief Justice Ellsworth I recommended Judge Patteson as his successor. The President objected to him, and assigned as his ground of objection that the feelings of Judge Cushing would be wounded by passing him and selecting a junior member of the bench. I never heard him assign any other objection to Judge Patteson, though it was afterwards suspected by many that he was believed to be connected with the party which opposed the second attempt at negotiation with France. The President himself mentioned Mr. Jay, and he was nominated to the Senate. When I waited on the President with Mr. Jays letter declining the appointment he said thoughtfully "Who shall I nominate now?" I replied that I could not tell, as I supposed that his objection to Judge Patteson remained. He said in a decided tone "I shall not nominate him." After a moments hesitation he said "I believe I must nominate you." I had never before heard myself named for the office and had not even thought of it. I was pleased as well as surprized, and bowed in silence. Next day I was nominated, and, although the nomination was suspended by the friends of Judge Patteson, it was I believe when taken up unanimously approved. I was unfeignedly gratified at the appointment, and have had much reason to be so. I soon received a very friendly letter from Judge Patteson congratulating me on the occasion and expressing ⟨his?⟩ hopes that I might long retain the office. I felt truely grateful for th⟨e⟩ real cordiality towards me which uniformly marked his conduct.

I have my dear Sir been much more minute and tedious in detail than ¶40 the occasion required, but you will know how to prune, condense, exclude, and vary. I give you the materials of which you will make some thing or nothing as you please — taking this only with you, that you will be sure to gratify me by pursuing precisely the tract you had marked out for yourself, & admitting nothing which may overload the narrative according to the original plan. Do not insert any thing from the suspicion that I may look for it because I have introduced it into my narrative.

It would seem as if new and perplexing questions on jurisdiction will ¶41 never be exhausted. That which you mention is one of the strongest possible illustrations, so far as respects the original act, of the necessity in some instances of controuling the letter by the plain spirit of the law. It is impossible that a suit brought by the U.S. can be within the intention of the exception. There is however great difficulty in taking the case out of the letter. The argument you state is very strong and I am much inclined to yield to it. As no private citizen can sue in a district court on a promissory note I am much inclined to restrain the exception to those district courts which have circuit court jurisdiction. But the difficulty is I think removed by the act of the 3d. of March 1815 and by the decision of the last term.[24] I speak of that decision however from memory as I have not yet received 12th. Wheaton.

Farewell. With the highest respect & esteem, I am your

J MARSHALL

ALS, MiU-C. Story's note in blank dateline: "(Written in 1827 / JS.)." Date assigned on basis of evidence presented in preceding editorial note. For JM's deletions and interlineations, see Textual Notes below.

1. Letter not found.

2. JM was actually born in southeastern Prince William County, which became part of the newly established Fauquier County in 1759.

3. In his 1818 letter to Delaplaine, JM gave a fuller account of his ancestry, including his grandparents on both sides. He also noted that he was the oldest of fifteen children (JM to Delaplaine, 22 Mar. 1818, *PJM*, VIII, 187, 188).

4. James Thomson.

5. In his 1818 sketch, JM identified the treasurer as Jaquelin Ambler and noted that he was the third son of Richard Ambler, "a gentleman who had migrated from England, & settled at York Town in Virginia" (ibid., 187).

6. Story declined to use this paragraph in his *North American Review* article.

7. The U.S. Circuit Court for Virginia originally met alternately at Charlottesville and Williamsburg. Richmond became the permanent meeting place in May 1791 (*U.S. Statutes at Large*, I, 75, 217).

8. *PJM*, II, 196–200.

9. JM alluded to his "Aristides" and "Gracchus" newspaper essays of 1793 (*PJM*, II, 201–7, 221–28, 231–38, 238–47).

10. The "intimate friend" was John Harvie, who represented Richmond in the House of Delegates in 1793 and 1794. Harvie's son Jaquelin later married JM's daughter Mary. The "infuriated politician" was probably William Foushee, who represented Richmond in the 1791 session (Earl G. Swem and John W. Williams, *A Register of the General Assembly of Virginia, 1776–1918* [Richmond, 1918], 36, 40, 42).

11. This meeting occurred in Apr. 1796 (*PJM*, III, 22–24).

12. After mentioning the meeting of Apr. 1796 in which he carried resolutions approving the president's conduct, JM here shifts the chronology back to Nov. 1795, when the Virginia legislature debated the constitutionality of the Jay Treaty.

13. Northern newspapers published an extract of a letter from Richmond, dated 20 Nov. 1795, containing this account of the debate: "The house of Assembly have been debating 3 days on the Constitutionality, and general policy of the treaty. . . Mr. Marshall has distinguished himself in a remarkable manner, and no language can do justice to his able remarks in favor of the treaty" (Philadelphia *Gazette of the United States,* 28 Nov. 1795; Boston *Independent Chronicle,* 7 Dec. 1795; Boston *Columbian Centinel,* 9 Dec. 1795).

14. Ware v. Hylton, argued in Feb. 1796 (*PJM*, III, 7–14; V, 317–29).

15. *PJM*, II, 319, 320.

16. This debate actually occurred in the Nov. 1795 session of the legislature. A motion proposed by the Federalists praised the president's "great abilities, wisdom, and integrity." A substitute motion, omitting "wisdom," passed the House of Delegates by a vote of 89 to 56. The Senate, however, restored the word and the House ultimately approved the Senate's amendment by a vote of 78 to 62. A similar debate also took place in the Nov. 1796 session, when the legislature prepared an address to the president on the occasion of his retirement from office. The Federalists moved a passage citing the president's conduct as "so strongly marked by wisdom in the cabinet, by valor in the field, and by the purest patriotism in both." The motion lost by eight votes, however, and the address adopted by the legislature omitted any reference to the president's "wisdom" (*Journal of the House of Delegates of . . . Virginia [1795]* [Richmond, Va., 1795], 28–29, 71–72; *Journal of the House of Delegates of . . . Virginia; 1796* [Richmond, Va.,1796], 65, 70, 71; *PJM*, III, 59; Richard R. Beeman, *The Old Dominion and the New Nation, 1788–1801* [Lexington, Ky., 1972], 150–51).

17. *PJM*, III, 31–33.

18. *PJM*, III, 86, 91.

19. *PJM*, III, 153–242.

20. *PJM*, III, 330–81.

21. *PJM*, III, 426–59.

22. *PJM*, III, 506, 508. This appointment was to replace James Wilson, who died in 1798. James Iredell died in 1799.

23. *PJM*, IV, 148–49.

24. The reference is to the case of U.S. v. Greene, which Justice Story decided at the Oct. 1827 term of the U.S. Circuit Court for Maine. In that opinion Story discussed the act of Mar. 1815 concerning the jurisdiction of the district courts and the Supreme Court's interpretation of that act in the 1827 case of Postmaster General v. Early (U.S. v. Greene, 26 Fed. Cas. 33; 12 Wheat. 144–52; *PJM*, X, 412–18).

Textual Notes

¶ 1	l. 6	conquer ~~this difficulty~~ ↑it↓ now, it
¶10	l. 4	1787, I was ~~again~~ elected
¶11	l. 5	time when ↑a love of↓ union and resistance
	ll. 18–19	instrumental in ~~pr~~ ↑aug↓ menting

	ll. 26–27	consequently a ~~decided~~ ↑determined↓ advocate
¶14	ll. 4–5	had become so ~~entirely~~ exasperated,
	l. 10	candidate for ~~the~~ Congress, and,
¶17	l. 1	1790 ~~during & I believe~~ & 1791
¶21	ll. 1–2	my brother who ↑though of the same political opinions with myself,↓ was the
	ll. 3–4	the election was ↑almost↓ suspended
¶22	l. 4	violence which ~~seemed to~~ set human
	l. 9	of the President ~~& I carrie~~.
¶24	l. 11	opinion took [erasure] place which
	l. 18	a commercial ~~question~~ ↑treaty↓ was
	ll. 23–24	inexpediency of the ~~inexpediency of the~~ treaty.
¶25	l. 9	Mr. Dexter ↑& Mr. Sedgewic,↓ of Massachusetts,
¶26	l. 1	a little ~~before~~ ↑after↓ this time
¶29	ll. 27–28	embarked for ~~Europe~~ Amsterdam.
¶30	ll. 5–6	generally known. ↑A journal which I kept exhibits a curious account of transactions at Paris.↓ As soon
	ll. 23–24	this answer ↑of the Minister.↓ We were
	l. 25	be ordered ~~out~~ to leave
	ll. 28–29	endeavouring to ~~force~~ ↑impose on↓ him
¶36	l. 3	war office ~~for the purpose of making~~ ↑ in order to make some↓ enquiries
	l. 4	military ↑friends,↓ and was
¶37	l. 20	events to ~~remove~~ ↑relieve ↓ me from
¶38	ll. 4–5	truely attached ~~I~~ ↑My conduct↓ soon
¶39	ll. 14–15	had not ~~myself~~ ↑even↓ thought of it.
	ll. 17–18	I believe ↑when taken up↓ unanimously
	ll. 20–21	on the ~~appointment~~ ↑occasion↓ and expressing
	l. 21	retain the ↑office.↓ I felt

To William T. Dwight

Sir[1]   Richmond August 7th. 1827.

I scarcely know how to apologize for having so long delayed my acknowlegements for your polite and flattering attention in transmitting me a copy of your oration before the Washington benevolent Society of Pennsylvania, delivered on the 22d of February last.[2] It reached this place during my absence on a visit from which I did not return till I was about to commence my circuit, and I have since been employed in official duties which were extended to an unusual length. I have now read your oration with pleasure and attention and thank you for the gratification you have given me.

The views you have taken of the character of our revolution, of the country in which it took place, of its era, of the character of the people who accomplished it, of its causes and of its consequences are entirely just and seem naturally connected with the Subject you were discussing[:] The character of that great man who contributed so essentially to one of the most interesting, perhaps the most interesting event in the history of the human race. Yet by introducing these views you have given Variety to the Subject which has been treated so frequently as to require no little ingenuity to suggest what has not been Said before.

Allow me to repeat my thanks for this flattering mark of your attention and to assure you that I am, with great respect, your obedt

J MARSHALL.

Tr, Beveridge-Marshall Papers, DLC. Addressed to Dwight in Philadelphia. Note by transcriber: "Copy of a letter written by John Marshall / Chief Justice of the United States to / William Theodore Dwight Esqre Philadelphia / Forwarded at the request of Mrs. Edward S. Dwight Smyrna, Delaware / The original being the property of his granddaughters / Mrs. Adele Dwight Garrison / Miss Elizabeth Bradford Dwight / 336 Sh. 15th. St / Philadelphia / Pa. / June 15th. 1913."

1. William Theodore Dwight (1795–1865), one of eight sons of Yale College president Timothy Dwight, graduated from Yale in 1813. After intermittently studying law and serving as a tutor at Yale, Dwight in 1819 went to Philadelphia to resume his law studies. He practiced law there until 1831, when he decided to enter the ministry. From 1832 to 1864 he was minister of the Third Congregational Church of Portland, Me. (Benjamin W. Dwight, *The History of the Descendants of John Dwight, of Dedham, Mass.* [2 vols.; New York, 1874], I, 205–6).

2. Dwight, *An Oration before the Washington Benevolent Society of Pennsylvania* (Philadelphia, 1827).

To Thomas S. Grimké

Sir[1]   Richmond August 7th. 1827

I had the pleasure of receiving some time past a copy of your Oration on the practicability and expediency of reducing the whole body of the law of South Carolina to a Code,[2] and sometime afterwards, your Address on the character and objects of Science delivered before the literary and philosophical Society of So: Carolina.[3] I trust you will excuse my not having made my acknowledgments for these marks of your polite consideration when I tell you that the first reached this place during my absence on a visit from which I did not return, till my circuit was about to commence & that I received the[m] while actually engaged in laborious official duties. I have now had leisure to read both with attention, & beg you to receive my thanks for the gratification you have given me. I concur entirely in the opinions that the body of the law, may be reduced to a Code, & that great advantages might result from this simplification of those rules which affect every Member of Society. The utility of the plan must depend on its execution, in which there is undoubtedly much difficulty. Those to whom the great work is committed, must select, condense,

& devise.[4] It will require the exercise of patient investigation, deliberation, & judgment, but the object is worth the effort.

You have presented in a strong point of view the influence of the Reformation on Science. I had always attached much importance to that great revolution in The human mind, but you have certainly given me new & more enlarged ideas on its effects. That it has increased the freedom of inquiry & discussion on subjects of the deepest interest is certain, & that freedom of discussion & inquiry invigorate the intellect is equally certain.

Allow me Sir, to repeat my acknowledgments for these flattering marks of polite attention, and to assure you that I am, With great respect, Your obt.

J MARSHALL

Tr, MiU-C. Tr of JM's letter followed by Tr of two other commendatory letters: from Samuel Gilman, "Cannonsborough," 15 June 1827, and from Whitemarsh B. Seabrook (1795–1855), "Edisto Island," 25 June 1827.

1. A graduate of Yale College (1807), Thomas Smith Grimké (1786–1834) was a South Carolina lawyer, educator, and reformer. He served as a state senator from 1826 to 1830. He advocated pacifism and higher education for women among other causes and supported the union during the nullification controversy.

2. *An Oration on the Practicability and Expediency of Reducing the Whole Body of the Law to the Simplicity and Order of a Code* (Charleston, S.C., 1827).

3. *An Address, on the Character and Objects of Science, and Especially the Influence of the Reformation on Science and Literature, Past, Present and Future, of Protestant Nations* (Charleston, S.C., 1827).

4. JM probably wrote "revise," which the copyist erroneously transcribed.

To Peter V. Daniel

Dear Sir   Warrenton Aug. 10th. 1827

Since my arrival at this place I find the Armory about to be erected in the neighborhood has excited a good deal of attention and produces of course a very respectable number of applications.[1] Some of my friends, leaning as is usual in such cases on any staff, and not *suspecting* its weakness, have applied to me to aid them. Although I am conscious of inability of [*sic*] serve them & have told them so, they press me to say something in their favour, & I cannot refuse to certify what is true.

Colonel Kemper wishes to undertake the building.[2] He is a man of great integrity and may I believe be depended on. I, of course, am not a judge of his skill as a workman, but he has lately built a jail at this place and his work has given entire satisfaction. I understand that it is generally thought to be remarkably well executed.

Mr. Fauntler[o]y is a lawyer of this place who is probably known to you as he was in the legislature a few years past.[3] He is a gentleman very generally esteemed and of a character entirely amiable & unexceptionable. He offers as a candidate for the superintendance of the institution. I do not know the title of the office. I am convinced that he is worthy of confidence.[4] With great respect, I am dear Sir your obedt.

J MARSHALL

Mr. Briggs is acquainted with both Colo. Kemper and Mr. Fauntleroy.

ALS, Vi. Addressed to Daniel at Richmond; postmarked (by hand) Warrenton, 12 Aug. Endorsed "Judge Marshall / in favour Col Kemper / and Mr Fauntleroy / Recd 20 Aug 1827."

1. An act adopted by the General Assembly in Mar. 1827 directed the executive "to purchase a site for the erection of one additional arsenal, and contract for the erection of suitable buildings for the same." Gov. William B. Giles and the executive council chose Warrenton "as the most eligible site" (*Supplement to the Revised Code of the Laws of Virginia* [Richmond, Va., 1833], 83–84; *Journal of the House of Delegates of the Commonwealth of Virginia* [Dec. 1827], 2).

2. Charles Kemper (1756–1841), of the prominent family whose seat was Cedar Grove (now Clovelly) in Fauquier County, was an officer of the Virginia Continental Line during the Revolution and later served as surveyor of the county (Willis Miller Kemper and Harry Linn Wright, eds., *Genealogy of the Kemper Family in the United States* [Chicago, 1899], 68–69; *DAR Patriot Index*, 381; *Fauquier County, Virginia* [Warrenton, Va., 1959], 76, 212–13).

3. Thomas Turner Fauntleroy (1796–1883) held a commission as lieutenant during the War of 1812, after which he studied law in Winchester and practiced in Warrenton. He was elected to the Virginia legislature in 1823, representing Fauquier County. In 1836 he embarked on a military career, serving as an officer in the U.S. Army until joining the Confederate service in 1861 (Lyon G. Tyler, ed., *Encyclopedia of Virginia Biography* [5 vols.; 1915; Baltimore, 1998 reprint], II, 214).

4. The proposed arsenal at Warrenton was never built. In his Dec. 1827 message to the legislature, Gov. Giles noted some "material difficulties" in purchasing the land for the arsenal "in consequence of some uncertainties in the title." Shortly thereafter, in Feb. 1828, the General Assembly repealed all acts providing "for erecting any arsenal or arsenals, not heretofore erected" (*Journal of the House of Delegates of the Commonwealth of Virginia* [Dec. 1827], 2; *Supplement to the Revised Code of Va.*, 90).

To Bushrod Washington

My dear Sir   Winchester Aug. 19th. 1827

I received the day before yesterday at my brother's your letter of the 7th.[1] and am much concerned to hear that your health has not been so good as I had been led to hope it was from what I had heard concerning it on your leaving Philadelphia. As your chills have left you we may however indulge the expectation that the Dyspepsy which has persecuted you will follow them or at least be greatly moderated.

I regret very much that it is not in my power to say with any certainty when I shall again be in this place. I set out to day for Romney where I must be to morrow. I hope to meet a gentleman there with whom I have business. Should he meet me I shall return on tuesday & shall be in Winchester on Wednesday in the forenoon. Should my hope of meeting this gentleman in Romney be disappointed I must proceed to Cumberland in Maryland, and cannot be in Winchester till late in the week.[2] I should feel much pleasure in diverging from my course for the pleasure of seeing you & Mr. Turner, but I am compelled by business to hasten my return to Fauquier.[3] I am to meet some persons at Fauquier court house on monday that is tomorrow week.

Should I not have the pleasure to see Mr. Turner, have the goodness to tell him that I hope we will be able to communicate by letter the subject on which he wishes to converse with me.

I received a packet from him last autumn for Mr. Gaston which I delivered. I should have mentioned its delivery to Mr. Turner but took it for granted that Mr. Gaston had written to him. It was my purpose to ask Mr. Gaston last spring for his commands to Mr. Turner, but he did not attend that session of the circuit court.[4] It will give me much regret if the restrictions on my time should prevent my seeing Mr. Turner and thereby produce any disappointment to him. I should feel great pleasure in doing anything within my reach for his accomodation.[5]

With the best wishes for your health & happiness I am my dear Sir affectionately your

J MARSHALL

ALS, DLC. Addressed to Washington at "Blakely near Charleston / Jefferson County"; postmarked Winchester, 20 Aug. Endorsed by Washington and forwarded with note dated 21 Aug. 1827: "My dear Sir / I send you this letter for / your information. I recd it this morning / Affecty Yrs / B. W."

1. Letter not found. JM probably received this letter at Happy Creek, James M. Marshall's home near Front Royal. Bushrod Washington was then staying at Blakely, home of his nephew John A. Washington, near Charles Town in Jefferson County (Charlotte Judd Fairbairn, *The Washington Homes of Jefferson County, West Virginia* [Ranson, W. Va., n.d.], 20–23).

2. JM's business in Romney and in Cumberland, Md., no doubt concerned his Hampshire County lands. The gentleman he hoped to meet was possibly Joseph Sprigg, his agent for collecting rents. See JM to Sprigg, 25 May 1829.

3. Mr. Turner was possibly Henry Smith Turner (1770–1834) of Jefferson County. He lived at Wheatlands, not far from Blakely. He and Bushrod Washington were sons-in-law of Col. Thomas Blackburn (ca.1740–1807) of Rippon Lodge, Prince William County (Horace Edwin Hayden, *Virginia Genealogies* . . . [Wilkes Barre, Pa., 1891], 601–3, 636–37; Charles Town [West Va.] *Virginia Free Press*, 24 July 1834).

4. William Gaston, the North Carolina lawyer who frequently argued cases in the U.S. Circuit Court for North Carolina.

5. Turner was evidently the person to whom Bushrod Washington forwarded this letter (see provenance note).

To Archibald D. Murphey

Dear Sir   Richmond October 6th. 1827

Your oration delivered in Person Hall, Chapel Hill, reached this place during a visit I had made to our mountain country.[1] It was taken out of the post office and placed on a general table among a number of papers and pamphlets received during my absence, and was not perceived till today. I mention this circumstance as an apology for having permitted so much time to elapse without making my acknowledgements for the gratification derived from its perusal.

I take a great deal of interest in your portraits of the eminent men of North Carolina who have now passed away from the theatre of action. It was my happiness to be acquainted with those of whom you speak as being known to yourself and I feel the justness of the eulogies you have bestowed upon them. I never heard Mr. Davie or Mr. Moore at the bar;[2] but the impressions they both made on me in private circles were extremely favorable, and I think you have given to the character of each its true colouring. Neither have I ever heard Mr. Stanly but I have known him also in private, and it was not possible to be in his company without noticing & being struck with his general talents, & most especially his vivacity his wit and his promptness. He appeared to be eminently endowed with a ready elocution & an almost intuitive perception of the subjects of discussion.[3] With Mr. Haywood and Mr. Henderson I was well acquainted & have heard them often at the bar. They were unquestionable among the ablest lawyers of their day.[4] I saw not much of Mr. Duffie as a professional man but thought him a very pleasing agreeable gentleman.[5] You have omitted one name which ranks I think among the considerable men of your state. It is that of the late Judge Iredell. I was well acquainted with him too, & always thought him a man of real talents.

In the rapid sketch you have taken of the colonial government some circumstances excite a good deal of surprize. The persecuting spirit of the high church party was still more vindictive than I had supposed, and the principle of limiting your laws to two years was I beleive peculiar to Carolina. The scarcity of books too which seems to have prevailed even since the revolution is a very remarkable fact. Although I concur perfectly in the opinion you express that much more advantage is to be derived from the frequent and attentive perusal of a few valuable books than from indiscriminate & multifarious reading, that cramming injures digestion, yet some books are necessary not only for ornament but use.

Allow me to thank you sir for the pleasure I have received from the perusal of your oration — for I must suppose that I am indebted to yourself for this mark of polite attention, and to express my particular acknowledgements for the flattering notice you have taken of the Life of Washington.[6] That work was hurried into the world with too much precipitation, but I have lately given it a careful examination & correction.

Should another edition ever appear it will be less fatiguing, & more worthy of the character which the Biographer of Washington ought to sustain.[7] With very great respect & esteem, I am Sir your Obedt

J MARSHALL

ALS, Nc-Ar. Addressed to Murphey at Haw River, N.C.; postmarked Richmond, 6 Oct. Endorsed by Murphey.

1. Archibald D. Murphey, *An Oration Delivered in Person Hall, Chapel Hill on the 27th June, 1827* (Raleigh, N.C., 1827). A 1799 graduate of the University of North Carolina, Murphey (1777–1832) was a distinguished lawyer, jurist, and statesman who advocated economic and social reform in his home state.

2. William R. Davie (1756–1820), a graduate of Princeton (1776), was a lawyer and Federalist politician. He attended the Federal Convention of 1787 and was a leader in securing ratification of the Constitution. Alfred Moore was briefly JM's colleague on the Supreme Court.

3. John Stanly (1774–1834), educated at Princeton, was a lawyer and Federalist member of Congress (1801–3, 1809–11). He also served many years in the North Carolina House of Commons.

4. John Haywood (1762–1826) was a lawyer, judge, and court reporter in North Carolina before moving to Tennessee in 1807, where he continued to lead a distinguished career in law. Archibald Henderson (1768–1822) served in Congress as a Federalist (1799–1803) and later served intermittently in the state legislature while maintaining a busy law practice in the state and federal courts.

5. William Duffy (d. 1810) had been Murphey's mentor in law when the two resided in Hillsborough. Duffy later moved to Fayetteville and served a term in the state legislature (W. J. Peele, *Lives of Distinguished North Carolinians* [Raleigh, N.C., 1898], 113; William Henry Hoyt, ed., *The Papers of Archibald D. Murphey*, in *Publications of the North Carolina Historical Commission* [2 vols.; Raleigh, N.C., 1914], I, 6 n. 3.

6. Murphey praised JM's *Life of Washington*, claiming that "the history of our revolution will never be so well written again. . . . There is no historical work in any language, that can be read with so much advantage such moral effect, by American youth . . . . They should read it with diligence, and read it often. They will never rise from the perusal of it, without feeling fresh incentives both to public and private virtue" (*Oration Delivered in Person Hall*, 11).

7. A second edition of Murphey's *Oration* published in 1843 included JM's letter to Murphey. The oration and JM's letter were reprinted in Peele, *Lives of Distinguished North Carolinians*, 128–49.

To Peter S. Du Ponceau

Dear Sir   Richmond Octr. 30th.⟨1827⟩

I have had the pleasure of receiving your eloquent eulogium in commemoration of the Honorable William Tilghman and thank you for the gratification afforded me by its perusal.[1] You have presented him to the world in lights in which he is equally respectable and amiable.

If his decisions have accomplished a union between the civil and common law so as to enable the same tribunal to respect in its judgements the principles of both, he has certainly confered a great benefit on his state, and in doing so, has achieved a work of real difficulty. He has improved your system at least as much as Lord Mansfield did that of England.

You have displayed his private virtues and domestic misfortunes in such a manner as deeply to interest the reader and to secure both his admiration and his sympathy. With very great respect and esteem, I am dear Sir your Obedt

J MARSHALL

ALS, PPAN (on deposit at PPAmP). Addressed to Du Ponceau in Philadelphia; post-marked Richmond, 30 Oct. Endorsed by Du Ponceau.

1. Peter Stephen Du Ponceau, *Eulogium in Commemoration of the Honourable William Tilgh-man* . . . (Philadelphia, 1827), delivered at the meeting of the American Philosophical Society on 11 Oct. 1827. An eminent Philadelphia lawyer, William Tilghman (1756–1827) was chief justice of the Pa. Supreme Court from 1806 to 1827 and president of the American Philosophical Society from 1824 until his death.

To Martin P. Marshall

My dear Nephew: Richmond, Nov. 7th. 1827

I have not heard from you since I transmitted your contract with my sister Taylor, and am consequently uncertain whether you have received it, and whether it answers your purpose. My sister is very desirous of knowing what is the progress of the suit, when it will probably terminate and what danger there is of losing any part of the land.[1]

I have lately received a letter from my sister Pollard which shows that she is greatly distressed. Mr. Pollard has also written to me informing me that some debtor of the estate of Mr. Davis is sued by his executors and could make an arrangement by which the debt to me would be secured.[2] I do not choose to meddle in the business because I may embarrass the suit, but if any arrangement could be made by which the debt would be secured in such manner that the interest should be paid to my sister during her life and the principal paid to my executors at her death, it would be very gratifying to me. Would it be imposing too much trouble on you to ask you to make some inquiries into this business? Mr. Pollard can give you the requisite information. I would write immediately to my nephew John but understand that he has removed out of the state, and as he has never given me the slightest information respecting my suit, I suppose he must have abandoned it.[3]

Your Aunt is, I hope, rather improving in her health, though she is still in a very melancholy situation. She sends her love to yourself and Mrs. Marshall, I am, my dear Nephew, Your affectionate Uncle,

J. MARSHALL

Tr (typescript), Collection of Thomas W. Bullitt, Louisville, Ky., 1971; Beveridge-Marshall Papers, DLC. Noted as addressed to Marshall in Flemingsburg, Ky.

1. For JM's previous correspondence concerning his efforts to assist Jane Marshall Taylor recover money through the sale of her Kentucky lands, see *PJM*, VIII, 138–40, 315–16, 364; IX, 61–62, 242; X, 260–61, 306–7.

2. Letters not found. Nancy Marshall Pollard, JM's sister, was married to William Pollard. Her first husband was the late Joseph Hamilton Daveiss, on whose estate JM had a claim (ibid., X, 119, 307).

3. John J. Marshall.

To Henry B. Bascom

Dear Sir,   RICHMOND, November 19, 1827.

Yesterday, on my return from North Carolina, I had the pleasure of receiving your favor of the 10th.[1] The question you proposed is one which I am not well qualified to answer.[2] It can scarcely be considered independently of accompanying circumstances. That agriculture is a science in which society is deeply interested, no man will deny; and that it may be greatly improved by scientific researches, will, I presume, be generally admitted. It is, however, a science in which much practice must be blended with theory, and in which theory itself varies with soil, climate, and a variety of circumstances. Much will, of course, depend on the professor, and much on the facility with which he may be enabled to make his experiments.

A student may certainly derive advantages from such a department, if well conducted, and may acquire a knowledge of principles that will be useful to him in after life. It seems to me to be connected with the department of chemistry, and, in some degree, with mechanics. Such a professorship may, I should think, furnish valuable information to the public.

How far it may be useful to the particular institution, may probably depend upon circumstances, among which the state of its funds ought not to be overlooked. With great respect, I am your obedient servant,

J. MARSHALL.

Printed, M[oses] M. Henkle, *The Life of Henry Bidleman Bascom* (Louisville, Ky., 1854), 194–95.

1. Letter not found. Henry Bidleman Bascom (1796–1850), a Methodist minister and future bishop, had recently been appointed president of Madison College in Uniontown, Pa. He previously preached on circuits in Ohio, Tennessee, and Kentucky, and from 1824 to 1826 was chaplain of the U.S. Congress. After resigning the Madison College presidency in 1829, he served as agent of the American Colonization Society and as president of Transylvania University in Lexington, Ky.

2. Besides JM, Bascom wrote James Madison, Charles Carroll of Carrollton, Henry Clay, DeWitt Clinton, and John Quincy Adams for their opinions on the creation of an agricul-

tural department and professorship at the college. Moses Henkle published the entire correspondence in his biography (ibid., 190–97).

To Horace Binney

Dear Sir   Richmond Novr. 19th. 1827

Yesterday, on my return from North Carolina, I received your eulogium on the late Chief Justice Tilghman, together with your letter of the 5th.[1] Its perusal has afforded me real gratification, and I am much obliged by this mark of your polite attention. My acquaintance with this gentleman, though transient, had been sufficient to prepare me to think well of him. I am greatly flattered by your assurance that he thought favorably of me.

It is impossible to read the portrait you have drawn without the highest respect for his official character, and love mingled with reverence for his private worth. The expression of deep feeling which pervades it constitutes of itself exalted praise.

In contemplating his arduous public duties I am particularly struck with the difficulty of engrafting the peculiar principles of equity on the stock of the common law. Having been accustomed to see them administered under different forms, if not by different tribunals, the task of applying the doctrines of a court of chancery to a case made up by pleadings according to the technical rules of common law, seems to me extremely arduous. The labors of the Judge must be enhanced, and I should think it an additional difficulty that such of the advantage of precedent must be lost by transferring such a cause to the jury.

Allow me to repeat my acknowledgement for the pleasure your discourse has given me, and to assure you that, I am with great and respectful esteem, Your Obedt

J MARSHALL

ALS, Schouler Collection, MHi. Addressed to Binney in Philadelphia. Postmarked Richmond, 20 Nov. Endorsed by Binney.

1. Letter not found. Horace Binney, *An Eulogium upon the Hon. William Tilghman, Late Chief Justice of Pennsylvania* (Philadelphia, 1827). Binney (1780–1875), a future eulogist of JM, graduated from Harvard in 1797, studied law, and then embarked on a legal career that brought him to the pinnacle of the Philadelphia bar. He argued important cases in both the Pa. Supreme Court and the U.S. Supreme Court. He also produced six volumes of *Reports of Cases Adjudged in the Supreme Court of Pennsylvania* (Philadelphia, 1809–15). After retiring from the bar, he wrote extensively on legal and biographical subjects.

To Henry M. Brackenridge

Sir   Richmond Novr. 19th. 27

I have received your letter respecting the office of Reporter of the cases decided in the Supreme court.[1]

As soon as it was understood that the office would probably become vacant I received an application from Mr. Peters of Philadelphia supported by warm recommendations from my friends Judges Washington and Peters.[2] Being much disposed to oblige these gentlemen and having no doubt of the capacity of the applicant, I assured them that I would favor his pretensions. I know that three Judges are pledged to support him. Whether he will succeed with a fourth I am unable to say.

Many other applications have been made; and I cannot doubt that every Judge has determined in favour of some on⟨e⟩ of them.

I think it right to give you this information as it may enable you to decide respecting your intermediate arrangements. With great respect I am Sir, your Obedt

J MARSHALL

ALS, PPiU. Addressed to Brackenridge (spelled "Breckenridge") in Washington; postmarked Richmond, 20 Nov. Address crossed through and readdressed in another hand "No. 216 Race Street / Philadelphia"; postmarked Washington, 4 Feb.

1. Letter not found. Henry Marie Brackenridge (1786–1871), son of jurist and writer Hugh Henry Brackenridge, was born in Pittsburgh and received his early education from his father. He embarked on a legal, judicial, diplomatic, and literary career that took him to Baltimore, St. Louis, New Orleans, South America, Florida, and eventually back to Pittsburgh. At this time he was a territorial judge for the West Florida District but had been absent since Nov. 1826, having traveled to Washington and then to Philadelphia on account of his wife's illness. Although criticized for leaving his judicial post, Brackenridge retained his appointment and returned to Florida, where he remained until 1832 (Benjamin D. Wright to John Q. Adams, 10 Nov. 1827; Brackenridge to Henry Clay, 26 Dec. 1827, Clarence Carter et al., eds., *The Territorial Papers of the United States* [28 vols.; Washington, D.C, 1934–75], XXIII, 935, 959–64).

2. See Richard Peters, Jr. to JM, 30 Sept. 1826; JM to Richard Peters, 2 Oct. 1826 (*PJM*, X, 305–6 and n. 1; 306 and n. 2).

To Timothy Pitkin

Dear Sir   Richmond Decr. 7th. 1827

I had the pleasure of receiving a few days past your letter of the 29th. of Novr.[1]

The resolutions of the House of Burgesses of Virginia concerning which you enquire were published at the time in the gazette of the day as stated in the 2d. vol. of the Life of Washington. They were also preserved in a work known by the name of Prior Documents, a collection of state papers preceding the war of our revolution which has been thought accurate. The Manuscript journal was lost & very few printed copies existed. Perhaps that which Mr. Wirt was fortunate enough to find is the only copy which exists. It is the only copy known to exist. I did not doubt the correctness of the resolutions as reported in a paper of the day published at the seat of government, and as preserved in the best collection extant. Opposed to them however is a printed journal. Every gentleman must weigh the evidence and judge for himself. I am inclined to think, though I find much difficulty in accounting for the difference, that the weight of evidence, so far as respects the resolutions actually passed by the house, is with the journal.[2] With very great respect & esteem, I am dear Sir Your Obedt

J MARSHALL

ALS, CSmH. Addressed to Pitkin in New Haven, Conn.; postmarked Richmond, [7?] Dec. Endorsed.

1. Letter not found. Pitkin (1766–1847), a graduate of Yale (1785), was then writing *A Political and Civil History of the United States from the Year 1763*, which was published in 1828. He had previously served as a Federalist member of Congress from Connecticut (1805–19). In 1816 he published *A Statistical View of the Commerce of the United States of America*, a second and third edition of which appeared in 1817 and 1835.

2. In 1815 William Wirt had written to JM about Patrick Henry's Stamp Act resolutions of 1765. Wirt noted that JM in the *Life of Washington* had presented an erroneous text of the resolutions as adopted by the House of Burgesses and sent him a copy of the printed journal containing four resolutions. He also sent a copy of the resolutions left by Henry at his death that contained an additional resolve said to have been adopted by the House but expunged from the journals the next day. Wirt again called attention to the error two years later in his *Sketches of the Life and Character of Patrick Henry*. In his *History of the Colonies*, published in 1824, JM presented a corrected text of five resolutions, which he copied from that in Wirt's biography. In the first edition of the *Life of Washington*, JM included six resolutions, stating that the first four passed and the two remaining were not agreed to. Pitkin was inclined to believe that this version was "the resolutions, as originally offered by Mr. Henry, before they were finally revised and modified by the assembly" (Wirt to JM, 7 Jan. 1815, *PJM*, VIII, 63–65 and nn.; Wirt, *Sketches of the Life and Character of Patrick Henry* [9th ed.; Philadelphia, 1836], 80, 81 n.; Pitkin, *Political and Civil History of the United States from the Year 1763* [2 vols.; New Haven, Conn., 1828], I, 176).

To Joseph Story

My dear Sir   Richmond Decr. 11th. 1827

I have a commercial question before me which puzzles me a good deal, on which as it is not going before the Supreme court I should be much gratified by your aid. The case is this. **A** carrying on trade in Petersburg in Virginia was accustomed to ship cotton to **B** carrying on trade in New York, and to send him bills of exchange on Europe to be sold. **A** drew bills on **B** as occasion required. In the course of this business, as is no uncommon thing with Virginians, **A** became the debtor. In the autumn of 1825 **A** being indebted to **B** remitted a bill of exchange on a house in England, which **B** sold on credit, and received in payment a note which fell due in March 1826. Notice of the sale was given to **A** & the note deposited in bank for collection. The maker and indorser of the note both failed, and the proper steps were taken by **B** to obtain the money but he gave no notice to **A** of the insolvency of the parties to the note, or that it had been dishonoured until three months afterwards. **A** insists that **B** has made the note his own, has made the credit absolute, and cannot exchange it to him in account. I have searched all my books respecting principals and agents and can find nothing applicable to this case. Is an agent in such case bound to give his principal the same notice of the dishonour of these notes as must be given by the holder of a bill of exchange or promissory note to the drawer or maker? Or is he bound only to use due diligence to collect the money, and to be answerable for such damage only, as may be sustained by his neglect to give notice? Does the law presume damage or must it be proved? You commercial men are familiar with these questions — to us agriculturists they are at least novel.[1]

Things are going on queerly in New York under the management of Messrs. VanBuren & Clinton. Do you suppose that a contract is made for the U.S. in reversion or remainder as well as for the present estate — that is speaking of the 4th. of March 1829 as the time present? Farewell — Yours truely

J MARSHALL

ALS, Keats-Shelley Memorial Association, Rome, Italy. Addressed to Story in Salem, Mass; postmarked Richmond, 13 Dec.

1. Hamilton, Donaldson & Company v. Cunningham, Opinion, 12 June 1828.

From Joseph Story

My dear Sir   Salem Decr. 15. 1827.

The North American Review for January 1828 will be published in a few days; & the Editor did me the favour to send me last Evening three copies of that part of it which contains the Review of your History of the Colonies.[1] In addition to what appears in it, I had made several extracts from the work itself for publication. But as it occupied the space of 40 pages, it was thought necessary to omit them. I pray your indulgence for what I have written, & shall feel amply repaid, if you should feel that this imperfect sketch is not wholly inadequate to its professed purpose. The consideration of what I owed to you as a living personage somewhat restrained my pen, & with the truest desire to do you justice, I am far from thinking, that I have succeeded. The copy, which I send you accompanying this letter will better enable you to judge, than any explanatory remarks I could make.

I hope to have the pleasure of meeting you in January, & I shall bring Mrs. Story along with me, to whom it will afford me very great gratification to introduce you.[2]

With my earnest wishes for the continuance of your life & health, believe me most truly & affectionately yours obliged friend

JOSEPH STORY

ALS, Marshall Papers. ViW. Addressed to JM in Richmond. Postmarked Salem, Mass., 17 Dec.

1. *North American Review,* XXVI (1828), 1–40.

2. Story had married Sarah Wetmore, his second wife, in 1808.

To Thomas S. Hinde

Dear Sir   *Richmond, December* 16. [1827?]

I received your letter by Mr. Doddridge.[1] I am truly sorry that I have not preserved the letters of recommendation which you transmitted through Mr. Rowan and colonel Johnson.[2] I suppose them to be intended only for the occasion, and after laying them before the judges, did not imagine that those which were not asked for were to be taken care of. At least one hundred letters and other testimonials were collected and presented for and by different applicants, and when we were not requested to return them, it was not expected that they would be afterwards applied for. As neither Mr. Rowan nor colonel Johnson indicated a wish that the testimonials in your favor should be returned, I did not suppose that it was desired. I shall regret it very much if this circumstance should be an inconvenience to you.[3] With great respect, I am your obedient, &c.

J. MARSHALL.

Printed, *American Pioneer,* II (1843), 415–16 (with facsimile signature); Tr, Marshall Papers, ViW.

1. Letter not found. Philip Doddridge (1773–1832), a lawyer and statesman who resided in Brooke County (now West Va.). He represented that county in the House of Delegates and later served in the U.S. Congress (1829–32). At the Virginia Convention of 1829–30, Doddridge was the leading spokesman for reformers seeking greater representation for the west in the legislature. He represented Hinde in the case of Mallow v. Hinde, heard at the 1827 term of the Supreme Court (12 Wheat. 193, 194).

2. Hinde wrote to JM in Dec. 1826, enclosing papers supporting his application as clerk of the Supreme Court. John Rowan and Richard M. Johnson (1780–1850) were U.S. senators from Kentucky (Hinde to JM, 28 Dec. 1826, *PJM,* X, 327).

3. Hinde appended the following note to JM's letter: "Note. The papers referred to were a certificate of qualification as a clerk, of the judges of the appellate court of Kentucky, general letter of recommendation, &c., from which you might have had all their autographs

together. I open the packet to make this note, and write without spectacles. Th: S Hinde."
Hinde was a collector of autographs, which he submitted to John S. Williams, editor of the
American Pioneer. Williams printed selected documents with facsimile signatures, including a
document signed by George Washington in addition to JM's letter to Hinde (*American
Pioneer,* II [1843], 415–21).

To [Jaquelin A. Marshall]

My dear Son   Richmond Decr. 18th. 27
   Your mother continues extremely uneasy about the situation of your
family. In my letters to your brothers I have desired them to keep us
informed so far as they have any information themselves on the subject.
But their letters are unsatisfactory. They tell us that when the last intelligence was received your son was supposed to be better but was not out of
danger.[1] Her uneasiness of course continues, and she desires me to ask
you to let her know precisely how he is, and what is the health of his
mother & yourself & the rest of the family. Our love to all. I am my dear
son your affectionate father

J MARSHALL

ALS, Collection of Frederick Marshall Ball, Mystic, Conn. Identity of recipient based on
internal evidence.

1. JM evidently referred to a son recently born to Jaquelin and Eliza Clarkson Marshall.
There is no record of this son, who presumably died shortly after birth. A daughter had
been born to the couple earlier in the year (Paxton, *Marshall Family,* 205).

To Samuel L. Southard

Dear Sir   Richmond Decr. 19th 1827
   Be pleased to accept my acknowledgements for your flattering recollection of me in transmitting me a copy of the Presidents message[1]
with the assurances of the respect and esteem with which I remain your
obliged & obedt. servt.

J MARSHALL

ALS, Southard Papers, NjP. Addressed to Southard in Washington; postmarked Richmond, Dec. Endorsed by Southard as received 21 Dec. "No Ans."

1. *Message from the President of the United States . . . at the Commencement of the First Session of the
Twentieth Congress* (Washington, D.C., 1827).

To Hugh D. Evans

Sir   RICHMOND, Dec. 27, 1827.

I have deferred making any acknowledgments for your Essay on Pleading, and for the very flattering letter which accompanied it, until the rising of the court should afford leisure for giving it an attentive reading.[1] That is now accomplished, and I have derived much gratification from the perusal.

You have certainly examined the science of special pleading, with the eye of a critic, who looks through the subject, for the purpose of becoming master of the object of its rules; and you have taken a just and truly common sense view of the whole.

The statutes of amendment have certainly accomplished much, and have left not a great deal to be done; but you have shown that they have left something. I confess I can perceive no reason why one thing should be averred, which is not essential, and consequently traversable, unless it were a narrative necessary to the understanding of the case.[2]

Be so good as to accept my thanks for this very polite mark of your attention, and be assured that I am, with great respect, your obedient servant,

J MARSHALL

Printed, Hall Harrison, *Hugh Davey Evans, LL.D.: A Memoir Founded upon Recollections Written by Himself* (Hartford, Conn., 1870), 156–57; ALS offered for sale by Goodspeed's Book Shop, Boston, Mass., 1938 (*The Flying Quill,* Jan. 1938, 25).

1. Letter not found. Hugh Davey Evans, *An Essay on Pleading with a View to an Improved System* (Baltimore, 1827). Evans (1792–1868), of Baltimore, was a lawyer and legal writer who devoted much of his later life to writing about the history and doctrines of the Protestant Episcopal Church.

2. JM's letter was included among testimonial letters from John Q. Adams, Joseph Story, and James Kent, which Harrison published in an appendix to his memoir (Harrison, *Hugh Davey Evans,* 155–56, 157).

To Joseph Story

My dear Sir   Richmond Decr. 30th. 1827

I have received your flattering letter[1] and the still more flattering Biography which accompanied it. You will not I am persuaded consider me as affecting diffidence when I express a consciousness that your friendship has given an importance to the incidents of my life to which they have no just pretensions.[2] This consciousness is mingled with a fear that many may ascribe to me such an excess of vanity as fully to counterbalance any good quality I may be allowed to possess. These fears however do not chill the warm and grateful sentiments with which I receive every mark of your good opinion. The belief that the writer of this sketch views me through a medium which magnifies whatever may deserve commendation, and diminishes those failings which others may deem[3] serious faults, is dearer to my heart than any impression which eulogy, were it even deserved, might make on others.[4] Mutual esteem and friendship confer reciprocally on those who feel the sentiment, one of the most[5] exalted pleasures of which the human mind is susceptible.

When[6] the Review appears I shall not name the author, because there is a part of it concerning which I wish to have some conversation with you. It is that which bestows negative praise by declaring the absence of certain qualities which are undoubtedly not very desirable.[7] I fear that this may be suspected to affirm the presence of these same qualities in another work which has produced a good deal of excitement.[8] You will readily conceive the effect of such a suspicion.[9] If therefore any of my particular friends should enquire, as possibly they may, what artist has drawn the portrait so flattering to myself,[10] I shall not name him for the present.

I congratulate you on the prospect of a more agreeable winter than you have heretofore passed[11] at Washington. I trust accomodations may be found for Mrs. Story at Mrs. Rapines,[12] and that she may be tempted by gracing our table to shed the humanizing influence of the sex over a circle which has sometimes felt the want of it.[13] She must however be forewarned that she is not to monopolize you, but must surrender you to us to bear that large portion of our burthens which belongs to you.

I have received your letter of the 22d. of December, and am greatly obliged by the examination you have given the subject concerning which I enquired.[14] I had hoped that the point was settled in the commercial towns.[15] My mind had a strong leaning in the direction which yours seems to have taken, and you confirm the opinion I was previously disposed to adopt.

I participate in the serious feelings which you suggest as growing out of the present contest for the Presidency. I begin to doubt whether it will be long practicable peaceably to elect a chief Magistrate possessing the powers which the constitution confers on the President of the United States, or such powers as are necessary for the government of this great country with a due regard to its essential interests.[16] I begin to fear that our constitution is not doomed[17] to be so long lived as its real friends have hoped. What may follow sets conjecture at defiance. I shall not live to witness and bewail the consequences of those furious passions which seem to belong to man.[18] Yours truely & affectionately

J MARSHALL

ALS, MiU-C; ALS (draft), ViW.

1. The draft reads "of the." See Story to JM, 15 Dec. 1827.
2. In the draft JM inserted a comma and continued the sentence with "mingled with a fear," etc.
3. The draft reads "think."

4. The draft reads "dearer to my heart than any other consideration connected with praise."

5. The draft reads "choice and."

6. In the draft this is the third paragraph. JM inserted "When the review appears &c" above the draft's second paragraph (beginning "I congratulate you") to indicate his intention to transpose the second and third paragraphs in making his fair copy.

7. The draft reads "It is that which negatives certain qualities which are undoubtedly not much to be admired."

8. In the draft this sentence reads "I fear that this may be suspected to affirm that these qualities belong to another."

9. In characterizing JM's authorship of the *History of the Colonies*, Story wrote: "He does not listen with implicit faith to every idle tale told by artless credulity or vulgar prejudice. He does not seek the title of superior wisdom by unsettling the truths of history, and proving, that all writers, but himself, have mistaken the facts and the characters of former times. He does not construct any new narrative of events, and in his own closet show how fields were lost or won, by drawing upon the resources of his own fancy. He does not dispute the veracity of persons nearest the scenes, simply because his own theory would be broken down by any admission in their favor. . . He does not obtrude his own reflections with a profuse and embarrassing pertinacity." JM was apparently concerned that this passage would give offense to Justice Johnson, whose biography of Nathanael Greene had recently drawn critical fire in the pages of the *North American Review* (*North American Review*, XXVI [1828], 38, 39; Timothy Pickering to JM, 14 Feb. 1827, *PJM*, X, 338–39, 349 n. 2, 350 n. 3).

10. The draft reads "If therefore my friends should enquire, as probably they may, what artist has drawn this flattering portrait."

11. The draft reads "spent."

12. Charlotte Rapine (d. 1835) was the widow of Daniel Rapine (ca.1768–1826), a former mayor of Washington and postmaster of the House of Representatives at the time of his death. Story and his wife Sarah actually stayed at the Pennsylvania Avenue boarding house run by Mrs. Ruth McIntyre (Allen C. Clark, "Daniel Rapine, The Second Mayor," *Records of the Columbia Historical Society*, XXV [1923], 194–215); Webster to Nathaniel Silsbee, 4 Jan. 1828, Charles M. Wiltse et al. eds., *The Papers of Daniel Webster, Correspondence*, II [Hanover, N.H., 1976], 267–68).

13. The draft reads "and that she will by gracing our table shed the humanizing influence of the sex over our not very polished circle."

14. Letter not found. See JM to Story, 11 Dec. 1827 and n. 1.

15. This sentence is not in the draft.

16. In the draft this sentence reads "I begin to doubt whether it will be practicable to elect a chief Magistrate possessing the powers which the Executive of the U.S. ought to possess."

17. This word is not in the draft.

18. In the draft this sentence reads "I shall not live to see and bewail the consequences of those furious passions which are breaking loose upon us."

From Timothy Pickering

My Dear Sir,   Salem Jany. 2. 1827 [1828].[1]

Judge Story's early departure, after he informed me of the day, prevented my addressing you by him. As he carries his wife with him, however, this letter may probably reach Washington before him. On his return last March, he delivered me your letter of the 15th of that month; for which I now make my acknowledgements.[2]

You say "It is not a little gratifying to us who are treading close upon your heels, to observe how firmly you step, & how perfectly you retain your recollection." I am grateful to the author of my being for its preservation through so many years, in the possession of vigorous health & strength of body, and much more for the continuance (to which your remark refers) of my mental faculties; which I please myself in thinking have yet sustained no fall from that moderate standard where my consciousness ever placed them. Their exercise will fill the space of my remaining life; & I hope without abatement. Of our bodily power it is proverbially said — "Use Stren[g]th and have it."[3] So I fondly wish — I am almost tempted to say I expect — that, being now free from constant manual labours (for I have quitted my farm) the steady & nearly exclusive exercise of the powers of my mind, may preserve their force. God forbid that I should survive my understanding. The amusing story of the Archbishop of Toledo, I hope will never be applicable to me.

Referring to the years we have lived, you remark, "that I am a *little* before you." But by the last number of the North American Review, which came to hand this day, I see that I am more than ten years in advance as you were born on the 24th of September 1755. My birth was on the 6th of July, old style, answering to the 17th new style in 1745; and I always mention my birth as on the 17th. I learn from Judge Story, that your Constitution is strong and your health good; and as you take daily exercise, to confirm both, I trust your country will enjoy the benefits of your judicial labours for a long period yet to come. I consider the public liberty, and the rights of individuals, as ultimately resting on the ability & independence of the Supreme Federal Judiciary. In its hands is placed the high Controuling *Authority*, the *Moral Sceptre*, of the *Nation*: and the Executive which shall ever put on that bench a man deficient in talents, integrity, and mental independence, will deserve execration.

The amicable tenor of your letter of the 14th of March was highly gratifying to me.[4] Remotely situated as we are from each other, it is not probable, as you remark, that we shall again be brought together: but I shall never cease to cherish your memory with sincere affection and very great respect.

I was happy that you took in good part my frank statement of facts respecting General Washington. Of his "firmness" in critical periods you doubtless found abundant proofs among his papers, as well as in your own observation of public occurrences. I recollect, in a cabinet consultation with the heads of departments, he once spoke to this effect — "Let me see my way clear, and nothing shall turn me aside." On this point you express precisely the idea I entertain of his character, where you say — "Though prizing popular favour as highly as it ought to be prized, he never yielded principle to obtain it, or sacrificed his judgement on its altar." Diffident of his own opinion, in public questions of importance, he always sought information, & thankfully received it, from those whom he thought entitled to his confidence. In his elevated public stations this was eminently useful; and especially in his civil administration, in which instant decision was not necessary. For he would diligently and patiently examine every such question; and aided by all attainable adventi[ti]ous lights, form his judgement; and this, therefore, would seldom be erroneous. All his views, indeed, being scrupulously directed to the promotion of the public welfare, correct judgements were justly to be expected.

I write you long letters: but without taxing you for answers of corresponding lenghth, it will always give me pleasure to know that I continue to live in your esteem.

T. PICKERING

ALS (draft), Pickering Papers, MHi. Inside address to JM.

1. Pickering or someone interlined "28" above "27."
2. JM to Pickering, 15 Mar. 1827, *PJM*, X, 411–12.
3. The quotation is evidently a variation of the proverb "Use legs and have legs" (*The Oxford Dictionary of English Proverbs* [3d. ed.; Oxford, 1970], 856).
4. Pickering meant the letter of 15 Mar. 1827.

To Henry Clay

Dear Sir   Richmond Jany. 5th. 1828

I thank you for the copy of your address on the charges made against you respecting the election of President, which I have read with the more pleasure because it combines a body of testimony much stronger than I had supposed possible, which must I think silence even those who wish the charge to be believed.[1]

With sincere wishes for the improvement of your health, and with real esteem, I am dear Sir your obedt

J MARSHALL

ALS, Clay Papers, DLC. Addressed to Clay in Washington; postmarked Richmond; date illegible. Endorsed by Clay.

1. Henry Clay, *An Address of Henry Clay to the Public, Containing Certain Testimony in Refutation of the Charges against Him, Made by Gen. Andrew Jackson, Touching the Last Presidential Election* (Washington, 1827). See Mary W. M. Hargreaves and James F. Hopkins, eds., *The Papers of Henry Clay*, VI (Lexington, Ky., 1981), 1394–96, for a summary and publication history. See also Robert V. Remini, *Henry Clay, Statesman for the Union* (New York, 1991), 320–21.

From John Randolph

My dear Sir   Washington Jan. 7. 1828.

Nothing was farther from my intention than to draw you into a correspondence & especially on *that* subject, and I beg to assure you of my entire innocence, in intention at least, of any such act of bad taste & ill breeding — not to say presumption.

I had heard of Col. P's almost solitary position among his former associates in Politicks, & I imputed it to the causes touched upon in my last,[1] & to another which I did not name — his regard for the memory of Fisher Ames; around whose grave the Messrs. A. prowled like the hyænas, or vampyres of the East.[2] The charge of traitorous misdemeanors against the N. E. federalists brought by Mr. A. junr. to Mr. Jefferson rests on the testimony of Mr. Giles, who related the whole to a friend of mine, minutely. That statement I read in the Senate, in my place, in 1826. The reporters did not print it: but Mr. G. does not & cannot deny one word of it. The disclosure was made by Mr. A. first to him, that he might lay it before Mr. J. He declined doing so, but was the means of bringing about the interview between Mr. A. & Mr. J. Mr. G.'s words are truly remarkable. It does not appear that he went with Mr. A. farther than the door, perhaps the gate, of the President's House — yet when Mr. A. made the disclosure to Mr. J. he says "& when he did so, Sir, I saw him." I can reconcile this in but one way, that Mr. G was in an adjoining apartment possibly behind a screen. This indeed is not at all creditable to Mr. G.

I hope you will pardon this intrusion upon you. I should not have made this statement but that my name has been used in the newspapers on the subject.

I told the Senate that I had no authority to read my correspondent's letter containing the detail of what passed between him & Mr. G. that I had apprized him of my intention so to use it: (not having time to consult him) that I knew the high responsibility which it involved; & that there was no reparation which he could ask & a gentleman could give that I would not make to atone for my fault, if he did not forgive it.

This letter will probably not reach you until after you shall have left Richmond: but I could not resist writing it. Once more, I ask your excuse & assure you, that I am with all possible esteem & regard Dear Sir, your obliged & faithful Servant

JOHN RANDOLPH OF ROANOKE

ALS, Gray-Glines Collection, Ct. Inside address to JM.

1. Letter not found. "Col. P." is Timothy Pickering.

2. In his speech of 1 Feb. 1828 on "Retrenchment and Reform," Randolph used strikingly similar language in speaking of the Adamses: "Who were the persecutors of Fisher Ames, whose very grave was haunted as if by vampyres?" (Powhatan Bouldin, *Home Reminis-*

JOHN RANDOLPH
Oil on canvas by Chester Harding, 1829.
Courtesy of the Corcoran Gallery of Art

cences of John Randolph of Roanoke (Danville, Va., 1878), 288). On this speech, see JM to Randolph, 6 Mar. 1828 and nn.; Randolph to JM, 16 Mar. 1828 and nn.).

To John Randolph

My dear Sir   March 6th. 1828

    I have not thanked you for the last copy of your eloquent and interesting speech on "retrenchment and reform," nor expressed my deep sense of the too flattering sentiment inscribed on it towards myself, because I intended to call on you, and accompany my enquiries concerning your health with some manifestation of the grateful feelings with which I receive these continued proofs of your kindness.[1] Indeed my dear Sir, it is with unaffected pleasure I perceive that no casual difference of opinion changes your regard for a man who, though he will not compare himself exactly to the animal who "crawls with some one of his hundred feet, always in contact with the subject on which he moves" ever has and ever will feel a just pride in the friendship of the "gallant horseman who at a flying leap clears both ditch and fence."[2]

    The pressure of official duties added to some what of the indolence of age has hitherto prevented my calling on you, and I therefore put on paper my earnest wishes for your health, and sincere assurances that I remain with real esteem and regard, Your Obedt

J MARSHALL

ALS, Collection of Association for the Preservation of Virginia Antiquities, ViHi. Addressed to Randolph and endorsed by him "That great master of the human heart."

1. John Randolph, *Substance of a Speech of Mr. Randolph, on Retrenchment and Reform, Delivered in the House of Representatives . . . on the First of February, 1828* (Washington, D.C., 1828). This was the first pamphlet edition of Randolph's celebrated speech, which the Virginia congressman prefaced with a dedication dated 29 Feb. 1828 to his constituents, "[w]hose confidence and love have impelled and sustained me under the effort of making it." The speech was a diffuse, often vituperative, attack on the Adams administration as well as a justification of his own conduct during a political career of thirty years. See Robert Dawidoff, *The Education of John Randolph* (New York, 1979), 288–92.

2. The pamphlet edition of the speech was annotated with footnotes and longer notes gathered in an appendix. To a passage where he expressed scorn for "dialecticians," who "after they had laid down their premises, and drawn, step by step, their deductions, sit down, completely satisfied, as if the conclusions to which they had brought themselves were really the truth," Randolph subjoined a footnote referring the reader to a note in the appendix, which reads: "A caterpillar comes to a fence; he crawls to the bottom of the ditch, and over the fence, some one of his hundred feet always in contact with the subject upon which he moves — a gallant horseman, at a flying leap clears both ditch and fence — [']Stop! says the caterpillar; you are too flighty — you want connexion and continuity: it took me an hour to get over — you can't be sure as I am, who have never quitted the subject, that you have overcome the difficulty and are fairly over the fence.' 'Thou miserable reptile, (replies our fox-hunter,) if, like you, I crawled over the earth slowly and painfully, should I ever

catch a fox? or be any thing more than a wretched caterpillar?'–N.B. He did not say 'of the law' " (*Substance of a Speech of Mr. Randolph, on Retrenchment and Reform*, 19, 29).

From John Randolph

My dear Sir   Thursday Mar. 6. 1828
    Horace, my favorite Horace long ago taught me that
    Principibus placuisse viris, non ultima laus est.[1] What then must be my gratification to receive, & with no stinted measure too; the praise of him, whose approbation I have been more desirous to win, than that of any other man living? whom I have strived most to please? Altho' the still burnt Kentucky whiskey is nauseous to my palate, I can yet enjoy the *aroma* of an exquisite glass of Madeira, or Paxarete, or Burgundy and I doubt whether my head would have been more affected by a bottle of Clos Vougeot, capped with another of real Sillery Champagne, than by your truly kind note. Fortunately however, certain sedatives from another quarter have preserved me from absolute intoxication. To drop the metaphor — "lest it may drop me" — you have made one very happy man today, my dear Sir; altho my vanity great as it is will not be blinded to one source of your kind & flattering approbation — that kindliness of nature which distinguishes you to your advantage (with many other great & good qualities) from your grateful & faithful servant

JOHN RANDOLPH OF ROANOKE.

ALS, Marshall Papers, ViW. Addressed to JM, "Chief Justice / of the / U.S."

1. Horace, *Epistles*, Bk. 1, Ep. XVII, l. 35: "to have won favour with the foremost men is not the lowest glory" (H. Rushton Fairclough, trans., *Horace: Satires, Epistles, and Ars Poetica* [Cambridge, Mass., 1961], 363).

From Timothy Pickering

Dear Sir,   Salem March 10. 1828.[1]
    Judge Wilson of Pennsylvania, a member of the National Convention, once told me, that after the Constitution had been finally settled, it was committed to him to be critically examined respecting its style; in order that the instrument might appear with the most perfect precision & accuracy of language. Such is my impression of his meaning. And perhaps no legal composition presents fewer points of disputable construction. In a copy of the Constitution printed for the use of the Senate, when I was a member, and also in the copy prefixed to the edition of the laws of the United States, in which John B. Colvin was employed, the first clause in the 8th section, Article I. is thus printed and pointed:

"Section 8. The Congress shall have power["]

"To lay and collect taxes, duties, imposts, and excises; to pay the debts and provide for the common defence and general welfare of the United States; but all duties, imposts, and excises, shall be uniform throughout the United States."[2]

It is a year or more since I thought this clause had been misconstrued in consequence of the punctuation; and I made in the margin of my copy, the following note:

"There should be a comma only after excises: for the meaning intended was evidently this: 'The Congress shall have power to lay and collect taxes, &c. & excises, to pay (i.e. in order to pay) the debts &c': and the closing passage, 'but all duties' &c. confirms this construction: and then the powers necessary 'to provide for the general welfare' are specified."

To-day, having occasion to look into the Journals of the Old Congress for 1787, after they had received the Constitution from the Convention, I observed that the clause in question had a comma only after the word excises, in the first line. My edition of the Journals is the first, as printed in 1787, under the eye of the accurate secretary, Charles Thompson.[3] Whether Courts, in construing laws, are ever governed by their punctuation, I do not know: but it would seem that the composition of laws should be clear, independently of the punctuation. I am however inclined to think that the semicolon after excises, has led some persons to view the clause as giving powers almost unlimited; to do any act which had for its object "the general welfare." The very form of the clause favours the construction I put upon it.

The second clause confers the power of borrowing money. And Congress being thus (by these two means, of taxing and borrowing) furnished with funds, sixteen additional powers are specifically given, showing how, in the application of those funds, Congress was "to provide for the general welfare."

The like remarks, with others respecting the tariff, I sent to the editor of the Boston Daily Advertiser, who published them in that paper some two months ago.

I observe a notice in the newspapers, of a speech of a very able man, Mr. Oakley of New York, in opposition to the making of roads and canals, under the authority of Congress, as not warranted by the Constitution.[4] Of one thing I am entirely satisfied, that if such a power had been explicitly proposed to be conferred on Congress, in the Constitution, it would never have been ratified by nine States, if even by any of them. And yet the exercise of this power seems to me to stand on the same ground with some others exercised without hesitation, under the specified power "to regulate commerce with foreign nations, and among the several states, and with the Indian Tribes." To give safety & facility to the maritime commerce with foreign nations and among the several states, light-houses, beacons, and piers have been erected, at great expense; and now a

"Break-Water," near the mouth of Deleware bay, is in contemplation; at the cost of some hundreds of thousands of dollars.[5] It would doubtless prove a highly useful work, by saving much property, and many lives. But would not similar extensive benefits result from providing for commerce among the several states, by opening a water-passage near the seacoast, by means of canals communicating with the bays and sounds? But such canals would cost a great deal of money! True: and this, probably, starts, or enforces the objections as to Constitutional powers.

But Mr. Oakley's idea of distributing the vast sums requisite for public roads & canals, among the several states (*to say nothing of the want of power in Congress to replenish state-treasuries*) is in the highest degree objectionable. The National objects of roads and canals are, to give general safety and facility of transportation by *continued communications, connecting the several states in the most useful manner.* But divide the same revenue among the states, to be applied at their discretion, and they will consult only their respective separate interests, regardless of the *National accommodation.* Nor do I believe the money would be expended more economically under state governments than under the general government. Such cases, I am aware, are prone to become mercenary jobs: but I would rather rely for able and honest agents appointed under the general government, than under the governments of the individual states, where there would be *more narrow minds,* and at least as many wanting in integrity. In some states the works would be faithfully executed — in others the reverse, the undertakers pocketing the money.

Hamilton, in his report on manufactures, "Article XI, on the facilitating of the transportation of commodities," — mentioning roads and canals, says — "There can certainly be no object more worthy of the cares of the local administrations; and it were to be wished, that there was no doubt of the power of the national government to lend its direct aid, on a comprehensive plan. This is one of those improvements which could be prosecuted with more efficacy by the whole, than by any part or parts of the Union." "There are cases in which the general interest will be in danger to be sacrificed to the collision of some supposed local interests. Jealousies in matters of this kind are as apt to exist, as they are apt to be erroneous."[6]

But the same canals and improved roads, while promoting commerce, would be a provision for the *national defence.* The Romans made expensive military roads to enable them to pass troops & stores, safely and expeditiously, to all parts of their immense empire. Such roads in the United States, if made at all, must be made in time of peace.

In reference to my observation, that if the Constitution offered to the consideration of the people, had contained an express provision for authorizing Congress to lay out roads and canals, and expend public revenue upon them, it would not have been accepted by nine states, if by any, I extract the following remark of Hamilton, in his celebrated argument on the Constitutionality of the National Bank. He says—"The secretary of state will not deny, that whatever may have been the intention of the framers of a constitution, or of a law, that intention is to be sought for in the instrument itself, according to the usual and established rules of construction. Nothing is more common than for laws to *express* and *effect* more or less than was intended."[7]

These suggestions on the construction of the Constitution, addressed to the highest judicial officer of the United States it is hoped will not be deemed an impertinent intrusion. They are respectfully submitted to his censure by, His faithful friend

T. PICKERING.

ALS (copy), Pickering Papers, MHi.

1. Pickering made this copy of the letter two months after sending it, as he explained in a headnote to the copy. On 17 May 1828 he read in a Boston newspaper a Massachusetts congressman's opposition to Thomas J. Oakley's plan "to have the money in the Treasury of the U. States, which might be applied to the making of roads & canals, distributed and paid over to the individual states, in the proportion of their respective representations in the National House of Representatives." This "brought to my mind a letter I had written to Chief Justice John Marshall, on the 10th of last March; in which, discussing the just construction of one part of the Federal Constitution, I adverted to this project of Mr. Oakley's; and as that letter is spread over several loose papers, & referred to passages in Hamilton's writings to be inserted in the fair letter to Marshal; I here copy the whole of it." Pickering had composed an earlier draft of this letter on 9 Jan., which began: "Will you permit *me* to intrude my ideas on the legal construction of any part of the National Constitution, of which the Court in which you preside can alone give an authoritative decision?" He crossed out the first two paragraphs and inserted a heading "Tariff" to the remainder. This became the draft of an essay by "A Free Inquirer," which Pickering enclosed in a letter to John Lowell on 14 Jan., requesting him to submit it to a newspaper. The essay was published in *Boston Daily Advertiser* on 19 Jan. 1828 ("The Tariff" [draft], 9 Jan. 1828; Pickering to John Lowell, 14 Jan. 1828, Pickering Papers, MHi).

2. The edition of the laws quoted by Pickering is *Laws of the United States of America, from the 4th of March, 1789, to the 4th of March, 1815* (5 vols.; Philadelphia and Washington, 1815), which was compiled by John B. Colvin, a State Department clerk.

3. Pickering had a set of the *Journals of Congress. Containing the Proceedings from Sept. 5, 1774 to [3d Day of November 1788]* (13 vols.; New York and Philadelphia, 1777–[1788]). He referred to volume XII of that edition, which has the individual title, *Journal of the United States in Congress Assembled: Containing the Proceedings from the Sixth Day of November 1786, to the Fifth Day of November, 1787* (Philadelphia, 1787). Charles Thomson (1729–1824) was secretary of the Continental Congress throughout its existence.

4. Oakley, a member of Congress from New York, stated in a speech of 1 Mar. 1828 on internal improvements "that a great portion of this House, and of the nation, doubt the existence of any power in Congress to enter upon a course of internal improvement, by constructing roads and canals." Even if a majority believed that Congress did have this power, Oakley continued, that majority should "act in a manner least offensive to the minority." Those portions of the People who question the power, would much prefer that the funds of the General Government, which might be spared for roads and canals, should be disbursed by the agency, under the immediate superintendence of the State authorities. Ought not, then, that principle to be adopted?" At the time Pickering wrote, the newspapers had not published Oakley's entire speech but had published the House journal for 1 Mar., which noted that the New Yorker addressed the House "on the propriety of dividing

the surplus fund of the government among the several states, to be by them applied to such objects of internal improvement as they might think proper" (*Register of Debates in Congress* . . . , IV [Washington, 1828], 1705; *Niles' Weekly Register* [Baltimore], 8 Mar. 1828).

5. A bill for erecting a breakwater near the mouth of Delaware Bay was then before the House and was approved by Congress on 23 May. The act appropriated $250,000 for this purpose (*U.S. Statutes at Large*, IV, 290–91).

6. Pickering might have quoted from a recent edition of Hamilton's 1791 report, *Alexander Hamilton's Report on the Subject of Manufactures* . . . (6th ed.; Philadelphia, 1827), 58–59. The report is reprinted in Harold C. Syrett et al., eds., *The Papers of Alexander Hamilton*, X (New York, 1966), 230–340 (quotation at 310–11).

7. Pickering placed an asterisk here and added a footnote that was probably not part of the original letter sent to JM: "*This argument of Hamilton's was addressed to President Washington, in Decr. 1790, in answer to Jefferson's objections, and to remove the doubts of the President, when the bill for establishing a National Bank, which had passed both Houses of Congress, was before him, for his approval or rejection. Jefferson, the Secretary of State, had puzzled Washington, always anxious faithfully to perform his duty. Hamilton's argument swept away Jefferson's objections, and the President approved the Bill." Pickering could have read Hamilton's opinion on the bank bill in various sources, including *The Works of Alexander Hamilton* . . . (3 vols.; New York, 1810), I, 111–55. The opinion is reprinted in Syrett et al., eds., *Papers of Hamilton*, VIII (New York, 1965), 97–134.

American Insurance Company v. Canter
Opinion
U.S. Supreme Court, 15 March 1828

On a voyage from New Orleans to France in February 1825 the French ship *Point à Petre* wrecked off the coast of Florida. Rescuers salvaged the cargo of cotton and carried it into Key West, where it was sold under a local court's decree. The purchaser was David Canter (1776–1829) of Charleston, South Carolina. The original owners of the cotton had abandoned the property to its New York insurers, the American Insurance Company and the Ocean Insurance Company. These companies claimed the property and filed their libel in the U.S. District Court of South Carolina in April 1825, shortly after Canter sold the cotton to a Charleston firm (which in turn sold it at public auction). The libelants contended that the sale at Key West was invalid because the local court had no jurisdiction over admiralty and maritime causes. The U.S. District Court in July 1825 ordered a partial restitution of the cotton to the libelants, from which decree both parties appealed to the U.S. Circuit Court in Charleston. Judge William Johnson subsequently reversed the district court's decree and upheld Canter's claim to all the cotton under the Key West sale. The insurance companies filed an appeal in the Supreme Court in March 1826. The case was argued on 8, 10, and 11 March 1828 by David Ogden for the insurance companies and by John Whipple (1784–1866) and Daniel Webster on behalf of the claimant Canter. Marshall's opinion of 15 March 1828 upholding the circuit court's decree is of interest for his comments on Congress's power to acquire and govern territories, on admiralty jurisdiction, and on the jurisdiction of federal courts under Article III of the Constitution (American Ins. Co. v. Canter, App. Cas. No. 1415, Record on Appeal, 1–2; 1 Fed. Cas. 658–63; U.S. Supreme Court Minutes, 8, 10, 11, 15 Mar. 1828; James William Hagy, *This Happy Land: The Jews of Colonial and Antebellum Charleston* [Tuscaloosa, Ala., 1993], 290–91; Henry E. Whipple, *A Brief Genealogy of the Whipple Families* . . . [Providence, R. I., 1873], 42–44).

The Atlantic Ins. Co. & The Ocean Ins. Co.
v
350 Bales of Cotton, David Canter Claimant

The plaintiffs filed their libel in this cause in the District court of South Carolina to obtain restitution of 356 bales of cotton, part of the cargo of the ship Point a Petre which had been insured by them on a voyage from New Orleans to Havre de Grace in France. The Point a Petre was wrecked on the coast of Florida, the cargo saved by the inhabitants and carried into Key West where it was sold for the purpose of satisfying the salvors; by virtue of a decree of a court consisting of a Notary and five jurors, which was erected by an act of the territorial legislature of Florida. The owners abandoned to the Underwriters who, having accepted the same, proceeded against the property, alleging that the sale was not made by order of a court competent to change the property. ¶1

David Canter claimed the cotton as a *bona fide* purchaser under the decree of a competent court which awarded 76 per cent to the salvors, on the value of the property saved. ¶2

The District Judge pronounced the decree of the territorial court a nullity, and awarded restitution to the libellants of such part of the cargo as he supposed to be identified by the evidence, deducting therefrom a salvage of 50 percent. ¶3

The Libellants and Claimants both appealed. The circuit court reversed the decree of the district court, and decreed the whole cotton to the claimant with costs, on the ground that the proceedings of the court at Key West were legal, and transferred the property to the purchaser. ¶4

From this decree the Libellants have appealed to this court. ¶5

The cause depends mainly on the question whether the property in the cargo saved, was changed by the sale at Key West. The conformity of that sale to the order under which it was made has not been controverted. Its validity has been denied on the ground that it was ordered by an incompetent tribunal. ¶6

The tribunal was constituted by an act of the territorial legislature of Florida, passed on the 4th. of July 1823 which is inserted in the record.[1] That act purports to give the power which has been exercised. Consequently the sale is valid if the territorial legislature was competent to enact the law. ¶7

¶8   The course which the argument has taken will require that, in deciding this question, the court should take into view the relation in which Florida stands to The United States.

¶9   The constitution confers absolutely on the government of the Union, the powers of making war, and of making treaties. Consequently that government possesses the power of acquiring territory either by conquest or by treaty.

¶10   The usage of the world, is, if a nation be not entirely subdued, to consider the holding of conquered territory as a meer military occupation, until its fate shall be determined at the treaty of peace. If it be ceded by the treaty, the acquisition is confirmed, and the ceded territory becomes a part of the nation to which it is annexed, either on the terms stipulated in the treaty of cession, or on such as its new Master shall impose. On such transfer of territory, it has never been held that the relations of the inhabitants with each other undergo any change. Their relations with their former sovereign are dissolved, and new relations are created between them and the government which has acquired their territory. The same act which transfers their country transfers the allegiance of those who remain in it; and the law which may be denominated political is necessarily changed, although that which regulates the intercourse and general conduct of individuals remains in force until altered by the newly created power of the State.

¶11   On the 2d. of Feb. 1819, Spain ceded Florida to The United States. The 6th. art of the treaty of cession contains the following provision; "The inhabitants of the territories which his Catholic Majesty cedes to The United States by this treaty shall be incorporated in the Union of The United States, as soon as may be consistent with the principles of the federal constitution, and admitted to the enjoyment of the privileges, rights and immunities of the citizens of The United States."[2]

¶12   This treaty is the law of the land, and admits the inhabitants of Florida to the enjoyment of the privileges rights and immunities of the citizens of The United States. It is unnecessary to enquire whether this is not their condition independent of stipulation. They do not however participate in political power, they do not share in the government, till Florida shall become a state. In the mean time, Florida continues to be a territory of The United States, governed by virtue of that clause in the constitution which empowers Congress "to make all needful rules and regulations respecting the territory or other property belonging to The United States." Perhaps the power of governing a territory belonging to The United States which has not by becoming a state, acquired the means of self-government, may result necessarily from the facts that it is not within the jurisdiction of any particular state, and is within the power and jurisdiction of The United States. The right to govern, may be the inevitable consequence of the right to acquire territory. Whichever may be the source whence the power is derived, the possession of it is unquestioned.

In execution of it, Congress in 1822 passed "an act for the establishment of a territorial government in Florida"; and on the 3d. of March 1823 passed another act to amend that of 1822.[3] Under this act, the territorial Legislature enacted the law now under consideration.

The 5th. section of the act of 1823 creates a territorial legislature which "shall have legislative powers over all rightful objects of legislation; but no law shall be valid which is inconsistent with the laws and Constitution of The United States.["] ¶13

The 7th. sec enacts "That the judicial power shall be vested in two superior courts and in such inferior courts, and justices of the peace as the legislative council of the territory may from time to time establish." After prescribing the place of session and the jurisdictional limits of each court, the act proceeds to say, "Within its limits herein described each court shall have jurisdiction in all criminal cases; and exclusive jurisdiction in all capital offences; and original jurisdiction in all civil cases of the value of one hundred dollars arising under and, cognizable by the laws of the territory now in force therein, or which may at any time be enacted by the legislative council thereof." ¶14

The 8th. sec. enacts "That each of the said superior courts shall moreover have and exercise the same jurisdiction within its limits, in all cases arising under the laws and constitution of The United States, which, by an act to establish the judicial courts of The United States approved the 24th. of September 1789, and an act in addition to the act entitled an act to establish he judicial courts of The United States, approved the 2d. of March 1793, was vested in the court of Kentucky district." ¶15

The powers of the territorial legislature extend to all rightful objects of legislation, subject to the restriction that their laws shall not be "inconsistent with the laws and constitution of The United States." As salvage is admitted to come within this description, the act is valid unless it can be brought within the restriction. ¶16

The counsel for the libellants contend that it is inconsistent with both a law and the constitution; that it is inconsistent with the provisions of the law by which the territorial government was created, and with the amendatory act of March 1823. It vests, they say, in an inferior tribunal a jurisdiction which is by those acts, vested exclusively in the superior courts of the territory. ¶17

This argument requires an attentive consideration of the sections which define the jurisdiction of the superior courts. ¶18

The 7th. Sec. of the act of 1823 vests the whole judicial power of the territory "in two superior courts, and in such inferior courts and Justices of the peace, as the legislative Council of the territory may from time to time establish.["] This general grant is common to the superior and inferior courts, and their jurisdiction is concurrent, except so far as it may be made exclusive in either, by other provisions of the statute. The jurisdiction of the superior courts is declared to be exclusive over capital ¶19 offences. On every other question over which those courts may take cognizance by virtue of this section concurrent jurisdiction may be given to the inferior courts. Among these subjects are "all civil cases arising under and cognizable by the laws of the territory now in force therein, or which may at any time be enacted by the legislative council thereof."

¶20 It has been already stated that all the laws which were in force in Florida while a province of Spain, those excepted which were political in their character, which concerned the relations between the people and their sovereign, remained in force, till altered by the government of The United States. Congress recognizes this principle by using the words "laws of the territory now in force therein.["] No laws could then have been in force but those enacted by the Spanish government. If among these a law existed on the subject of salvage, and it is scarcely possible there should not have been such a law, jurisdiction over cases arising under it was conferred on the superior courts, but that jurisdiction was not exclusive. A territorial act conferring jurisdiction over the same cases on an inferior court, would not have been inconsistent with this section.

¶21 The 8th. sec. extends the jurisdiction of the superior courts in terms which admit of more doubt. The words are "That each of the said superior courts shall moreover have and exercise the same jurisdiction within its limits, in all cases arising under the laws and constitution of the United States, which by an act to establish the judicial courts of The United States," "was vested in the court of Kentucky district."

¶22 The 11th. Sec. of the act declares "That the laws of the United States relating to the revenue and its collection," "and all other public acts of The United States not inconsistent or repugnant to this act, shall extend to and have full force and effect in the territory aforesaid."

¶23 The laws which are extended to the territory by this secti⟨on⟩ were either for the punishment of crime, or for civil purposes. Jurisdiction is given in all criminal cases by the 7th. section but in civil cases that section gives jurisdiction only in those which arise under and are cognizable by the laws of the territory. Consequently all civil cases arising under the laws which are extended to the territory by the 11th. Sec. are cognizable in the territorial courts by virtue of the 8th. Section: and in those cases the superior courts may exercise the same jurisdiction as is exercised by the court for the Kentucky district.

¶24 The question suggested by this view of the subject on which the case under consideration must depend, is this.

¶25 Is the Admiralty jurisdiction of the District courts of The United States vested in the superior courts of Florida under the words of the 8th. Sec. declaring that each of the said courts "shall moreover have and exercise the same jurisdiction within its limits, in all cases arising under the laws and constitution of The United States" which was vested in the courts of the Kentucky district?

¶26 It is observable that this clause does not confer on the territorial courts all the jurisdiction which is vested in the court of the Kentucky district, but that part of it only which applies to "cases arising under the laws and constitution of The United States." Is a case in Admiralty of this description?

The constitution and laws of The United States give jurisdiction to the ¶27 District courts over all cases in Admiralty, but jurisdiction over the case does not constitute the case itself. We are therefore to enquire whether cases in Admiralty and cases arising under the laws and constitution of The United States are identical.

If we have recourse to that pure fountain from which all the jurisdic- ¶28 tion of the federal courts is derived we find language employed which cannot well be misunderstood. The constitution declares that "The judicial power shall extend to all cases in law and equity arising under this constitution, the laws of The United States, and treaties made or which shall be made under their authority; to all cases affecting ambassadors, other public ministers and consuls; to all cases of admiralty and maritime jurisdiction."

The constitution certainly contemplates these as three distinct classes ¶29 of cases; and, if they are distinct, the grant of jurisdiction over one of them does not confer jurisdiction over either of the other two. The discrimination made between them in the constitution is we think conclusive against their identity. If it were not so, if this were a point open to enquiry, it would be difficult to maintain the proposition that they are the same. A case in Admiralty does not in fact arise under the constitution or laws of The United States. These cases are as old as navigation itself, and the law, admiralty and maritime, as it has existed for ages, is applied by our courts to the cases as they arise. It is not then to the 8th. Sec. of the territorial law that we are to look for the grant of Admiralty and maritime jurisdiction to the territorial courts. Consequently if that jurisdiction is exclusive, it is not made so by the reference to the District court of Kentucky.

It has been contended that by the constitution, the judicial power of ¶30 The United States extends to all cases of Admiralty and maritime jurisdiction; and that the whole of this judicial power must be vested "in one Supreme court and in such inferior courts as Congress shall from time [to time] ordain and establish." Hence it has been argued that Congress cannot vest admiralty jurisdiction in courts created by the territorial legislature.

We have only to pursue this subject one step farther to perceive that this ¶31 provision of the constitution does not apply to it. The next sentence declares that "The Judges both of the supreme and inferior courts shall hold their offices during good behavior." The Judges of the superior courts of Florida hold their offices for four years. These courts then are not constitutional courts in which the judicial power conferred by the constitution on the general government can be deposited. They are incapable of receiving it. They are legislative courts created in virtue of the general right of sovereignty which exists in the government, or in virtue of that clause which enables Congress to make all needful rules and regulations respecting the territory belonging to the United States. The jurisdiction with which they are invested is not a part of that judicial power which is defined in the 3d. article of the constitution, but is conferred by Congress in the execution of those general powers which that body possesses over the territories of The United States. Although admiralty jurisdiction can be exercised in the states in those courts only which are established in pursuance of the 3d. article of the constitution, the same limitation does not extend to the territories. In legislating for them, Congress exercises the combined powers of the general and of a state government.

¶32   We think then that the act of the territorial legislature erecting the court by whose decree the cargo of the Point a Petre was sold, is not "inconsistent with the laws and constitution of The United States,["] and is valid. Consequently, the sale made in pursuance of it changed the property, and the decree of the circuit court awarding restitution of the property to the claimants ought to be affirmed with costs.[4]

AD, American Insurance Company v. 356 Bales of Cotton, David Canter, Claimant, Appellate Opinions, RG 267, DNA; printed, Richard Peters, Jr., *Reports of Cases Argued and Adjudged in the Supreme Court of the United States . . .* , I (Philadelphia, 1828), 541–46. For JM's deletions and interlineations, see Textual Notes below.

1. American Ins. Co. v. Canter, Record on Appeal, 6–8. This act was commonly known as the "Wreckers Act" (1 Pet. 532). See Dorothy Dodd, "The Wrecking Business on the Florida Reef, 1822–1860," *Florida Historical Quarterly,* XXII (1944), 178–81.

2. Hunter Miller, ed., *Treaties and Other International Acts of the United States of America,* III (Washington, 1933), 8.

3. *U.S. Statutes at Large,* III, 654–59, 750–54.

4. In consequence of the Supreme Court's mandate, the case was again put on the docket of the U.S. Circuit Court, which on Canter's application directed a court officer to inquire into and fix the amount of his damages. The libelants protested against this reference on the ground that the mandate gave no authority to inquire into damages; that no damages had in fact been awarded by the decrees of the various courts that had heard the case; and that they were not liable for any damages. The circuit court nevertheless asserted its right to ascertain damages, though ultimately it disallowed any damages except for a small amount arising from incidental expenses. Canter took an appeal of this decree to the Supreme Court, which after overruling a motion to dismiss the case for want of jurisdiction affirmed the circuit court's decree at the 1830 term. Justice Story delivered the Court's opinion. In the meantime, the territorial wrecking act of 1823 had been declared invalid, first by the Florida Superior Court in 1825 and then by Congress in 1826 (American Ins. Co. v. Canter, 1 Fed. Cas. 664–65; Canter v. American Ins. Co., 2 Pet. 554–55; 3 Pet. 307–19; Dodd, "Wrecking Business," 181–82; *U.S. Statutes at Large,* IV, 138).

Textual Notes

	Title	The ~~American~~ ↑Atlantic↓ Ins.
¶ 1	l. 6	was sold ↑for the purpose of satisfying the salvors↓ by
	l. 8	legislature of ~~Georgia~~ ↑Florida.↓ The

	ll. 9–10	abandoned ~~the~~ ↑to↓ the Underwriters, who ↑having accepted the same↓ proceeded
¶ 2	l. 1	the ~~property~~ ↑cotton↓ as
	l. 2	per cent ↑~~on the value of the property saved~~↓ to the
¶ 3	l. 1	District ~~court~~ Judge
¶ 4	ll. 3–4	proceedings ↑of the court↓ at Key
¶ 6	ll. 4–5	by an ~~tribunal~~ incompetent
¶10	ll. 13–14	regulates the ~~com~~ intercourse
¶12	l. 2	privileges ~~of the~~ rights
	l. 6	mean time, ~~it is governed by Congress under the~~ Florida
	ll. 11–12	not ↑by↓ becoming a state, ↑acquired ~~with~~ the means of self government,↓ may
	l. 14	States. ~~It~~ ↓The right to govern,↓ may
	ll. 15–16	territory. ~~F~~ Whichever may be the source ~~from which~~ ↑whence↓ the
	l. 19	act, the ~~law~~ territorial
¶13	l. 2	rightful ~~powers~~ ↑objects↓ of
¶14	l. 2	courts, and ~~t~~ justices
	ll. 3–4	establish." ~~The pl~~ After
¶17	l. 1	libellants ~~contended~~ ↑contend↓ that
	ll. 1–2	both ~~the law~~ ↑a law↓ and ↑the↓ constitution;
	ll. 2–3	the law ~~under~~ ↑by↓ which
¶18	l. 1 beg.	~~The 7th. Sec. of the act of 1823 vests the judicial~~ This argument
¶19	ll. 5–6	as it ~~is~~ ↑may be↓ made
	l. 8	offences, ~~and in no other case. That of the inferior~~ on every
¶23	l. 5	all civil ~~which~~ ↑cases↓ ~~arise~~ ↑arising↓ under
¶24	l. 1	The question ~~was~~ suggested
	l. 1	of the ~~case~~ subject on
	l. 2	is this. ~~1st. Is the jurisdiction so far as it was exclusive in the Kentucky district court exclusive also in the superior courts of the territory?~~
		~~2d. Is the Admiralty jurisdiction of that court conferred on the superior courts of the territory as "a case arising under the laws and constitution of The United States."~~
		~~1st. It has been argued at the bar and the argument has great weight, that the exclusiveness of jurisdiction does not affect its operation or its extent. Its completeness in a court which exercises it, does not depend on the inability of any other court to exercise the same jurisdiction. The language of the 8th. sec is not that the superior courts shall exercise ↑the↓ jurisdiction in the cases it confers, exclusively of those courts which partake generally of the judicial power, but that it shall exercise the same jurisdiction. The jurisdiction is the same though it be not exclusive. Exclusiveness acts upon other courts, not on that which takes cognizance of the cause. The district court of Kentucky for example has exclusive jurisdiction of all suits for penalties and forfeitures incurred under the laws of The United States. The jurisdiction in any~~

~~such suit is not enlarged by being exclusive, nor would it be diminished if The United States were permitted to sue for a penalty in any other court.~~

~~— In describing the jurisdiction of the superior courts of the territory Congress has made it exclusive where such was their intention. It is exclusive in all capital cases. We have no reason for supposing that it would not be made expressly exclusive in such other cases as congress intended to confide to the superior courts only. The district courts of The United States have exclusive jurisdiction cognizance exclusive ↑of the courts↓ of the several states over crimes and offences cognizable under the authority of The United States where no other punishment than whipping not exceeding thirty stripes, a fine not exceeding one hundred dollars, or a term of imprisonment not exceeding six months, is to be inflicted. Jurisdiction over these crimes and offences is given to the superior courts of the territory by the 7th. sec. of the act, but it is not exclusive. In criminal cases this exclusive jurisdiction of the is confined to those which are capital. In this instance then jurisdiction which is exclusive in the district court of Kentucky is not exclusive in the superior courts of the territory.~~

~~— 2d. If the grant of jurisdiction to the district of court of jurisdiction ↑court in any↓ case had been complete; and the legislature had ad ↑ded in by distinct sentence↓ is the admiralty jurisdiction of the district court conferred by the 8th se of the Act? that no other court should take jurisdiction of the same case the jurisdiction ↑of the district court↓ would have been as entirely exclusive as it now is. Would the grant to a territorial court of the same jurisdiction in the particular case which was vested in the district court, without the prohibitory clause, make that jurisdiction exclusive? We think it would not, because the exclusion of ↑other↓ courts constitutes no part of the jurisdiction of a particular court. If it would not in a distinct sentence we do not perceive any solid distinction between the declaration of that exclusiveness in the same sentence and in a different sentence.~~

¶25   l. beg   ~~2d~~

          ll. 2–3   Sec ↑declaring↓ ~~That~~ ↑that↓ each of

¶27   l. 2   courts over ~~the~~ ↑all↓ cases ↑in Admiralty,↓ but

          ll. 3–4   enquire whether ~~they~~ cases

¶28   l. 2   we find ~~it expressed in terms~~ language

          l. 3   misunderstood. The [*erasure*] constitution

¶29   l. 9   the law, ~~of the~~ admiralty

          ll. 9–10   maritime ~~applied to the cases as it~~ ↑they↓ as it has existed for ages, it as it has existed for ~~ever~~ ages,

¶30   ll. 6–7   territorial legislature. ~~We have only to pur~~

¶32   l. 1   the act ~~by which the court which [erasure]~~ ↑of the territorial legislature↓ erecting

          l. 5   awarding ~~restitution of~~ ↑restitution of↓ the

To Peter S. Du Ponceau

Dear Sir   Washington March 16th. 1828

I have deferred returning my thanks to you and through you to Mr. Laussat, for his very interesting "Essay on Equity in Pennsylvania," till I could borrow time enough from our professional duties to read the work.[1] I have now done so at intervals, and have felt much gratified at the perusal. You have certainly done a great deal — more than I supposed possible — to supply what had appeared to me to be a most serious defect in your judicial system. Accustomed myself to a court of Chancery, I had always supposed it indispensable to the administration of justice upon the principles of our jurisprudence. Mr. Laussat has proved that it is not so indis⟨pens⟩able as I supposed it to be. I still lean however to my old opinions, and cannot help thinking that some embarassment must attend the administration of the powers belonging to courts of equity through the agency of Juries. While reflecting on this subject, I attended an exhibition of the deaf and dumb in our capitol, and was never more astonished or gratified than I was at the wonderful progress they had made, by the high improvement of their other senses, in compensating for their inability to hear, and consequent inability to speak.[2] By the aid of organs more directly adapted to other purposes, they had become capable of receiving the ideas generally conveyed by sounds, and of communicating those which are usually communicated by speech. Their condition is wonderfully improved by this admirable substitution; Yet I must think it would be better had they been endowed with the sense of hearing.

I perceive very plainly that both Mr. Laussat and yourself prefer your system to ours. I am not sure you are mistaken, though I cannot concur in the opinion.[3] Whoever may be right I beg you to believe that I am with respectful esteem, your obedt

J. MARSHALL

ALS, New York Society Library. Endorsed by Du Ponceau. Addressed to Du Ponceau in Philadelphia. Address has been cut from cover and attached to foot of second page.

1. Antony Laussat, *An Essay on Equity in Pennsylvania* (Philadelphia, 1826). Laussat (1806–33), then nineteen, wrote this essay in the spring of 1825 as a dissertation for the Law Academy of Pennsylvania. It addressed the question whether in Pennsylvania a separate court of chancery was "indispensably necessary." After completing his studies, Laussat led a successful career in law and politics that was cut short by his premature death. In addition to his essay, Laussat prepared an edition of Fonblanque's *Treatise on Equity* (John Pringle Jones, *An Eulogium upon Antony Laussat, Esquire . . .* [Philadelphia, 1834], 7, 10–16).

2. An exhibition of pupils of the Pennsylvania Institution for the Education of the Deaf and Dumb took place in the House of Representatives chamber on 16 Feb. 1828. Lewis Weld (1796–1853), principal of the Philadelphia institution, hoped the exhibition would raise awareness of the progress in educating the deaf and gain financial support. Also attending the event was Thomas H. Gallaudet (1787–1851), then principal of a school for the deaf in Hartford, Conn., in whose honor Gallaudet College (now University) was named. President Adams attended as well and recorded a detailed account in his diary

(Washington *Daily National Intelligencer*, 16 Feb. 1828; Lewis Weld, *An Address Delivered in the Capitol, in Washington City, February 16th, 1828, At an Exhibition of Three of the Pupils of the Pennsylvania Institution for the Education of the Deaf and Dumb* [Washington, 1828]; Charles Francis Adams, ed., *Memoirs of John Quincy Adams,* VII [Philadelphia, 1875], 434–37).

3. JM apparently wrote another letter (not found) to Du Ponceau about Laussat's work. In an 1834 eulogy for Laussat, JM is quoted as writing to Du Ponceau that "if any thing could move his prejudices in favour of the 'separation of the Courts of Common Law and Equity, it would be the argument of this essay' " (Jones, *Eulogium upon Antony Laussat,* 12).

From John Randolph

My dear Sir   Sunday 16th. [March 1828]

I am so unreasonable as to tax you with another copy of my *thing,*[1] and to beg that you will run your eye over the passages marked in pages 9. 11. (& the short note G. at the end.) 25–26 a curious historical fact — 31. 33. & the Post Script.[2]

The whole will not take 20 minutes. Can I see you at your lodgings before you go & when? Most respectfully & gratefully — your obliged & faithful

J. R. OF R.

ALS, Collection of the Association for the Preservation of Virginia Antiquities, ViHi. Addressed to JM. Date assigned on basis of internal evidence.

1. Randolph had just published a new edition of his speech on retrenchment and reform containing additional passages in the body, some new notes, and a "Postscript, in Lieu of a Preface," dated 4 Mar. 1828 (*Substance of a Speech of Mr. Randolph on Retrenchment and Reform, Delivered in the House of Representatives . . . , February 1, 1828* [2d. ed.; Washington, 1828]). This version is reprinted in Powhatan Bouldin, *Home Reminiscences of John Randolph of Roanoke* (Danville, Va., 1878), 271–320.

2. The first of the marked passages dealt with Everett's complaint that the salaries of U.S. diplomats were too small, to which Randolph responded: "There is one touchstone of such a question — it is the avidity with which those situations are sought — I will not say by members of this House — we are hardly deemed of sufficient rank to fill them." At this point the Virginia congressman added a new passage on page 9: "A Receivership or Inspectorship of the Land Office must do for us; ay, even for such of us as, by our single vote, have made a President. Sir, the generous steed by whose voice the son of Hystaspes was elevated to the throne of Persia, was better recompensed, as he deserved to be, than the venal asses whose braying has given a ruler to seven millions of freemen, and to a domain far surpassing in power, as well as extent, that of the Great King — the Grand Monarque of antiquity!" (*Substance of a Speech of Mr. Randolph on Retrenchment and Reform,* 9).

On page 11 Randolph spoke of "the old Republican party in New England — the worthy successors of John Langdon," to which in the new edition he subjoined a footnote directing the reader to the note G in the appendix. This new note reads: "With this venerable friend and sterling patriot, Mr. R. believes that 'the great body of the people of New England are genuine Republicans, of steady and virtuous habits, unsurpassed by any other people upon earth. But they are too often hoodwinked by the Priesthood and the Press in the interest of the Aristocracy' " (ibid., 11, 34).

The "curious historical fact" was presumably that related in a note on the embargo, which Randolph added in the second edition. It concerned Randolph's motion in May 1809 to approve the Madison administration's attempts to restore commercial intercourse with Great Britain. The motion was eventually adopted by a small majority, but "all the decided friends of the administration" opposed it. From this vote, Randolph concluded that the administration meant to go to war with Great Britain (ibid., 25–26).

Yet another addition Randolph made in the second edition was to a note in which he castigated certain judges of the Virginia Court of Appeals for participating in anti-Jackson politics. He undoubtedly directed JM's attention to a passage in which he professed his "respect for the Ermine": "Yes, I respect the *pure* Ermine of Justice, when it is worn as it ought to be—and as it is, by the illustrious Judge who presides in the Supreme Court of the United States, with modest dignity and unpretending grace" (ibid., 31).

In the postscript, Randolph advised his readers that there was "much in the foregoing pamphlet that was not spoken on the floor of the House of Representatives" and that some passages were "reported not as the speaker said them." He then urged his fellow southerners to reject Adams and support Jackson, "an uniform, unwavering, tried Republican, who had fought in the war of our Revolution, and shed his stripling blood for his country; and who, in the second war with England, had crowned himself and her with imperishable renown" (ibid., 35).

To Timothy Pickering

Dear Sir   Washington March 18th. 1828[1]

I had yesterday afternoon the pleasure of receiving your letter of the 10th. I have always supposed there must be an error in pointing the section you recite. I have always supposed that there ought to be a comma instead of a semicolon after the word excises. I have never beleived that the words "to pay the debts and provide for the common defence and general welfare of The United States" were to be considered as a substantive grant of power, but as a declaration of objects for which taxes &c might be levied. I am much gratified by the information you give that in your copy of the journals of the Old Congress for 1787 that the clause in question was pointed as we both think it ought to have been. The information is new to me and I am much obliged by your giving it.

I have no doubt of the correctness of your opinion that a general power to make internal improvements would not have been granted by the American people. But there is a great difference between a general power and a power to make them for military purposes or for the transportation of the mail. For these objects the power may be exercised to great advantage and, there is much reason for thinking, consistently with the constitution; farther than this, I know not why the government of The United States should wish it, nor do I beleive it is desired.

I concur entirely with you on the proposition to replenish the treasuries of the States from the treasury of The United States. If our revenue should exceed the wants of the government the ready mode for extricating ourselves from the difficulty is to diminish the taxes. I can scarcely reconcile the arguments in favor of taxing for the use of the States with the argument that you cannot tax for the general welfare. And yet they sometimes proceed from the same quarter.

We closed a laborious session yesterday, and I am on the wing for Virginia.

It gives me great pleasure to hear from you and greater still to know that you still retain your powers of body and mind. Except yourself I know no man who was active in our revolution that is older than I am. With respectful and affectionate esteem,
I am dear Sir your Obedt

J MARSHALL

ALS, Pickering Papers, MHi; copy, Pickering Papers, MHi. Addressed to Pickering in Salem, Mass. Endorsed by Pickering "recd. 24th / agrees with my construction / of the Constitution."

1. Pickering copied the ALS and placed it immediately following the copy of his letter to JM of 10 Mar. 1828, with the following note at the head of his copy of JM's reply: "To the preceding letter I received the following answer from Chief Justice Marshall; which I insert in order to present, in one view, our corresponding opinions on some questions of National importance."

From John Randolph

My dear Sir   Wednesday morning, March 20. [19] 1828[1]
I must relinquish the pleasure of being your companion in the Potowmack.[2] It is with great reluctance that I give it up. By great exertion I had made all the necessary arrangements for my departure. This caused me to pay a visit of duty as well as of inclination after Sunset. It was past nine, when I got home. The consequence has been a night of *Croup* & almost suffocation, that I am well persuaded if it had been passed on board a Steam boat would have been my last. It is the only night in which I have been compelled to break my Servant's rest.

I have the pleasure to know the revd. Mr. Shepherd.[3] He, I have no doubt, has "given a good account of our Jacobin Banker's Clerk.["] H — n is an adroit man of business: *habile* & *bien instruit* — a Gallatin without Mr. G's powers of debate. He was bred in a *Swiss* Banking House at Paris — was a member of the most ferocious Clubs at the outset of the Revolution. Want of capacity in England & his industry have made him what he is.[4]

Mr. Shepherd is a most respectable Clergyman of the Church of England — a man of fortune & one who has long had the lead of the whig interest in the neighbourhood of Liverpool, where he has repeatedly supported the Sefton (Molineaux) Interest against Canning & Huskisson.[5]

And now my dear Sir wishing you a pleasant voyage, a happy meeting with your family & every earthly & unearthly blessing here & hereafter; now & forever. Your faithfully attached friend & Servant

J. R OF ROANOKE

ALS, Marshall Papers, ViW. Addressed to JM.

1. Randolph wrote on Wednesday, 19 Mar., not Thursday, 20 Mar. (see n. 2).

2. The steamboat *Potomac* ran between Washington and Richmond, leaving the former every Wednesday at three in the afternoon and arriving at the latter on Friday evening (*Daily National Intelligencer,* 19 Mar. 1828).

3. The reference is possibly to William Shepherd (1768–1847), a Liverpool dissenting minister, writer, and local Whig political activist. If so, then Randolph was mistaken in describing Shepherd as "a most respectable Clergyman of the Church of England."

4. William Huskisson (1770–1830), the prominent liberal Tory statesman, advocate of free trade and representative of the mercantile interests in Parliament. In 1827 he became leader of the House of Commons and entered the government as head of the colonial office. Conflict with the duke of Wellington (the prime minister) forced him to resign from the government in May 1829. In his youth Huskisson lived in Paris, where he witnessed the early years of the French Revolution.

5. The Molyneux family were earls of Sefton, whose seat was north of Liverpool. George Canning (1770–1827) had been British foreign secretary, 1807–9 and 1822–27, and served briefly as prime minister in 1827. He was closely associated with Huskisson in promoting liberal Tory policies.

To Joseph Story

My dear Sir   [Richmond, 26 March 1828]

I beg you to accept my portrait for which I sat in Washington to Mr. Harding, to be preserved when I shall sleep with my Fathers as a testimonial of sincere and affectionate friendship. The remaining hundred dollars you will be so good as to pay to Mr. Hardin[g] for the head and shoulders I have bespoke for myself.[1] I shall not wish the portrait designed for myself to be sent to Richmond till I give directions for it to be accompanied by the head Mr. Greenaugh means to cast for me.[2] You will very much oblige me by letting me know when those castings are accomplished what is the price at which he sells them, because if they should not be held higher than I think my head worth I may probably order more than one of them.

I hope Mrs. Story & yourself have had a pleasant journey & have found your little family in perfect heal[t]h. I congratulate you both on this anticipated happiness. I had a pleasant sail through a smooth sea to Norfolk & thence to Richmond. I have seen scarcely any person out of my own family since my return but, if I may credit appearances there is rather a more stormy and disturbed atmosphere on land than I encountered in the Bay. The spirit of party is understood to be more bitter than I could have supposed possible. I am however on the wing for my friends in the upper country where I shall find near and dear friends occu⟨pied⟩ more with their farms than with party politics

I had one of your fish dressed yesterday and found it excellent. I am dear Sir with real regard and esteem, Your Obedt

J MARSHALL

I had nearly forgotten to say that I received today under cover from Mr. Webster Mr. McGruders letter announcing the loss of my surtout.[3] I thank for the trouble you have taken as much as if it had terminated more successfully. Once more farewell, Your

JM

ALS, Story Papers, MHi. Addressed to Story in Salem, Mass.; postmarked Richmond, 26 Mar. and franked.

1. Chester Harding (1792–1866), the New England portraitist, painted most of the eminent Americans of his day. He was then in Washington, where he took portraits of JM and the other Supreme Court justices and also of President John Quincy Adams. Of this sojourn, Harding wrote: "My visit to Washington . . . has been one of profit and pleasure. I have had the gratification of seeing a good deal of the great men of the age, particularly Judge Marshall. I am convinced that I shall feel through life that the opportunity to paint the Chief Justice, and at the same time hear his converse, would be ample compensation for my trouble in accomplishing these objects." The portrait JM gave to Story was bequeathed to Harvard on the latter's death in 1845. It is now at the Harvard Law School. The other 1828 Harding portrait, that intended for JM himself, has not been positively identified apart from another portrait the artist executed in 1829 (Andrew Oliver, *The Portraits of John Marshall* [Charlottesville, Va., 1977], 64–71.

2. Horatio Greenough (1805–1852), the Boston-born sculptor and graduate of Harvard (1825), spent most of his adult life in Italy. He was then in Washington, where he sculpted President Adams and also obtained sittings with JM. "I had this morning the first sitting from Chief-Justice Marshall," wrote Greenough on 28 Feb. 1828. "Judge Story says that any one would recognize my sketch; that it is capital." At least one other sitting took place on 12 Mar. Greenough apparently never completed his bust of JM. In 1901 the sculptor's younger brother wrote that "Horatio may have modelled a bust of C. J. Marshall but I do not recall any such work. In any case, if he did, it is highly improbable that any cast of it is in existence" (ibid., 179–80).

3. Letter not found.

To John H. Pleasants

On 29 March 1828 Chief Justice Marshall read in the *Richmond Whig* the following passage from the Baltimore *Marylander:*

> We hear that JUDGE MARSHALL, Chief Justice of the Supreme Court, a few days since, in conversation with a gentleman observed, "I HAVE NOT VOTED FOR TWENTY YEARS, BUT I SHALL CONSIDER IT A SOLEMN DUTY I OWE MY COUNTRY, TO GO TO THE POLLS AND VOTE AT THE NEXT PRESIDENTIAL ELECTION-FOR," ADDED HE IN HIS IMPRESSIVE MANNER, "SHOULD JACKSON BE

ELECTED, I SHALL LOOK UPON THE GOVERNMENT AS VIR-
TUALLY DISSOLVED."

Marshall then wrote the letter below, addressed to John Hampden Pleasants
(1797–1846), editor of the *Richmond Whig*. The *Whig* strongly supported
the reelection of John Quincy Adams in 1828, as did the *Marylander*, which
was edited by Edward Coote Pinkney (1802–1828), a lawyer and poet who
was a son of the late William Pinkney. After quoting Marshall's alleged remarks, Pinkney added his own editorial commentary:

Judge Marshall is as pure and disinterested a patriot as ever lived, and
is so acknowledged by all who know him. He was one of those dauntless
ones to whom we are indebted for our present free institutions.

When one so illustrious for his talents, learning and virtues, and so
venerable for his age, feels himself impelled by the highest of all duties,
to openly declare so laudable a determination, his example will not be
lost upon his countrymen.

In reprinting the *Marylander* piece, Pleasants likewise seized the opportunity to editorialize about the approaching election. Observing that the
opinion of the chief justice was "worth as much as the united opinions" of
those politicians who supported Andrew Jackson, the *Whig* editor added:

We are not of the political school of Gen. Marshall—but we have lived
long enough to surmount the prejudices of party, and to learn to
despise their nick names, their cant, and their slang. We know that
this great man—great in public and in private—practices more republicanism, than the thousands of demagogues who have democracy
perpetually on their tongues, and intolerance in their hearts and actions. . . . If the people are to be swayed by great names—if they are
to be invoked to follow the colours borne by a Calhoun and a Van
Buren—we hold up this name, the greatest of all, and ask them what
safer guide they can have, than one whose whole life is a pledge of his
sincerity, whose acquaintance with public men and public affairs, is
superior to any living, and whose station in the government, elevating
him alike above hopes and fears, from either party, is a guarantee of his
disinterestedness?

The *Marylander* story, along with Marshall's letter to Pleasants disavowing
its accuracy, was widely reprinted in the newspapers of the day. The origin of
the publication, as the chief justice discovered on a visit to the upper country in April, lay in remarks made by his nephew in a conversation at Baltimore, the circumstances of which Marshall fully recounted in a letter to
Story (*Richmond Whig*, 29 Mar. 1828; JM to Story, 1 May 1828).

SIR: *March* 29, 1828.

I perceive in your paper of to-day a quotation from the Marylander, of
certain expressions ascribed to me respecting the pending election for
the Presidency of the United States, which I think it my duty to disavow.
Holding the situation I do under the government of the United States, I
have thought it right to abstain from any public declarations on the
election; and were it otherwise, I should abstain from a conviction that
my opinions would have no weight.

I admit having said in private that, though I had not voted since the establishment of the general ticket system,[1] and had believed that I never should vote during its continuance, I might probably depart from my resolution in this instance, from the strong sense I felt of the injustice of the charge of corruption against the President and Secretary of State: I never did use the other expressions ascribed to me.

I request you to say that you are authorised to declare that the Marylander has been misinformed. Very respectfully, your ob't.

J. MARSHALL.

Printed, *Richmond Whig*, 2 Apr. 1828.

1. Virginia, as did most states by this time, elected presidential electors on a general ticket, having used this method since 1800. Those qualified to vote were allowed to vote for as many electors as were allotted to the state. Before 1800, the election was by geographical district, with each qualified voter voting only for one person who resided in the district (Hening, *Statutes*, XIII, 536–41; Shepherd, *Statutes*, II, 197–200; Charles O. Paullin, *Atlas of the Historical Geography of the United States* [1932; Westport, Conn., 1975 reprint], 88–93).

From Henry Clay

Dear Sir   Washington 8h. April 1828

In yielding to the impulse of my own feelings, by expressing to you my grateful acknowledgments for your late note to the Editor of the Whig, I hope you will excuse the liberty I take. I know that you were moved, on that occasion, by your well known love of truth and justice; but that does not abate the force of my personal obligation to you. On your own account, indeed, I regret that it became necessary that you should have to say publicly one word on the agitating topic of the day, because it will subject you to a part of that abuse which is so indiscriminately applied to all and to every thing standing in the way of the elevation of a certain individual.

Anxious to preserve your favorable opinion of me, I have requested our friend Mr. Call to shew you confidentially Copies of two letters of mine to Mr. Blair of K. about which you may happen to have observed some comments in the prints.[1] I have to bespeak your indulgence for the levity and pleasantry which characterize them. My apology is that they were written in the familiarity and confidence of private intercourse and friendship.[2] I am with great respect, faithfully Your obt. Servant

H CLAY

ALS, Collection of the Association for the Preservation of Virginia Antiquities, ViHi. Inside address to JM.

1. See Daniel Call to Henry Clay, 12 Apr. 1828, Robert Seager II et al., eds., *The Papers of Henry Clay*, VII (Lexington, Ky., 1982), 224–25. At the time Clay was circulating among his

friends copies of his letters to Francis P. Blair written in Jan.1825, which contained candid comments about the presidential candidates in the 1824 election. Clay was pondering whether to publish these letters, which he believed would absolve him of the "corrupt bargain" charge but could also prove embarrassing if their contents were revealed to the public (ibid., 144–46, 151–52, 154, 191–92, 194–95; Robert V. Remini, *Henry Clay: Statesman for the Union* [New York, 1991], 322).

2. For the letters to Blair, 8 Jan. 1824 [25] and 29 Jan. 1825, see James F. Hopkins, Mary W. Hargreaves, et al., eds., *The Papers of Henry Clay,* IV (Lexington, Ky., 1972), 9–11, 46–48.

To Henry Clay

DEAR SIR: RICHMOND, *May* 1, 1828.

A visit to my friends in the upper country, from which I returned yesterday, prevented my receiving your letter of the 8th of April, at an earlier day. The note you mention, was drawn from me very unwillingly, and the opinion it expressed, was the necessary result of evidence on a mind not predisposed to condemn. If it draws upon me a portion of that scurrility, which has been lavished on others, I must console myself with the reflection, that I have not voluntarily intruded myself upon a controversy, which has been carried on with such unexampled virulence.

Mr. Call looked in upon me yesterday afternoon, and showed me your two letters to Mr. Blair. We have indeed 'fallen upon evil times,' if the seal of confidence is to be broken, and such letters to be shown, for the purpose of injuring the writer. No fair mind can misunderstand them, or pervert their light and sportive language into a confession of dishonorable views. I know not how Mr. Blair can abstain from a public vindication of your conduct, so far as it is developed in those letters.

With great and respectful esteem, I am, dear sir, your obedient servant,

J. MARSHALL

Printed, Calvin Colton, *The Life of Henry Clay,* I (New York, 1855), 389.

To Joseph Story

My dear Sir Richmond May 1st. 1828

Yesterday on my return from a visit to my sons in our upper country I had the pleasure of receiving your very friendly letter of the 10th. of April.[1] The kind partiality you have always manifested towards me has been ever most grateful to my heart. No gratification is more pure or more exalted than the regard of those we esteem. I received at the same time a letter from Mr. Harding dated the 6th. of April[2] informing me that he should leave Washington within a fortnight from that day and requesting me to direct the disposition he should make of the portrait I had requested him to draw for my use. As he had left Washington ten days before his letter reached me I could give no directions on the subject, and have not written to him. I presume he is in Boston. Will you have the goodness to let him know that his letter was not answered because it was not received & that I will thank him if he has left the portrait in Washington to let me know with whom it remains; and, if it is with him to deliver it to you. I shall rely on you to give it house room till the representation of the court in Costume is prepared when I must make arrangements to have both, together with the head in plaister, conveyed to this place. I believe I said something on this subject to you in my last letter.[3]

I was a good deal provoked at the publication in the Marylander — not because I have any objection to its being known that my private judgement is in favor of the reelection of Mr. Adams, but because I have great objections to being represented in the character of a furious partisan. Intemperate language does not become my age or office and is foreign from my disposition and habits. I was therefore not a little vexed at a publication which represented me as using language which could be uttered only by an angry party man. As I knew I had never conversed on the subject except confidentially with friends I was persuaded that the communication to the printer could not have been direct, and that it had been a good deal metamorphosed in its journey to him. On my late visit to the upper country I was informed that this was the fact. One of my Nephews for whom I feel great regard and who was on the Adams convention was asked in Baltimore by a gentleman of that place if he knew my opinion respecting the candidates for the Presidency.[4] On his answering that I seldom mentioned the subject, but that he had heard me say that though I had not voted for upwards of twenty years I should probably vote at the ensuing election, the gentleman observed then he supposed I should consider the election of Jackson as a virtual dissolution of the government. This observation was received with a smile & some light expression of its extravagance, and upon the strength of this circumstance a communication was made which produced the publication in the Marylander. On seeing it my nephew wrote to a friend in Baltimore requesting him to enquire whether it was made on the strength of his communication, and if it was, enclosing a publication denying that he had ever authorized it or had ever heard me use such language as had been ascribed to me. The editor of the Marylander was in a situation when the letter was received, to prevent the enquiry which was directed, and his death has put an end to that part of the business.[5] My Nephew stated the affair to me while in the mountain country, and was too much chagrined for me to add to his mortification by blaming him. I must bear that newspapers scurrility which I had hoped to escape, and which is generally reserved for more important personages than myself. It is some consolation that it does not wound me very deeply.

I am glad to hear that Mrs. Story and yourself had a prosperous journey homeward. The epidemic you mention has prevailed extensively in Richmond and has in some instances been fatal. I am happy to hear that it has not been so in your famil⟨y⟩.

You will soon be on your spring circuit if ⟨not⟩ already engaged on it. I wish you a pleasant t⟨rip⟩ and am with affection and esteem, Your

J MARSHALL

ALS, MHi. Addressed to Story in Salem, Mass., postmarked Richmond, 2 May.

1. Letter not found.
2. Letter not found.
3. In addition to his portrait of JM, Harding also drew likenesses of the other justices and had begun a picture of the Supreme Court "as in session." That painting, if ever completed, has not been found (Andrew Oliver, *The Portraits of John Marshall* [Charlottesville, Va., 1977], 65–66).
4. The nephew was evidently Thomas M. Colston, who attended a convention of Virginians opposed to the election of Andrew Jackson held in Richmond in Jan. 1828. Colston was a delegate from Berkeley County. JM's son, James K. Marshall, also attended the convention, representing Fauquier County (*Richmond Enquirer,* 10 Jan. 1828).
5. Edward C. Pinkney, editor of the *Marylander,* died on 11 Apr. 1828.

To Samuel L. Southard

Dear Sir   Richmond May 4th. 1828

On my return a day or two past from a visit to my friends in the upper country I had the pleasure of receiving your "Anniversary Address" delivered before The Columbian Society at Washington.[1] I have read it with much gratification as well as interest.

Permit me to thank you for the pleasure its perusal has given me and to assure you that I am with great and respectful esteem, Your Obedt

J MARSHALL

ALS, NjP, Southard Papers. Addressed to Southard in Washington and franked; postmarked Washington, 4 May. Endorsed by Southard as received on 6 May.

1. Southard, *Anniversary Address Delivered before the Columbian Institute, at Washington* (Washington, D.C., 1828).

To [Levi Woodbury]

Sir   Richmond May 20th. 1828

On my return from the court in North Carolina I received your eloquent speech on the bill for the relief of the surviving officers of the revolution which I have read with real pleasure.[1] I thank you for this mark of your politeness and attention and beg you to be assured that I am with respect and esteem, Your obedt

J MARSHALL

ALS, DLC, Montgomery Blair Papers. Identity of recipient based on internal evidence.

1. Levi Woodbury, *Remarks by Mr. Woodbury, of New-Hampshire, on the First Decision of the Bill for the Relief of the Surviving Officers of the Revolution* (Washington, D.C., 1828). Woodbury (1789–1851), of New Hampshire, was a member of the U.S. Senate from 1825 to 1831. He subsequently served as secretary of the navy and as secretary of the treasury in the Jackson and Van Buren administrations. Elected to the Senate again in 1841, Woodbury resigned in 1845 to accept an appointment as associate justice of the Supreme Court, replacing Joseph Story.

To Edward Everett

Dear Sir   Richmond, May 21st. 1828

On my return from North Carolina I received your speech on the subject of retrenchment for which I am much obliged to you.[1] I had seen it previously in the papers, but have read it a second time with pleasure, and am gratified at the opportunity of preserving it in a pamphlet form. If any fair mind had received impressions unfavourable to the President on the points which you notice, those impressions must have been removed by your explanations and arguments. With great respect and esteem, I am Sir your Obedt

J MARSHALL

ALS, MHi. Addressed to Everett in Washington and franked; postmarked Richmond, 21 May. Endorsed by Everett.

1. *Speech of Mr. Everett, of Mass. on the Subject of Retrenchment: Delivered in the House of Representatives of the United States, Feb. 1, 1828* (Washington, D.C., 1828). Everett's speech brought forth John Randolph's celebrated speech of the same day.

Wright v. Stanard
Opinion
U.S. Circuit Court, Virginia, 23 May 1828

In December 1824 Philadelphia merchants Samuel G. Wright and David Cooke obtained a judgment in an action of assumpsit against John King of Richmond. In pursuance of this judgment they sued out a writ of elegit in November 1825 against King's Richmond real estate. At the same time this property was being extended under the elegit, Robert Stanard purchased the same property under a March 1825 decree of the state Superior Court of Chancery in Richmond. Wright and Cooke then brought an action of ejectment against Stanard in the federal court in December 1826. A jury issued a special verdict on 16 December 1826, on which Marshall pronounced the following opinion (U.S. Cir. Ct., Va., Rec. Bk. XVI, 39–40; XVIII, 467–86).

Wright & Cook
v
Stannard

This cause comes on upon a special verdict found in an ejectment ¶1 brought to obtain possessi⟨on⟩ of a lott in the city of Richmond which was taken by virtue of a writ of elegit issued on a judgement of this court. The ejectment being the prescribed mode for obtaining actual possession in such a case, the question is, Was this lott subject to the writ when it was exe[c]uted.

The judgement was rendered in favour of the plaintiffs against John ¶2 King on the 16th. day of December in the year 1824. The writ of elegit issued on the 14th. of November 1825.[1] The special verdict finds that John King was seized in fee of the lott on which the inquisition was taken, on the 30th. of September 1819, on which day he conveyed a part of the premisses to John Gibson and John McCrea in trust for the security of a debt in the deed mentioned. On the 9th. of October he conveyed the residue of the premisses to the same trustees also for the benefit of a creditor in that deed mentioned.[2]

The debt secured by the deed of September 1819 was payable by instal- ¶3 ments, the last of which fell due on the 16th. day of Jany. 1832; and the deed stipulated that the said King should retain the possession and re- ceive the profits until default should be made in the last payment.

The debt secured by the deed of october was also payable by instal- ¶4 ments, the last of which fell due on the 24th. day of Jany. 1825, and the trustees were to sell if on that day any part of the debt should remain unpaid.

The interest of the said John King so far as it was a present interest, was ¶5 unquestionably subject to an elegit. It remains then to enquire whether this interest has been so transferred as to be placed out of the reach of that writ.

On the 22⟨d⟩. of March 1820 John King & Helen S. King his wife in ¶6 pursuance of an agreement to make a reasonable provision for the dower of the said Helen S. which is recited in the deeds, conveyed the dower right of the said Helen S. to certain real estate which had been previously conveyed by the said John King in trust for certain creditors in the said deeds mentioned.[3]

On the 30th. of March 1820 John King conveyed certain real property ¶7 including the premisses in the declaration mentioned to Peter V. Daniel & James Rawlings in trust for his said Wife.[4] This deed professes to be made in consideration of the agreement recited in the deed of the 22d.

RICHMOND CITY HALL
Designed by Robert Mills and constructed, 1816–18. U.S. Circuit
Court sat here beginning in the 1820s.
Courtesy of the Library of Virginia

of the same month; and after its execution the trustees received the rents of the said tenement for the benefit of the said Helen S. The Jury find that at the date of this deed John King was greatly embarassed in his circumstances, and had conveyed great part of his property in trust for his creditors. They also find that the dower right conveyed in the deed of the 22d. of March was worth $1016.67 and that the dower right of the said Helen S. in other property conveyed by her husband but not by herself was worth $1777; and that th⟨e⟩ property conveyed by the deed of the 30th. of March in satisfaction of dower released by the deed of the 22d. of March was worth $3040.[5]

The defendant claims under a sale made in pursuance of an interlocutory decree of the court of chancery for the state, which was pronounced on the 26th. day of March 1825 in a suit brought by Mollin Rankin & Gallop, creditors of the said John King to set aside the deed of the 30th. of March 1820 as being fraudulent as to creditors.[6] ¶8

The plaintiffs were not parties to this suit, and, consequently, are not bound by the decree. They have therefore a right to reexamine the validity of the deed which was the subject of that decree. Having obtained their judgement before the decree was pronounced, and having issued their writ of elegit while that judgement was in force, the decree, however correct in its principles, must leave the property subject to the lien, if any, which was created by the judgement. ¶9

If the deed of the 30th. of March 1820 was absolutely void, then the interest which the deed of the 22d. of the same month left in John King was liable to his creditors and was bound by the plaintiffs' judgement. If that deed was valid no interest remained in John King other than an equity of redemption. ¶10

The dower relinquished by Mrs. King certainly constituted a valid consideration for a deed which should settle on her a fair equivalent for that right. But the dower which she relinquished was worth but little more than one third of the property conveyed to her as that equivalent. A court of chancery may very properly, and does, consider such a deed as being held in trust for the wife to the value of the dower she has released, and for the creditors as to the residue. But how is such a deed treated in a court of common law? ¶11

At law the deed cannot be sustained in part only, but must be entirely good or entirely void. ¶12

The statute of frauds avoids all covinous conveyances made with the intent to delay hinder or defraud creditors, but does not extend to conveyances which are made on good consideration and in good faith. It has been already said that the dower released by Mrs. King under an agreement to make an adequate settlement on her, was a *good* consideration in the sense in which the word is used in the act, and I can find no case in which a court of law has ever held a deed of settlement on a wife to be absolutely void because the estate conveyed was worth more than the ¶13 price for which it was conveyed. Meer inadequacy of price may be so great as to be evidence of fraud to be submitted to a jury, but has never been determined to be, in itself, a fraud upon which a court will pronounce a deed to be absolutely void. In this case, the jury has not found fraud. There is no secret trust for the benefit of the husband. On the contrary, the trustees were put in possession of the property and received the profits for the separate use of the wife.

¶14   The plfs. contend that though the jury have not found fraud, they have found facts which amount to fraud, and have submitted the question to the court whether upon those facts the law be for the plaintiffs.

¶15   Without affirming or denying that a verdict may present a case to the court which, though it does not contain a specific finding that the deed is covinous or fraudulent, or made to deceive or delay creditors, may contain such equivalent matter as will in point of law show the deed to be void. I will hazard the opinion that meer evidence of fraud, circumstances which may or may not accompany coven, do not constitute such a case. The court will consider those circumstances on which the plaintiffs rely as amounting in themselves to a fraud.

¶16   1st. The first is the difference between the value of the dower which has been relinquished, and the property which has been settled in compensation for that dower.

¶17   The court has already said that this difference, if the conveyance be made with a real intent to pass the property, does not of itself, vitiate the deed in a court of law. If the value of the dower had been a few dollars or cents less than the value of the property conveyed in satisfaction of it, no person would suppose the deed to be a nullity on that account. And if a small difference of value would not avoid it, what is the difference that will? Where does the law stop? The difference may be so great as to satisfy the conscience of the jury that the conveyance is intended to cover the property from the just claims of creditors; but as a meer question of law, I can find nothing in the books which will justify a court in saying that a deed otherwise unexceptionable, is void because the consideration is of less value than the property conveyed.

¶18   2.The other circumstance on which the plaintiffs rely is that the deed of the 30th. of March conveys all the property of John King, which property still remained in his possession.

¶19   The verdict finds the deed, but does not find that it comprehended all his property. On this subject the jury say "We find that at the date of the deed last mentioned, the said King was greatly embarassed in his circumstances, and the greater part of his property was conveyed by deeds of trust to secure the debts in those deeds specified." This finding certainly does not show that the whole of his property was comprehended in the deed of the 30th. of March 1820. The jury find a subsequent deed dated on the 24th. of May in the same year which purports to convey other property to trustees for his creditors.[7] The deed of the 30th. of

March certainly stipulates for the surplus money arising from his property which was conveyed in trust, but only the greater part of his property was so conveyed.

Neither does the verdict show that King retained possession of the property. The deed itself does not stipulate for his retaining possession; and it authorizes the trustees to receive the rents for the separate use of the wife. It authorizes her residence in any tenement she might elect which was not rented out, but this is not a stipulation for the possession even of that tenement, much less of the whole property, but the husband. The verdict does not show that this privilege was even exercised, or could have been exercised. ¶20

It appears to me that the deed of the 30th. of March 1820 was valid at law, and conveyed the interest which was left in the said John King by the deed of the 30th. of September 1819. ¶21

It remains to enquire how far the proceedings in chancery can affect this cause. ¶22

The court of chancery sustained the deed to the extent of the consideration which moved from Mrs. King but no farther, and directed the property to be sold and the residue of the money to be paid to the creditor at whose suit the sale was decreed. The plaintiffs in this cause were not parties to that suit, and were consequently not bound by the decree. But if they would avail themselves of it, they must admit its validity. They cannot take a part and reject a part of it. ¶23

The decree ascertains the value of the dower right of Mrs. King and limits her claim under the deed to that value, which amount was received before the service of the elegit. ¶24

The sale under the decree was made while the Marshal of this court was taking the inquisition for the extent of the lot, and the chancellor has directed a conveyance to be made to the purchaser.[8] ¶25

The counsel for the plaintiffs has taken several exceptions to the proceedings in chancery, which would be considered if the verdict showed a title at law in the plaintiffs independent of the decree of the court of chancery. But the verdict I think does not show such a title, and I do not think that this is a case in which the decree can be taken in part and rejected in part. ¶26

I am therefore of opinion that the law on this second[9] verdict is for the defendant. ¶27

PPAmP; printed, John W. Brockenbrough, *Reports of Cases Decided by the Honourable John Marshall . . .* , II (Philadelphia, 1837), 312–17. For JM's deletions and interlineations, see Textual Notes below.

1. Special verdict, 16 Dec. 1826, U.S. Cir. Ct., Va., Rec. Bk. XVIII, 483.

2. Ibid., 469–72. JM misstated the date of the second conveyance, which should be 4 Oct. 1819. It was recorded on 9 Oct.

3. Ibid., 472–75.

4. Ibid., 475.

5. Ibid., 478.

6. The plaintiffs in this suit in the Richmond Superior Court of Chancery were Stuart Mollan, John Rankin, and Alexander Gallop, partners in the merchant firm of Mollan, Rankin, and Gallop. The defendants, in addition to King and his wife, were Daniel and Rawlings. As the clerk noted, he did not insert the record of the state chancery suit into the record book because the original papers had been returned to the chancery court after the trial "and no copy of the record has ever been filed." However, a copy of the special verdict in the case papers does have the the the record of the chancery suit appended to it (ibid., 482–83; special verdict, [16 Dec. 1825], Wright and Cooke v. Stanard, U.S. Cir. Ct., Va., Ended Cases [Unrestored], 1828, Vi).

7. U.S. Cir. Ct., Va., Rec. Bk. XVIII, 478–82.

8. The sale under the decree took place on 14 Nov. 1825, the date of the writ of elegit. The chancery court confirmed the sale and directed a conveyance on 14 Jan. 1826 (special verdict, [16 Dec. 1825], Wright and Cooke v. Stanard).

9. Brockenbrough has "special," which JM evidently intended to write.

Textual Notes

¶ 1	l. beg.	~~This is~~ ↑This cause comes on upon a special verdict found in↓ an
	ll. 2–3	was taken ~~by the proper officer and~~ by virtue
	l. 4	prescribed ~~remedy~~ ↑mode↓ for obtaining
¶ 2	l. beg.	The ~~verdict~~ judgement was rendered in
	l. 2	the year 182 [erasure] ↑4↓. The
	l. 3	November 1825 ~~and~~. The special
	ll. 6–7	trust for ~~certain creditors~~ ↑the security of a debt↓ in the
	ll. 8–9	the benefit of ~~his~~ ↑a↓ creditor in
¶ 3	l. beg.	The [erasure] ↑debt↓ secured by
¶ 4	l. beg.	The ↑debt secured by the↓ deed of october was
	ll. 3–4	sell if ~~default should be made in the payment by that day of any part of the whole debt.~~ ↑on that day any part of the debt should remain unpaid.↓
¶ 5	l. 1	interest ~~which remained in~~ ↑of↓ the said
¶ 6	ll. 2–3	an agreement ↑to make a reasonable provision for the dower of the said Helen S. which is↓ recited
¶ 7	l. 4	agreement ~~in~~ recited
	ll. 13	satisfaction of dower ~~conveyed~~ ↑released↓ by
¶ 8	l. 3	brought by ~~Mollan~~ ↑Mollin↓ Rankin
	l. 5	March 1820 as ↑being↓ fraudulent
¶10	ll. 4–5	John King ~~:~~ ↑other than an equity of redemption.↓
¶12	ll. 1–2	but must be ↑entirely↓ good or
¶13	l. 3	consideration and ~~bona fide~~ in good faith
	l. 7	settlement ↑on a wife↓ to be
	l. 8	because the ~~land~~ ↑estate↓ conveyed
	ll. 10–11	jury, but ~~is not~~ ↑has never been determined to be↓, in itself
	l. 12	void. ~~In Roe v Mitton 2 Wils. 356~~ In this
	l. 13	There is no ↑secret↓ trust
¶15	l. beg.	~~I do not~~ Without affirming
	l. 2	though it ~~may~~ ↑does↓ not contain

	ll. 5–6	evidence of a fraud, ~~facts~~ ↑circumstances↓ which may or may not accompany [*erasure*] coven,
¶17	ll. 5–6	if a small ~~sum~~ difference
¶18	ll. 2–3	King, ~~and yet However retains the possession of it~~ which property
¶19	ll. 9–12	creditors. ↑The deed of the 30th. of March certainly stipulates for the surplus money arising from his property which was conveyed in trust, but only the greater part of his property was so conveyed.↓
¶21	l. 1	30th. of March ↑1820↓ was
¶23	l. 1	deed to the ~~extend~~ extent of the
¶25	l. 2	inquisition for the ~~extend~~ extent of
¶26	l. beg.	~~The finding~~ The counsel for the

United States v. Graves
Opinion
U.S. Circuit Court, Virginia, 24 May 1828

This case arose from the delinquency of Thomas B. Ellis of Surry County, U.S. collector of direct taxes and internal duties for the fifteenth collection district of Virginia. In May 1819 U.S. Attorney Stanard brought an action of debt in the U.S. District Court at Richmond on Ellis's performance bond, executed in February 1816 and signed by Charles H. Graves and three other sureties. The United States obtained judgment on the bond in April 1820, Ellis having died in the meantime. After execution was levied on this judgment, Graves and others gave a forthcoming bond for the delivery of slaves at a certain date in satisfaction of the judgment. On the failure to deliver this property, the U.S. attorney obtained judgment on the forfeited forthcoming bond in April 1823. In July 1825 he applied to the equity side of the U.S. Circuit Court, seeking payment of Graves's share of the judgment out of lands in Surry County sold by Graves or conveyed to trustees after the commencement of the original suit on the performance bond. The U.S. attorney claimed that under federal law a lien attached to those lands from the time that suit began. In addition to Graves and his trustees or purchasers of his lands, the defendants in the equity suit were Ellis's administrator and the other sureties or their representatives. Their answers were filed in December 1825 and January 1826. In June 1826 the court, reserving a decision on the liability of the purchasers of Graves's lands, ordered the commissioner to make a report on what estate Graves possessed or controlled at the time the bill was filed. These proceedings delayed a final decision until the May 1828 term (U.S. Dist. Ct., Va., Rec. Bk. IV, 304–9; V, 53–56; U.S. Cir. Ct., Va., Ord. Bk. XII, 116, 146, 234; bill in chancery, 28 July 1825; answers in chancery, 1, 8 Dec. 1825, Jan. 1826, 23 May 1826, U.S. v. Graves, U.S. Cir. Ct., Va., Ended Cases [Unrestored], 1828, Vi).

The United States

v

Graves & al

¶1   In the year 1813 Thomas B Ellis was appointed collector of the internal taxes in one of the districts of Virginia, and gave bond for the performance of his duty with Charles H Graves, James Wilson, Nathaniel Cocke, and Bartholomew D Henly as his sureties. Having failed to account for the monies he had collected, his bond was put in suit; and, on the 5th. of April 1820, a judgement was rendered against Graves, Wilson, and Cocke, the surviving obligors. On a settlement at the treasury, it appears that the actual deficiency is $7000.

¶2   The bill alleges that Thomas B. Ellis is dead insolvent, that the sureties, except the defendant Graves, have paid, or are ready to pay their aliquot parts of the debt; & that Graves was, when the suit was instituted, seized of two tracts of land which he has since conveyed away to satisfy creditors.[1]

¶3   This suit is brought against the said Graves and the other obligors or their representatives, and against the purchaser of the land said to have been in his possession, for the purpose of subjecting it to the payment of his portion of the debt.

¶4   The answer of Graves insists that Ellis left a considerable estate both real and personal. That an execution was issued on the judgement, which was levied on six negroes the property of some of the defendants and a forthcoming bond given which was forfeited. That at the rendition of the judgement, the defendant was in possession of personal estate sufficient to satisfy it. It insists on the want of due diligence on the part of The United States, and resists the lien claimed for them.[2]

¶5   The purchasers insist that the lien, if any was created by the act of Congress, does not bind the land in their hands; that the lien is conditional — dependent on a deficiency of personal estate; that the personal estate of those against whom the judgement was rendered was at the time, and is now, sufficient to satisfy it; & the plaintiffs have a plain remedy at law. They deny the insolvency of Graves, and also that of Ellis. They deny also the continuance of the lien created by the judgement; but the plaintiffs do not rely on this.[3]

¶6   The Exr. of Ellis denies that his estate is sufficient to satisfy the judgement.[4]

¶7   In June 1826 this court directed an account of the property in possession of the defendant Graves or in the possession of others in trust for his use.[5]

¶8   The report dated the 15th. of May 1827, shows that Graves has taken the oath of an insolvent debtor; but that some real and a few inconsiderable articles of personal property were continued in his schedule, and that deeds have been made of other real estate which was in his possession when the bill was filed.[6]

If this real estate is chargeable with that part of the debt which ought to ¶9 be paid by graves, some farther account must be taken. If it is not so chargeable, the account would be useless. It is therefore proper now to examine the question of lien which has been made by the defendants who are purchasers.

v. 4th. p 627. Sec. 6. The act of Congress declares "that the amount of ¶10 all debts due to The United States by any collector of internal duties" &c.[7]

The first part of this section unquestionably charges the lands and real ¶11 estate of the collector and his sureties with the amount of all debts due to The United States from the institution of the suit. The effect of this lien is I think as little to be doubted as its existence. It does not indeed pass the estate; but it binds the land as effectually as a mortgage can bind it. A mortgage binds by force of law, and a lien created by statute has all the force law can give it. It commences with the suit, and, as its object is to secure the land as a fund from which the debt may be satisfied, it terminates only when that object is accomplished.

Had the enactment terminated with that part which creates the lien, ¶12 the plaintiffs case would be relieved from the most serious difficulty which opposes the relief claimed by the bill. But the section proceeds with a provision for the execution of the lien. That provision is that the land may be sold in the manner prescribed by the act in a particular state of things which is also prescribed. Although then the creation and the continuance of the lien be certain, the enquiry remains whether that state of things exists in which it may be enforced.

In pursuing this enquiry, it may be useful to consider the subject on ¶13 which the law was to operate. In every state of the Union, I believe, except Virginia, lands may be taken in execution for the payment of debts.[8] Consequently in every state except this, the forms of executions are such that lands may be siezed to satisfy them; and these forms are adopted for the courts of The United States. These laws however varied in the different states. I am not acquainted with the different regulations which prevailed, but believe that in some instances the land could not be sold till the personal estate was exhausted; in some perhaps it might be seized immediately; and in some it might be delivered at a valuation. But in all, I believe, an alienation pending the suit, would convey a secure title to the purchaser.

This section then has two objects. The first, to overreach any inter- ¶14 mediate conveyance between the issuing of the original writ and the service of the execution; the second, to prescribe a uniform course for proceeding against lands under all judgements obtained by The United States against delinquent collectors and their sureties.

In a state where land may be taken in execution, and may, in pursuance ¶15 of the act of Congress, be sold at public auction, no reason can be assigned for coming into a court of equity unless there be some fraudulent alienation before the original writ was issued. If the land may be taken in

execution & sold under the judgement there is no ground for the interposition of equity.

¶16   Under what circumstances may this execution and sale take place? The
law answers when there is a "want of goods and chattels or other personal
effects of such collector or his sureties to satisfy any judge[ment] which
shall or may be recovered against them respectively." This want of goods
and chattels then is a state of things which must exist before the land can
be sold to satisfy the judgement. Congress intended that the personal
estate should be first exhausted.

¶17   If the suit had been instituted against only one of the obligors, it will
not be contended that his land might be sold while personal estate remained to satisfy the judgement. An officer who should sell the land in
the first instance would violate the law, would probably be restrained by
the court, and would certainly expose himself to the action of the injured party. It may well be doubted whether the title he could make
would be valid.

¶18   Is any distinction to be taken between a judgement against one obligor
and a judgement against all of them? I can perceive no reason for such a
distinction. The judgment is one entire thing which affects all equally.
The execution also, is entire, and affects equally the property of all. If it
possess an intrinsic quality which postpones its capacity to reach land
until the personal estate liable to it shall be exhausted, that intrinsic
quality adheres to it and applies to its operation when emanating on a
judgement against several, as completely as when emanating on a judgement against one. On a joint judgement then, the personal estate of all
liable to the execution must be exhausted, before land can be sold unless
there be something in the language of the act of Congress which shall
require a different construction. I find nothing in that act which varies
the general principle; nothing which may enable a court or its officer, for
the sake of equality, to sieze the lands of one of the debtors while personal
estate remains which is liable to the execution, although that personal
estate may belong to another who has paid his aliquot part of the debt.

¶19   If this construction be correct, then The United States do not, under
this act of Congress, possess the power to sell at discretion, for the purpose of equality, or for any purpose, the land of one of the parties against
whom judgement has been obtained, while the execution may be satisfied by the personal property of others. A court of equity cannot give
this right in states where the judgement is to be satisfied out of land by
legal process.

¶20   Can a different rule exist in the state of Virginia?

¶21   The act of 1789 rendered perpetual by the act of 1792 adopts the
forms of writs and executions then in force in the states respectively.[9]
Although in Virginia lands could not be taken in execution by creditors
generally, they were liable to executions issued on certain judgements
rendered in favour of the Commonwealth.[10] When then the act of Con-

gress declared that the lands of their debtors might be sold in certain cases to satisfy the debt due to The United States, the process act adopted the form of execution issued by the Commonwealth in the state of Virginia. Could this be doubted, the process act provides for the case by subjecting the forms of writs and executions "to such alterations and additions as the said courts (of The United States) respectively shall in their discretion deem expedient." There is then I think, the same remedy at law against the lands of delinquent collectors and their sureties in Virginia as in other states.

Were this otherwise, Were it understood that the process act did not ¶22 adopt for The United States the execution against lands which might be issued by the Commonwealth on judgements in favor of itself, and that the omission of the court to make the requisite alteration in and addition to the form of the execution rendered an application to equity necessary, still equity could interpose so far only as to remedy the omission and carry the intention of Congress into execution in Virginia as in the other states. That is to subject the lands of those against whom judgement has been rendered where there is a deficiency of personal estate.

It is not alleged that such deficiency exists in this case, and therefore ¶23 no foundation is laid for proceeding at law against the lands.

Has any thing occurred which authorizes a court of equity to interpose ¶24 and subject lands which were not liable at law, to the payment of this debt.

The execution which issued on the original judgement was levied and ¶25 a forthcoming bond given which was forfeited. The bond was returned to court and execution was awarded on it.

It is contended on the part of Graves and those who claim title to lands ¶26 held by him when the original suit was instituted on the part of The United States, that these proceedings discharge the lien created by issuing the original writ.

The state courts, by whose decisions on this point this court is bound, ¶27 have undoubtedly determined that a forthcoming bond when forfeited is a payment of the judgement on which the execution issued; and that no farther proceedings can be founded on that judgement. The forthcoming bond is substituted for the judgement, and the recourse of the plaintiff is against the parties to that bond.[11]

The forthcoming bond being considered as a satisfaction of the judgement, Graves and those who claim under him contend that it is necessarily a discharge of the original debt and consequently of the lien created by the act of Congress. ¶28

As the opinion has been already expressed that this lien cannot be ¶29 enforced against the real estate while personal estate remains, and as the personal estate cannot be considered as exhausted until the forthcoming bond shall be shown to be unproductive, it is not necessary at present to decide this very doubtful question. I certainly think it a doubtful question; for the bond though a technical is not actual satisfaction; and, though it arrests all farther proceedings on the judgement, I am not entirely convinced that it extinguishes the original claim. Be this as it may, the fact that it prevents a sale of the lands under the judgement cannot empower a court of equity to enforce the lien until the impossibility of obtaining satisfaction from the bond shall be shown. Whether equity can, even in that state of things afford the aid which is requested is a point on which I have not formed an opinion.

¶30   The relief prayed in the bill has been supported on distinct ground from that which has been considered. It has been contended that sureties who pay the debt may assert the claim of The United States upon the principal, and that the equitable right which sureties have against each other for contribution may induce the court to decree in this suit against those who will be ultimately bound to the parties who shall pay more than their just proportion of the debt.

¶31   Though both these propositions are true I do not think either of them can avail the plaintiff or those for whose benefit the principle is advanced.

¶32   The United States can impart to a surety no other right than The United States could assert for themselves. Having no right to enforce the lien on the lands in the present state of things, they cannot impart this right to sureties.

¶33   The same consideration restrains this court from decreeing in this cause on the principle of contribution. The right to contribution grows out of the equitable relations of the parties with each other. If a claim exist against several defendants, and from any circumstance one ought to pay more than another, or if one defendant would have a right to proceed against another for any sum he may be decreed to pay, the court will adjust the equity between the parties and decree in the first instance according to their ultimate liabilities. But in this case the plaintiff has a right to recover against any of the parties brought before the court. If the decree against one person gives him a right upon another against whom the plaintiff could not sustain a suit in the first instance then I think the court ought not to settle this controversy between the defendants unless it could entertain jurisdiction in a suit between the parties brought for the purpose of settling their equities. If the decree which the plaintiff asks against the lands which form the subject of the present controversy cannot be made for the benefit of The United States, then I think it cannot be made in the name of The United States for the benefit of a surety. If the judgement against such surety gives him claims upon others, those claims must be asserted in a court which has jurisdiction of them. I do not think that the bill so far as it asserts the right of The United States to enforce their lien upon the lands of any of the defendants can be sustained at present.

¶34   The counsel for The U.S. having admitted that the estate of Ellis had been exhausted by process in a distinct suit, and that the debt might be satisfied from the forthcoming bond, it is ordered that the bill be dismissed without prejudice.[12]

AD, Marshall Judicial Opinions, PPAmP; printed, John W. Brockenbrough, *Reports of Cases Decided by the Honourable John Marshall . . .* , II (Philadelphia, 1837), 379–87. For JM's deletions and interlineations, see Textual Notes below.

1. Bill in chancery, 28 July 1825, U.S. v. Graves.

2. Answer of Charles H. Graves, 23 May 1826, ibid.

3. Answer of Richard H. Edwards, 8 Dec. 1825, ibid.

4. Joint and several answers of William Dobie, administrator of Nathaniel Cocke, James Wilson, and Joseph Barham, administrator of Thomas B. Ellis, 22 Nov. 1825, ibid.

5. U.S. Cir. Ct., Va., Ord. Bk. XII, 116.

6. Commissioner's report, 15 May 1827, U.S. v. Graves.

7. JM cited the 1813 act "making further provision for the collection of internal duties" (*U.S. Statutes at Large*, III, 82, 83). His source was *Laws of the United States of America, from the 4th of March, 1789, to the 4th of March, 1815* (5 vols.; Philadelphia and Washington, 1815), IV, 627.

8. Although in Virginia lands could not be sold on execution, the writ of elegit enabled a creditor to take temporary possession of one-half a debtor's lands to satisfy his debt (*PJM*, V, l–li; William Griffith, *Annual Law Register of the United States*, III [1822; New York, 1972 reprint], 335).

9. This was the act to regulate processes (*U.S. Statutes at Large*, I, 93, 275–76).

10. This provision had been in effect since 1787 (Hening, *Statutes*, XII, 558–59; *Revised Code of Va.*, II, 51).

11. Brockenbrough's note cites the opinions of Judge William H. Cabell in Cooke v. Piles, 2 Munf. 153 (Va. Ct. App., 1811) and of Judge Spencer Roane in Lusk v. Ramsay, 3 Munf. 454 (Va. Ct. App., 1811). This subject is discussed in Conway Robinson, *The Practice in the Courts of Law and Equity in Virginia* (3 vols.; Richmond, Va., 1832–39), I, 597, citing these and other cases.

12. The formal decree of 24 May 1828 is recorded in U.S. Cir. Ct., Va., Ord. Bk. XII, 234.

Textual Notes

¶ 2	l. 3	that Graves [*erasure*] ↑was,↓ when
¶ 5	l. 5	plaintiffs have ~~consequently~~ a plain
	l. 8	do not ~~contend for~~ ↑rely on↓ this.
¶10	l. 2	duties" shall ~~"be a lien upon the lands and real estate of such collector and of his sureties" "from the time when suit shall be instituted for recovering the same."~~
		~~— The opinion of the court does not turn exclusively on this claim of enacting part of the section taken unconnected with the qualifications which follows; but as the question which arises upon it has been argued with great earnestness, and is of considerable interest, I shall not pass it by, unnoticed.~~
		~~— It has been truely said that a lien upon an estate is not the estate itself, but a tie which binds it. This tie however binds the estate to the full amount to secure which it is created. The act of Congress, as applied to this particular case~~ ↑&c.↓
¶11	l. 9	that object is ~~eff~~ accomplished.
¶13	l. 1	to consider ~~the state of~~ the subject
	l. 4	every state ↑except this,↓

¶15	l. 1	where land ~~might~~ ↑may↓ be taken in execution, and ~~might~~ ↑may↓, in pursuance
	ll. 4–5	taken in execution ↑& sold↓ under the
¶16	l. 1 beg.	~~When~~ ↑Under what circumstances↓ may
¶17	l. 6	It may ~~be~~ well be doubted
¶18	ll. 6–7	intrinsic quality ↑adheres to it and↓ applies
¶19	l. 1	The United States ~~could~~ do not,
	ll. 4–5	be satisfied [*erasure*] ↑by↓ the personal
¶20	l. 1	of Virginia ~~where lands generally cannot be taken in execution for debt, and where the act of Congress which adopts the forms of writs and executions then in force in the states respectively, has not been supposed to furnish any execution against lands~~ ↑?↓
¶21	l. 3	Although ↑in Virginia↓ lands could not
	l. 7	to satisfy [*erasure*] ↑the↓ debt due to ~~the~~ ↑The↓ United
	l. 11	States) ~~shal~~ ↑respectively↓ shall
¶22	l. 1	Were it ~~to~~ understood that
	l. 6	remedy the ~~defec~~ omission and
¶23	l. 1 beg.	~~It does~~ It is not alleged
¶24	l. 1	occurred ~~in this case~~ which authorizes
	ll. 1–2	interpose and ~~subject~~ subject
¶25	ll. 1–2	was levied ~~on the personal estate of one of the parties, who gave what is termed a forthcoming bond~~ ↑and a forthcoming bond given↓ which was
¶27	l. 2	that ~~their~~ a forthcoming
	l. 3	payment of [*erasure*] the judgement
¶28	l. 1	as a ~~technical?~~ satisfaction
	ll. 3–4	consequently of ~~th~~ ↑the↓ lien created
¶29	l. 11	satisfaction from [*erasure*] the bond
¶30	l. 5	decree in this ~~first inst~~ suit against
¶33	ll. 9–10	If the ~~plain~~ decree against
	l. 13	entertain jurisdiction [*erasure*] in a suit
¶34	l. beg.	↑The counsel for The U.S. having admitted that the estate of Ellis had been exhausted by process in a distinct suit, and that the debt might be satisfied from the forthcoming bond, it is ordered that [*erasure*] the bill be dismissed without prejudice.↓

To [Edward Bates]

Dear Sir   Richmond May 29th. 1828

On my return from North Carolina I had the pleasure of receiving your letter accompanying the amendment you propose to the bill then depending before the House of Representatives respecting the Judiciary of The United States.[1] I beg you to receive my acknowledgements for the kind and flattering sentiments you express towards myself.

I have avoided declaring an opinion respecting our judicial establish-ment, having no other desire than to aid, while I remain in office, in the faithful execution of any system which the wisdom of Congress may de-vise. I was myself a member of the House of Represe⟨n⟩tatives when the act of 1801 was first introduc⟨ed⟩ and gave it my hearty support.[2] It did not pass till the subsequent session. The idea of adjourning questions to the supreme court on which the Judges at the circuits might be divided had not then occurred, and it was supposed that the circuit court ought to consist of three Judges. I am now satisfied that it may very well consist of two, and that the appointment of one circuit Judge for each circuit would be sufficient.

I presume your plan is to embrace all the states in the Union in the same system. Consequently the circuits must be enlarged. How far this may be practicable in the western states I am unable to determine. I presume that all of those states cannot be comprehended in one circuit. Consequently the present arrangement must be so changed as to bring the Atlantic states into fewer circuits, or extend them to the west.

The calculation I presume is that, by transferring the original business of the circuit to . . .

AL[S], ViW. One or more pages missing. For identity of recipient, see n. 1.

1. Letter not found. The context points to Edward Bates (1793–1869) as JM's correspon-dent. Bates was a Missouri congressman who later served as U.S. attorney general during the Civil War. On 4 Feb. 1828 Philip P. Barbour, chairman of the House Judiciary Commit-tee, reported a bill "further to amend the Judicial System of the United States." This bill proposed to increase the number of Supreme Court justices and judicial circuits from seven to ten. On 18 Feb. Bates submitted an amendment, in effect a new bill, proposing to transfer the original jurisdiction of the existing circuit courts to the district courts, abolish the present circuit courts, and establish new circuit courts consisting of a Supreme Court justice and all the district court justices within a circuit. Bates's amendment retained the existing number of circuit courts (seven), whose jurisdiction would now be exclusively appellate over the district courts (H.R. 144, 20th Cong. [1828]).

2. See *PJM,* IV, 117–18.

United States v. Moore
Opinion
U.S. Circuit Court, Virginia, 3 June 1828

This was an action of debt against Samuel McDowell Moore (1796–1875), son and administrator of Andrew Moore (1752–1821) of Rockbridge County. The elder Moore had been a member of the House of Representa-tives (1789–1797) and Senate (1804–9) and served as U.S. marshal (1810–21). Then a member of the state legislature, Samuel McDowell Moore later served a term (1833–35) in Congress. In April 1827 U.S. Attorney Robert Stanard brought an action of debt on Andrew Moore's performance bond as marshal, executed in January 1815. The defendant filed a plea of conditions performed in December 1827, to which the plaintiff replied, assigning four breaches of the condition of the bond. In May 1828 the defendant pleaded the act of limitations, but the court sustained the plaintiff's demurrer and overruled this plea. A jury then returned a conditional verdict, which brought forth this opinion from Marshall on 3 June 1828 (U.S. Cir. Ct., Va., Rec. Bk. XVIII, 533–36).

The United States

v

Moores admr.

¶1   This is an action of debt brought upon the official bond of the Marshall of this district, the intestate of the defendant, upon which the jury have found a verdict which assesses contingent damages dependent on a case stated by the parties. This case is so stated as to require the court to take into view the instructions which would have been given to the jury at the trial had instructions been asked.

¶2   The first breach assigned in the replication is that monies were received by the deputy of the Marshall for The United States on executions placed in his hands which money has never been paid over. On this breach no controversy arises.[1]

¶3   The second breach assigned is that two writs of capias ad respondendum were issued against debtors of The United States which were placed in the hands of the same deputy who neglected to execute them or either of them, or to return them or either of them, "whereby The United States were prevented from recovering judgement against each of the said debtors and the said debts and each of them have been and are totally lost to The said United States.["][2]

¶4   Damages are assessed to the amount of these two debts.[3]

¶5   The case stated is that two writs of capias ad respondendum against two several debtors of The United states were placed in the hands of the deputy who instead of executing them received the sums due from the several defendants, and made return thereof on the writs after which the suits were dismissed. The United States have never received this money and they now claim it from the estate of the Marshall. The defendant denies his liability for this claim.

¶6   In this first[4] assignment of breaches the receipt of the money is not brought into view. The neglect of duty in not serving the process is the fault alleged to have been committed by the officer, and for this neglect his principal is unquestionably liable. But what is the extent of his liability?

¶7   But one general answer can be given to this question. As in all other instances of neglect, he is liable to the extent of the injury producd thereby. This is to be ascertained by a jury. The replication alleges that the debt has been lost thereby; and if this fact be as alleged, the amount of the debt is the measure of damages. But this is a subject for the consideration of the jury. It was not submitted to the jury, and has been transferred to the court. If the loss of the debt was the direct and necessary legal consequence of this neglect, the verdict ought to stand; but if this be a subject on which the judgement of the jury under the instruction of the court ought to be exercised, then it would be improper in the court to decide upon it until that judgement shall be exercised.

It is too obvious to require discussion that the loss of a debt is not the ¶8 necessary consequence of neglecting to serve the first process which comes to the hands of the officer. The law provides for new process; and the question whether that new process may not be as available to the plaintiff as the original process depends on circumstances of which the jury must judge.

If in this case the plaintiff has been prevented from issuing new process ¶9 by the act of the officer, that is not alleged in this part of the replication. If it may be given in evidence on this general assignment, then we must look into the act which is alleged to have arrested further proceedings.

That act is the receipt of the money due to The United States. ¶10

If the officer was not authorized to receive this money, his receipt of it ¶11 could not bind The United States nor prevent further proceedings according to law; if he was authorized to receive it, the defendant will admit that the plf. could proceed no farther and that the loss of the debt is the consequence of not serving the process and receiving the money. This question will be properly considered under the third breach assigned in the replication.

3d. The 3d. breach is that the officer did arrest the said debtors as ¶12 commanded by the said process who thereupon "respectively paid to the said deputy the full amounts of their respective debts aforesaid and in consideration thereof the said deputy did then and there discharge the said debtors from the arrests aforesaid, and willfully failed to make due return of the said arrests or either of them, or to account for and pay the amounts so received from said debtors or any part thereof too the said United States whereby the said United States was prevented from obtaining judgements against their said debtors for their said debts, and the said debts were and are wholly lost to the said United States."[5]

To support this breach it would be necessary to show in the first in- ¶12 stance that the debtors were arrested.

This is not proved; but may and perhaps ought to be assumed by the ¶13 jury from the facts admitted in the case. The material enquiry then presents itself—Was the receipt of the money an official act? Was it authorized by the mandate of the writ?

We are decidedly of opinion that it was not. The mandate of the writ ¶14 was to take the person of the defendants mentioned ther[e]in and to have them before the court to answer the United States in a plea of debt

&c. A controversy exists between the parties which is to be adjusted, not by the officer, but by the court. His duty is ministerial, not judicial. It is to bring the debtor into court to receive its judgement, not to render that judgement.

¶15   The sum actually due is generally less than that demanded in the writ; and in these cases it was considerably less. The officer does not know officially the real amount of debt, and consequently cannot adjust it, & receive the money. If he is not authorized to ascertain the sum due and to receive that sum neither is he authorized to receive the whole sum mentioned in the writ and to discharge the persons arrested. His dut⟨y⟩ is prescribed by the words of the writ. He is to obey its mandate. It would be time misapplied to enter into a consideration of the consequences of permitting the Officer to depart from the mandate of the writ, and to make himself accountable to The United States when not authorized by law so to do. It is enough to say that the writ did not authorize him to receive the money, and that its receipt was not an official act.

¶16   Since the money was not received by virtue of the writ with the execution of which the Deputy was entrusted, his principal cannot be chargeable by the legal force of that receipt. If he is chargeable, it is in consequence of the official acts performed or omitted by his deputy.

¶17   The act performed is making his return which is "Debt and cost satisfied." The charge in the replication is that upon receiving the money he discharged the debt⟨or⟩s.

¶18   That this proceeding is a misfeasance in office which subjects the principal to the action of The United States is not controverted. But on this breach as on the 2d., the amount of damages depends on the amount of injury. The return of the officer did not estop The United States from taking such farther stop as is warranted by law. If the return shows service of the process the plaintiff might proceed again⟨st⟩ the defendant and the Marshal for want of bail; if it does not show service, or if it shows a discharge, the plf. might sue out new process. The return that the debt was satisfied did not bind The United States. The amount of injury therefore depends on all the circumstances, and those circumstances must be weighed by a jury.

¶19   The counsil for the United States insists that the money received by the deputy is in the measure of damage sustained by The United States; that the deputy is responsible for the sum so received, and, as he received by color of his office the principal is also responsible to the same extent.

¶20   But if the receipt of this money did not estop The United States, if it was not an official act authorized by the process or by law, the loss of the debt does not appear to be a necessary consequence from the return on the writ, or the neglect to take bail.

4th. The 4th. breach assigned is the nonpayment of the money received under sundry executions mentioned in the first breach and the money mentioned in the second and third breaches for which it is supposed that the district court has adjudged the Marshal to be liable.[6]

AD, Marshall Judicial Opinions, PPAmP; printed, John W. Brockenbrough, *Reports of Cases Decided by the Honourable John Marshall . . .*, II (Philadelphia, 1837), 320–24. For JM's deletions and interlineations, see Textual Notes below.

1. The first breach concerned an execution issued in May 1816 from the U.S. District Court at Norfolk on a judgment for $1,548.85, with interest from 14 Jan. The execution was placed in the hands of Moore's deputy, William P. Foster, who failed to account with the U.S. for the money collected on the execution. The conditional verdict assessed damages to the amount of the judgment (U.S. Cir. Ct., Va., Rec. Bk. XVIII, 534, 536).

2. The first writ was dated 18 May 1816 for the sum of $922.95; the second was dated 2 July 1816 for the sum of $185.36 (ibid., 534–35).

3. Ibid., 536. The total was $1108.31.

4. Brockenbrough corrected this to read "second." JM wrote paragraphs six through thirteen on a separate sheet, which he marked for insertion at this point.

5. The conditional verdict on this breach awarded damages to the same amount as assessed on the second breach (ibid., 534–35, 536).

6. Ibid., 535. On this breach the conditional verdict awarded damages of $2,657.16, the total amount of the judgment mentioned in the first breach and the two debts mentioned in the second breach. The verdict further stated that if the court found for the plaintiff on the fourth breach, then the jury finds for the defendant on the other breaches. If, however, the court was of opinion that the plaintiff was not entitled to judgment on the fourth breach but was entitled to recover either on the second or third breach, then the jury finds "for the defendant on that one of the said second or third breaches, on which Judgment shall not be entered so that in any event, the total amount of damages assessed against the defendant . . . shall not exceed the amount above assessed on the fourth breach" (ibid., 535, 536).

Brockenbrough omitted the passage on the fourth breach, which JM apparently left unfinished. The court set aside the conditional verdict as "too imperfect to enable the court to render Judgment upon it" and ordered a new trial. On 4 June a jury returned a verdict for the plaintiff on the first breach, awarding damages of $1,548.85, with interest from 14 Jan. 1816; for the defendant on the second breach; for the plaintiff on the third breach, awarding damages of one cent; and for the defendant on the fourth breach, having been instructed by the court that "the matters stated in that breach" were not "in point of law a breach of the condition of the bond."

In addition to this suit, the U.S. also brought an action of debt suggesting devastavit (that the administrator had wasted the estate) and a suit in chancery. These cases were dismissed in June 1832 on notice from the solicitor of the U.S. treasury that Andrew Moore's accounts had been settled (ibid., 537; XIX, 417–18, 457–61).

Textual Notes

¶ 1	l. 3	verdict which ~~gives~~ assesses
¶ 2	ll. 2–3	on executions ~~when~~ placed in
¶ 3	l. 3	deputy who ~~failed~~ ↑neglected↓ to
¶ 5	ll. 1–2	ad respondendum ~~were~~ against two ↑several↓ debtors of
	ll. 4–5	which the ~~wri~~ suits were
	l. 7	claim. ~~In considering this point the first question which presents itself is, was the receipt of the money an official act? Was it authorized by the mandate of the writ? We~~

¶ 7 l. beg.   But one ~~an~~ general answer
¶ 8 l. 3   comes to ↑the↓ hands
¶11 l. 1   officer was ↑not↓ authorized
     l. 3   the ~~defendants~~ ↑defendant↓
¶15 l. 6   the writ and to ~~forbear the service of the process~~ ↑discharge
                 the persons arrested.↓ His
¶18 l. 2   The United States is ↑not↓ controverted.
     l. 7   the Marshal ↑for want of bail;↓ if it
¶20 ll. 2–3   by law, ~~it~~ ↑the loss of the debt↓ does not
     ll. 3–4   the return ~~of~~ ↑on↓ the writ, or the
     ll. 5–6   received under ~~th~~ ↑sundry↓ executions

Hamilton v. Cunningham
Opinion
U.S. Circuit Court, Virginia, 12 June 1828

In April 1827 Hamilton, Donaldson & Company, commission merchants of
New York City, brought an action of assumpsit against Alexander Cunningham, a Petersburg merchant. Cunningham was accustomed to shipping
cotton to the New York firm and sending bills of exchange drawn in Europe
to be sold. In the course of trade Cunningham drew bills of exchange on
Hamilton, Donaldson, becoming debtor to the company, "as is no uncommon thing with Virginians," Marshall observed. The transactions that gave
rise to the present case began in November 1825, when Cunningham, then
indebted to Hamilton, Donaldson, remitted two bills on Liverpool merchants to be sold and the proceeds placed to his credit. The New York firm
sold the bills, receiving payment partly in cash and partly in two promissory
notes payable in March 1826. Hamilton, Donaldson attempted to collect
payment at that time, but both the maker and indorser of the notes had
become insolvent. The company did not inform Cunningham of the notes'
dishonor until three months after the fact. The Petersburg merchant contended that the New Yorkers had assumed ownership of the promissory
notes and that he should have full credit for their amount. Trial of the
case took place over five days in December 1827, at the conclusion of which
a jury returned a special verdict on a case stated. The verdict awarded a
greater or lesser sum for the plaintiff depending on the court's opinion as to
which party was liable for the amount of the promissory notes. Finding
nothing in the authorities on principal and agent "applicable to this case,"
the chief justice turned to his colleague Story for advice: "You commercial
men are familiar with these questions—to us agriculturists they are at least
novel." The New Englander's reply (not found), wrote Marshall in acknowledgment, confirmed "the opinion I was previously disposed to adopt." The
court's judgment and Marshall's accompanying opinion were given on 12
June 1828 (U.S. Cir. Ct., Va., Rec. Bk. XVIII, 538–71; JM to Story, 11,
30 Dec. 1827).

Hamilton Donalson & Co
v
Cunningham

Before I proceed to the point on which this cause appears to me to ¶1
depend, it may be proper to notice some incidental questions which have
been suggested in its progress, or in the argument on the case agreed.

It was contended by the defendant at the trial before the jury, that the ¶2
plaintiffs, by mingling the property of the defendant, with that of others
in a joint note, so as to deprive him of that perfect controul over it which
his interest might require, or at least to embarass the exercise of that
controul, had so misconducted themselves in their agency as to become
liable for the debt. I was inclined to this opinion; but placed it upon the
usage at New York. The case states that usage, so as to justify the conduct
of the agents, and this is no longer a question in the cause; but I think it
proper to declare that I satisfied myself as soon as I looked into the
subject that my first impression was an erroneous one, and that the usage
of New York conforms to the general rule. 1. Liv. on agency 85. He quotes
Malynes Lex Merc. 81. 82 Molloy B. 3. ch. 8. Sec. 4. 2d. Dal 136 id. 134 4
Dal 136.[1] Beawes in his lex merc. p 36. of 6th. Dub. ed in his ch. of Factors
&c says "One and the same factor may and generally does act for several
merchants who must run the joint risk of his actions though they are
meer strangers to one another; as if five merchants shall remit to one
factor five distinct bales of goods and the factor make a joint sale of them
to one man who is to pay one moity down and the other at six months
end; if the buyer breaks before the second payment, each man must bear
a proportional share of the loss, and be contented to accept of their
dividend of the money advanced."[2]

That the bills were sold upon credit has not been urged against the ¶3
agents as misconduct because they gave notice thereof to their principals
who acquiesced in the sale. Independent of this fact, the sale upon credit
was necessary and usual at the time, and was within the power to sell. But
the defendants do insist on the fact that their agents received notes in
payment for the bills which notes had been given some time before and
were not indorsed by the purchasers of the bills.

These circumstances are said to be such as cast suspicion on the notes, ¶4
and ought to have restrained the agent from taking them.

What influence these circumstances connected with others might have ¶5
on a jury, it is not for me to say. They are presented to the court in the case
agreed by the parties, connected with no other circumstance than this,
that the makers of the note were at the time considered as good. If **A** and
B give their note to **C** on account of any transaction with him, and before
it becomes payable **C** wishes to negotiate it, I have never understood that,
in a commercial city, this is an unusual circumstance which ought to

discredit the note. If I am correct in this, I can perceive no distinction between taking this note having three months to run, and taking the note of **C** the purchaser with **D** as his surety on the same credit. The whole depends on the relative credit of the parties. If **A** & **B** are as trustworthy at the time as **C** & **D** I can perceive no solid reason for distinguishing between their notes. The same reasoning excuses the agent for not insisting on the indorsement of the purchaser. A man may be unwilling to put his name on any paper, and this might render doubtful notes still more doubtful, but ought not, I think, to discredit the notes of men whose mercantile standing was solid at the time. The circumstances that the bills were sold for a note of previous date, on which the purchaser did not place his name are not I think *per se* sufficient to weigh down the fact that the maker and indorser were at the time in good credit.

¶6   Some stress has been laid on the fact that the nam⟨e⟩ of the purchaser has not been communicated to the defe⟨nd⟩ants. But the purchaser was not responsible, and the agent could have no motive for communicating it. Had it been demanded, suspicion might have been justified by withholding it; but no importance ought I think to be attached to the simple omission to communicate it when no enquiries were made on the subject.

¶7   A point of more difficulty has been very much pressed in the argument. It is the omission of the agent to give notice of the non payment of the notes. It is laid down generally by Paly and Chitty that it is the duty of an agent in whose hands a bill is placed for collection to give immediate notice of its dishonour. Both Paly and Chitty adopt the rule from Beawes Lex Merc, in his chapter on bills of exchange &c fig 117 (6th. Dub. ed. p 373).[3] The passage in Beawes is in the following words "It is incumbent on him to whom a bill is remitted in commission 1st. to endeavour to procure acceptance; 2dly. on refusal, to protest (if not forbidden) though not expressly ordered; 3dly to advise the remitter of the receipt, acceptance, or protesting it, and in case of the latter, to send the protest to him; and 4thly. to advise any third person that is or may be concerned in it; and all this by the posts return, without farther delay."

¶8   The counsel for the defendants insists that a neglect of the duty thus prescribed subjects the agent for the amount of the bill if the debt should be lost. The plaintiffs contend that such neglect subjects him only to compensation for the injury actually sustained from that cause.

¶9   It is plain from the language of the sentence that the author could not mean to say that the failure of the agent in any part of the duty thus prescribed would subject him under all circumstances to the payment of the whole bill if it should be dishonoured by non payment on the part of the drawee. It is declared to be equally the duty of the agent to advise the remitter of the receipt, acceptance, or protest. These are placed in the text on the same footing. But it will not be pretended that the omission to give notice of the receipt of the bill or of its acceptance would render the agent liable for its amount on the failure of the acceptor to pay.

The defendants however do not put the case so strongly as to insist that ¶10 the agent, by neglecting any particular part of his duty, becomes responsible for the whole debt, should the acceptor fail. They contend that he is in the same situation as the holder of a bill, or as if he had been a party to the note, and incurs the same responsibility for any neglect of duty as such person would have incurred. The plaintiffs controvert this proposition.

The general rule appears to me to be that a person acting on commis- ¶11 sion, who by his misconduct has brought loss upon his principal, is responsible to the precise extent of the loss produced by that misconduct. The rule is very well expressed by Mr. Livermore in his valuable treatise on agency v1 st. p 398. He says "The loss which the principal has sustained by reason of the negligence of his agent, I should take to be the true measure of damages in an action founded upon that negligence. This appears to follow from the very definition of damages, being a recompence given by the jury for the injury or wrong done to the party."[4] And Beawes in his chapter on factors &c says "A factor is but a servant to the merchant, and receives from him in lieu of wages a commission" &c. "He ought to keep strictly to the tenor of his orders, as a deviation from them, even in the most minute particular exposes him to make ample satisfaction for any loss that may accrue from his non observance of them." Again he says "A factor should always be punctual in the advices of his transactions, in sales, purchases, affreightments, and more especially in draughts by exchange, for if he sells goods on trust without giving advice thereof; and the buyer breaks; *he is liable to trouble for his neglect;* and if he draws without advising his having so done, he may justly expect to have his bill returned protested."[5] The rule which governs human transactions generally is that compensation shall be apportioned to the injury, and that rule is I think applicable to principal and agent. 2 Wils. 325 3 Johns. NY. rep. 185.[6]

From this general rule there are some exceptions. The law merchant ¶12 has made one which stands on reasons peculiar to itself. This exception relates to commercial paper. For the benefit of trade, and to avoid endless contention respecting liabilities on paper of that description, a set of positive rules prescribing with precision the exact course to be pursued by the holder, and measuring the damage in every case of deviation, has been substituted by merchants instead of the general rule of law that the person chargeable with negligence shall be responsible for the damages actually produced by his misconduct. This exception applies to all those whose names are on the paper, and to a person who has induced an indorser to take a bill by a written promise to accept but has not I think been carried farther. I do not think it has been extended to an agent to whom commercial paper is transmitted for collection, but who does not make himself a party to that paper by putting his name upon it. I find no case which establishes this principle.

¶13   Beawes in his chapter on bills of exchange &c fig. 18 says "When any person has bills sent him to procure an acceptance with directions to return them or hold them at the order of the seconds, &c and the person to whom they are sent either forgets or neglects to demand acceptance, or if he suffers the party on whom they are drawn to delay their acceptance, and the drawer in the interim fail, he is certainly very blame worthy for his carelessness and disregard of complying with his obligation; though this will not subject him to payment of their value." Mr. Beawes adds "But if he should be urged and pressed to procure acceptance and payment of a bill sent to him, and should protract or defer the getting it done, and the acceptant, being ignorant of the drawers circumstances, declares he would have accepted it had it been timely presented; the person guilty of the neglect will be obliged to make good the loss that has happened to his correspondent purely through his omission and carelessness."[7]

¶14   Both these cases show very clearly the distinction supposed by Mr. Beawes to exist between an agent to whom a bill is remitted for collection, and an indorser. If the liability of an agent to his principal was the same with that of a holder to his indorser, there can be no doubt that the loss would be his in the first case put; nor that it would be equally his in the last case put although the drawee should not declare "that he would have accepted it had it been timely presented."

¶15   The same author in the same chapter fig 97 says "If a remitter in commission stands *del credere* for the remisses, he acts indiscreetly if he has the bills made payable to himself or order that he may indorse them." Among other reasons for this opinion one is 2dly. that "the remitter by this means makes himself liable not only to answer all damages &c to his principal, but also to every possessor and indorser of the bill after him. 3dly. By indorsing the bill, he makes it his own, and obliges himself on the account of his principal, not only for the value by him received, but for all other charges and reexchanges.[8]

¶16   And though a remitter by commission does not stand *del credere,* he acts with equal imprudence in having the bills made payable to himself or order, and then indorses them, for thereby he effectually engages himself to stand *del credere* without reaping any advantage therefrom."[9]

¶17   These passages show that Mr. Beawes takes a clear distinction between the relation in which an agent for collection stands to his principal, and that in which the holder of a bill stands to the drawer or indorser. The same negligence or omission which will deprive the holder of all recourse against the drawer or indorser will not subject the agent to his principal to the extent of the bill placed in his hands for collection. His name is not on the bill and the law merchant does not apply to him.[a][10]

¶18   The case of Bridges vs Berry 3 Taunton 130 was a bill drawn by the defendant himself.[11] The decision that the neglect of the holder to give

[a]8th. East 242

notice to the drawer of its dishonour deprived the holder of his recourse against the drawer for a preexisting debt as a security for which this bill was given belongs to a different and a much more difficult question which I am about to examine.

The main question in the cause, and I will not affect to consider it a ¶19 clear one, is this. Have the plaintiffs by their conduct respecting these notes made them an absolute payment towards the discharge of the debt due to them from the defendant? Have they made the notes their own?

The parties stood towards each other in the double relation of princi- ¶20 pal and agent; and of debtor and creditor. This double relation does not sink either character, nor lessen the obligations imposed by either. That these notes were not applied in part payment of a preexisting ascertained and fixed debt, but to the credit of the defendant in a running account in which he was uniformly the debtor, is not I think a material circumstance. The transaction was not a sale of the bills of exchange, or of the notes by the defendant to the plaintiffs, but an application of those bills, and of the notes for which they were sold to his credit with them in the ordinary way in which such paper is credited; that is provisionally, to become absolute on their payment, or on such other event as may authorize the debtor to consider them as paid.

It is admitted to be incumbent on the person receiving negotiable ¶21 paper under these circumstances to use due diligence to obtain its acceptance and payment; and that negle[c]t in these respects, converts the provisional into an absolute payment. But due diligence, it is alleged, has been used in this case; and the charge against the agent & creditor is that he did not give notice that the notes were dishonoured. Mr. Chitty p 1 26. says "The effect of taking a bill of exchange or promissory note in satisfaction of a precedent debt is that the creditor cannot proceed in an action for such debt without showing that he has used due diligence to obtain acceptance or payment; and also showing if the defendant was a party thereto, or delivered it to the plaintiff, that the defendant had due notice of the dishonour."[12]

Elementary writers sometimes state general rules as if they were univer- ¶22 sal; and do not always make those discriminations which a comparison of the cases themselves show ought to be made, nor trace results to the true principle which produces them. Chitty is undoubtedly a very respectable writer; but when he carries a rule farther than the cases have carried it, the proposition he states rests upon his own authority entirely; and when the dictum stands alone unaccompanied by the principle on which it is founded, there is the more reason for searching out the principle and enquiring whether that will comprehend the case which the dictum will comprehend. If it will not, we may conclude that the writer has expressed himself carelessly, and may withhold our assent from his proposition in the broad terms in which he states it. In this case Mr. Chitty makes it indispensable that the defendant should have due notice of the dishon-

our of a note given provisionally in payment of a debt. In general, the
person who delivers such note has his recourse against some other person, and that recourse may be lost if immediate measures be not taken to
enforce the claim. In any such case there is an actual loss or the law
supposes a loss of the debt, and throws the hazard on him whose negligence has produced it. Mr. Chitty lays down the rule as if it did not
depend on the fact that there were other persons whose responsibility
might be affected by the want of notice. The authorities on which he
relies for this broad proposition are an act of Parliament passed in the
4th. year of the reign of Queen Anne, & Bridges v Berry 3d. Taunton
130.[13] The act of Parliament is not supposed to affect this case.[14] It may
however be proper to advert to it. It enacts that if any person accept
any bill for and in satisfaction of any former debt &c the same shall be
esteemed a complete payment of such debt if the person do not take
his due course to obtain payment thereof" &c.[15] Mr. Chitty may have
founded himself on his construction of this statute. So far as he has done
so his authority is inapplicable to this case. Bridges v Berry was an action
brought against the acceptor of a bill of exchange who, when the bill fell
due obtained time and gave the holder a bill drawn and indorsed by
himself on one Ivory payable two months after date. This bill was dis-
honored and the plaintiff omitted to give notice of its nonpayment to the
drawer. At the trial it was admitted that the plaintiff could not recover
upon it, but he insisted that it constituted no bar to a recovery of the
original debt. The court determined that it was a bar; and if no reason
had been given for the opinion, I should admit that the case supported
the principle for which it is cited. But the court does give a reason. It is
that the defendant himself had a right to sue other persons, and that the
plaintiff, by not giving him due notice of its dishonour had put it out
of his power to recover what was due thereupon. This is not an argument mixed up with other arguments conducing to the judgement of the
court, but is the very principle of that judgement. It is the distinction
taken between that case and one cited in argument. It is the very foundation of the judgement, a fact without which the judgement would not
have been rendered.

¶23   I will take the liberty to say that this decision, if not inconsiderately
made, has been very careless reported. The defendant was the drawer
and indorser of the bill which was dishonoured. His recourse upon it
therefore could have been only against the acceptor. His right to recover
against the acceptor depended on having funds in his hands, and the
ability to recover could be lost only by the insolvency of the acceptor.
Neither of these essential facts is stated in the report, but the opinion of
the court is founded on them, and in applying the case we must suppose
their existence. Here then is an actual loss sustained by the debtor to the
amount of the bill, and his exoneration from the original debt is made to

depend on that loss. The case therefore does not support the broad principle which Mr. Chitty has extracted from it.

I cannot forbear noticing the distinction taken between the right to recover on the bill which had been dishonoured and on the original debt. It was admitted that no suit could be sustained on the dishonoured bill—Why? Because the law merchant applied to it, and the doctrine of notice discharged the drawer and indorser. If this necessarily applied to the debt on account of which the bill was given, then there could be as little question in a suit for that debt as on the bill. The law merchant would settle the one case as positively as the other. But while the claim on the bill was abandoned as desperate, that for the original debt was defeated only by the consideration of actual loss sustained in consequence of the negligence of the creditor who was holder of the bill. ¶24

This distinction is still more strongly marked in Bishop v Rowe & same v Bayly 3. Maul & Selwin 362.[16] ¶25

The suit against Rowe was on a bill of exchange drawn & indorsed by himself and accepted by J Bayly. It was also indorsed by the plaintiff and was discounted at bank for Tucker. The bill was dishonoured and due notice given. The money was in part paid and for the residue amounting to £100, Tucker drew a bill on Lewis payable to the plaintiff which the plaintiff indorsed and carried to the bank. This bill was also dishonoured, but no notice was given to Tucker. It was insisted that, because the remedy on the substituted bill was lost, no action could be maintained on the original debt. A verdict was taken for the plaintiff, and a rule to show cause why a new trial should not be granted was discharged. Lord Ellenborough laid some stress on the circumstance that the name of Tucker, though the person for whom the original bill was discounted, and who was consequently the debtor in fact, was not on it. Tucker was therefore a person intervening, and his bill was accepted not "for and in satisfaction of a former debt["] under the statute of Anne, but for the chance of its being productive. The plaintiff might have returned it presently or within a reasonable time; and when the bill is dishonoured, unless it had been received in satisfaction of a former debt, he was not bound to go farther. Lord Ellenborough expressed great doubt but was finally of opinion that the original creditor was not bound to prove that notice was given to the drawer of the substituted bill especially where the name of that drawer was not on the bill which constituted the original debt for which the suit was brought.[17] ¶26

Le Blanc J was of opinion that no action could have been maintained on the substituted bill for want of notice; but that the substituted bill was no payment of the original bill unless something had been done to discharge the party to that bill. If he could have shown that, by the laches of the plaintiff in the course of this negotiation he had lost 100£ or that he had been prevented from suing on the £100 bill, he might have made out a defence.[18] ¶27

¶28   Bayly J. was of opinion that if the defendant had proved that Tucker drew on funds in the hands of the drawee, the defence might have been sustained, but not having shown this fact, he had not made out his defence.[19]

¶29   This was undoubtedly a case in which the inclination of the court might be excusably in favour of the plaintiff, for justice was plainly and strongly with him. The principle of this case, as in Bridges and Berry, is, that if a bill be received as provisional payment, the omission to give due notice of its dishonour deprives the creditor of his action on that bill, but does not compel him to take it as absolute payment, or deprive him of his action on the original debt, farther than damage has been sustained, actually, or in legal supposition, by the debtor. In both cases, the possible damage was the loss of the funds which the drawer might have in the hands of the drawee. The court of Common pleas seems to have assumed the existence of such funds; the court of Kings bench required proof of the fact. They both show how entirely the question whether a provisional becomes an absolute payment depends on circumstances, and how carefully all those circumstances are to be considered.

¶30   Both these cases turn singly on the omission to give notice, unaccompanied with any positive act on the part of the creditor. Circumstances may undoubtedly raise a legal presumption against the person who is creditor, or agent, or both, which may charge him with the loss if he is meerly an agent, or convert a provisional into an absolute payment if he is a creditor. Some strong cases of this description have been cited which, though decisions at *nisi prius,* are not to be absolutely disregarded.

¶31   In Edgar v Bumstead 1st. Campb. n. p. c. 411 the plf. an insurance broker had paid money to the assured for an insolvent under writer, not knowing his insolvency at the time. Lord Ellenborough was of opinion that it could not be recovered back. This opinion was placed on the known course of dealing between the insurance broker, the merchant and the underwriter. The agent, if not acting *del credere,* would certainly not have been liable for the insolvency of the under writer; yet the act of voluntary payment, though made by mistake, fixed the debt due from the underwriter on him and made it his own.[20]

¶32   In Jamison & another v Swainstone 2 Campb. N.P. C. 546, the plfs. who were insurance brokers had effected a policy for the defendant on a vessel which was afterwards stranded, and the plaintiffs advanced considerable sums of money to refit her for the voyage.[21] An average loss was adjusted in May 1806 upon which the plfs. transmitted an account to the defendant debiting him with their advances and giving him credit for the average loss due from the underwriters. The balance due on this account was immediately paid. In the month of August following, which was the usual time of settling between the brokers and the underwriters, the plfs. called upon the underwriters, some of whom refused to pay on the ground of insolvency. Different applications were afterwards made but without success. In August 1808, the plaintiffs transmitted another account to the defendant claiming the sum due from the insolvent underwriters. On their refusal to pay a suit was instituted, and at the t[r]ial Mansfield Ch. Just. said he was of opinion that after so great a lapse of time between rendering the two accounts, the brokers as between themselves and their principal must be presumed either to have received actual payment from the underwriters or to have settled with them some other way. For the purpose of recovering from the defendant, they should have apprised him in Aug. 1806 of the state of the underwriters, who, he was naturally led to suppose, had settled with the brokers, and their silence had deprived him for the space of two years of all opportunities of enforcing the policies of insurance. The verdict was for the defendant.[22]

This is a case of simple agency. The delay will be admitted to have been ¶33 such as to justify the opinion of the assured that the money had been received by the brokers. But the language of the judge shows clearly that immediate notice of the failure of the underwriters ought to have been given; and we are left to conjecture for what length of time the laches of the agent might have been excused.

These cases, as well as those of Andrew v Robinson & al. 3 Campb. N.P. ¶34 C. 199; and Ovington v Bell & another ib. 237. show on what nice circumstances these questions turn.[23]

In the case under consideration a bill of exchange was remitted by the ¶35 defendant who was a debtor to the plaintiffs in a letter of the 28th. of Novr. 25 directing them to sell it, and to place the proceeds to his credit with them.[24] This bill was sold on the 7th. of Decr. partly for cash and partly for negotiable notes payable in March 1826 which were indorsed to the plfs. and placed by them in bank for collection. Notice of the sale was given to the defendant the succeeding day, and an account transmitted to him on the 13th. of Jany. 1826 in which he was credited for the proceeds of the bill. The money and the notes constituted two distinct items of credit.

Thus far the conduct of the agent was unexceptionable. The bill was ¶36 transmitted to him to be converted into available funds, and, if he sold it upon credit, the notes might have been made payable to the defendant in which case they must have been transmitted to him to be indorsed, and returned for collection, or might be made immediately payable to himself. The latter course was more convenient to the parties, but it subjected the agent, however correct in itself to any disadvantage connected with it.

In March 1826, the notes were regularly protested for non payment. ¶37 According to commercial usage, the plfs. ought to have given the defendant immediate notice of their dishonour, and thus have put it in his power to direct such measures as his view of circumstances might suggest. No doubt he would have been guided by the advice of the plaintiffs; but he had a right to the exercise of his judgement, and the plaintiffs ought to have enabled him to exercise it. The correspondence between the parties was regular and frequent, yet no hint was given of the non payment of these notes until the 30th. of June 1826. From the silence of the plaintiffs respecting these notes through the whole of this correspondence the defendant had certainly a right to presume that they were paid, and had undoubtedly a claim upon the plaintiffs commensurate with their actual damages. The rule by which these damages would be ascertained is not now the question. The defendant insists that the payment has become absolute without entering upon this enquiry. If the case stopped at this point I believe my opinion would be against him. But it does not stop at this point.

¶38   It is unnecessary to discuss the intricate questions which would arise in this stage of the cause, the notes being negotiable paper, because my opinion turns chiefly on the acts of commission on the part of the plaintiffs taken in connexion with this act of omission, and with another which will be hereafter noticed.

¶39   On the 21st. of April 1826 James Hamilton visited the defendant in Petersburg and received from him a very considerable payment on account of his debt to them, without mentioning the non payment of the notes. This fact is a strong circumstance to show that the plaintiffs relied on the notes. It is said not to be shown that Hamilton was the partner who transacted the business, or that he was acquainted with the fact. This might be an important enquiry in a criminal prosecution; but in a civil action brought by the firm of Hamilton Donaldson & Co. both partners as residents of New York, must I think be presumed unless the contrary be shown, to be residents, to be active partners, and to be acquainted with the whole transaction. The silence of Mr. Hamilton is the silence of the firm.

¶40   A still more important fact remains to be considered. On the 5th. of May 1826 the plaintiffs wrote a letter to the defendant concerning their increased responsibilities for him, in which they recognize the account transmitted in Jany. and restate the balance between them upon the principle that the notes were paid. This is I think equivalent to an account in which unconditional credit should be given for the notes. They were then dishonoured. The plfs. give no notice of this dishonour, but credit the defendant for them. Had the relation between the parties been meerly that of principal and agent, and the plfs. instead of crediting the defendant for the notes had paid their amount, the case would have been much stronger than that of Edgar v Bumstead, because the money would have been paid, not through mistake, but with full knowledge of the insolvency of the parties to the notes. Between the payment of the money by a meer agent, and the transmission of what is equivalent to an acknowledgement of the payment of the notes by a person who is at the same time age⟨nt⟩ and debtor, the distinction I think cannot easily be drawn.

I have said that there is still another act of omission which has consider- ¶41
able influence on this case. That is the failure to enforce the judgement
which has been obtained or to show otherwise the insolvency of those
who are liable for them.[25]

I readily admit that in general, it is sufficient for him who has received ¶42
negotiable paper as a provisional payment to present it for acceptance
and to demand payment; and that, on its being dishonoured, he may return it, and recur to his original claim. Had these notes stood in the name
of the defendant this course would have been sufficient. But they are in
the name of the plaintiffs, and have been put in suit in their name. If
the notes had been sent to the defendant with the name of the plaintiffs
on them, they would according to the cases have been responsible. Le
feavre v Floyd reported in 1st. Marshall 318 & 5th. Taunton 749 is expressly in point.[26] They have by putting the notes in suit placed their
names upon them, & have disabled themselves from striking them off.
They have taken upon themselves to collect the money by suit and
ought to show their inability to do so before they can come against the
defendant.

The defendant has been prevented from exercising any power over ¶43
these notes by compromise or otherwise by the acts and omissions of the
plaintiffs. The plaintiffs have undertaken to collect the money by suit.
Under these circumstances, I think they cannot recover the amount of
the notes in this action. Judgement must be entered for the lesser sum
found by the jury.

AD, Marshall Judicial Opinions, PPAmP; printed, John W. Brockenbrough, *Reports of
Cases Decided by the Honourable John Marshall . . .* , II (Philadelphia, 1837), 363–79. For JM's
deletions and interlineations, see Textual Notes below.

1. Samuel Livermore, *A Treatise on the Law of Principal and Agent; and of Sales by Auction* (2
vols.; Baltimore, Md., 1818), I, 85, citing: Gerard Malynes, *Consuetudo, vel, Lex Mercatoria: Or,
The Ancient Law-Merchant . . .* (3d ed.; London, 1686), 81, 82; Charles Molloy, *De Jure
Maritimo et Navali, or, A Treatise of Affairs Maritime and of Commerce* (4th ed.; London, 1690),
Bk. 3, ch. 8, sec. 4, p. 422; Schenkhouse v. Gibbs, 2 Dall. 136 n. (Pa. Sup. Ct., 1794);
Ingraham v. Gibbs, 2 Dall. 134 (Pa. Sup. Ct., 1791); Schenkhouse v. Gibbs, 4 Dall. 136 (Pa.
Sup. Ct., 1794).

2. Wyndham Beawes, *Lex Mercatoria Rediviva; or, The Merchant's Directory . . .* (6th ed.;
Dublin, 1773), 36. This title should be distinguished from later versions of Beawes's work,
entitled *Lex Mercatoria Rediviva, or, A Complete Code of Commercial Law. . . .*

3. Beawes, *Lex Mercatoria Rediviva; or, The Merchant's Directory . . .* , 373–4; William Paley, *A
Treatise on the Law of Principal and Agent* (4th Am. ed.; New York, 1856), 4–5; Joseph Chitty,
*A Practical Treatise on Bills of Exchange, Checks on Bankers, Promissory Notes, Bankers' Cash Notes,
and Bank Notes* (Philadelphia, 1821), 37. Paley and Chitty cite Beawes, *Lex Mercatoria Rediviva, or, A Complete Code of Commerical Law* (6th ed.; Dublin, 1795), 431.

4. Livermore, *Principal and Agent*, I, 398.

5. Beawes, *Lex Mercatoria Rediviva; or, The Merchant's Directory*, 36, 38.

6. Russell v. Palmer, 2 Wils. K.B. 325, 95 Eng. Rep. 837 (K.B., 1767); Smedes's Executors
v. Elmendorf, 3 Johns. Rep. 185 (N.Y. Sup. Ct., 1808).

7. Beawes, *Lex Mercatoria Rediviva, or, The Merchant's Directory*, 363.

8. Ibid., 371. A *del credere* agent is one who is obligated to indemnify his principal in the event of loss to the principal as a result of credit extended by the agent to a third party.

9. Ibid., 371–72.

10. Warrington v. Furbor, 8 East 242, 103 Eng. Rep. 334 (K.B., 1807).

11. Bridges v. Berry, 3 Taunt. 130, 128 Eng. Rep. 51 (C.P., 1810).

12. Chitty, *Treatise on Bills of Exchange*, 126.

13. Ibid., 126 n., citing the statute of 3 and 4 Anne, c. 9, sec. 7 (1704?) and Bridges v. Berry (cited in n. 11, above).

14. Here JM inserted a note "B. see sep. paper." On a separate sheet he wrote the next four sentences of his opinion, which he directed "To be inserted at B. 2d. page of 2d. sheet."

15. Chitty *Treatise on Bills of Exchange*, 662–65, reprinted this statute in an appendix. JM freely quoted sec. 7 (at 665).

16. Bishop v. Rowe, Bishop v. Bayly, 3 Mau. & Sel. 362, 105 Eng. Rep. 647 (K.B., 1815).

17. 3 Mau. & Sel. 365–66, 105 Eng. Rep. 648–49.

18. 3 Mau. & Sel. 366–68, 105 Eng. Rep. 649.

19. 3 Mau. & Sel. 368–69, 105 Eng. Rep. 649–50.

20. Edgar v. Bumstead, 1 Camp. 411, 170 Eng. Rep. 1003 (N.P., 1808).

21. Jameson v. Swainstone, 2 Camp. 546 n, 170 Eng. Rep. 1247 n (N.P., 1809).

22. 2 Camp. 547 n., 170 Eng. Rep. 1247 n.

23. Andrew v. Robinson, 3 Camp. 199, 170 Eng. Rep. 1354 (N.P., 1812); Ovington v. Bell, 3 Camp. 237, 170 Eng. Rep. 1367 (N.P., 1812).

24. JM's account of the transactions between the parties is taken from the case stated (U.S. Cir. Ct., Va., Rec. Bk. XVIII, 541–46).

25. The plaintiffs obtained a judgment on the protested notes in May 1827 but had not sued out an execution on this judgment (ibid., 565–71).

26. Le Fevre v. Floyd, 5 Taunt. 749, 128 Eng. Rep. 886 (C.P., 1814), also reported in Sir Charles Marshall, *Reports of Cases Argued and Determined in the Court of Common Pleas* (2 vols.; London, 1815–17), I, 318.

Textual Notes

¶ 2	l. 2	mingling ~~his interest~~ ↑the property of the ~~defendants~~ defendant,↓ with
	ll. 3–4	deprive ~~them defendants~~ ↑him↓ of that perfect controul ↑over it↓ which ~~their~~ ↑his↓ interest
	l. 5	misconducted ~~himself~~ ↑themselves↓ in ~~his~~ ↑their↓ agency
	ll. 5–6	as to ~~take~~ ↑become liable for↓ the debt ~~upon himself.~~
	l. 8	of the ~~agent~~ agents, ↑and this is no longer a question in the cause;↓ but
	l. 9	declare ~~myself~~ ↑that I↓ satisfied
	ll. 10–11	and that ↑the usage of New York conforms to↓ the general rule ~~conforms.~~
	ll. 11–12	agency 85. ↑He quotes↓ Malynes
	l. 13	Dal 136 ~~id 34~~ id. 134
¶ 3	l. 4	necessary ↑and usual↓ at the
¶ 5	ll. 1–2	might have on ~~the~~ ↑a↓ jury,
	l. 15	paper, ~~but this ought not to~~ and this might ~~dou~~ render
	l. 18	for a note ~~not~~ ↑of↓ previous

	l. 20	good credit. ~~I doubt whether an agent could justify~~ I doubt wheth
¶ 6	l. 4	demanded, ~~suspicion~~ suspicion
	l. 5	it; but ~~the simple~~ no importance
¶ 7	ll. 1–3	much pressed ~~in at~~ in the argument. ↑It is the omission of the agent to give notice of the non payment of the notes.↓ It is
	ll. 9–10	though not ↑expressly↓ ordered;
¶ 8	l. 4	from that ~~neglect~~ cause.
¶ 9	l. 8	acceptance would [*erasure*] render
¶10	ll. 1–2	insist that ~~an~~ ↑the↓ agent,
	ll. 4–5	bill, or ↑as if he had been↓ a party
¶11	ll. 17–18	without giving ~~notice~~ ↑advice↓ thereof,
	ll. 20–23	protested." [*erasure*] ↑The rule which governs human transactions generally is that compensation shall be apportioned to the injury, and that rule is I think applicable to principal and agent. 2 Wils. 325 3 Johns. NY. rep. 185.↓
¶12	ll. 1–2	general rule ↑there are some exceptions.↓ The law merchant has made ~~a single exception~~ ↑one↓ which stands
	l. 4	description, ~~merchants have substituted~~ a
	ll. 6–8	deviation, ↑has been substituted by merchants instead of↓ ~~for~~ the general rule of law that the ~~wrong de~~ person ~~guilty~~ ↑chargeable↓
	ll. 10–12	on the paper, ↑and to a person who has induced an indorser to take a bill by a written promise to accept↓ but has not I think ~~as a general rule,~~ been
¶13	l. 1	exchange &c ↑fig. 18↓ says
	ll. 6–7	for his ~~careless~~ ↑carelessness↓ and
	l. 10	sent [*erasure*] to him
¶14	l. beg.	~~This ca~~ Both these cases
	l. 3	indorser. ~~The~~ ↑If↓ the liability
¶15	l. 4	opinion one is ↑2dly.↓ that
¶16	l. 3	for thereby ~~the~~ ↑the↓ effectually
¶17	ll. 1–2	between the ~~relations~~ ↑relation↓ in which
	l. 3	stands to [*erasure*] ↑the↓ drawer
	ll. 6–7	collection. ↑His name is not on the bill and the law merchant does not apply to him.[a]↓
¶18	l. 3	deprived the ~~dra~~ ↑holder↓ of his
	l. 6	about to ~~consider~~ ↑examine.↓
¶19	l. 3	discharge of the ~~original~~ debt
¶20	l. 1	double ~~charac~~ relation of
	l. 2	debtor and ~~character~~ ↑creditor.↓
¶21	l. 3	respects, ~~makes~~ ↑converts↓ the
¶22	l. 9	that will ~~embrace~~ ↑comprehend↓ the
	l. 10	we may conclude ~~rather~~ that
	l. 14	note given ↑provisionally↓ in payment of debt. ~~Generally~~ ↑In general↓ the
	l. 22	proposition are [*erasure*] an act
	l. 31	when the [*erasure*] bill fell
	l. 42	recover what ~~his~~ ↑was↓ due thereupon.

¶23   l. 1   this decision, ~~was~~ if not
      ll. 4–5   acceptor. ~~Want of notice did a His want of~~ ↑His right to
                 recover against the acceptor↓ ~~depends~~ ↑depended↓ on
                 having
      ll. 7–8   but the ~~good~~ opinion of the court ~~assumed~~ ↑is founded↓ on
                 them
¶24   l. 6   which the bill ↑was↓ given,
¶26   ll. 4–5   for the residue ↑amounting to £100,↓ Tucker
      l. 11   circumstance that ~~Tucker~~ the name
      l. 13   was not on ~~the original bill~~ ↑it.↓
      ll. 14–15 was accepted ↑not "for and in satisfaction of a former debt["]
                 under the statute of Anne, but↓ for the
      l. 17   it had been ~~accepted~~ ↑received↓ in
¶27   l. 5   he had lost ~~the original debt~~ ↑100£↓ or that
¶29   ll. 2–3   was plainly ↑and strongly↓ with him.
      ll. 4–5   to give ↑due↓ notice
      ll. 7–8   has been ~~actually~~ sustained, ~~or is supposed by law to have
                 been sustained~~ ↑actually or in legal supposition,↓ by the
      l. 14   be considered. ~~Both these cases turn singly on the omission~~
¶30   l. 2   the creditor ~~, or agent~~. Circumstances
      l. 7   though ~~nisi~~ decisions
¶31   l. 2   paid money ~~by mistake~~ ↑to the assured↓ for
      l. 4   recovered back ~~in an . . . . fo?~~. This
¶32   l. 5   plfs. transmitted ↑an account↓ to the
      l. 8   August following, ~~when~~ ↑which was↓ the
      ll. 14–15 at the t[r]ial ~~Lord~~ Mansfield Ch.
      ll. 21–22 settled with the ~~underwriters~~ ↑brokers,↓ and their
¶35   l. 1   consideration ~~the bill~~ ↑a bill of exchange↓ was
      ll. 2–3   defendant ~~on the 28th of Novr. 1825~~ who was a debtor to the
                 plaintiffs ~~who were creditors~~ in a letter ↑of the 28th. of Novr.
                 25↓ directing them
      l. 4   was sold ↑on the 7th. of Decr.↓ partly
      l. 5   notes ↑payable in March 1826↓ which
      l. 6   placed by them in [erasure] ↑bank↓ for collection. ~~notice~~
                 ↑Notice↓ of the sale
      l. 7   the defendant ↑the succeeding day↓, and an
      ll. 7–8   transmitted to him ↑on the 13th. of Jany. 1826↓ in
¶37   ll. 3–4   put it in ~~their~~ ↑his↓ power
      l. 4   measures as ~~their~~ ↑his↓ view
      l. 9   notes until ~~the 22d. of July 1826 when another account
                 current was inclosed to him adding their amount to his debit~~
                 ↑the 30th. of June 1826.↓ From
      l. 10   this correspondence ~~the whole of this correspondence~~ the
      ll. 11–12 paid, and had ~~unquestionably~~ ↑undoubtedly↓ a claim
¶38   ll. 1–2   would arise ↑in↓ this stage
¶39   l. 4   notes. ~~He ought~~ This fact is
      ll. 8–9   partners ↑as residents of New York,↓ must
¶40   l. 9   meerly that of ~~creditor and debtor~~ ↑ principal and agent,↓
                 and the

	l. 9	instead of ~~paying~~ ↑crediting↓ the
	l. 13	Between the ~~advance~~ ↑payment↓ of
	l. 14	transmission of ↑what is equivalent to↓ an
¶41	l. 3	to show [*erasure*] ↑otherwise↓ the
¶42	l. 2	present [*erasure*] it for
	l. 7	notes had ~~come~~ ↑been↓ sent to the defendant with the ↑names of the↓ plaintiffs
	l. 10	in point. ~~He~~ They have
¶43	l. 2	the acts ↑and omissions↓ of the plaintiffs

Bank of the United States v. Winston
Opinion
U.S. Circuit Court, Virginia, [19 June 1828?]

This case arose from the indebtedness of George Winston (1759–1826) to the Bank of the United States and other creditors. Winston, a Richmond resident and head of a prominent Quaker family, executed a deed of trust in August 1820 to secure his debts, giving priority to a debt due to the commonwealth of Virginia. The bank brought suit on the chancery side of the federal court against Winston and the trustees, seeking satisfaction of its claims. Pleasant Winston (1792–1876), a son of George Winston, was a defendant in this suit. The court had previously issued orders and interlocutory decrees in June 1821, December 1822, June 1824, and June 1825. The facts of the case are sufficiently set forth in Marshall's opinion, which apparently was given at the May 1828 term (see n. 1) (U.S. Cir. Ct., Va., Ord. Bk. XI, 143–44, 319, 470–71, 488, 489–90; XII, 38; *Richmond Whig*, 28 Feb. 1826; Edward Pleasants Valentine, [comp.], *The Edward Pleasants Valentine Papers* [4 vols.; Richmond, Va., 1927], III, 1752–57; Alfred Sumner Winston III, comp., *The Winstons of Hanover County, Virginia and Related Families, 1666–1992* [Baltimore, 1992], 9, 31).

The Bank of The U.S. & al

v

Winstons exrs. and others[1]

This is an application on the part of Pleasant Winston to be allowed the sum he has paid The Commonwealth as surety for G. Winston on a judgement obtained by The Commonwealth.   ¶1

In the year 18   The Commonwealth of Virginia obtained a judgement against G. W for the sum of $.[2] No execution has ever issued on this judgement. Soon after its rendition, an act was passed directing that execution should be delayed on G. W.'s giving sufficient surety for the payment of the debt by instalments. In pursuance of this act bonds for the whole debt were executed with P. W. as surety.[3] Before the first instalment became due judgements were obtained by the Bank of The U. S.   ¶2 and by several other creditors against G. W. He made a deed of his property for the payment of his debts giving priority to the debt due to the state of Virginia, which has been set aside by a decree of this court as fraudulent.[4] It being understood that the Commonwealth asserted a lien on this property under its original judgement and also under the deed, and the Commonwealth having declined becoming a party to the suit in this court, no sale was ordered, but the Marshal was directed to receive the rents and profits and to hold them subject to the order of the court. Afterwards in the year 1824, The Commonwealth instituted suits on the bonds given by G & P. W. and obtained judgements, some of which have been paid by P. W. He claims to stand in the place of the Commonwealth, and to be paid his debt before those creditors who obtained judgements in the intervening time between the original judgement of the State against G. W. and the subsequent judgements against G. & P. W. He contends that the lien created by the original judgement still continues, that by paying a subsequent judgement on a bond given in consideration of the first, he is to be considered as having paid so much in discharge of the first, and consequently to be entitled to a preference over the other creditors. This claim is resisted by the other creditors on various grounds some of which will be considered.

¶3   As the lien created by a judgement is given by the statute which authorizes an elegit, it is settled in this country that the lien depends on the right to sue out an elegit. 2 Call 125. 4 H & M. 57.[5] This is not controverted, but it is insisted by P. W. that the Commonwealth may now sue out an elegit on the original judgement against G. W. and that he is entitled to the priority which that right gives to the Commonwealth.

¶4   When this idea was first suggested it occurred to me and I stated to the bar that the doctrine of subrogation or substitution was confined to sureties, and had never been applied to a meer volunteer. If an assignable instrument be transferred, its obligation at law and in equity remains. If a security not assignable be discharged by a surety whom it binds, equity keeps it in force in his favor, and puts such surety in the place of the original creditor. But I think there is no case in which this has been done in favour of a person not bound by the original security, who discharges it as a voluntier. I will not say that it may not be done; but if it may equity will consider all the circumstances and impose equitable terms. The decision of this point is not I think essential to the cause.

¶5   Were it admitted that P. W. has a right to rank on the fund in the power of the court according to the original judgement in favor of the commonwealth, the enquiry would be whether that judgement is still a lien. The counsel for P. W. contend that it is, 1st. Because the proceedings under that judgement on the part of The Commonwealth do not amount to a stay of execution; 2dly. If they do, the execution may now issue and will relate to the date of the judgement.

¶6   I shall not unnecessarily decide the first question. That may hereafter arise in a case which will depend entirely on it. I do not think this does. The second has been already decided in this court. In the case of Scriba & Deanes this court determined that the lien of a judgement on which execution is stayed, dates, not from its rendition, but from the time when execution may be sued out.[6] I have not changed this opinion. If then P W could claim the lien created by the original judgement, his lien would be postponed to that of other creditors whose judgements were obtained before the expiration of the time during which execution was suspended, unless it should be decided that the Commonwealth could have sued out an elegit, notwithstanding the act of Assembly under which the bonds were taken which bind P. W. I have said it is unnecessary to decide this point at present. My reason is this. I think it too clear for controversy that The Commonwealth and those who claim under her, must abandon or abide by her original judgement. Equity cannot give all the advantages of both. If she or her substitute claim under the elegit, the party so claiming must be content with what the elegit will give. If, waiving the elegit, The Commonwealth pursues her remedy on the bonds which she has taken instead of her original judgement, and thereby obtains more than that judgement would yield, equity will not aid her in the attempt to come in under the original judgement also. Waiving every other objection to the claim of P. W. this is insurmountable. The debt to the Commonwealth is augmented by having recourse to the bonds which have been given in satisfaction of the judgement, and the fund for other creditors is diminished to the same amount, if she still retains her priority. Equity will not, to effect such an object, tack that priority to the subsequent judgements which augment the debt. I think then, if every other objection to the claim of P W. could be removed, it must fail unless he could comply with the condition a court of equity ought to impose, the reduction of the claim of The Commonwealth to the amount of its judgement.[7]

AD, Marshall Judicial Opinions, PPAmP; printed, John W. Brockenbrough, *Reports of Cases Decided by the Honourable John Marshall . . .* , II (Philadelphia, 1837), 252–56. For JM's deletions and interlineations, see Textual Notes below.

1. Although Brockenbrough assigned this opinion to the May 1825 term, the decree given at that term does not pertain to the opinion. The decree of 19 June 1828 also does not appear to fit with the opinion, though a notation below JM's docket indicates that it was given at the May 1828 term (U.S. Cir. Ct., Va., Ord. Bk. XII, 254–55). The case is not listed in Index to Ended Causes, U.S. Cir. Ct., Va., 1790–1861, Vi, and no case papers have been found.

2. Virginia obtained a judgment against George Winston in the General Court on 19 June 1818 for $18,000 (U.S. Cir. Ct., Va., Ord. Bk. XII, 38; Commonwealth v. Winstons, 5 Rand. 546 (Va. Ct. App., 1827).

3. In Mar. 1819 George Winston obtained an act of the Virginia Assembly allowing him five, six, and seven years to pay off the debt by equal installments. He executed a bond to the commonwealth in June 1819, conditioned to pay the debt in three installments due in Mar. 1824, Mar. 1825, and Mar. 1826 (Commonwealth v. Winstons, 5 Rand. 546 (Va. Ct. App., 1827).

4. For this decree of 21 June 1824, see U.S. Cir. Ct., Va., Ord. Bk. XI, 470–71.

5. Wayles's Executors v. Randolph, 2 Call 125 (Va. Ct. App., 1799); *PJM*, V, 117–60; Nimmo's Executor v. Commonwealth, 4 H. & M.. 57 (Va. Ct. App., 1809).

6. Scriba v. Deanes, 1 Brock. 166 (1810); *PJM*, VII, 262–68.

7. The case was still on the docket in 1831, the last year covered by the surviving order books (U.S. Cir. Ct., Va., Ord. Bk. XII, 387, 410, 419).

Textual Notes

¶1	l. 1	Winston ~~for~~ ↑to be allowed↓ the
	l. 2	paid ~~the~~ The Commonwealth
	l. 3	by ~~the~~ The Commonwealth
¶2	l. 1	18 ~~the~~ The Commonwealth
	l. 4	giving ♭ sufficient
	ll. 9–10	debts ↑giving priority to the debt due to the state [*erasure*] of Virginia,↓ which
	l. 13	declined ~~bringing its claim~~ ↑becoming a party to↓ the suit
	l. 15	to the ~~disp~~ ↑order↓ of the
¶3	ll. 4–5	may now sue [*erasure*] out an
¶4	ll. 2–3	substitution ↑was confined to sureties, and↓ had never
	l. 5	assignable be ~~trans~~ discharged
¶5	l. 1 beg.	~~It has been denied~~ Were it
	l. 3	would be [*erasure*] whether
¶6	l. 5	dates, not from [*erasure*] its
	l. 8	postponed [*erasure*] to that
	ll. 13–14	clear for [*erasure*] controversy that ~~the~~ The Commonwealth
	ll. 16–17	the [*erasure*] elegit, the party ↑so claiming↓ must
	ll. 17–18	elegit, ~~the~~ The Commonwealth
	ll. 22–23	Commonwealth is ~~swelled~~ ↑augmented↓ by
	l. 26	priority to ↑the↓ subsequent
	l. 30	claim of ~~the~~ The Commonwealth

To John Pitman

Dear Sir[1]   Richmond June 25th. 1828

I had the pleasure of receiving in Washington your opinion in the case of Gardner v Collins.[2] I was too much occupied during the term to read it as it deserves, and left Richmond immediately after the rising of the court at Washington for our mountains whence I did not return till my circuit was about to commence which is just finished. I mention these circumstances as my apology for not acknowledging the receipt of your letter of the 14th. of Feby.[3] I postponed its acknowledgement until I could give the opinion it inclosed an attentive perusal. I have now done so and certainly think the argument one which deserves the most deliberate consideration. I shall lay it before the Judges in our consultations on the case.[4]

It is to be regretted that the question has not been settled in the state courts. We are much more inclined to receive than to give the construction on the legislative acts of a state, especially where they affect individuals so vitally as the law of descents necessarily must.[5]

I receive pleasure in being recollected by you and beg you to be assured that I am with great respect, Your obedt

J MARSHALL

ALS, Pitman Papers, RPB. Addressed to Pitman in Providence, R.I. Postmarked Richmond, 26 June.

1. John Pitman (1785–1864), of Rhode Island, graduated from Brown University in 1799, studied law, and practiced in New York City; Kentucky; Providence; Salem, Mass.; and Portsmouth, N.H., before settling permanently in Providence. He served as U.S. attorney for Rhode Island from 1821 to 1824, when he was appointed judge of the U.S. District Court. He sat on this court until his death (History of the Federal Judiciary [http://www.fjc.gov], Federal Judicial Center, Washington, D.C., Nov. 2000).

2. The case of Gardner v. Collins was then pending in the Supreme Court. It began in the U.S. Circuit Court for Rhode Island in May 1825 as an action of trespass and ejectment. In Nov. 1826 the judges (Story and Pitman) divided on an agreed statement of facts, and the case came to the Supreme Court by a certificate of division. An earlier case between the same two parties had been decided on circuit in June 1824, Story giving the opinion in favor of the plaintiff (Gardner v. Collins, appellate case file, App. Cas. No. 1462; 9 Fed. Cas. 1162).

3. Letter not found.

4. The case was argued in the Supreme Court in Jan. 1829 and decided for the plaintiff, Story giving the opinion (U.S. Sup. Ct. Dockets, App. Cas. No. 1462; 2 Pet. 58, 84–95).

5. As Story stated at the outset of his opinion, the case depended "altogether upon the true construction of the statute of descents of Rhode Island of 1822" (2 Pet. 84).

To Willis Cowling, James Sizer, and James Gray

Gentlemen[1]   Richmond June 28th 1828

I acknowledge with grateful sensibility your very kind invitation to join the members of the Sabbath Schools of Richmond & Manchester on the 4th of July in a procession to be formed on the Capitol Square at half past eight and from thence to proceed to Trinity Church where an appropriate address will be delivered at ten.

I beg you to believe that no person estimates more highly than I do the purity of the motives by which the members of those schools are actuated, or the value of the objects which they seek to attain. I cannot be more perfectly convinced than I am, "that virtue & intelligence are the basis of our independence and the conservative principles of national & individual happiness" nor can any person believe more firmly that the institutions you patronize are devoted to the promotion of both.

I should not hesitate to manifest the sincerity of these opinions by attending the procession you propose, were I not prevented by unavoidable absence from Richmond. I am compelled by the feeble health of Mrs. Marshall to leave this place on the 3d of July and not to return till the 5th.[2]

I intreat you to make my most respectfull acknowledgements to the societies you represent & to receive yourselves my grateful thanks for the kind & flattering terms in which you have communicated their invitation.[3] With great respect I am Gentlemen Yr Obt Servt

JOHN MARSHALL

Tr, Marshall Papers, ViW; printed, *American Sunday School Union Magazine* (Aug. 1828), 238. Tr endorsed above dateline: "Chief Justice Marshall's Letter."

1. Willis Cowling (d. 1828) was described in a death notice as "a bright ornament of the Methodist Church." James Sizer (1784–1867), a member of the First Baptist Church of Richmond, served as deacon of the church from 1829 until his death. He was also a trustee of the Baptist seminary that later became Richmond College. James Gray (1788–1855), a prosperous Richmond merchant, was a ruling elder of the Presbyterian Church on Shockoe Hill (*Richmond Enquirer,* 22 Aug. 1828; Lewis H. Mundin, *A Genealogy of the Sizer and Dickerson Families of Caroline County, Virginia* [Richmond, 1982], 4; *Richmond Portraits,* 81).

2. On occasions of noisy celebrations in Richmond, JM and his wife retreated to their Chickahominy farm.

3. For an account of the procession, which included officials, teachers, and pupils of the Sabbath Schools associated with the Methodist, Presbyterian, and Baptist churches of Richmond and various public dignitaries, see *Richmond Enquirer,* 8 July 1828.

Black v. Scott
Opinion
U.S. Circuit Court, Virginia, 30 June 1828

The purpose of this equity suit was to obtain a decree for the distribution of the estate of John Lesslie (d. 1818), a member of the community of Scots merchants residing in Richmond. The original plaintiffs were Isabella Black and her children, British subjects living in Scotland who were creditors of Lesslie. The defendants were James Scott, Lesslie's executor, and Andrew Lesslie and Jane Lesslie, Lesslie's children and devisees. Except for order book entries, no traces of this case have been found in the records and papers of the U.S. Circuit Court. At some point William L. Myers, for whom Lesslie had served as guardian, became a party plaintiff by petition. Myers was presumably the son of Ann Myers, widow of Lewis Myers, whom Lesslie had married in 1803. The court's decree of 30 June 1828 was based on three chancery commissioner's reports of December 1821, December 1826, and January 1828. Marshall's opinion accompanying the decree dealt only with the claim of William L. Myers (U.S. Cir. Ct., Va., Ord. Bk. XII, 35, 67, 235, 259–63; Muir v. Brown's Executors, U.S. Cir. Ct., Va., Rec. Bk. XIX, 461; *Virginia Magazine of History and Biography,* XXXIV [1926], 163, 168; *Richmond Enquirer,* 24 Dec. 1818).

Black & al

v

Scott exr. of Lesslie & al

This is an application on the part of John Forbes exr. of William L   ¶1
Myers[1] for an order that he shall receive the amount of his claim which
has been established by a decree of the court of chancery of the state, out
of the proceeds of the real estate of John Lesslie decd. which are now in
the possession of this court for distribution among his creditors.

William L Myers was a ward of John Lesslie, and priority is claimed for   ¶2
him over all other creditors out of the real estate of his guardian. This
priority is claimed under the 12th. sec. of the act "to reduce into one the
several acts concerning Guardians, orphans, curators, infants, Masters
and apprentices,["] which is in these words "The estate of a guardian or
curator, appointed under this act, not under a specific lien, shall after the
death of such guardian or curator, be liable for whatever may be due from
him or her, on account of his or her guardianship, to his or her ward,
before any other debt due from him or her."[2]

This clause has, in the argument been considered in connexion with   ¶3
the 60th. sec. of the act "reducing into one the several acts concerning
wills, the distribution of intestates estates, and the duty of executors and
administrators," which was passed at the same session. That section is in
these words "The executors and Administrators of a Guardian, of a committee, or of any other person who shall have been chargeable with, or
accountable for, the estate of a ward, an ideot or a lunatic, or the estate of
a dead person committed to their testator or intestate by a court of
record, shall pay so much as shall be due from their testator or intestate to
the ward, idiot, or lunatic, or to the legatees or persons entitled to distribution, before any proper debt of their testator or intestate."[3]

It has been truely said that these two acts having been passed at the   ¶4
same session respecting the dignity of claims on the estates of deceased
persons ought to be considered together, and that the two sections ought
to be construed as if they were contained in the same act. It has been
added, not I think with the same correctness, that the one ought to
restrain and limit the extent of the other.

I have to regret that these two sections, which are certainly very inter-   ¶5
esting to the people of Virginia, have not received a settled construction
in the state courts, and that this court should be required to hazard an
opinion on any point which may not heretofore have arisen in them. It is
however my duty to state my view of the subject, which I shall be ready to
correct if a different view of it shall be taken in the state.

In doing this I shall first consider the 60th. sec. of the act concerning   ¶6
wills &c as if it stood alone. The words of that section are applicable
exclusively to the conduct of exrs. or Admrs. in disbursing the assetts of
their testator or intestate which come to their hands in their official

character. The language of the section will admit of no other interpretation. It applies to no other part of the decedents estate and regulates the conduct of no other person. The section is addressed to exrs. & admrs. and prescribes their duty in the case it describes. That case is the existence of a debt due from their testator or intestate to the estate of a Lunatic, or of any deceased person which may have been committed to his charge. These claims have priority to any proper debt of their testator or intestate and must be paid by such exr. or admr. out of the assetts which may come to his hands. I think it cannot be doubted that as between themselves, these debts have equal dignity.

¶7   The language of the 12th. section of the act concerning guardians &c is entirely different. It does not address itself to the personal representatives of the deceased, nor prescribe their duty, nor does it comprehend all the persons who are described in the 60th. section of the act concerning wills &c. It affects the estate of the deceased not under a specific lien, and provides for the single claim of a ward on the estate of his curator or guardian. The language of this section reaches the real estate and must have been so intended. It provides that such estate, not being under any specific lien shall be liable for such debt before any other debt due from him or her.

¶8   A question might arise whether this section gave priority to a ward on the personal estate over other persons enumerated with him in the 60th. sec. of the act concerning wills &c. If it did give such priority the two acts would be inconsistent with each other. The one would give the ward a preference over persons whom the other in express words placed on an equal footing with him. The rule which requires that acts *in pari materia*[4] should be construed together requires that the persons enumerated in the 60th. sec. of the act concerning wills &c should stand equal in their claims on the personal estate and that the 12th. sec. of the act concerning Guardians &c should apply only to real estate. The same rule however requires that it should apply to real estate.

¶9   In making this application I cannot doubt that the debt due to the ward is to be preferred to any bond debt due from the testator or intestate on his own account. The language of the act is imperative and explicit.

¶10   It has been said that heirs commit no devastavits. From this it is inferred that one claim can have no priority over another. I shall not examine this proposition. If its truth be admitted the inference is not of course.

¶11   In England all bond debts binding the heir, unless it be the debt to the King, are equal. In Virginia they are not equal. A debt due to the ward has a prior claim on the estate of his guardian to any other debt due to a proper creditor of the guardian; and though I will not say that the heir or devisee may or may not commit a devastavit, that he may or may not plead a debt due to a ward to an action by a bond creditor I think it may be said that where both claims come before a court administering legal assets, that which the law prefers is entitled to preference from a tribunal which expounds and applies the law.

¶12 A question of more difficulty is on the operation which this statute has on the land of the guardian. Does it create a lien? If it does, the land would be bound in the hands of a purchaser. This has never been supposed, and would be an alarming construction. It would, contrary to the general policy of the law, set up a secret lien which would be a restraint on alienations not imposed by express words, and not required by any necessary construction of the section.

¶13 Does it without giving a lien on the land itself create a liability of the heir or devisee to pay the debt due to the ward in consideration of the land descended or devised, or does it meerly give preference to an existing liability?

¶14 The language of the section would indicate that priority alone was in the mind of the legislature. Its object does not seem so much to enable the ward to obtain satisfaction out of the real estate, as to give an existing claim on that estate a preference to other existing claims. The estate shall be liable to it "before any other debt due from" the guardian. The legislature would seem to have in its mind debts for which the estate is liable, and to decide on the dignity of those debts. If, according to the existing state of the law all debts due to wards from the estates of their guardians, which have preference under this section, have a right to claim satisfaction from heirs and devisees to the extent of the estate descended or devised, the statute may be construed, not as giving the right, but as giving priority to that right. But if the section applies to cases where no antecedent right exists, it would be difficult to resist that construction of the words which gives the right as well as the priority. The words of the section which describe the estate to which it applies are "The estate of a guardian or curator, appointed under this act &c." If the words "appointed under this act["] apply to a guardian as well as a curator, then priority is given to the wards of statutory guardians only, not to the wards of testamentary guardians; and all statutory guardians are required to give bond. If they apply to a curator only and give equal priority to a debt due to a ward whether his guardian was created by testament or by statute, then priority is given in a case where no antecedent right existed. Testamentary guardians are not required to give bond if the testator has otherwise directed by his will. At least this appears to me to be the proper construction of the 2d. & 5th. sections of the act compared with each other.

¶15 If the words, "The estate of a guardian or curator appointed under this act" "shall be liable" &c be read with a comma after the word "Guardian," the words appointed under this act would apply solely to the Curator. But in the printed code, the comma is placed after the word "curator," so as to connect the guardian with the curator, and apply the subsequent words equally to both. I am however aware that not much stress is to be laid on this circumstance, and that the construction of a sentence in a legislative act does not depend on its pointing. The legislature can scarcely be supposed to have intended to distinguish between remedies for debts due from testamentary and statutory guardians, and I am therefore disposed to read the act with the comma after the word "Guardian."

¶16   But although the act directs bonds to be given by Guardians, it does not prescribe the form of the bond, or that the heir shall be bound in it. The usage undoubtedly is to bind the heirs; and it is not probable that any court would be inattentive to this circumstance. The legislature may be presumed to have had such a bond in contemplation, and to have legislated on the idea that the heirs were uniformly bound in it. But suppose a court should neglect to take a bond, or should take a bond in which the heirs were not named, would the general provision of the act that the estate of the guardian shall be bound to satisfy the debt due to his ward before any proper debt of his own, be defeated by this omission? I should feel much difficulty in answering this question in the affirmative.

¶17   The history of the legislative enactments on this subject has been referred to in argument.

¶18   The act of 1705 for the distribution of intestates estates &c. subjects the estate of any person who shall die chargeable with the estate of any person deceased or with any orphans estate to the payment of such debt in the first instance, in terms which would apply to real as well as personal estate. The same act may be construed to require bond from testamentary guardians, or from those only to whom the orphans estate may be committed by the court.[5]

¶19   In the year 1748 a revisal of the laws was made. The act "for the better management and security of orphans and their estates," gives the debt due from the Guardian to his ward priority against the personal estate only, and requires bond from those guardians only to whom the estates of orphans have been committed by order of court.[6] As this revisal is understood to have been the work of the ablest lawyers of that day, it is probable that this act contains the received construction of the act of 1705.

¶20   The laws were again revised in 1779 and the bills prepared by the revisors were enacted in 1785. The 50th. sec. of the act concerning wills &c gives the same priority against the personal estate which is given by the act of March 1819.[7] The first section of the "act concerning guardians, infants, masters, and apprentices," renders the estate of every guardian liable in the first instance for any debt due to his ward on account of his guardianship, but requires no bond from any guardian not appointed by the court.[8]

¶21   The revisal of 1792 reenacts the provisions contained in the acts of 1785.[9]

¶22   In Decr. 1794, for the first time, an act was passed requiring a testamentary guardian to give bond before he exercises any authority over the minor or his estate, "unless it is otherwise directed by the testators will."[10] This act took effect on the first day of March 1795. From the first day of Jany. 1787 then when the law of 1785 went into operation, until the first day of March 1795, the law gave priority against the real estate of Guardians to debts not secured by bond. Upon a review of the whole subject I am inclined to think, contrary to my first impression, that the act of 1819 ought to be construed as making the estate of a Guardian liable to a debt due to his ward on guardianship account, and not as meerly giving priority to such debt. I am not sure that this is material to the main question now before the court.

In this case the Guardian had given a bond in which his heirs were bound; and the question is whether the ward can now assert in this court the priority given by the statute and by his bond. ¶23

The simple contract creditors maintain that he cannot, because under the will of John Lesslie the real estate has been converted into equitable assetts. ¶24

The following are the material clauses in the will. "In the first place I desire that all my just debts may be paid, and for this purpose I subject my whole estate real and personal. In case it should be necessary for the purpose of paying my debts to sell any part of my real estate, I give to my executors afternamed the power of so doing" "and authorize my said exrs. or such of them as may act to make conveyances to the purchaser or purchasers." He then gives some legacies which he charges on his whole estate and adds "all the rest and residue of my estate after the payment of my debts and legacies as aforesaid I give to my two children Andrew and Jane." The devisees of the residue are his heirs at law. ¶25

It is contended on the part of Myers that he is entitled to preference 1st. as a creditor by bond in which the heirs are bound. ¶26

2d.ly, Under the act of Assembly. ¶27

1st. I will first consider the general proposition that under this will bond creditors may assert a prior claim upon the real estate. ¶28

It must be admitted that specialty creditors have no lien upon the lands. The heir, being bound by the contract of his ancestor, is liable to the amount of assetts which he takes by descent from that ancestor, and no farther. The ancestor could devise his lands, and the devisee not being bound by the contract held them exonerated from the creditor, or the heir could alien them and thus also defeat the creditor, because the lands, not being specifically bound, could not be reached, and the heir, at the time the writ issued, held nothing by descent. ¶29

It being thus clearly settled that the creditor had no lien on the lands of his debtor, even after his decease, and that the heir was liable for the contract of his ancestor in regard of lands actually held by descent at the time the writ issued only to the amount of the land so descended, let us apply these principles to the case under consideration. ¶30

¶31   John Lesslie by his will subjects his whole estate to the payment of his debts, and empowers his exrs. or such of them as may act to sell his lands and convey to the purchaser.

¶32   The validity of this devise in a court of equity, has not been questioned. If it be valid, then it would seem in reason to affect the land in the same manner as a disposition of the land itself limited to the same objects. The actual interest of the heir in the land is no greater than if it had been devised to be sold so far as was necessary to pay his debts and after the payment of debts to descend.

¶33   What then does the heir take beneficially by descent, supposing the will to go no farther than this clause? Obviously nothing more than what remains after payment of debts. This then is the amount of the real assetts which he holds liable to the contracts of his ancestor. Suppose this devise, instead of being for the payment of debts generally, had been for the payment of a portion to a child in pursuance of a marriage contract, or of debts due by simple contract. These devises would have been unquestionably valid, and the land would have been subject to them in equity. What then would have descended to the heir? Clearly so much only as would remain after payment of the charge. It would seem then in reason that to an action at law by a specialty creditor the heir ought to have been permitted to show in his plea the land that had descended and the charge upon that land and that in such a case the judgement should be only for the value after the discharge of the incumbrance. Suppose in such a case the heir were to pay off the portion due by marriage settlement or the simple contract debts charged on the land as a court of equity would I think compel him to do, and a suit were then to be instituted by a specialty creditor, can it be doubted for a moment that the heir would be allowed to offset these payments against the sum for which he was chargeable in consideration of the lands descended if a court of law could take notice of the charge? These seem to me to be corollaries from the propositions that before the statute against fraudulent devises, the ancestor might devise his lands in whole or in part so as to defeat creditors, and that a charge upon lands, being valid, affects them to the full extent of the charge, and diminishes *pro tanto* the real assetts in the hands of the heir.

¶34   But in England courts of common law do not take up the subject in this reasonable point of view because they do not take cognizance of a trust, nor have they ever sustained a suit brought by a simple contract creditor against an heir to whom lands have descended charged with the debts of his ancestor, nor have they, so far as I have observed, ever considered such charge in the decision of any question brought before them unless the heir has been also executor. When the two characters are united, so that suits at law could be sustained by simple contract creditors, the courts of common law, excluding the trust from their view, have considered the whole as legal assets. This limited view of the subject is probably to be ascribed to their limited jurisdiction.

I have considered the question as if the real estate had descended to the heirs. But the testator has devised it to them, and the words of the devise rather strengthens the argument. They are "All the rest and residue of my estate, after payment of my debts and legacies aforesaid I give devise and bequeath to my two children Andrew and Jane their heirs exrs. and admrs. to be equally divided between them." ¶35

What is given to them by this will? If the words of the testator are worth any thing, he gives only the residue of his estate after payment of debts and legacies. ¶36

I will now advert to the "act for the relief of creditors against fraudulent devises."[11] ¶37

This act recognizes the power of persons indebted by specialties in which themselves and their heirs are bound, who die seized of lands "to dispose of or *charge* the same by their wills or testaments;" "in such manner as such creditors have lost their debts." To remedy this mischief the 2d. sec. enacts "that all wills and testaments, limitations, dispositions, and appointments of or concerning any messuages" &c shall be utterly void as to creditors; and the 3d. sec. gives the creditor the same remedy against the heir and devisee as he would have had against the heir had the land descended to him. ¶38

The 4th. sec. provides that where there shall be "any limitation or appointment *devise or disposition* of or *concerning* any messuages &c" "for the raising or payment of any real and just debt or debts" &c "the same and every of them shall be in full force." The case comes within the very words of this part of the proviso. The will of Mr. Lesslie is "a devise or *disposition* of or *concerning* lands" "for the raising or payment of just debts." I do not think the subsequent part of the proviso can vary the construction. The 5th. sec. of the act applies exclusively to cases where lands not charged by the ancestor with his debts have been sold by the heir. In the case of Freemoult v Dedire 1. P.W 429 the Lord Chancellor obviously so understood them.[12] ¶39

This case then stands as it stood before the statute was enacted; and that statute has no other influence on the cause than to furnish an argument in favour of the validity of the charges made in the will by its recognition of their validity. ¶40

I will now consider the question on the English decisions. ¶41

At law the books furnish I believe no case in which the rights of a simple contract creditor have been taken into view. To actions of debt brought against the heir on the bond of his ancestor, he has generally pleaded "nothing by descent," and has relied on a will devising lands to him charged with debts to support his plea. The single enquiry made by the court has been whether he holds at law by descent or by purchase. In Cr. ¶42

Ch. 161 & 2d. Mod. 286 he was considered as a purchaser;[13] but in 1st. L. R. 728 & 2d. Strange 1270, which last case is also reported in 1st. Bl. 22, it was decided that he held by descent.[14]

¶43   If in a court of law which has no jurisdiction over trusts, this issue had been found in favour of the heir, the creditor would have been without remedy. A will charging his debt on land devised to the heir would, before the statute against fraudulent devises, have been construed to be a will depriving him of all recourse against the fund.

¶44   In cases where the character of heir and executor were combined in the same person, the construction by the courts of law that the whole fund was to be considered as constituting legal assets seems also to result from the incompetency of those courts to act upon trusts. Common law can reach the case but partially; and its decisions therefore ought not to bind a court conclusively, which is so constituted as to enter into the whole subject, investigate it thoroughly, and decide upon it in all its relations.

¶45   For a time the court of chancery seems to have followed the rule of law, but it is matter of surprize that any hesitation should ever have been made by that court in considering the heir as a trustee, and compelling him to execute the trust according to the principles of equity. In Hargrave v Tindal reported in a note in 1 Br. C. C. 136, Lord Hardwicke held an estate which descended to an infant heir charged with debts by the will of his ancestor, to be equitable assets;[15] and the case is still stronger if the estate be devised to the heir so charged.

¶46   The principle is well settled in chancery where lands descend or are devised to an heir who is simply heir, subject to the payment of debts. The question was longer unsettled where the will gave a power to exrs. to sell. The law uniformly considered the estate as legal assets where the exrs. were the trustees. Equity followed the law in this respect, even where the land was devised to the exrs. to be sold. But in Lewin v Oakly 2d. Atk. 50 Lord Cambden decided that, in such a case the assets were equitable, not legal.[16] A distinction, not very well founded in reason, was taken between a power given to exrs. to sell, and a devise of the lands to be sold by executors. The descent was considered as broken in one case, not in the other. This distinction derives countenance from the great authority of Lord Coke; but is I think assailed in the notes of Hargrave and Butler with arguments not easily to be refuted.[17] However this may be at law, it is I think completely overruled in Chancery.

¶47   This whole subject is fully considered in the case of Silk and Prime reported in a note in 1st. Br. C. C. 138.[18]

¶48   The testator charged all his real estate, except a part devised to his mother, with his debts, and directed that Prime and Maxon who were his executors, or the survivors of them, or his heirs, should sell so much of it as might be necessary for their payment. In this case the land was devised to his wife and two daughters, which two daughters were his heirs, and the words of the will give a naked power to the executors and the heirs of the survivour to sell. The Chancellor, after great deliberation and a thorough examination of the cases, determined that the lands were equitable assetts.

In giving his opinion he enters into a full investigation of the subject in which he says that he can hardly suggest a case in which the assetts would be legal but where the exr. has a naked power to sell *qua* executor.[19] It was held that the naked power was not *qua* executor in that case because the power might be executed by the heirs of the survivor in whose hands the produce of the sales could not be assetts, nor could the creditor maintain an action at law against him. ¶49

As Mr. Lesslie has not given the power to the heirs of the executor, it may be supposed that the decision in Silk & Prime is inapplicable to the case before the court and is rather an authority in favor of treating the assetts as legal. This makes it proper to proceed somewhat farther with Silk & Prime. ¶50

The Chancellor obtains two rules from the dissertation he had concluded. ¶51

1st. "It is a good rule in expounding wills to make them speak in favour of equitable assets if it may be done.

2d. That if you can lodge the assetts in the hands of the trustees, the court will never put them in the hands of the executors, and when [a] person is invested with both characters, the trustee shall be preferred."

In applying these rules to the particular case, the Chancellor undoubtedly rests much in the extension of the power to the heir of the executor, but he does not rest on this principle solely. He relies also on other parts of the will which, I think, would have been deemed sufficient had the power to sell not been extended to the heirs of the surviving executor. His language in this part of his opinion is impressive. It is ¶52

1st. "The testator's will does most emphatically direct the payment of all his just debts. ¶53

I can never think that a man who does repeatedly and so anxiously provide for the payment of *all,* could ever mean by legal preference, to pay some and leave the rest unpaid." ¶54

2d. The second relates to the extension of the power to the heir of the surviving executor. ¶55

3d. "This is the case of a charge upon the lands. ¶56

They are devised to the testators wife and daughters subject to this charge. In this respect it is a trust, and no more to be sold than what is necessary for this purpose. ¶57

The power then to sell is meerly consequential, the testator having named the exr. for this purpose. The court would have compelled the devisees. Whoever sells to satisfy a charge must be a trustee because a charge is a trust. ¶58

¶59   To make the case still clearer, the rents and profits in the hands of the devisees are assetts before the sale, legal assetts they cannot be for the exr. has no right to receive them. They must therefore be equitable assetts. And if it be once admitted that any one part of the land is equitable assetts, the whole must be the same; for the trust is one and the same trust through out."

¶60   These reasons exist in all their force in the case under consideration. No testator could display more anxiety for the payment of all his debts than is displayed by Mr. Lesslie.

¶61   This too is a charge on lands. They are devised to the daughters subject to this charge. That the devisees are the heirs at law can make no difference in the question now under consideration of this court, or which was under the consideration of the English court. That question was not and is not whether the descent was broken by the devise, but whether the naked power to the exrs. to sell converted the estate into legal assetts. That question is the same in this court as in that, and the language of the chancellor is as applicable as if a third person had been a devisee with the two daughters. In this therefore the charge is also a trust, and no more of the land is to be sold than is necessary for the purpose.

¶62   In this case too the court would compel the devisees to sell; and the power therefore to sell "is meerly consequential, the testator having named the exrs. for this purpose." The devisees would have sold under the order of the court as trustees.

¶63   In this case too, had the heirs received the rents and profits before the sale, they would have been equitable assetts subject to the trust.

¶64   I cannot read this part of the opinion without being convinced that the chancellor would have decreed the assetts to be equitable although the heir of the exr. had not been named.

¶65   In the case of Newton & al. v Bennet & al. 1 Br. c. c. 135 the testator after making provision for his wife desired "that all his estates in Kent should be sold forthwith and (after payment of several sums of money) that the remainder might be vested in his executors for the payment of his debts."[20]

¶66   Lord Bathurst decided that these were equitable assetts. Upon a re-hearing by consent Lord Thurlow expressed the same opinion. He said "the devise was tantamount to giving the exr. a power to sell and to apply the money to payment of debts." In noticing the argument at the bar that the descent was not broken, he adverts, certainly not with approbation, to the distinction taken by Lord Coke between a devise of land to be sold by his exrs. and a dry power to sell. He concludes with saying "I think the descent is broken and that these are equitable assetts &c."

¶67   It has been contended that this case turned entirely on the question whether the descent was broken, and is an authority in favour of equitable assetts in no case unless the descent be broken. This argument is founded on the following words which the reporter has ascribed to Lord

Thurlow "I think the descent is broken, and that these are equitable assetts on the authority of Sir Joseph Jekyle 3 P.W 341."[21]

The proof that these words were not uttered by Lord Thurlow is very ¶68 strong. In two cases mentioned in a note to the report, the mistake is stated on evidence which appears to be conclusive.[22] The opinion itself seems to me to prove that Lord Thurlow could not have put the case on this point. If, as he says, "the devise was tantamount to giving the exr. a power to sell, then the descent could not be broken according to the construction put on such devises by those who contend for legal assetts. The reference to the case in 3 PW 341 in the very sentence in which this declaration is said to be made, and following that declaration as if furnishing the authority of making it, is also of some weight, because that case turns on a different question. Lord Thurlow also says "The only matter urged was that where money to be raised by the sale of lands was given to exrs., it was made personal, and must be applied in a course of administration"; "but that doctrine has not been adopted in later times, and must imply that a testator meant differently in giving to an exr. than if he had given to any other trustee."[23]

But if the will is properly stated in the report, these words giving them ¶69 the full effect claimed for them, would make no difference in the effect of that case on the present. If in the will of Thomas Tryon as stated in Newton v Bennet, the descent was broken, then it is broken in this case also, and in every case where a power is given to sell.

The case of Pope v Gwyn mentioned in 8th Vez 28 was on a will in which ¶70 the testator directs that his real and personal estates should be liable for all his debts of what sort so ever. Lord Thurlow held the real estate to be equitable assetts.[24]

These cases were decided before the passage of the act establishing the ¶71 judiciary of The United States, which adopts the principles of Chancery as the rule in cases of equity in the federal courts.

In Baily v Ekins 7th. Vez. 319 William Garrett charged his real & per- ¶72 sonal estate with the payment of his debts, and devised his lands to his exrs. their heirs &c in trust to sell and pay his debts, and apply the residue to the support & education of his heir until he should attain his age of 21 when he gave the money and real estates to his heir.[25]

It was contended that the descent was not broken, and that a charge ¶73 did not make the estate equitable assets.

In this case the devise is to the exrs. & their heirs, but this circumstance ¶74 is not relied on or mentioned in the argument of counsel, or in the opinion of the court. The Chancellor did not decide the question whether the descent was broken. He said "that Hargrave v Thomas and Batson v Lindegreen were authorities that a charge upon real estate does make it equitable assetts.["][26] He said "the rule cannot be accurate when it is stated that the descent ought to be broken. It would be more accurate to state it thus, that it must appear upon the will that the testator meant the descent to be broken. Suppose a devise to trustees in trust to pay debts; &, all the trustees dying in the life of the testator, the estate descends upon the heir; would not that be equitable assetts?" He says again "a meer charge is no legal interest. It is not a devise to any one, but that declaration of intention upon which a court of equity will fasten; and by virtue of which they will draw out of the mass going to the heir or to others, that quantum of interest which will be sufficient for the debts.["]

¶75   In Shippard v Lutwidge 8th. Vez. 28 Henry Lutwidge devised his estate to his heir charged with the payment of his debts. The chancellor determined that the heir was a trustee and that the estate was equitable assetts.[27]

¶76   This question, where the estate passes to the heir, or where the power to sell is given to the exr. and his heirs, appears to be completely settled in England. The only doubt, if there be a doubt, is where a naked power to sell is given to the exrs. without mentioning their heirs. I think the case of Silk & Prime together with the subsequent cases, decides that even under such a will the assets are equitable.

¶77   In Nimmos exr. v The Commonwealth 4th. H & M 57 the testator had directed his lands to be sold for the payment of debts. I have searched the record but the will is not in it. The Judges all speak of it as a charge and it is to be presumed that the sale was made by the exr. because the price of the lands is introduced into his account. The Judges all say that it is equitable assets and that the judgement of the Commonwealth gave no priority. That those assets should be pursued in chancery.[28]

¶78   I proceed now to consider the operation of the act of Assembly on this case. It declares that the estate of a guardian or curator shall, after his death, be liable for whatever is due to his ward on account of his guardianship before any other debt due from him or her.

¶79   It has been already said that this section gives priority and creates liability if it did not before exist, but does not create a lien. The words imply a liability for other debts. One estate cannot properly be said to be liable for one debt before others if it be not liable for others. Although then the section may charge lands with a debt with which they were not previously chargeable, it does not follow that it charges land in a condition not to be charged by existing law. The language of the section is comparative. It compares the charge it creates, if it does create one with other charges, and gives it the priority over them. This can apply only to an estate in a condition to be reached by some other debts.

¶80   Previous to the passage of the act against fraudulent devises, lands devised were not liable for any debt whatever. Lands devised for the payment of debts, being exempted from the operation of that statute, pass as they did before it was enacted, and still remain exempt from all legal liabilities. By this exemption the statute protects the trust and leaves the estate to its operation.

¶81   I felt much difficulty in deciding whether the words of the section do not apply to equitable as well as legal assetts. But legislation is rarely intended to act upon and controul the equitable principles which are applied by a court of chancery, unless its language be such as to leave no doubt of the intended application. Even after forming an opinion on this point, I felt the pressure of the question whether a case in which the lands were to be sold under a power given to the exr. did not constitute an exception applicable to this case. After bestowing the best consideration in my power on the English cases I have come to the conclusion that wherever the assets are equitable, the equitable principle must prevail.

That the right of the ward to priority where the assets are equitable, has never been asserted in this country, is not without its weight in the consideration of this case. ¶82

In the case of Jones v Hobson 2d. Randolph 488 the court of appeals determined after an elaborate argument as I have understood, and a profound consideration of the subject, that the sureties of an exr. were not bound for money which came to his hands on account of lands sold for the payment of debts.[29] In delivering the opinion of the court Judge Green in commenting on the act which provides that the bond shall be put in suit until the will be fulfilled as far as lies in the exrs. to fulfil the same says "This expression is understood to relate to the fulfilment of so much of the will as it belongs to the exrs. in their character of exrs. merely, to fulfil, and not to any superadded duty imposed upon them by the will as trustees or otherwise." Again he says "At the common law, in whatever order the exr. might be bound at law or in equity to apply the proceeds of land to the payment of debts, he acted in relation to that subject only as trustee. It was a trust superadded to the office of executer, and not inseparable from it."[30] ¶83

He concludes so much of this very able opinion as relates to this subject with saying "Upon this point we are of opinion that the proceeds of land devised to be sold are not and never were a testamentary subject; that exrs. hold such proceeds not in their character of exrs., but as trustees; that the literal terms of the executors oath & bond bind him only in relation to the goods chattels and credits of his testator; that there is nothing in our legislation on this subject which indicates an intention that the obligation should have a greater extent but the contrary: and that the sureties of an exr. are not responsible for the proceeds of lands sold by him."[31] ¶84

This opinion was given in a case in which the will of the testator in all its material features resembled that of John Lesslie. It decides positively that in such a case the court of appeals considers the exr. as holding the money arising from land sold by the exr. under a power given by the will, as trustee; and consequently that they are equitable assets. ¶85

The conclusion to which I am brought by a consideration of the cases in England and this country is that the exr. of Myers is entitled only to his equal proportion of the fund arising from the real estate.[32] ¶86

AD, Marshall Judicial Opinions, PPAmP; printed, John W. Brockenbrough, *Reports of Cases Decided by the Honourable John Marshall . . .*, II (Philadelphia, 1837), 327–48. For JM's deletions and interlineations, see Textual Notes below.

1. On Myers's death, Forbes was made a party plaintiff by order of the court (U.S. Cir. Ct., Va., Ord. Bk. XII, 235).

2. *Revised Code of Va.*, I, 405, 408.

3. Ibid., 375, 389.

4. *In pari materia* ("upon the same matter or subject").

5. Hening, *Statutes*, III, 371, 375.

6. Ibid., V, 449, 450, 453.

7. Ibid., XII, 140, 152.

8. Ibid., 194–97.

9. Shepherd, *Statutes*, I, 88, 97, 103–6.

10. *Revised Code of Va.*, I, 406. This provision of the 1794 act was reenacted in 1819.

11. Ibid., 391–93.

12. Freemoult v. Dedire, 1 P.Wms. 429, 431–32, 24 Eng. Rep. 458–59 (Ch., 1718).

13. Gilpin's Case, Cro. Car. 161, 79 Eng. Rep. 740 (K.B., 1629); Brittam v. Charnock, 2 Mod. 286, 86 Eng. Rep. 1076 (C.P., 1679).

14. Emerson v. Inchbird, 1 Raym. Ld., 91 Eng. Rep.1386 (K.B., 1701); Allam v. Heber, 2 Str. 1270, 93 Eng. Rep. 1174 (K.B., 1748); also reported in 1 Black., W. 22, 96 Eng. Rep. 12.

15. Hargrave v. Tindal, 1 Bro. C. C. 136, 140 n., 28 Eng. Rep. 1036, 1037 n. (Ch., 1753).

16. Lewin v. Okeley, 2 Atk. 50, 26 Eng. Rep. 428 (Ch., 1740). The chancellor who gave this opinion was Lord Hardwicke, not Lord Camden.

17. Edward Coke, *The First Part of the Institutes of the Laws of England: or, A Commentary upon Littleton* (18th ed.; 2 vols.; London, 1823), I, 112–13 and n. 2. This annotated edition of the *Institutes* was prepared by Francis Hargrave and Charles Butler.

18. Silk v. Prime, 1 Bro. C. C. 138 , 140 n., 28 Eng. Rep. 1036, 1037–40 (Ch., 1768).

19. Here and below JM quotes from Lord Chancellor Camden's opinion at 1 Bro. C. C. 140 n., 28 Eng. Rep. 1039–40.

20. Newton v. Bennet, 1 Bro. C. C. 135, 28 Eng. Rep. 1035 (Ch., 1782).

21. 1 Bro. C. C. 137, 28 Eng. Rep. 1036; Case of the Creditors of Sir Charles Cox, 3 P. Wms. 341, 24 Eng. Rep. 1092 (Ch., 1734). Sir Joseph Jekyll was Master of the Rolls.

22. Newton v. Bennet, 1 Bro. C. C. 140 n., 28 Eng. Rep. 1037 n. The first note to this case reads: "The report of the judgment in this case is materially wrong; since 'Lord *Thurlow* is represented as intimating that the descent must be broken. *Lord* Thurlow *said no such thing; but considered a charge sufficient.*' " The quotation is from counsel's argument in Bailey v. Ekins, 7 Ves. 322, 32 Eng. Rep. 131 (Ch., 1802).

23. 1 Bro. C. C. 138, 28 Eng. Rep. 1036.

24. Pope v. Gwyn, 8 Ves. 28, 29, 30 n., 32 Eng. Rep. 260 and n. (Ch., 1787).

25. Bailey v. Ekins, 7 Ves. 319, 32 Eng. Rep. 130 (Ch., 1802).

26. 7 Ves. 322–23, 32 Eng. Rep. 132. JM garbled Lord Chancellor Eldon's citation of cases. These were Hargrave v. Tindal (cited in n. 15, above), Burt v. Thomas, and Batson v. Lindegreen .

27. Shiphard v. Lutwidge, 8 Ves. 26, 28–30, 32 Eng. Rep. 259, 260 (Ch., 1802).

28. Nimmo's Executor v. The Commonwealth, 4 H. & M. 57 (Va. Ct. App., 1809).

29. Jones v. Hobson, 2 Rand. 483 (Va. Ct. App., 1824).

30. 2 Rand. 497, 498–99. John W. Green (1781–1834), of the prominent Culpeper County family, was appointed to the bench of the Virginia Court of Appeals in 1822, having formerly served as chancellor of the Williamsburg chancery district. He served in the Virginia Convention of 1829–30 (Philip Slaughter, *A Brief Sketch of the Life of William Green, LL.D.* . . . [Richmond, Va., 1883], 13, 64; *Richmond Enquirer,* 11, 13, 25 Feb. 1834).

31. 2 Rand. 501–2.

32. The decree of 30 June 1828 distributing Lesslie's estate included a dividend to Forbes, Myers's executor, in the amount of $2,340.46 (U.S. Cir. Ct., Va., Ord. Bk. XII, 262).

Textual Notes

¶ 1	ll. 2–3	his claim ↑with↓ ~~with~~ which has been
	l. 4	decd. which ~~have been sold and~~ are now
¶ 2	ll. 2–3	guardian. This ~~claim~~ ↑priority↓ is
¶ 3	l. 1	argument been ~~taken into viewcon~~ ↑considered↓ in connexion
	l. 7	estate of a ↑ward,↓ an ideot
	l. 9	from their ↑testator or↓ intestate
¶ 4	l. 2	same session ~~regulating~~ ↑respecting the dignity of↓ claims
¶ 6	l. 1	this I shall ↑first↓ consider
	l. 7	person. ~~The language is~~ ↑The section is↓ addressed to
	ll. 8–10	existence of a ~~claim against the estate on the part~~ ↑debt due from their testator or intestate to the estate↓ of a Lunatic, or ~~the estate~~ of
	l. 13	may come to ~~their~~ ↑his↓ hands.
¶ 7	l. 3	nor does it ~~pres~~ comprehend all
	l. 6	the single ~~case~~ ↑claim↓ of a
¶ 8	l. 10	real estate. The ↑same↓ rule
¶ 9	ll. 1–2	that the debt ~~of~~ ↑due to↓ the ward is
¶10	ll. 1–2	devastavits ~~and therefore~~ ↑. From this it is inferred that↓ one claim
	ll. 3–4	be admitted ~~it will not affect the case~~ ↑the inference is not of course.↓
¶11	l. 3	prior claim ~~to~~ ↑on↓ the estate
	ll. 3–4	guardian to any ↑other↓ debt due to a ↑proper↓ creditor
	ll. 5–6	devisee may ↑or may not↓ commit a devastavit, ↑that he may or may not plead a debt due to a ward to an action by a bond creditor↓
	ll. 7–8	a court ↑administering legal assets,↓ that
¶12	l. 1	difficulty ↑is↓ on the operation
	l. 4	an alarming ~~consequence~~ ↑construction.↓ ~~I do not think the words of the act require it. They are direct that the estate shall be liable to the ward before any other debt due from the Guardian~~ It would,
¶13	l. 1	without ~~a making~~ ↑giving↓ a lien on the land
	l. 3	does it ↑meerly↓ give
¶14	l. beg.	~~The act itself directs that a bond shall~~ The language
	l. 4	existing claims. ~~His debt~~ The estate
	ll. 12–13	where no ~~prior~~ ↑antecedent↓ right
	l. 15	describe the ~~parce~~ estate to
¶15	l. 9	between ↑remedies for↓ debts due
	ll. 10–11	guardians ~~;~~ ↑and I am therefore disposed to read the act with the comma after the word "Guardian."↓
¶16	l. 9	guardian shall be ~~bond~~ ↑bound↓ to

¶21 l. beg.   ~~In the~~ ↑The↓ revisal of 1792
¶22 ll. 3–4   testators will." ↑This act took effect on the first day of March
            1795.↓
     l. 5   law of 1785 ~~took~~ went into
     ll. 11–12 main question ↑now↓ before the court.
¶23 l. 2   the question ↑is↓ whether the
¶25 l. 1   The ~~testator will begin with the following clause~~ ↑following
            are the material clauses in the will↓ "In
¶29 l. 3   amount of ~~the assets~~ assetts which
     ll. 4–5   the devisee ↑not being bound by the contract↓ held them
     l. 6   and thus ↑also↓ defeat
     l. 8   the time ~~of his plea~~ ↑the writ issued,↓ held nothing
¶30 l. 1   that the ~~lands~~ ↑creditor↓ had no
     ll. 2–3   was liable ~~in consideration~~ ↑for the contract of his ancestor in
            regard↓ of lands
     ll. 3–4   the time ~~of his plea pleaded~~ ↑the writ issued↓ only to
¶31 l. 1   Lesslie ↑by his will↓ subjects his whole
¶32 l. 1   devise ↑in a court of equity,↓ has not
     l. 2   then it ~~must~~ ↑would seem in reason to↓ affect the
     ll. 3–4   objects. The ↑actual↓ interest of
¶33 l. 1   heir take ↑beneficially↓by descent
     ll. 6–7   contract, or ~~for~~ of debts due by ~~marriage~~ ↑simple↓ contract.
     ll. 8–9   valid, ↑and the land would have been subject to them in
            equity.↓ What
     ll. 10–11 charge. ~~Can it be doubted~~ ↑It would seem then in reason↓
            that to
     ll. 11–12 the heir ~~might~~ ↑ought to have been permitted to↓ show in
     ll. 13–14 that land ~~?Can it be doubted~~ ↑and↓ that in such a case the
            judgement ~~would~~ ↑should↓ be only
     ll. 16–17 the land ↑as a court of equity would I think compel him to
            do,↓ and a
     l. 18   creditor, ~~↑as a Court of equity would I think compel him to
            do↓~~ can it
     ll. 20–21 descended ↑if a court of [erasure] law could take notice of the
            charge?[erasure]↓ These
     ll. 22–23 propositions that ↓before the statute against
            fraudulent devises,↓ the ancestor ~~may~~ ↑might↓ devise
            ~~A distinction has been taken between a power . . . . cult to with
            hold our assent from his remarks. But it is not necessary to
            inquire into the solidity of this distinction, because, admits it
            full force, it cannot affect the land after the execution of the
            power, and in this case the power has been executed.~~
¶34 l. 1   courts of ↑common↓ law
¶35 l. 1   if the ~~land~~ ↑real estate↓ had
     l. 6   and admrs. ↑to be↓ equally ~~to be~~ divided
¶36 l. 3   and legacies. ~~Had there been no power to the executors to
            sell, then had the heirs entered immediately, they would have
            held as trustees for creditors and legatees, and a court of
            chancery must have enforced the trust. I will not therefore~~

~~enquire whether under this will they take by descent or~~
~~purchase, although, if it were material I should find it very~~
[*erasure*] ~~difficult to resist the argument in favour of~~
~~considering them as purchasers.~~

¶39	l. 3	raising or ~~paying~~ ↑payment↓ of any
	ll. 7–8	construction. ~~This case stands as it stood~~ The 5th.
	l. 10	case of ~~Freeman~~ ↑Fremoult↓ v Dedire ↑1 P.W↓
¶40	l. 3	charges made ~~by~~ ↑in↓ the will
¶42	l. 3	he has ↑generally↓ pleaded
	l. 5	with debts ↑to support his plea.↓
	ll. 6–7	purchase. ~~The enquiry~~ In Cr. Ch.
¶43	l. 1	no jurisdiction ~~of~~ ↑over↓ trusts,
¶44	l. beg.	~~The question~~ In cases
	ll. 2–3	the whole ↑fund↓ was
¶45	l. 4	to execute ~~his~~ ↑the↓ trust
	ll. 5–6	Hardwicke held ~~a will~~ an estate which ~~was devised~~ ↑descended↓ to an
¶46	l. 2	to an heir ↑who is simply heir,↓
	ll. 2–3	debts. ~~Those questions have~~ ↑The question↓ was
	l. 5	this respect, ~~and~~ even where [*erasure*] the
	ll. 8–9	was taken ~~was taken~~ between
	ll. 13–14	at law, ~~This~~ ↑it↓ is I think
¶48	ll. 4–5	the land ~~descended to the~~ ↑was devised to his wife and two
		daughters, which two daughters were his↓ heirs,
	l. 7	after [*erasure*] great deliberation
¶49	l. beg.	~~The chancellor in~~ In giving his opinion ↑he↓ enters
	ll. 4–5	the power ~~was given to~~ ↑might be executed by↓ the
¶50	l. 4	makes it proper to ~~pursue~~ proceed
¶52	ll. 5–6	surviving executor. ~~There are~~ His
	l. 6	impress ↑ive. It is↓
¶55	ll. 1–2	↑2d. The second relates to the extension of the power to the
		heir of the surviving executor.↓
¶61	l. 1	on lands ~~which is a trust that the court [wants?]~~ ↑.↓ They are
	l. 3	in the ~~case~~ ↑question now↓ under consideration ↑of this
		court,↓ or which
¶65	l. 1	Bennet &al. ↑1 Br. c. c. 135↓ the
¶66	l. 2	Thurlow ~~gave~~ ↑expressed↓ the same
	l. 8	assetts &c." ~~copy to the~~
¶67	l. 4	founded on the ↑following↓ words ↑which↓ the
¶68	ll. 1–2	very strong. ~~The reporter was not present when the decree~~
		~~was pronounced.~~ In two
¶69	ll. 3–4	If in ↑the will of Thomas Tryon as stated in↓ Newton v
¶70	l. beg.	~~But the whole~~ The case of Pope v ~~Gwin~~ ↑Gwyn↓ mentioned
	ll. 1–2	on a will ~~directing~~ in which the
¶71	l. 3	as the rule ~~of law~~ in cases
¶72	ll. 1–2	Garrett ~~devised to his exrs. & their heirs &c. his real~~ charged
		his real ↑& personal↓ estate
¶73	l. 2	the estate ~~real~~ ↑equitable↓ assets.
¶74	l. 1	this case ~~as in Silk v Prime~~ the devise

l. 2   not relied ↑on↓ or mentioned ~~by~~ ↑in↓ the argument ↑of counsel,↓ or in

¶75   l. 1   Vez. 28 ↑Henry Lutwidge↓ devised

¶76   ll. 1–2   where the ~~devise is~~ ↑power to sell is given↓ to the

¶77   ll. 5–7   his account. ↑The Judges all say that it is equitable assets and that the judgement of the Commonwealth gave no priority. That those assets should be pursued in chancery.↓

¶79   l. 3   other debts. ~~Lands~~ ↑An estate↓ can not

      ll. 8–9   one with ~~previously~~ other charges,

      l. 10   an estate ~~capable of being~~ ↑in a condition to be↓ reached

¶80   ll. 1–2   devises, ~~an estat~~ ↑lands↓ devised ~~was~~ ↑were↓ not liable

¶81   ll. 6–7   the lands were ↑to be↓ sold

      l. 9   on the ↑English↓ cases ~~in the E~~ I have

¶83   l. 2   elaborate argument ↑as I have understood,↓ and a

¶84   ll. 4–5   as trustees; ~~that the literal~~ that the

¶85   l. beg   ~~In~~ ↑This↓ opinion

      ll. 1–2   testator in all ↑its↓ material ~~circumstances~~ ↑features↓ resembled

The Charlottesville Convention
Memorial and Resolutions
Charlottesville, Virginia, 16–17 July 1828

EDITORIAL NOTE

From 14 July to 18 July 1828 John Marshall attended a convention in Charlottes-ville held to revive interest in internal improvements. According to the memorial printed below, the convention arose from "a spontaneous effort in several coun-ties" to urge upon the General Assembly the importance of continuing the work of facilitating transportation and improving internal commerce. After a promis-ing beginning, Virginia's internal improvement program had begun to languish, hampered by the great expense of constructing canals and turnpike roads and by sectional conflicts over the distribution of funds for this purpose. Marshall had long been an active supporter of this program, notably as the head of a commis-sion in 1812 to survey a water-and-land route to connect the eastern and western regions of the state. His report to the legislature laid the foundation for Vir-ginia's flagship internal improvement project, the James River waterway, which ultimately promised to establish an unbroken commercial route linking the Ohio River with the Chesapeake Bay. Dissatisfaction with the efforts of the James River Company to make timely progress on this project had led in 1823 to the state's taking over the entire enterprise. By 1825 the James River Canal extended twenty-seven miles above Richmond to Maiden's Adventure Falls in Goochland County, and three years later a seven-mile canal through a gap in the Blue Ridge Mountains was completed. The two canals remained unconnected, however, and completion of this work was accorded highest priority among the recommenda-tions of the Charlottesville convention.[1]

The convention was composed of delegates from thirty-nine of Virginia's counties and from its six incorporated towns, along with members of the state Board of Works and the state's chief engineer, Claudius Crozet. Among the delegates were eminent citizens of the commonwealth, including former Presidents James Madison and James Monroe, who were also in Charlottesville for the meeting of the University of Virginia's Board of Visitors. Marshall headed the Richmond delegation of six members who had been chosen at a meeting of interested citizens on 26 May. Joining him in this delegation were John Brockenbrough, Joseph Marx, Jaquelin B. Harvie (Marshall's son-in-law), Robert Stanard, and Benjamin W. Leigh.[2]

At the opening session Marshall seconded Madison's nomination as president of the convention, noting that "he was satisfied he expressed the earnest wishes of the whole body, in making the request, that he would take the chair." After being assured he could call any other member to the chair in case his duties as rector of the University of Virginia prevented him from presiding, Madison was unanimously chosen president. The next important business took place on 15 July, with the appointment of a committee "to take into consideration, the subject of Internal Improvement" and to recommend measures "to effect that Improvement." Madison appointed Monroe to head this committee of thirteen, which also included Marshall (the second named), James Barbour, and John Coalter. The next day, 16 July, the committee presented a draft of a memorial addressed to the General Assembly, which was read and ordered to be printed. On 17 July Marshall submitted eight resolutions that summarized the committee's recommendations and were "added to and considered a part of the Report presented on yesterday." The last two days of the convention were devoted to considering and amending the report and resolutions. In November 1828 Madison transmitted a copy of the proceedings of the convention and the amended memorial and resolutions to Governor Giles for presentation to the General Assembly.[3]

Marshall had a larger role in the Charlottesville convention than has previously been acknowledged. In addition to presenting the eight resolutions of 17 July, the chief justice almost certainly drafted the memorial that the committee of thirteen reported on 16 July. Although Monroe headed this committee, his appointment was made "from respect of years and station, . . . not from any expectation that he will take upon himself the labor of preparing the Report." In feeble health, he was described as looking "exceedingly wasted away."[4] Responsibility for chairing the committee thus fell largely to Marshall, the second named, who for that reason alone would have been closely involved in drawing the report. Moreover, as the author of the 1812 report, he was a logical choice to compose the memorial. The style of the memorial, which blends a broad appeal for the support of internal improvements as essential to promoting civilization and prosperity with practicable recommendations grounded in a realistic appreciation of the commonwealth's limited financial resources, is reminiscent of the 1812 report. Marshall's known connection with the resolutions of 17 July, which became part of the memorial, and his amendments to the wording of the memorial on 19 July also appear to point to his authorship. At least one Virginia newspaper noted at the time that the memorial "was generally supposed to be from the pen of the Chief Justice of the United States."[5]

BENJAMIN WATKINS LEIGH
Oil on canvas by John Wesley Jarvis, 1828.
Courtesy of the Virginia Historical Society

1. *PJM*, VII, 355–79; Wayland Fuller Dunaway, *History of the James River and Kanawha Company* (New York, 1922), 48–91; Ronald E. Shaw, *Canals for a Nation: The Canal Era in the United States, 1790–1860* (Lexington, Ky., 1990), 112–14.

2. "Proceedings of the Charlottesville Convention," *Journal of the House of Delegates of the Commonwealth of Virginia [1828–29]* (Richmond, Va., 1828), app., 35–44; *Richmond Enquirer*, 30 May 1828.

3. Charlottesville *Virginia Advocate*, 17 July 1828; "Proceedings of the Charlottesville Convention" and "Memorial of the Charlottesville Convention," *Journal of the House of Delegates [1828–29]*, app., 35, 45.

4. *Richmond Enquirer*, 18 July 1828.

5. "Proceedings of the Charlottesville Convention," *Journal of the House of Delegates [1828–29]*, app., 44; Fredericksburg *Political Arena*, 22 July 1828. The Washington *Daily National Intelligencer*, 24 July 1828, and *Niles' Weekly Register* (Baltimore), 26 July 1828, also named the chief justice as the penman, probably on the basis of the report in the Fredericksburg paper.

TO the Honorable the Speakers and Members of the Senate and House of Delegates of Virginia, the memorial of the Convention assembled at Charlottesville, on the subject of Internal Improvement, most respectfully represents; That the immense importance of facilitating the transportation of the produce of the soil to market, and of improving the means of intercourse between those parts of the state which have a natural connexion with each other, have impressed themselves so deeply on the minds of many of their fellow citizens as to produce a spontaneous effort in several counties to communicate their sentiments and feelings to the legislature of their country, in a more solemn manner than could be effected by the expression of individual opinions. For this purpose thirty nine counties, and the towns of Norfolk, Williamsburgh, Petersburgh, Richmond, Fredericksburgh, and Lynchburgh, have deputed your memorialists to meet in Charlottesville, for the purpose of interchanging with each other the opinions which prevail in their respective districts, and of submitting the result of their consultations to those to whom Virginia has confided her government.

It is scarcely possible to turn our attention to this interesting subject without adverting to its influence on the prosperity of nations. In almost every part of the civilized world, internal improvements have produced or have been the offspring of civilization and wealth. They have most usually been the harbingers of an increased degree of power and greatness to society, and of comfort to the individuals who compose it. We cannot turn our eyes towards Europe without perceiving the advantages in every country which has applied its means to their attainment. In Great Britain and in Holland especially, the benefits derived from these sources almost bid defiance to calculation. In France they have been very great; and her late Emperor, who meditated the useful as well as the grand and magnificent, had formed vast plans for internal improvement, which yielded only to that all devouring ambition of which he was at length the victim.

If national power and wealth, or the happiness and comfort of individuals produced by successful industry, be the legitimate objects of government, the experience of other countries shows how much these objects are promoted by the judicious and persevering applications of national and individual wealth to roads and canals — emphatically termed the veins and arteries of the body politic.

If we turn our eyes from other countries to our own, we find ample evidence of that important truth which has been so fully disclosed and demonstrated by the experience of Europe. A sister state, whose original advantages were undoubtedly great, has multiplied those advantages to an amount already exceeding any previous estimate; and is advancing so rapidly as to justify the belief that the produce accumulating for transportation through her canals, will be limited only by the capacity of those channels of communication to convey it to its appropriate market. The great canal of New York has not only given a most powerful impetus to the commerce and agriculture of that state, but has attracted to its metropolis a large portion of the commerce of the West. Other States stimulated by the imposing example, are endeavouring to improve their natural advantages, and to turn them to the best account. Virginia does not behold the exertions of others without making any for herself. She does not remain the passive spectator of the activity of her sister states. She cannot consent to be stationary while they are advancing. She cannot look on unmoved while her neighbours are securing not only that commerce which belongs naturally[1] to them, but that which ought to seek the markets of Virginia. It is not her policy to compel her citizens to abandon her markets, and seek for connexions elsewhere. Such is not her antient policy. The legislature of Virginia was among the first to take up this interesting subject: among the first to commence internal improvements. The improvement of the upper navigation of the James and Potomac rivers was suggested and recommended by the wisest of her sons; by those, whose intelligent patriotism she may long contemplate with satisfaction and with pride.

Neither the knowledge nor the resources of the country justified, at that time, the attempt to execute those great works on a scale that would be productive of all the advantages that ought to be derived from them. Increased knowledge and enlarged resources extended our plans of improvement. Virginia entered upon this course with eagerness, and pursued it for sometime with animation. She has however in some measure desisted from the pursuit; and, if she has not abandoned, has at least suspended the execution of her greatest work — that from which the most important advantages were anticipated. Will true wisdom justify the continuance of this policy?

We have only to cast our eyes on the map of the United States to be assured that the natural advantages of Virginia are very great. The Chesapeake, one of the noblest bays of the world, receives her magnificent rivers and pours them into the Atlantic. Independent of other valuable streams, her northern frontier is washed by the Potomac, her southern by the Roanoke, and her centre is pierced by the James. These great rivers penetrate the Alleghany Mountains, and afford the shortest channel of water communication with several of the western states. They pass through a country rich in mineral and vegetable productions, which the labour and ingenuity of man could not fail to turn to valuable account, if those means of transportation were afforded him,[2] which these waters in an improved state, would unquestionably furnish. Why then is Virginia less populous and opulent than many of her sister states? Why is the trade of the Chesapeake transferred entirely to a neighbour?

Perhaps even the number of our rivers may have had some tendency to prevent the accumulation of capital at any one place and perhaps the policy of our predecessors may have contributed to give trade a direction to other channels. But without vainly repining the past, it is the part of true wisdom to adopt and pursue that system which is best for the present and the future.

What then is the course which is most advisable for Virginia? Does sound policy, does a judicious survey of our situation in all its aspects[3] recommend the total abandonment or even further suspension of those plans of improvement which are now in progress, especially that of our most important river, or does it recommend an immediate resumption of them, modified perhaps by that instruction which our experience has furnished?

The advantages of an improved navigation of our rivers are too obvious, and too universally admitted, to require that they should be shown or enforced by argument. That this improvement is in itself a positive good, the acquisition of which is greatly to be desired, is a truth which all acknowledge and assert. The only objection which the immediate pursuit of this good has encountered, is the enormous expense with which it is attended. It has been urged, and, in the opinion of many, successfully, that its advantages do not compensate for its price; that neither the public nor individuals have a prospect of remuneration for the money expended.

That the past gives too much countenance to this objection, is acknowledged and lamented. If the same scale of expence were to be attached inseparably to any plan which might be devised, Virginia might pause and enquire whether prudence and a regard to her real interests would justify perseverance in her course.

But in the commencement of a great and untried work, many errors may be expected which will not recur in its progress. Experience corrects much; and, among its other valuable results, ascertains the price of labour; and suggests the best and cheapest mode of applying it to its object. The last report of the principal Engineer contains a suggestion on this subject which is worthy the attention of those who may be entrusted with the execution of this business, should it be revived.[4]

But, independent of the beneficial changes which may be made in the mode of applying labor to the object, a change of plan has been suggested which is recommended by its diminution of expence. We may therefore dismiss all calculations founded on the enormous expenditure made on that part of the work which has been already executed, and direct our views to that cheaper system of operation which is suggested in the last report of the principal Engineer. On his estimates we may, it is presumed, safely rely. They appear to be made with fairness; without any intention of presenting a too flattering view of the subject. Assuming them to be correct, may not Virginia proceed with some confidence to the completion of those improvements which are already in progress? Are not her resources adequate to the object, and does not the soundest policy advise the application of them?

In reflecting on these momentous questions, it will readily occur to the legislature that money invested in a productive fund may be replaced at the will of the proprietor. He does not acquire a dead capital, but a subject capable of circulation, capable of being again converted into money at pleasure. It will be at the option of the legislature to retain the property, in which case the dividends, if any reliance is to be placed on the estimates of the Principal Engineer, will meet the interest; or to sell so much stock as will discharge the principal. A loan then thus employed, does not impose a continuing burthen on the people, but becomes and active fund, having the double operation of reproducing itself, and of dispensing benefits to the state at large, as well as to a great number of its inhabitants.[5]

This convention will not engage in the task for which perhaps it is not well fitted, of calculating the expense or the productiveness of the improvements which we recommend. These calculations have been made officially by the person whose duty it is to obtain the requisite information, and whose professional talents ought to enable him, and we believe do enable him, to decide upon the subject. To them, we refer, and the judgment of the legislature will be exercised upon them. To that judgment we submit with implicit confidence.

There is however one obvious circumstance to which we will take the liberty to advert.

In every proposition to commence a more expensive and more beneficial system of improvements, the legislature will undoubtedly, take into its view the comparative value of the object with the expense of its attainment. In making this comparison, future disbursements would be opposed to future advantages, and no other item would be brought into the amount.[6] Even in these cases, an enlarged policy which contemplates the future as well as the present, would, we persuade ourselves, perceive in the pecuniary returns which might reasonably be expected, and still more in the vast accommodation to its citizens, and the consequent increase of articles for market and of the general prosperity, a full remuneration for present advances. All experience shows that judicious and permanent improvements of internal navigation, continually disclose new sources of wealth, furnish additional employment for industry, and thus add to the population and strength of a country.

But, as respects the navigation of James river we are not now about to commence the more expensive and more beneficial system. It is already begun, and a very large sum of money has been expended on it. The canal from Richmond to Maiden's Adventure has cost, as appears from the last report of the Principal Engineer, $640,000, and that through the mountain section 365,000. The value of these works, of the lower canal especially, depends essentially on uniting them. All those who commence transportation at or below the head of the canal are undoubtedly benefitted by it, because freights are lessened by the addition to the cargo. But those who enter the river above, derive no advantage from the canal below, because their cargoes and their moving power must be adapted to the state of the upper navigation. If the improvement stops at its present point, upwards of one million of dollars are wasted.[7] We can avail ourselves of this expenditure only by extending the improvement. From our estimates of the advantages and disadvantages of its extension, this item ought not to be excluded. If it be taken into the amount,[8] its influence, unless every estimate which has been made is deceptive, must be decisive in favour of prosecuting this work.

So imperfect is the navigation of this river above the head of the lower canal, that in one state of the water, a boat cannot bring half a load; and in another, it is liable to be wrecked on the voyage. The vast importance of completing this improvement must be obvious to all. The river in its whole course from Covington passes through a fertile country, abounding in landing places where boats take in their cargoes; so that every step of improvement, on its advance up the river, gives to an additional tract of country, the whole benefit of the lower canal. To us then it seems apparent, that the extension of a safe navigation to this point is recommended by the soundest policy; and we submit this opinion with great deference to the legislature of our country.

If the real interest of the state requires that this part of the work should be completed, that the present expensive and dangerous navigation should be rendered cheaper and safer, the strongest motives operate against all avoidable delay. While our fellow-citizens still labour under the difficulties which the present state of the river opposes to transportation, the Commonwealth loses the interest of the money already expended.

It is too, worthy of consideration that the present cheapness of labour is peculiarly auspicious to the prosecution of great public enterprizes.

The accomplishment of this important part of the work will enlarge the fund applicable to other improvements.

Unless the calculations submitted by those who have been selected for their professional skill, be fallacious, the tolls after its navigation shall have been improved will be sufficient to liberate the fund which has been appropriated to this object from its present burthens.

Our observations have been applied more particularly to James river, because we consider it as claiming eminently the immediate attention of the legislature for several reasons.

It passes in its whole extent though the centre of the State, and accommodates a greater number of our fellow citizens than any other river.

It is the exclusive property of the State, and the whole produce of the tolls may either be brought into the treasury or applied to other improvements.

It promises more than any other, to be auxiliary to the extension of the commerce of Virginia and the West.

The improvement of its navigation will contribute greatly to the augmentation of our commercial capital.

And lastly, it will save a large sum already expended on that part of the work which has been accomplished.

If we persist in an almost infinite sub-division of our funds, nothing great will be completed. If we apply them first to the most important objects, they will be accomplished; and their accomplishment will enable us to proceed with others. It cannot, we think, be doubted that by rendering each work in which we engage productive, we shall be enabled to move on progressively until the whole shall become so.

Although then the patronage of the legislature should be directed to James River, it does not follow that the improvement of other rivers should be out of view.

The Potomac and the Roanoke having their sources, as well as the James, in the Alleghany mountains, affords facilities to the inhabitants of a vast tract of country, and the means of intercourse between the Atlantic and the Western states. They are all of them rivers of the first class, and the strongest motives exist for the improvement of their navigation.

The Roanoke is understood to contain more water than the James, and its navigation between the falls near Halifax and the Blue Ridge, is not supposed to be so difficult or so dangerous. It is also understood that a fund is obtained for a canal around the falls, so as to connect the upper with the lower navigation. The report to which reference has frequently been made, shows, that the Dismal Swamp canal will be completed this summer, after which the same vessels may pass in safety from the falls of Roanoke to Norfolk. The legislature, we think, cannot be charged with neglecting the interests of this river, if farther advances in the improvement of its navigation, be postponed for a short time.

A slight attention to the map of Virginia, demonstrates, indeed, that as the Alleghany recedes from the Ocean, in its extension from North to South, the Southern rivers which rise in that mountain, are lengthened in their course to the Atlantic.[9] But increased length, which enables a river to accommodate a greater extent of country, serves, in some degree, as the measure of the probable productiveness of the capital vested in its improvement; and, the more especially, when penetrating successive ranges of mountains, and crossing deep vallies, as well as elevated table lands, it derives additional importance from the number & variety of the productions which it bears to a common market. It thus assures a more steady employment to the capital of that market, as well as a more stable profit upon its own navigation.

Among the great rivers of Virginia a new interest has been recently imparted to the Roanoke, by the discovery of the practicability of uniting its waters, with those of James River, and both rivers with the waters of Greenbrier and New River, and by their instrumentality, with those of the great Kenawha. West of the Alleghany, this river and the Monongahela occupy the first rank, and it is fortunate for the union of the resources of the Commonwealth, in promoting their improvement, that it connects itself with that of the three great rivers of the Atlantic.

The Potomac, considered apart from its principal branches, is a border river, but the Shenandoah, now imperfectly navigable for two hundred miles, and the South branch for one hundred, give to the Potomac, the character of a Virginia river; its branches bearing towards its stem, the relation of all the commercial channels of the Commonwealth, to their great estuary, the Chesapeake.

Happily for the early improvement of this river, a continued canal is now in progress, from its tide towards the base of the Alleghany Mountain, so that a contribution to the capital employed in this enterprise, not exceeding that of a sister and bordering state, will fulfil, at a cost easily provided, the correspondent obligations of the Commonwealth to her own citizens. Indeed, a comparison of the relative interest of Maryland and Virginia in this great work, establishes, incontestibly, the superior importance to the latter of its successful and speedy accomplishment. Expedited as the progress of this canal will be, by the present subscription of $3,600,000 to its stock; the sum proposed to be added to that amount by the Commonwealth of Virginia will ensure its speedy completion and render its stock immediately productive.

The Monogahela will constitute to the North as the great Kenawha to the South, the western termination of these great channels of commerce binding together not only the eastern and western territory, but the two great divisions of the United States.

Under the general denominations of the preceding rivers are comprehended such of their tributaries as can be rendered navigable; but the growth of their branches must follow that of their stems.[10]

The rivers of Virginia which are not comprised in the first class, have their origin in the Blue Ridge or the range of mountains running nearer the Ocean. To some,[11] the Commonwealth has already extended her patronage, and to others, the same spirit, enlightened by experience, will hereafter dispense its beneficent influence.

From the improvement of the rivers of the Commonwealth, the Convention pass to the subject of roads.

So numerous are these, as to suggest a rigorous[12] restriction of the public wealth, to the construction of such as are of prime necessity, for social, commercial and political purposes. No error, in relation to the success of any system of *Internal Improvement* would be more injurious, as has been intimated in an earlier part of this memorial, than that of dispersing *its funds*, over many minor objects. But, looking to the map of the territory of this Commonwealth, three leading[13] roads are suggested: having in view, a connection of its western, with its eastern frontier, across those natural barriers, which, under a less auspicious system of state and federal government would threaten its separation. However strong those ties may be knit by affection, wisdom suggests the expediency of confirming them, by the unceasing and steady support of interest.

In this view, roads from the political and commercial centre of the State, from some point upon, or near her central line of water communication, southwestwardly towards the county of Lee, northwestwardly towards the county of Brooke, at the opposite extreme of the State, and westwardly, to some position between them on the Ohio river, merit, in the opinion of the convention, the early consideration, and efficient patronage of the General Assembly.

In relation to one of these roads, a sense of the importance of its prolongation from its present eastern and western extremes, is suggested by the aid which the Legislature has already afforded to its construction, and the great benefits[14] derived from it. The Convention is also apprised, that while its cost is likely to be amply repaid, by its increasing utility; its extension, which will certainly and profitably augment its use may be effected, at an expense much below that which has attended the part of it, already constructed. This consideration, alike applicable to the two other routes here proposed, enhances the facility and the expediency of their execution.

These are objects of immense importance to Virginia. All feel and acknowledge their magnitude. But the fund devoted to their attainment is already charged to the full extent of its present capacity. The probability is that its productiveness will be in some measure increased by the completion of several public works[15] which are in progress; but this augmentation cannot be considerable. It is gradually liberating itself from the burthens imposed upon it, and will probably after the present year yield some surplus in addition to the execution of its existing engagements. After the year 1830, it may undoubtedly be considered as very productive. Its operation, if it even be directed[16] to important objects will be sensibly felt. But as it consists of stock the dividends on which may fluctuate, the necessity may arise, especially if the immediate objects of improvement must be multiplied, for[17] some addition to the taxes, or a sale of some of its disposable funds, or an admission of other stockholders to participate in the tolls of such works as have been or may be begun, or extending any loan which may be effected to the interest upon it, at least for the first year. A loan to some extent will be required; and till the fund for Internal Improvement shall be enabled to meet the interest on this loan, resort may be necessary[18] to one or the other of these measures. We can perceive no other alternative. On such a subject, on the choice between these measures, this convention will not presume to hazard a suggestion.

Such are some of the leading objects of Internal Improvement and such the means of their accomplishment, which the Convention most respectfully recommend to the favourable regard of a paternal Legislature. But they would not acquit themselves of the obligation which they owe to their immediate constituents and to the Commonwealth, if they did not add, that after completing these great works, their value, if it does not essentially depend upon, will be greatly augmented by a judicious and efficient system of common roads. The happiness, because it is, itself, dependent on the social intercourse of the people of any country, must rest very much upon the improvement of those numerous highways, which conduct them, and the productions of their land and labour to the leading channels of internal and external commerce. What a vast waste of time, of industry, and of resource,[19] does a bad system of common roads occasion in any country, which may have the misfortune to feel its oppression. Candour as regards the entire Commonwealth, justice to those who suffer most grievously from the present road system of Virginia, call upon the Convention to pronounce it unequal, in the burthens which it imposes upon the people, and inefficient in its results.

Bearing, in any system of Internal Improvement, the relation to the great avenues of trade, which the daily offices of social feeling, have to the public virtues, a good system of common roads makes up, in the frequency of its use, what it may seem to want, to superficial observers, in dignity.[20] In a comprehensive system of Improvement, the General Assembly will assign to a just and effectual provision for the county roads, a rank proportioned to the enjoyments which it dispenses, and thus heal one source of dissatisfaction in the Commonwealth, which has, in truth, but one interest, that of diffusing every where the spirit of social contentment.

[Resolutions]

Mr. Marshall offered the following resolutions, which on his motion, were added to, and considered a part of the Report presented on yesterday.

We submit most respectfully to the Legislature, the following opinions as the result of our deliberations.

1st. That the best interests of Virginia will be promoted by persevering in that system of Internal Improvement, which has been so wisely begun.

2d. That the improvement of the navigation of the James River is an object of great importance to the State, and to a large number of its inhabitants, and is indispensable to the value of those works which have been already executed, and to the preservation of that money which has already been expended.[21]

3d. That a just attention to the interests of our fellow citizens on our northern frontier, requires that the State should subscribe to the Stock of the Chesapeake and Ohio Canal, the amount to be payable in five annual instalments.[22]

4th. That the improvement of the navigation of the Shenandoah after the Potomac Canal shall have reached Harper's Ferry on such principles and terms as the wisdom of the Legislature may devise, is an object of vital importance to the inhabitants of that part of the country, and is entitled to a share of the public patronage.[23]

5th. That the improvement of the navigation of the great Kenhawa from the falls to its mouth, recommends itself to the Legislature not only by its intrinsic importance to the inhabitants who will participate in its immediate benefits, but as a link in that chain of connexion which, passing through Virginia, may unite the Ohio to the Chesapeake.

6th. That the farther improvement of the navigation of the Roanoke is an object of deep interest both to Virginia and North Carolina, on which both states will, we trust, act in concert, so soon as their funds will enable them to act effectively.

7th. That the extension of the Kenhawa road westward to the Ohio river, and eastward towards the eastern frontier of our state, is a measure dictated by sound policy; and that the construction of similar roads to connect the central navigation of Virginia with the north and south western extremes of her territory, is a measure of like importance; both of which are recommended to the attention of the legislature, so soon as means can be acquired to proceed on them with effect.

8th. That an improvement of the common roads founded upon the authority of the several county courts of the Commonwealth, is an object essential to the enjoyment by the people, of all the benefits of an enlarged plan of Internal Improvement.[24]

Printed, *Virginia Advocate* (Charlottesville, Va.), 17, 19 July 1828.

1. "Naturally belongs" in the official proceedings and in the final version of the memorial ("Proceedings of the Charlottesville Convention" and "Memorial of the Charlottesville Convention," *Journal of the House of Delegates[1828–29]*, app., 38, 46).

2. "Her" in the official proceedings and in the final version of the memorial (ibid.).

3. "Respects" in the official proceedings but "aspects" in the final version (ibid.).

4. This and other references below are apparently to Claudius Crozet, *Report of C. Crozet on the Continuation of the Canal from Maiden's Adventure Falls to the Mouth of Dunlap's Creek*

(Richmond, Va., 1826). In obedience to a resolution of the General Assembly of 9 Mar. 1827, Crozet prepared a subsequent report, which was to be considered "as a complement" to the 1826 report. See Claudius Crozet, *Report on the Survey of James River* [Richmond, 1828?], 1.

5. On 19 July John Lewis of Spotsylvania County moved to strike the preceding paragraph, but the motion lost ("Proceedings of the Charlottesville Convention" and "Memorial of the Charlottesville Convention," *Journal of the House of Delegates [1828–29]*, app., 44).

6. "Account" in the official proceedings and in the final version (ibid., 39, 47).

7. On 19 July, Chapman Johnson of Augusta County successfully moved to strike "are wasted" and insert "will be comparatively unproductive" (ibid., 44).

8. On the basis of the above correction (see n. 6), this should probably be "account," but no correction was made.

9. The map referred to may be *A Map of the State of Virginia Reduced from the Nine Sheet Map of the State* . . . . (Richmond, Va., 1827). See Earl G. Swem, comp., *Maps Relating to Virginia in the Virginia State Library* . . . (Richmond, Va., 1914), 109.

10. On 19 July, on Johnson's motion, the preceding three paragraphs (beginning with "Happily for") were stricken out and the following passage inserted: "The improvement of this river may be considered as already in progress. Roads have been provided, which, according to the estimates of those who best understand the subject, will go far towards the completion of the eastern section of that great work. If Virginia, pressed as she is, for means to prosecute improvements, depending solely on herself, should decline co-operating at this time with those who are engaged in it, her conduct cannot be attributable to any indifference to the navigation of this truly important river, or to the interests of its inhabitants. To us it appears, that she will attend most effectually to the interests of many of them, by such exertions as it may be in her power to make on the Shenandoah and the South Branch of the Potomac, as soon as the canal leading up the main river shall reach their mouths respectively" ("Proceedings of the Charlottesville Convention"and "Memorial of the Charlottesville Convention," *Journal of the House of Delegates [1828–29]*, app., 44).

11. "Of them" added in the official proceedings and in the final version (ibid., 40, 48).

12. "Rigorous"omitted in the official proceedings and in the final version (ibid.).

13. "Leading" omitted in the official proceedings and in the final version (ibid.).

14. "Benefit" in the official proceedings and in the final version (ibid.).

15. "Turnpike roads" replaced "public works" in the official proceedings, but on JM's motion of 19 July "public works" was reinstated (ibid., 41, 44).

16. On JM's motion of 19 July, "it even be directed" was stricken and replaced by "limited" (ibid.. 44).

17. This passage was not in the official proceedings but was added on JM's motion of 19 July in place of this passage: "Yet there is much reason to fear that the Legislature cannot proceed immediately, even with the most pressing of these works, without" (ibid., 41, 44).

18. In the official proceedings "must be had" replaced "may be necessary." On JM's motion of 19 July "may be necessary" was reinstated (ibid.).

19. In the official proceedings and in the final version "private revenue" replaced "resource" (ibid., 41, 49).

20. In the official proceedings and in the final version this passage reads "seem, to superficial observers, to want in dignity" (ibid., 41, 49).

21. The convention in committee of the whole on 17 July amended this resolution by (on Leigh's motion) adding "future productiveness" after "value" and by (on Johnson's motion) striking out the words after "executed." The convention formally approved these amendments the next day (ibid., 42–43).

22. On 18 July the committee of the whole (on Johnson's motion) dropped the third resolution. The convention approved this amendment later the same day on a roll call vote of 61 to 57, JM voting in the minority to retain the resolution (ibid.).

23. On 18 July the committee of the whole (on Johnson's motion) added a new resolution to follow the fourth: "That the improvement of the navigation of the South Branch of

the Potomac, after the Potomac canal shall have reached the mouth of the said South Branch, on such principles and terms as the wisdom of the Legislature may devise, is an object of vital importance to the inhabitants of that part of the country, and is entitled to a share of the public patronage." The convention approved this amendment, which became the fourth resolution in the final version. The original fourth resolution became the third (ibid., 42, 43, 49).

24. On 18 July Leigh moved this additional resolution: "That a wise and just policy requires, that it should be adopted as a general principle, (subject of course to occasional exceptions,) that all disposable means which the Commonwealth now possesses, or can prudently command, should be concentrated and applied to some one of the great objects of Internal Improvement, which shall be deemed objects of primary importance, such as the Legislature shall in its wisdom select; and that being accomplished, the same should then in like manner be concentrated and applied to other works of the same kind, each in succession, in such order as shall be deemed most advisable." This resolution was defeated on a roll call vote of 58 to 49, JM voting in the majority (ibid., 43).

To William B. Sprague

Revd. Sir[1]   Richmond July 22d. 1828

Yesterday on my return from an excursion into the country I found your letter of the 4th., together with the two sermons which accompanied it.[2] I am equally flattered by the request conveyed in your letter, and by the manner in which it is communicated. Be assured it would give me real pleasure to furnish the autographs you are in search of were it in my power. But the letters I may have received of the description you mention have either not been preserved, or contain such communications as are private in their nature.

I have read your very valuable sermons with great pleasure and attention. That which respects the duties of civil rulers is a compendium of what belongs to that important subject.[3] You notice towards the conclusion what has frequently attracted my serious attention — "the support of religious institutions." We do not regard this subject in Virginia as you do in New England. Previous to the revolution we had an established church and all were taxed for its support. From one extreme we passed to the other, and individual contributions purely voluntary, were substituted for those which had been imposed by law. Soon after the conclusion of the war, an attempt was made to pass a bill for a general assessment — that is a small tax levied on property generally, for the support of the ministers of religion, each individual being at liberty to declare the person to whom his contribution should be paid. This bill failed; and it supporters incurred so much popular odium that no person has since been found hardy enough to renew the proposition.[4]

I have been peculiarly gratified with your sermon on intemperance.[5] This dangerous and destructive vice requires the union of all good men for its extirpation. I wish the influence of the pulpit was more frequently

exerted against it. Drunkenness and gambling are the most deadly enemies of religion, morals, and human happiness. The whole sermon, the
introductory part especially is remarkably well adapted to the subject.
With very great respect, I am Sir your Obedt

J MARSHALL

ALS (draft), Marshall Papers, ViW. Inside address to Sprague in West Springfield, Mass.

1. William B. Sprague (1795–1876), a graduate of the Yale class of 1815, was then pastor
of the Congregational Church of West Springfield, Mass. A prolific writer of sermons and
author of works on various subjects, particularly history and biography, Sprague was also a
noted collector of autographs, amassing some 40,000 during his lifetime.

2. Letter not found. This letter may have contained a request similar to that in a letter to
James Madison, in which Sprague wrote on behalf of an English clergyman who was interested in the autographs of "some of our most distinguished men, particularly of our several Presidents, and of the signers of the Declaration of our Independence" (Sprague to
Madison, 5 July 1828, Madison Papers, DLC).

3. William B. Sprague, *The Claims of Past and Future Generations on Civil Rulers: A Sermon,
Preached at the Annual Election, May 25, 1825* . . . (Boston, 1825).

4. The general assessment bill was introduced in the 1784 session of the Virginia legisla-
ture and carried over to the 1785 session. It was backed by Patrick Henry and Richard
Henry Lee, among others, but was defeated by the organized opposition led by James
Madison. The campaign against the bill produced Madison's celebrated "Memorial and
Remonstrance." At the time, JM predicted the bill would "miscarry," though he apparently
favored the measure (Robert A. Rutland, et al., eds., *The Papers of James Madison*, VIII
[Chicago, 1973], 295–306; *PJM*, I, 131).

5. Sprague, *Intemperance, A Just Cause for Alarm and Exertion: A Sermon, Preached at West
Springfield, April 5th, 1827* . . . (New York, 1827).

To Edward Everett

Dear Sir   Richmond August 3d. 1828
    I am indebted to you for the pleasure derived from reading your ora-
tion delivered before the citizens of Charlestown on the 4th. of July last,
and can pay you only with thanks.[1] You have not meerly effaced completely the blot with which a late writer in the London Quarterly Review
has endeavoured to stain the original settlement of our country;[2] You
have shed a degree of briliancy on that page of our history which enables
us to reflect on it with just pride. With great respect and esteem, I am
your obedt

J MARSHALL

ALS, Everett Papers, MHi. Addressed to Everett in Boston; postmarked Richmond, 4
Aug. Endorsed by Everett: "Acknowledging my Oration."

1. Everett, *An Oration Delivered before the Citizens of Charlestown on the Fifty-second Anniversary
of the Declaration of Independence* (Charlestown, Mass., 1828), reprinted in Edward Everett,
Orations and Speeches on Various Occasions (2d. ed.; 2 vols.; Boston, 1850), I, 150–72.

2. Everett referred to an article in the *London Quarterly Review* of Jan. 1828, in which the writer (in Everett's words) stated "that the original establishment of the United States, and that of the colony of Botany Bay, were pretty nearly modelled on the same plan. The meaning of this slanderous insinuation is, that the United States were settled by deported convicts, in like manner as New South Wales has been settled by transported felons" (Everett, *Orations and Speeches*, 158).

To Joseph Hopkinson

My dear Sir   Richmond Aug. 10th 1828

My friend and neighbour Doctor Brockenborough is about to place Miss Randolph, a Grand daughter of Mrs. Brockenbrough, in some French family in Philadelphia, principally for the purpose of making her mistress of the French language, though she goes with a view to education generally.[1] Both Mr. & Mrs. Brockenbrough are anxious that she should mix with the genteel young female society of the place, and, as I suppose it probable that you may be blessed with a daughter near Miss Randolphs age, I take the liberty to introduce this young lady to you and to your family as one who will I am persuaded be found an agreeable and pleasing companion for the younger part of it.

I wish you as much happiness & comfort as it is possible to enjoy in this hot weather and am dear Sir with affectionate esteem Your Obedt

J MARSHALL

ALS, Hopkinson Papers, PHi. Addressed to Hopkinson in Philadelphia.

1. Dr. John W. Brockenbrough (1774–1852), a native of Essex County, was educated as a physician at the University of Edinburgh but practiced only briefly. He was then president of the Bank of Virginia in Richmond, an office he held for forty years. His wife was the former Gabriella Harvie (older sister of Jaquelin B. Harvie, JM's son-in-law), who was first married to Thomas Mann Randolph, Sr., of Tuckahoe. Her granddaughter was Mary Gabriella Randolph (d. 1837), who later married John B. Chapman of Philadelphia (*Richmond Whig*, 4 July 1837; Mary Wingfield Scott, *Houses of Old Richmond*, [New York, 1941], 147–48; Kenneth Shorey, ed., *Collected Letters of John Randolph of Roanoke to Dr. John Brockenbrough, 1812–1833* [New Brunswick, N.J., 1988], xxi–xxii).

To [Edward C. Marshall] and Thomas Marshall

My dear Son   Aug. 29th. 1828

As I passed through Fredericksburg I read the decree obtained by Mrs. Clarke against Swan, and find the land cannot be sold under it as it now stands.[1] If the purchase money is in part unpaid the decree might have been for an immediate sale, but it is not so framed. The probability is that the suit was meerly for rent in assise on account of dower. It is in

Mr. Pollards power to take possession of the dower and to take a moity of the land by *elegit* to satisfy the decree. When he shall have done so you can judge what it will be proper for you to do. Under the elegit the land must be valued by a jury and Mr. Pollard must ⟨ . . . ⟩ annual rent at which the jury ⟨ . . . ⟩ ⟨w⟩ill be able to judge ⟨ . . . ⟩ his interest or to rent it from him at a reasonable rent including the dower as well as the moity taken by elegit. I would not however be concerned with it except with a view to an ultimate purchase.

I suggested to you the propriety of having no farther communication with Mr. Swan. He has no idea of that frank dealing to which I am accustomed. He cannot conceive that the offer I make is all I mean to give. Should he say any thing farther to you on the subject, let h⟨im⟩ know that my offer having been rejected I consider it as withdrawn & that I most certainly will not give the same sum with the same terms of payment unless you have possession so as to seed the land this fall.[2]

Mrs. Colston[3] is better, your mother as usual and your friend ⟨ n lle⟩ are well. ⟨ . . . ⟩

⟨J MARSHALL⟩

For my son Thomas

Mr. Fisher has written to you that he can lend money for Mrs. Carrington.[4] I mention it for the purpose of saying that if you take it you must direct immediately in what manner it is to be remitted. A check can certainly be sent on Winchester or Fredericksburg, and probably on Alexandria.

Your Mothers love to all. Your affectionate ⟨Fa⟩ther

J. M.

I wish any good opportunity to be em⟨ploy⟩ed for sending down my horses, one at a time if two persons be not coming down. I will pay the riders stage hire back to Fredericksburg. It is probable Charles Smith or Mr. Colston[5] may chuse to ride one of them down.

ALS (privately owned; on deposit, Marshall-Hayden Collection, ViU, 1967). Identity of recipient based on ownership by descendant of Edward C. Marshall. One or two lines missing owing to tear at bottom of first sheet.

1. The case of Sarah Clarke v. Charles Swann was heard in the Fredericksburg Superior Court of Chancery. A provisional decree of 18 May 1826 ordered commissioners to allot one-third part of a tract of land that John Clarke (Sarah Clarke's late husband) had conveyed to Swann and further ordered the defendant to render an account of the rents and profits of this land from the time of John Clarke's death. The final decree of 14 May 1828 awarded Sarah Clarke the sum of $776.73, with 6 percent interest on $555.33 of this amount from 1 Jan. 1828 (Fredericksburg Superior Court of Chancery, Ord. Bk., 1825–27, 179; 1827–29, 159 [microfilm], Vi).

2. A deed from JM to Edward C. Marshall, dated 8 Apr. 1828, for one thousand acres in Fauquier County describes its boundaries as being adjacent to "Swann's land" (Irwin S.

Rhodes, ed., *The Papers of John Marshall: A Descriptive Calendar* [2 vols.; Norman, Okla., 1969], II, 320).

3. Probably Elizabeth Marshall Colston, JM's sister and widow of Rawleigh Colston.

4. George Fisher (d. 1857) of Richmond was the husband of Ann Ambler Fisher (1772–1832), Polly Marshall's younger sister. Elizabeth Jaquelin Ambler Carrington (1765–1842), widow of Edward Carrington, was Polly Marshall's older sister (Louise Pecquet du Bellet, *Some Prominent Virginia Families* [1907; 4 vols. in 2; Baltimore, 1976 reprint], I, 47, 51).

5. Probably Thomas M. Colston, JM's nephew. He lived in Berkeley County but might have been coming to Richmond to visit his wife's family. Elizabeth Fisher Colston (1798–1845) was the daughter of George Fisher and Ann Ambler Fisher (ibid., I, 51).

To Martin P. Marshall

My dear Nephew   Richmond Septr. 2d. 1828

I have just received your letter of Aug. 11th. enclosing one from Mr. Triplett and am willing to allow that gentleman the percentage he asks as a commission on the money he may collect from the estate of Mr. Daviess.[1] It is 20 percent.

I presume from the fact that the execution was levied on the reversion of dower slaves, that the law of Kentucky authorizes this proceeding. Should this be settled, and no debts or other mode of making the money can be found that, it would be advisable to again to seize this reversionary interest & purchase it in for me. I would however consider this as the last resort even if the law be clear, and would not be concerned with the reversion if the law be doubtful. I will thank you to let Mr. Triplett know immediately that I assent to his proposal respecting his commission.

I am desirous of remitting my sister[2] one hundred dollars but your letter leaves me in some uncertainty how to act. The pressure on me for money in consequence of my liability for others is such that I never have at my disposal more than is necessary. As your letter leaves it doubtful whether you may not draw on me, tho not through the bank of The United States, I feel in doubt as to a remittance, because your draft might find me not provided with funds to take it up. I receive money the 1st. of January April, July & october. If you draw on me I could wish to receive the draft about those periods or to receive positive notice so that I may certainly reserve the money. If you do not draw I will remit you a draft on the bank of The U.S. in Kentucky or in some other manner.

I observe that some costs have been incurred in serving the execution on the dower slaves. I have no recollection of having paid this. Be so good as to inform me on this subject that I may do now what I ought to have done sooner.

I am happy to hear that the division respecting the election of the President has not interrupted the harmony of the family. The election, though of deep present interest will pass away and be forgotten. Family feuds are lasting and the pain they inflict is real. In this state as in Kentucky the people in mass are favorable to General Jackson. Those who court their favour are also his partisans. A great portion of the intelligent and unambitious are in ⟨fa⟩vour of the reelection of Mr. Adams. Th⟨ey⟩ constitute a decided minority in Virginia.

We rejoice in the health an⟨d⟩ ⟨happiness?⟩ of your family. Your aunt thinks and speaks of you often. I am my dear Nephew, Your affectionate Uncle

J MARSHALL

ALS, James Schoff Collection, MiU-C. Addressed to Marshall in Flemingsburg, Ky.; postmarked Richmond, 2 Sept.

1. Letters not found. JM had a claim on the late Joseph Hamilton Daveiss's estate. Triplett may have been John Triplett, who in 1829 was listed along with Martin Marshall as among Fleming County's large slaveholders (JM to Martin Marshall, 7 Nov. 1827 and n. 2.; Robert S. Cotterill, *History of Fleming County: The First One Hundred Years, 1780–1880* [n.p, n.d.], 226).

2. Nancy Marshall Pollard.

To [Edward C. Marshall]

My dear Son   Richmond Septr. 16th. 1828

Your letter of the 13th. reached me yesterday.[1] I shall be enabled to borrow $1000 for the payment of Swan.

In your previous letter you said the money was to be paid him the last of Novr. If I do not hear farther from you I shall suppose that it will be in time, if remitted by the last of that month and will take care to forward a draft to you on the Bank of Winchester unless you should prefer one on Fredericksburg. If you have made any new arrangement by which the money is to be paid sooner you will give me the necessary information. If I do not hear from you I shall be assured that the draft will be in time if received in November.

The sooner you receive the title the better. It will be advisable to look into the clerks office for any deed Swan may have made, for the title ought to be safe & previous examination may save much future trouble & perhaps loss.

I am glad to hear you are pleased with the quality of the land. The purchase was extremely desirable. Your Mothers health improves. Her love to all the families, Your affectionate Father

J MARSHALL

ALS (privately owned; on deposit, Marshall-Hayden Collection, ViU, 1967). Identity of recipient based on internal evidence.

1. Letter not found.

To James K. Marshall

My dear Son   Richmond Septr. 25th. 182[8]

Your letter of the 19th. reached me yesterday.[1] I am extremely sorry that I did not know while in Fauquier that an arrangement might probably be made with Mr. Moorehead for Johnsons land.[2] I have given a promise for a lease for my life at 100$ per annum. I would most chearfully let Moorehead have the land in exchange if it was unincumbered provided he would come to reasonable terms. Of this however I should almost despair. You do not hint at what he would ask or be willing to give and therefore I am not sanguine that a bargain could be made were it even in my power to get off my promise to Johnson. If a contract could be made with Moorehead I would willingly give 100$ to be released from my agreement with Johnson.[3] I would not however even then consent to part with the land to Moorehead but on reasonable terms, and I think the probability very much against his consenting to such. You of course would have nothing to do with the lea⟨se⟩ on my brothers land.

Wheat has continued to look up. I hope it may continue near its present price. Flour is also very well at present. If my grain or flour was in market I should not hold up for a better price, but it is dangerous to sell before delivery because few can be depended on in the event of a declining market.

Your Mothers love to claudia & Mary[4] and her Grand children. Your affectionate Father

J Marshall

ALS, Collection of the Association for the Preservation of Virginia Antiquities, on deposit at ViHi. Addressed to James K. Marshall at "Moreland / near Oak Hill / Fauquier"; postmark torn. Endorsed.

1. Letter not found.

2. George Morehead was a Fauquier landowner, with whom JM previously had dealings (*PJM*, IX, 270–72 and n. 1; X, 302, 430).

3. In 1812 JM had contracted to sell a lot in Leeds Manor to George S. Johnson but in Aug. 1828 canceled this contract and agreed to lease the lot for life (Bond, 1 Dec. 1812 [owned by Mrs. James R. Green, Markham, Va., 1971; Agreement, 22 Aug. 1828 and n. 1 [App. II, Cal.]).

4. Claudia Burwell Marshall was James K. Marshall's wife. Mary Harvie, JM's daughter, was then visiting her Fauquier relatives.

From Thomas Marshall

My dear father,   Oak Hill, Septr 26. 1828

The mail of to-day brought your very acceptable letter of the 21st inst.[1] Margaret is rejoiced to hear of the birth of her little nephew, and that her sister was doing well.[2] Mr Lewis has just returned from a trip to Washington, where he has made a contract for the delivery of his barley crop. His health is much improved. Little Robert is likewise well.[3] They are to set out on the 29th, weather permitting, for the lower country. My children, who were affected by the whooping cough, are now well. The rest enjoy good health. Margaret desires me to return her acknowledgments to my mother & yourself for kindly informing her of the late interesting event.

There has been a great fluctuation in the Alexa flour market. Flour was up to $6.50 on monday last, but soon fell. It is now $5.50 I am told. I think it can hardly fall below that price; but dread the consequences of premature speculation.

At present we are so dry in this part of the country, that we should be glad of an opportunity to obtain a supply of corn meal. Flour is out of the question. The fluctuation of the market does not affect us sensibly.

Some of our farmers have commenced seeding. I expect to begin tomorrow. My preparation for a crop has been a laborious one. I am delighted with the operation of a large roller which I have had made since you were here. It will give to our corn fields the degree of compactness requisite for a wheat crop, and which I think they have always wanted. I have manured about 16 or 17 acres, and expect to manure perhaps 34 more for wheat. The whole quantity of ground prepared for a crop does not exceed 180 acres; of which 112 are fallow.

My sister Mary & her children, except Mary who is here, have gone to Prospect Hill.[4] They will return probably in a few days. Please remember me kindly to Mr Harvie. I should be happy to see him at Oak Hill.

I am anxious for an opportunity to send your horses down, and also one which I have sold to Aunt Carrington. Mr Lewis would take one of them to Richmond; but the horse on which his servant rides is attached to the gigg by an out-licker. Mr Chas B. Smith has been applied to but without success. Mr Colston has been here but once for several weeks, and did not intimate any intention of going below shortly. If I were not busily engaged in seeding I w⟨ou⟩ld send all three horses to Richmond by one of my hands, and divide the travelling expenses with you.

Mr Lewis wishes me to attend the sale at Westover on the 21st October.[5] I may contrive to get them down about that time, & let the boy ride my horse back part of the way, if an earlier opportunity should not present itself.

I am, my dear father, with tender recollection of my dear mother, your affectionate son

THOMAS MARSHALL

P.S. Margaret means to write to Eleanor by her father.

ALS, Marshall Papers, ViW. Addressed to JM in Richmond. Handwritten postmark "Oak Hill Septr 27 1828."

1. Letter not found.

2. Margaret Lewis Marshall (1792–1829), a daughter of Fielding Lewis (1763–1834) of Weyanoke, in Charles City County, married Thomas Marshall in 1809. Her younger sister Eleanor Lewis Douthat was the widow of Richmond lawyer Robert Douthat (ca. 1796–1828), who had died the preceding May. She had just given birth to William Douthat, who died in Sept. 1829 while visiting Oak Hill with his family (Paxton, *Marshall Family*, 90, 95–96; Merrow Edgerton Sorley, comp., *Lewis of Warner Hall: The History of a Family* [Columbia, Mo., 1935], 103–5, 110, 123–24; *Richmond Enquirer*, 23 May 1828; *Richmond Whig*, 23 Sept. 1829).

3. Robert Douthat (b. 1820), oldest son of Robert and Eleanor Douthat, frequently visited his Oak Hill cousins in the summer and early fall. In 1841 he married Mary Ambler Marshall (1820–1862), JM's granddaughter (Paxton, *Marshall Family*, 204; Maria Newton Marshall, comp., *Recollections and Reflections of Fielding Lewis Marshall: A Virginia Gentleman of the Old School* [Orange?, Va., 1911], 27).

4. Prospect Hill was the home of Jaquelin A. Marshall. Mary Harvie's daughter Mary Marshall Harvie (1815–1873) was then thirteen (*Fauquier County, Virginia, 1759–1959* [Warrenton, Va., 1959], 187; Paxton *Marshall Family*, 207).

5. Westover, on the James River in Charles City County, was the seat of the late Robert Douthat. It was scheduled to be sold on 22 Oct. 1828 for the payment of Douthat's debts as secured by two deeds of trust. The estate then consisted of one thousand acres. In addition to the land and buildings, the sale was to include all the livestock and forty to fifty slaves (*Richmond Enquirer*, 2 Sept. 1828).

To Andrew Smith

Dear Sir[1]   [ca. 20 October 1828]

I should feel much pleasure in promoting your views were it in my power to do so. Your general character during your long residence in Richmond, as well as my own personal observation has given me such favourable impressions respecting your capacity, attention to business, and integrity — that I feel much confidence in the fidelity with which you would discharge the duties of any situation in which you might be placed. With great respect, I am Dr. Sir, Your Obt Servt.

J MARSHALL

Copy, RG 59, Letters of Application and Recommendation during the Administration of Andrew Jackson (file of Andrew Smith), DNA. Date assigned on basis of circumstantial evidence (see n. 1).

1. Andrew Smith was formerly a Richmond merchant whose firm Smith & Riddle went bankrupt in 1823. After unsuccessful attempts to recoup his fortunes in New York and in Washington, he made repeated efforts to secure employment with the federal government. He eventually obtained a position in the Treasury department under the Jackson administration. The copy of JM's undated letter is filed with other letters on Smith's behalf in his application to the Jackson administration. It is probably the same copy that was filed with Smith's application to the Adams administration, which was returned to Smith at the close of that administration. In his earlier application Smith listed JM as a reference in a letter to Sec. of State Clay, 23 Oct. 1828, and enclosed a copy of JM's letter in a letter to Clay, 4 Nov. 1828 (RG 59, Letters of Application and Recommendation during the Administration of

John Quincy Adams [file of Andrew Smith]; Letters of Application and Recommendation during the Administration of Andrew Jackson [file of Andrew Smith]).

To Francis Scott Key

Dear Sir   Richmond, Oct. 24th. 1828

I had an application yesterday from a man of colour in this place which induces me to address this letter to you as one of the Managers of the Colonization society.

The applicant is at the head of a numerous family and appears to have some education. I think his name is Shepherd. He says he has had some correspondence with Mr. Gurley. His statement is that from the advantageous opinion he has formed of Liberia on the representations made by the agents and other members of the society he had determined to remove his family thither; and that several other free people of colour in this place had resolved to accompany him. Under the assurance that a vessel would receive him this fall which was to be expedited by the society he had disposed of his little property and changed or suspended those pursuits by which he supported his family and will be really injured if he shall be unable to procure a passage. He appears much alarmed at a report that the vessel in which the coloured people of this place had hoped to sale [sic] will not be provided and that they will be disappointed. I could give him no information but promised to make enquiry and to communicate the result to him. Will you my dear Sir have the goodness to say what is the prospect on this subject, and whether, should no vessel sail from Norfolk, a passage could be granted to this family and to how many others, in any vessel which may sail from a different port?[1] I am dear Sir with great esteem and regard, Your Obedt

J MARSHALL

ALS, American Colonization Society Records, DLC. Addressed to Key in "George Town / Dist. of Columbia"; postmarked Richmond, 26 Oct. Endorsed "Answered Nov 4th. 1828" [not found].

1. An application on behalf of Joseph Shepherd in Apr. 1828 described him and his family of five as "excellently qualified to be useful." In July 1828 Shepherd made his own application for thirteen people. As of Dec. 1828 some seventy prospective emigrants from Richmond were awaiting passage on a vessel to Liberia. Shepherd, aged forty-two, was among those who embarked on the *Harriet* from Norfolk in Feb. 1829 (Applicants for Emigration, Benjamin Brand, 1 Apr. 1828; Joseph Shepherd, 12 July 1828; Brand to James Laurie, 13 Dec. 1828, American Colonization Society Records, DLC; *Niles' Weekly Register* [Baltimore], 7, 14 Feb. [supplement] 1829).

To Joseph Story

My dear Sir   Richmond Oct. 29th., 1828

I have just finished the perusal of your centennial discourse on the first settlement of Salem, and while fresh under its influence, take up my pen to thank you for the pleasure it has given me.[1] You have drawn a vivid portrait, and I believe a faithful likeness of those extraordinary men who first peopled New England; and my feelings as well as my judgement have accompanied you in your rapid sketch of the character and conduct of their descendants. I wish the admonitory part may have its full effect on others as well as on those to whom it was particularly addressed. Some of our southern friends might benefit from the lesson it inculcates.

But I have been still more touched with your notice of the red man than of the white. The conduct of our Fore Fathers in expelling the original occupants of the soil grew out of so many mixed motives that any censure which philanthropy may bestow upon it ought to be qualified. The Indians were a fierce and dangerous enemy, whose love of war made them sometimes the aggressors, whose numbers and habits then made them formidable, and whose cruel system of warfare seemed to justify every endeavour to remove them to a distance from civilized settlements. It was not until after the adoption of our present government that respect for our own safety permitted us to give full indulgence to those principles of humanity and justice which ought always to govern our conduct towards the aborigines when this course can be pursued without exposing ourselves to the most afflicting calamities. That time however is unquestionably arrived; and every oppression now exercised on a helpless people depending on our magnanimity and justice for the preservation of their existence, impresses a deep stain on the American character. I often think with indignation on our disreputable conduct (as I think it) in the affair of the Creeks of Georgia; and I look with some alarm on the course now pursuing in the North west. Your observations on this subject are eloquent, and are in perfect accordance with my feelings.[2] But I turn with most pleasure to that fine passage respecting the lady Arabella Johnson. I almost envy the occasion her sufferings and premature death have furnished for bestowing that well merited eulogy on a sex which so far surpasses ours in all the amiable and attractive virtues of the heart—in all those qualities which make up the sum of human happiness, and transform the domestic fireside into an elysium.[3] I read the passage to my wife, who expresses such animated approbation of it as almost to excite fears for that exclusive admiration which husbands claim as their peculiar privilege. Present my compliments to Mrs. Story and say for me that a lady receives the highest compliment her husband can pay her when he expresses an exalted opinion of the sex, because the world will believe that it is formed on the model he sees at home.

I have read with much interest the character you have drawn of our deceased friend and brother the lamented Judge Trimble. Most richly did he merit all you have said of him. His place I fear cannot be completely supplied. I was desirous of having the character republished in our papers; but was restrained by the flattering introduction of my name. My modesty was alarmed by the apprehension that the request for its publication might be ascribed as much to vanity as to my deep feeling for departed worth.[4]

Most cordially do I congratulate you on the appointment of our friend Hopkinson.[5] With affectionate esteem I am dear Sir your

J MARSHALL

ALS, Story Papers, MHi. Addressed to Story in Salem, Mass.; postmarked Richmond, 2 Nov.

1. Story, *A Discourse Pronounced at the Request of the Essex Historical Society, on the 18th of September, 1828 in Commemoration of the First Settlement of Salem* . . . (Boston, 1828); reprinted in William W. Story, ed., *The Miscellaneous Writings of Joseph Story* (1852; New York, 1972 reprint), 408–74.

2. Story devoted a section of his discourse to considering how the founders grappled with the question, "How far was it lawful to people this Western world, and deprive the Indians of that exclusive sovereignty over the soil which they had exercised for ages beyond the reach of human tradition?" While excusing the New England forefathers of forcefully expelling the Indians "upon any pretence of European right," the Massachusetts jurist lamented the fate of the native Americans: "What can be more melancholy than their history? By a law of their nature, they seem destined to a slow, but sure extinction. Everywhere, at the approach of the white man, they fade away. We hear the rustling of their footsteps, like that of the withered leaves of autumn, and they are gone forever. They pass mournfully by us, and they return no more" (Story, ed., *Miscellaneous Writings*, 457–65 [quotations at 457, 462–63]).

3. Lady Arabella (or Arbella) Johnson, daughter of the earl of Lincoln, accompanied her husband Isaac Johnson to the Massachusetts Bay Colony in 1630. The admiral ship of Winthrop's fleet was named the *Arbella* in her honor. She died in Aug. 1630, two months after arriving, and her husband died a month later. Of her Story wrote: "What, indeed, could be more touching than the fate of such a woman? What example more striking than hers, of uncompromising affection and piety? Born in the lap of ease, and surrounded by affluence; with every prospect which could make hope gay, and fortune desirable; accustomed to the splendors of a court, and the scarcely less splendid hospitalities of her ancestral home; she was yet content to quit, what has, not inaptly, been termed this paradise of plenty and pleasure, for 'a wilderness of wants,' and with a fortitude superior to the delicacies of her rank and sex, to trust herself to an unknown ocean and a distant climate, that she might partake, with her husband, the pure and spiritual worship of God." The author went on to use her example as an occasion for praising the virtues of the female sex (ibid., 424–26).

4. Story's sketch of Justice Robert Trimble, who had died in August, was published in the Boston *Columbian Centinel*, 17 Sept. 1828 (reprinted in William W. Story, ed., *Life and Letters of Joseph Story* [2 vols.; Boston, 1851], I, 541–43). "In constitutional law," Story wrote, "he belonged to that school, of which Mr. Chief Justice Marshall (himself a host) is the acknowledged head and expositor. He loved the Union with an unfaltering love, and was ready to make any sacrifice to ensure its perpetuity."

5. JM had recommended Joseph Hopkinson as U.S. District Judge for Pennsylvania as early as Mar. 1827 amid rumors that Richard Peters, Sr., the incumbent judge, was about to retire. After Peters died in Aug. 1828, President Adams made a recess appointment of

Hopkinson on 23 Oct., which became permanent at the next session of Congress (*PJM*, X, 419 and n. 1; Robert Seager II et al., eds., *The Papers of Henry Clay*, VII [Lexington, Ky., 1982], 484; JM to Hopkinson, [ca. 18 Mar. 1829] and n. 1).

To Henry Clay

My dear Sir   Richmond Novr. 28th. 1828

In consequence of my inattention to the post office I did not receive your letter of the 23d. till yesterday afternoon.[1] I need not say how deeply I regret the loss of Judge Trimble. He was distinguished for sound sense, uprightness of intention, and legal knowledge. His superior cannot be found. I wish we may find his equal. You are certainly correct in supposing that I feel a deep interest in the character of the person who may succeed him. His successor will of course be designated by Mr. Adams because he will be required to perform the most important duties of his office before a change of administration can take place.

Mr. Crittenden is not personally known to me, but I am well acquainted with his general character. It stands very high. Were I myself to designate the successor of Mr. Trimble, I do not know the man I could prefer to him. Report, in which those in whom I confide concur, declares him to be sensible, honorable, and a sound lawyer. I shall be happy to meet him at the supreme court as an associate. The objection I have to a direct communication of this opinion to the President arises from the delicacy of the case. I cannot venture, unasked, to recommend an associate justice to the President, especially a gentleman who is not personally known to me. It has the appearance of assuming more than I am willing to assume. I must then, notwithstanding my deep interest in the appointment, and my conviction of the fitness of Mr. Crittenden, a conviction as strong as I could well feel in favour of a gentleman of whom I Judge only from general character, decline writing to the President on the subject.[2] With great and respectful esteem I am my dear Sir, Your Obedt.

J MARSHALL

ALS, Clay Papers, DLC. Addressed to Clay in Washington and franked; postmarked Richmond, 28 Nov. Endorsed by Clay.

1. Letter not found.

2. In his diary for 2 Dec. 1828, Adams wrote: "Mr. Clay read me a letter from Chief-Justice Marshall, speaking very favorably of J. J. Crittenden to fill the office of Judge of the Supreme Court, but declining to write to me. I had offered the place to Mr. Clay, who declined it." Adams nominated Crittenden on 17 Dec. 1828, but on 12 Feb. 1829 the Senate, which was controlled by the Democrats, resolved not to act on the nomination during the present Congress. On 6 Mar. President Jackson nominated John McLean (1785–1861), postmaster general under Adams, to succeed Trimble on the Supreme Court. The Senate confirmed the appointment the next day (Charles Francis Adams, ed., *Memoirs of John Quincy Adams*

[Philadelphia, 1876], VIII, 78; *Journal of the Executive Proceedings of the Senate*, III [Washington, 1828], 622, 636; 644; IV [Washington, 1887], 6, 7 ; Warren, *Supreme Court*, I, 700–707).

Kirkpatrick v. Gibson
Opinion
U.S. Circuit Court, Virginia, 10 December 1828

The plaintiffs in this suit, British subjects residing in Scotland, were legatees of the late John Gibson (d. 1807), a Scots merchant who resided at Prospect Hill, near Dumfries, in Prince William County. They included the executors (William Kirkpatrick and others) of Mary Heasty, Gibson's sister; Agnes Brown, daughter of Mary Heasty, and her husband; and the children of Peter Gibson and Hugh Gibson, John Gibson's brothers. The original defendants, executors of John Gibson, were James Reid (d. 1821), a Dumfries merchant, and Dr. John Spence (1766–1829), of Belle Aire in Prince William County. Spence, a native of Scotland, was educated at the University of Edinburgh and led a distinguished career as a writer on medical subjects, notably vaccination. The suit began in April 1818 with the filing of the plaintiffs' bill in chancery. After the defendants filed their joint answer in December 1818, depositions were taken in Liverpool and in various cities in Scotland in 1819 and 1820. Since that time the court had issued several interlocutory decrees, most recently in June 1827 directing the commissioner in chancery to settle the account of the administration of Gibson's estate to ascertain what remained for distribution among his legatees. The commissioner's report of May 1828 was the basis of Marshall's opinion and decree of 10 December 1828 (U.S. Cir. Ct., Va., Rec. Bk. XIX, 520–618; U.S. Cir. Ct., Va., Ord. Bk. XII, 190–91, 287; *Prince William: The Story of Its People and Its Places* [Richmond, 1941], 83, 87).

Kirkpatrick & al
v
Gibsons exrs.

The material question in this cause is the amount of the security which ¶1 the plaintiffs who are legatees in the will of —— Gibson deceased ought on receiving their legacies, to give to the defendants, his exrs., as an indemnity against the claims of such creditors as may hereafter appear. The counsel for the plaintiffs insists that the amount of this security is within the discretion of the court, and is to be regulated by the circumstances of the case. The counsel for the defendants contends that the security ought to cover the whole sum paid, & that any less sum would not be an indemnity.

The act of assembly which is considered as regulating this subject is in ¶2 these words "nor shall an administrator be compelled to make distribution at any time, until bond & security be given by the persons entitled to distribution, to refund due proportions of any debts or demands which may afterwards appear against the intestate, and the costs attending the recovery of such debts."[1]

¶3   The act of Parliament of the 28 & 29 Ch. 2 contains the same provision.[2]

¶4   In England the rule is settled that the amount of the security to be demanded by the exr. is to be regulated by the sound discretion of the court. I have not seen any case declaring that a different rule is applicable to administrators.

¶5   It is contended that the court of appeals has construed this act as comprehending exrs. though only Administrators are named, and that it must be so expounded as to require a bond equal in amount to the sum which the distributees may possibly be required to refund.

¶6   The uniform course of the courts of the United States is to adopt that construction of the acts of a state legislature which the courts of the state have given to it. If therefore the courts of Virginia have construed this law to embrace exrs. in its provisions, & to require that bond shall, in every case, be given by the legatee to the amount of the legacy received, this court has only to conform to those decisions.

¶7   In the cases of Clay v Williams 2 M. 105 & Rootes v Webb 4 Mun. 77 the court only decides that bond & security is demandable by the executor, but is silent respecting the amount, & indicates no opinion respecting the application of the act of assembly to the case.[3] In Stovall's exr. v Woodson & wife the decree of the chancellor is declared "to be erroneous in this, that the appellees are not directed to give bond & security according to the provisions of the act of Assembly in such case provided."[4]

¶8   I should be much better satisfied that I understand this decree correctly if it was accompanied with some explanation of the principle on which it was made. But the report neither gives us the argument of counsel nor the opinion of the court. We have simply the decision in the words above quoted.

¶9   In the construction of ancient statutes, courts, in search of the intent, often went far beyond the words. But in modern times, this practice has been a good deal restrained. Courts still construe words liberally, to reach that intention which the words themselves import, but seldom insert a description of persons omitted by the statute, because, in the opinion of the court, there is the same reason for comprehending those persons within its provision, as for comprehending those who are actually enumerated. I should therefore be much disposed to the opinion that the court of appeals rather adopted the principle of the act & applied it to a case confessedly within judicial discretion, than construed the act to comprehend that case. It must however be admitted that the words "according to the provisions of the act of assembly in such case provided," rather favor a different opinion. But be this as it may, the case of Stovalls exr. v Woodson & wife is silent as to the amount of the security.

This point was again under the consideration of the court in the case of Dandridge's admr. v Armstead & others. The propriety of requiring security was again asserted, and the court said that bond & security should be required by the chancellor "to the satisfaction of the court."[5] These words may imply that the amount in which bond & security should be given, should be "to the satisfaction of the court" or meerly that the court should be satisfied as to the sufficiency of the security to pay the sum in which the bond must necessarily be given. I rather suppose the first to be the correct construction. The words imply it. Every court taking bond with security requires of course to be satisfied that the security is competent to the payment of the sum mentioned in the bond. The discretion which the words indicate would seem to be something more than would be comprehended in the sentence had they been omitted. They indicate that discretion respecting the sum which is, according to usage, exercised by a court of equity.   ¶10

I think then that the decisions of the court of appeals, taken all together, have not adopted a construction of our act of assembly essentially different from the construction which the chancellor of England had previously given to the same statute in England. I am the more inclined to this opinion because it is reasonable to suppose that whenever a British statute is reenacted in this country we adopt the settled construction it has received as well as the statute itself. And such I believe has been the course of every court in the union.   ¶11

In this case then I think the amount of the bond is within the legal discretion of the court, to be governed by circumstances; and that the length of time which has intervened, the means which have been used to give notice to creditors, and the probability of outstanding debts are circumstances which ought to influence its opinion. If after due publication & notice, creditors will still lie by, all courts ought to protect the exr. from any claims beyond the indemnity which a court of competent jurisdiction has directed.[6]   ¶12

AD, Marshall Judicial Opinions, PPAmP; printed, John W. Brockenbrough, *Reports of Cases Decided by the Honourable John Marshall . . .*, II (Philadelphia, 1837), 388–91. For JM's deletions and interlineations, see Textual Notes below.

1. JM quoted from sec. 58 of Virginia's comprehensive statute concerning wills, intestacy, distribution of intestates' estates, and the duty of executors and administrators. This provision was first enacted in 1705 (*Revised Code of Va.*, I, 389).

2. The marginal note in the *Revised Code of Va.* states this section was derived from the English statute of 22 and 23 Ch. II, c. 10 (1671).

3. Clay v. Williams, 2 Munf. 105 (Va. Ct. App., 1811); Rootes v. Webb, 4 Munf. 77 (Va. Ct. App., 1813).

4. Stovall's Executors v. Woodson, 2 Munf. 303, 304 (Va. Ct. App., 1811).

5. Dandridge's Administrator v. Armistead, unreported, was an appeal from an 1816

decree of the Superior Court of Chancery at Williamsburg. JM quoted from the decree pronounced in this case by the Court of Appeals on 11 Dec. 1821 (Va. Ct. App. Ord. Bk. X, 190–92).

6. The accompanying decree sent the report back to the commissioner with various directions and ordered Spence to pay and distribute the proceeds of a certificate for U.S. stock among the several plaintiffs "without their giving bond with sureties to refund the same as insisted upon for the defendant Spence." After Spence's death, the case was revived against his executor. The court issued a final decree on 1 June 1832 (U.S. Cir. Ct., Va., Ord. Bk. XII, 287; U.S. Cir. Ct., Va., Rec. Bk., XIX, 548–60).

Textual Notes

¶ 1	ll. 2–3	ought ↑on receiving their legacies,↓ to give
	ll. 4–5	appear ~~on receiving their legacies~~. The
	ll. 5–6	the amount ~~in which~~ ↑of↓ this security ~~is to be directed ought~~ is within
¶ 5	ll. 3–4	the sum which ~~may p~~ the
¶ 6	ll. 4–5	shall ↑in every case,↓ be given
¶ 7	ll. 3–4	no opinion ~~that~~ ↑respecting↓ the application
¶ 9	ll. 10–11	the act to ~~apply to~~ ↑comprehend↓ that case.
¶10	l. 5	that the ~~court sh~~ amount in which
¶12	l. 6	still lie by, ~~the~~ ↑all↓ courts ought

To James K. Marshall

My Dear Son: RICHMOND, Dec. 14, 1828.

Your hogs arrived on Wednesday evening. I had twelve of them killed on Friday morning. They weighed 1891. The remaining thirteen will be killed as soon as the weather will permit, perhaps to-morrow, but the weather I fear is too hot. I fear you will be disappointed in the price. It is four dollars only. An immense quantity has come in from the West. I shall give you four and a quarter, and take myself what I cannot sell at that price. As I can know nothing about the title to the land in question, I presume your object is to make some inquiries respecting the characters of Mr. M. and Mr. A. Of Mr. A., I know nothing. Mr. M. is a lawyer of eminence, who was formerly a judge. He unfortunately engaged in some purchases in the mad times that have gone by, which wasted his fortune, in consequence of which he resigned his seat on the bench and returned to the bar. He is a sensible man, and I should place confidence in what he says. Were it my business I should procure the information he asks and give him a moiety of the land if he will prosecute the claim at his own expense. I should have feared that the act of limitations was already a bar, but Mr. M.'s judgment may be relied on. Your mother's love to the family. I am, my dear son, Your affectionate father,

J. MARSHALL.

Printed, Sallie E. Marshall Hardy, "John Marshall," *Green Bag*, VIII (1896), 485–86.

To [James K. Marshall]

My dear Son   [Richmond, ca. 21 December 1828]

Above is the weight of your hogs. Several of them were too large for this market, & I should have found much difficulty in selling the large ones at four dollars.[1] Mr. Fisher took five of them weighing about 750. He refused to take more and on showing the weights to some others they were declined as being too large. The Parkinson breed is not preferred, and if you think of raising hogs as a business, you will do well to change it.[2] The opinion is that the bacon is not so sweet as the common wood hog. I wrote to you that I had paid Mary forty dollars & Miss F. Burwell twenty.[3] Miss Fanny's purchases came to one dollar more which was paid her by Mary. The list of articles purchased by Mary including ten dollars paid for Miss Maria Willis, and one dollar to Miss Fanny Burwell amounted to $25.84 beyond the 40 you directed me to pay her. These sums added to the 20 I enclosed to you amount to $105.84 leaving $68.75 in my hands which I will pay to Mr. Blair subject to the order of Miss Maria Willis as you directed.[4]

I am surprized as well as grieved at the magnitude of your debts. This fortunate year will enable you to pay a part of them, and I hope the next will enable you to liberate yourself entirely or so nearly as to bring the sum you owe under your controul. I do not think any of my sons, unless it be the Doctor[5] feel the proper horrour at owing money which cannot be paid. I should be glad to hear that John also was paying off debts instead of spending his money at Baltimore and other places of, what he thinks, amusement.[6]

AL[S], Marshall Papers, ViW. Second page missing. Addressee and date assigned on basis of internal evidence (see n. 1). At top right of page JM wrote "Seymour Hudgins."

1. At the top of the letter, turning the sheet ninety degrees to the right from the bottom, JM wrote a list of figures representing the weight of each of the twenty-five hogs that James had recently sent to Richmond. In his letter of 14 Dec. JM reported having had a dozen of these slaughtered weighing a total of 1,891 pounds. This total, added to the weight of the remaining thirteen hogs, came to 4,108 pounds. Having promised to buy them at $4.25 a hundredweight, JM calculated the amount to be $174.59.

2. The "Parkinson breed" probably originated with Richard Parkinson (1748–1815), the British agriculturist who came to America and rented one of George Washington's farms. He wrote a number of agricultural works, including *A Tour in America in 1798, 1799, and 1800 . . .* (2 vols.; London, 1805) and *Treatise on the Breeding and Management of Live Stock* (2 vols.; London, 1810).

3. Frances P. ("Fanny") Burwell (b. 1790) was the daughter of Lewis Burwell (1764–1833) and Judith Kennon Burwell (1770–1849) of Richmond and cousin of Claudia Marshall, wife of James K. Marshall. She was a communicant of the Monumental Church in Richmond and a teacher in the Sunday school. In 1835 she married Henry Alexander of Monroe County (Stuart E. Brown, *Burwell: Kith and Kin of the Immigrant Lewis Burwell [1621–1653]* [Berryville, Va., 25, 26; George D. Fisher, *History and Reminiscences of the Monumental Church, Richmond, Va., from 1814 to 1878* [Richmond, 1880], 105, 163, 169;

Richmond Whig, 27 Aug. 1833; Norfolk *American Beacon and Norfolk and Portsmouth Daily Advertiser,* 8 June 1835).

4. In his calculations at the top of the page, JM deducted $105.84 from $174.59, leaving $68.75. Blair was possibly John H. Blair, administrator of Nathaniel Burwell's estate (*PJM,* IX, 202 and n. 1).

5. Jaquelin A. Marshall.

6. JM evidently continued his letter on a second sheet that has not been found.

To John Randolph

My dear Sir   Richmond Decr 24th. 1828

I have deferred making my acknowledgements for the message and other public documents for which I am indebted to you,[1] in the hope of being enabled to accompany my thanks for this flattering attention — not with any information of what is passing in our legislature, for the papers communicate every thing, but with some speculations on the future which might possibly amuse. I despair however of making even this return for your kindness. On the all engrossin⟨g⟩ subject of the convention, there is so much dive⟨rsity as w⟩ell as contrariety of opinion that even those ⟨who m⟩ingle freely with the members, and converse ⟨intim⟩ately with them, can only conjecture what will be the result of legislative deliberation respecting it.[2] A man who has not these advantages, who has heard the sentiments only of the few, can scarcely hazard even a conjecture.

It is supposed, and with some reason, that the principle on which the convention may be constituted will have no inconsiderable influence on the character of that body, and consequently on the character of the constitution it may devise. You have seen the plan recommended by the committee. It assumes the principle on which the state has been divided into congressional districts as the basis of representation in convention. The delegates from the great slave holding counties consider this proposition as an advance on their part which ought to be met by the tramontaine gentlemen. The members from the West think very differently. In their opinion the free white population is the only legitimate basis of representation, and they consider themselves as having advanced to the extreme limit which can be marked by the spirit of conciliation when they offer to elect the members of the convention from Senatorial districts. On one sid⟨e the⟩y adhere to the representation by coun⟨ty⟩ and on the ⟨other⟩ a representation according to ⟨numbers⟩ computing ⟨only free?⟩ male adults. These however will ⟨most⟩ probably join the standard of the friends of the one dis⟨trict⟩ system or the other. Which of these systems will triump⟨h⟩ cannot at present even be conjectured. One prediction may be made with some confidence. This foundation for a new arrangement of political power will not be laid without much exasperation and discontent. We cannot foresee the extent to which this discontent will be pressed. It is certainly very doubtful whether such a portion of it may not reach the people as to make it a problem not easy of solution whether this great movement may not prove abortive, or result only in angry contest and increased ill temper.[3]

I wish you health enough to enjoy the festivities of the ⟨sea⟩son and beg you to believe that I remain with great and respectful esteem, Your Obedt

J MARSHALL

ALS, NIC. Addressed to Randolph in Washington and franked; postmarked Richmond, 24 Dec. Endorsed by Randolph.

1. Randolph had probably sent President Adams's message of 2 Dec. (*Message from the President of the United States to Both Houses of Congress, at the Commencement of the Second Session of the Twentieth Congress* [Washington, 1828]).

2. The question of whether to call a convention to revise the state constitution had been submitted to Virginia's freeholders (those eligible to vote under the constitution) in the spring of 1828 and approved. The present session of the General Assembly was considering various plans for organizing the convention (Alison Goodyear Freehling, *Drift Toward Dissolution: The Virginia Slavery Debate of 1831–1832* [Baton Rouge, La., 1982], 45–46).

3. The plan finally adopted was a district system in which the freeholders in each of the state's twenty-four senate districts were to elect four convention delegates (ibid., 47–48).

From Timothy Pickering

My Dear Sir,   Salem Dec. 26. 1828.

To old age the Sun performs his annual round apparently in one fourth of the time in which early youth observed his course. Our yearly exchange of a letter seems now to be a frequent occurrence. And on my part it is an *enjoyment,* from the pleasure of assuring you of the continuance of my sincere respect & esteem — a pleasure which will end only with my life.

When a vacancy occurs in the Bench of the Supreme Court of the United States, I feel a deep solicitude that it may be filled not merely with ability & learning, but with INDEPENDENCE; for without the latter, *honesty* in ordinary cases, involving no political consequences, is an essentially defective virtue. My solicitude for an able and independent Supreme Judiciary, arises from my considering it as the guardian of public liberty — as holding the Moral Sceptre of the Union. In this regard, therefore, I earnestly hope Mr. Adams may close his political course with an act distinguished for its high national importance, like that of his father's at the completion of *his* contracted cycle of four years. For himself it would be a redeeming act.

In the present year, there has been published in London the third volume of Governor Hutchinson's History of Massachusetts; bringing it down from 1750, which was the conclusion of his second volume, to June

1774, when he departed, with his family, for England; where he died, in 1780.[1]

The subject of this volume was too local to warrant a publication in England, as a literary work, with any prospect of indemnity to the publisher. And his family, or the individual possessed of the manuscript, was unwilling to hazard its passage over the Atlantic; and perhaps more fearful of some unfair management, if printed in Boston, where the author, in that last period of his public life, had become so obnoxious. Hence it remained unpublished, until the Massachusetts Historical Society (as I have understood) engaged to defray the expense of its publication in London. It is an interesting work; and I doubt not substantially correct. For however exceptionable his conduct, after the commencement of our controversy with the Mother Country (dating from the Stamp Act) — I have never heard of Governor Hutchinson's veracity being called in question.

In this volume Hutchinson gives the characters of the most distinguished popular leaders, in that Controversy. Those of the two Adamses are conspicuous. Of Samuel Adams, the Governor says — "He was for near twenty years, a writer against government, in the publick news papers; at first but an indifferent one: long practice caused him to arrive at great perfection, and to acquire a talent of artfully & fallaciously insinuating into the minds of his readers a prejudice against the characters of all whom he attacked, beyond any other man I ever knew. This talent he employed in the messages, remonstrances, and resolves of the house of representatives, most of which were of his composition; and he made more converts to his cause by calumniating governors, and other servants of the crown, than by strength of reasoning."

"John Adams (says the Governor) was a distant relation and intimate acquaintance of Mr. Samuel Adams." — "He is said to have been at a loss which side to take." (I am disposed to absolve John Adams from this *on dit* suggestion.) — "He joined in opposition. As the troubles increased, he increased in knowledge, and made a figure, not only in his own profession, but as a patriot; and was generally esteemed as a person endowed with more knowledge than his kinsman, and equally zealous in the cause of liberty; but neither his business nor his health would admit of that constant application to it, which distinguished the other from all the rest of the province. In general, he may be said to be of stronger resentment upon any real or supposed personal neglect or injury than the other; but in their resentment against such as opposed them in the cause in which they were engaged, it is difficult to say which exceeded."

"His ambition was without bounds, and he has acknowledged to his acquaintance that he could not look with complacency upon any man who was in possession of more wealth, more honours, or more knowledge than himself."[2]

This anecdote is so perfectly characteristic, as, with me, to need no collateral evidence of its truth: But enough is to be found, even in his own writings. I have, in my Review of his Correspondence with Cunningham, quoted two passages on the subject of ambition; or the inordinate love of praise — a near relative, if not the same. On *this* passion in him, I remarked (at page 3) that it could bear no opposition, or even lukewarmness, in regard to the means of gratifying it; & that he had himself described it in language that would not have occurred to any man who had not felt it, in its utmost intensity. "The desire of the esteem of others, (says he) is as real a want of nature as hunger; and the neglect & contempt of the world, as severe a pain as the gout or the stone." And in pp. 99–100, I quote another passage. He says — "Ambition strengthens at every advance, and at last takes possession of the whole soul so absolutely, that the man sees nothing in the world of importance to others, or himself, but in this object." And in the next sentence, combining the love of gold and the love of praise with Ambition, he says these three passions are capable of "subduing all others, & even the understanding itself, if not the CONSCIENCE too, until they become absolute and imperious masters of the whole mind." The "subtlety" of these three passions, even in their excesses, he, very composedly, calls "a curious speculation."[3]

Altho' you will deem this letter quite long enough already, I am disposed to extend it by giving you a couple of anecdotes.

When in Philadelphia, about ten years ago, I called to see Thomas Willing. He tho' in good health, was confined to his house; being a cripple in consequence of having broken his thigh some two years before. He was 86 or 87; but in good spirits and in the full enjoyment of his mental faculties. Looking back to former times, & the commencement of our Revolution War, he told me that he was then (1775) a member of Congress for Pennsylvania; where no hostile act had yet occurred; although an army was assembled at Cambridge. I suppose that Saml. Adams, in particular, was extremely solicitous, that by the war brought to her own door — by actual fighting within her own waters, the citizens of that great and wealthy State, should be roused & animated to a more zealous cooperation in the common cause. The Philadelphians had built a number of gunboats for their river defence. It was known that a British armed vessel was below; and the squadron of gunboats had descended. Mr. Willing said, that Sam Adams, who had been walking in the State House yard, and heard the report of cannon hastily entered the room where Congress held its sessions, and where members were then assembled, and skipping along, and snapping his fingers exclaimed, "The ball's begun — the ball's begun — thank God, the ball's begun!" I wish, said Mr Willing, (sitting at the time by the side of Joseph Hews, a delegate from No. Carolina, and enfeebled by a consumption) "I wish, (said Willing) that man was in Heaven!" "Oh! Recall that wish! (answered Hewes) I expect to be there myself in three weeks — and I should be unwilling to meet with him."

In the year 1820, a Convention of Delegates from all the towns in

Massachusetts, was called, to revise and amend its constitution: Judge Story was a delegate from Salem. John Adams & another represented Quincy. Declining the presidency of that assembly, on account of his great age, he stayed with them but a few days; in the course of which, however, he made a short, but very good speech, on the constitution of the Senate — to retain it as originally established; the representative of *property;* while, as nearly all the citizens were taxed, it was combined with population: for the number of Senators in each district was proportioned to its direct taxes to the State revenue — and not to its population.[4] Some democrats desired that the number of Senators in the respective Senatorial districts, should be apportioned not according to the taxation, but exclusively, to the population. This, Mr. Adams, and all the most intelligent, & considerate members opposed. But some busy democrats of Salem procured a regular town meeting to be called, for the purpose of instructing its delegates to urge the abolition of the existing constitutional rule, and to substitute an apportionment *per capita.* Among these *wise* Constitution-mongers, was Benjamin W. Crowninshield — once secretary of the Navy (of whom, in that character, perhaps you may recollect what John Randolph said of him, in the last session of Congress —) and now a member of the House from Essex.[5] In reference to the sentiments which Mr. Adams had expressed, he closed his flippant remarks with exclaiming "Shame — Shame!"

Viewing the sentiments of Mr. Adams as perfectly correct and salutary, I defended them and him against Crowninshield's reproaches, especially as uttered against a man who, I remarked, had read and thought more on the subject of government than perhaps any other citizen in the United States.

I was followed by another townsman on the same side; and the question was decided against the conceited innovators, by an indefinite postponement of their resolution.

The intelligent editor of the Salem Gazette (since deceased) being present at the discussion, introduced into his next paper, an account of the town meeting, with the substance of the speeches. This paper soon came to Mr. Adams's hands — perhaps forwarded by some one who thought it extraordinary that *I* should step forth an advocate for John Adams. Be that as it may — the Old Gentleman was highly pleased, as Mrs. Quincy informed me; and — taking one of his sudden flights — exclaimed — that "He should be willing to meet me in Heaven!"

In truth, my dear sir, though sufficiently sensible to injuries, & ready to appear in my own vindication, I am not aware that I am blind to the valuable qualities and useful acts of any man; whatever ground he gives for my resentment. Towards Mr. Adams, indeed I felt no resentment; and in the sense of the poet, I can cheerfully repeat — "E'en in a Bishop I can spy desert."[6]

My remarks on the Judiciary have brought to mind Mr. Jefferson's letter to lieutenant Governor Barry, which is inserted in the Appendix to my Review.[7] I have just read it again — and with increased indignation at the virulent spirit displayed towards Federalists; while the weakness of his reasoning on the judiciary exposes himself to contempt.

Why has it been deemed essential to a free government, that the legislative — executive, and judicial authorities should be carefully separated? And to what end separated, unless, in the exercise of their constitutional powers, they are independent? Only, in our limited government, subjecting the Executive and the judges to impeachment. But Mr. Jefferson said "impeachment is not even a scarecrow." What then is to check the transgressions, however atrocious, of the President himself? It was indeed, judged necessary, considering the great powers of the President, especially in respect to his command of the physical force of the country, & his extensive influence in selecting candidates for offices, that his negative on the laws should not be absolute. But very different is the situation of the Judges: they can oppose no previous check on any attempts to encroach on their jurisdiction: they were therefore most wisely rendered absolutely independent of the other branches of the government: and I would imprecate the wrath of Heaven on those who shall attempt the subversion of the system.

Altho' I, in common with many others, have for a long period considered Mr. Jefferson as a visionary statesman; and therefore can read his absurd notions about the judiciary without astonishment; yet I am inclined to ascribe them, as exhibited in his letter to Barry, as much to passion as to wrongheadedness. To me they appear strongly marked with resentment, after the lapse of so many years, still rankling in his bosom, from the escape of Judge Chase from the vengeful impeachment instigated, I believe, by him, & virulently prosecuted by his partisans. Recollect the haste with which he pardoned the scoundrel Callender — his able agent in calumnies against his political opponents — and his peremptory order to the marshall to restore the sum paid for the fine imposed by the sentence of Judge Chase: a restoration as unwarrantable as if he had put his hand directly into the public treasury & thence drawn the money. Chase had also sentenced to death the rebel leader of the whiskey drinkers Jefferson's friends and efficient supporters in raising him to the President's Chair. How the latter culprit after two convictions, escaped the hangman's noose, I have elsewhere shown; though fruitless in regard to the object of the pardoning Chief.[8]

May I venture to fill the vacant space, in this miscellaneous letter, with some notice of Patrick Henry? From Mr. Wirt's Life of that distinguished man (tho' the biographer deals too much in hyperboles) I infer that he was truly a virtuous & religious man. Of his *eloquence*, Mr. Jefferson once told me, that it surpassed that of any man he had ever heard speak. But his speeches in the Virginia Convention, on the Constitution, (two or three of which I have read) appear more declamatory than solid. He seems to have been terrified and he strove to excite the like terror in others with apprehensions of the eventual overthrow of the public liberty, if it should be adopted: seeming to have over-looked the simple fact, that the legislators & all the officers provided for in the Constitution, derived, directly or indirectly, their appointments, like those of the several State-governments, in which he reposed entire confidence, from the *People;* and could be displaced in like manner, if they proved unfaithful to their trusts. Farewell!

T. PICKERING

ALS (draft), Pickering Papers, MHi. At top of first page Pickering wrote "To John Marshall now and for near / thirty years past, Chief Justice of the U States."

1. Thomas Hutchinson, *The History of the Province of Massachusetts Bay, from 1749 to 1774* (London, 1828). The third volume of Hutchinson's work was compiled and edited by John Hutchinson, the author's grandson. The first two volumes originally appeared in 1764 and 1768 and were published in an American edition as *History of Massachusetts from the First Settlement Thereof in 1628, until the Year 1750* (3d ed.; 2 vols.; Boston, 1795). The most recent edition is Lawrence Shaw Mayo, ed., *The History of the Colony and Province of Massachusetts-Bay, by Thomas Hutchinson . . .* (3 vols.; Cambridge, Mass., 1936).

2. Mayo, ed., *History of the Colony and Province of Massachusetts-Bay*, III, 212, 213–14.

3. Timothy Pickering, *A Review of the Correspondence between the Hon. John Adams, Late President of the United States, and the Late Wm. Cunningham, Esq., Beginning in 1803 and Ending in 1812* (Salem, Mass., 1824), 3–4, 100.

4. Adams's speech at the Massachusetts Convention in Dec. 1821 is excerpted in Merrill D. Peterson, ed., *Democracy, Liberty, and Property: The State Constitutional Conventions of the 1820's* (Indianapolis, Ind., 1966), 75–77.

5. In his speech on "Retrenchment and Reform" of 1 Feb. 1828 Randolph scornfully referred to Crowninshield, Madison's secretary of the navy, as "the Master Slender—no, the Master Silence of Ministers of State. Shakespeare himself could go no lower" (Powhatan Bouldin, *Home Reminiscences of John Randolph of Roanoke* [Danville, Va., 1878], 316–17).

6. Alexander Pope, *One Thousand Seven Hundred and Thirty Eight. Dialogue II* (London, 1738), 7.

7. Pickering, *Review of the Correspondence*, 184–85, reprinting Jefferson's letter to William T. Barry, 2 July 1822.

8. Pickering alluded to the treason trials of John Fries, who was sentenced to death in 1800 but was pardoned by President Adams.

From Timothy Pickering

Dear Sir, Salem Decr. 26. 1828.

I have already given to Judge Story my anniversary letter for you. I now trouble you with a short one.

In looking to-day for a sample of General Hamilton's hand-writing, in some letter that I could part with, for Judge Story, I met with a copy of one of my own letters to a Virginia gentleman, of the date of 1817, to obtain authentic information concerning an anecdote recited at Mr. Catlett's table in Alexandria, where I was a guest, "That Patrick Henry once said, 'that he could forgive every thing else in Mr. Jefferson, but his corrupting Mr. Madison.'" I could not recollect by which of the guests the anecdote was recited; nor could another guest, the one to whom I wrote. But both he & his brother (they were Henry and Thomas Turner) said it was a current report: and from their expressions, I supposed it was a generally believed fact.[1]

I have myself long believed, that if Mr. Jefferson had died in Paris — or never seen Madison after his return from France — He and Hamilton would have co-operated in the administration of the government organized under the Constitution, in the framing and adoption of which they were cordial & successful fellow-labourers; Madison becoming, from a friend, a virulent persecutor.

If you favour me with a letter, on Judge Story's return from Washington, let me request you to bear the above recited anecdote in mind. I am, as ever, most truly yours

T. PICKERING

ALS (draft), Pickering Papers, MHi. Addressed to "General Marshall."

1. Pickering's correspondence with the brothers Thomas Turner of Prince William County and Henry Turner of Alexandria took place in Feb. 1817. Henry Turner informed Pickering that he believed John Hopkins was the source of the story. Hopkins, however, claimed not to have remembered making the statement at that time, but (according to Turner) did recall hearing "the anecdote ten years ago and frequently seen that printed, and has no doubt that the declaration in question was made by Mr. Henry" (Pickering to Thomas Turner, 14 Feb. 1817; Thomas Turner to Pickering, 24 Feb. 1817; Henry Turner to Pickering, 21 Feb. 1817, Pickering Papers, MHi).

From Henry Clay

My dear Sir   Washington Decr 27. 1828
                                               (Confidential)

After the liberty which I took in addressing you on the subject of a successor to Judge Trimble, I ought before now to have informed you that I took the further liberty of shewing your answer to my letter to the President; and that he subsequently nominated Mr. Crittenden to the Senate, before which the nomination is yet pending. It's fate is uncertain, as that of all nominations are in the present Condition of public affairs. I shall regret very much if the appointment should not be confirmed because I am persuaded that a better could not be made from the section of the Union which under any circumstances will I presume supply the vacancy. I am with the highest respect, Your faithful & ob. Servt.

H. CLAY

ALS, Gray-Glines Collection, Ct. Addressed to JM in Richmond and franked. Postmarked Washington, 29 Dec.

To Alexander Smyth

DEAR SIR: Richmond, Jan. 1st, 1828. [1829][1]

I have received your speech on the resolution amendatory of the Constitution, and thank you for sending it to me.[2] I have read it with great attention, and think the argument against the re-eligibility of the President, very strong. Public opinion is, I believe, taking a decided direction towards this point; and, I am disposed to think, in its favor. Some difference may exist respecting the time for which the Chief Magistrate ought to be elected—more, perhaps, than on the propriety of his being re-eligible.

The question is one of great interest and delicacy; and is not without difficulty. We may perceive the inconvenience of the present arrangement much more clearly than those which may result from any new and untried system. In a great and powerful republic, nothing is more difficult than the disposition of the Executive power. Yet, though not very fond of experiments, I should be disposed to try the effect of confining the Chief Magistrate to a single term.

With great respect, I am, sir, your obt. servt.

J. MARSHALL.

Printed, *Daily National Intelligencer* (Washington, D.C.), 5 January 1829. Inside address to Alexander Smyth, Washington.

1. The correct date is 1829, as is clear from the context. The editor (presumably Joseph Gales) introduced the text of the letter with these remarks: "The following letter is published under a belief that the distinguished patriot and statesman, by whom it was written, will have no objection that his fellow citizens should know his opinion; and a confidence that they will allow that opinion the weight to which it is entitled."

2. Alexander Smyth, *Speech of Alexander Smyth, of Virginia, on the Resolution Amendatory of the Constitution* . . . (Washington, 1828). Smyth delivered this speech on 18 Dec. 1828 in the House of Representatives in support of his resolution proposing amendments to the Constitution concerning the election of the president. The most important of these provided that after 3 Mar. 1829 no person elected president would be again eligible to hold that office. The House eventually tabled Smyth's motion on 20 Feb. 1829 (*Register of Debates in Congress* . . . , V, [Washington, 1830], 119–25, 320–21, 322, 361–71).

From Timothy Pickering

Dear Sir, Salem Jany. 7. 1829.

Although I wrote you two letters by Judge Story, I hope you will pardon a third, following so closely at their heels.

Last evening I took up the   number of the North American Review just published. In it is a review of the Life of the Renound *Elbridge Gerry;* 520 pages Octavo! And this is only the *first part* of the life of that

Great Personage! terminating with the Revolutionary War. The second volume (probably to occupy as many more pages) is in progress; for the rest of his life; & will consequently display his diplomatic talents. I have not seen the book. It was written by his son-in-law, Thomas Trecothick Austin, a lawyer of Boston.[1] The Reviewer, I am told, is Edward Everett, whom you must know at Washington; a gentleman distinguished for ability, and his great literary acquirements; but who as an ambitious aspirant, in the Adams Train, must have felt a terrible damper in the issue of the recent Presidential Election. He possesses; however — the blandishments of a Courtier; and will not be irreconcilable to the New Political Power. Such is my opinion of this gentleman. His soft, winning manners, and his talents, qualify him to conciliate esteem and respect. With such abilities to do extensive good, I sincerely wish his desire to please, and his ambition, were accompanied with a high minded, determined independence.

It seems that Mr. Austin has introduced many letters to Mr. Gerry from gentlemen whose names are familiar in our revolutionary story. He mentions those of "John & Samuel Adams, Washington, Jefferson, Knox, Dana, King"; and refers to "other distinguished men of that day." These letters, the Reviewer says, "are sufficient to stamp the highest degree of importance on the volume." It is probable that some of them may be useful historical documents. He adds — "There are fewer of Mr. Gerry's letters than we could have wished."[2] I observe that in referring to him, he carefully calls him "the vice-president.["]

In page 49 of the Review, you will see Mr. Everett's remarks on the public characters of Jefferson — Franklin, Washington, and John Adams. Of the two former he says — "Mr. Jefferson & Dr. Franklin exercised the purely philosophical influence (but that of the highest order), over American affairs; the latter (of the two) long before the crisis of the revolution came on, the former more eminently in the succeeding stages of our political progress." It was, my dear sir, this lofty eulogy on *Jefferson* which suggested to me the writing of this letter. Where was this philosophical influence, of the highest order, over American affairs, displayed by Mr. Jefferson? Where are the evidences of it? Has Mr. Everett seen any written documents of Mr. Jefferson's, to authorize his panegyrick? What politico-philosophical pamphlets did he write prior to the commencement of our revolution war, and during its existence, to enlighten, & guide, and animate his countrymen? I presume there must have been some; though I was never so fortunate as to light on any of them: and I should be much gratified to see them. William Lewis, that eminent Philadelphia lawyer, once told me that he assisted Mr. Jefferson in his correspondence with Mr. Hammond: I suppose on points of law (public & municipal) and authorities to be produced of decisions thereon.[3]

I suspect, that Everett has made his round assertion: without resting on any particular evidence. Could he refer to the measures of his administra-

TIMOTHY PICKERING
Oil on wood by James Frothingham, 1820.
Courtesy of the Peabody-Essex Museum

tion—detestable as it was? and in which his embargo alone produced more loss and injury to the U. States than all the French spoliations immense as these were.

Mr. Everett cannot resist, he says, the temptation of quoting from Gerry's Life, one letter from John Adams. The subject—the Cincinnati Societies; the imaginary dangers from which continued to harrass his pure republicanism as late as April 1785, the date of his letter.[4] It bears few marks of sagacity or wisdom. It is rather the offspring of that jealousy in Mr. Adams, which, as Hamilton said, "was capable of discolouring every object;"[5] and of that corroding Envy which rendered unhappy the person who "could not look with complacency upon any man who was in possession of more wealth, more honours, or more knowledge than himself."[6] In the same letter he says—"While reputations are so indiscreetly puffed, while thanks and *statues* (Washington's equestrian) are so childishly awarded, and the greatest real services (his own) so coldly received, I had almost said censured, we are in the high road to have no virtue left, and nothing but ambition to reward."[7]—"Awful, my friend, is the task of the intelligent advocate for liberty." — "It is a constant warfare from the cradle to the grave, without comfort, thanks, or rewards, and is always overcome at last." The conclusion of the whole is—"It is not worth the while for you and me to die martyrs to singular notions. You are young and may turn fine gentleman yet. I am too old, and therefore will retire to Pen's Hill,"

'The world forgetting, by the world forgot.'

Poor Man! Think of his ambition displayed more than twenty years afterwards, to obtain the president's chair, a second time! When his principle was—"Flectere si nequeo superos, Acheronta movebo."[8]

The date of the letter from which the above quotations are made (April 25. 1785) must be erroneous; for just two months before (Feby. 24th) he had been elected minister plenipotentiary to represent the United States at the Court of Great Britain.

Permit me to say a few words concerning that mighty Bugbear, the Cincinnati Association. In his letter to Gerry, Mr. Adams intimates that it might have originated with two foreign officers who served in the American Army, the Marquis de la Fayette & Baron Stuben, persons born and bred among titled societies, and accustomed to decorations there deemed honourable. But its putative father was General Knox. I recollect, that when the institution became unpopular, I heard of a petty controversy between Steuben & Knox; the latter ascribing its origin to Stuben; and he affirming that it originated with Knox.

I will now state to you, what I have never before committed to writing, my own objection to the institution, at the time it was formed. This was— not its *formidable* nature; but, in relation to its first & leading principle, its *real insignificance*. That principle was—"An incessant attention to preserve inviolate those exalted rights and liberties of human nature, for which they have fought and bled."[9]

This (savouring of the natural pomposity of Knox) was the *assumption of an importance* in the actual population & the certain increasing millions of the people of the United States, that disgusted me; and compared with whom, the Cincinnati were and would be but as a drop in the bucket. I knew the general character of the officers, from the generals to the sub-alterns. So far as fighting was concerned they had done, & would again do their full share of duty. But among them, small was the number of enlightened minds competent to discern, and time⟨l⟩y to guard against, the approaches of danger to the public liberty; while such characters, in comparison, abounded, and would more abound in the Nation. When, therefore, I concluded to subscribe the general association, it was *to avoid singularity*. Had I declined, I should have probably stood alone.

You will read Mr. Adams's letter. He said — "This Cincinnati Institution was the deepest piece of *cunning* yet attempted" against "our first princi-ple, equality." *Cunning* ascribed to the pure mind of Washington, the Head of the Society, and to the open hearted Knox!

But I fatigue you with my long scribbles — and here I stop; requesting only that you will bear in mind my wish to be furnished with some evi-dence, if any remain, or ever had existence, of Mr. Jefferson's "purely philosophical influence, and that of the highest order, over American affairs." That he acquired & exercised an immense influence over them, is true; but of little connection with philosophy or patriotism.[10] Most sincerely yours.

T. PICKERING

ALS (draft), Pickering Papers, MHi. Noted as addressed to JM "(Chief Justice)."

1. James T. Austin, *The Life of Elbridge Gerry. With Contemporary Letters. To the Close of the American Revolution* (Boston, 1828). A second volume, subtitled "From the Close of the American Revolution," was published in 1829. Austin (1784–1870), whose wife Catherine was Gerry's daughter, was a prominent Boston lawyer, politician, and writer. The review of the first volume appeared in the *North American Review*, XXVIII (1829), 37–57.

2. *North American Review*, XXVIII (1829), 53.

3. As secretary of state, Jefferson enlisted the help of William Lewis in preparing his reply to British minister George Hammond, 29 May 1792, concerning infractions of the peace treaty of 1783 (Lewis to Jefferson, 1 Jan. 1791, Julian P. Boyd et al., eds., *The Papers of Thomas Jefferson*, XVIII [Princeton, N.J., 1971], 461–71; Jefferson to Hammond, 29 May 1792, Charles T. Cullen et al., eds., *The Papers of Thomas Jefferson*, XXIII [Princeton, N.J., 1990], 551–613).

4. The review (pp. 55–57) reprinted Adam's letter to Gerry, 25 Apr. 1785, citing pp. 427–31 of Austin's *Life of Gerry*.

5. Pickering quoted Alexander Hamilton's "Letter . . . Concerning the Public Conduct and Behavior of John Adams," [24 Oct. 1800], (Harold C. Syrett et al., eds., *The Papers of Alexander Hamilton*, XXV [New York, 1977], 190).

6. Pickering again quoted Thomas Hutchinson's characterization of Adams, as he had done in a recent letter to JM (Pickering to JM, 26 Dec. 1828 [first letter] and n. 2).

7. Pickering again quotes Adams's letter to Gerry, 25 Apr. 1785 (see n. 4). The parenthetical phrases are his own insertions.

8. Virgil, *Aeneid,* Bk. VII, l. 312: "If I cannot move the gods, I shall stir up hell" (translation from James Morwood, *A Dictionary of Latin Words and Phrases* [New York, 1998], 67).

9. Pickering quoted the first of the "immutable" principles that were to "form the basis for the Society of the Cincinnati" (Minor Myers, *Liberty Without Anarchy: A History of the Society of the Cincinnati* [Charlottesville, Va., 1983], 259).

10. Pickering died on 29 Jan. 1829.

To Mary W. Marshall

My dearest Polly   Washington Feby. 1st. 1829

Our sick Judges have at length arrived and we are as busy as men can well be. I do not walk as far as I formerly did, but I still keep up the practice of walking in the morning. We dined on friday last with the President, and I sat between Mrs. Adams and the lady of a member of Congress whom I found quite agreeable as well as handsome.[1] Mrs. Adams was as cheerful as if she was to continue in the great house for the ensuing four years. The President also is in good health and spirits. I perceive no difference in consequence of the turn the late election has taken.

General Jackson is expected in the city within a fortnight, and is to put up in this house. I shall of course wait on him. It is said he feels the loss of Mrs. Jackson very seriously.[2] It would be strange if he did not. A man who at his age loses a good wife loses a friend whose place cannot be supplied.

I dine tomorrow with the British minister[3] and the next day again with the President. I have never before dined twice with the President during the same session of the court. That on friday was an official dinner. The invitation for tuesday is not for all the other Judges and I consider it as a personal civility.[4] Tell Mr. Call all the secretaries are sick and Mr. Clay among them. He took cold by attending the colonization society and has been indisposed ever since.

The town it is said was never so full as at present. The expectation is that it will overflow on the 3d. of March. The whole world it is said will be here. This however will present no temptation to you to come. I wish I could leave it all and come to you. How much more delightful would it be to me to sit by your side than to witness all the pomp and parade of the inauguration.

I hear very little from Richmond but I adhere to my old rule of beleiving that every body dear to me, and especially the one dearest to me is well.

Tell Mr. Harvie I am greatly obliged by his letter.[5]

Farewell my dearest Pol⟨ly⟩ with the most ardent wish for your happ⟨iness⟩ I am your ever affectionate

J MARSHALL

ALS, Marshall Papers, ViW. Addressed to Mrs. Marshall in Richmond; postmarked Washington, 3 Feb.

1. The dinner party on the evening of 30 Jan. was described by Adams in his diary as "the last entertainment of my political Life and given to the Judges of the Supreme Court of the United States." The "agreeable" guest seated next to JM may have been Charlotte Gray Everett, wife of Edward Everett (John Quincy Adams Diary, 30 Jan. 1829, MHi).

2. Rachel Donelson Jackson (1767–1828) died on 23 Dec. 1828.

3. Charles Richard Vaughan (1774–1849) served as British minister to the U.S. from 1825 to 1835.

4. JM accepted an invitation to dine with President and Mrs. Adams on 3 Feb. The only other Supreme Court justice attending this dinner was Story (JM to John Quincy Adams, [ca. 1 Feb. 1829], Adams Papers, MHi; John Quincy Adams Diary, 3 Feb. 1829, MHi).

5. Letter not found.

From Henry Clay

Dept. of State Washington 11 Feby. 1829.

The Secretary of State presents his compliments to the chief Justice Marshall and in answer to his Note of yesterday[1] concerning Leland B. Rose, convicted of a misdemeanor before the Circuit Court of the United States for the District of Virginia, and sentenced to a term of imprisonment for the same, has the honor to inform him, that a copy of the record in the case of Rose, was received here on the 14th. of January from Mr. Jefferies, Clerk of the Court, and immediately submitted to the President, for his decision upon the recommendation, which it contained, of the Court and Jury, in behalf of the Prisoner; and that on the same day the President returned to this Department the copy referred to with his decision subjoined, a transcript of which is herewith respectfully communicated to the Chief Justice.[2]

Letterbook copy, RG 59, DNA.

1. Letter not found.

2. Rose, of Westmoreland County, was a mail carrier on the route between Westmoreland Courthouse and Kilmarnock in Lancaster County. At the Nov. 1828 term of the U.S. Circuit Court, he was convicted of stealing a bank note from a letter posted at Lyell's Store in Richmond County. The jury accompanied its guilty verdict with a unanimous recommendation for mercy for Rose "in consequence of his extreme youthful appearance." The court subsequently agreed that Rose was an "object of mercy" and that it would make this recommendation to the president of the U.S. President Adams decided to refer the recommendation to his successor, though at the same time he stated his reasons why the crime should not have the penalty remitted. Noting that the only reason assigned for mercy was the prisoner's "youthful appearance," Adams declared that he had "never felt myself at liberty to remit any part" of the punishment for this crime. "Persons employed in the transportation of the mail," he went on, "are so accessible to temptation; the crime is so easy of commission; so sheltered from detection; so distressing in its effects upon the sufferers by its perpetration; so subversive of public confidence in the security of communications . . . that the only protection to these inestimable interests is in the *certainty* with which the

penalties of the law are inflicted. . . ." Accordingly, "clemency to the transgressor is cruelty to the innocent—pardon to one is punishment to Millions." On 10 Mar. 1829, Congressman John Taliaferro, acting on behalf of Rose's parents, wrote to President Jackson asking him to act on the case. Presumably, the request for mercy was denied, for there is no record of a pardon or remission (Indictment, U.S. v. Rose, U.S. Cir. Ct., Va., Ended Case [Unrestored], 1828, Vi; U.S. Cir. Ct., Va., Ord. Bk. XII, 266, 267, 279; Case File No. 393, Petitions for Pardon and Related Briefs, 1800–49, RG 59, DNA).

Foster and Elam v. Neilson
Notes on Arguments
U.S. Supreme Court, [17–18] February 1829

Mr. Jones[1]

Can eject. be maintained on a naked Spanish grant.
Does not admit the necessity of examining the extent of the treaty.
That is for the political department
When private individuals come into court and ask the enforcement of the treaty against the sovereign doubts the propriety

No reservation for any individual in the treaty of 1803 with France. There is a general stipulation for property. Any infringement by the sovereign of this stipulation justifies an appeal to the other.

The U.S. have maintained that the treaty of cession transferred to them the territory in question. After long negotiation they took possession of it. Is it for their court to say this was an act of violence without right?

1st   Had the British any right to territory on the East side of the Mississipi? Discovery & settlement.

1680   Father Hennepen penetrated as far as the river Illinois. A governor of Canada fitted out an expedition which found the river and descended it Lasalle proceeded to France and formed the immense plan of uniting Louisiana with Canada.

Never a minute territorial dispute respecting the boundary of Louisiana or Florida.

France when the war of 56 commenced was in possession of Louisiana lying on both sides the Mississipi.

The endeavour to do away the right gained by Lasalle is founded on the charter to ⟨G.?⟩C.[2]

Spain cedes Florida. What was Florida? She had but two settlements St. Augustine and Pensacola.

Eng. held both the spanish & French title.

Eng. was compelled to retrocede to Spain the Florida which she
had acquired from France as well as what she had received from
Spain

Spain retroceded Louisiana as France had held it.

Can the words respecting the extent of Louisiana Such as France
possessed it &c. be meer surplusage? Why not stop with retroced-
ing as it was ceded by France? Why refer possession of France
exclusively to her possession after 62? As it should be after treaties
&c What treaties? Only the treaty's settling the limits of Florida.
Retrocession — May not assignee retrocede to his assignor what
that assignor had ceded to another who ceded to him?

Obj.   Admission on part of The U.S. that Louisiana had been delivered
& His message to Congress. Sent a special mission in 1804 to Paris
& Madrid.

The occupation of The U.S. was under a claim or right and an
exertion of it.

In 1812 the place where the lands lie was incorporated with Louisiana.

In 1817 it was divided between Louisiana and Mississipi.

St. Pa. V. 12³ No preliminary basis as to the extent of Louisiana & Florida.

1819   Claim of Spain Firmly repelled by The U.S. A quit claim of what
she did not hold legally; a cession of what she did not hold — "All
that belonged to Spain east of Mississipi.["]

This land on the same ground with the land north of 31st. degree.

Can this court annul any act of Congress passed in relation to its
concerns with a foreign government?

The document on which the plf. below sustained his title.
The caption of the grant Dist. Of Louisiana — parish of Baton
rouge speaks of himself as Intendant of Louisiana. Identifying
baton rouge with Louisiana.

This grant emanated pending the conferences at Aranjuez.
L.L. 981[4]

AD, Foster and Elam v. Neilson, Appellate Case No. 1463, RG 267, DNA.

1. On the background of this case see Foster and Elam v. Neilson, Opinion, 9 Mar. 1829.
Walter Jones argued for the defendant David Neilson on 17 and 18 Feb. (U.S. Sup. Ct.
Minutes, 17, 18 Feb. 1829; 2 Pet. 279–93).

2. This is apparently a reference to Anthony Crozat, who in 1712 received a grant to
Louisiana from the King of France. The printed report of Jones's argument mentions
Crozat at 2 Pet. 285.

3. *State Papers and Publick Documents of the United States* . . . (3d ed.; 12 vols.; Boston, 1819).
See Foster and Elam v. Neilson, Opinion, 9 Mar. 1829, and nn.

4. The abbreviation is apparently for "Land Laws," which counsel cited at 2 Pet. 263, 266,
273, 278. This was a short title for *Laws of the United States, Resolutions of Congress under the
Confederation, Treaties, Proclamations, and Other Documents Having Operation and Respect to the
Public Lands* (Washington, D.C., 1817).

To Mary W. Marshall

My dearest Polly   Washington Feb. 19th. 1829
    I send you inclosed a letter to Mr. Payne which I wish sent to him as
soon as convenient. I hope it may reach you in time to go out on sunday.[1]
I imagine Oby has carried out the clover seed which was in the cellar, and
perhaps what Mr. Harvie was to have purchased from Mr. Lewis for me.

    The day after writing my last I received a letter from my son James
containing the painful intelligence that you were not quite so well as
usual.[2] I shall be very uneasy till I hear again from you. Do my dearest
Polly let me hear from you through someone of those who will be willing
to write for you. I will ⟨fl⟩atter my self that your indisposition is meerly
temporary and that it has passed away. Yet I cannot be easy till my hope⟨s⟩
are confirmed.

    I wrote a day or two past to our son and have made a feeble attempt to
console him.[3]

    I have received a letter from our son Jaquelin[4] informing me that he
has a very fine son and that Eliza is as well as could be expected. His
son is named after himself. His daughters he says are a little indisposed
in consequence of confinement during the excessive bad weather they
have had.[5]

    Farewell my dearest Polly, that Heaven may bless and preserve you is
the unceasing prayer of your

                                   J MARSHALL

ALS, Marshall Papers, ViW.

1. Letter not found. Payne was possibly the overseer at JM's Chickahominy farm. JM knew that his wife would be going to the farm on Sunday the twenty-second to escape the noisy celebrations of Washington's birthday.

2. Letter not found.

3. Letter not found. Margaret Lewis Marshall, wife of Thomas Marshall, died on 2 Feb. 1829, giving birth to a son who also died. For an account of her death and burial at Oak Hill, see Maria Newton Marshall, comp., *Recollections and Reflections of Fielding Lewis Marshall: A Virginia Gentleman of the Old School* [Orange?, Va., 1911], 12–15.

4. Letter not found.

5. Jaquelin Ambler Marshall was born on 9 Feb. 1829. His two sisters at this time were Mary Ambler Marshall and Eliza Marshall (Paxton, *Marshall Family*, 204–5).

To [Peter B. Porter]

Sir[1]   Washington Feb. 24th. 29

I received a letter last fall from an old soldier of the revolution named William Kearns informing me that he had made an application for the advantages allowed old soldiers by the late act of Congress and requesting me to forward to the department a certificate of his service.[2] I do not recollect whether I wrote to the department on receiving the letter, or deferred it till I should come to this place. William Kearnes enlisted in 1776, in the autumn of that year as I believe, in the company then commanded by Captain William Blackwell and afterwards by myself in the 11th. Virginia regiment on continental establishment. I was at that time first lieutenant in the company and all the soldiers were enlisted for three years or during the war. I knew William Kearnes very well and know that he served faithfully at least three years. I am very respectfully Your obedt

J MARSHALL

ALS, RG 15 (file of William Kernes), DNA. Addressed to the secretary of war. Endorsed "respectfully referred to / the Secretary of the / Treasury. / Dep of War / Feby 25 1829."

1. Peter B. Porter (1773–1844) of New York, a former member of Congress (1809–13, 1815–16), had been secretary of war since June 1828.

2. Letter not found. William Kernes (also spelled Kerns or Kearns), then a resident of Kentucky, applied for a pension under the act of 15 May 1828 "for the relief of certain surviving officers and soldiers of the army of the revolution" (*U.S. Statutes at Large*, IV, 269–70; Declaration of William Kernes, 13 Oct. 1828, RG 15 (file of William Kernes), DNA; *PJM*, I, 6 and n. 7).

To Mary W. Marshall

My dearest Polly   Washington Feb. 28th 1829

I have looked eagerly through this week for a letter from some one of our friends giving me some information respecting you but have been disappointed. In spite of my firm resolution always to hope for the best,

I cannot suppress my uneasiness about you. Your general health is so delicate, your spirits so liable to depression that I cannot controul my uneasiness. I was never more closely occupied than I have been since my arrival at this place, yet my mind wanders to that dear fire side at which is seated what is most dear to me on earth.

I believe I mentioned in my last that I had received a letter from Edward, and that he thinks himself very happy, yet amidst all his happiness he thinks of and grieves for his brother.[1] I received a few days past a long letter from our son.[2] It is serious and very religious. His heavy loss has given his mind a still stronger impulse in that direction than it had previously received. He says that he is very much occupied with his children and I hope that will gradually restore him to happiness. He retains John with him and superintends his education.[3]

Farewell my dearest wife — that Heaven may protect and bless you is the constant prayer of your ever affectionate

J MARSHALL

ALS, Collection of the Association for the Preservation of Virginia Antiquities, ViHi. Addressed to Mrs. Marshall in Richmond; postmarked Washington, 1 Mar.

1. Letter not found. Edward C. Marshall had married Rebecca C. Peyton on 12 Feb. 1829 (Paxton, *Marshall Family*, 103).

2. Letter from Thomas Marshall not found. This was probably the letter of 21 Feb. acknowledged in JM to Thomas Marshall, 20 Mar. 1829.

3. John Marshall (1811–54) was Thomas Marshall's oldest son. He later attended the University of Virginia and inherited the Oak Hill estate (ibid., 194–95).

Poem

[Washington, February 1829][1]

Written, on the request of a lady[2] to inscribe my name in her book of Autographs; but withheld from the apprehension that such an effusion might be thought light and unbecoming[3]

In early youth when life was young,
   And spirits light and gay,
When music breathed from every tongue
   And every month was may;
When buoyant hope in colours bright
   Her vivid pictures drew,
When every object gave delight
   And every scene was new;
My heart with ready homage bowed
   At lovely woman's shrine,

And every wish that she avowed
　　Became a wish of mine.
Now age with hoary frost congeals
　　Gay fancy's flowing stream,
And the unwelcome truth[4] reveals
　　That life is but a dream;
Yet still with homage true I bow
　　At Womans sacred shrine
And if she will a wish avow
　　That wish must still be mine[5]

AD, TxU; note in unknown hand: "Lines written by Ch: Justice Marshall in February *1829*, while at Washington." AD, Marshall Papers, ViW. Slight variations in texts noted below.

1. There is evidently a third version of the poem in JM's hand, published in Frances Norton Mason, *My Dearest Polly* (Richmond, 1961), 300–1. This version, the original of which was "among the papers found at Leeds Manor," is identical to the ViW text except for the heading, "Lines written for a lady's album," and a concluding line (see n. 5).

2. In ViW text "that I would" replaces "to."

3. In ViW text this passage reads: "but withheld, in the apprehension that it might be thought light and unbecoming the gravity of seventy three."

4. In TxU text JM deleted "cruelly the" and interlined "the unwelcome."

5. The text in Mason, *My Dearest Polly*, 301, has this concluding line: "My old wife! My youth grown rich and tender with years!"

From Andrew Jackson

March 2d. 1829

Genl Jackson presents his respects to Chief justice Marshall and would be gratified to be informed by him whether it will suit his convenience to administer the oath prescribed by the Constitution for the President of the United States before he enters upon the duties of office, on Wednesday next at 12 oclock, and at such place as the senate may designate.

Letterbook copy, Jackson Papers, DLC.

To Mary W. Marshall

My dearest Polly   Washington March 5th [1829]

I have been much releived by hearing from several persons who came through or from Richmond, that there was no report in town of your being indisposed. I will resume my old confidence that you are well since I do not hear the contrary.

We had yesterday a most busy and crowded day. People have flocked to Washington from every quarter of the United States. When the oath was administered to the President the computation is that 12 or 15,000 people were present — a great number of them ladies. A great ball was given at night to celebrate the Election. I of course did not attend it. The affliction of our son would have been sufficient to restrain me had I even felt a desire to go.

I am told by several that I am held up as a candidate for the convention. I have no desire to be in the convention and do not mean to be a candidate. I should not trouble you with this did I not apprehend that the idea of my wishing to be in the convention might prevent some of my friends who are themselves desirous of being in it from becoming candidates. I therefore wish you to give this information to Mr. Harvie.

I had hoped yesterday that we were about to have good weather which would enable you to take proper exercise, but today makes me fear that my hope will be disappointed.

Farewell my dearest Polly. Your happiness is always nearest the heart of your

J MARSHALL

Tr, Beveridge-Marshall Papers, DLC. Noted by transcriber as addressed to Mrs. Marshall in Richmond. Transcriber's note: "This letter was copied from the original in the possession of Mrs. Claudia Jones-Navy Yard Washington D.C. on May 30th 1913."

Foster and Elam v. Neilson
Opinion
U.S. Supreme Court, 9 March 1829

James Foster (1752–1835) and Pleasants Elam, residents of Adams County, Mississippi, claimed a tract of land under a title originating in a grant from the King of Spain in 1804. According to the plaintiffs' petition filed in the U.S. District Court for Eastern Louisiana in November 1825, the land lay within what was then the Spanish province of West Florida. The petition complained that David Neilson of Louisiana had taken possession of the land and refused to give it up. In March 1826 Neilson filed exceptions to the petition, one of which stated that the petitioners did not show any right to the land in question because before the grant of 1804 that land had been ceded by Spain to France and by France to the United States. The district court upheld this exception in March 1827, whereupon the plaintiffs obtained a writ of error to bring the case to the Supreme Court. The appeal was argued over three days in February 1829, Richard S. Coxe (1792–1865) and Daniel Webster for the plaintiffs and Walter Jones for the defendant. The case turned on the construction of the treaty of 1803 by which the United States acquired the territory of Louisiana from France. The extent of that purchase, notably the boundary between Louisiana and West Florida, had long been a disputed point in relations between the United States and Spain (Foster and Elam v. Neilson, App. Cas. No. 1463; U.S. Sup. Ct. Minutes, 17, 18, 21, Feb., 9 Mar. 1829; *Biographical and Historical Memoirs of Mississippi* [2 vols.; Chicago, 1891], I, 758–59).

Foster & Elam

v.

Neilson

¶1   This suit was brought by the plaintiffs in errour in the court of The United States for the Eastern District of Louisiana, to recover a tract of land lying in that district, about thirty miles east of the Mississipi, and in the possession of the defendants. The plaintiffs claimed under a grant for 40,000 arpents of land made by the Spanish Governour on the 2d. of January 1804 to Jayme Jorda, and ratified by the King of Spain on the 29th. of May 1804. The petition and order of survey are dated in September 1803, and the return of the survey itself was made on the 27th. of October in the same year. The defendant excepted to the petition of the plaintiffs, alleging that it does not show a title on which they can recover; that the territory within which the land claimed is situated, had been ceded, before the grant, to France, and by France to The United States; and that the grant is void, being made by persons who had no authority to make it. The court sustained the exception, and dismissed the petition. The cause is brought before this court by a writ of errour.

¶2   The case presents this very intricate and at one time very interesting question; to whom did the country between the Iberville and the Perdido rightfully belong when the title now asserted by the plaintiffs was acquired?[1]

¶3   This question has been repeatedly discussed with great talent and research by the government of The United States and that of Spain. The United States have perseveringly and earnestly insisted that by the treaty of St Ildefonso made on the first of October in the year 1800, Spain ceded the disputed territory as part of Louisiana to France, and that France, by the treaty of Paris signed on the 30th. of April 1803 and ratified on the 21st. of October in the same year, ceded it to The United States. Spain has with equal perseverance and earnestness maintained that her cession to France comprehended that territory only which was at that time denominated Louisiana, consisting of the island of New Orleans and the country she received from France West of the Mississipi.

¶4   Without tracing the title of France to its origin, we may state with confidence that, at the commencement of the war of 1756, she was the undisputed possessor of the p⟨rovin⟩ce of Louisiana, lying on both sides the Mississipi, and extending eastward beyond the bay of Mobile. Spain was at the same time in possession of Florida; and it is understood that the river Perdido separated the two provinces from each other.

Such was the state of possession and title at the treaty of Paris con- ¶5
cluded between Great Britain, France and Spain on the 10th. day of
February 1763. By that treaty France ceded to Great Britain the river and
port of the mobile, and all her possessions on the left side of the river
Mississipi, except the town of New Orleans and the island in which it is
situated; and by the same treaty Spain ceded Florida to Great Britain. The
residue of Louisiana was ceded by France to Spain in a separate and
secret treaty between those two powers.

The King of Great Britain being thus the acknowledged sovereign of ¶6
the whole country east of the Mississipi except the island of New Orleans,
divided his late acquisition in the south, into two provinces, East and West
Florida. The latter comprehended so much of the country ceded by
France as lay south of the 31st. degree of North latitude, and a part of that
ceded by Spain.

By the treaty of peace between Great Britain and Spain, signed at ¶7
Versailles on the 3d. of September 1783 Great Britain ceded East and
West Florida to Spain; and those provinces continued to be known and
governed by those names as long as they remained in the possession and
under the dominion of his Catholic Majesty.

On the first of October in the year 1800 a secret treaty was concluded ¶8
between France and Spain at St Ildefonso, the 3d. article of which is in
these words "His Catholic Majesty promises and engages on his part to
retrocede to the French republic six months after the full and entire
execution of the conditions and stipulations relative to his royal highness
the duke of Parma, the colony or province of Louisiana, with the same
extent that it now has in the hands of Spain, and that it had when France
possessed it, and such as it should be after the treaties subsequently
entered into between Spain and other states."[2]

The treaty of the 30th. of April 1803 by which The United States ¶9
acquired Louisiana, after reciting this article, proceeds to state that "The
first Consul of the French republic," "doth hereby cede to The United
States, in the name of the French republic forever and in full sovereignty,
the said territory with all its rights and appurtenances as fully and in the
same manner as they have been acquired by the French republic in virtue
of the above mentioned treaty concluded with his Catholic Majesty."

The 4th. article stipulates that "there shall be sent by the government ¶10
of France a Commissary to Louisiana to the end that he do every act
necessary as well to receive from the officers of his Catholic Majesty the
said country and its dependencies, in the name of the French republic, if
it has not been already done, as to transmit it in the name of the French
republic, to the commissary or agent of The United States."[3]

On the 30th. of November 1803, Peter Clement Laussatt, Colonial ¶11
Prefect and Commissioner of the French republic authorized by full powers dated the 6th. of June 1803, to receive the surrender of the province
of Louisiana, presented those powers to Don Manuel Salcedo Governour

of Louisiana and West Florida, and to the Marquis de Casa Calvo Commissioners on the part of Spain, together with full powers to them from his Catholic Majesty to make the surrender. These full powers were dated at Barcelona the 15th. of October 1802. The act of surrender declares that in virtue of these full powers the Spanish Commissioners Don Manuel Salcedo, and the Marquis de Casa Calvo "put from this moment the said French Commissioner, the citizen Laussatt in possession of the colony of Louisiana and of its dependencies, as also of the town and island of New Orleans in the same extent which they now have, and which they had in the hands of France when she ceded them to the royal crown of Spain, and such as they should be after the treaties subsequently entered into between the states of his Catholic Majesty and those of other powers."[4]

¶12   The following is an extract from the order of the King of Spain referred to by the commissioners in the act of delivery. "Don Carlos by the grace of God" &c "Deeming it convenient to retrocede to the French republic the colony and province of Louisiana I order you as soon as the present order shall be presented to you by General Victor or other officer duely authorised by the French republic to take charge of said delivery, you will put him in possession of the colony of Louisiana and its dependencies, as also of the city and island of New Orleans with the same extent that it now has, that it had in the hands of France when she ceded it to my royal crown, and such as it ought to be after the treaties which have successively taken place between my states and those of other powers."[5]

¶13   Previous to the arrival of the French Commissioner, the Governour of the provinces of Louisiana and West Florida and the Marquis de Casa Calvo had issued their proclamation, dated the 18th. of May 1803 in which they say "His Majesty, having before his eyes the obligations imposed by the treaties, and desirous of avoiding any disputes that might arise, has deigned to resolve that the delivery of the colony and island of New Orleans which is to be made to the General of division Victor, or such other officer as may be legally authorized by the government of the French republic, shall be executed in the same terms that France ceded it to his Majesty in virtue of which the limits of both shores of the river St Louis or Mississipi shall remain as they were irrevocably fixed by the 7th. article of the definitive treaty of peace concluded at Paris the 10th. of February 1763 according to which the settlements from the river Manshac or Iberville to the line which separates the American territory from the dominions of the King, remain in possession of Spain and annexed to West Florida."[6]

¶14   On the 21st. of October 1803 Congress passed an act to enable the President to take possession of the territory ceded by France to The United States,[7] in pursuance of which commissioners were appointed to whom Monsieur Laussatt the Commissioner of the French Republic surrendered New Orleans and the province of Louisiana on the 20th. of December 1803. The surrender was made in general terms; but no actual possession was taken of the territory lying east of New Orleans. The government of The United States, however soon manifested the opinion that the whole country originally held by France, and belonging to Spain when the treaty of St Ildefonso was concluded, was by that treaty retroceded to France.

On the 24th. of February 1804 Congress passed an act for laying and ¶15 collecting duties within the ceded territories which authorized the President, whenever he should deem it expedient, to erect the shores &c of the bay and river Mobile, and of the other rivers, creeks &c emptying into the gulph of Mexico east of the said river Mobile, and west thereof to the Pascaguola inclusive into a separate district, and to establish a port of entry and delivery therein.[8] The port established in pursuance of this act was at fort Stoddert, within the acknowledged jurisdiction of The United States; and this circumstance appears to have been offered as a sufficient answer to the subsequent remonstrances of Spain against the measure. It must be considered, not as acting on the territory, but as indicating the American exposition of the treaty, and exhibiting the claim its government intended to assert.

In the same session, on the 26th. of March 1804, Congress passed an ¶16 act erecting Louisiana into two territories. This act declares that the country ceded by France to the U.S. South of the Mississi[ppi] territory, and south of an east and west line to commence on the Mississipi river at the 33d. degree of North latitude and run west to the western boundary of the cession, shall constitute a territory under the name of the territory of Orleans. Now the Mississipi territory extended to the 31st. degree of North latitude, and the country south of that territory was necessarily the country which Spain held as West Florida; but still its constituting a part of the territory of Orleans depends on the fact that it was a part of the country ceded by France to The United States. No practical application of the laws of The United States to this part of the territory was attempted, nor could be made, while the country remained in the actual possession of a foreign power.

The 14th. sec. enacts "That all grants for lands within the territories ¶17 ceded by the French republic to The United States by the treaty of the 30th. of April 1803, the title whereof was at the date of the treaty of St. Ildefonso in the crown, government, or nation of Spain, and every act and proceeding subsequent thereto of whatsoever nature towards the obtaining any grant title or claim to such lands, and under whatsoever authority transacted or pretended, be, and the same are hereby declared to be, and to have been from the beginning, null, void, and of no effect in law or equity." A Proviso excepts the titles of actual settlers acquired before the 20th. of December 1803, from the operation of this section. It was obviously intended to act on all grants made by Spain after ⟨h⟩er retrocession of Louisiana to France; and, without deciding on the extent of that retrocession, to put the titles which might be thus acquired, through the whole territory whatever might be its extent, completely under the controul of the American government.[9]

¶18   The President was authorized to appoint Registers or Recorders of land titles who were to receive and record titles to lands acquired under the Spanish and French governments, and boards of Commissioners who should receive all claims to lands, and hear and determine in a summary way all matters respecting such claims. Their proceedings were to be reported to the Secretary of the treasury, to be laid before Congress, for the final decision of that body.[10]

¶19   Previous to the acquisition of Louisiana, the Ministers of The United States had been instructed to endeavour to obtain the Floridas from Spain. After that acquisition, this object was still pursued, and the friendly aid of the French government towards its attainment was requested. On the suggestion of Mr. Talleyrand that the time was unfavourable, the design was suspended. The government of The United States however soon resumed its purpose; and the settlement of the boundaries of Louisiana was blended with the purchase of the Floridas, and the adjustment of heavy claims made by The United States for American property condemned in the ports of Spain during the war which was terminated by the treaty of Amiens.

¶20   On his way to Madrid, Mr Monroe, who was empowered in conjunction with Mr. Pinckney the American minister at the court of his Catholic Majesty, to conduct the negotiation, passed through Paris, and addressed a letter to the Minister of exterior relations, in which he detailed the objects of his mission, and his views respecting the boundaries of Louisiana. In his answer to this letter, dated the 21st. of December 1804, Mr. Talleyrand declared in decided terms that by the treaty of St Ildefonso Spain retroceded to France no part of the territory east of the Iberville which had been held and known as West Florida, and that in all the negotiations between the two governments Spain had constant[ly] refused to cede any part of the Floridas, even from the Mississipi to the Mobile. He added that he was authorized by his Imperial Majesty to say that at the beginning of the year 1802, General Bournonville had been charged to open a new negotiation with Spain for the acquisition of the Floridas; but this project had not been followed by a treaty.[11]

¶21   Had France and Spain agreed upon the boundaries of the retroceded territory before Louisiana was acquired by The United States, that agreement would undoubtedly have ascertained its limits. But the declarations of France made after parting with the province cannot be admitted as conclusive. In questions of this character, political considerations have too much influence over the conduct of nations, to permit their declarations to decide the course of an independent government in a matter vitally interesting to itself.

¶22   Soon after the arrival of Mr. Monroe at his place of destination the negotiations commenced at Aranjuez. Every word in that article of the treaty of St. Ildefonso which ceded Louisiana to France was scanned by the ministers on both sides with all the critical acumen which talents and zeal could bring into their service. Every argument drawn from collateral circumstances connected with the subject, which could be supposed to elucidate it was exhausted. No advance towards an arrangement was made, and the negotiation terminated leaving each party firm in his original opinion and purpose. Each persevered in maintaining the construction with which he had commenced.[12] The discussion has since been resumed between the two nations with as much ability and with as little success.[13] The question has been again argued at this bar with the same talent and research which it has uniformly called forth. Every topic which relates to it has been completely exhausted; and the court by reasoning on the subject could only repeat what is familiar to all.

We shall say only that the language of the article may admit of either construction, and it is scarcely possible to consider the arguments on either side without believing that they proceed from a conviction of their truth. ¶23

The phrase on which the controversy mainly depends, that Spain retrocedes Louisiana with the same extent "that it had when France possessed it," might so readily have been expressed in plain language, that it is difficult to resist the persuasion that the ambiguity was intentional. Had Louisiana been retroceded with the same extent that it had when France ceded it to Spain, or with the same extent that it had before the cession of any part of it to England, no controversy respecting its limits could have arisen. Had the parties concurred in their intention, a plain mode of expressing that intention would have presented itself to them. But Spain has always manifested infinite repugnance to the surrender of territory, and was probably unwilling to give back more than she had received. The introduction of ambiguous phrases into the treaty which power might afterwards construe according to circumstances, was a measure which the strong and the politic might not be disinclined to employ. ¶24

However this may be, it is we think incontestible that the American construction of the Article, if not entirely free from question, is supported by arguments of great strength which can not be easily confuted. ¶25

In a controversy between two nations concerning national boundary, it is scarcely possible that the courts of either should refuse to abide by the measures adopted by its own government. There being no common tribunal to decide between them, each determines for itself on its own rights; and if they cannot adjust their differences peaceably, the right remains with the strongest. The judiciary is not that department of the government to which the assertion of its interests against foreign powers is confided; and its duty commonly is to decide upon individual rights according to those principles which the political departments of the nation have established. If the course of the nation has been a plain one, its courts would hesitate to pronounce it erroneous. ¶26

¶27   We think then, however individual Judges might construe the treaty of St. Ildefonso, it is the province of the court to conform its decisions to the will of the legislature, if that will has been clearly expressed.

¶28   The convulsed state of European Spain affected her influence over her colonies; and a degree of disorder prevailed in the Floridas at which The United States could not look with indifference. In October 1810, the President issued his proclamation directing the Governour of the Orleans territory to take possession of the country as far east as the Perdido, and to hold it for The United States.[14] This measure was avowedly intended as an assertion of the title of The United States; but as an assertion which was rendered necessary in order to avoid evils which might contravene the wishes of both parties, and which would still leave the territory "a subject of fair and friendly negotiation and adjustment."

¶29   In April 1812[a] Congress passed "an act to enlarge the limits of the state of Louisiana." This act describes lines which comprehend the land in controversy, and declares that the country included within them shall become and form a part of the state of Louisiana.[15]

¶30   In May of the same year another act was passed annexing the residue of the country West of the Perdido to the Mississipi territory.[16]

¶31   And in February 1813, the President was authorized "to occupy and hold all that tract of country called West Florida which lies west of the river Perdido, not now in possession of The United States."[17]

¶32   On the 3d. of March 1817 Congress erected that part of Florida which had been annexed to the Mississi[ppi] territory into a separate territory called Alabama.[18]

¶33   The powers of government were extended to and exercised in those parts of West Florida which composed a part of Louisiana and Mississipi respectively, and a separate government was erected in Alabama.

¶34   In March 1819 Congress passed an act to enable the people of Alabama to form a constitution and state government;[19] and in December 1819, she was admitted into the union and declared one of The United States of America. The treaty of Amity settlement and limits between The United States and Spain was signed at Washington on the 22d. day of February 1819, but was not ratified by Spain till the 24th. day of October 1820, nor by The United States until the 22d. day of February 1821. So that Alabama was admitted into the union as an independent State in virtue of the title acquired by The United States to her territory under the treaty of April 1803.

¶35   After these acts of sovereign power over the territory in dispute, asserting the American construction of the treaty by which the government claims it, to maintain the opposite construction in its own courts would certainly be an anomaly in the history and practice of nations. If those departments which are entrusted with the foreign intercourse of the

[a]U.S.L. v 4. 409

nation, which assert and maintain its interests against foreign powers, have unequivocally asserted its right of dominion over a country of which it is in possession and which it claims under a treaty; if the legislature has acted on the construction thus asserted, it is not in its own courts that this construction is to be denied. A question like this respecting the boundaries of nations, is, as has been truely said, more a political than a legal question; and, in its discussion, the courts of every country must respect the pronounced will of the legislature. Had this suit been instituted immediately after the passage of the act for extending the bounds of Louisiana, could the Spanish construction of the treaty of St. Ildefonso have been maintained? Could the plaintiff have insisted that the land did not lie in Louisiana but in West Florida, that the occupation of the country by The United States was wrongful, and that his title under a Spanish grant must prevail, because the acts of Congress on the subject were founded on a misconstruction of the treaty? If it be said that this statement does not present the question fairly, because a plaintiff admits the authority of the court, let the parties be changed. If the Spanish grantee had obtained possession so as to be the defendant, could a court of The United States maintain his title under a Spanish grant made subsequent to the acquisition of Louisiana, singly on the principle that the Spanish construction of the treaty of St Ildefonso was right, and the American construction wrong? Such a decision would we think have subverted those principles which govern the relations between the legislative and judicial departments, and mark the limits of each.

¶36 If the rights of the parties are in any degree changed that change must be produced by the subsequent arrangements made between the two governments.

¶37 A "treaty of amity, settlement and limits between The United States of America and the King of Spain" was signed at Washington on the 22d. day of February 1819. By the 2d. Article "his Catholic Majesty cedes to the United States in full property and sovereignty all the territories which belong to him, situated to the Eastward of the Mississipi known by the name of East and West Florida."

¶38 The 8th. article stipulates that "all the grants of land made before the 24th. of January 1818 by his Catholic Majesty or by his lawful authorities in the said territories ceded by his Majesty to The United States shall be ratified and confirmed to the persons in possession of the lands to the same extent that the same grants would be valid if the territories had remained under the dominion of his Catholic Majesty."[20]

¶39 The court will not attempt to conceal the difficulty which is created by these articles.

¶40 It is well known that Spain had uniformly maintained her construction of the treaty of St Ildefonso. His Catholic Majesty had perseveringly insisted that no part of West Florida had been ceded by that treaty, and that the whole country which had been known by that name still belonged to him. It is then a fair inference from the language of the treaty that he did not mean to retrace his steps, and relinquish his pretensions but to cede on a sufficient consideration all that he had claimed as his, and consequently in the 8th. Article to stipulate for the confirmation of all those grants which he had made while the title remained in him.

¶41   But The United States had uniformly denied the title set up by the Crown of Spain, had insisted that a part of West Florida had been transferred to France by the treaty of St Ildefonso, and ceded to The United States by the treaty of April 1803, had asserted this construction by taking actual possession of the country; and had extended its legislation over it. The United States therefore cannot be understood to have admitted that this country belonged to his Catholic Majesty, or that it passed from him to them by this article. Had his Catholic Majesty ceded to The United States "all the territories situated to the eastward of the Mississipi known by the name of East and West Florida,["] omitting the words "which belong to him," The United States in receiving this cession might have sanctioned the right to make it, and might have been bound to consider the 8th. article as coextensive with the second. The stipulation of the 8th. article might have been construed to be an admission that West Florida to its full extent was ceded by this treaty.

¶42   But the insertion of these words materially affect the construction of the article. They cannot be rejected as surplusage. They have a plain meaning, and that meaning can be no other than to limit the extent of the cession. We cannot say they were inserted carelessly or unadvisedly, and must understand them according to their obvious import.

¶43   It is not improbable that terms were selected which might not compromise the dignity of either government, and which each might understand consistently with its former pretensions. But if a court of The United States would have been bound under the state of things existing at the signature of the treaty to consider the territory then composing a part of the State of Louisiana as rightfully belonging to The United States, it would be difficult to construe this article into an admission that it belonged rightfully to his Catholic Majesty.

¶44   The 6th. article of the treaty may be considered in connexion with the second. The 6th. stipulates that "the inhabitants of the territories which his Catholic Majesty cedes to The United States by this treaty, shall be incorporated in the Union of The United States as soon as may be consistent with the principles of the federal constitution." This article, according to its obvious import, extends to the whole territory which was ceded. The stipulation for the incorporation of the inhabitants of the ceded territory into the Union is coextensive with the cession. But the country in which the land in controversy lies was already incorporated into the Union. It composed a part of the State of Louisiana which was already a member of the American confederacy.

¶45   A part of West Florida lay east of the Perdido; and to that the right of his

Catholic Majesty was acknowledged. There was then an ample subject on which the words of the cession might operate, without discarding those which limit its general expressions.

Such is the construction which the court would put on the treaties by ¶46 which The United States have acquired the country east of New Orleans. But an explanation of the 8th. article seems to have been given by the parties which may vary this construction.

It was discovered that three large grants which had been supposed, at ¶47 the signature of the treaty, to have been made subsequent to the 24th. of January 1818 bore a date anterior to that period. Considering these grants as fraudulent, The United States insisted on an express declaration annulling them. This demand was resisted by Spain; and the ratification of the treaty was for some time suspended. At length his Catholic Majesty yielded, and the following clause was introduced into his ratification, "Desirous at the same time of avoiding any doubt or ambiguity concerning the meaning of the 8th. Article of the treaty in respect to the date which is pointed out in it as the period for the confirmation of the grants of lands in the Floridas made by me, or by the competent authorities in my royal name which point of date was fixed in the positive understanding of the three grants of land made in favour of the Duke of Alagon, the Count of Punon rostro, and Don Pedro de Vargas being annulled by its tenor, I think it proper to declare that the said three grants have remained and do remain entirely annulled and invalid; and that neither the three individuals mentioned, nor those who may have title or interest through them, can avail themselves of the said grants at any time or in any manner; under which explicit declaration the said 8th. Article is to be understood as ratified."[21] One of these grants, that to Vargas, lies west of the Perdido.

It has been argued, and with great force, that this explanation forms a ¶48 part of the article. It may be considered as if introduced into it as a proviso or exception to the stipulation in favor of grants anterior to the 24 of January 1818. The article may be understood as if it had been written that "All the grants of land made before the 24th. of January 1818 by his Catholic Majesty or his lawful authorities in the said territories ceded by his Majesty to the United States, except those made to the Duke of Alagon, the Count of Punon Rostro, and Don Pedro de Vargas, shall be ratified and confirmed" &c.

Had this been the form of the original article, it would be difficult to ¶49 resist the construction that the excepted grants were withdrawn from it by the exception, and would otherwise have been with its provisions. Consequently that all other fair grants within the time specified were as obligatory on The United States as on his Catholic Majesty.

One other Judge and myself are inclined to adopt this opinion. The ¶50 majority of the court however thinks differently. They suppose that these three large grants being made about the same time, under circumstances strongly indicative of unfairness, and two of them lying east of the Perdido, might be objected to on the ground of fraud common to them all, without implying any opinion that one of them which was for lands lying within The United States, and most probably in part sold by the government, could have been other wise confirmed. The government might well insist on closing all future controversy relative to these grants, which might so materially interfere with its own rights and policy in its future disposition of the ceded lands, and not allow them to become the subject of judicial investigation; while other grants, though deemed by it to be invalid, might be left to the ordinary course of the law. The form of the ratification ought not, in their opinion, to change the natural construction of the words of the 8th. article, or extend them to embrace grants not otherwise intended to be confirmed by it. An extreme solicitude to provide against injury or inconvenience from the known existence of such large grants by insisting upon a declaration of their absolute nullity, can, in their opinion, furnish no satisfactory proof that the government meant to recognize the small grants as valid, which, in every previous act and struggle, it had proclaimed to be void, as being for lands within the american territory.

¶51   Whatever difference may exist respecting the effect of the ratification, in whatever sense it may be understood, we think the sound construction of the 8th. article will not enable this court to apply its provisions to the present case.

¶52   The words of the article are that "All the grants of land made before the 24th. of Jany. 1818 by his Catholic Majesty &c shall be ratified and confirmed to the persons in possession of the lands, to the same extent that the same grants would be valid if the territories had remained under the dominion of his Catholic Majesty." Do these words act directly on the grants so as to give validity to those not otherwise valid, or do they pledge the faith of The United States to pass acts which shall ratify and confirm them?

¶53   A treaty is in its nature a contract between two nations, not a legislative act. It does not generally effect of itself the object to be accomplished, especially so far as its operation is infraterritorial, but is carried into execution by the sovereign power of the respective parties to the instrument. In The United States a different principle is established. Our constitution declares a treaty to be the law of the land. It is consequently to be regarded in courts of justice as equivalent to an act of the legislature whenever it operates of itself without the aid of any legislative provision. But where the terms of the stipulation import a contract, where either of the parties engage to perform a particular act, the treaty addresses itself to the political, not to the judicial department, and the Legislature must execute the contract before it can become a rule for the court. The article under consideration does not declare that all the grants made by his Catholic Majesty before the 24th. of January 1818 shall be valid to the same extent as if the ceded territories had remained under his dominion. It does not say that those grants are hereby confirmed. Had such been its language, it would have acted directly on the subject, and would have repealed those acts of Congress which were repugnant to it. But its language is that those grants shall be ratified and confirmed to the persons in possession &c. By whom shall they be ratified and confirmed? This seems to be the language of contract; and if it is, the ratification and confirmation which are promised, must be the act of the legislature. Until such act shall be passed, the court is not at liberty to disregard the existing laws on the subject. Congress appears to have understood this article as it is understood by the court. Boards of Commissioners have been appointed for East and West Florida to receive claims for lands; and on their reports titles to lands not exceeding ⟨ ⟩oo acres have been confirmed to a very large amount. On the 23d. of May 1828, "an act was passed supplementary to the several acts providing for the settlement and confirmation of private land claims in Florida, the 6th. Sec. of which enacts that "all claims to land within the territory of Florida embraced by the treaty between Spain and The United States of the 22d. of Feby. 1819, which shall not be decided and finally settled under the foregoing provisions of this act, containing a greater quantity of land than the Commissioners were authorized to decide, and which have not been reported as antedated or forged, &c shall be received and adjudicated by the Judges of the superior court of the district within which the land lies upon the petition of the claimant" &c "Provided that nothing in this section shall be construed to enable the Judges to take cognizance of any claim annulled by the said treaty or the decree ratifying the same by the King of Spain, nor any claim not presented to the Commissioners or register and Receiver.["] An appeal is allowed from the decision of the Judge of the District to this court. No such act of confirmation has been extended to grants for lands lying west of the Perdido.[22]

¶54 The Act of 1804 erecting Louisiana into two territories has been already mentioned. It annuls all grants for lands in the ceded territories, the title whereof was, at the date of the treaty of St Ildefonso, in the crown of Spain. The grant in controversy is not brought within any of the exceptions from the enacting clause.

¶55 The legislature has passed many subsequent acts previous to the treaty of 1819, the object of which was to adjust the titles to lands in the country acquired by the treaty of 1803. They cautiously confirm to residents all incomplete titles to lands for which a warrant or order of survey had been obtained previous to the 1st. day of October 1800.

¶56 An act passed in April 1814 confirms incomplete titles to lands in the state of Louisiana for which a warrant or order of survey had been granted prior to the 20th. of Decr. 1803 where the claimant or the person under whom he claims was a resident of the province of Louisiana on that day, or at the date of the concession, warrant or order of survey, and where the tract does not exceed 640 acres. This act extends to those cases only which had been reported by the board of Commissioners, and annexes to the confirmation several conditions which it is unnecessary to review because the plaintiff does not claim to come within the provisions of the act.[23]

¶57   On the 3d. of March 1819 Congress passed an act confirming all complete grants to land from the Spanish government contained in the reports made by the Commissioners appointed by the President for the purpose of adjusting titles which had been deemed valid by the Commissioners; and also all claims reported as aforesaid founded on any order of survey, requette, permission to settle or any written evidence of claim derived from the Spanish authorities which ought in the opinion of the commissioners to be confirmed, and which by the said reports appear to be derived from the Spanish governments before the 20th. day of December 1803 and the land claimed to have been cultivated and inhabited on or before that day.[24]

¶58   Though the order of survey in this case was granted before the 20th. of December 1803, the plf. does not bring himself within this act.

¶59   Subsequent acts have passed in 1820, 1822, and 1826.[25] But they only confirm claims approved by the Commissioners, among which the plaintiff does not allege his to have been placed.

¶60   Congress has reserved to itself the supervision of the titles reported by its commissioners, and has confirmed those which the commissioners have approved, but has passed no law withdrawing grants generally for lands west of the Perdido from the operation of the 14th. Sec. of the act of 1804, or repealing that section.

¶61   We are of opinion then that the court committed no errour in dismissing the petition of the plaintiff, and that the judgement ought to be affirmed with costs.

AD, Foster and Elam v. Neilson, Appellate Opinions, RG 267, DNA; printed, Richard Peters, *Reports of Cases Argued and Adjudged in the Supreme Court of the United States* . . . , II (Philadelphia, 1829), 299–317. For JM's deletions and interlineations, see Textual Notes below.

1. JM here inserted a note, "(reinstate the following paragraph)," referring to the third paragraph, which he had originally struck through. In the left margin opposite the third paragraph, someone wrote "reinstated."

2. The third article of the Treaty of St. Ildefonso is embodied in the first article of treaty of 1803 by which the U.S. acquired Louisiana (Hunter Miller, ed., *Treaties and Other International Acts of the United States of America*, II (Washington, 1931), 499. JM could have used the text as printed in *Laws of the United States of America, from the 4th of March, 1789, to the 4th of March, 1815* (5 vols.; Philadelphia and Washington, 1815), I, 134–140.

3. Miller, ed., *Treaties and Other International Acts*, II, 500, 501. The tenth paragraph was written on a separate sheet of paper and marked for insertion at the appropriate point.

4. This and the two subsequent documents quoted by JM had also been quoted in argument by Coxe, who noted that they had "recently been submitted to Congress in a communication from the President, and will shortly constitute a part of the history of the nation" (2 Pet. 270–71). He referred to President Adams's message of 11 Feb. 1829 informing Congress that a translation of all Spanish and French ordinances concerning land titles in Florida and other territories formerly belonging to France and Spain had been deposited at the state department. This compilation was made by Joseph M. White (1781–1839), Florida's delegate to Congress, and was printed as *Message from the President of the United States, Transmitting Information in Relation to the Execution of the Act of 23d May Last, "Supplementary to the Several Acts Providing for the Settlement and Confirmation of Private Land Claims in Florida," &c.* (U.S. House, 20th Cong., 2d sess., 1829, H. Doc 121). The act of delivery of Louisiana by Spain to France, 30 Nov. 1803, is document No. 22 in White's compilation (ibid., 165–66). Neither Coxe nor JM appears to have used this source, however, for their quotations from the French and Spanish documents do not exactly match the translations in White.

5. Document No. 20 in White's compilation (ibid., 161–63).

6. Document No. 21 in White's compilation (ibid., 163–65).

7. *U.S. Statutes at Large*, II, 245. This act passed on 31 Oct. 1803.

8. Ibid., 251, 254.

9. Ibid., 283, 287–89.

10. The reference is to the act of 2 Mar. 1805 "for ascertaining and adjusting the titles and claims to lands, within the territory of Orleans, and the district of Louisiana" (ibid., 324, 326–27).

11. Monroe to Talleyrand, 8 Nov. 1804; Talleyrand to Monroe, 21 Dec. 1804 (*State Papers and Publick Documents of the United States . . .* [3d ed.; 12 vols.; Boston, 1819], XII, 197–202, 203–5; *ASP, Foreign Relations*, II, 634–35, 635–36). In *ASP* Talleyrand's letter is correctly stated to be addressed to John Armstrong, the American minister in Paris.

12. JM referred to the negotiations in 1805 between Monroe and Charles Pinckney and Spanish foreign minister Pedro de Cevallos (*State Papers and Publick Documents*, XII, 206–326; *ASP, Foreign Relations*, II, 636–69).

13. Further negotiations took place in 1817 and 1818 between Secretary of State Adams and Spanish minister Don Luis de Onís (*State Papers and Publick Documents*, XII, 5–195; *ASP, Foreign Relations*, II, 441–79).

14. President Madison's proclamation of 27 Oct. 1810 (*State Papers and Publick Documents*, VII, 480–82; J. C. A. Stagg et al., eds., *The Papers of James Madison: Presidential Series*, II [Charlottesville, Va., 1992], 595–96).

15. *U.S. Statutes at Large*, II, 708–9. JM's note cited the 1815 edition of *Laws of the United States of America*, IV, 409.

16. *U.S. Statutes at Large*, II, 734.

17. This act of 12 Feb. 1813 was among a series of acts concerning the occupation of the Floridas that were enacted in secret sessions of Congress in 1811 and 1813 and were not promulgated until the publication of the session acts of the Fifteenth Congress ending in Apr. 1818 (ibid., II, 713 n.; III, 472).

18. Ibid., III, 371–73

19. Ibid., 489–92.

20. The definitive text of the treaty is in Hunter Miller, ed., *Treaties and Other International Acts of the United States of America*, III (Washington, 1933), 3–18. A contemporary publication of the treaty was included in *Laws of the United States of America: From the 4th of March, 1815, to the 4th of March, 1821* (Washington, 1822), 614–31. This was a continuation of the five-volume edition of the laws published in 1815 and was thus volume VI of the ongoing series.

21. Miller, ed., *Treaties and Other International Acts*, III, 18–20.

22. *U.S. Statutes at Large*, IV, 284–86.

23. Ibid., III, 121–23.

24. Ibid., 528–32

25. The acts of 11 May 1820, 8 May 1822, and 31 Mar. 1826 (ibid., 573–75, 707–8; IV, 152).

Textual Notes

¶ 1	l. 1	errour ~~against~~ in the
	l. 2	States ~~for~~ ↑for↓ the
	ll. 4–5	grant ↑for 40,000 arpents of land↓ made
	l. 8	the ↑return of the↓ survey
	l. 15	cause is ~~now~~ ↑brought↓ before this court ~~on~~ ↑by↓
¶ 2	l. 1	and ↑at one time very↓ interesting
¶ 3	ll. 1–2	research ~~between~~ ↑by↓ the
	l. 5	territory ↑as part of Louisiana↓ to
	l. 6	Paris ~~made~~ signed on
	ll. 8–9	earnestness ~~insisted~~ ↑maintained↓ that
¶ 4	ll. 4–5	bay of ~~mobile~~ ↑Mobile.↓ Spain was
¶ 6	l. 1	acknowledged ~~proprietor~~ ↑sovereign↓ of
	l. 3	divided ~~Florida into~~ ↑ the ↓ ~~the~~ ↑his late acquisition in the south, into↓ two
	l. 4	comprehended ↑so much of↓ the country
¶ 7	l. 3	provinces ~~were~~ continued
	l. 5	dominion of ~~Spain~~ his Catholic
¶ 8	l. 2	Ildefonso, ~~by~~ the 3d.
¶ 11	ll. 1–2	Laussatt, ↑Colonial Prefect and↓ Commissioner
	l. 2	republic, ~~empowered~~ ↑authorized↓ by full
	l. 3	1803, to ~~receive~~ ↑receive↓ the
	l. 4	Louisiana, ~~from~~ presented those
	l. 13	which they ↑now↓ have ~~at this time~~ and
¶ 13	l. 2	Florida ~~in the following terms. "His Majesty having before his eyes~~ and the
	l. 16	Florida." ~~Th Monsieur Laussatt the French Commissioner for receiving and delivering the province, delivered it to The United States on the 20th of December 1803~~
¶ 14	ll. 4–5	the French ~~Laussatt~~ ↑republic↓ surrendered
	ll. 6–7	December 1803. ~~no actual surrender was made~~ ↑The surrender was made in general terms; but no actual possession was taken↓ of the territory
	ll. 7–8	Orleans ~~, but the~~ ↑. The↓ government
	l. 8	States, ↑however↓ soon
	l. 9	that the ↑whole↓ country ~~went~~ originally
¶ 15	ll. 7–8	act was ~~however~~ ↑at fort Stoddert,↓ within
	ll. 9–10	States; and ~~when, in the subsequent negotiations between the two powers, Spain~~ complained of it, this circumstance ~~was offered and . . . .~~ ↑appears to have been offered as a sufficient answer to the subsequent remonstrances of Spain against the measure.↓ It
¶ 16	ll. 2–3	the country ↑ceded by France to the U.S.↓ South of
	l. 4	line to ~~begin commence~~ commence on the Mississipi ~~territory~~ river at

	ll. 9–10	still its ~~annexation to~~ ↑constituting a part of↓ the
	l. 11	France to ~~the~~ The
	l. 12	The United States ~~was~~ to this
¶17	l. 2	ceded by ~~France~~ the French
	ll. 9–10	settlers ~~from the oper~~ acquired before
	l. 10	section. ~~The 16th. Sec~~ extends ↑continues↓ ~~the act enabling the President to take possession of the territories ceded by France until the first day of the following October.~~ ↑The island of↓ New Orleans, ~~and Louisiana West of the Mississipi, were already in possession of The United States. This section therefore could be intended only for the country east of that river.~~
	l. 12	Louisiana to ~~Spain~~ ↑France↓; and
	ll. 13–14	retrocession, ~~whatever might be the extent of the territory~~ to put the titles which might be thus acquired, ↑through the whole territory whatever might be its extent,↓ completely
¶18	l. 1	appoint ~~regis~~ ↑Registers↓ or Recorders
	l. 3	and ~~boards~~ boards of Commissioners
¶19	l. 9	States ~~on Spain~~ for American
¶20	l. 2	minister at ~~Madr~~ the
	ll. 13–14	had been ~~authorized~~ ↑charged↓ to
	l. 14	with Spain ~~relative~~ for the
¶22	l. 3	Ildefonso ~~by~~ which ↑ceded↓ Louisiana
	ll. 3–4	scanned ↑by the ministers↓ on both
	ll. 10–11	The ~~subject~~ ↑discussion↓ has since been ~~revived~~ ↑resumed↓ between
¶24	l. 8	intention, ~~it is not probable that~~ a
	l. 11	probably ↑unwilling to↓ give
	l. 13	circumstances, ~~is~~ ↑was↓ a measure ~~of~~ which
¶25	l. 3	arguments ~~which have~~ of great
¶26	l. 1	concerning ~~their~~ ↑national↓ boundary,
¶28	l. 2	prevailed in ~~the colo~~ the
	l. 6	This ~~step~~ ↑measure↓ was
¶29	l. 4	Louisiana. ~~In Feby. 1813 Congress passed an act authorizing the President "to occupy and hold all that tract of country called West Florida which lies west of the river Perdido, not now in possession of The United States."~~
¶30	l. 2	Mississipi ~~country~~ ↑territory.↓
¶32	l. 3	called ~~Al~~ Alabama.
¶33	l. 1 beg	~~The powers Government~~ The powers of government
	l. 2	parts of ↑West↓ Florida
¶34	l. 3	1819 ~~Alabama was~~ she was
	l. 9	States ↑to her territory↓ under the
¶35	l. 10	denied. ~~A dist~~ A question
	l. 11	has been [*erasure*] truely said,
	l. 13	Had this ↑suit↓ been instituted
	l. 22	grantee ~~shall have~~ ↑had↓ obtained
	l. 23	could ~~an . . .~~ a court of
¶37	l. 1 beg.	~~The~~ ↑A↓ "treaty of

¶38 l. 3   by his ~~said~~ Majesty

¶40 ll. 5–7   that he ~~understood himself to cede all that~~ ↑ did not mean to
                retrace his steps, and relinquish his pretensions but to cede
                on a sufficient consideration all that↓ he

     ll. 7–8   consequently ~~understood~~ ↑in↓ the

¶41 l. 3   ceded ~~by France~~ to The United

     l. 8   article. ~~Had the cession been~~ Had his

     l. 11   cession ~~would~~ ↑might↓ have

     l. 12   and ~~must~~ ↑might↓ have been

     l. 14   article ~~must~~ ↑might↓ have been construed ~~on the~~ ↑to be an↓
                admission

¶44 ll. 5–6   constitution." This ~~stipulation~~ ↑article↓, according

¶45 l. 1 beg ~~So the 7th article stipulates~~ A part of

¶46 l. 1   is the ~~—~~ construction which

     l. 3   explanation ↑of the 8th. article↓ seems

¶47 l. 1 beg ~~Three~~ ↑It was discovered that↓ three

     l. 5   demand was ~~for some time~~ resisted

     ll. 20–21 as ratified. ↑One of these grants, that to Vargas, lies west of
                the Perdido.↓

¶48 ll. 1–2   forms ~~as entirely~~ a part of the article. ↑It may be considered↓
                as

     l. 4   1818. ~~That~~ The article ~~must~~ ↑may ~~and ought to~~↓ be
                understood as

     l. 5   grants ~~which~~ of land

     l. 7   United ↑States,↓ except

¶49 l. 1   the form ~~of the original article, ↑the argument must have . . .
                ↓ the construction ↑it . . . ↓must have been that the excepted
                grants were with drawn from the article by the exception.
                That made to Don Pedro de Vagas is understood to lie west of
                the Perdido and would otherwise have been confirmed by it.
                One other Judge and myself are much inclined to adopt this
                opinion.~~ of the original

     l. 4   other ↑fair↓ grants

¶50 l. 9   controversy ~~with respect~~ ↑relative↓ to

     ll. 21–22 within the ~~American~~ american territory

¶51 l. 1   difference ~~might~~ ↑may↓ exist

¶52 l. 1   land made ~~by his Catholic Majesty &c~~ before

¶53 l. 7   equivalent to ~~a legisla~~ an act

     ll. 12–13 court. ~~In the case~~ ↑The article↓ under

     l. 13   declare that ↑all↓ the

     ll. 15–16 dominion. ↑It does not say that those grants are hereby
                confirmed.↓ Had

     l. 22   which ~~is~~ ↑are↓ promised, must

     l. 23   such ~~acts~~ ↑act↓ shall be

     l. 27   titles ↑to lands not exceeding [?]oo acres↓ have been

     ll. 38–39 nothing in this ~~act~~ ↑section↓ shall

     ll. 41–42 Spain, ↑nor any claim not presented to the Commissioners or
                register and Receiver.["]↓ An

     l. 43   District to ~~the~~ this court

¶54 l. 4   within ↑any of↓ the
¶55 l. 2   titles ~~for~~ to lands
¶56 ll. 1–2   to lands ~~for which~~ in the
     ll. 5–6   survey, ↑and where the tract does not exceed 640 acres.↓ This
¶57 l. 3   the ~~government~~ ↑President↓ for
     l. 5   claims ↑reported as aforesaid↓ founded
¶58 l. 2   1803 the ↑plf.↓ does not
¶60 l. 3   passed no ~~general~~ law
     l. 4   of the ↑14th. sec. of the↓ act

To Joseph Hopkinson

My dear Sir   [Washington, 18 March 1829]
I received some time past a small packet from Mrs. O Sullivan which she requested me to return, and I now take the liberty of doing it through you. I should not give you this trouble did I not fear that a letter addressed to her might miscarry, and she expresses a strong desire to have the papers it incloses again in her possession.

Among the many friends who rejoice at your late appointment, there is not one who takes a more sincere and lively interest in it than myself. I had at first supposed it impossible that the Senate could hesitate to give the President good advice, at least on this occasion; but I soon found I was mistaken, and the apprehension produced by the first delay was strengthened by all the intelligence which rumour gave us. We were told that a great principle, the principle of **R E F O R M,** must be established, that the public will required it should be universal, and we feared that not even you could escape from its all comprehensive operation. The gratification received from the dissipation of our fears was not a little increased by learning the decided majority by which the nomination was approved. Notwithstanding the strength and violence of the current, we are told that scarcely a Senator about whose good opinion you would be very solicitous, voted against you. This is pleasant, and I congratulate you upon it.[1]

You hear from others and see in the papers more than I can tell you respecting the transactions of this lately busy place. Rumour tells us more I would hope than is true. The President it is said is not himself inclined to proscription. This I am inclined to believe, because I think a President of The United States will always be more disposed to conciliate than exasperate; and must always feel some reluctance at inflicting injury; But he is brought in by a hungry and vindictive party frequently, who do not feel his responsibility, and who demand pay for their services. His better judgement and better feelings too often yield to their importunities.

My principles lead me to wish every administration to do well, because I love the government and wish it to be well administered. I therefore hope as long as hope can find any thing to feed on. Yet I perceive much more to fear than to hope for the future. I do not mean to apply this meerly to the existing President. Farewell; That you may be happy and that Providence may continue to take care of our country is the constant prayer of your affectionate friend

J MARSHALL

ALS, Hopkinson Papers, PHi. Addressed to Hopkinson in Philadelphia. Endorsement on address leaf in hand of Bushrod Washington: "Forwarded by / Yr friend / B. Washington / Mansion house 3d St." Date assigned on basis of JM to Barbara O'Sullivan, 18 Mar. 1829.

1. President Adams made a recess appointment of Hopkinson as U.S. District judge in Oct. 1828 and subsequently nominated him on 11 Dec. More than two months elapsed between his nomination and confirmation by the Senate on 23 Feb. 1829. A motion to postpone the nomination until 4 Mar. was defeated by a vote of 28 to 15 (JM to Story, 29 Oct. 1828 and n. 5; *Journal of the Executive Proceedings of the Senate* [3 vols.; Washington, D.C., 1828], III, 621, 650).

To Mary W. Marshall

My dearest Polly   Washington March 18th. 29

As the time for the rising of our court approaches I grow beyond measure impatient to see you. I now think we shall rise on saturday, and in that event I hope to be with you on monday. Should any thing occur to detain us longer I will write to you; but should the court rise on saturday I shall not write again. We have had a very laborious session. This however does not distress me. I anticipate with the more pleasure the happiness of being with you in Richmond.

Farewell my dearest Polly. I hope to find you in as good health as when we parted, I am your ever affectionate

J MARSHALL

Facsimile of ALS, Paul C. Richards, Catalog No. 202 (Templeton, Mass., 1986), item #72. Described as "one full page, quarto" and as having address leaf bearing Washington postmark.

To Barbara O'Sullivan

Madam[1]   Washington March 18th. 1829

I now return you under cover to Mr. Hopkinson the letters you trans-mitted me in yours of the 11th. of February.[2] That from Mr. Hopkinson is written with the gentlemanly good feeling and kindness of heart which those who know him alway⟨s⟩ look for and always find. If the other is from you⟨r⟩ son and daughter it cannot be read without deep regret. But the ties between parent and child are too strong to be absolutely severed, and the hope may be cherished that the return of better feelings and a just sense of duty may restore harmony between you and them.[3] Very respectfully I am Madam Your Obedt

J MARSHALL

ALS, Collins Collection, CoCCC. Addressed to Mrs. O'Sullivan in Philadelphia with the note "The attention of / The Honble Mr. Hopkinson." Endorsed: "March 18. 1829 / from Marshal." Another endorsement: "court of Human Relations."

1. Barbara O'Sullivan (1783–1851), also known as Barbara O'Sullivan Addicks, was of the Irish Catholic family O'Sullivan or O'Sullivan-Beare. She then resided in Philadelphia, having led a peripatetic life on two continents. She was the daughter of Thomas Herbert O'Sullivan (d. 1824), who while serving in the British army in New York City in 1782 married Mary McCready, daughter of a local merchant. After separating from and then divorcing his wife, Thomas O'Sullivan placed his daughter in a convent in Montreal, where she remained until 1798. She then returned to New York, apparently at her mother's behest. In 1799 she married Joseph Lee, a Philadelphia merchant, by whom she had a son and two daughters. In 1813 Lee obtained a divorce from her after she became involved with John Edward Addicks, a German merchant then living in Philadelphia. She married Addicks in 1813 and had two sons and a daughter by him. In 1816 she and her second husband went to Germany, where she lived for the next eight years. By 1824 she was in New Orleans, where her husband died. Her father also died in 1824, and she seems to have dropped "Addicks" from her name (only to reinstate it some years later) in order to obtain her share of her father's estate.

O'Sullivan's wanderings during the next several years brought her (now a widow with young children in tow) to Nashville, Cincinnati, Charlottesville, Richmond, and, most recently, Washington, D.C. She had resumed her peculiar practice (begun while in Europe) of wearing men's clothing, evidently for practical reasons of personal safety when traveling alone. By her own admission, she strove "to obtain the notice of great men," to whom she turned for financial aid and subscriptions for her book projects. In the summer of 1827 she spent a night at the home of James Madison, whose aid she sought in meeting expenses incurred at Charlottesville. In August of that year she was in Richmond, where she met JM, who headed a subscription list for her book (subscribing for two copies at ten dollars). The next year she was in Washington importuning President Adams, who acidly recorded the encounter in his diary: "Mrs. O'Sullivan came again with her tale of misery and distress, her children, her man's attire, and her book, for which she is soliciting subscriptions. It is a difficult thing to persevere in kindness with a half-insane man—with a half-insane woman, impossible. She wrote me a long letter some days since, offering, if I would supply her wants of money, to resume her female raiment. I now told her that I knew not why she renewed her application to me, as I had several months since given her a definite answer, more than once repeated. She said she was sensible of the extreme prejudices in this country against her male clothing; and I told her that I partook of those prejudices. I gave her a five-dollar bill, and entreated her not to come to me again."

Despite this rebuff, O'Sullivan persisted in her undertakings and achieved some success. At the time she was working on a French grammar for children, which she translated from German and published in 1831 (under the name of Barbara O'Sullivan Addicks) as *An Elementary Practical Book for Learning to Speak the French Language.* This text went through many editions during the next two decades. The same year, in Philadelphia, she launched an unsuccessful effort to create a weekly journal the *Psyche,* intended "principally for the female portion of the community." Her aim was "to advocate the practice of the milder virtues, cultivate the mind, improve the manners, and dispose the heart to kindly affections." Earlier in 1831 she delivered a lecture on education at the Franklin Institute in Philadelphia, a copy of which she sent to Adams and received a polite reply. In 1837 she published this and other lectures in a pamphlet, *Essay on Education; in Which the Subject Is Treated as a Natural Science.* She dedicated this work "to the memory of the late right honorable John Marshall, Chief Justice of the United States," having obtained his reluctant permission a few months before his death. Her eccentric personality passed down to her grandson, John Edward O'Sullivan Addicks (1841–1919), a gas tycoon, philanderer, and aspiring politician who in the late nineteenth century launched a protracted and unsuccessful attempt to purchase a U.S. Senate seat from the Delaware legislature (The O'Sullivan Family, V: The Major's Daughter, Barbara O'Sullivan Addicks, Ms, PHi; Barbara O'Sullivan to James Madison [two letters, June or July 1827], Madison Papers, DLC]; Barbara O'Sullivan to Nicholas Trist, 25 Aug. 1827, Trist Papers, DLC; Barbara O'Sullivan to John Quincy Adams, 16 Feb. 1828; John Quincy Adams to Barbara O'Sullivan Addicks, 25 Sept. 1831, Adams Papers, MHi; Charles Francis Adams, ed., *Memoirs of John Quincy Adams Comprising Portions of His Diary from 1795 to 1848,* VIII [Philadelphia, 1876], 56–57; Bertha Monica Stearns, "Philadelphia Magazines for Ladies:1830–1860," *Pennsylvania Magazine of History and Biography,* LXIX [1945], 208).

2. Letter not found.

3. The son and daughter mentioned by JM evidently refer to her children by Joseph Lee. In 1813 Joseph Hopkinson represented Barbara O'Sullivan Addicks (as she was then known) in a legal case that sheds light on the circumstances of her marriage and divorce from Lee and subsequent marriage to John Edward Addicks. Lee brought a habeas corpus action to gain custody of his two daughters, who had lived with their mother since birth. The couple's son remained with his father after Barbara separated from her husband around 1809. Owing to financial setbacks, Lee made no provision for her support and that of her daughters. Lee obtained a divorce from her in June 1813 on grounds of adultery with Addicks, with whom she had been living for several years and borne a son the preceding December. A few days after the divorce, Barbara married Addicks, apparently unaware of a Pennsylvania law prohibiting "the party who is guilty of adultery, from marrying with the paramour, during the life of the former husband." Although expressing its "disapprobation of the mother's conduct," the court found no fault in her treatment of her children and "considering their tender age" concluded that they should remain with their mother (The O'Sullivan Family, V: The Major's Daughter, Barbara O'Sullivan Addicks, Ms, PHi; Commonwealth v. Addicks and Wife, 5 Binn. 520–22 [Pa. Sup. Ct., East. Dist. 1813]).

To [Robert] H. Small

Sir[1]   Washington March 18th. 1829

I received your letter of January 9th. respecting the copies of the Am Colonies in your possession, but have deferred writing to you on the subject till now.[2]

The price of the book was too high at first, and it is probable that difficulty would now be found in disposing of it even at a reduced price. If you can do any thing with it, I am content with any disposition you may make showing you half the profits as a commission. If nothing else can be done I wish them packed away if it can be done without inconvenience to yourself and remain a year or two when I may perhaps have it in my power to do something with them. I should be willing to exchange them for other books. I am Sir respectfully, Your Obedt

J MARSHALL

I have some idea they would sell in the west. But I have too little information on these subjects to rely on any opinion I might form.

ALS (owned by James Marshall Plaskitt, Upperville, Va., 1973). Addressed to "Richard H. Small" in Philadelphia. Endorsed incorrectly "March 14th 1829."

1. The addressee was not "Richard" but Robert H. Small, presumably a son or relation of Abraham Small, publisher of JM's *History of the Colonies*. In a subsequent letter to the same correspondent, which JM addressed to "R. H. Small," an endorsement identifies the recipient as Robert H. Small (JM to Robert H. Small, 3 Dec. 1829). This is probably the same Robert H. Small who published *A Catalogue of Law Books: Published and for Sale by Robert H. Small* (Philadelphia, 1857).

2. Letter not found.

Weston v. The City Council of Charleston
Opinion
U.S. Supreme Court, 18 March 1829

In February 1823 the city council of Charleston, South Carolina, adopted an ordinance laying a tax on 6 and 7 percent stock of the United States. Plowden Weston and others, holders of United States stock, immediately applied to Judge Elihu Hall Bay for a writ of prohibition to restrain the city council from imposing the tax on the ground that the ordinance was repugnant to the Constitution. After hearing arguments in chambers, Judge Bay ordered the issuing of the writ of prohibition on 22 April 1823. The city council then appealed to the Constitutional Court of South Carolina, which in May 1824 reversed Judge Bay's order and upheld the constitutionality of the ordinance by a vote of four to three. Judge John S. Richardson (1777–1850) delivered the majority opinion, while Judge Daniel Huger (1779–1854) delivered the minority opinion. These opinions, along with Judge Bay's opinion accompanying his order for the writ of prohibition, were entered on the record that went up to the Supreme Court by writ of error in 1825. The case was submitted to the Court without argument on 3 February 1827. In the meantime doubts arose about the Supreme Court's jurisdiction under section 25 of the Judiciary Act. At the 1829 term, on 28 February and 10 March, the Court heard arguments on the jurisdiction and then on the merits. Robert Y. Hayne represented the plaintiffs; Hugh S. Legaré and Henry N. Cruger appeared for the defendants. Marshall delivered the Court's opinion on 18 March 1829 (Weston v. City Council of Charleston, App. Cas. No. 1326; City Council v. Weston, Harp. 340–54 [Const. Ct., S.C., 1824]; John Belton O'Neall, *Biographical Sketches of the Bench and Bar of South Carolina* [2 vols.; 1859; Spartanburg, S.C., 1975 reprint], I, 140–42 ; U.S. Sup. Minutes, 28 Feb. 1829, 10 and 18 Mar. 1829).

Weston & al

v

The city Council of Charleston[1]

¶1   This case was argued on its merits at a preceding term; but a doubt having arisen with the court respecting its jurisdiction in cases of prohibition, that doubt was suggested to the bar and a reargument was requested. It has been reargued at this term.

¶2   The power of this court to revise the judgements of a state tribunal depends on the 25th. section of the judicial act. That section enacts "that a final judgement or decree in any suit in the highest court of law or equity of a state in which a decision in the suit could be had," "where is drawn in question the validity of a statute of or an authority exercised under any state on the ground of their being repugnant to the constitution, treaties, or laws of The United States and the decision is in favour of such their validity," "may be reexamined and reversed or affirmed in the Supreme court of The United States."[2]

¶3   In this case the city ordinance of Charleston is the exercise of an "authority under the state of South Carolina," "the validity of which has been drawn in question on the ground of its being repugnant to the constitution," and "the decision is in favour of its validity." The question therefore which was decided by the constitutional court, is the very question on which the revising power of this tribunal is to be exercised, and the only enquiry is whether it has been decided in a case described in the section which authorizes the writ of errour that has been awarded. Is a writ of prohibition a suit?

¶4   The term is certainly a very comprehensive one, and is understood to apply to any proceeding in a court of justice by which an individual pursues that remedy in a court of justice which the law affords him. The modes of proceeding may be various but if a right is litigated between parties in a court of justice, the proceeding by which the decision of the court is sought is a suit. The question between the parties is precisely the same as it would have been in a writ of replevin or in an action of tresspass. The constitutionality of the ordinance is contested; the party aggrieved by it applies to a court, and at his suggestion, a writ of prohibition, the appropriate remedy is issued. The opposite party appeals; and, in the highest court, the judgement is reversed and judgement given for the defendant. This judgement was we think rendered in a suit.

¶5   We think also that it was a final judgement in the sense in which that term is used in the 25th. section of the judicial act. If it were applicable to those judgements and decrees only in which the right was finally decided, and could never again be litigated between the parties, the provisions of the section would be confined within much narrower limits than the words import, or than Congress could have intended. Judgements in actions of ejectment, and decrees in Chancery dismissing a bill without prejudice, however deeply they might affect rights protected by the constitution laws or treaties of The United States, would not be subject to the revision of this court. A prohibition might issue restraining a collector from collecting duties, and this court could not revise and correct the judgement. The word "final" must be understood in the section under consideration as applying to all judgements and decrees which determine the particular cause.[3]

We think then that the writ of errour has brought the cause properly before this court. ¶6

This brings us to the main question. Is the stock issued for loans made to the government of The United States liable to be taxed by States and corporations? ¶7

Congress has power "to borrow money on the credit of The United States." The stock it issues is the evidence of a debt created by the exercise of this power. The tax in question is a tax upon the contract subsisting between the government and the individual. It bears directly upon that contract while subsisting and in full force. The power operates upon the contract the instant it is framed, and must imply a right to affect that contract. ¶8

If the states and corporations throughout the Union possess the power to tax a contract for the loan of money, what shall arrest this principle in its application to every other contract? What measure can government adopt which will not be exposed to its influence? ¶9

But it is unnecessary to pursue this principle through its diversified application to all the contracts and to the various operations of government. No one can be selected which is of more vital interest to the community than this of borrowing money on the credit of The United States. No power has been conferred by the American people on their government the free and unburthened exercise of which more deeply affects every member of our republic. In war, when the honour, the safety, the independence of the nation are to be defended, when all its resources are to be strained to the utmost, credit must be brought in aid of taxation, and the abundant revenues of peace and prosperity must be anticipated to supply the exigencies, the urgent demands of the moment. The people, for objects the most important which can occur in the progress of nations, have empowered their government to make these anticipations, "to borrow money on the credit of The United States." Can any thing be more dangerous or more injurious than the admission of a principle which authorizes every state and every corporation in the union which possesses the right of taxation, to burthen the exercise of this power at their discretion? ¶10

If the right to impose the tax exists, it is a right which in its nature acknowledges no limits. It may be carried to any extent within the jurisdiction of the state or corporation which imposes it, which the will of each state and corporation may prescribe. A power which is given by the ¶11 whole American people for their common good, which is to be exercised at the most critical periods for the most important purposes, on the free exercise of which the interests certainly, perhaps the liberty of the whole may depend may be burthened impeded, if not arrested, by any of the organized parts of the confederacy.

¶12   In a society framed like one, with one supreme government for national purposes, and numerous state governments for other purposes, in many respects independent, and in the uncontrouled exercise of many important powers, occasional interferences ought not to surprize us. The power of taxation is one of the most essential to a state, and one of the most extensive in its operation. The attempt to maintain a rule which shall limit its exercise, is undoubtedly among the most delicate and difficult duties which can devolve on those whose province it is to expound the supreme law of the land in its application to the cases of individuals. This duty has more than once devolved on this court. In the performance of it we have considered it as a necessary consequence from the supremacy of the government of the whole, that its action in the exercise of its legitimate powers should be free and unembarassed by any conflicting powers in the possession of its parts. That the powers of a state cannot rightfully be so exercised as to impede and obstruct the free course of those measures which the government of the States united may rightfully adopt.

¶13   This subject was brought before the court in the case of McCullough against the State of Maryland[a] when it was thoroughly argued and deliberately considered. The question decided in that case bears a near resemblance to that which is involved in this. It was discussed at the bar in all its relations, and examined by the court with its utmost attention. We will not repeat the reasoning which conducted us to the conclusion then formed, but that conclusion was that "all subjects over which the sovereign power of a state extends are objects of taxation; but those over which it does not extend, are upon the soundest principles exempt from taxation." "The sovereignty of a state extends to every thing which exists by its own authority, or is introduced by its permission"; but not "to those means which are employed by Congress to carry into execution powers conferred on that body by the people of The United States." "The attempt to use" the power of taxation "on the means employed by the government of the Union in pursuance of the constitution, is itself an abuse because it is the usurpation of a power which the people of a single state cannot give." The court said in that case that "the states have no power, by taxation or otherwise, to retard, impede, burden, or in any manner controul the operation of the constitutional laws enacted by Congress to carry into execution the powers vested in the General government."[4]

¶14   We retain the opinions which were then expressed. A contract made by

[a]4th. Wh 316

the government in the exercise of its power to borrow money on the credit of The United States, is undoubtedly independent of the will of any state in which the individual who lends may reside, and is undoubtedly an operation essential to the important objects for which the government was created. It ought therefore on the principles settled in the case of McCullough against the state of Maryland, to be exempt from state taxation, and consequently from being taxed by corporations deriving their power from states.

It is admitted that the power of the government to borrow money can not be directly opposed, and that any law directly obstructing its operation would be void; but a distinction is taken between direct opposition, and those measures which may consequentially affect it. That is, that a law prohibiting loans to The United States would be void, but a tax on them to any amount is allowable. ¶15

It is we think impossible not to perceive the intimate connexion which exists between these two modes of acting on the subject. ¶16

It is not the want of original power in an independent sovereign state to prohibit loans to a foreign government, which restrains the state legislature from direct opposition to those made by The United States. The restraint is imposed by our constitution. The American people have conferred the power of borrowing money on their government, and by making that government supreme, have shielded its action in the exercise of this power from the action of the local governments. The grant of the power is incompatible with a restraining or controuling power, and the declaration of supremacy is a declaration that no such restraining or controuling power shall be exercised. ¶17

The right to tax the contract to any extent when made, must operate upon the power to borrow before it is exercised, and have a sensible influence on the contract. The extent of this influence depends on the will of a distinct government. To any extent, however inconsiderable it is a burthen on the operations of government. It may be carried to an extent which shall arrest them entirely. ¶18

It is admitted by the counsel for the defendants that the power to tax stock must affect the terms on which loans will be made; but this objection it is said, has no more weight when urged against the application of an acknowledged power to government stock, than if urged against its application to lands sold by The United States. ¶19

The distinction is we think apparent. When lands are sold no connexion remains between the purchaser and the government. The lands purchased become a part of the mass of property in the country with no implied exemption from common burthens. All lands are derived from the general or particular government, and all lands are subject to taxation. Lands sold are in the condition of money borrowed and repaid. Its liability to taxation in any form it may then assume is not questioned. The connexion between the borrower and the lender is dissolved. It is no ¶20 burthen on loans, it is no impediment to the power of borrowing, that the money, when repaid, loses its exemption from taxation. But a tax upon debts due from the government, stands we think on very different principles from a tax on lands which the government has sold.

¶21   The[5] Federalist has been quoted in the argument, and an eloquent and well merited eulogy has been bestowed on the great statesman who is supposed to be the author of the number from which the quotation was made. This high authority was also relied upon in the case of McCullough against the State of Maryland, and was considered by the court. Without repeating what was then said, we refer to it as exhibiting our view of the sentiments expressed on this subject by the authors of that work.[6]

¶22   It has been supposed that a tax on stock comes within the exceptions stated in the case of McCullough agt. The State of Maryland.[7] We do not think so. The Bank of The United States is an instrument essential to the fiscal operations of the government, and the power which might be exercised to its destruction was denied. But property acquired by that corporation in a state was supposed to be placed in the same condition with property acquired by an individual.

¶23   The tax on government stock is thought by this court to be a tax on the contract, a tax on the power to borrow money on the credit of The United States, and consequently to be repugnant to the constitution.

¶24   We are therefore of opinion that the judgment of the Constitutional court of the state of South Carolina reversing the order made by the court of Common pleas awarding a prohibition to the city council of Charleston to restrain them from levying a tax imposed on six and seven per cent stock of The United States under an ordinance to raise supplies to the use of the city of Charleston for the year 1823, is erroneous in this, that the said constitutional court adjudged that the said ordinance was not repugnant to the constitution of The United States; whereas this court is of opinion that such repugnancy does exist. We are therefore of opinion that the said judgement ought to be reversed and annulled and the cause remanded to the constitutional court for the state of South Carolina that farther proceedings may be had therein according to law.[8]

AD, Weston v. City Council of Charleston, Appellate Opinions, RG 267, DNA; printed, Richard Peters, *Reports of Cases Argued and Adjudged in the Supreme Court of the United States . . . ,* II (Philadelphia, 1829), 463–69. Numbers in margin of MS indicate passages selected for reporter's headnote. For JM's deletions and interlineations, see Textual Notes below.

1. JM began the draft with a sentence addressed to the reporter: "State the case as in the printed statement omitting the words enclosed in brackets showing the division of the court."

2. *U.S. Statutes at Large,* I, 85–86.

3. The argument against jurisdiction focused principally on the Supreme Court's inability to enforce a judgment of reversal in proceedings on a writ of prohibition. In his dissenting opinion, Justice Johnson denied that proceedings in prohibition constituted a suit within the meaning of section 25 of the Judiciary Act. A prohibition, he contended, was

not a case in which there could be a final judgment; nor was it a suit in which the Supreme Court could enter judgment or award execution. Justice Thompson, also dissenting, declined to inquire into the question, which he believed to be "of minor importance." The Supreme Court, he said, did "not claim the power of enforcing its judgment," and the Charleston ordinance would remain in effect unless the city council "voluntarily" repealed it. The Supreme Court's judgment on the point of jurisdiction was "no more than an opinion expressed upon an abstract question" (2 Pet. 470–72, 474).

4. McCulloch v. Maryland, 4 Wheat. 429, 430, 436 (1819); *PJM*, VIII, 275, 278. JM wrote this sentence on a separate sheet and marked it for insertion at this point.

5. JM wrote this paragraph on a separate sheet and marked it for insertion at this point.

6. The reported argument on behalf of the Charleston City Council does not mention *The Federalist*. In McCulloch v. Maryland the Court quoted and commented on *The Federalist* No. 31 by Hamilton. Thompson's dissenting opinion in the present case quoted a passage from *The Federalist* No. 32, also by Hamilton, in which the author acknowledged the states' "independent and uncontrollable authority to raise their own revenues for the supply of their own wants" — excepting only duties on imports and exports (4 Wheat. 433–34; *PJM*, VIII, 277; 2 Pet. 477).

7. The majority opinion of the Constitutional Court of South Carolina, the argument of Legaré and Cruger on behalf of the city council, and Thompson's dissenting opinion all quoted or cited this passage in McCulloch v. Maryland: "This opinion does not deprive the States of any resources which they originally possessed. It does not extend to a tax paid by the real property of the bank . . . nor to a tax imposed on the interest which the citizens of Maryland may hold in this institution, in common with other property of the same description throughout the State" (4 Wheat. 436; *PJM*, VIII, 279; Harp. 343; 2 Pet. 462, 479).

8. Johnson and Thompson, in dissent, maintained that Charleston's tax on U.S. stock was a tax on income that did not directly interfere with the general government's power to borrow money. Johnson thought it was "a very unwise and suicidal tax" but that it did not amount to a "masked attack upon the powers of the general government." Thompson could perceive no distinction between a state tax on the interest of stock of the Bank of the U.S., which was permissible under the McCulloch rule, and a tax on the interest of U.S. stock. The McCulloch principle, he said, "must be understood as referring to a direct tax upon" the means employed by the general government in executing its powers (2 Pet. 473, 479).

Textual Notes

¶ 1	l. 3	bar and ~~the case~~ a reargument
¶ 2	l. 1	The ~~jurisdiction~~ ↑power↓ of this
	ll. 4–5	"where is ~~the~~ drawn
¶ 3	ll. 8–9	Is a ↑writ of↓ prohibition a
¶ 4	ll. 2–3	individual ~~is by by a course of law~~ pursues that
	ll. 6–7	is precisely ~~the~~ the same
	l. 8	is contested; ~~and~~ the
	l. 9	to a ~~judge~~ ↑court↓, and at
¶ 5	ll. 2–3	it were ~~applied~~ ↑applicable↓ to those
¶ 7	l. 1	Is ~~government~~ ↑the↓ stock issued
	l. 2	taxed by ~~the~~ States
¶ 8	l. 2	evidence of ~~the~~ ↑a↓ debt
¶ 9	l. 2	of money, ~~the same~~ what shall
¶10	l. 2	the contracts ~~of~~ and to the
	l. 5	conferred ~~on~~ ↑by↓ the
	ll. 14–15	be more ↑dangerous or more↓ injurious

¶11   l. 2   limits. ~~It is carried~~ ↑It may be carried to any extent↓ within
¶12   l. 1   In a ~~government constituted~~ ↑society framed↓ like
      ll. 6–7   The attempt to ↑maintain a rule which shall↓ limit
      l. 11   considered it as ~~the~~ ↑a↓ necessary
      l. 17   adopt. ~~The admission of the principle that the will of the part may at any time~~ ↑controul and↓ ~~defeat the will of the whole~~
¶13   ll. 15–16 an abuse ~~of the~~ ↑it↓ power because it is the
      ll. 17–20 give." ↑The court said in that case that "the states have no power, by taxation or otherwise, to retard, impede, burden, or in any manner controul the operation of the constitutional laws enacted by Congress to carry into execution the power vested in the General government."↓
¶14   l. 1   opinions which ~~was~~ ↑were↓ then
¶15   ll. 1–2   money ~~could~~ ↑can↓ not be directly
      ll. 2–3   obstructing ~~it~~ ↑its operation↓ would
      l. 3   void; but ~~it is insisted that a power which a state undoubtedly possesses ought not to be restrained because in its exercise it may consequentially affect the meas~~ a distinction
      l. 4   affect ~~the power~~ ↑it.↓ That is,
      ll. 5–6   but a tax ↑on them↓ to any amount ~~on those loans~~ is allowable.
¶16   l. 2   subject. ~~subject; and the difficulty of sustaining the~~ ↑right↓ ~~power of taxation~~ ↑taxing loans when made↓ ~~by any course of reasoning which might not also sustain the power of direction opposition~~ ↑right of opposing them in the first instance.↓ ~~The general power of taxation is acknowledged. We hold it sacred. But it does not reside in a state more certainly than the power of future legislation over future contracts. The power to make future contracts void in law is one which the states exercise at their discretion. They settle the rate of interest, and prescribe the forms by~~ ↑without↓ ~~which contracts have no validity.~~
¶17   ll. 2–3   restrains ~~a~~ ↑the↓ state ~~legislation~~ ↑legislature↓ from
      l. 3   opposition to ~~loans~~ ↑those↓ made
¶18   l. beg.   ~~If~~ ↑The right to tax↓ the contract ~~may be taxed~~ to any
      l. 4   extent, ↑however inconsiderable↓ it is
¶19   ll. 2–3   but this ↑objection↓ it is said, ~~has~~ ↑has↓ no more
      l. 4   power to ↑government↓ stock, than
¶20   ll. 4–5   derived from ↑the general or particular↓ government.
      l. 11   debts due ~~by~~ ↑from↓ the
¶ 21 l. 1 beg. ↑The Federalist has been quoted in the argument, and an eloquent and well merited eulogy has been bestowed on the great statesman who is supposed to be the author of the number from which the quotation was made. This high authority was also relied upon in the case of McCullough against the State of Maryland, and was considered by the court. Without repeating what was then said, we refer to it as exhibiting our view of the sentiments expressed on this subject by the authors of that work.↓

¶22 l. 1 beg.   ~~It has been said, for the purpose we presume of showing that~~
~~no privilege is attached to debts due from The United States,~~
~~that even its domain is exempted from taxation by compact.~~
~~But the compacts alluded to are~~ ↑do↓ ~~not~~ ↑stipulate↓ ~~for the~~
~~protection of the domain of The United States. They stipulate~~
~~for the exemption of lands actually sold for a specified term~~
~~of years after the sale has been made.~~
   l. 2   case of ~~the State~~ McCullough
   l. 7   individual. ~~So with respect to~~
¶24 ll. 7–8   said ordinance ~~ought~~ was not

From Committee of Richmond Citizens

SIR   RICHMOND, 19th March, 1829.

In compliance with a resolution adopted by a Meeting of the Citizens of Richmond, held at the Capitol, on the 16th inst., we have the pleasure of announcing your nomination as one of the delegates to represent this district in Convention, and requesting your assent to serve if elected.[1]

We avail ourselves of the occasion, to add our individual solicitations upon this subject, and to assure you of the high gratification we shall experience in the event of your election. Yours, very respectfully,

> *John Rutherfoord,*[2]
> *John Hayes,*[3]
> *Gurdon H. Bacchus,*[4]
> *Robert G. Scott,*
> *Wm. H. Fitzwhylsonn,*[5]
> *Richard A. Carrington,*[6]
> *Wm. H. Richardson,*[7]
> Committee.

Printed, *Richmond Enquirer,* 31 March 1829.

1. A committee of Richmond citizens met in the Capitol on 16 Mar. and nominated JM, John Robertson, John B. Clopton, and William Chamberlayne as delegates. The same letter was addressed to the other nominees (ibid., 20 Mar. 1829).

2. John Rutherfoord (1792–1866) then represented Richmond in the House of Delegates. He was later (1841–42) acting governor of Virginia. He also served as president of the Mutual Assurance Society (*William and Mary Quarterly,* 1st ser., I, [1893], 175; Earl G. Swem and John W. Williams, *A Register of the General Assembly of Virginia 1776–1918* [Richmond, Va., 1918], 425; Mary Wingfield Scott, *Houses of Old Richmond* [New York, 1941], 75).

3. John Hayes (1790–1834) was a Richmond physician (*Richmond Enquirer,* 12 Dec. 1834; R. Bolling Batte Papers, Vi).

4. Gurdon H. Bacchus (ca. 1789–1834) was a Richmond attorney (*Richmond Enquirer,* 11 December 1834).

5. William Fitzwhylsonn (ca. 1767–1837) a native of Wales, moved to Richmond before 1790. He ran an English school for young men and women " 'to teach the English tongue

grammatically,' " and also established a bookstore, "where 'literature in general, music and bookbinding came within his scope.' " In 1817 he became mayor of the city (ibid., 27 June 1837; *Richmond Portraits*, 65–66).

6. Richard A. Carrington (1797–1855) was a Richmond physician (R. Bolling Batte Papers, Vi).

7. William H. Richardson (1795–1876) was then clerk of the Virginia Council of State and served as the first secretary of Commonwealth, 1832–52. He organized the Virginia State Library (now Library of Virginia) and was its first librarian, 1828–52 (R. Bolling Batte Papers, Vi).

To Thomas Marshall

My dear Son   Washington March 20th. 1829

Your letter of the 21st. of Feby. reached me in course of post, and afforded me that melancholy satisfaction which is inspired by the belief that a friend whom we tenderly love and who is labouring under heavy affliction, does not absolutely sink under its pressure, but struggles with it, and invokes the only aids which Heaven holds out to us — Religion and Reason.[1] I am consoled with the conviction that you have not forgotten the duties which we owe to those around us, and are mindful of the claims of those whom Providence has bestowed upon you for your happiness, and who are greatly dependent on your continuing attentions and exertions. Continued occupation is a duty both to them and yourself. It assuages mental pain, and cooperating with time pours balm into the wounded heart.

I am glad to hear that you have retained John at home for both the reasons you mention. I have no doubt of the consolation his society affords you, and believe it will be rather advantageous than injuriou⟨s⟩ to him. Our intelligence from the University at Charlottesville is very distressing. Several young men have been seized with the fever after leaving it.[2] A son of General Jones of this city is now very ill, and his life is thought in great danger.[3]

We are now approaching the end of a laborious term, and I hope soon to be in Richmond. My last letters inform me that your mothers health is as usual. Some previous hints had given me a good deal of uneasiness.

The city has been full of applicants for office. The numbers who think their services entitle them to reward are immense. The President would be unable to gratify them all were he even to remove every man in office who did not take an active part in support of his election. Great discontents are of course.

On the subject of removals some difference prevails in the reports of the day. On one side we hear that proscription is the order of the day — that it will be very comprehensive if not universal; On the other, we are told that the peculiarly offensive only will be removed. A good deal has already been done north of us; and I have fears for the few friends of mine who hold office in Virginia. My old friend Mr. Swan amiable and estimable as he is, will it is said give place to a less worthy and less capable man. He had on one occasion dropped a careless but offensive expression which was noted and communicated.[4] The system of espionage will in such times be pursued by hunters after office even if not encouraged by the person to whom the retailers of scandal would wish to pay their court.

The ground is now covered with snow. I count on leaving this tomorrow. Farewell my dear son, I am your affectionate Fathe⟨r⟩

J MARSHALL

ALS, Collection of the Association for the Preservation of Virginia Antiquities on deposit at VHi. Addressed to Thomas Marshall at Oak Hill, Fauquier County; postmarked Washington, D.C., 21 Mar. Endorsed "Answered."

1. Letter not found.

2. During the winter of 1829 an outbreak of typhoid fever occurred at the University of Virginia, forcing the school to suspend classes between 1 Feb. and 1 Apr. (Philip Alexander Bruce, *History of the University of Virginia: 1819–1919*, II: *The Lengthened Shadow of One Man* [New York, 1920], 240–42).

3. Walter Jones (1776–1861), a prominent member of the Supreme Court bar, had been commissioned as a brigadier general of the militia in 1821. By his wife Ann Lucinda Lee he had three sons and eleven daughters. Their son, Walter Jones, Jr., died on 4 Apr. at the age of eighteen (*Richmond Enquirer*, 10 Apr. 1829).

4. Thomas Swann (1789–1845), U.S. Attorney for the District of Columbia since 1821, was nominated and confirmed for a third term in Jan. 1829. After the expiration of Swann's commission in Jan. 1833, Jackson nominated Francis S. Key in his place. Swann lived in Alexandria, where in addition to practicing law he was a merchant and bank president (*Journal of the Executive Proceedings of the Senate*, III [Washington, D.C., 1828], 236–37, 401, 405, 623, 629; IV [Washington, D.C., 1887], 302; T. Michael Miller, comp., *Artisans and Merchants of Alexandria, Virginia: 1780–1820* [2 vols.; Bowie, Md., 1991–92], II, 164–65).

Willson v. Black Bird Creek Marsh Company
Opinion
U.S. Supreme Court, 20 March 1829

Under the authority of a Delaware act of 1822, the Black Bird Creek Marsh Company built a dam across Black Bird Creek in New Castle County. In March 1824 the company brought an action of trespass in the Supreme Court of Delaware against Thompson Willson and others, owners and crew of the sloop *Sarah* for destroying the dam. The sloop was a coasting vessel enrolled and licensed under the federal coasting act of 1793. The defendants pleaded that the creek was a navigable public creek open to all citizens for the purposes of unobstructed navigation and that the company had wrongfully erected the dam. The court in November 1825 gave judgment to the plaintiff on a demurrer to this plea. The Delaware High Court of Errors and Appeals affirmed this judgment in June 1826. Counsel for the defendants (now the plaintiffs in error) filed an appeal in the Supreme Court in February 1828. In argument on 17 March 1829 Richard S. Coxe for the plaintiffs in error and William Wirt for the defendant presented two questions for decision: (1) whether the record presented a case for the Supreme Court to take jurisdiction under section 25 of the Judiciary Act; (2) whether the Delaware law authorizing construction of the dam was unconstitutional as repugnant to the commerce clause. The chief justice delivered the Court's opinion on 20 March (Willson v. Black Bird Creek Marsh Co., App. Cas. No. 1504; U.S. Sup. Ct. Minutes, 17, 20 Mar. 1829).

Willson

v

The Blackbird creek Marsh Com

¶1   The defendants in errour deny the jurisdiction of this court, because, they say, the record does not show that the constitutionality of the act of the legislature under which the plaintiff claimed to support his action was drawn into question.

¶2   Undoubtedly the plea might have stated in terms that the act, so far as it authorized a dam across the creek, was repugnant to the constitution of The United States; and it might have been safer, it might have avoided any question respecting jurisdiction, so to frame it. But we think it impossible to doubt that the constitutionality of the act was the question and the only question which could have been discussed in the state court. That question must have been discussed and decided.

¶3   The plaintiffs sustain their right to build a dam across the creek by the act of assembly. Their declaration is founded upon that act. The injury of which they complain is to a right given by it. They do not claim for themselves any right independent of it. They rely entirely upon the act of assembly.

¶4   The plea does not controvert the existence of the act, but denies its capacity to authorize the construction of a dam across a navigable stream in which the tide ebbs and flows, and in which there was, and of right ought to have been, a certain common and public way in the nature of a high way. This plea draws nothing into question but the validity of the act; and the judgement of the court must have been in favour of its validity. Its consistency with or repugnancy to the constitution of The United States, necessarily arises upon these pleadings, and must have been determined.[1] This court has repeatedly decided in favour of its jurisdiction in such a case. Martin v Hunters lessee[a] Miller v Nicholls[a] & Williams v Norris[a] are expressly in point.[2] They establish as far as precedents can establish any thing, that it is not necessary to state in terms on the record,

[a]1 Wh. 355. [a]4 Wh. 311. [a]12 Wh. 117.

that the constitution or a law of The United States was drawn in question. It is sufficient to bring the case within the provisions of the 25th. Section of the judicial act, if the record shows that the consti[tution] or a law or a treaty of The United States must have been misconstrued or the decision could not be made. Or as in this case, that the constitutionality of a state law was questioned, and the decision has been in favour of the party claiming under such law.

The jurisdiction of the Court being established, the more doubtful ¶5 question is to be considered whether the act incorporating the Blackbird Creek Marsh company is repugnant to the constitution so far as it authorizes a dam across the creek. The plea states the creek to be navigable, in the nature of a high way, through which the tide ebbs and flows.

The act of Assembly by which the plaintiffs were authorized to con- ¶6 struct their dam shows plainly that this is one of those many creeks passing through a deep level marsh adjoining the Delaware, up which the tide flows for some distance. The value of the property on its banks must be enhanced by excluding the water from the marsh, and the health of the inhabitants probably improved. Measures calculated to produce these objects, provided they do not come into collision with the powers of the general government, are undoubtedly within those which are reserved to the states. But the measure authorized by this act stops a navigable creek, and must be supposed to abridge the rights of those who have been accustomed to use it. But this abridgement, unless it comes in conflict with the constitution or a law of The United States, is an affair between the government of Delaware and its citizens, of which this court can take no cognizance.

The counsel for the defendants[3] insist that it comes in conflict with the ¶7 power of The United States "to regulate commerce with foreign nations and among the several states."

If congress had passed any act which bore upon the case, any act in ¶8 execution of the power to regulate commerce the object of which was to controul state legislation over those small navigable creeks into which the tide flows, and which abound throughout the lower country of the middle and southern States, we should feel not much difficulty in saying that a state law coming in conflict with such act would be void. But Congress has passed no such act. The repugnancy of the law of Delaware to the constitution is placed entirely on its repugnancy to the power to regulate commerce with foreign nations and among the several states—a power which has not been so exercised as to affect the question.[4]

We do not think that the act empowering the Blackbird creek Marsh ¶9 Company to place a dam across the creek, can, under all the circumstances of the case, be considered as repugnant to the power to regulate commerce in its dormant state, or as being in conflict with any law passed on the subject.

There is no errour and the judgement is affirmed.   ¶10

AD, Willson v. Black Bird Creek Marsh Company, Appellate Opinions, RG 267, DNA; printed, Richard Peters, *Reports of Cases Argued and Adjudged in the Supreme Court of the United States . . .* , II (Philadelphia, 1829), 250–52. Numbers in margin of MS indicate passages selected for reporter's headnote. For JM's deletions and interlineations, see Textual Notes below.

1. Entered on the record of the appeal in the Delaware High Court of Errors and Appeals is a copy of an agreement, dated 19 Feb. 1824, signed by the counsel who argued the case in the state court. Among other things, counsel stipulated, "No advantage on either side to be taken of the pleadings in the above case but the constitutional question on which the case turns to be fairly and fully brought before the Court." Also, "Neither party to be precluded from taking the case to the Supreme Court of the United States if they have the right to do so" (Willson v. Black Bird Creek Marsh Co., App. Cas. No. 1504).

2. Martin v. Hunter's Lessee, 1 Wheat. 304 (1816); Miller v. Nicholls, 4 Wheat. 311 (1819); Williams v. Norris, 12 Wheat. 117 (1827). JM's citation of Martin v. Hunter's Lessee refers to a page (355) of Story's opinion rather than to the first page of the report. See also Craig v. Missouri, Opinion, 12 Mar. 1830, where JM repeated this citation. In the left margin opposite this footnote JM or someone wrote "8."

3. Someone (Peters?) inserted "Plaintiffs in error" above "defendants," a correction embodied in the printed report.

4. On this occasion the Court discerned no conflict between the state law and the federal coasting act, as it did in voiding New York's monopoly laws in Gibbons v. Ogden (1824).

Textual Notes

¶ 1	l. 1. beg.	~~State the case from the printed statement.~~
¶ 3	l. 1	plaintiffs ~~sustains his~~ ↑sustain their↓ right to [*erasure*] build a dam
	ll. 3–4	do not ~~complain~~ ↑claim↓ for themselves
¶ 4	l. 7	constitution of ~~the~~ The
	ll. 8–9	have been ~~decided~~ ↑determined.↓ This
	l. 10	Hunters lessee ~~Miller~~ Miller v Nicholls
	ll. 17–18	state law ~~must have been~~ ↑was↓ questioned,
¶ 5	l. 2	question ↑is to be considered↓ whether
	l. 3	company is ~~unconstitutional~~ ↑repugnant to the constitution↓ so
¶ 6	l. 2	one of those ↑many↓ creeks passing
	l. 7	they do not ~~impinge~~ come
¶ 8	l. 7	no such act. The ~~unconstitutionality~~ ↑repugnancy of↓ the [*erasure*] law of
¶ 9	l. 4	dormant state, or as ↑being↓ in conflict with any ~~Case~~ ↑law↓ passed

To Committee of Richmond Citizens

Gentlemen   Richmond March 25th. 1829

I have received with sentiments of profound respect your communication of my nomination by the citizens of Richmond as one of the delegates to represent this district in convention. This distinguished mark of the continuance of that favorable opinion of which I have received so many proofs commands my warmest gratitude, and will be cherished in my recollection while memory exists.

No man feels the importance of the approaching convention more than I do, or looks forward to its proceedings with more anxious solicitude. No man would more readily contribute his exertions towards the attainment of the great object Virginia now pursues — the improvement of her constitution — if I beleived it to be in my power to render those essential services which my constituents, were I to be elected, would expect from me. I beg you and them to beleive that my declining to become a candidate does not arise from indifference to the great subject on which the convention is to deliberate, or from insensibility to the kindness of my fellow citizens; but is to be ascribed exclusively to a conviction that I do not retain those physical powers which would enable me to take that part on the floor of the convention which my constituents would expect, and which their interests might require. I must therefore request that the attention of the district may be directed to some other person whose age and powers are more adequate to the important duties to be performed.

I pray you gentlemen and my fellow citizens of Richmond to be assured of the sensibility with which I receive this additional mark of their favour, and to beleive that I am with real and affectionate respect, Your and their Obedt. Servt

J Marshall

ALS, MH-H; printed, *Richmond Enquirer,* 31 March 1829. ALS addressed to John Rutherfoord, John Hayes, Gurdon H. Bacchus, Robert G. Scott, William H. Fitzwhylsonn, Richard A. Carrington, and William H. Richardson. Endorsed by Rutherfoord.

From Committee of Richmond Citizens

SIR   RICHMOND, 27th March, 1829.

We have been much disappointed by the receipt of your communication of the 25th inst., since it devolves upon us the painful duty of announcing to our fellow-citizens, your reluctance to serve in the Convention. We trust, however, that you may be prevailed upon to re-consider your determination, and yield your assent to what we confidently believe to be the unequivocal wish of the district. We fully appreciate the motives and feelings which induced you to request, "that the attention of the district may be directed to some other person, whose age and powers are more adequate to the important duties to be performed." But, we deem the unimpaired vigor of high mental faculties, united with integrity and experience, of so much importance on the present occasion, that your constituents would, no doubt, make due allowance for the want of "those physical powers, which would enable you take part on the floor of the

Convention." No one would be so unreasonable as to expect of you, at your advanced period of life, the exertion of the same powers of debate, which, under other circumstances, justice to yourself, and due regard to the interests of the Commonwealth might require. But, your presence, your opinions and advice, upon the important questions which will engage the attention of that assembly, could not fail to have their due weight. Believing that the future tranquillity of the State materially depends upon the ratification of the Constitution which may be submitted to the people, we consider it highly important, that it should emanate from the wisest heads, the purest hearts, and the most unsuspected patriotism. If there ever be an occasion when all the talent, and virtue, and experience of Virginia are required, that occasion is now presented. And, while all eyes are anxiously directed to our most enlightened and distinguished men, for the approaching crisis, you must excuse us for saying, that Virginia looks to *you* as one of the few surviving sages and patriarchs of the land, in whose purity of intention, and ability to serve her, all parties repose the most unbounded confidence. We feel assured, that your refusal to serve in the Convention, will be a serious disappointment, not only to your fellow-citizens of Richmond, but to the district and State. We do not ask you "to become a candidate,"—but earnestly desire that you will not withhold your services if elected. This is probably the last call that will be made upon you by your native state, and, considering the magnitude of the occasion, we anxiously hope that the appeal will not be unavailing.

We duly estimate the kind manner of your communication, and beg leave to assure you of our profound respect and affection.

> *John Rutherfoord,*
> *John Hayes,*
> *Gurdon H. Bacchus,*
> *Robert G. Scott,*
> *Wm. H. Fitzwhylsonn,*
> *Richard A. Carrington,*
> *Wm. H. Richardson,*
> Committee.

Printed, *Richmond Enquirer,* 31 March 1829.

To John Rutherfoord

Dear Sir   Richmond March 28th. 29

The flattering letter from the committee with which I was yesterday honoured, has received my most serious attention. Although my unwillingness to appear at this advanced period of life, in a popular assembly, however composed, and whatever may be its object, cannot be entirely overcome, it shall yield to the arguments and representations of your letter, and to the opinions of some other friends. Should the counties of the district concur in the opinion which has been expressed by the city of Richmond, I shall, to the best of my ability, discharge the trust confided to me. At the same time I shall be well pleased should they direct their attention to some other person.

You mentioned last night the publication of the letters between the committee and myself. As the counties may not concur with the city in sentiment, the publication of our correspondence at present would not be desirable. Should the election terminate according to your anticipations I leave it to the committee to act as the members shall chuse.

I inclose you my answer to the last letter of the committee and am with great respect & esteem, Your Obedt. Servt

J MARSHALL

ALS, Rutherfoord Papers, NcD. Addressed to Rutherfoord and endorsed by him.

To Committee of Richmond Citizens

Gentlemen Richmond March 28th. 1829

I have received your letter of the 27th. with emotions which the sentiments it communicates cannot fail to excite in a mind feelingly alive to the esteem and approbation of friends. I dare not indulge the hope that my services, in any situation, can have the value which your partial favour attaches to them; and, therefore cannot, without real difficulty, change the resolution I had deliberately formed respecting my course as regards the convention. That deference however which I have always felt for the judgement and wishes of those whom I respect, and of my fellow citizens generally, will still influence my conduct; and, if I should, on this great and last occasion, be the choice of the district, my repugnance to becoming a member of the convention shall yield, and my services, such as they are, shall be at their command.[1] I am Gentlemen with great respect and esteem, Your Obedt. Servt

J MARSHALL

ALS, Rutherfoord Papers, NcD; printed, *Richmond Enquirer*, 31 March 1829. ALS enclosed in JM to Rutherfoord, 28 Mar. 1829. Addressed to John Rutherfoord, John Hayes, Gurdon H. Bacchus, Robert G. Scott, William H. Fitzwhylsonn, Richard A. Carrington, and William H. Richardson

1. The elections took place in May in each of Virginia's twenty-four senatorial districts. JM was a candidate for the district composed of the counties of Charles City, Elizabeth City, James City, Henrico, New Kent, Warwick, York, and the cities of Richmond and Williams-

burg. He led the list of candidates with 794 votes, followed by John Tyler with 571, Philip Norborne Nicholas with 490, and John Clopton with 471 (*Richmond Enquirer,* 5 June 1829).

To William B. Giles

Dear Sir   Richmond May 7th. 1829

While I was absent from this place your speech made in the House of Delegates in January 1827 "concerning a convention" was brought in and thrown on a table among numerous papers and pamphlets so that I did not see it till to day.[1] I have read it with equal pleasure and attention. Your views respecting the county court system are peculiarly gratifying to me. Allow me to hope that you will as a member of the convention be more successful in supporting the opinions you avow than you have been in opposing a convention. In the supposition that I am indebted to you for this mark of polite attention permit me to thank you for it and to assure you that I am with great respect, Your Obedt

J MARSHALL

ALS, Charles Roberts Autograph Letters Collection, PHC. Addressed to Giles and endorsed by him "About the Convention question." Giles also wrote another note: "Mr. Jones will be pleased to send this note from Judge Marshall to Thomas — The Judge wishes well to my election, and goes all lengths with my speech."

1. Giles, *The Bill, "Concerning a Convention"* . . . [Richmond, Va., 1829?]. Giles delivered this speech in the House of Delegates on 26 Jan. 1827. It was published in the *Richmond Enquirer* in Mar. 1827 and had recently been republished in pamphlet form (*Richmond Enquirer,* 1, 3 Mar. 1827; 7 Apr. 1829).

To [James M. Garnett]

Dear Sir   Richmond May 20th. 1829

On my return from North Carolina I received your letter of the 10th.[1]

My private judgement is certainly in favor of founding the right of suffrage on the basis of an interest in land. I have no objection to extending the present rule to a reversionary interest; and to leases for such a term of years as may give the lessee actual property in the soil. The state of society in a part of our country suggests this extension. Tenants in the upper part of the state are numerous; and the migratory spirit of our people creates such difficulty in ascertaining the expiration of leases for lives, as to excite some unwillingness on the part of land holders, to execute leases of that description.

I have never thrown my ideas on this subject in the shape of an argument; and they are very well expressed in your "reply to the enquiries of a free holder."[2]

I have never, in reflecting on it, allowed all the weight which is generally ascribed by my countrymen, to the natural rights of Man. These rights exist in a state of nature, but are surrendered, as it seems to me, when he enters into a state of society, in exchange for social rights and advantages. If any original natural rights were retained (I speak not of those with which society has no concern, the exercise of which cannot affect others, such as freedom of thought, breathing the atmosphere, using our senses &c) we should expect them to be those of life and liberty. Yet both are at the disposition of society. All natural rights therefore of this description may be controuled by society, and are exercised by its permission. The wanton use of this power by the imposition of unnecessary restraints, would certainly be an abuse of it. Still the power exists, and its exercise must be regulated by the wisdom of society. On no other principle can the exclusion of females, minors, free people of colour &c from the polls be sustained.

If, as I think cannot be denied, a voice in the government of a country be the exercise of a social, not of a natural right, society must judge of the extent to which it ought to be granted, and of the individuals on whom it may be safely and beneficially conferred. It is a question of expediency, not of right.[3]

Considering it as a question of expediency, we ought, it would seem to me, in solving it, to take into view all the great objects for which government is instituted. One of primary magnitude — security against external force devolves mainly on the government of the Union. State legislation embraces taxation for state purposes, and every thing relative to persons and property.

Personal security is undoubtedly an object of the first importance; but it is obvious to all, and has been repeatedly observe⟨d⟩ that this is an object in which all have an equal interest. However the legislature may be elected, personal liberty will be equally secure, because the legislator must be equally intent on its preservation. All persons must be equally subject to the laws; and no difference or opposition of interest can exist in this respect.

But the laws which affect our persons constitute a small portion of the code of every nation. The great mass of legislation respects property. Is it wise, is it safe, in framing the legislature, to exclude property altogether from our consideration? If power and property be separated entirely from each other, is there not reason to fear that they may be reunited by means which cannot be avowed?

To me it seems true wisdom so to constitute the legislature as to furnish the best attainable security that its opinions will lead to the preservation of the great subjects of legislation — persons and property. If it be true, as I think it is, that any representation of the people which public opinion would tolerate, or any statesman of the day could suggest, would sedulously and with equal vigilance guard our persons, we ought not entirely

LETTER TO JAMES MERCER GARNETT
First page of letter to James Mercer Garnett, 20 May 1829.
Courtesy of the Gilder Lehrman Collection at the Pierpoint Morgan Library.

to overlook the safety of our property. This is I think but done by beginning at the foundation — at the right of suffrage. In the representative we may expect to see the image — the improved image, but still the image, of his constituents; and if we would form a representative body both wise and faithful, we must give its full effect, as far as human provisions can give it, to the sense of the honest yeomanry of the country — the real people — by removing the in⟨flu⟩ence of those whom it would be unsafe to trust.

I know very well that among the most destitute of the human race may be found intelligence, honour, and inflexible principle; bu⟨t⟩ we have no means of distinguishing them by law; and, in framing a constitution must act on general principles. It is generally true that the opposite qualities may be too often looked for among those who would be excluded from the right of suffrage by the rule which has been mentioned.

If any property qualification be required, the arguments in favour of an interest in land are so obvious and have been so often mentioned that they need not be repeated. It is so easily acquired that no person of any property who values the right of suffrage will be without it. If any discrimination be made, this is recommended additionally by the fact that we are accustomed to it.

While I express my individual judgement I must say that public opinion has, I suspect, decided the question differently. If we are to trust what we see in the papers, the disposition to abandon the principle we have hitherto maintained, and to make the right of suffrage universal, or to depend on a small property qualification, has become very extensive. Beyond the blue ridge this opinion appears to be universal. Immediately east of that mountain, it has been adopted by many. It has derived great support from the sentiments ascribed to Mr. Jefferson.

Should the friends of the present system, or of something very like it be outvoted, the question will be whether any, and if any, what other test shall be substituted in its place. The payment of taxes presents itself as the most obvious; but there is great difficulty in fixing the amount.

I am also in favour of estimating our slave population in apportioning our representation.

Most of the observations already made apply to this question as strongly as to freehold suffrage. It is among the most productive funds for taxation, it bears a great portion of the burthens of government, and has peculiar claims to consideration in the formation of that body which is to be entrusted with the power of imposing taxes. The fact that they are unequally distributed in different sections of the state gives additional strength to the claims of those who possess it to have on this account some increased weight in the legislature. It is the best, perhaps the only certain security against oppressive taxation. I would add that slaves though property, are also persons. They constitute a part of the real effective population of the country. They exclude a white population to the same extent.

Although incapable of exercising the right of suffrage themselves, why may it not be exercised for them by that active part of the society which exercises the same right for others equally incapable of acting for themselves. Females, minors &c are excluded from the polls, but are included in the enumeration of persons on whom representation is apportioned.

The obvious unfitness of this sketch for publication will secure it from the public view. It is designed for your private eye. I shall of course perform that part which my duty as a citizen may require, but am not willing as a meer voluntier to emerge from that privacy and retirement to which my period of life has doomed me. I do not give this hint from any apprehension of the publication of this letter but to suggest my unwillingness that the use you mention should be made of it. Indeed this is an unnecessary precaution, as neither its matter nor its manner fit it for your purpose.

I look with anxiety for the elections in your district in the earnest hope that Virginia will have the aid of your services in the convention.[4] With great and respectful esteem, I am dear Sir your Obedt

J MARSHALL

ALS, Gilder Lehrman Collection, NNPM. Addressee identified by internal evidence (see n. 2).

1. Letter not found.

2. James M. Garnett, *A Reply to the Inquiries of a Freeholder, . . . on the Subject of the Convention* (Richmond, 1829). Garnett wrote in reply to "A.B.," a freeholder in the senatorial district composed of the counties of King and Queen, King William, Essex, Caroline, and Hanover. Writing in the *Richmond Enquirer* of 31 Mar. 1829, "A.B." asked Garnett and a half-dozen other prospective convention candidates in that district to state "whether, if elected, they are disposed to serve; and if so disposed, that they respectively and distinctly state the fundamental principles which they are for laying down for our future government." In particular, the candidates were asked to give their views concerning the right of suffrage, legislation and taxation, the election of a governor and his duties, the election of judges and their tenure of office, and the county courts. Garnett's reply, dated 8 Apr. 1829, first appeared in the *Enquirer* of 17 Apr. 1829. On the right of suffrage, Garnett believed "it should be founded on the possession of land," though he was "willing to extend this right to such as had a sufficient reversionary interest, or leases for lives, or for a long term of years in the same" (*Reply to the Inquiries of a Freeholder,* 4).

3. JM echoed Garnett, who said that the question concerning the right of suffrage was "neither more nor less, than one of *mere expediency,* having little more to do with what are truly natural rights, than an exclusive claim would have had, set up by either party to a larger portion of brains, than the other" (ibid., 5).

4. Garnett was elected in his district along with John Roane, Richard Morris, and William P. Taylor (Hugh Blair Grigsby, *The Virginia Convention of 1829–30* [1854; New York, 1969 reprint], 101).

To Joseph Sprigg

Dear Sir   Richmond May 25th. 1829

Yours of the 16th. has just reached me and I regret very much to hear of the ill health of your family.[1] Sickness so early in the year is unusual, and you must be careful to avoid a relapse. I am sorry too to hear that you have not sold your crop of wheat. I had hoped that you had secured the good price of last winter.

I do not recollect what passed between Doctor Dunn and myself respecting the repairs of the house, but will certainly comply with my promise whatever it may have been. I have no doubt but that what Captain Dunn says is correct.[2]

I would send the title bond for the land sold to Mr. Dunn but expect to visit Hampshire again in August and will then settle the business.[3]

Major Collins charged me a most unreasonable price for his seed wheat; but I did not like to have a dispute.[4] He charged me too most enormously as I thought for the work done on the bank; but he said it was all necessary. As the price of wheat ⟨has⟩ fallen I suppose Mr. Singleton will prefer taking the wheat on shares to paying the sum charged by Major Collins. I wish him however to say at once which he prefers. I do not desire you to take the trouble of going to see him on this account, but when you do fall in with him, if you think of it, I wish you to mention it.

I hope Mrs. Sprigg and your family as well as yourself are now in health, and am dear Sir with great regard, Your Obedt

J Marshall

ALS, ViHi. Addressed to Sprigg at "Swan ponds / near Cumberland / Allegheny county / Maryland."

1. Letter not found. Joseph Sprigg (1793–1864) of Cumberland, Md., across the Potomac River from Hampshire County (now West Va.), was JM's tenant and agent for collecting rents on his Swan Ponds tract in Hampshire County. Sprigg's son, Joseph Sprigg, later served as attorney general of West Virginia. A brother, Michael Cresap Sprigg (1797–1841), served in the U.S. House of Representatives from Maryland (1827–31); another brother, James Cresap Sprigg (1797–1852), represented Kentucky in the U.S. House of Representatives for one term (1841–43) (Sharon J. Doliante, *Maryland and Virginia Colonials: Genealogies of Some Colonial Families* [2 vols.; Baltimore, 1998], II, 932–34). On 31 Oct. 1837, Joseph Sprigg received $414 from James K. Marshall, JM's executor, for expenses incurred between 1827 and 1833 (account [May 1827–1833], collection of Mrs. James R. Green, Markham, Va., 1971).

2. Lewis Dunn of Frankfort, Hampshire County, was possibly a tenant on Swan Ponds. A probate of Dunn's will on 25 Aug. 1837 lists several receipts by Joseph Sprigg as Marshall's agent. Capt. Ephraim Dunn was administrator of Lewis Dunn's will (*http://www.rootsweb.com/7Ewvminera/dunnwill.html* [11 Oct. 2001]).

3. JM made periodic trips to Hampshire County by way of Cumberland, Md. (*PJM*, IX, 240; JM to Bushrod Washington, 19 Aug. 1827).

4. The reference is possibly to Thomas Collins, who served as a militia officer, magistrate, and sheriff of Hampshire County (Vicki Bidinger Horton, comp., *Hampshire County Minute Book Abstracts* [2 vols.; Green Spring, W. Va., 1993–94], I, 21, 26, 82, 98; II, 8).

Bank of the United States v. McKenzie
Opinion
U.S. Circuit Court, Virginia, 29 May 1829

This case originated in a note made by Michael W. Hancock of Richmond on 24 October 1821, promising to pay $4,000 to the order of Samuel Perkins in sixty days. The note was payable and negotiable at the Richmond branch of the Bank of the United States. Perkins on the same day endorsed the note to Donald McKenzie, who in turn endorsed it to the bank, where it was discounted for a fixed value. On failing to receive payment after the note became due in December 1821, the bank in January 1822 sued Hancock in the federal court and obtained a judgment at the May 1822 term. Execution on this judgment failed to produce any effects. In August 1828 Robert Stanard, attorney for the bank, brought an action of assumpsit against McKenzie and an identical action against Perkins. In May 1829 Benjamin W. Leigh for the defendant filed two pleas: (1) the general issue, denying the defendant's liability for the debt; (2) the act of limitations, alleging that the plaintiff did not bring the suit within five years from the time the cause of action accrued. The plaintiff replied to the second plea that the bank was a Pennsylvania corporation whose members were citizens of that state and therefore exempt from Virginia's act of limitations. The defendant rejoined that the plaintiff at the time had a branch office in Richmond whose members were Virginia citizens and therefore came within the operation of the act of limitations. At this point the record states that the plaintiff "surrejoined generally," the defendant "joined issue," and the case went to a jury, which returned a verdict for the plaintiff on the first plea but found for the defendant on the second issue. Marshall's opinion was a ruling on a demurrer, which is not mentioned in the record. It is placed under date of 29 May 1829, when the pleas, replication, and rejoinder were entered (U.S. Cir. Ct., Va., Rec. Bk. XV, 293–95; XIX, 213–15).

The Bank of The U.S.

v

McKenzie

¶1   This suit is brought on a note discounted by the bank of The U.S. at its branch in Virginia. The defendant pleads the act of limitation. The plf replies that the debt was contracted at the office in Virginia the President and Directors of which reside in the state and are members of the corporation. The demurrer to the replication makes the question whether this plea is a bar to the action.[1]

¶2   The 4th. sec. of the act for the limitation of actions is copied from the English statute on the same subject and enacts that "all actions of trespass" &c "shall be commenced and sued within the time and limitation hereafter expressed and not after; that is to say; The said actions upon the case other than for slander" "within five years next after the cause of such action or suit, and not after."[2]

It has been observed by English Judges, and if the observation had ¶3 never been made the truth would be obvious to all, that if the act had contained no other clause than this, it would have barred every action it enumerates, whatever might be the character or condition of the plaintiff. It would have barred the rights of infants, femes covert, persons non compos or beyond the sea, as well as of corporations. The enacting clause does not contemplate the character of the plaintiff but looks singly to the action itself. This being an action on the case is within the enacting clause of the statute, and must be barred by it unless the plaintiff can be brought within the exception.

The 12th. sec. provides "that if any person or persons that is or shall be ¶4 entitled to any such action of trespass" &c "be or shall be at the time of any such action given or accrued, fallen or come within the age of twenty one years, feme covert, non compos mentis imprisoned, beyond the seas or out of the country that then such person or persons shall be at liberty to bring the same actions so as they take the same within such times as are before limited after" such disability shall be removed.[3]

The counsel for the plaintiff contends ¶5
1st. That this section limits the words of the enacting clause so as to restrain them from operating on debts due to corporations.
2d. That if this be against him then the plaintiff is within the saving of the exception.

The argument in support of the first point is substantially this. A corpo- ¶6. ration aggregate is not liable to any of the disabilities which are enumerated in the 12th. Sec.; not even to that of being beyond sea, because, being a meer legal entity, being entirely incorporeal, it can have no place of residence. Since it cannot be brought within the 12th. sec. it ought not to be comprehended in the enactment of the 4th. because the savings of the statute must be construed to extend to every description of persons who are the objects of the enacting clause.

This argument is, I think, anticipated and answered in the observation ¶7 made on the words of the 4th. sec. They do not take into view the character of the plaintiff but of the action. In construing this section it is entirely unimportant by whom the suit is brought. The action is equally barred by length of time whoever may be the plaintiff. The plain words of the statute are decisive. Nor does any reason of justice or policy exist which should take a corporation out of these words. The legislature could have no motive for limiting the time within which a suit should be brought by an individual which does not apply with equal force to a suit brought by a corporation.

We find no words in the exception intimating the intention to make it ¶8 coextensive with the enacting clause, or to limit the general provision of the enacting clause to such general classes of persons as may furnish individuals for whom justice would require the savings of rights which are found in the 12th. Section. An exception is not coextensive with the provisions from which it forms the exception; and if a corporation cannot be brought within any of the savings of the statute, the inference is, not that a corporation is withdrawn from the enacting clause, but that the legislature did not think it a being whose right to sue required a prolongation beyond the legal time given for suitors generally.

¶9   2d. The proposition that the plaintiff is within the saving of the rights of persons out of the country, is one of more difficulty, which requires more consideration.[4]

¶10   The enacting clause, it has been said, looks to the action only. The proviso which gives farther time to those whose particular situation was supposed by the legislature to require it looks to persons only. Its language is "if any person or persons that is or shall be entitled to any such action, be or shall be at the time of any such cause of action given or accrued, within the age of 21 years" &c "that then such person or persons shall be at liberty t ⟨o⟩ bring the same actions["] &c.

¶11   The plaintiff to come within the letter of the exception, must be considered as a person or persons. This a corporation aggregate, in its capacity as a body politick, in which alone it acts, cannot be. But the statute of Virginia is taken almost verbatim from the English statute, and therefore the construction which had prevailed in England may be considered as adopted with the words on which that construction was made. Long before the statute of Virginia was enacted, the courts of England had extended the construction of this very section so as to embrace cases within its equity though not within its words. This decision was not indeed made in a case relating to the character of the plaintiff, but in one relating to the character of the cause which does not stand on stronger reason. In Chandler vs Vilett 2 Saunders 120, it was decided that an action on the case came within the equity of the saving of the statute, though it is omitted in the enumeration of actions to which that saving applied.[5] The 12th. sec. of the act of Virginia likewise omits this action, but I have no doubt that the courts of the state would so construe th⟨at⟩ section as to bring that action within it. The question I believe has never been raised although the occasion for raising it has frequently occurred. Upon this principle of liberal construction I think the 12th. section ought to be extended so as to comprehend in its provisions any plaintiff actually affected by the impediments it recites. If then the present plaintiff really comes within the equity of the 12th. sec. I should be much inclined to allow him its benefits. But if the plaintiff claims the advantages allowed to persons, there is some reason for subjecting him to the consequences resulting from the character in which those advantages are claimed.

¶12   The plaintiff is a corporate body acting by the name and style of "The President Directors and Co. of the bank of The United States," and consisting of the original subscribers to the said bank or their assignees. The

Presid⟨ent⟩ and Directors are to be stockholders and are to be elected annually at the banking house in the city of Philadelphia at which place they are to carry on the operations of the said bank. They are authorized to establish offices of discount and deposit wherever they may think fit and to commit the management of the said offices and the business thereof to such persons and under such regulations as they may think proper. The President and Directors transacting the business of the Bank at Philadelphia have in pursuance of the power given in the charter established an office of discount and deposit at Richmond to transact the business of the bank at that place. At this office as at every other the whole business is necessarily conducted in the name of the corporation, and the President and Directors at this office as at every other are as much the agents of the corporation as the President and Directors doing business at Philadelphia. The President and Directors at Philadelphia are neither the nominal nor real plaintiffs. The nominal plaintiffs are the President Directors and company; the real plaintiffs are all the stockholders. The President and Directors transact so much of the business of the company as is proper for them, at their banking house in Philadelphia; but so much of the business of the company as is proper for the President and Directors of the office at Richmond is transacted at their banking house in Richmond. The contract on which the present suit is founded was made with the company acting by its agents in Richmond.

¶13   To bring the plaintiff within the letter or the spirit of the saving in the 12th. section locality must be given to the corporation. A place of residence must be assigned to it, and that place of residence must be out of the commonwealth of Virginia. The counsel for the plaintiff contends that the corporation resides in Philadelphia. How is this to be sustained? The corporate body consists of all the stockholders, and acts by a name comprehending all the stockholders. These stockholders reside all over The United States; but being in their corporate capacity, in which alone they act, a meer legal entity, invisible, inaudible, incorporeal, they act by agents. It may well be doubted, and is doubted, whether the residence of these agents, or their place of doing business can fix the residence of the corporation. If it can, these agents are divided into distinct bodies, residing in different states and doing business at distinct places in those different states. The banking house of the President and Directors of the office at Richmond is as fixed and as notorious as the banking house at Philadelphia. The agents of the company acting at Richmond are as notoriously and as completely its agents as those who act in Philadelphia. If then the residence of the corporate body is fixed and ascertained by the residence of its agents or their place of doing business, it resides in Richmond as truely as in Philadelphia. So far as respects this particular contract, it may with entire propriety be said to reside in Richmond. The contract was made here with agents who reside here at a banking house established here, and is to be performed at this place. In equity and in reason the plaintiff cannot I think, as to this contract if as to any, be placed in Philadelphia.

¶14 When it is recollected that we resort to the equity of the statute to bring the plaintiff or the action on the case within the terms or the operation of the 12th. section, the reason is I think the stronger for considering this case as excluded from it, and within the enacting clause.

¶15 The case of the Bank of The United States v Deveaux & al. 5. Cr. 61 decides this case in principle.[6] In that case the court determined that it might look behind or through the name of the corporation and see the individuals who were the actual plaintiffs, who constituted that legal entity in whose name the corporation acted. It is very much under the sanction of that decision that the plaintiff is brought within the 12th. Sec. of the act; and that decision makes the plaintiff a resident of every place where any member of the corporation resides. However difficult it might be to apply the principle of that case in reason and in justice to a contract made by an individual residing and sued in a state where no office or banking house existed and where a straggling corporator was to be found, no difficulty can exist in applying it to a case like this, where a suit is brought in the state in which the contract was made, in which it was to be performed, and in which the agents and members of the corporation with whom the debt was contracted and to whom it was to be paid, resided.

¶16 The plaintiff also insists that the act does not apply to this case because The United States, being a member of the corporation; is a party plaintiff.

¶17 This argument has I think been fully met at the bar by the counsel for the defendant. In support of the argument urged at the bar, some decisions made by the Supreme court may I think be urged. It may well be doubted on the authority of those cases, whether the privileges, the prerogative if I may use the term, of The United States as a sovereign belong to a case in which it does not appear in its sovereign capacity. In the Post Master General vs. Early 12 Wh. 136.[7] the jurisdiction of the court was denied, although the suit was brought for a debt confessedly due to the United States. It was sustained because, in the opinion of the Judges it was given by an act of Congress. If jurisdiction could not be maintained without an act of Congress much difficulty would certainly be felt in applying the prerogative of government to such a suit so as to withdraw the bar of the statute of limitations.

¶18 In the case of the bank v Deveaux & al it was not even alleged that The United States was a party because a member of the corporation, and that jurisdiction could be taken on that ground.

¶19 In the bank of The U.S. v The Planters bank of Georgia 9th. Wh. 904 the defendant pleaded to the jurisdiction of the court because the state of Georgia was a corporator.[8] The Judges of the circuit court being divided on the question, it was referred to the supreme court. In this case the question whether a sovereign becoming a membe⟨r⟩ of a trading corporation carries its sovereign prerogatives with it was brought directly before the court. The court said "It is we think a sound principle that when a government becomes a partner in any trading company, it devests itself, so far as concerns the transactions of that company, of its sovereign character, and takes that of a private citizen. Instead of communicating to the company its privileges and its prerogatives, it descends to a level with those with whom it associates itself, and takes the character which belongs to its associates, and to the business which is to be transacted. Thus many states of this Union who have an interest in banks, are not suable even in their own courts; yet they never exempt the corporation from being sued. The state of Georgia, by giving to the bank the capacity to sue and be sued voluntarily strips itself of its sovereign character, so far as respects the transactions of the bank, and waives all the privileges of that character. As a member of a corporation a government never exercises its sovereignty. It acts merely as a corporator, and exercises no other power in the management of the affairs of the corporation, than are expressly given by the incorporating act.

The government of the Union held shares in the old bank of The U.S.; ¶20 but the privileges of the government were not imparted by that circumstance to the bank. The U.S. was not a party to suits brought by or against the bank in the sense of the constitution, so with respect to the present bank. Suits brought by or against it are not understood to be brought by or against The U.S. The government by becoming a corporator, lays down its sovereignty, so far as respects the transactions of the corporation and exercises no power or privilege which is not derived from the charter."[9]

This case has I think fully decided the question whether any prerogative of The U.S. is imparted to the bank. ¶21

In the Bank of Kentucky v Wister & al 2. Peters 31⟨2⟩ it appeard that the ¶22 state of Kentucky was the sole proprietor of the stock of the bank.[10] Yet it was determined by the court that the case was decided by the case of the Planters bank of Georgia in 9th. Wheaton.

This point then is completely settled as I think in the Supreme court. ¶23
The law is for the defendant and judgement is to be given for him.[11] ¶24

AD, Marshall Judicial Opinions, PPAmP; printed, John W. Brockenbrough, *Reports of Cases Decided by the Honourable John Marshall . . .*, II (Philadelphia, 1837), 395–402. For JM's deletions and interlineations, see Textual Notes below.

1. JM confounded the plaintiff's replication with the defendant's rejoinder. The demurrer most likely was submitted by the plaintiff in response to the rejoinder. Brockenbrough omitted JM's first three sentences, substituting his own prefatory statement that the plaintiff demurred to the rejoinder.

2. *Revised Code of Va.*, I, 488–89.

3. Ibid., 491.

4. JM interlined "reflection" above "consideration" but did not delete the latter.

5. Chandler v. Vilett, 2 Wms. Saund. 120, 85 Eng. Rep. 836 (K. B., 1670).

6. Bank of the U.S. v. Deveaux, 5 Cranch 61 (1809); *PJM*, VII, 196–202.

7. Postmaster General v. Early, 12 Wheat. 136 (1827); *PJM*, X, 412–18.

8. Bank of the U.S. v. Planter's Bank of Georgia, 9 Wheat. 904 (1824); *PJM*, X, 83–87.

9. 9 Wheat. 907–8; *PJM*, X, 85.

10. Bank of Kentucky v. Wister, 2 Pet. 318 (1829).

11. In stating that judgment was to be given for the defendant, JM was evidently over-ruling the plaintiff's demurrer and declaring that the defendant's rejoinder was legally sufficient. Presumably, at this point the plaintiff surrejoined and the case went to jury. A year later, on 10 June 1830, the parties again came into court, the plaintiff insisting that it was entitled to judgment despite the jury's verdict for the defendant on the second plea. When each party announced a determination to take the case to the Supreme Court, the circuit court gave a pro forma judgment for the defendant. The same pleadings, verdict, and judgment were entered in the case against Perkins. There is nothing in the Supreme Court records to indicate that the parties in either case pursued an appeal (U.S. Cir. Ct., Va., Rec. Bk. XIX, 216; U.S. Cir. Ct., Va., Ord. Bk. XII, 300–301, 354).

Textual Notes

¶ 1	l. 1	discounted at ↑by↓ the bank of
	ll. 2–5	limitation. and the ↑The plf replies that the debt was contracted at the office in Virginia the President and Directors of which reside in the state and are members of the corporation.↓ The demurrer
¶ 2	ll. 1–2	from the 2d. of Ja English statute
¶ 3	ll. 3–4	every action it enumerated ↑enumerates↓, whatever
	l. 6	as well as ↑of↓ corporations. The
¶ 4	l. 4	covert, non [*erasure*] compos mentis
¶ 6	l. 4	entity, ↑being entirely incorporeal,↓ it can
	ll. 5–6	sec. it ↑ought↓ not to be
	l. 7	construed to comprehend ↑extend to↓ every
¶ 7	l. 3	plaintiff but the form of the action.
	l. 4	action is ↑equally↓ barred by
¶ 8	l. 6	it forms an ↑the↓ exception; and if
¶ 9	l. 2	is one of of more
¶10	ll. 4–5	any such ↑action,↓ be or shall
¶11	l. 1 beg.	To bring the ↑The↓ plaintiff ↑to come↓ within the letter
	l. 2	as a person ↑or persons.↓ This
	ll. 7–8	the courts ↑of England↓ had extended
	ll. 8–9	cases within the ↑its↓ equity though
	ll. 19–20	section ought to be construed ↑extended↓ so as to
	ll. 23	inclined to bring him within ↑allow him↓ its benefits
	ll. 25–26	from the consideration of the persons who compose ↑character in which those advantages are claimed.↓
¶12	l. 1	by the name ↑and style↓ of "The
	l. 3	of the ↑original↓ subscribers to the said bank ↑or their assignees.↓ The
	ll. 20–21	transact the particular ↑so much of the↓ business which ↑of the company as↓ is proper for

	l. 23	Directors ↑of the office↓ at Richmond
¶13	ll. 1–2	the letter ~~of~~ ↑or↓ the spirit of the saving ↑in the 12th. section↓ locality
	l. 6	stock holders, and ~~this body~~ acts by
	l. 12	these ~~residents~~ ↑agents↓ are divided
	ll. 24–25	this contract ↑if as to any,↓ be placed
¶14	ll. 1–2	statute to [*erasure*] bring the plaintiff
	ll. 2–3	the terms ↑or the operation↓ of the
	l. 4	case as ↑excluded from it, and↓ within
¶15	ll. 10–11	an individual residing ↑and sued↓ in a state where no office ↑or banking house↓ existed
	l. 14	the agents ↑and members↓ of the corporation
¶16	ll. 2–3	party plaintiff. ~~In the~~
¶17	l. 2	defendant. In ~~addition to~~ ↑support of↓ the argument
	l. 12	to such a ~~case~~ ↑suit↓ so as to
¶18	ll. 1–2	that ~~the~~ ↑The↓ ~~suit v~~ United States
¶21	l. 1	question whether [*erasure*] any

To William B. Sprague

Reverend and dear Sir: RICHMOND, *June 11th*, 1829.

I had the pleasure of receiving a few days past a copy of "Letters from Europe in 1828," for which I am indebted to your goodness.[1] Being at the time engaged in official duties I could not immediately give my time and attention to its perusal, and deferred acknowledging the obligation till I should have more leisure. The first moments, after closing the court, have been devoted to this object, and I have read your letters with real interest. Your animated description of the country and of the magnificent edifices you had seen almost brought them before my view.

The *maison carré* at Rheims is the model in imitation of which the capitol of Virginia was constructed.[2] We have deducted from the beauty as much as we have added to the convenience of the building, by turning the attic into a basement story, for offices, and by showing chimneys on the summits of the sidewalks. But however much I may be pleased with the topographical part of the work, I am still more interested in your description of living character.

The reading world, in the United States, has long possessed a general knowledge of Mr. Wilberforce and Miss Hannah More, and this general knowledge, accompanied as it universally is with admiration, increases the gratification of being introduced to them in their private and retired scenes.[3] But no persons excite my wonder so much as Mr. Hill, and Mr. Wilkes. That they should preserve such mental vigour and physical strength to the age they have attained, is a prodigy peculiarly, perhaps deceptively, encouraging to those who are approaching the same period.[4]

I pray you to receive my thanks for this very gratifying mark of your consideration, and my grateful acknowledgments for the more than polite letter which accompanied it. With great respect I am, Your obedt servt

J. MARSHALL

Printed, *Collector: A Magazine for Autograph and Historical Collectors,* XXII (1909), 109–10. ALS offered for sale by Kenneth W. Rendell, Inc., 1995 (Catalogue 248 *Historical Letters, Manuscripts, and Documents,* 41); described as "one and two-thirds pages, quarto," and as addressed to William B. Sprague in West Springfield, Mass.

1. *Letters from Europe, in 1828* (New York, 1828). Sprague originally published these letters in the *New-York Observer* between May and Oct. 1828.

2. The Maison Carré at Nîmes, in southern France, was the model for the Virginia Capitol. "Rheims" may be a transcription error.

3. For Sprague's meetings with William Wilberforce and Hannah More, see *Letters from Europe,* 93–98, 114–20.

4. Rowland Hill was eighty-nine and Matthew Wilkes eighty-one when Sprague visited them. Both were still active preachers (ibid., 75–78).

To Joseph Story

My dear Sir   Richmond June 11th. 1829

I had the pleasure some time past of receiving your letter inclosing a copy of that which transmitted a copy of his commission to our friend Judge Hopkinson.[1] I am the more gratified by the flattering terms of the letter when I recollect by whom the copy was taken. I am sure you told her in my name by anticipation how much I was delighted by such a letter copied by such a hand.

I am almost ashamed of my weakness and irresolution when I tell you that I am a member of our convention. I was in earnest when I told you that I would not come into that body, and really believed that I should adhere to that determination; but I have acted like a girl addressed by a gentleman she does not positively dislike, but is unwilling to marry. She is sure to yield to the advice and persuasion of her friends.

I wrote from Washington signifying my wish not to be brought forward, and desiring that the attention of the district might be directed to some other person; but the letter was mentioned to very few, and those few advised that it should not be communicated, but that I should remain free to act on my return as my judgement might direct.

The committee appointed at this place to nominate had written to me at Washington but the letter reached that place the day of my departure or the day afterwards, and of course was not received. A duplicate was transmitted to me a few days after my arrival in Richmond, which I answered immediately, acknowledging my grateful sense of the favorable opinion which had led to my nomination, but declaring my unwillingness to become a member of the convention, and declining the honour intended me. The Committee would not act upon this letter; but in the meantime it was rumoured in the town that I declined being voted for, in consequence of which I was pressed so earnestly on the subject by friends whose opinions I greatly value that my resolution began to stagger. It was said that whether I took any part in debate or not my services were counted on as of real importance. The committee addressed a second letter to me, containing assurances of their anxious desire that I would reconsider the resolution I had formed, and assent to what they were certain was the general wish of the district. As is usual, I yielded, and gave a reluctant consent to serve if I should be elected. Such is the history of the business. I assure you I regret being a member, and could I have obeyed the dictates of my own judgement, I should not have been one. I am conscious that I cannot perform a part I should wish to take in a popular assembly; but I am like Moliere's *Medicin malgré lui.*

The body will contain a great deal of eloquence as well as talent, and yet will do I fear much harm with some good. Our freehold suffrage is I believe gone past redemption. It is impossible to resist the influence, I had almost said contagion of universal example. With great esteem and affection, I am my dear Sir your Obedt

J Marsh⟨all⟩

ALS, Story Papers, MHi. Addressed to Story in Salem, Mass.; postmarked Richmond, 12 June.

1. Letter not found.

To Samuel D. Ingham

Sir[1]   Richmond July 2d. 1829

Frequent applications are made to me to certify the services of officers engaged in the war of our revolution. I gave one yesterday to a captain Sutton who was a paymaster in one of the Virginia Regiments which was ordered to the south while the residue of the Virginia line including the regiment in which I served remained in the north.[2] I gave it in some haste while some friends were waiting for me, and on reflection in the afternoon am induced to suspect that a fact may be implied from the certificate which I did not intend. The fact to which I allude is that Capt. Sutton was captured in Charleston. I did not mean to convey this idea. I meant to say that I beleived he still belonged to the regiment when it was captured, not that he was then personally with it. I beleive he was not with it. We had more officers than were necessary and some whose services were not required for the time remained either as supernumerary or to follow after the regiment. I am induced to beleive that this was Captain Suttons case. I do not understand that he ever resigned. I do not suppose that

Capt. Sutton will attempt to represent himself as having been a prisoner; but to obviate the possibility of misinterpreting my certificate I have thought it proper to give this explanation.

If the subject does not belong to your department I hope you will pardon the trouble I give when I request that this letter may be transmitted to the person before whom the certificate may be laid. Very respectfully, I am Sir your Obedt

J MARSHALL

[Certificate]

July 1st. 1829

I was very well acquainted with Captain John Sutton during the war of our revolution. He was pay master to one of the Virginia regiments on continental establishment. He says the first, and I have no doubt it was the first. He continued in the service as well as I recollect until it was ordered to the south and I believe marched with it from the northern army where I remained. The regiment was captured in Charleston. I never heard that Captain Sutton resigned.

J MARSHALL

City of Richmond to Wit:

This day Chief Justice John Marshall personally appeared before me an Alderman for the city aforesaid and made oath, that the above Certificate so far as he knows or believes, is true. Given Under my hand this 1st. day of July 1829.

JAMES RAWLINGS

ALS, RG 15 (file of John Sutton), DNA. Addressed to the secretary of the treasury in Washington and franked; postmarked Richmond, 2 July. Endorsed as received 6 July.

1. Samuel D. Ingham (1779–1860) of Pennsylvania was secretary of the treasury from Mar. 1829 to June 1831. He had previously served in Congress from 1813 to 1818 and again from 1822 to 1829

2. John Sutton of Caroline County was described in a pension application of 1832 as "aged about eighty eight" (affidavit, 10 Aug. 1832, RG 15 [file of John Sutton], DNA; T. Dix Sutton, *The Suttons of Caroline County, Virginia* [Richmond, Va., 1941], 8).

To Joseph Story

My dear Sir   Richmond July 3d. 1829

Your favour of the 23d. of June accompanying "Mr. Brazer's discourse at the interment of Doctor Holyoke," and your very interesting address to the bar of Suffolk at their anniversary on the 4th. of Septr. 1821, reached me a few days past.[1] It is impossible to read the first without strong impressions of the worth both of Doctor Holyoke and Mr. Brazer.

Your address was of course read with pleasure and attention. It takes, as is your *custom* a very comprehensive view of the subject — of the law and of the distinguished persons who have adorned it. It presents strong incentives to exertion.

Directly after writing my last letters I saw your appointment to the Dane professorship, and anticipated your acceptance of it.[2] The situation imposes duties which I am sure you will discharge in a manner useful to others, and conducive to your own fame. I did not however anticipate that the labour would immediately press so heavily on you as your letter indicates. Four octavo volumes in five years is a heavy requisition on a gentleman whose time is occupied by duties which cannot be neglected. I am confident that no person is more equal to the task than yourself; but I cannot help thinking that the publication may be postponed to advantage. I presume the work will be in the form of lectures; and I suspect you will find it advisable to postpone the publication of them till they have been revised for a second course. Precipitation ought carefully to be avoided. This is a subject on which I am not without experience.[3]

I hope your attention has been turned to the two great cases we have under advisement. I wish you would place your thoughts upon paper. I am the more anxious about this as I have myself not considered them, and fear that I shall be prevented from bestowing on them the attention they ought to receive. Mr. Thompson I presume will look thoroughly into that from New York and be prepared in it; but if the majority of the court should not concur with him, it will be necessary that preparation should be made for such an event.[4]

We shall have a good deal of division and a good deal of heat, I fear, in our convention. The free hold principle will I beleive be lost. It will however be supported with zeal. If that zeal could be successful I should not regret it. If we find that a decided majority is against retaining it I should prefer making a compromise by which a substantial property qualification may be preserved in exchange for it. I fear the excess incident to victory after a hard fought battle contested to the last extremity may lead to universa⟨l⟩ suffrage or to something very near it. What is the property qualification for your senate? How are your senators apportioned on the state? And how does your system work?

The question whether white population alone, or white population compounded with taxation shall form the basis of representation, will excite perhaps more interest than even the free hold suffrage. I wish we were well through the difficulty. Farewell. I am my dear Sir affectionately & truely, Your

J MARSHALL

ALS, Story Papers, MHi. Addressed to Story in Salem, Mass.; postmarked Richmond, 3 July.

1. Letter not found. The enclosed publications were John Brazer, *A Discourse Delivered in the North Church, in Salem, on Saturday, 4th of April 1829 . . . at the Interment of Edward Augustus Holyoke* (Salem, Mass., 1829) and Joseph Story, *An Address Delivered before the Members of the Suffolk Bar . . . on the 4th of September, 1821* (Boston, 1829). The latter was published as the lead article in the first issue of the *American Jurist and Law Magazine* in Jan. 1829. Story had declined to publish the address when he first delivered it in 1821 (JM to Story, 18 Sept. 1821, *PJM*, IX, 184, 185 n. 5; *American Jurist and Law Magazine*, I [1829], ii, 1–34). The address, entitled "Progress of Jurisprudence," was republished in William W. Story, ed., *The Miscellaneous Writings of Joseph Story* (1852; New York, 1972 reprint), 198–241.

2. JM read of Story's appointment in the newspaper. On the occasion of Josiah Quincy's inauguration as president of Harvard in June 1829, Nathan Dane made a donation of $10,000 to establish a professorship of law at the university. On 11 June the Harvard Corporation appointed Story as the first Dane professor, as the donor had requested (*Richmond Enquirer,* 12 June 1829; *Niles' Weekly Register* [Baltimore], 20 June 1829; William W. Story, ed., *Life and Letters of Joseph Story* [2 vols.; Boston, 1851], II, 3–6).

3. JM often regretted that his *Life of George Washington* "was composed with too much precipitation" (JM to Gales & Seaton, 22 Feb. 1825, *PJM*, X, 147).

4. The New York case was Inglis v. The Trustees of The Sailor's Snug Harbour, which had been argued at the Jan. 1829 term and held under advisement. Thompson delivered the opinion of the court at the Jan. 1830 term. In separate opinions Johnson concurred and Story concurred in part and dissented in part. Another case held under advisement from the Jan. 1829 term was Shanks v. Dupont, which came up from the South Carolina Supreme Court of Appeals. Story delivered the opinion of the court at the Jan. 1830 term, and Johnson dissented (3 Pet. 101,112–35, 135–45, 145–88, 243–50, 250–67)

To [James] Rawlings

Dear Sir[1]   Richmond, July 25th. 1829

The distressed I might say distracted situation of my wife at length forces me very reluctantly to make a direct application to you, and to state to you her real situation. The incessant barking of your dog has scarcely left her a night of quiet since the beginning of summer. During this spell of hot weather she has been kept almost perpetually awake. Last night she could not sleep two hours. Her situation is deplorable, and if this state of things continues she cannot live.

Rather than ask what it may be disagreeable to you to do, I would without hesitation abandon my house, and have proposed it to her; but our little place in the country affords her only a confined and hot chamber in which she thinks she cannot live. She therefore insists on my communicating her situation directly to you in the hope that when it is known the cause may not be continued. It is most painful to me that any thing in the circumstances of my family should interfere in the slightest degree with the inclination of a neighbour, and I have refrained as long as possible from applying to you on this irksome subject. Very respectfully, Your Obedt

J MARSHALL

We should take refuge among our friends in the upper country, but my wife cannot travel, and cannot sleep in a house with a family.

ALS (draft), Marshall Papers, ViW. Inside address to "Mr. Rawlings."

1. The addressee was probably James Rawlings (ca.1788–1838), a Richmond alderman and principal agent of the Mutual Assurance Society from 1815 to 1837. At the time of his death, Rawlings was president of the Farmers' Bank of Virginia (*Richmond Enquirer*, 17 Feb. 1838; John B. Danforth and Herbert A. Claiborne, *Historical Sketch of the Mutual Assurance Society of Virginia* [Richmond, Va., 1879], 127.

To Daniel Webster

Dear Sir   Richmond Aug. 9th. 1829

Mr Williams a respectable member of our bar and of our legislature visits the north in quest of health.[1] He purposes passing through Boston and wishes particularly to look in at your courts, should any of them be in session. Will you pardon the liberty I take in presenting him to you, and in asking your aid to furnish those facilities which will enable a stranger to observe with some advantage your mode of proceeding. With great respect and esteem, I am dear Sir your Obedt

J MARSHALL

Copy (owned by George C. Whipple III, Carmel, N.Y. 1972); Tr, NhHi. Copy addressed to Webster in Boston.

1. John G. Williams (d. 1833) served three terms in the House of Delegates from Henrico County, beginning in 1829. In addition to practicing law, Williams was also president of the Richmond Common Hall (Earl G. Swem and John W. Williams, comps., *A Register of the General Assembly of Virginia, 1776–1918* [Richmond, Va., 1918], 446; *Richmond Enquirer*, 24 Dec. 1833).

To Thomas G. Marshall

My dear Nephew: Richmond, Sept. 7th. 1829.

I received a letter from you before my late visit to Fauquier, which, by some unaccountable accident, I had attributed to Major Ambler, and directed my answer to him.[1]

I am greatly in advance for my brother's estate, but have determined not to interfere with the rents for the lands in Fauquier and Frederick. There has been some mistake as to the past. I have now requested W. Smith to make a separate rent roll of the rents on the land belonging to Colo Ambler[2] and my brother's heirs and to act according to their directions as to those rents. About two years rents, including I believe the present year's, are in arrears, and I have directed him to account with Colo. Ambler and my brothers heirs for those rents. I have not settled my accounts with Mr. Smith, and do not know what I may have received from him, but I have resolved to account with my brothers heirs for what I might have ⟨ . . . ⟩ to settle with Mr. Smith.

The annual rents due the estate for the Fauquier
lands is   [£] 23.78
For the Frederick land   [£] 27.5.6
                                                                     [£] 51.0.6

My brother has been dead thirteen years.
Deduct the two years rent now due there
remain 11 years   11
                                                                     [£]561.5.6
     Equal to $1870.08
     Deductions for collecting   112.
                                                                     4) 1758.08
     W. Markley's part   439.52
     Paid through Mr. Smith   340.
                                                                          99.52

I could not make an accurate calculation at the court house and directed Mr. Smith to pay you for Mr. Granly $340. I then thought my brother had died in 1807. On looking into my papers I find he died in 1816. I then supposed the two years of rent ⟨ . . . ⟩ excluded the rent to ⟨ . . . ⟩ this fall. On looking more accurately into Mr. Smith's statement I incline to think that the rent ⟨ . . . ⟩ includes the rents which will accrue this fall. Then two circumstances enlarge the sum to which Mr. B ⟨ . . . . is entitled, and I wish Mr. Smith to pay you for ⟨illegible⟩ as it ⟨illegible⟩ collecting an additional ⟨illegible⟩dred dollars. This letter will ⟨illegible⟩ for this purpose. I had made ⟨illegible⟩ for my ⟨ . . . ⟩, but intended them at the time as presents, and I do not purpose to change them now.

Your brother William is considerably indebted. If any person will administer on his estate I will pay him the same sum which I pay Mr. ⟨illegible⟩. If you administer you will be entitled to a commission.

I hope your family is in good health, and am your affectionate

J. MARSHALL

Tr, Beveridge-Marshall Collection, DLC. According to transcriber, letter addressed to Thomas Marshal, Locust Hill, Fauquier County. Angle brackets enclose words transcriber unable to read.

1. Letters not found. Thomas Marshall, son of JM's late brother William Marshall, had recently moved to Fauquier. "Major Ambler" was Thomas M. Ambler, another of JM's nephews who also resided in Fauquier (*PJM*, X, 120, 119 n. 1; *Old Homes and Familes of Fauquier County Virginia* [Berryville, Va., 1978], 591–92).

2. John Ambler, father of Thomas M. Ambler.

To Hugh S. Legaré

Dear Sir[1]   Richmond Septr 21. 1829

I am much flattered by the very gratifying mark of your recollection with which you have favd me in transmitting the 7th. No of the So Rev. I had heard it advantageously mentioned, but had never the pleasure before of seeing it. Whatever may have been my anticipations, they have been more than equalled by the perusal of this Number and I have contributed my mite towards the spread of its reputation within my narrow circle. My first attention was directed of course, to the two Essays which were designated by a pencil mark, both of which I read with pleasure. The criticism on the translation of Cicero de Repuba by Mr Featherstonhaugh has no inconsiderable literary merit. The Translator is certainly not much indebted to the critic — but if the citations are a fair specimen of the work, the criticism has as much justice as severity.[2]

While reading the observations on my friend Hoffman's ["]Outlines" I could not help reproaching myself as an example of that latent tendency to ill nature which has been charged on poor human nature. I truly respect both Mr. Hoffman & his lectures.[3] The passage selected from them has my full approbation. Yet I could enjoy the remarks made by the writer in the revw. on his introduction of matter, the relevency of which it would require more ingenuity to discover than to understand any proposition in his Book — So much more apt are we to taste the playful wit, which amuses itself on a friend than if directed to ourselves.[4] With great & respectful esteem, I am yr Obt Svt

J MARSHALL

Tr, South Caroliniana Collection, ScU. Tr in hand of Mary S. Bullen (Legaré's sister), who wrote at top: "Copy of a letter from Chief Justice Marshall to H S Legaré." Below signature, she wrote: "I send you this copy & have retained the original wh. together with letters of John Randolph — Albert *Gallatin Roger Sherman* I have been fortunate in finding *all directed,* to my brother personally." ALS offered for sale by Goodspeed's, Boston, 1957 (*Flying Quill* [July–Sept. 1957], 4).

1. Hugh Swinton Legaré (1797–1843), of Charleston, was a lawyer, politician, and man of letters. He was then a member of the South Carolina legislature and later served as attorney general of the state and as U.S. attorney general in the administration of John Tyler. In 1828 he became editor of the *Southern Review* and was its chief contributor until it ceased publication in 1832.

2. The article, "Cicero de Republica," was a review of G. W. Featherstonhaugh, *The Republic of Cicero, Translated from the Latin and Accompanied with a Critical and Historical Introduction* (New York, 1829), in *Southern Review,* IV (1829), 136–76. It was reprinted in a posthumous collection of Legaré's writings edited by his sister (Mary S. Bullen, ed., *Writings of Hugh Swinton Legaré* . . . [2 vols.; Charleston, S.C., 1846], II, 216–53). JM's use of the phrase "fair specimen" echoes the lead sentence of the review: "We should be very sorry to consider this pretended *translation* of Cicero's Republic . . . as a fair specimen of the scholarship of New-York."

3. "Hoffman's Legal Outlines," a review of David Hoffman, *Legal Outlines, Being the Sub-*

stance of a Course of Lectures Now Delivering in the University of Maryland (Baltimore, Md., 1829), in *Southern Review,* IV (1829), 47–69.

4. Legaré took Hoffman severely to task for the "the enormous mass of irrelevant matter" in the volume. Hoffman's wanderings into topics outside law, he wrote, could "neither directly nor indirectly, neither in business nor in speculation, neither at the bar nor in the closet, nor yet in the moot-club . . . be made to answer any one practical good purpose." Still, the reviewer did take "great pleasure" in praising Hoffman "as a lecturer on legal principles," quoting at length "the very judicious and philosophical remarks upon jurisdiction in Lect. vi" (ibid., 47, 48, 61, 62–63).

From Daniel Webster

Dear Sir   Boston Sep. 24 1829
    Mr Smith of New Hampshire, a Gentleman of our Profession, & son of Mr. Smith late Ch. Justice of that State is about to travel Southward for the improvement of his health.[1] If he should visit Richmond, he will hand you this, as he will be anxious to enjoy the means of seeing to advantage the interesting scene which Richmond is expected to exhibit, I beg to commend him to your kindness, as a well informed & respectable man.
Yrs always truly

DAN'L. WEBSTER

Tr, NhHi.

1. William Smith (1799–1830), son of Chief Justice Jeremiah Smith (1759–1842) of New Hampshire (Charles H. Bell, *The Bench and Bar of New Hampshire . . .* (Boston, 1894), 651.

To Joseph Story

My dear Sir   Richmond Septr. 30th. 1829
    I have read with great pleasure your discourse pronounced as Dane Professor of law in Harvard University.[1] It is in your best style of composition.
    You have marked out for yourself a course of labour which is sufficiently arduous; but I beleive you love to struggle with difficulty, and you have generally the good fortune or merit to overcome it. At seventy four you will find indolence creeping over you. But we will not anticipate evil.
    You have not spared the students of law more than the Professor. You have prescribed for them a most appalling course. Our southern youths would stumble at the threshhold and think such a task too formidable for even a commencement. You Yankees have more perseverance, or think more justly on the proposition that he who attempts much may accomplish something valuable, should his success not be complete.

I hope I shall live to read your lectures. They will form an exception to the plan of life I had formed for myself, to be adopted after my retirement from office — that is to read nothing but novels and poetry.

Our convention approaches. I still feel vain regrets at being a member. The chief though not the only cause of these regrets is that *non sum qualis eram*[2] — I can no longer debate. Yet I cannot apply my mind to anything else. Farewell — with affectionate esteem I remain your

J MARSHALL

ALS, Story Papers, MHi. Addressed to Story in Boston. Readdressed in another hand to Cambridge; postmarked Richmond, 30 Sept. Endorsed by Story.

1. Joseph Story, *A Discourse Pronounced upon the Inauguration of the Author, as Dane Professor of Law in Harvard University, on the Twenty-fifth Day of August, 1829* (Boston, 1829). The discourse, entitled "Value and Importance of Legal Studies," was reprinted in William W. Story, ed., *The Miscellaneous Writings of Joseph Story* (1852; New York, 1972 reprint), 503–48.

2. "I am not what I used to be."

To Mary Barney

Dear Madam[1]   Richmond October 1st. 1829

I have just received your letter and the packet transmitted by Mr. Harding.[2] It was impossible for me, attached as I truly am to the memory of your Father, and sincerely wishing your happiness, to read your impressive letter of the 5th. of June without the most lively sympathy. I need not tell you how deeply and how sincerely I lament the state of things you so feelingly describe and regret the cause which has produced it. I cannot however advise any publication of the case. I do not perceive any advantage which can be expected from it. You will of course take such measures as your own judgement and that of your nearest friends may suggest and approve; but when my opinion is asked I can only say that I cannot advise a publication.[3] With very sincere wishes for your happiness I am Madam with great respect Your obedt

J MARSHALL

ALS (owned by the Barcelo Family, Princeton, N.J., 2002). Addressed to Mrs. Mary Barney in Baltimore, Md.; postmarked Richmond, 1 Oct. Endorsed "Judge Marshall."

1. Mary Chase Barney (d. 1872) was the daughter of the late Justice Samuel Chase. She was married to William B. Barney, son of Joshua Barney (1759–1818), a naval hero of the Revolutionary War and the War of 1812. In 1832 she published a memoir of her father-in-law (Jane Shaffer Elsmere, *Justice Samuel Chase* [Muncie, Ind., 1980], 318–19; Mary Barney, ed., *A Biographical Memoir of the Late Commodore Joshua Barney* [Boston, 1832]). She also edited the *National Magazine; or, Lady's Emporium*, a Baltimore publication that had a brief existence in 1830–31.

2. Letter and packet not found. The artist Chester Harding had recently arrived in Richmond to draw portraits of delegates to the state constitutional convention.

3. The "case" referred to concerned William B. Barney, who with the advent of the Jackson administration had been dismissed from his post as naval officer for the port of Baltimore. Barney had held this office since 1818 (succeeding his father) and been re-appointed by Presidents Monroe and Adams. In response to her husband's dismissal, Mary Barney wrote an impassioned letter to President Jackson, dated 13 June 1829, accusing him of unjustly punishing Barney for supporting Adams's reelection and thereby cruelly and knowingly reducing the family to poverty. Jackson, she wrote, "knew the dependence of eight little children for food and raiment upon my husband's salary." Presumably, Mrs. Barney was soliciting JM's views about the propriety of publishing this letter. If so, his advice was not heeded, for the letter eventually appeared in newspapers in May 1830 and "large editions" of the letter were also separately "printed on satin." Earlier, in Mar. 1830, the Senate rejected a resolution requesting the president to inform the Senate of the reasons for Barney's removal (*Journal of the Executive Proceedings of the Senate*, III [Washington, 1828], 155, 156, 312, 315, 551, 554; IV [Washington, 1887], 79; *Niles' Weekly Register* [Baltimore], 15, 29 May 1830; *Mrs. Barney's Letter to President Jackson* [n.p., 1829]).

The Virginia Convention

EDITORIAL NOTE

In response to a referendum of eligible voters in the spring of 1828, a convention of delegates assembled in the capitol at Richmond in October 1829 to write a new constitution for Virginia to replace the one enacted in 1776. Reform had been brewing for several decades amid growing dissatisfaction with a system of repre-sentation that in the lower house of the legislature allotted two delegates to each county regardless of population. With the increase of white population occurring more rapidly in the western parts of the state, this arrangement gave ever more disproportionate political power to the older sections of the commonwealth east of the Blue Ridge Mountains. The freehold suffrage requirement (ownership of fifty acres of unimproved land, twenty-five acres and a dwelling in the country, or one-quarter-acre lots in towns) also came under attack.

Reform sentiment was strongest in the Shenandoah Valley and in the trans-Allegheny region that included most of present-day West Virginia. In the develop-ing west free labor and independent farming predominated, distinguishing it from the static plantation slave society of eastern Virginia. The convention was essentially a contest for political power between two distinctive regions, pitting democratic, reform-minded westerners against conservative easterners. It has aptly been called "the last of the great constituent assemblies in American his-tory," in which the commonwealth's most distinguished statesmen past and pres-ent brilliantly debated fundamental political ideas. In this contest for power, the issue of democracy was inextricably bound up with the question of slavery, as slaveholders perceived a direct threat to their property in reform proposals that apportioned representation according to white population and extended the vote to nonfreeholders.[1]

Among those in Richmond for this historic gathering were former presidents James Madison and James Monroe, who along with Chief Justice Marshall formed a living link with Virginia's revolutionary beginnings. A poignant symbolic mo-ment occurred on the opening day, 5 October, when Madison and Marshall escorted Monroe to the president's chair. Other notables attending the convention were Governor William B. Giles, Speaker of the U.S. House of Representatives Philip P. Barbour, Congressman John Randolph, a host of other federal and state legislators, and eminent members of the bench and bar.

At the age of seventy-four Marshall feared he was no longer physically able to participate in the floor debates of a popular assembly. It had been thirty years (as a member of Congress) since he had participated in such a body. He therefore politely declined the nomination extended by a committee of Richmond citizens the preceding March. The committee asked him to reconsider, assuring him that he would not be expected to take part on the floor but that his opinions and advice "could not fail to have their due weight." Flattery and an appeal to duty this time elicited a reluctant consent to become a candidate.[2] Privately, the chief justice regretted that his vanity had overcome a resolution formed by his better judgment. "I was in earnest," he confided to Story, "when I told you that I would not come into that body, and really believed that I should adhere to that determination; but I have acted like a girl addressed by a gentleman she does not positively dislike, but is unwilling to marry. She is sure to yield to the advice and persuasion of her friends."[3] In the May elections Marshall headed the list of the four successful candidates elected from his senatorial district.

Reluctant as he was to serve, Marshall became fully absorbed in the subject of constitutional reform as the convention approached. His views were those of a republican of the old school, though always inclined to pragmatic statesmanship and compromise rather than to dogmatic adherence to ideological principle. He remained attached to freehold suffrage but recognized that it was "gone past redemption." If the freehold principle could not be preserved, he preferred "making a compromise by which a substantial property qualification may be preserved in exchange for it."[4] Marshall set down the most elaborate statement of his views on suffrage in a letter written four months before the convention. Here he expressed his willingness to extend the freehold principle "to a reversionary interest; and to leases for such a term of years as may give the lessee actual property in the soil." Suffrage was a "social" not a "natural" right, a privilege to be granted only on considerations of "expediency." The wisest course was "so to constitute the legislature" as would best provide for the security of "the great subjects of legislation — persons and property." This was to be accomplished by confining the right of suffrage to property holders, particularly those who owned land, "the honest yeomanry of the country." Public opinion in Virginia, he suspected, no longer endorsed this once orthodox republican view and under Thomas Jefferson's influence appeared to be moving toward universal white manhood suffrage.[5]

Marshall did his part to bring the views of the disenfranchised to the attention of the convention by presenting "The Memorial of the Non-Freeholders of the City of Richmond" on 13 October. After it was read, he took the further step of moving that the memorial be referred to the committee on the legislative department, noting that "however gentlemen might differ in opinion on the question discussed in the memorial, he was sure they must all feel that the subject was one of the deepest interest, and well entitled to the most serious attention of this body."[6] It soon became clear, however, that a majority at the convention was not inclined to make a radical departure from the ancient system. Realizing that universal suffrage was unattainable, democratic reformers urged that the right to vote be extended to all taxpaying citizens. Conservatives resisted, extolling the virtues of the freehold principle. Marshall's sympathies were with them, but he himself did not rise in convention to defend freehold suffrage, perhaps an indication of a lack of ideological zeal. Silently, the chief justice voted with the majority in rejecting extension of the franchise to taxpayers. In the end, the convention did break the freehold principle but only modestly broadened the suffrage to include leaseholders (of property of the annual value or rent of twenty dollars) and housekeepers (heads of families who paid taxes).[7]

The suffrage issue was of decidedly secondary importance to the intractable question of the basis of representation, which revolved around the demographic shift of white population to the westward that had been occurring since the late eighteenth century. Reformers urged that the legislature be apportioned according to white population, which would increase representation of the western regions—the Valley and trans-Allegheny—to around forty-five percent of the delegates in the House of Delegates. On this basis the Tidewater region (where most of the slave property was concentrated) would see a decrease in its representation from thirty-five percent under the present system of equal county representation to twenty-four percent. In place of equal county representation (which had little support), conservatives proposed a basis combining white population and taxation. Since most state taxes fell on land and slaves, they believed this mixed basis would would protect slaveholding interests. Under this compound basis, Tidewater representation would rise to thirty percent while western representation would fall to thirty-five percent.[8]

The debates on these apportionment plans and various compromise positions occupied the largest portion of the published reports of the proceedings. In the same letter containing his thoughts on suffrage, Marshall stated his preference for "estimating our slave population in apportioning representation." Much of the reasoning in support of freehold suffrage applied as forcefully to this question as well, he said. Because slave property was "among the most productive funds for taxation" and bore "a great portion of the burthens of government," it had "peculiar claims to consideration in the formation" of the legislature. The increased representation enjoyed by slaveholders was "perhaps the only certain security against oppressive taxation." Slaves were also "persons" who constituted "a part of the real effective population of the country" and therefore should be counted like others—females and minors—disqualified from voting but "included in the enumeration of persons on whom representation is apportioned."[9]

Marshall made only a few appearances on the convention floor in the debate over representation. As an old republican, the chief justice believed "the soundest principles of republicanism" sanctioned "some relation between representation and taxation."[10] Although aligning himself with eastern conservatives opposed to the white basis, he largely refrained from rhetoric that linked republicanism to the defense of minority interest. And he most certainly did not sympathize with the conservative argument that likened the stand of eastern Virginia to the commonwealth's defense of state rights within the federal system. Marshall instead focused his efforts on bringing about a workable compromise. "Give me a Constitution," he said, "that shall be received by the people: a Constitution in which I can consider their different interests to be duly represented, and I will take it, though it may not be that which I most approve."[11] Genuine compromise necessarily entailed the sacrifice of theory, mutual and equal concession, the identification of a true "middle ground" on which the parties could meet. For him that middle ground was representation in both houses of the legislature on a compound basis of white population and three-fifths of the slaves ("federal numbers"). When this compromise failed, Marshall voted with the majority for a plan that apportioned representatives and senators equitably among the geographical regions of the state. Approval of this plan was a bitter defeat for the reformers and secured the continuing political ascendancy of Virginia's slaveholders.[12]

Marshall directed most of his attention at the convention to the judiciary department. As chairman of the judiciary committee, the chief justice prepared a draft report that, as amended in committee, he presented to the convention on 20 October. His first proposed resolution announced the two principal goals he hoped to accomplish: to give constitutional status to the county courts and to secure the principle of judicial independence. The county courts had no explicit recognition under the constitution of 1776, but venerable tradition had firmly entrenched them as local governing bodies. In recent years these oligarchic, self-perpetuating bodies of magistrates had come under increasing attack from democratic reformers. With equal passion conservative defenders of the old order extolled the county courts as the principal pillar of the Old Dominion's wise and beneficent system of governance. Although critical of the county court establishment as a state legislator in the 1780s, Marshall in 1829 enlisted his support for preserving this system of local government.[13]

The assault on the county courts began in the deliberations of the judiciary committee, which by a narrow majority first removed and then reinstated their designation as constitutional courts. When the judiciary report came up for consideration by the committee of the whole on 30 November, Thomas M. Bayly moved to strike the county courts from the list of constitutional courts. This motion prompted Marshall to rise in praise of these tribunals as largely responsible for the internal tranquillity that prevailed in Virginia. "There is no part of America," he said, "where less disquiet and less of ill-feeling between man and man is to be found than in this Commonwealth, and I believe most firmly that this state of things is mainly to be ascribed to the practical operation of our County Courts." After two days of debate a decided majority signified its agreement with the chief justice in voting to reject Bayly's motion.[14]

More important to Marshall than saving the county courts was preserving judicial independence. In addition to providing for judicial tenure during good behavior, his report specified that "no modification or abolition of any Court shall be construed to deprive any Judge thereof of this office." To this clause the judiciary committee added "but such Judge shall perform any judicial duties which the Legislature shall assign him." The motive behind this provision was to guard against a possible construction founded on Congress's 1802 repeal of the Judiciary Act of 1801. The repeal had abolished the federal circuit courts composed of sixteen new federal judgeships appointed under the 1801 act. When the clause came before the committee of the whole on 11 December, Philip P. Barbour moved to strike it, precipitating a spirited debate in which Marshall tenaciously and eloquently defended the independence of the judiciary. Barbour opposed the clause as preventing the legislature from carrying out an efficient reorganization of the court system by reducing the number of judges necessary to administer justice. Attention then shifted to an amendment proposed by Littleton W. Tazewell to change the name of the "Court of Appeals" to "Supreme Court." By adopting the language of the federal Constitution, said Tazewell, the proposed Virginia constitution would have the same construction, which according to him was that the Supreme Court alone was a constitutional court and only its judges were beyond the reach of Congress. According to this understanding, the effect of Barbour's motion would be confined to inferior courts, and, if the legislature chose to abolish such a court, it also abolished the office of a judge of that court. Like others who supported Barbour's motion, Tazewell raised the specter of a class of judicial pensioners receiving salaries while performing no duties.

Marshall regarded Barbour's motion and especially Tazewell's amendment as a direct blow against judicial independence. In response he patiently tried to explain why an uncompromising adherence to this principle was vitally necessary: "Advert, sir, to the duties of a Judge. He has to pass between the Government and the man whom that Government is prosecuting: between the most powerful individuals in the community, and the poorest and most unpopular. It is of the last importance, that in the exercise of these duties, he should observe the utmost fairness. Need I press the necessity of this? Does not every man feel that his own personal security and the security of his property depends on that fairness? The Judicial Department comes home in its effects to every man's fireside: it passes on his property, his reputation, his life, his all. Is it not, to the last degree important, that he should be rendered perfectly and completely independent, with nothing to influence or to controul him but God and his conscience?" The principle should apply not only to supreme court judges but to all judges "who try causes between man and man, and between a man and his Government." There was also a practical consideration. Unless judicial independence was firmly implanted in the constitution, the judiciary department would not be able to attract the most knowledgeable and talented lawyers to the bench. "But if they may be removed at pleasure," he asked, "will any lawyer of distinction come upon your bench? No, Sir. I have always thought, from my earliest youth till now, that the greatest scourge an angry Heaven ever inflicted upon an ungrateful and a sinning people, was an ignorant, a corrupt, or a dependent Judiciary. Will you draw down this curse upon Virginia?"[15] Marshall's resort to such an uncharacteristic rhetorical flourish showed that the debate over judicial tenure roused his deepest feelings, engaging his mind and heart in equal measure.

The large majorities by which the committee of the whole defeated Barbour's and Tazewell's motions suggest that Marshall's words had their effect. The battle was far from over, however, and resumed on 23 December when the convention formally considered the clause that Marshall believed was necessary to protect the independence of the judiciary. This time Lucas P. Thompson moved to strike it, and William B. Giles took the lead in supporting the motion. Again the chief justice rose in reply, reaffirming his adherence to the distinction between a court, which the legislature might abolish, and the office of a judge, which was to be held during good behavior. The effect of the motion, he urged, was to make judicial tenure in fact depend on the will of the legislature. The convention voted to retain the clause, though by a smaller majority than had prevailed in the committee of the whole. On 29 December the convention approved an addition to the clause that spoke to the nagging concern about paying salaries to surplus judges. It now read: "No modification or abolition of any Court, shall be construed to deprive any Judge thereof of his office; but such Judge shall perform any Judicial duties which the Legislature shall assign him; but if no Judicial duties shall be assigned to him by the Legislature, he shall receive no salary in virtue of said office." Marshall in vain objected that the addition made the tenure of judges depend on the legislative will. He tried to reassure the delegates of the moral impossibility of a situation in which there would be no judicial duties to be assigned a judge whose court had been abolished. The amendment was therefore not only unnecessary but needlessly put in jeopardy the principle of judicial independence.

When the select committee submitted its draft constitution to the convention on 4 January 1830, the entire clause was dropped, leaving judicial tenure to rest solely on the declaration that judges were to hold their offices during good behavior. Marshall himself was a member of that committee and no doubt proposed omitting the clause. The select committee, he later explained, agreed that the provision stating that no abolition of a court was to deprive a judge of office was "in utter repugnance" to that permitting the legislature to withhold a judge's salary by refusing to assign him any judicial duties.[16] As the convention neared its conclusion, Marshall was uneasy about his colleagues' commitment to an independent judiciary. "A strong disposition to prostrate the judiciary has shown itself and has succeeded to a considerable extent," he wrote Story. The chief justice postponed his trip to Washington for the Supreme Court session in order to be present for a final debate on the judiciary that took place on 13 January.[17]

With the clause now dropped from the constitution, the convention took up the question of how the judiciary article was to be interpreted. Tazewell and Giles restated their view that abolition of a court terminated the office of a judge of that court, both citing Congress's 1802 repeal of the 1801 Judiciary Act as giving the true interpretation of the federal Constitution, whose language was adopted by the proposed Virginia constitution. Marshall denied that the Constitution had been "definitively expounded by a single act of Congress," particularly one that had "passed in times of high political and party excitement." At the same time he insisted that neither his opinion nor those of any member of the convention ought to influence the construction of the constitution, a task that should be left to future judicial decision. The constitution "ought to be construed *in its words:* and not in the opinion any member might have expressed upon it. . . . Let the Constitution speak its own language: and be construed by those whose office it was to construe it."[18] Ultimately, the convention reinstated the clause in an amended form that read: "No law abolishing any court shall be construed to deprive a Judge thereof of his office, unless two-thirds of the members of each house present, concur in the passage thereof: But the Legislature may assign other duties to the Judges of courts abolished by any law enacted by less than two-thirds of the members of each house present." Marshall voted with the majority in adopting this amendment.

After more than three months of deliberations the convention had produced a constitution that was (wrote Marshall) "not precisely what any of us wished, but is better than we feared."[19] The chief justice himself could rest satisfied that the judiciary article survived substantially as he had originally proposed it. His performance in the debate on judicial tenure belied his doubts that he was no longer equal to the challenge of participating in public assemblies. Despite a weakened voice and awkward delivery, Marshall commanded attention by the force of his still vigorous intellect, his cogent reasoning, and his patriarchal wisdom. He spoke infrequently and not at great length but always to good effect, carefully choosing his moment for entering the debate. His appearance was "revolutionary and patriarchal." Dressed "in a long surtout of blue," he possessed "a face of genius, and an eye of fire." Because his voice was "extremely feeble," as soon as he rose to speak his fellow delegates "would press towards him, and strain with outstretched necks and eager ears, to catch his words." While acknowledging the power of his reasoning and the lucidity of his arguments, observers were particularly struck by Marshall's "intense earnestness," his animation and even passion when speaking: "He has a song in speaking to which his right arm harmonises with a most ungracious swing. He leans forward in speaking; and pours his whole feelings in his speech."[20]

When the convention was not in session, Marshall hosted dinners at his house near the capitol. No record of these dinners and attending guests exists, though a letter to Madison withdrawing an invitation on account of the death of Bushrod Washington suggests that they were a regular occurrence. Visiting family members who stayed at the house included Thomas Marshall, the chief justice's recently widowed son, who attended the convention debates first as an observer and later as a delegate from the Fauquier district. Another house guest was Thomas Francis Marshall, a nephew from Kentucky.[21] Besides entertaining, Marshall spent hours in the studios of the portrait artists who flocked to Richmond for the occasion. Chester Harding, Robert Sully, and James Wattles executed portraits of the chief justice based on sittings during the convention. Also in town was George Catlin (1796–1872), who produced his monumental painting of the convention in the style of Trumbull's *Declaration of Independence.*[22]

The proceedings and debates of the convention were published in the pages of the *Richmond Enquirer.* Editor Thomas Ritchie hired Arthur J. Stansbury of Washington, reporter of Congress, to report the debates. From his stenographic notes and from the speakers' own notes and drafts, Stansbury prepared a daily sketch of the proceedings and speeches, which Ritchie printed within a few days of their occurrence. Longer speeches that could not fit into the daily sketch were also eventually published in full. Seven months after the convention adjourned, Ritchie and his partner John L. Cook published the debates as *Proceedings and Debates of the Virginia State Convention, of 1829–30,* a closely printed volume exceeding nine hundred pages. Marshall presumably relied on notes for his longer utterances, though no papers in his hand relating to the convention have been found. In at least one instance, the chief justice supplied Ritchie with materials for printing a corrected version of his speech.[23] The texts of his speeches and remarks published below are taken from the reports as printed in the newspaper.

1. Merrill D. Peterson, ed., *Democracy, Liberty, and Property: The State Constitutional Conventions of the 1820s* (Indianapolis, Ind., 1966), 271–74; Alison Goodyear Freehling, *Drift Toward Dissolution: The Virginia Slavery Debate of 1831–1832* [Baton Rouge, La., 1982], 36–81.

2. Committee of Richmond Citizens to JM, 27 Mar. 1829; JM to Committee of Richmond Citizens, 28 Mar. 1829.

3. JM to Joseph Story, 11 June 1829.

4. JM to Joseph Story, 11 June 1829, 3 July 1829.

5. JM to James M. Garnett, 20 May 1829.

6. *Proceedings and Debates,* 25–31.

7. Peterson, ed., *Democracy, Liberty, and Property,* 279–81; *Proceedings and Debates,* 25–31, 368, 383.

8. Freehling, *Drift Toward Dissolution*, 49–50, 271.

9. JM to James M. Garnett, 20 May 1829.

10. Speech on Apportionment, 30 Nov. 1829 (288, below).

11. Speech on Apportionment, 30 Nov. 1829 (289, below)

12. Speech on Apportionment, 4 Dec. 1829 (303, below); Peterson, ed., *Democracy, Liberty, and Property*, 277–79; Freehling, *Drift Toward Dissolution*, 66–70.

13. Peterson, ed., *Democracy, Liberty, and Property*, 282–83; *PJM*, I, 124.

14. Speech on County Courts, 30 Nov. 1829 (293, below).

15. Debate on Judiciary, 11 Dec. 1829 (317, below).

16. Debate on Judiciary, 13 Jan. 1830 (337, below).

17. JM to Joseph Story, 8 Jan. 1830.

18. Debate on Judiciary, 13 Jan. 1830 (338, below).

19. JM to Thomas W. Griffith, 7 Feb. 1830.

20. [Charles Campbell], "Convention of Virginia," *Southern Literary Messenger,* III (1837), 238; [Lucian Minor], "Chief Justice Marshall," *Southern Literary Messenger,* II (1836), 188; Hugh Blair Grigsby, *The Virginia Convention of 1829–30* (1854; New York, 1969 reprint), 15–16; Grigsby, "Sketches of Members of the Constitutional Convention of 1829–1830," *Virginia Magazine of History and Biography,* LXI (1953), 322–23.

21. JM to James Madison, 30 Nov. 1829; Earl G. Swem and John W. Williams, *A Register of the General Assembly of Virginia, 1776–1918* (Richmond, 1918), 245; JM to Mary W. Marshall, 31 Jan. 1830 and n. 3.

22. JM to John Randolph, ca. Nov. 1829 and n. 1; JM to John Vaughan, 10 Sept. 1830 and n. 1; JM to James Madison, ca. Oct. 1829 and n.1; Andrew Oliver, *The Portraits of John Marshall* (Charlottesville, Va., 1977), 113–20.

23. Speech on Apportionment, 4 Dec. 1829 and n. 1.

Debate on Committees
Virginia Convention
9 October 1829

Mr. Mercer then moved the following resolution:

Resolved, That so much of the twenty-fourth rule of the Convention, as limits the number of a Select Committee to thirteen, be suspended, for the purpose of enlarging the three Committees required by the preceding resolutions, to such extent, as that each Committee shall comprehend one member from every Senatorial District, and composing the Committee required by the fourth resolution of such members as may not be placed on the preceding Committees.[1]

Mr. M. now replied to the objections before stated by Mr. Leigh,[2] and referred to precedents in the Journals of the House of Delegates, to shew that Committees of twenty, of thirty-three, and one of forty-three members, had been appointed on important subjects. No great evil, he thought, arose from the formal mode of discussion, pursued in large Committees, though he acknowledged, that he should prefer the colloquial mode of debate.

A desultory conversation ensued, in which Messrs. Leigh, Stanard, Mercer, Fitzhugh and Doddridge took part, and in which several modifications of the resolution were proposed. Mr. Marshall enquired of Mr. Mercer, if he intended to bring forward, at all, the two resolutions he had read yesterday?[3]

Mr. Mercer replying in the negative,

Mr. Marshall said, that if he had brought them forward, he should have thought, that one Committee of twenty-four was sufficient; as the subject to be referred to it, was geographical in its nature, and had a bearing on members, according to the part of the State where they resided. In such a Committee, twenty-four members might be required, in order to collect the opinions of every part of the State; but this was not equally necessary on questions not geographical in their nature. When the measure proposed, was to affect all the citizens alike, there was not the same reason for a difference of opinion, in different districts. Still, if no objection arose from the proposed number of members in the Committee, Mr. Marshall said, he should have submitted to the arrangement; but there was an objection, and a serious one, which did arise from it: it was the wish, he presumed, of every member, that at least some portion of the business before the Convention, might be entered upon and completed as soon as practicable. But it must be obvious, that if each of the Committees were to consist of twenty-four members, more time would be consumed in preparing their reports, than if the number were smaller. If, for example, the Committees should consist of thirteen members, the reports, though he hoped not less considered, would be considered and reported upon in less time.

Mr. Scott moved to amend the resolution, by striking out the word "three," so as to read, "the first of the Committees," instead of "the first *three* of the Committees."

Mr. Mercer observed in reply to Judge Marshall, that there was not a part of the Constitution, in which all parts of the Senate were not deeply interested. How could the Convention know the opinions of the people, for instance, respecting the Executive Department of Government, but by consulting the people? and how could it consult them, but through their representatives? So respecting the Judiciary; he could assure the honorable and venerable gentleman that that was a question of a local character; there did exist on that subject, evils of very great magnitude; but those evils were not universal, but local in their extent. The gentleman was ready to admit that the principle involved in the first of the resolutions was such as required a Committee from all parts of the State; he believed the same principle would be found to apply to all the other resolutions. Mr. M. then stated the reasons why he should not offer his two resolutions, and concluded by a compliment to the judgment and standing of the gentleman from Richmond.

Mr. Marshall rejoined. If his friend had understood him to say that every part of the community was not interested in every part of the Constitution, he had greatly mistaken his meaning. But the interest they take in the other parts of the Constitution not geographical in their bearing, was not local or geographical in its kind. Gentlemen on one side of James River, for instance, had the same interest in the Executive Department of the Government, as those on the other side. That interest did not depend at all upon their residence: on that Department, therefore, he could see no reason for a Committee taken from all parts of the State; but the case was very different when the question of the basis of representation was involved. As that subject was not necessarily separated by the Legislative Department, he saw no need of reporting on it by a separate Committee. As there was nothing geographical in the Executive or Judicial Departments of government, to consider them; and as a large Committee was likely to be slow in reporting, he preferred one of more limited numbers.[4]

Printed, *Richmond Enquirer*, 10 October 1829.

1. The convention on this day adopted a series of resolutions to appoint committees on the legislative, executive, and judicial departments, and a fourth committee to consider matters not referred to the preceding committees.

2. In response to Mercer's previous notice that he would move for the enlargement of the committees to twenty-four members each, Leigh objected that such large committees "would be so many debating societies" (*Proceedings and Debates*, 20).

3. On 8 Oct. Mercer gave notice that he would move for committees to consider the questions of suffrage and the basis of representation (ibid., 10).

4. Scott's amendment lost, and Mercer's resolution was adopted.

Draft of Report of Judiciary Committee
Virginia Convention
12 October 1829

On 9 October the convention ordered the establishment of four committees to consider amendments to the present constitution, one each on the legislative, executive, and judicial departments, and one on the bill of rights and on other matters not referred to the preceding committees. These committees of twenty-four were named the following day. Marshall, as chairman of the judiciary committee, submitted the following propositions on 12 October (*Richmond Enquirer*, 13, 15 Oct. 1829).

That the Judicial power shall be vested in a Court of Appeals, in such Inferior Courts as the Legislature shall from time to time ordain and establish, and in the County Courts;[1] the jurisdiction of these tribunals to be regulated by law. The Judges of the Court of Appeals, and of the Inferior Courts, shall hold their offices during good behaviour, or until removed in the manner prescribed in this Constitution; and no modification or abolition of any Court shall be construed to deprive any Judge thereof of this office. The present Judges remain in office,[2] and all vacancies shall be

supplied by   ; but if any vacancy shall occur during the recess of the
            the Governor, or other person performing the duty of Governor,
may appoint a person to fill such vacancy, who shall continue in office
until the end of the next succeeding session of the   .[3] That the
Judges of the Court of Appeals, and of the Inferior Courts, shall receive
fixed and adequate salaries, which shall not be diminished during their
continuance in office. That on the creation of any new County, Justices of
the Peace shall be appointed in the first instance, as may be prescribed by
law. When vacancies shall occur in any County, or it shall for any cause be
deemed necessary to increase their number, appointments shall be made
by the Governor, on the recommendation of their respective County
Courts.[4] That the Judges of the Court of Appeals, and of the Inferior
Courts, offending against the State, either by mal-administration, corruption, or neglect of duty, or by any other high crime or misdemeanor, shall
be impeachable by the House of Delegates; such impeachment to be
prosecuted before the Senate. If found guilty by a majority of   of
the whole Senate, such person shall be removed from office. That Judges
may be removed from office by a vote of the General Assembly, but a
majority of   of each House must concur in such vote, and the cause
of removal shall be entered on the Journals of each. The Judge, against
whom the Legislature is about to proceed, shall receive notice thereof,
accompanied with a copy of the charges against him, at least
before the day on which either House of the General Assembly shall act
on such charge.

Printed, *Richmond Enquirer,* 15 October 1829.

1. During its first two days of deliberations, on 13 and 14 Oct., the committee removed
the county courts from their designation as constitutional courts. That left the Court of
Appeals as the only constitutional court; the inferior courts, including the county courts,
were to be regulated by the will of the legislature. However, on 15 Oct., the committee
reinstated the county courts to constitutional status. The circumstances of the reinstate-
ment were recounted by Alexander Campbell of Brooke County in his speech of 1 Dec.
According to Campbell, Robert Stanard "moved for a reconsideration, a member being
then present who was absent when they were rejected — they were then carried by one of a
majority, one of the friends of reform being absent" (ibid., 15 Oct. 1829; *Proceedings and
Debates,* 525).

2. The committee also at an early stage decided that "the Commissions of the present
Judges should cease with the *present* Constitution, and that all the judges should be re-
elected with the new Constitution." As amended, the resolution provided for the present
judges "to remain in office until the expiration of the first session of the legislature held
under the new Constitution and no longer." On 17 Oct. John Scott, Jr., of Fauquier County
moved to add the words, "But the Legislature shall cause to be paid to such of them as shall
not be reappointed, such sums, as from their age, infirmities and past services, shall be
deemed reasonable." This motion lost by a vote of 12 to 10, but a second amendment,
substituting "may cause to be paid" in place of "shall cause to be paid," prevailed by a vote
of 13 in favor. A motion by Robert B. Taylor of Norfolk to exempt the present Court of
Appeals judges from being vacated by the new constitution was unsuccessful (*Richmond
Enquirer,* 15, 20 Oct. 1829).

3. This section on filling judicial vacancies was subsequently attached to a separate resolution providing for the mode of electing judges, which JM did not include in his draft. Debate on this question centered on whether to retain the present method of electing by joint ballot of both houses of the legislature or of election by the senate on nomination by the executive. On 16 Oct. the committee narrowly approved retaining the former mode, JM breaking a 10 to 10 tie by casting his vote in favor (ibid., 15, 17 Oct. 1829).

4. On 17 Oct. Campbell offered a substitute motion providing for counties, cities, and boroughs to be divided into wards for apportioning justices and for election of justices for a term of years by persons qualified to vote for members of the legislature. The committee rejected this alternative. At the same time the committee approved Scott's resolution providing for county clerks to be appointed by their respective courts and their tenure of office to be regulated by law (ibid., 20 Oct. 1829).

Report of Judiciary Committee
Virginia Convention
20 October 1829

Mr. Marshall, from the Committee on the Judiciary Department of Government, made the following report from the Committee:[1]

1. Resolved, That the Judicial power shall be vested in a Court of Appeals, in such Inferior Courts, as the Legislature shall from time to time ordain and establish, and in the County Courts. The Jurisdiction of these tribunals shall be regulated by law. The Judges of the Court of Appeals and of the Inferior Courts, shall hold their offices during good behaviour, or until removed in the manner prescribed in this Constitution; and shall, at the same time, hold no other office, appointment, or public trust: and the acceptance thereof, by either of them, shall vacate his judicial office. No modification or abolition of any court, shall be construed to deprive any judge thereof of his office; but such Judge shall perform any judicial duties which the Legislature shall assign him.

2. Resolved, That the present Judges of the Court of Appeals, Judges of the General Court, and Chancellors remain in office until the expiration of the first session of the Legislature, held under the new Constitution, and no longer. But the Legislature may cause to be paid to such of them, as shall not be re-appointed, such sum as, from their age, infirmities, and past services, shall be deemed reasonable.

3. Resolved, That Judges of the Court of Appeals and Inferior Courts, except Justices of the County Courts, and the Alderman or other Magistrates of corporation Courts, shall be elected by the concurrent vote of both Houses of the General Assembly, each House voting separately, and having a negative on the other; and the members thereof voting *viva voce*. The votes of the members shall be entered on the Journals of their respective Houses. Should the two houses, in any case, fail to concur in the election of a judge, during the Session, the Governor shall decide the

election, by appointing one of the two persons who first received a majority of votes in the Houses in which they were respectively voted for. But if any vacancy shall occur, during the recess of the General Assembly, the Governor, or other person performing the duty of Governor, may appoint a person to fill such vacancy, who shall continue in office until the end of the next succeeding session of the General Assembly.

4. Resolved, That the Judges of the Court of Appeals, and of the Inferior Courts shall receive fixed and adequate salaries, which shall not be diminished during their continuance in office.

5. Resolved, That on the creation of any new county, Justices of the Peace shall be appointed, in the first instance, as may be prescribed by law. When vacancies shall occur in any county, or it shall, for any cause, be deemed necessary to increase their number, appointments shall be made by the Governor, by and with the advice and consent of the Senate, on the recommendation of their respective County Courts.

6. Resolved, That the Clerks of the several Courts shall be appointed by their respective Courts, and their tenure of office be prescribed by law.

7. Resolved, That the Judges of the Court of Appeals and of the Inferior Courts, offending against the State, either by mal-administration, corruption, or neglect of duty, or by any other high crime or misdemeanor, shall be impeachable by the House of Delegates, such impeachment to be prosecuted before the Senate. If found guilty by a majority of two-thirds of the whole Senate, such persons shall be removed from office. And any Judge so impeached shall be suspended from exercising the functions of his office until his acquittal, or until the impeachment shall be discontinued or withdrawn.

8. Resolved, That Judges may be removed from office by a vote of the General Assembly: but two thirds of the whole number of each House must concur in such vote, and the cause of removal shall be entered on the Journals of each. The Judge against whom the Legislature is about to proceed shall receive notice thereof, accompanied with a copy of the causes alleged for his removal, at least twenty days before the day on which either House of the General Assembly shall act thereupon.

The report having been read, on motion of Mr. Marshall, it was laid upon the table.[2]

Printed, *Richmond Enquirer*, 22 October 1829.

1. The resolutions JM presented on this day were adopted by the judiciary committee on 19 Oct. (*Richmond Enquirer*, 20 Oct. 1829).

2. The report was taken up by the committee of the whole beginning on 30 Nov.

Debate on Mode of Proceeding
Virginia Convention
21 October 1829

Mr. Marshall, from the Committee on the Judicial Department of Government, then rose and said, that although it was not probable the Convention would take up any one of the reports of the Select Committees which had been appointed, until the reports of all those Committee should have been received, yet, with a view to put the reports which had been rendered in a way to be acted upon by the Convention, if such should be its pleasure, he moved that the report made by the Committee on the Judicial Department, be referred to a Committee of the Whole Convention, and be made the Order of the Day for to-morrow.

Mr. Upshur of Accomack, said, that he had understood a wish to be entertained by some members of the House, that a smaller Committee than a Committee of the Whole, should be raised for the purpose of receiving and digesting the reports of the Select Committees, and laying the whole before the Convention to receive its action thereon. Should such a course be adopted after the report of the Judicial Committee had gone to a Committee of the Whole, it would have again to be withdrawn from their hands and put with the rest under the care of the Sub-Committee. He would, therefore, very respectfully suggest to the member from Richmond, whether it would not be expedient to withdraw for the present the motion which he had made. Mr. U. said that he was the rather induced to this course, by observing that the Chairman of the Committee on the Executive (Mr. Giles) was not in his place, and he knew that it was not the wish of that Committee, that their resolution should take the course now proposed.

Mr. Marshall said, that he was by no means solicitous that the motion he had made should be adopted: his only object had been to put business in such a train, that it might be taken up and acted upon whenever the house should wish to consider it. The Reference of the report to a Committee of the Whole, implied no sort of necessity that the report should be immediately acted upon. As to the suggestion of the gentleman from Accomack, (Mr. Upshur) if the House should agree to refer all the reports to a Select Committee before the Committee of the Whole should have perfected its action on the particular report which was the subject of his motion; all that would have to be done, would be to discharge the Committee of the Whole from the further consideration of it: the motion he had made, would not be at all in the way of such a course. It seemed to him very possible, and extremely probable, that the House would not refer the respective reports to a Select Committee, until they should have received some report from the Committee of the Whole: nevertheless, he was entirely willing to withdraw his motion, if the gentleman insisted upon it.

Mr. Doddridge of Brooke, observed that if the suggestion of the gentleman from Accomack, (Mr. Upshur) had been occasioned by any thing that had fallen from him, (Mr. D.) the gentleman had certainly misunderstood him. The course he had desired to see pursued, was that each report should be referred to a separate Committee of this House, and after all the reports should then have been considered and fully discussed in Committee of the Whole, they be finally referred to one general Committee, which might properly be called a Copying Committee, who should transcribe and report the whole to the Convention.

Mr. Upshur, after a few words of explanation, withdrew the suggestion he had made, and the question having been taken on the motion of Mr. Marshall, it was decided in the affirmative, and the report of the Judicial Committee was accordingly referred to a Committee of the Whole Convention, and made the Order of the Day for to-morrow.

Printed, *Richmond Enquirer*, 22 October 1829.

Remarks on Judiciary Report
Virginia Convention
24 October 1829

Mr. Marshall observed, that it was obviously convenient, that all the reports from the Select Committees, should be before the same Committee of the whole; and as he believed, though he was not entirely sure, that the report of the Committee on the Judicial Department, had been referred to a particular Committee of the whole, distinct from that recognized in the resolution this day adopted, he moved, if that were the case, that the particular committee of the whole, to which the report had gone, might be discharged from the farther consideration of it, and that the report might take the same direction, as had been given to those from the other Select Committees. The motion prevailed, and the report from the Judicial Committee was thereupon referred to the Committee of the whole.[1]

Printed, *Richmond Enquirer*, 27 October 1829.

1. JM's remarks followed the adoption of resolutions referring the reports of the legislative and executive committees to a committee of the whole. The report of the judiciary committee had previously been referred to a committee of the whole on 21 Oct.

To James Madison

Dear Sir   [Richmond, ca. October 1829]

Mr. Wattles is an artist from Baltimore who is desirous of taking your portrait.[1] Although I am sensible of the numerous applications of the same character to which you are exposed, I cannot refuse to introduce this additional applicant for the same favour. Mr. Wattles has placed me on canvass, and the likeness is thought remarkably good.[2] With great and respectful esteem, I am your Obedt

J MARSHALL

ALS, ViU. Inside address to "Mr. Madison." For dating, see n. 1.

1. James Wattles, a self-taught portrait painter, was active in Baltimore from 1829 to 1854. He was then in Richmond to draw the members of the convention. In July 1835, shortly after JM's death, Wattles wrote to Madison in quest of a copy of JM's letter to Madison written "pending the session of the Virginia Convention in Richmond." Madison replied that he could not find the letter though he recollected "such a letter was certainly presented to me, and left an impression very favorable to your talent in taking likenesses" (George C. Groce, *The New-York Historical Society's Dictionary of Artists in America, 1564–1860* [New Haven, Conn., 1957], 665; Gregory R. Weidman et al., *Classical Maryland, 1815–1845: Fine and Decorative Arts from the Golden Age* [Baltimore, Md., 1993], 75–76; *Richmond Enquirer*, 2 Oct. 1829; Wattles to Madison, 13 July 1835; Madison to Wattles, 18 July 1835, Madison Papers, DLC).

2. As he explained in his 1835 letter to Madison, Wattles was trying to gather testimony praising his likeness of the chief justice because the Baltimore bar "desired to procure a portrait." Surviving records indicate that the Bar Library of Baltimore purchased Wattles's portrait of JM before Mar. 1840 and that the portrait was still hanging in the courthouse in Baltimore in the 1940s. The portrait was damaged during renovation of the courthouse in the 1950s and subsequently vanished. Only a photograph (taken in 1938) of the original survives (Andrew Oliver, *The Portraits of John Marshall* [Charlottesville, Va., 1977], 85–87; James F. Schneider, *The Story of the Library Company of the Baltimore Bar* [Baltimore, Md., 1979]).

To George C. Washington

My dear Sir   Richmond Novr. 29th. 1829

I am much obliged by the kind attention manifested by your letter of the 26th. inst.[1] The intelligence it communicates is indeed to me most afflicting. I had few friends whom I valued so highly as your Uncle, or whose loss I should regret more sincerely.[2] I had flattered myself when we parted last spring, that I should leave him on the bench when retiring from it myself; but Heaven has willed otherwise. We have been most intimate friends for more than forty years, and never has our friendship sustained the slightest interruption. I sympathize most truely with Mrs. Washington.[3] With great and respectful esteem I am dear Sir your Obedt

J MARSHALL

JOHN MARSHALL
Oil on canvas by James Wattles, ca. 1829.
Courtesy of the Baltimore Courthouse and Law Museum

ALS (owned by Thomas F. Overlander, Austin, Tex., 1997). Addressed to Washington in Georgetown, D.C.; postmarked Richmond, 29 Nov. Endorsed by Washington.

1. Letter not found. George Corbin Washington (1789–1854), grandnephew of George Washington, represented Maryland in the U.S. Congress from 1827 to 1833 and again from 1835 to 1837.
2. Bushrod Washington died in Philadelphia on 26 Nov. 1829 after completing his New Jersey circuit (*Niles' Weekly Register* [Baltimore], 5 Dec. 1829).
3. Ann Blackburn Washington was with her husband during his final illness, but she herself died two days later on her way home from Philadelphia to Mount Vernon (ibid.).

To James Madison

Dear Sir   Richmond Novr. 30th. 1829

I have just received information of the death of my friend Judge Washington. I need not say how much I regret his loss. The official and friendly connexion between us would I think make it improper in me immediately to receive company. For this reason I have felt myself compelled to embrace the embarassing part of withdrawing the invitation I gave for wednesday next. With great and respectful esteem, I am dear Sir your Obedt.

J MARSHALL

ALS, Montague Collection, NN. Endorsed by Madison. Note at foot of page: "Presented by Mrs. Madison."

Speech on Apportionment
Virginia Convention
30 November 1829

On 24 October the select committee on the legislative reported as its first resolution that representation in the House of Delegates should be apportioned on the basis of the white population. In committee of the whole on 27 October, John W. Green moved to amend this resolution so as to base representation on white population and taxation combined. This motion set off a lengthy debate between reformers led by Philip Doddridge, John R. Cooke, and Chapman Johnson and conservatives led by Abel P. Upshur and Benjamin W. Leigh. Green's motion lost by the casting vote of President Monroe on 14 November. Leigh, on 16 November, proposed to base representation on "federal numbers," that is, white population and three-fifths of the slaves. After rejecting this plan by a vote of 49 to 47 (JM voting with the minority), the committee of the whole took up other parts of the select committee's report before resuming the subject of apportionment on 30 November. On this day Upshur submitted a compromise proposition to apportion both houses of the General Assembly according to an average of the ratios of the three plans that had been debated: white population only, white population combined with taxation, and federal numbers. Leigh followed with a proposal differing only slightly from Upshur's, in which both branches of the legislature would be apportioned by a combination of white population and federal numbers. Cooke then offered a compromise favored by many of the reformers: representation in the House according to white population and representation in the Senate according to federal numbers. Alexander Campbell, a reformer from the western county of Brooke, presented a plan that retained white population as the basis of representation in both houses while attempting to protect the east against excessive taxation or appropriations (*Proceedings and Debates*, 39, 53, 321, 322, 341–42, 344, 494–97; Merrill D. Peterson, ed., *Democracy, Liberty, and Property: The State Constitutional Conventions of the 1820s* [Indianapolis, Ind., 1966], 274–79).

Mr. PRESIDENT: No person in the House can be more truly gratified than I am, at seeing the spirit that has been manifested here to-day: and it is my earnest wish that this spirit of conciliation may be acted upon in a fair, equal and honest manner, adapted to the situation of the different parts of the Commonwealth, which are to be affected. As to the general propositions which have been offered, there is no essential difference between them. That the Federal numbers and the plan of the white basis shall be blended together so as to allow each an equal portion of power, seems to be very generally agreed to. The difference is, that one party applies these two principles separately, the one to the Senate, the other to the House of Delegates, while the other party propose to unite the two principles, and to carry them in their blended form through the whole Legislature. One gentleman differs in the whole outline of his plan. He seems to imagine that we claim nothing of republican principles, when we claim a representation for property.[1] Permit me to set him right. I do not say that I hope to satisfy him or others, who say that Republican Government depends on adopting the naked principle of numbers, that we are right; but I think I can satisfy him that we do entertain a different opinion. I think the soundest principles of republicanism do sanction some relation between representation and taxation. Certainly no opinion has received the sanction of wiser statesmen and patriots. I think the two ought to be connected. I think this was the principle of the revolution: the ground on which the Colonies were torn from the mother country and made independent States.

I shall not, however, go into that discussion now. The House has already heard much said about it. I would observe that this basis of Representation is a matter so important to Virginia, that the subject was reviewed by every thinking individual before this Convention assembled. Several different plans were contemplated: The basis of white population alone; the basis of free population alone; a basis of population alone; a basis compounded of taxation & white population, (or which is the same thing, a basis of Federal numbers;) two other bases were also proposed, one referring to the total population of the States, the other to taxation alone. Now, of these various propositions, the basis of white population, and the basis of taxation alone are the two extremes. Between the free population, and the white population, there is almost no difference: Between the basis of total population and the basis of taxation, there is but little difference. The people of the East thought that they offered a fair compromise, when they proposed the compound basis of population and taxation or the basis of the Federal numbers. We thought that we had republican precedent for this—a precedent given us by the wisest and truest patriots that ever were assembled: but that is now past. We are now willing to meet on a new middle ground beyond what we thought was a middle ground, and the extreme on the other side. We considered the Federal numbers as middle ground, and we may, perhaps, now carry that proposition. The gentleman assumed too much when he said that question was decided. It cannot be considered as decided, till it has come before the House. The majority is too small to calculate upon it as certain in the final decision. We are all uncertain as to the issue. But all know this, that if either extreme is carried, it must leave a wound in the breast of the opposite party which will fester & rankle, and produce I know not what mischief. The majority, also, are now content once more to divide the ground, and to take a new middle ground. The only difficulty is, whether the compromise shall be effected by applying one principle to the House of Delegates, and the other to the Senate, or by mingling the two principles, and applying them in the same form to both branches of the Legislature? I incline to the latter opinion. I do not know, and have not heard, any sufficient reason assigned for adopting different principles in the two branches. Both are the Legislature of Virginia, and if they are to be organized on different principles, there will be just the same divisions between the two, as appears in this Convention. It can produce no good, and may, I fear, produce some mischief. It will be said, that one branch is the representative of one division of the State, and the other branch of another division of it. Ought they not both to represent the whole? Yet I am ready to submit to such an arrangement, if it shall be the opinion of a majority of this House. If this Convention shall think it best that the House of Delegates shall be organized in one way and the Senate another, I shall not withhold my assent. Give me a Constitution that shall be received by the people: a Constitution in which I can consider their different interests to be duly represented, and I will take it, though it may not be that which I most approve.

While I agree in the main to the proposition offered by the gentleman from Chesterfield,[2] there are some slight objections to it. It is not perfectly equal, if you take the census of 1820, as the basis of computation. I have prepared no plan to be laid before the House, but have made some calculations as a guide for my own judgment, going to shew what the apportionment ought to be on the basis he has assumed. His ground is that the ratio ought to be an exact compromise of the principle of white population, and that of the Federal numbers. I have endeavoured to calculate the result of such a ratio. The whole white population being 603,031 and the House of Delegates consisting of 126, each member will represent 4,791 white persons. The country west of the Blue Ridge having 133,100, will be entitled to 27 members and a large fraction: I have therefore allowed them 28. The Valley containing 121,096 white persons will be entitled to 25 members. The country between the Blue Ridge and tide-water, having 189,356 free-whites, will be entitled to 39 and a large fraction: I therefore allow that part of the State 40 delegates. The tide-water country containing 159,517, will be entitled to 33 delegates. This will be the ratio, taking the free white population as the basis.

Let us now assume as the basis the Federal numbers. The whole State contains 895,003 Federal persons. Each member will, therefore represent 7,031 Federal persons. The western district containing 142,147 of such persons, will be entitled to 20 delegates. The Valley containing 142,083, will also be entitled to 20 Delegates. The Middle Country 330,025, will be entitled to 45 and a large fraction, say 46. The tide-water country, containing 280,619, will be entitled to 39.

Now, Sir, I added these several results of the white basis, and of Federal numbers, and I divided the amount by 2, which gave me the following as the average of the two ratios:

For the Western District, 24 delegates.

For the Valley, 22½, say 23.

For the Middle Country, 43½, say 43.

For the tide-water Country, 36.

I think if we do adopt an exact compound of these two ratios, we ought to carry the principle through, and take the above numbers, unless I have committed some arithmetical error — it is possible I may, but I think I have not. The principle, then, which I propose as a compromise is, that the apportionment of representation shall be made according to an exact compound of the two principles of the white basis and of the Federal numbers, according to the census of 1820. There can be but one objection to this calculation. It is that the Census of 1820 is not the Census of 1829. I admit it. But every thing of the population of 1829 considered as a basis is so much conjectural, that it will be difficult to come to any satisfactory result. I take the Census of 1820, as preferable to such a conjectural basis. If it produces injustice, that injustice will be temporary and of short duration. The proposition of the gentleman from Chesterfield which has my perfect approbation with this exception, allows an immediate increase of numbers to that part of the State which must suffer by the census of 1820. It cannot do permanent injustice to them; perhaps not for a moment; and even if it should, the other part of the plan will effectually remove it. Should there by any injustice, it must speedily be removed by a new Census. I wished to avoid going into the detail of the apportionment in each county. That may be left to the first Legislature which shall assemble under the amended Constitution. Let the first H. of Delegates be constituted of 5 Representatives from each senatorial district, you will then have a House consisting of 120 Delegates, who will be more competent than ourselves, to apportion the total representation among the counties, and who can more appropriately perform that office. I should regret to see the time of the Convention wasted in balancing the controversies of the counties. I barely throw this out, however, for consideration. I only wish, that the calculations may be understood by the Convention, together with the principles on which they have been made. It will be necessary to carry the substance of this calculation in mind, before we form a definite judgment on the estimates which differ from it.[3]

Mr. LEIGH's *Plan is a House of 126 Members.*

White population amounts by the Census of 1820, to				603,081
In a House of 126, each member will represent persons,				4,791
West of the Alleghany,	133,100	27–3,743	28	
Between the Alleghany and Blue Ridge	121,096	25–1,321	25	
Between the Blue Ridge and Tide Water	189,356	39–2,507	40	
On Tide Water	159,517	33–1,414	33	
	603,069	124	126	
Federal numbers amount to				895,003
Each member will represent persons,				7,031
West of the Alleghany,	142,147	20–1,527	20	
Between the Alleghany and Blue Ridge	142,083	20–1,463	20	
Between the Blue Ridge and Tide Water	330,025	46–6,599	47	
On Tide Water	280,619	39–6,410	39	
	894,974	125	126	

To divide the apportionment between white population and Federal numbers:

West of the Alleghany,

White,	{ 28	
Federal,	{ 20	
	48	24

Between the Alleghany and Blue Ridge,

White,	{ 25	
Federal,	{ 20	
	45	23

Between the Blue Ride and Tide Water,

White,	{ 40	
Federal,	{ 47	
	87	43

On Tide Water

	White,	$\left\{\begin{array}{l} 33 \\ \underline{39} \end{array}\right.$	
	Federal		
		72	36
			126

The white population and Federal numbers added, and then divided give   220,063

If the country on Tide Water be entittled to 36 members, then each member will represent   6,113

	Whites	Fed. Nos.	
The Henrico dist. Contains	21,885	40,395	
Its share of 36 members, is	4–3,001	5–4,240	9–7,241
			4–8,620

Printed, *Richmond Enquirer,* 1 December 1829.

1. Campbell rejected the scheme of admitting federal numbers as forcing westerners "to compromise a principle, which, as republicans we can never, without apostasy from our faith, and a renunciation of our principles, yield. Our brethren of the east have as they think to compromise, no republican principle: they admit, that the principle for which we contend is a just principle and a republican principle, were there no peculiar property, or peculiar interest in the way" (*Proceedings and Debates,* 497).

2. Leigh.

3. The editor of the *Richmond Enquirer* gave this account of JM's speech: "The scene was animated by the appearance of Chief Justice Marshall for the first time on the floor. His views differed in some respects from the details of Mr. Leigh's plan, though he agreed in the general principle. He spoke, for some time, with great emphasis—invoking the spirit of conciliation, and showing the concession which the East was willing to make for the sake of compromise" (*Richmond Enquirer,* 1 Dec. 1829).

Speech on County Courts
Virginia Convention
30 November 1829

After the presentation of the compromise proposals on representation, the convention went into committee of the whole and took up the first resolution of the judiciary committee, the first sentence of which declared that "the Judicial power shall be vested in a Court of Appeals, in such Inferior Courts, as the Legislature shall from time to time ordain and establish, and in the County Courts." Thomas M. Bayly of Accomac County moved to strike out "and in the County Courts." In his accompanying speech, Bayly stated that his resolution would not abolish the county courts but merely place them within the power of the General Assembly to preserve, alter, or abolish them as it deemed appropriate. He went on to criticize the county court system as contrary to "republican principles" by uniting legislative, executive, and judicial powers in a single self-perpetuating body. He further contended hat the county justices were generally "very unfit to exercise chancery or common law jurisdiction." Marshall then spoke against Bayly's motion (*Proceedings and Debates*, 502–4).

Mr. Marshall rose in opposition. The question now before the committee is substantially the question, whether the county Courts shall continue to exist or not. Any objection to the details of the system is not sufficient, to induce us to strike out the clause which is the subject of the present motion. If the jurisdiction of these courts is considered as defective, let the system be so modified, as to make their jurisdiction more perfect. The matter is perfectly open, and will continue to be perfectly open, if this clause is permitted to stand. If the motion succeeds, either the County Courts must be abandoned, or the article modified. The article, as it stands, purports to enumerate all the courts, in which the judicial power of the Commonwealth is to be vested. County Courts form one of these depositories. If we expunge County Courts from this list, we shall virtually deny to them any part of the judicial power of the State: it follows, that no objection to the jurisdiction of those courts as at present exercised, ought to induce us to consent to the proposed amendment, unless it is our purpose that County Courts shall not continue to constitute any part of our Judiciary system. The article, as it now stands, leaves the whole subject open to the Legislature.[1] They may limit or abridge the jurisdiction of all the courts as they please. If the Legislature choose to give them all Chancery jurisdiction, or if they shall think fit, to limit their jurisdiction in common law cases to a specific sum, the Legislature can do so. The whole subject of jurisdiction is submitted, absolutely and without qualification, to the power of the Legislature. The only effect therefore of the amendment will be, to abolish the County Courts. Is the Committee prepared for this? I certainly am not. The County Courts may be for some causes, an ill organized tribunal. It may be, for instance, unfit for Chancery jurisdiction: but that is no reason why such courts should not exist. We must have a County Court of some kind: its abolition will affect our whole internal police. I am not in the habit of bestowing extravagant eulogies upon my countrymen. I would rather hear them pronounced by others: but it is a truth, that no State in the Union, has hitherto enjoyed more complete internal quiet than Virginia. There is no part of America, where less disquiet and less of ill-feeling between man and man is to be found than in this Commonwealth, and I believe most firmly that this state of things is mainly to be ascribed to the practical operation of our County Courts. The magistrates who compose those courts, consist in general of the best men in their respective counties. They act in the spirit of peace-makers, and allay, rather than excite the small disputes and differences which will sometimes arise among neighbours. It is certainly much owing to this, that so much harmony prevails among us. These courts must be preserved: if we part with them, can we be sure that we shall retain among our justices of the peace the same respectability and weight of character as are now to be found? I think not. But my main object in rising, was to remind the Committee that there was no need of striking out the clause, if all we seek is some change in the jurisdiction of the courts.[2]

Printed, *Proceedings and Debates of the Virginia State Convention* (Richmond, Va., 1830), 504–5; summary, *Richmond Enquirer,* 1 Dec. 1829.

1. The first resolution provided that the jurisdiction of all the enumerated tribunals was "to be regulated by law."

2. Debate on Bayly's motion took up the remainder of the day. After JM, Thomas R. Joynes, Bayly's eastern shore colleague, spoke in favor of the motion, as did Bayly again and Richard H. Henderson. Philip P. Barbour, Giles, Johnson, and Leigh opposed the motion *(Proceedings and Debates,* 505–16).

To John Randolph

My dear Sir   [ca. November 1829]
    Mr. Harding will call on me to day and I will inform him that I will attend you to his room at any hour you may designate.[1] You may name the hour when I see you and I can give him the information this afternoon when I am to sit for him to retouch my portrait.[2] I am my dear Sir, very truely your

                                                            J MARSHALL

ALS (owned by Charles H. Ryland, Warsaw, Va., 1993). Endorsed with note "Mr Chief Justice / During the sitting of / the Convention."

1. The artist Chester Harding went to Richmond in the fall of 1829 "with the intention of *taking off the heads* of the Convention." During his three-month stay, he painted eighteen portraits, including JM's and John Randolph's. Harding presented a letter of introduction to Randolph "with considerable trepidation knowing something of his peculiarities, but my fears were groundless. I was most graciously received, and was assured that it would give him great pleasure to sit to me." (Harding to Samuel F. Lyman, 25 Feb. 1830, in Margaret E. White, ed., *A Sketch of Chester Harding, Artist* [Boston, 1929], 149–51).

2. While in Richmond, Harding was invited to attend a Barbecue Club meeting with JM and his fellow quoit players. The artist left a memorable account of the chief justice drinking a tumbler of mint julep and getting "down on his knees, measuring the contested distance with a straw, with as much earnestness, as if it had been a point of law" (ibid., 147).

THE VIRGINIA CONSTITUTIONAL CONVENTION OF 1829–1830
Oil on a walnut panel by George Catlin, 1829–1830. Marshall is seated in front row, behind James Madison, standing. *Courtesy of the Virginia Historical Society.*

Debate on County Courts
Virginia Convention
1 December 1829

Debate resumed on Bayly's motion of the previous day to remove the county courts from being designated as county courts. Henderson supported the motion in a speech that was highly critical of the legal competence of the county tribunals. Philip Doddridge of Brooke County also spoke in favor of the motion, observing that the question was not whether those courts ought to be abolished but whether they should exist independent of the legislative will. Marshall spoke after Doddridge (*Proceedings and Debates,* 520–24).

Mr. MARSHALL wished to offer a few observations merely with a view to put gentlemen on a right footing, as to the nature of the question. They spoke of the county courts as if the report of the Legislative Committee proposed to perpetuate them on precisely their existing form, and with their present powers. They speak of the unfitness of those courts for all the jurisdiction they now possess; and if they prove, or think that they prove that the present organization of those courts, can be improved, they think they have thereby proved that this clause ought to be stricken out. But the whole jurisdiction of the county courts, is submitted to the Legislature; the Legislature may take away the whole of it, and leave them to exist in form only. What injury will ensue? no salaries will be taken away. The form of a county court will be left in existence, but without any power. Can they do any injury? But, if they cease to be nominal, they cease to be real. While they exist, they are capable of receiving any jurisdiction, the Legislature may choose to give them. But if they do not exist, they can have no jurisdiction. Gentlemen, therefore, mistake the question, and speak to a matter not before the Committee, when they shew that these courts can be modified to advantage. Some gentlemen are opposed to the mode of appointment in these courts; but that question is not before the committee. For myself, I prefer the existing mode, others may differ from me. Let the mode of continuing them be changed, still the courts themselves will be preserved. We have not reached the resolution which provides for that; when we shall reach it, if gentlemen wish the general system preserved, but the mode of appointment changed, they can give their opinions then. That question is not now before the Committee. The only question is, whether the form of the county courts shall be preserved. When gentlemen say that to strike this clause from the resolution amounts to nothing, and that the courts nevertheless may still be preserved, I beg leave to repeat, that if the form of the resolution remains and you strike out the words "and the County Courts," you take away from those courts all capacity to receive judicial power, and do not leave the Legislature power to vest in them any jurisdiction. I speak of the resolution as it now stands. It may indeed be altered, so as to leave all the jurisdiction in the power of the Legislature, and I wish they would suggest such an alteration. But as the resolution is now drawn, if you strike out this clause, you leave the county courts incapable of receiving any judicial power whatever. You enumerate all the tribunals which are to possess judicial power, and tribunals not in the resolution can have none. Let it be recollected that all the various services performed by these courts, and which were enumerated by the gentleman from Chesterfield, (Mr. Leigh,) are portions of judicial power.

Mr. DODDRIDGE asked what it was that rendered it impossible that these courts could receive judicial power, if the express mention of them were stricken out.

Mr. MARSHALL replied that it was because the resolution professes to enumerate all the courts in which the judicial power of the commonwealth was to be reposed. If county courts are stricken out from that enumeration, they will be incapable of receiving any part of that power. Why should this be done?

Mr. HENDERSON said he differed from the opinion just expressed. Supposing the clause to be stricken out, the county courts would still be included under the words of the clause immediately preceding, viz: "such inferior courts as the Legislature shall from time to time, ordain and establish."

Mr. MARSHALL said he was truly sorry so often to trouble the committee, but he wished to remove a misunderstanding which seemed to have obtained. If gentlemen would look at the residue of the resolution, they would perceive that it goes on to give salaries to all the judges of the inferior courts. This, surely, does not extend to county courts.

It was plain, therefore, that the resolution does not comprehend county courts, when it speaks of "other inferior courts," but means to designate them by the specific and appropriate term.[1]

Printed, *Richmond Enquirer*, 3 December 1829.

1. Alexander Campbell followed with a long speech in support of the motion in which he contended that the county courts as presently constituted were contrary to republican principles. The committee then voted against the motion, those in favor numbering twenty-two. Campbell moved to strike out "the" before "County Courts." Some discussion ensued, with JM remarking that the motion "could do no harm, and if it tended to reconcile any gentleman to the resolution, it had better be adopted." Campbell's motion carried by a vote of 48 to 42, the reporter noting that Madison, Monroe, and JM voted in the affirmative. The clause of the resolution accordingly now read, "*Resolved,* That the Judicial power shall be vested in a Court of Appeals, in such inferior Courts as the Legislature shall from time to time ordain and establish, and in County Courts" (*Proceedings and Debates,* 525–31).

Amendments to First Resolution of Judiciary Report
Virginia Convention
2 December 1829

Mr. MARSHALL said there were some additional provisions he wished to have introduced into the Resolution, and which he had not yet suggested. The Resolution professes to enumerate all the depositories of the Judicial power of the Commonwealth — and, therefore, all intended to be included must be enumerated. Justices of the Peace when not upon the bench but acting singly exercise an important portion of the Judicial power: The trial of warrants was a considerable part of the Judicial Power of the Commonwealth: He, therefore, moved to amend the resolution by adding the following clause after the words "County Courts":

In the 3rd line of the first resolution of [the] Judicial Committee, strike out the word "and" — And 2dly at the end of the same line insert "and in the Justices of the Peace who shall compose the said Courts."

The amendment was agreed to.

Mr. MARSHALL then proposed to add still farther to the enumeration. Corporation Courts constituted a necessary part of the judicial system, and should not be omitted. He at first proposed to insert the amendment after the words "County Courts," but some gentlemen whom he had consulted, felt apprehensive that such a location might render these Corporation Courts, Constitutional tribunals — and though he had no such apprehension himself, for caution sake he would not propose to insert them there, but so introduce the amendment that it should be impossible to consider them as courts constitutionally established; he then moved the following:

"The Legislature may also vest such jurisdiction as shall be deemed necessary in Corporation Courts, and in the Magistrates who may belong to the Corporate body."

This amendment was also agreed to.

Printed, *Richmond Enquirer,* 3 December 1829.

Debate on County Courts
Virginia Convention
2 December 1829

Alfred H. Powell of Frederick moved for a reconsideration of the previous day's vote to delete "the" before "County Courts." Removing the definite article, he believed, would require the legislature to reconstruct anew the county court system. John Randolph supported the motion for reconsideration with a speech extolling the virtues of the county courts. Marshall spoke in reply to Randolph (*Proceedings and Debates,* 531–33).

Mr. Marshall said, he could assure the gentleman from Charlotte, that that gentleman was not a greater friend to the County Courts than he was, nor was he a greater friend to the mode in which the justices are now appointed than he; and whenever the Committee should reach that part of the report which applied to this particular question, the gentleman would find him following in his track, not closely perhaps, but at some distance, yet certainly following. He was disposed to make a great sacrifice to secure that object.

He would now call the attention of the Committee to the fifth resolution of the report, and which he trusted would be suffered to remain in it. It disposed of the subject the gentleman from Charlotte appeared to be so much concerned about. (Here Mr. M. read the fifth resolution in the following words: "*Resolved,* That on the creation of any new county, justices of the peace shall be appointed in the first instance as may be prescribed by law. When vacancies shall occur in any county, or it shall, for any cause, be deemed necessary to increase their number, appointments shall be made by the Governor, by and with the advice and consent of the Senate, on the recommendation of their respective County Courts.")

If the Convention should leave to the Governor an Executive Council, then he was ready to say, let the appointment of justices be made by the Governor, by and with the advice of the Council, as is now provided by the Constitution. But, if it should be contrary to the will of the Convention that a Council be retained, then let the appointment be made with the advice of the Senate, on the recommendation of the County Court. It was his purpose to offer an amendment, which would give still more importance to the recommendation of the County Court. He would not suggest it at present, but he should most certainly so endeavor. He did not, however, suppose it to be necessary to re-instate the article *"the"* in order to effect all that gentleman wished, and which he wished as strongly as the gentleman. When the word was stricken out, it was apprehended that the effect might be to have some new court constituted and called "a County Court," and which might displace *the* County Courts as at present established. Mr. M. said, he should be dissatisfied with such a change; but he did not apprehend it could result from omitting the article. The amendment which had been adopted rendered such a thing impossible. It directed that the justices of the peace should constitute the County Courts; and if so, what was there to fear? He perceived nothing. But with respect to the County Courts as now established, and the mode of their appointment, there was not a member of the Convention more strongly disposed to retain them than he.

Mr. Randolph rose to supply the omission of a fact which he had intended to state when last up, which was, that he never had been, was not then, and never should be, a magistrate; nor was there a magistrate connected with him by blood or marriage, within his own county, or as far as he knew, any where else.

Mr. Marshall said, that he hoped he had not been considered as insinuating any such motive as having actuated the gentleman from Charlotte. It would really give him more pain than he could express. No person could be more fully satisfied that that gentleman uttered his own opinions, and that what he said flowed from him in a manner the most spontaneous and impartial.

Mr. Randolph replied, that it was impossible that what he had now stated could have had the remotest connexion with the remarks of the distinguished gentleman from Richmond, because he had intended to have said it when up before, and had omitted to do so only through inadvertence: that gentleman was the last man in the world that he could suspect of intending to make any injurious insinuations whatever. He knew that like my uncle Toby "he would not hurt a fly."[1]

Printed, *Proceedings and Debates of the Virginia State Convention* (Richmond, Va., 1830), 533–34.

1. After Powell, Leigh, and Johnson urged adoption of Powell's motion, the committee of the whole voted 53 to 41 to reconsider. Upshur argued against, and Johnson for, reinstating "the." The committee then voted 50 to 44 to retain "the," with Madison, Monroe, and JM voting against striking out the word (ibid., 534–37).

To Robert H. Small

Sir   Richmond Decr. 3d. 1829

Your letter of the 25th. of Novr. reached me a few days past and ought to have received an immediate answer.[1] The pressing duties of a court and convention both in session will I trust afford some apology for the delay.

I have revised the life of Washington and purpose to offer it as soon as the copy right of Mr. Wayne shall expire, to Mr. Cary of Philadelphia.[2] As profit is not my object I wish only to receive about twenty copies to distribute among my particular friends. Should that work sell it may create some demand for the history of the colonies. In that event I purpose to turn that over likewise to Mr. Cary. Whatever it may raise over the sum I have actually expended will be his. Should he be dissatisfied with this he may name his own terms. Have the goodness to show Mr. Cary this letter and if he accedes to the proposition, be also obliging enough to place the copies of the history in his possession. Should Mr. Cary decline this proposition I must ask the favour of you to have the copies boxed up and sent to Richmond to my address. I leave this early in Jany. for Washington. Any expense which may be incurred shall be immediately repaid. With great respect, I am Your Obedt

J MARSHALL

ALS, Dreer Collection, PHi. Addressed to "R. H. Small esquire" in Philadelphia; postmarked Richmond, 4 Dec. Note on cover that letter was "given me / by Robt H Small Esqr / 1852 F J Dreer."

1. Letter not found.

2. Caleb P. Wayne purchased the copyright for the *Life of George Washington* in 1802 and renewed it in 1817 (*PJM*, VI, 220; IX, 196 n. 3). The revised edition was published in 1832 by the Philadelphia firm of Carey & Lea. "Mr. Cary" was either Mathew Carey (1760–1839) or Henry Charles Carey (1793–1879), his eldest son, both of whom were prominent Philadelphia publishers and economists. Father and son were partners in the publishing business, as was Isaac Lea (1792–1886), Mathew Carey's son-in-law.

Speech on Apportionment
Virginia Convention
4 December 1829

The committee of the whole resumed consideration of the apportionment issue on 2 December by taking up the various compromise plans, beginning with that proposed by Upshur. Although there was agreement that "federal numbers" should be a basis of representation along with white population, the members sharply divided on whether to combine the bases in both branches or to apply them separately. Leigh vigorously opposed Cooke's plan of separate bases, contending that a federal basis for the Senate was insufficient security for eastern Virginians. At the end of the day on 3 December William F. Gordon of Albemarle proposed an amendment that equitably distributed representatives and senators among four principal regions: Tidewater, Piedmont, Valley, and trans-Allegheny. The next day, 4 December, Gordon withdrew his amendment, which left Upshur's plan as the formal question before the committee. After Chapman Johnson spoke in favor of Cooke's plan, Marshall rose to speak (*Proceedings and Debates*, 537–59, 560–61).

Two propositions respecting the basis of representation have divided this Convention almost equally.[1] One party has supported the basis of white population alone, the other has supported a basis compounded of white population and taxation; or which is the same thing in its result, the basis of federal numbers. The question has been discussed until discussion has become useless. It has been argued until argument is exhausted. We have now met on the ground of compromise. It is now no longer a question whether the one or the other shall be adopted entirely but whether we shall, as a compromise, adopt a combination of the two, so as to unite the House on something which we may recommend to the people of Virginia, with a reasonable hope that it may be adopted.

Now, when on the subject of compromise, two propositions are again submitted to the Committee; one of them is, that the two principles originally proposed shall remain distinct; one of them constituting the basis of the House of Delegates, and the other of the Senate. The other proposition is, that the two principles shall be combined and made the basis of both Houses. This latter proposition presents the exact middle ground between white population exclusively, and the basis of white population combined with taxation, or what has been denominated the basis of federal numbers.[2]

The motion of the gentleman from Augusta, (Mr. Johnson) to strike out the word "Resolved," from the proposition offered by the gentleman from Northampton, (Mr. Upshur) is intended to substitute for the combined ratio, which is the foundation of that gentleman's scheme, the proposition of the gentleman from Frederick, (Mr. Cooke) which is to introduce white population exclusively as the basis of the House of Delegates, and white population and taxation combined as the basis of the Senate. This is the question now before the Committee.

We are engaged on the subject of compromise, a compromise of principles which neither is willing to surrender. The very term implies mutual concession. Some concession must be made on both sides, but the quantum to be made by each must depend on the relative situation of the parties, and this must be considered before a right judgment can be formed on the subject. Let us enquire, then, what is the real situation of the parties on this question. On this enquiry will depend the reasonableness of any compromise that may be proposed.

The past discussion shows conclusively the sincerity with which each principle has been supported. There can be no doubt of the honest conviction of each side, that its pretensions are fair and just. The claims of both are sustained with equal sincerity, and an equally honest conviction, that their own principle is correct, and the adversary principle is unwise and incorrect. On the subject of principle nothing can be added, no advantage can be claimed by either side, for no doubt can be entertained of the sincerity of either. To attempt now to throw considerations of principle into either scale, is to add fuel to a flame which it is our purpose to extinguish. We must lose sight of the situation of parties and state of opinions, if we make this attempt.

What is that situation?

A question has been taken in the Committee on the proposition first submitted to us, and it has been carried by a majority of two.[3] Is it possible under existing circumstances, that any confidence can be reposed in this decision? Can either the majority or minority feel any confidence that the same question will hereafter be again decided precisely in the same manner? Can we be blind to the actual working of public opinion? Do not gentlemen believe it to be more probable that at least some one of the members of this majority, may change his opinion and thus leave the House equally divided? Is it not even probable that a still greater change may take place, so as to place the present scanty majority, with the same paucity of numbers on the other side? Can any gentleman be confident how this question will be ultimately decided? None of us can be certain that its result in the House will be the same that it has been in Committee?

But let us decide one way or the other, if the majority shall be so small, if the opinions of the Convention shall be so nearly balanced, the Constitution will go forth to the people, deriving very little additional weight from the recommendation of this body. The majority and minority will have almost equal weight, and the Constitution will rest on itself. Is it possible to conceal from ourselves, that the powerful arguments of the minority conveyed to the people through the press, supported by the co-operating interest of a large district of country whose weight has been placed in the opposite scale, may produce great effect? The endeavor would be vain to conceal the fact that in a part of the Eastern country — that lying upon and South of James river near the Blue Ridge, there are interests which must and will operate with great force unless human nature shall cease to be what it has been in all time. It is impossible to say what may be the influence of those interests abroad, though they may exert none on the members of this convention. It is impossible to say how far they may affect the adoption or rejection of the Constitution. But it is by no means certain that this change in public opinion will not be felt in this body also. Admitting gentlemen to retain their theories — theories which they maintain with perfect sincerity, still there exists another theory equally republican and which they equally respect the theory, that it is the duty of a representative to speak the will of his constituents. We cannot say how far this may carry gentlemen. Neither can we say what will be the ultimate decision of this House or of the people.

Taking this view of the state of parties, it is manifest that to obtain a just compromise, concession must not only be mutual — it must be equal also. The claims of the parties are the same. Each ought to concede to the other as much as he demands from that other, and thus meet on middle ground. There can be no hope that either will yield more than it gets in return.

What is that middle ground?

One party proposes that the House of Delegates shall be formed on the basis of white population exclusively, and the Senate on the mixed basis of white population and taxation, or on the federal numbers. The other party proposes that the white population shall be combined with Federal numbers, and shall, mixed in equal proportions, form the basis of Representation in both Houses. This last proposition must be equal. All feel it to be equal. If the two principles are combined exactly, and thus combined, form the basis of both Houses, the compromise must be perfectly equal.

Is the other proposition equal? I ask the gentleman who make it if they think it so?

The party in favor of the compound basis in both Houses have declared their conviction that there is no equality in the proposition. They at least think it unequal. How can they accede to a proposition as a compromise which they firmly believe to be unequal? Do gentlemen of the opposite party think it equal? If they do, why refuse to take what they offer to us?

They consent that the Senate shall be founded on the mixed basis, and the House of Delegates on the white basis. If this be equality, why will they not take the Senate? There can be only one reason for rejecting it—they think the proposition unequal. If the Senate would protect the East, will it not protect the West also? If the proposition is equal when the Senate is tendered by them to us, is it not equal when tendered by us to them? If it is equal, it must be a matter of absolute indifference to which party the Senate is assigned. If a difficulty arises, it is because the proposition is unequal, and if it be unequal, can gentlemen believe that it will be accepted? Ought they to wish it?

After the warm language (to use the mildest phrase) which has been mingled with argument on both sides, I heard with inexpressible satisfaction propositions for compromise proposed by both parties in the language of conciliation. I hailed these auspicious appearances with as much joy as the inhabitant of the polar regions hails the re-appearance of the sun after his long absence of six tedious months. Can these appearances prove fallacious? Is it a meteor we have seen and mistaken for that splendid luminary which dispenses light and gladness throughout creation? It must be so, if we cannot meet on equal ground. If we cannot meet on the line that divides us equally, then take the hand of friendship, and make an equal compromise; it is vain to hope that any compromise can be made.[4]

Printed, *Richmond Enquirer,* 8 December 1829.

1. An earlier report of JM's speech appeared in the newspaper on 5 Dec. On that day editor Thomas Ritchie wrote a note to JM apologizing for the garbled presentation of his remarks, to which the chief justice graciously replied that it was "quite possible and even probable that the confusion in language is imputable to myself rather than to the stenographers." Ritchie printed a corrected version on 8 Dec.with this explanation: "From the late hour on Friday night, at which our Reporter sketched the Remarks of Judge Marshall in the Convention, on Friday last, we had not the opportunity of presenting them with Judge M's revisions—Some errors having crept into the original Report, we seize the earliest occasion of laying the following authentic Sketch of it before our readers" (JM to [Thomas Ritchie], ca. 6 Dec. 1829; *Richmond Enquirer,* 5, 8 Dec. 1829).

2. The "confusion in language" is evident in this passage as printed in the newspaper on 5 Dec. It reads: "But now, on the subject of compromise, two propositions are again presented to the Committee. The one of these is, that the two principles originally proposed shall be made the bases of representation in one House of the Legislature, and the other in the other House: the other proposition is that the two principles shall be combined together and made the basis of both Houses. This latter proposition contains a middle principle between the basis of white population exclusively and the basis of white population and taxation combined" (*Richmond Enquirer,* 5 Dec. 1829).

3. JM referred to the vote of 16 Nov., in which the committee of the whole rejected by a vote of 49 to 47 Leigh's motion to base representation in the House of Delegates on federal numbers (*Proceedings and Debates*, 322, 341–42).

4. On 5 Dec. Gordon revived his amendment proposing an equitable distribution of representatives and senators among the various regions. The committee of the whole approved his plan by a vote of 49 to 43, JM voting with the majority (ibid., 569–75).

To [Thomas Ritchie]

Dear Sir   [ca. 6 December 1829]

I received your note of saturday respecting my remarks of the preceding day in the house.[1] I never suspected you of an inclination to present me to the public in a less favorable dress than that in which I had presented myself.[2]

It is undoubtedly true that the idea I had intended to convey appeared in a form rather more unintelligible than that in which I had supposed it to be communicated to the convention; but it is quite possible and even probable that the confusion in language is imputable to myself rather than to the stenographers. Having been very long out of the habit of mixing in public debate it is quite probable that rising unexpectedly to myself on the spur of the occasion, I may have expressed myself in an indistinct as well as hurried manner. At all events the affair is too unimportant to require explanation, or to be recollected. Very respectfully I am Your Obedt

J MARSHALL

ALS (owned by Carl A. Przyborowski, McHenry, Ill., 1992). For identification of recipient, see n. 2.

1. Letter not found.

2. The context of this letter points to Thomas Ritchie, editor of the *Richmond Enquirer*, as JM's correspondent. On Saturday, 5 Dec., the newspaper published a somewhat confusing report of JM's convention speech of 4 Dec. See Speech on Apportionment, 4 Dec. 1829 and n. 1.

Debate on Judiciary
Virginia Convention
10 December 1829

On this day the committee of the whole resumed consideration of the report of the judiciary committee. After some discussion, the committee adopted the second resolution and amended the third and fourth resolutions. It then took up the fifth resolution, "*Resolved*, That on the creation of any new county, justices of the peace shall be appointed in the first instance, as may be prescribed by law. When vacancies shall occur in any county, or it shall for any cause be deemed necessary to increase their number, appointments shall be made by the Governor, by and with the advice and consent of the Senate, on the recommendation of their respective County Courts." Samuel Claytor moved to strike out the latter part of the resolution beginning with "appointments," with a view to giving the legislature the power to fill vacancies. The motion to strike out was defeated 48 to 44, JM voting against (*Proceedings and Debates*, 600–604).

Mr. Marshall said, that the fate of the motion just made, shewed it to be very decidedly the sense of the Committee, that vacancies in the number of Justices were to be filled by the Executive, on the recommendation of the County Courts; but this mode of appointment could be preserved in its purity and perfection only, by requiring the Executive in nominating and the Senate in deciding on his nomination, to act on all the recommendations of a county court taken as a whole. If this were not required, the Governor might select one, or two, or more, of the names recommended, get these persons appointed, and commissioned, and thus very materially change the character of the court which made the recommendations; and effect the same thing as by the original power of appointment without any recommendation by the county court. By requiring him to take the whole, if any, you retain, said Mr. M., those magistrates which the Court wished to see appointed, and thus give full effect to their nomination.

If the Executive needs, as is conceded, to be instructed as to who are proper candidates to be nominated and who not, from whom is he to ask that instruction rather than from the county court Magistrates themselves? They are dispersed through the county: they know when vacancies occur; and they know better than any one else who are fit persons to fill them. To whom shall the Governor appeal rather than to them? If the nomination is to be made by the Executive, all must agree there is no source of information so valuable to him, or which can furnish such correct and certain intelligence.

Suppose it left in the choice of the Executive to leave out some of the persons recommended to him, and retain others, how is he to learn whom to admit and whom to refuse? All gentlemen feel that it is impossible the Governor, personally, should possess such knowledge of men in the various counties throughout the Commonwealth, and such an acquaintance with all the individuals they may recommend, so as to be able to select such as are the most fit among them. He must receive information from others, either privately or publicly communicated to him; and none can make a communication which the Executive can more rely upon than on theirs. It is possible that some individual whom they have recommended may be unworthy: he may have been guilty of some offence, even after being recommended. In that case let the whole recommendation be returned to be revised and corrected, and let the court strike out such names as they please. The courts themselves can alone know how to select proper individuals: Unless, indeed, the election of Magistrates is to be made by the People: but that is a point not presented by the present proposition. The question now is, on the recommendation by the courts and the action of the Executive upon that recommendation. Let him be required to act upon the whole recommendation, and either nominate all or none of the individuals it contains.

It may be said, that if the Governor recommends the whole, the subject may then be left to the discretion of the Senate, and they may advise the appointment of some and not of others of those nominated. What will be the effect? The Senate will derive the information on which it acts from that member of its own body who comes from the District in which the appointments are to be made; and will you rather submit the question to him to decide than to the county courts? If the Senate reject some of the persons nominated, they must do so on some information, probably that of one of their own members: but all know how many various influences may operate on that member, which do not upon the county courts. He has his supporters and his opponents, his friends and his enemies; but this can have no influence on the justices of the county court. They have no motive to action which is calculated to lead them to make improper recommendations.

I, therefore, move you, sir, to amend the resolution as follows.

"But the whole number recommended at any one time shall be commissioned[1] or rejected."[2]

Printed, *Richmond Enquirer*, 12 December 1829.

1. The *Enquirer* has "recommended," an error that was corrected in the subsequent publication of the debates (*Proceedings and Debates*, 605).

2. After Leigh noted some inconveniences that might result from this amendment, JM withdrew it temporarily and moved to strike out "by and with the consent of the Senate," which was approved. John Macrae then moved as a substitute for JM's previous amendment, "*Provided, however,* That if any person be recommended to fill any such vacancy, or new appointment, and shall be disapproved by the Governor, such person shall not be again recommended to fill the same vacancy, or new appointment." JM opposed this amendment "as going to disqualify forever, a man, against whom any objection was once made. The Governor might send back a recommendation, simply because it contained too many persons: yet according to Mr. Macrae's proposition, they were all to be disqualified and among them, perhaps the fittest man in the county." The committee then rejected both Macrae's and JM's amendments. Macrae then offered another amendment, which provided for the removal of justices of the peace for misbehavior, crime, neglect, and insolvency. This proposition also failed to carry. The committee then approved the sixth, seventh, and eight resolutions of the judiciary committee (ibid., 605–7).

Debate on Judiciary
Virginia Convention
11 December 1829

The committee of the whole resumed consideration of the judiciary committee's report, turning its attention to the first resolution. Philip P. Barbour
of Orange moved to strike out, "no modification or abolition of any court
shall be construed to deprive any Judge thereof of his office; but such Judge
shall perform any judicial duties which the Legislature shall assign him." He
contended that this provision was predicated on the mere possibility the
legislature would abuse its power to get rid of an obnoxious judge. The
greater evil, however, was that it would prevent the legislature from carrying
out a beneficial reform that would require a fewer number of judges than
presently employed. He denied that this case was embraced by the eighth
resolution, which provided for the removal of judges on a two-thirds vote of
each house of the legislature. After Richard Venable and Robert Stanard
spoke against the motion, Richard Morris proposed to meet Barbour's objection with the following amendment: "*Provided, however,* That if upon the
modification or abolition of any court, any Judge or Judges should not be
directed to perform other Judicial duties, it shall be competent to the General Assembly, two-thirds of the whole number of each House concurring
therein, to vacate the commission or commissions of such Judge or Judges."
Barbour remarked that this amendment still made it necessary for two-
thirds of each house to remove superfluous judges. (*Proceedings and Debates,*
608–11).

Mr. MARSHALL said he did not intend to enter into the debate at this
time. Had the gentleman from Orange been content with the amendment, he should have said nothing; but as he had not seemed satisfied
with it, he could not help suggesting to the gentleman from Hanover
(Mr. MORRIS,) whether it was proper to press the amendment. There was
not the slightest possible necessity for it as an explanation of the resolution: with great respect said Mr. M., for the opinion of the gentleman
from Orange, if I can understand his language he both mis-quoted and
mis-understood the eighth Resolution when he supposed it to require the
construction he puts upon it. He has used throughout his argument the
word *office* instead of *Court,* and it was that which produced the confusion
into which he has fallen, and which alone leads to the slightest suppos-
able difficulty. He says that the eighth Resolution does not apply to the
case provided against in the clause he would strike out, because it uses
the term office, and he says the Legislature cannot remove a man from an
office which office does not exist — that no abolition of the office can be
construed as a removal of the Judge — and that a Judge cannot be removed from an office that he does not hold, because the office has been
abolished.

Now, the language of the clause in the 1st resolution, speaks of the abolition of a *Court,* not of an *office*: but the abolition of a court is not the abolition of the office of the Judge. The office of a Judge is his capacity to administer justice: not to administer it in one court only. The former Judges of the General Court have been advanced to another Court since: yet the Judge remains, though he was appointed a Judge of the General Court. There is no necessity, whatever, for the proposition of the gentleman from Hanover. It is impossible the resolutions should be misunderstood so far as that the application of the 8th resolution, to the case provided for by the 2nd, cannot be seen — but if it was possible so far to misunderstand it, the language might be slightly changed. But it is obvious for the two taken together, that change the courts as you please, the Judge remains in office and is ready to receive any duty which the Legislature may assign to him. I suggest to the gentleman the propriety of withdrawing his proviso.

Mr. BARBOUR said, that the gentleman from Richmond had (not intentionally he was very sure) done him injustice, when he charged him with mis-quoting. He read from the printed pamphlet in his hand. The argument he had intended to urge was this, that though the court should be abolished and the office remain, still he questioned whether the removal of a useless Judge was within the scope of the 8th resolution. He would submit another reason for this opinion. By that resolution it was provided, that the Judge was to be served with a copy of the causes alleged against him.

Now, supposing the Legislature has abolished the court and wishes to remove one of the Judges. What are "the causes" to be shown in this case? Are they to say to the Judge, we want your services no longer, and you must come and dispute before us, whether your office ought or ought not to be continued? To my mind the 8th "resolution" imports the idea not that the Legislature wish to remove the office, but that against A. or B. some imputation has been brought, and that he is to be summoned to answer the charges.

Mr. MARSHALL rose in reply. I still say the gentleman has totally misrepresented the meaning of the resolution. He still says that it speaks of charges alleged *against him,* and asks if the abolition of the office is any charge *against* the Judge. No; it is not. I did not say it was. But I say, and I say it with great confidence, that as the terms of the resolution are expressed, it does not require that any cause shall be alleged against the Judge; whatever may operate as a cause for his removal comes within the Resolution: it may be assigned as such by the Legislature, and it does not imply that he has committed any offence. We must not confound the clause providing for the impeachment of a Judge with the clause providing for his removal from office; for crimes and offences, he is to be impeached, and the impeachment is to be tried before the Senate. But when the Legislature shall say that he is useless, and that there is cause for his removal, he may be removed. The resolution requires the cause to be assigned and recorded. The Legislature may say, as that cause, that the Judge is useless; that the number of Judges is too great, and that part of them may be dispensed with: and then the resolution applies entirely. It may be a question with the Legislature whether he has not been rendered useless by themselves in the abolition of his Court; but that is a question for them only and for nobody else. If they choose to designate it as the cause of his removal, they can act upon it.[1]

Printed, *Richmond Enquirer,* 12 December 1829.

1. Morris insisted on keeping his amendment on the floor, but it was not approved. Debate then resumed on Barbour's amendment (*Proceedings and Debates,* 612).

Debate on Judiciary
Virginia Convention
11 December 1829

Johnson spoke against Barbour's amendment. Tazewell then moved to replace "a Court of Appeals" with "one Supreme Court." His object was to adopt the same language as used in the U.S. Constitution and to "have the benefit of the settled interpretation put upon that phrase." He believed that the principle of judicial independence could be satisfied by making the judges of the Supreme Court independent. By changing the phraseology as he proposed, said Tazewell, the effect of Barbour's amendment would be confined to inferior court judges, who were properly subject to legislative control. Benjamin W. Leigh opposed Tazewell's motion, observing that the clear intent of the judiciary committee as expressed in the first, second, and eighth resolutions of the report was to leave the jurisdiction of the state tribunals to be regulated by law and to establish judicial tenure on the basis of good behavior (*Proceedings and Debates,* 608–11, 612–15).

Mr. MARSHALL now rose and addressed the committee in nearly the following terms:

The gentleman from Chesterfield, has understood the language of these resolutions correctly. No doubt was entertained in the judicial committee that the whole subject of the jurisdiction of the courts and the change of their form should be submitted entirely to the Legislature. There was no question on the subject. When I first heard the amendment of the gentleman from Norfolk, I had no objection to it except that this court of appeals had been long known to the Constitution of Virginia, and ought to be retained, unless there was some utility in the change. As to the consideration that there had been a regular and fixed construction of the Constitution of the U. States for a great length of time, that was no reason to change the title of court of appeals, because the Constitution of Virginia, had been in existence for a still longer time. But though my original objection to the change had been only that it was unnecessary, when I heard the gentleman's argument I felt more.

I shall not enter on the question, whether the construction of the Federal Constitution by the Congress of the U. S. is correct, or whether it will be adhered to or not. That question I shall not touch — it is not before the Committee. We act on the presumption, that that construction might be adopted, and we have provided against it. The argument of the gentleman goes to prove not only that there is no such thing as Judicial independence, but that there ought not to be no such thing: that it is unwise and improvident to make the tenure of the Judge's office to continue during good behaviour. That is the effect of his argument. His argument goes to prove, not only that there is no such thing, but that it is unwise that there should be. I have grown old in the opinion, that there is nothing more dear to Virginia, or ought to be dearer to her Statesmen, and that the best interests of our country are secured by it. Advert, sir, to the duties of a Judge. He has to pass between the Government and the man whom that Government is prosecuting: between the most powerful individuals in the community, and the poorest and most unpopular. It is of the last importance, that in the exercise of these duties, he should observe the utmost fairness. Need I press the necessity of this? Does not every man feel that his own personal security and the security of his property depends on that fairness? The Judicial Department comes home in its effects to every man's fireside: it passes on his property, his reputation, his life, his all. Is it not, to the last degree important, that he should be rendered perfectly and completely independent, with nothing to influence or to controul him but God and his conscience? You do not allow a man to perform the duties of a Juryman or a judge if he has one dollar of interest in the matter to be decided: and will you allow a judge to give a decision when his office may depend upon it? when his decision may offend a powerful and influential man? Your salaries do not allow any of your Judges to lay up for his old age: the longer he remains in office, the more dependant he becomes upon his office. He wishes to retain it, if he did not wish to retain it, he would not have accepted it. And will you make me believe that if the manner of his decision may affect the tenure of that office, that the man himself will not be affected by that consideration? But suppose he is not affected by it: if the mere repeal of a law, and the making some change in the organization of his Court, is to remove him, that these circumstances will not recur perpetually? I acknowledge that, in my judgment, the whole good which may grow out of this Convention, be it what it may, will never compensate for the evil of changing the tenure of the Judicial office.

The gentleman from Orange placed his argument upon this ground — that to impose such a restraint upon the legislature was to make an imputation upon the legislature which he would not make — he did not suppose it possible they would act in that manner, and he would not provide against it. For what do you make a Constitution? If your confidence is complete & no provision is necessary against misdoing, and no imputation is to be cast upon the legislature, why are we making another Constitution? Consider how far this argument extends in the 10th resolution of the Legis. Co, you say that no bill of attainder or *ex post facto* law shall be passed. What a calumny is here upon the Legislature, of the gentleman's native state! Do you believe that the Legislature will pass a bill of attainder, or an *ex post facto* law? Do you believe that they will pass a law impairing the obligation of contracts? If not, why provide against it? Does not the principle of the gentleman from Orange apply as much to this case as to the other? You declare that the Legislature shall not take private property for the public use without just compensation. Do you believe that the Legislature will put forth their grasp upon private property, without compensation? Certainly I do not. There is as little reason to believe they will do such an act as this, as there is to believe that a Legislature will offend against a Judge who has given a decision against some favourite opinion and favourite measure of theirs, or against a popular individual who has almost led the Legislature by his talents and influence. I am persuaded there is at least as much danger that they will lay hold on such an individual, as that they will condemn a man to death for doing that which when he committed it was no crime. The gentleman says it is impossible the Legislature should ever think of doing such a thing. Why then expunge the prohibition? He replies the benefit to be obtained is this, that it is possible the Legislature may create Judges whom they afterwards discover to be useless: they discern their error, but if this clause is retained, they cannot retrace the step and abolish their own work. Is this probable? In the history of this country, Judges are known to be charged with duties they are scarcely equal to. There are no surplus Judges. The office does not descend to the family, and multiply with it. All the Judges are created by a Legislative act: and they may as well abolish a court to get rid of a Judge, as create a court to make a Judge. There can be no just fear that unnecessary Judges will be created—it is not the tendency of our situation and our Government. (The danger that they will be left dependent, is more probable:) but if it does arise, it is provided against by the 8th resolution.

I see no utility in the amendment of the gentleman from Norfolk. It will change the established appellation of the court, long settled in our own Constitution. Be this, however, as it may, nothing can be in my apprehension more mischievous than to expunge that clause with the views that gentleman entertains. His design is professedly and avowedly, to leave all the Judges: but the Judges of the Court of Appeals, (and them too, as I believe will be the fact) to the power of the Legislature. There is this difference: The removal of a Judge is an unpleasant task—it usually occasions some reluctance: but, merely to take away the foundation on which he stands, and to let him drop, is another thing: this occasions very little compunction: and as little to re-elect others and leave him un-provided for.

I feel strongly, that this Convention can do nothing that would entail a more serious evil upon Virginia, than to destroy the tenure by which her Judges hold their offices.

Mr. TAZEWELL rose in reply:[1]

The gentleman from Chesterfield, said he, urges as an objection, that the jurisdiction of that Court of Appeals is merely appellate, and gives this as a reason why he will not vote to change the name of the Court. Has the gentleman adverted to the 4th line of the resolution, which declares that "the jurisdiction of these tribunals shall be regulated by law?" If the Legislature is to regulate the jurisdiction of all the courts, and this among the rest, what becomes of the ground he has taken, that the present jurisdiction of this court is appellate only? It is called "The Court of Appeals" and *ex vi termini* it must be appellate; but its jurisdiction may be altered by law in any way the Legislature shall direct. I do not know that it is so desirable, that its jurisdiction shall be appellate *only.* The distinction between original and appellate jurisdiction, is not perfectly clear. It runs into *apices juris.*[2] I know of no argument to show, that we ought to exclude all jurisdiction, other than appellate. I think there are many cases, where it ought to be original also. I therefore apprehend there is no force in the objection of the gentleman from Chesterfield.

The gentleman from Richmond tells us, that he is unwilling to adopt the change of denomination proposed by my amendment—First, be-cause it may cause the Constitution of Virginia to read *totidem verbis,* as the Constitution of the United States does: and the Constitution of Virginia is older, in its date, than the Federal Constitution, and is more certain in its interpretation. It will be seen by a repetition of the words, that the terms of the Federal Constitution are not repeated—they are changed; but if they were identically the same, what interpretation has been put on this Constitution, which should induce us to prefer it? What did the Constitu-tion do? Appoint Judges of the Court of Appeal? No—Judges of other Courts were made Judges of the Court of Appeals until 1788, when the District Court system was adopted. When that system was adopted, the Legislature thought there must be a Court of Appeals, and they then erected a District[3] Court with that name, and so it has remained ever since. So far the Constitution of Virginia has had no settled decision which bears upon the subject. The Court of Appeals was composed of the Judges of three other Courts, and a subsequent Legislature pronounced it to be a Constitutional Court. But no such difficulty has ever occurred respecting the Constitution of the United States. I am told there may be different constructions of that Constitution. I care not how many dif-ferent constructions may be put upon it *hereafter.* If the Convention adopt its language now, it adopts it as *now* construed: and after that, I do not care if they shall change the construction fifty times. I am for adopting the words as they are *now* understood: and it was for that reason that I moved the amendment. I would take the words "a Supreme Court," under the construction held by every Department of the Federal Government — that the "Supreme Court" is a Constitutional Court, and its Judges beyond the reach of Congress itself. If we adopt the term under this construction, we adopt the construction itself; and thus the Court of Appeals becomes consecrated as much as the Supreme Court of the United States. And with respect to the Inferior Courts, change but one word, and your Constitution will be precisely the same, on this subject, as the Constitution of the United States. The construction always was, that Congress may change and abolish them at pleasure; and the construction has been acquiesced in to the present time. By adopting the same words with the Federal Constitution as to both the Superior and Inferior Courts, all difficulty will be avoided for all time to come. This was my sole reason for wishing to have the amendment adopted.

But it seems that, because of this, I am supposed to be opposed to the independence of the Judiciary. Sir, if I know myself, there is no member of this Convention more sincerely attached to that independence than I am. But I have no idea of making the Judiciary independent of the law. I want a constitutional tribunal which the Legislature cannot abolish; and you get that when you get a Supreme Court: When it is said that every judgment of your Judicial Department shall, if required, be passed under the revision of this tribunal, you have got all that ought to be desired. If you go beyond this rule, where are you to stop? If every officer of every Court is not to be declared constitutional, at what point are you to stop? Create a forum which shall be as distinct and independent a department of your Government, as the Legislative or the Executive. You then have your three great Departments, and that is enough. The Inferior Courts must be subject to the Legislative control. It must be so. It always has been so in every country in the world but Virginia. Then I wish to know whether it is desirable that the judges should remain free from this control? The gentleman is for allowing the Legislature to act on the tribunal itself; but he wants to secure the preservation of the judge. What Judge? The Judge of what Court? When you say that he retains the capacity to receive another judicial office, it is saying nothing: because he would have that capacity just as much if he was no Judge at all. It is only to declare that the Judge shall continue to *receive his salary*. But for what? for nothing. If this is necessary to secure the independence of the Judiciary, why, in the name of Heaven, let it be so. You can't buy that independence too dear. But you have that, when you said there shall be a Supreme Court. The Constitution of the United States says the same thing, and it has worked well: the independence of the Federal Judiciary has not been impaired. As to the duty which a judge is called to perform, it certainly ought to influence the Legislature. It always has. The gent. from Chesterfield is mistaken, when he says, that the Constitution of the U. States, sinks the boat under the Judge. Three Judges became useless; but at that precise period, the old system of assize was got up in 1780, and brought in, in 1788: and then the Legislature appointed the three Judges of the court of Admiralty, to be Judges of the General Court. They were so commissioned, that they might be made Judges of the Court of Appeals. There was no obligation on the Legislature to elect these particular persons: but they were selected, because they had been Judges: this was the over-ruling motive, which prevailed in their election. I never can agree to introduce into any Constitution, a principle, which virtually declares, that a sinecure shall be created, to support a man, without employment, because he has been a Judge. I never will or can agree to create a band of judicial pensioners, call them what you will. He who performs a duty, should be paid for performing it; and he should not be paid, unless he does perform it. I never will consent to depart from this rule, be the consequences what they may.

But, how is the independence of the Judiciary affected, by declaring that the Judge, whose Court has been abolished, shall still retain his office? It is said, that he "shall perform *any* judicial duties, which the Legislature shall assign him." What now becomes of his independence? You may not sink the boat from under him; but you may pile up jurisdiction to any extent you please, til you sink the Judge, boat and all. Here is a Judge who resides, say in Accomac: (one of these Judges *in posse,* not *in esse,*) and you require him to hold a Court in Lee, or Monongalia, two, three, or four times a year. Is not this striking at his independence, as much as if you took away his office? You say he shall keep the office; but, then, you may lay upon him any amount of duty you choose. You have only to suppose *mala fides,* in your Legislature (and the provisions in your resolution go to the hypothesis of *mala fides* and profess to guard against it,) and your Judge is just as much at its mercy, as he would have been in the other case. You have only to suppose your Legislature wicked, and they can destroy any Judge they please.

As to the last clause, moved to be stricken out, by my friend from Orange, (Mr. BARBOUR,) I would abandon my opinions respecting it, if I could be satisfied, that when I have got a Supreme Court, I have not got an independent Judiciary: but I know that I have it, for I have seen it in the Federal Constitution, for 40 years; I want no more, and no better.

Mr. MARSHALL rejoined:

I trust the great importance of this subject, will be deemed a sufficient apology for my again troubling the Committee. Some observations have fallen from the gentleman from Norfolk, which I feel it incumbent upon me to notice. The gentleman has said, that it is sufficient for the independence of the Judiciary Department, that the Judges of the Supreme Court be independent: and that there is no country on earth, where the independence of the Judges of the other Courts is secured. I will refer him to the country with which I am best acquainted—I mean Great

Britain. What is the Supreme Court of Great Britain? It is the House of Lords. And are not the Judges of the Court of Common Pleas independent? Do they not hold their office during good behaviour? Yet these are Inferior Courts. I do not know so well the condition of other countries in this respect; but I believe the independence of the courts is preserved in France.

The independence of all those who try causes between man and man, and between a man and his Government, can be maintained only by the tenure of their office. Is not their independence preserved, under the present system? None can doubt it. Such an idea was never heard of in Virginia, as to remove a Judge from office. You may impose upon him any duty you please. You may say, that the Court of Appeals shall sit every day, from the 1st of January to the last of December. The Judge of a County Court may be called on to perform his duty on the bench, for a whole year: Yet he holds his office during good behaviour.

The Legislature can have no motive to impose unreasonable duties on a Judge — he may be required to do all he can do, and he can do no more. If the Judges in commission, are incompetent to the duty which is to be performed, the Legislature will create more Judges: it is within the ordinary province of Legislative action. Their independence is not impaired, by their being required to do all they can. That is their acknowledged duty.

We have heard about sinecures and judicial pensioners. Sir, the weight of such terms is well known here. To avoid creating a sinecure, you take away a man's duties, when he wishes them to remain — you take away the duty of one man, and give it to another: and this is a sinecure. What is this, in substance, but saying, that there is no such thing as judicial independence? You may take a Judge's duties away, and then discard him. What is this but saying, that there is, and can be, and ought to be, no such thing as judicial independence? The gentleman says, he is a great friend to an independent Judiciary, and his friendship extends to the Supreme Court only. The whole circuit duty is now in the Inferior Courts; would he be very willing to transfer it to the Court of Appeals? It is impossible for him to answer but in the negative. He would then have the whole criminal jurisdiction of the State, entrusted to Judges, removable from office by the Legislature at its pleasure. What would then be the condition of the court, should the Legislature prosecute a man, with an earnest wish to convict him? But more. The great mass of controversy existing in the Commonwealth, must always be decided in the Inferior Courts. We had an example in the Old General Court. What would be the consequence of giving original jurisdiction to an Appellate Court? Such a mass of causes accumulated in that court, that the great grandson of no man then living, would have seen the trial of the last cause on the docket. This will be the inevitable consequence: business will accumulate to an extent, that it will be impossible to pass through. The Inferior Courts will, therefore, try the great mass of causes, and reserve an appeal on questions of law. The gentleman would leave all these Judges unprotected by the Constitution. He declares himself a friend to Judicial Independence, and gives independence to those only, who have no criminal jurisdiction. I understand by Judicial Independence, the independence of all the members of the Judicial Department, whatever be their situation. He asks, are you to make every petty officer independent? I answer, no: but, is that the question? Are your Judges to be likened to every petty officer? Would he liken the Judges to them?

Will the gentleman recollect, that in order to secure the administration of justice, Judges of capacity, and of legal knowledge, are indispensable? And how is he to get them? How are such men to be drawn off from a lucrative practice? Will any gentleman of the profession, whose practice will secure him a comfortable independence, leave that practice, and come to take an office, which may be taken from him the next day? You may invite them, but they will not come. You may elect them, but they will not accept the appointment. You don't give salaries that will draw respectable men, unless by the certainty of permanence connected with them. But if they may be removed at pleasure, will any lawyer of distinction come upon your bench? No, Sir. I have always thought, from my earliest youth till now, that the greatest scourge an angry Heaven ever inflicted upon an ungrateful and a sinning people, was an ignorant, a corrupt, or a dependent Judiciary. Will you draw down this curse upon Virginia? Our ancestors thought so: we thought so till very lately — and I trust the vote of this day will shew that we think so still.[4]

Printed, *Richmond Enquirer,* 12 December 1829.

1. Tazewell's reply and JM's rejoinder were published in the 17 Dec. 1829 issue of the *Enquirer.*

2. *Apices juris non sunt jura* ("Extremities, or mere subtleties of law are not rules of law").

3. Both the *Enquirer* and *Proceedings and Debates* have "District," though Tazewell apparently said (or meant to say) "distinct."

4. Tazewell's motion lost by a vote of 56 to 29. Stanard moved to insert "Supreme" before "Court of Appeals," which was agreed to. The committee then rejected Barbour's amendment, 53 to 36, thus retaining the clause proposed by the judiciary committee. After observing this day's debate, a diarist recorded that he "heard a most able discussion between The Chief Justice & Mr. Tazewell on the question of the independence of the Judiciary. It was the battle of the Giants. The old Chief appeared to greater advantage than I ever heard him — his voice was clear and audible, his manner animated and most imposing. In all my life I never felt more veneration for any human being than for him at that moment" (*Proceedings and Debates,* 619–20; Joanne L. Gatewood, ed., "Richmond during the Virginia Constitutional Convention of 1829–1830: An Extract from the Diary of Thomas Green, October 1, 1829, to January 31, 1830," *Virginia Magazine of History and Biography,* LXXXIV [1976], 318).

To [Frederick W. Porter]

Sir   Richmond Decr. 21st. 1829

I have received your letter informing that the managers of "The Sunday School Union" have done me the honour to elect me as the successor of my much lamented friend the late Judge Washington.[1] I pray you to accept and to communicate to the board my assurances of the grateful sensibility with which I receive this mark of their favourable opinion.

No man estimates more highly than I do the real worth of your society or the intrinsic value of the objects it pursues. I am much very much gratified at the success which your letter informs me has thus far attended its philantropic meritorious and well directed labours. I hope and believe that the future will not form a contrast with the past. If any motive could induce me to decline the station which has been assigned me in the society by its partial favour it would be the consciousness of my utter inability to contribute by any advice or communication, to its usefulness. With the truest wishes for the prosperity of the institution and with great respect for yourself I am, Your Obedt. Servt

J MARSHALL

ALS (draft), Marshall Papers, ViW. Recipient identified by internal evidence (see n. 1).

1. Letter not found. JM's correspondent was Frederick W. Porter, corresponding secretary for the American Sunday-School Union, founded in Philadelphia in 1824. JM was elected to succeed Bushrod Washington as one of the Union's honorary vice-presidents. An excerpt from JM's letter (the second paragraph) was published in the Union's report for 1830 indicating that the recipient was the corresponding secretary. The same excerpt was also published in the Union's magazine (*The Sixth Report of the American Sunday-School Union* [Philadelphia, 1830], 7, 24; *American Sunday School Magazine*, VII [1830], 91).

Debate on Judiciary
Virginia Convention
23 December 1829

The convention on this day took up the judiciary report as amended in the committee of the whole. After the delegates approved the smaller amendments to the first resolution, Bayly moved to strike out "and in the County Courts, and in the justices of the peace, who shall compose the said courts." Henderson proposed to strike out "the" before "County Courts." After some debate, the convention rejected Henderson's amendment 56 to 40 and Bayly's amendment 68 to 27. It then agreed to amendments to the second and third resolutions. The fourth resolution, providing for the salaries of the judges of the Court of Appeals and of the inferior courts, had been amended to except county court justices and the aldermen and magistrates of the corporation courts. Marshall opposed this amendment "on the ground that County Courts and Corporation Courts, not being included within the term Inferior Courts, by any just construction, to except them was improper, because the exception would imply, that they were in their nature included in that phrase, and would be so in fact, if not taken out of it by this exception." The convention accordingly did not concur in this amendment. On agreeing to the amendment to the fifth resolution, the convention completed consideration of the amendments to the judiciary report as proposed in the committee of the whole. It then took up the amended resolutions in turn, beginning with the first. Lucas P. Thompson moved to strike out the last clause, which read "No modification or abolition of any court, shall be construed to deprive any Judge thereof of his office; but, such Judge shall perform any Judicial duties, which the Legislature shall assign him." Giles found this clause to be "highly objectionable," observing that it would create a "privileged order" of judges who would continue to draw their salaries even after their offices were abolished (*Proceedings and Debates,* 723–27).

Mr. MARSHALL said, he should regret to renew the debate, were he not pleased with the opportunity of saying, that in casting his eyes over the last debate on this subject, as it had been reported by the press, he felt displeased with one expression which had fallen from himself on that occasion. A word had escaped him, which might be understood as derogating from the high respect he entertained for the character and talents of a gentleman, (Mr. Barbour) who had been opposed to him. He hoped that gentleman and the Convention would believe him incapable of having intended to insinuate any thing that might have such a bearing. He well knew that gentleman to be entirely incapable of intentionally misquoting or misrepresenting any resolution that might be the subject of discussion.[1]

With respect to the argument the House had now heard, he did not mean, in any notice he should take of it, to utter one sentiment respecting what had been done in Congress in the removal of any Judge from office, nor on the provision reported by the Judicial Committee, for the removal of Judges by two-thirds of the Legislature. When the House should direct its attention to that clause, he thought he should find little difficulty in satisfying it that that provision was abundantly sufficient for the end it had in view. But that was not now the question.

Mr. M. said he felt so much difficulty in delivering his sentiments on the subject, that he should be compelled to confine himself to the straight and narrow path that led directly to the object before him, without departing from it to notice any of the subjects which had been incidentally presented by the gentleman from Amelia.

The question was, whether that clause of the 1st resolution of the Judicial Committee should be stricken out, which declares that no modification or abolition of any court shall be construed to deprive any Judge thereof of his office; but that such Judge should perform any judicial duties which the Legislature should assign him. To that single question he should confine himself in what he had now to say.

The gentleman from Amelia, (Mr. Giles) had referred to the office of a Judge and the court in which he sat as being, for some reason, indissolubly united. Are office and court, asked Mr. M., synonymes? Is it impossible to separate them? Can they, by no effort, be sundered? And if it be possible, is it not done in the present case? The resolution makes office to depend on good behaviour; and it expressly declares that the court may be abolished, and yet the office remain. Why cannot language separate them?

The constitution means to declare, that though the court may be abolished, the Judge shall continue to hold his office, and shall still perform the duties of a Judge. In what does the office of a Judge consist? I have always understood that it consists in his constitutional capacity to receive Judicial power, and to perform Judicial duties: that he is brought into office in the manner prescribed by the Constitution, and can perform the duties of his office, however the court may be changed. Whatever may be the situation of the court—however it may be named, still he holds the office, and if the Constitution shall declare that when the court is abolished, he shall still hold it, there is no inconsistency in the declaration. The gentleman says, that if a person be commissioned as a Judge of the General Court, and the General Court shall be abolished, his office is abolished with it—and he is the Judge of nothing. But the General Court under the present system is a constitutional court and cannot be abolished. We know that Judges who were Judges of the General Court at one time, became district Judges, and then Judges of the Superior court in the county. Should the General Court be abolished and by consequence the office with it, the question would occur, whether the Judges would perform any other duties; but if you declare in the Constitution that they shall be thus capable, the difficulty is removed. And will gentleman say, that this is impracticable? But the difficulty does not arise under the Constitution as it shall be, but as it is; the Constitution now declares that there shall be a General Court. The Legislature can no more abolish the General Court than the Court of Appeals. But the Constitution we are now engaged in making, does not say there shall be a Court of Appeals and a General Court: it says that the Judicial power shall be vested in a Court of Appeals, in such *Inferior Courts* as the Legislature shall from time to time ordain and establish, and in the county courts.

How will the commission of the Judges be made out? as Judges of the Inferior Courts—and if so, the Legislature may declare in which of the Inferior Courts they shall discharge their Judicial duty. Does, then, a change of that particular court, affect the office in any way? What creates the office? First an election by the Legislature as the Constitution directs: 2nd. a Commission by the Governor, or in such other form as the Constitution enjoins. When these acts have been performed, the Judges are in office. Now, if the Constitution shall say that his office shall continue and he shall perform Judicial duties, though his Court may be abolished, does he, because of any modification that may be made in that Court, cease to be a Judge of the Inferior Courts?

Suppose that the present Constitution had appointed Judges of the Inferior Courts, instead of the General Court, and their District Courts had been abolished, and Superior Courts of counties had been established in their place, would the Judge of the District Court thereby go out of office? You diversify his duties, and, therefore, his office is to be abolished! If I understand the Constitution a-right, the Legislature cannot, by law, create the *office* of a Judge. It can create *Courts,* and may change them at will: it may give them one name or another name, it may assign them one Judge, or two Judges, or three Judges: it may order them to sit here, or to sit there — it may give them a District of several Counties, or may direct them to sit in every county: still they will continue to be "Inferior Courts," and the Judges must perform any duties the Legislature shall assign them.

Where is the difficulty?

The question constantly recurs — do you mean that the Judges shall be removable at the will of the Legislature? The gentleman talks of responsibility. Responsibility to what? to the will of the Legislature? can there be no responsibility, unless your Judges shall be removable at pleasure? will nothing short of this satisfy gentlemen? Then, indeed, there is an end to independence. The tenure during good behaviour, is a mere imposition on the public belief — a sound that is kept to the ear — and nothing else. The consequences must present themselves to every mind. There can be no member of this body who does not feel them. If your Judges are to be removable at the will of the Legislature, all that you look for from fidelity, from knowledge, from capacity, is gone and gone forever. All chance of bringing men upon the bench, who know as much as lawyers at the bar, must be given up: there is an end to it. No respectable lawyer will come to the bench, if, for the slightest cause, so soon as he has separated himself from the bar — so soon as he has incapacitated himself to earn a comfortable support for his family there, he may be thrown out of an office he had been told was to be permanent, and driven away to poverty and all the humiliating consequences that must ensue.

Mr. M. said, he was well assured this was not what the Convention wished to do. But will it not, asked he, produce this state of things, if by any change or modification of the court, the Judge may be put out of office? What necessity can there be for this? do gentlemen believe that the duties of the inferior courts will diminish? that there will not always be as much Judicial duty as you will have Judges to perform it. If this is the fact, and surely it is, if we may reason from past experience, why make a mere transfer of duties to work a removal from office?

Can any gentleman say that the Legislature will never act in this manner? Look at what we are doing. This Convention is removing every Judge from office at one sweep. Are gentlemen sure the Legislature will never do the same thing? Is there any call directed to us which will not sound as loud in the ears of the Legislature? Can we, while at one blow we are dashing every Judge in the State from his office, say that the Legislature will never remove them in like manner hereafter? Sir, we should soon see realized the fears which are entertained by some amongst us.

I cannot sit down without noticing the morality of the course recommended by this measure. Gentlemen talk of sinecures, and privileged orders—with a view, as it would seem, to cast odium on those who are in office. You seduce a lawyer from his practice, by which he is earning a comfortable independence, by promising him a certain support for life, unless he shall be guilty of misconduct in his office. And after thus seducing him, when his independence is gone and the means of supporting his family relinquished, you will suffer him to be displaced and turned loose on the world with the odious brand of sinecure—pensioner—privileged order—put upon him, as a lazy drone who seeks to live upon the labour of others. This is the course you are asked to pursue.

Some allusion has been made to the tenure of office during good behaviour in England; and to the power of Parliament. In England they have no written Constitution; and yet the Judges consider themselves quite as secure as they are here, where we have one. Parliament will always maintain their independence, in order to save the people from the power of the crown. The crown is the source of apprehension: and the Legislature will never unite with it in removing the Judges from their office.

We have been told this arrangement will destroy all responsibility in the Judges. Are there no other means to make a Judge responsible, but to make him removeable from office at the will of the Legislature? If the provisions of the 7th and 8th resolutions are not sufficient to secure responsibility, we can make them so when they shall be the object of our attention. They are not at present before us. I believe they are now sufficient for that end; if not, they can be made so. But is it not new doctrine to declare, that the Legislature by merely changing the name of a court or the place of its meeting, may remove any Judge from his office?

The question to be decided is, and it is one to which we must come, whether the Judges shall be permanent in their office, or shall be dependent altogether upon the breath of the Legislature.

Mr. Giles rose again, and after an apology for troubling the House, said, that if he had had any doubts before, of the impropriety of the clause, the gentleman who had just taken his seat had relieved him from them all. He felt for the learning and standing and personal excellence of that gentleman so high a degree of respect, that he was willing to throw himself into the back ground, as to any weight to be attached to his opinion, and rely exclusively on the merits he could shew pertained to it, and thus he would endeavour to do so plainly, as not to be misunderstood. The gentleman from Richmond had told the Convention that an office during good behaviour, was an office for life. This he denied. There was no such word in a Judge's commission.

No such pledge was given him: was that the real tenure of his office? No, it was good behaviour and the continuance of the office. So long his salary was to be sure, and no longer.

He thought the gentleman had not succeeded in showing that it was not an anomaly to have the court out of being, and an office pertain to the court in being. The gentleman had asked if there were no terms by which this could be done? He answered, no: it was an anomaly in terms. He had, however, such high respect for that gentleman's standing, that he always doubted his own opinion when put in opposition to that of the gentleman. The gentleman had undertaken to show that a man may be a Judge of the District Court after the General Court, of which he had been a Judge, should be at an end. He told the Convention that the General Court was a Constitutional Court; but was it not surrendering the argument to go back to the old Constitution? By the Constitution now proposed, the Legislature was not to be trammelled. The gentleman had asked whether Judges of the General Court would not perform District Court services?

Judge Marshall here explained: he had, he perceived, been totally misconceived. He had said, that under the existing Constitution the General Court was a Constitutional court and could not be abolished: but that under the new Constitution the Judges of the inferior courts would continue to be such, though some change might be made in their sphere of action — and he had asked whether, because they should cease to perform District Court service, they must, therefore, cease to hold their office?

Mr. Giles resumed: He was very sorry he had misconceived the gentleman: but, after listening to the explanation he had now given, the impression on his mind remained the same still. He insisted that they were not to reason from the General Court existing under a former Constitution, to a Constitution containing no such court within its provisions; and one great object of forming which Constitution, was to get rid of that court. He denied that a Judge *could* perform duty in any other court but that to which he was commissioned. He could not have his commission to one court and his duties in another. Supposing the Judge to be incompetent, (as was known to be the case, and long to have been the case with at least one Judge whom he should not name,) could the Legislature assign such a Judge duties to perform in another court — duties to an incompetent Judge? What duties? Could he receive any at all? None; then his office was *vox et praeterea nihil.*[2]

He begged to call the attention of the House to what was the real genuine independence of a Judge in Great Britain. It was the security that his compensation should not be diminished during his continuance in office. Judges in England were deemed to be very independent even before the reign of William and Mary, when their offices expired with the demise of the crown. The law had since been changed, and they now survived — but it was perfect independence to be assured of an undiminished support during the continuance of their office. This was the true independence of a British Judge. Strike out the present clause, and a Judge in America would still be in a better situation than those of England.

But as the gentleman had spoken of hardships should the clause be stricken out, he would offer the amendment he had before read. It was no great favourite of his, but he was willing to go that far, and it was farther than any provision had ever gone on this subject under the sun.

The gentleman seemed to think that he had used terms calculated, if not intended, to throw reproach upon the Judges in office. He was not conscious of having used any terms that reflected in the least degree on their honour and integrity. But it did seem to him, that by the resolutions taken together, responsibility was rather avoided than sought to be secured. Had the gentleman told the House in what it consisted? Where was it? If there was such a thing, he presumed it was describable. For himself he could not see even a shadow of it. The gentleman had insisted that there was the same responsibility in this, as in other cases: and here was the greatest point of difficulty between the worthy gentleman and himself. When a representative returned to his constituents, did they cite him? did they give him twenty days notice to appear and answer? No such thing. They told him at once — Sir, we don't like you. And that was enough — they turned him out forthwith, and held themselves bound to assign no reason to him for so doing. But, in the case of a Judge there must be a majority of two-thirds of both Houses of the Legislature, and sixty days notice; and by the time the Judge appeared, the session would be over. The resolution first laid down a principle and then defeated it. But in the case of a representative, the responsibility was real — and its operation prompt and efficient. The voter might say to the representative as Tom Brown said to Dr. Fell,

> I do not like thee, Dr. Fell
> The reason why I cannot tell:
> But 'tis a fact I know full well,
> I do not like thee, Dr. Fell.[3]

He was willing to risk his liberty thus far — (and if human being existed, who was more jealous of it, he had yet to see him,) if a Judge became odious to the people, let him be removed from office.

Mr. G. concluded by this remark, that the House had exhibited on the other side the very *acme* of Judicial talent in the country; and yet it had produced no conviction in his mind, and, he believed, would not in theirs; on the contrary, it had but rivetted all the impression he had previously entertained.[4]

a majority, and as he believed would continue to receive it. It would remove much of the difficulty which attached to the general subject, and would seem to convey the assurance, that the body would be able yet to agree upon something. He did not, at this time, feel as if this had been so far settled. The vote in favour of the plan of the gentleman from Albemarle[2] — (and to which he presumed the gentleman from Fauquier alluded) — had been given, while another proposition, providing for future apportionment, was still before the House. The gentleman seemed to take that vote as an expression of the opinion of a very decided majority, that there should be no future apportionment provided for: but he did not so consider it. And when the proposition of the gentleman from Northampton, (Mr. Upshur,) was afterwards voted out, he considered that, not as a vote, declaring, that the Convention would lay down no plan for future apportionment: but only as rejecting that particular form of it. No vote whatever, as he understood, had yet been given, directly on that point: nor had the plan, proposed by the Legislative Committee itself, yet been rejected by the Convention.

The question, in relation to a future apportionment of representation, was, therefore, yet undetermined. And he could not say, that any proposition, containing a proposal on that subject, would certainly be rejected by the House.

While that question remained open, he felt great difficulty in saying how the House might vote on the present proposition, should some plan for future apportionment be finally agreed upon. Should such plan be adopted, it must of course be looked to in all other measures on the general subject; but if it was to be taken as certain, that no plan for the future was to be admitted, then the House could act upon that knowledge. He had no such knowledge, and could not act upon it. He did not know but he might prefer the present proposition to any which had been offered, if a plan was to be agreed upon respecting the future: but if none was to be agreed to, then he might vote *against* this as a present arrangement. In the one case he had to compare one plan for the future, with another plan for the future and to choose between them: but in the other case, he had to choose between a proposition for future apportionment, and rising without doing any thing. He should act very differently in the one case from what he should in the other. It was impossible to look without extreme reluctance, and extreme mortification and apprehension to the rising of the Convention without having been able to effect any thing. It behoves them all to consider the situation in which they were placed. The eyes of the world, (that is of so much of the world as cared for matters of this kind,) were turned in a considerable degree toward that Convention. The question whether men were capable of framing a form of Government for themselves in some measure depended for its solution upon the decisions of that body: certainly the general opinion on that question must be affected by them. But were the eyes of the union alone fixed upon them, it was a serious subject of reflection. Those eyes looked at them with great solicitude. The eyes of Virginia with an anxiety still greater, as was manifest from her having placed in this body men in whom she had long reposed her utmost confidence; and which must be the result, should such a body rise and do nothing. It could not be because there was nothing to do. There are none who pretended to say that—all admitted that great changes, or at least considerable changes might be made in the constitution for the better. All seemed to think there was much to do. If they rose, therefore, having done nothing, it would be manifest and undeniable that it was because they were unable to agree on any thing. How humiliating! He repeated, therefore, that if the question were put to him, "Shall the Convention rise without adopting any thing, or shall it adopt any plan of future apportionment?" he should be very differently situated from what he would be if asked "whether this plan or that plan of future apportionment were to be preferred?"

Mr. Randolph said, he had nothing to do with what disposition the House might make of the question; but he rose as one individual, the humblest member of the body, solemnly to deny that he ever had admitted, or ever could admit that the Government of Virginia as at present existing, required *great* changes. He admitted that it might need some very *small* changes—and had so declared more than once. He had now risen to take himself out of the general and sweeping assertion of the gentleman who had just taken his seat. He had never, at any time, made the admission which the gentleman had ascribed to all the members of the body.

Mr. MARSHALL said he must have misunderstood the gentleman from Charlotte—and he certainly had misunderstood him, as to the meaning of the terms *great* and *small*. He should not have ventured to include that gentleman in any general declaration, unless he had understood him as so expressing himself. The gentleman had said he was content to strike off one half the number of the Legislature: he had also said that he was content to make changes, which he had not defined in the Judicial Department. Now, said Mr. M., I confess that when I said there was no gentleman who did not admit that great, or at least considerable changes ought to be made in the Constitution, I did understand the gentleman from Charlotte, as having proposed very considerable changes. If he did not so understand them, then I attached to the changes an importance which he did not. I have no doubt there is no member of the body unwilling to make what I consider very considerable changes in the Constitution.[3]

Mr. MARSHALL said, that nothing was more obvious than that the proposition of the gentleman from Richmond co. (Mr. Neale) would not at present receive the support of any part of the House. He tho't it was not difficult for any one to say that it would be decided in the negative. Now, he was not willing it should be negatived until he should better know what would be the future course of the Convention; he wished it to lie on the table until that could be determined. If obliged to vote now, he should vote against it: at a future moment he might be willing to vote in its favour.[4]

Printed, *Richmond Enquirer,* 29 December 1829.

1. John Scott.
2. William F. Gordon.
3. Following JM, Randolph, Giles, and Coalter made brief remarks. William H. Fitzhugh of Fairfax then asked what object JM had in mind in making his resolution (*Proceedings and Debates,* 759–60).
4. After further discussion, JM withdrew his motion, and Neale withdrew his amendment (ibid., 760–62).

Debate on Judiciary
Virginia Convention
29 December 1829

The convention resumed consideration of the judiciary report, at this point having approved the third, fourth, fifth, and sixth resolutions and tabled the first, second, seventh, and eighth resolutions. The delegates once again turned their attention to the first resolution, the last clause of which declared that no abolition of any court "shall be construed to deprive any Judge thereof of his office; but such judge shall perform any Judicial duties which the Legislature shall assign him." Benjamin W. S. Cabell moved to add, "but if no Judicial duties shall be assigned to him by the Legislature, he shall receive no salary in virtue of said office" (*Proceedings and Debates,* 762).

Mr. MARSHALL said, that if the amendment had declared, that if there were no judicial duty, which the Legislature *could* assign to the Judge, none which he *could* perform, that then he should receive no salary, he should feel no objection to its adoption: but it was impossible not to see, that the amendment in its present form, revived the old question, as to the dependence of the continuance of a Judge's office, on the will of the Legislature. Whenever it should be the will of the Legislature to take away the employment of a Judge, by abolishing the court in which he served, and to take away his support, by assigning him no other duties, it was perfectly in their power to do so. If the amendment had required no more, than that a Judge should receive no salary, when there were no judicial duties to be done, which might be assigned to him, he should be content; but if it rested on the will of the Legislature, to assign him any duties or not, undoubtedly, the tenure of such a Judge's office, was a tenure during pleasure merely.

Mr. Cabell said, he should not be so presumptuous, as to oppose himself in argument to the venerable gentleman from Richmond; nor was it necessary for him to do so. He had been induced to offer the amendment, by a sacred regard to his duty to his constituents; and he was perfectly confident, that if the Constitution was eventually to contain such a feature in it as the first resolution contained, and which it was the object of his amendment to strike out, it would not be voted for by thirty men in all the District from which he came. They would regard such a clause as evincing an attempt to establish a band of civil pensioners; and he was well assured they never would tolerate it. So long as an officer performed his duties, they were very willing he should receive his salary; but when, for any cause, physical or moral, that officer should be unable to perform the duty he had convenanted to do, they would not consent that he should receive the emoluments of office. Mr. C. insisted, that his amendment in no degree attacked the independence of the Judiciary Department. He should certainly be the last man in that Assembly, who would offer to do any thing that would have such a tendency. But, he thought if the Judiciary Department was secure, they who presided in it must be sufficiently so. When the public interest should require the abolition of a court, the Legislative body, coming from all parts of the Commonwealth, and being acquainted with the interests and feelings of the whole State would soon discover the necessity of the case, and would abolish it accordingly. And when a Judge was discharged from the necessity of performing any work, he could not conceive that he was entitled to receive his salary. The idea that his office remained after his court was abolished, was so very metaphysical, that he was really unable to comprehend it. He had always presumed that the office of a Judge was incidental to the court of which he was a Judge, and when the court was abolished, it fell of course: that the office of a Judge ceased as soon as the things he was to judge of, were withdrawn. But, he should not attempt to pursue the argument, or amplify the ideas he had suggested.

Mr. Claytor asked, that the question should be taken by ayes and noes, and they were ordered by the House.

Mr. Madison said he availed himself of the remark of the gentleman from Richmond, to enquire whether it would not be proper to vary the amendment, so as to say, that if there were no duties properly assignable to the Judge by the Legislature, that then he should receive no salary. He believed this would meet the distinction which the gentleman had suggested; and if no body else moved it as an amendment, he would himself do so.

Mr. M. accordingly moved as an amendment to the amendment of Mr. Cabell, to strike out the words "if no duty shall be assigned him," and insert in lieu thereof, "if there shall be no duties properly assignable to him."

Mr. Johnson rose to enquire, how, should the amendment be adopted, it was to be determined whether there were any duties thus "properly assignable," or not? If the Legislature should ever be induced to abolish a court with a view to get rid of a Judge, and then it was to be referred to the same body to say, whether there were any duties properly assignable to him, on the performance of which his salary was to be continued, it was not possible there could be any other than one decision of the question. The Legislature, which had taken the first step in abolishing his court, would assuredly take the second, and declare there were no duties which it could with propriety assign to him. In such a case, there was no umpire between the parties, and thus the amendment would leave the case just where it was.

Mr. Doddridge said, that the gentleman from Augusta looked only to the rare and very extreme case, where a court should be abolished for the sake of disposing of an obnoxious Judge; but he seemed to forget that it might often happen, that that body might abolish a court *bona fide*, because it was useless, and could be dispensed with. He hoped the amendment of the gentleman from Orange would prevail.

Mr. Nicholas opposed the amendment of Mr. Cabell, as putting the Judge at the mercy of the Legislature. It could rarely happen, that the modification of a court would render the services of the existing Judges unnecessary; and if there even were one or two surplus Judges, to maintain these would be far better than putting the whole corps into the power of the Legislature.

Mr. MARSHALL said, he wished to submit to the gentleman from Orange (Mr. Madison,) for whose opinion he need not say that he entertained a very profound respect, some reasons which he thought would satisfy him that it was morally impossible such a state of things could occur, in which there should be no Judicial duties which could, with propriety, be assigned to a Judge thrown out of employment, by a modification or abolition of one of the courts: Supposing such Judge to belong to the Court of Appeals or to the Inferior Courts between that court and the County Courts, was it possible such a state of things could arise, in which there would be no duties properly assignable to either? 1st Take the Court of Appeals. When could the case occur when there should be no Court of Appeals? Would the original courts ever be made final as well as original? Would any man leave that discretionary with any body whatever? Would any gentleman say there should be no Court of Appeals? That there should be as many expositions of law as there were Inferior Courts? There were upwards of one hundred Inferior Courts in Virginia: Would any man say there ought to be an hundred and odd constructions of law in the Commonwealth? He was satisfied there was none who would say so. There must be then a Court of Appeals. And if so, could the time ever come when there would be no judicial business for the Court of Appeals? Modify that court as they pleased, there must be appellate duties to perform.

Then as to the Inferior Courts: He prayed gentlemen to consider what he had attempted over and over to impress upon their attention, that the question would no longer occur as to a man who had been commissioned as the Judge of a particular court: Should the resolution be agreed to as it now stood, Judges could be commissioned as Judges of the Inferior Courts of the Commonwealth, and their commission would extend to every court between the Court of Appeals and the County Courts; courts which exercised among them all the criminal jurisdiction of the country, and all of the civil too, which did not come before the county courts. Could this business ever cease? Could the time ever arrive when there would be no such duty to perform? No gentleman could look at the dockets of these courts and possibly think that there ever could occur such a state of things as was provided for by the last amendment. That amendment stated an impossible case — a case where there should be no controversies between man and man, and no crimes committed against Society. It stated a case that could not happen: and would the Convention encounter the real hazard of putting almost every Judge in the Commonwealth in the power of the Legislature, for the sake of providing for an impossible case? He hoped not. But were it even possible that such a case could arise, would it not be more wise to pay a Judge's salary for a short time, than to leave it at the mere pleasure of the Legislature, to say whether a Judge should retain his office or not? But the case was impossible: and therefore he saw no reason for adopting either of the amendments.[1]

Printed, *Richmond Enquirer,* 31 December 1829.

1. After Tazewell spoke for and Stanard against, Madison's amendment was voted down. Stanard then proposed his own amendment to Cabell's motion, which "gave rise to a long and animated debate." JM "declined entering into the argument — but briefly assigned his reason for voting against Mr. Stanard's amendment." That amendment was overwhelmingly rejected. The convention then approved Cabell's amendment by a vote of 59 to 36, JM voting against. As amended, the first resolution was adopted. A lengthy debate then ensued on the second resolution, which provided that the present judges should remain in office "until the expiration of the session of the first Legislature elected under the new Constitution, and no longer. But the Legislature may cause to be paid to such of them as shall not be re-appointed, such sum as from their age, infirmities, and past services, shall be deemed reasonable." JM briefly "gave his reasons for believing that there would be no suspension of Judicial duties on the adoption of the Constitution. As the second resolution provided the time when the Judges were to go out of office, he presumed the implication was, that they were to retain their office until that time. The Constitution would change nothing but what was *expressly* changed." The convention subsequently struck out the clause concerning compensation for judges who were not reappointed. The vote was 50 to 43, JM voting against. A motion to strike out the entire resolution lost by a vote of 32 to 59, JM voting in favor (*Proceedings and Debates,* 764–77).

Remarks on Judiciary
Virginia Convention
7 January 1830

On 30 December a select committee of seven was appointed to draft a new constitution. The members of this committee were Madison (chairman), Marshall, Doddridge, Johnson, Benjamin W. Leigh, Tazewell, and Cooke. On 4 January Madison presented a draft constitution, which first underwent consideration in the committee of the whole before being formally submitted to the convention. Stanard on 7 January proposed an amendment that would vest judicial power in the judges as well as the courts on which they sat. Henderson requested Marshall's opinion on this amendment (*Proceedings and Debates*, 777, 792–97, 818–20, 821).

Mr. Marshall said, that being thus called out, it was not in his power to remain wholly silent. His opinion was that the amendment was a proper one. There was the same reason, in part, though not entirely, for making a declaration respecting the power of a Judge when out of court, as there was for that of justices in addition to the power of the County Courts. The acts performed by Judges out of court had been very properly enumerated by the gentleman from Spottsylvania. The awarding of writs of *habeas corpus* especially, was always done out of court.

The subject had not occurred to the Judicial Committee, or it would have been attended to by them in making their report. If acts of Judicial power were performed by Judges out of court, the Judges as well as the courts ought certainly to be mentioned in the enumeration of the depositories of that power.[1]

Printed, *Richmond Enquirer,* 9 Jan. 1830.

1. The amendment was adopted.

To Joseph Story

My dear Sir   Richmond Jany. 8th. 1830
   I am under absolute uncertainty concerning the time of my attendance in Washington, and that is a circumstance which gives me great concern. The crisis of our constitution is now upon us. A strong disposition to prostrate the judiciary has shown itself and has succeeded to a considerable extent. I know not what is in reserve. The most important principles will be determined this week or early in the next. I had determined to abandon every thin⟨g⟩ and had taken my seat in the stage of saturday. Those who concur with me in opinion have pressed me so earnestly to remain with them a few days that I have consented to postpone my jurney, and shall not be present at the meeting of the court. I am

extremely anxious to hear from you. If you make a court I can remain a very few days without delaying the public business. If only three Judges attend I must quit the convention immediately whatever may be the state of those great questions on which I wish to vote.[1]

Present me affectionately to my brethren and write to yours truely

J MARSHALL

ALS, Story Papers, MHi. Addressed to Story in Washington; postmark illegible.

1. The court term opened on 11 Jan., with Justices Johnson, Duvall, Story, Thompson, and McLean attending. JM took his seat on 18 Jan. (U.S. Sup. Ct. Minutes, 11–18 Jan. 1830).

To [Thomas S. Grimké]

Dear Sir   Jany. 11th. 1830

I received some time past the pamphlet containing your oration on the 4th. of July 1809, and your speech in Decr. 1828 "on the constitutionality of the Tariff, and on the true nature of state government."[1] My acknowledgements of this flattering mark of your regard has been delayed much longer than I wished because the pressure of various avocations prevented my reading these speeches with the attention which they merit. I have now given them both a serious perusal and assent with my full judgement to the sentiments they contain.

Your argument delivered in the Senate is, without a compliment, the ablest I have ever seen on the subject which it discusses. It is supported by a body of facts and precedents which seem to me to speak a language which is irresistable. Is it possible that South Carolina can withstand so powerful an appeal to her reason her patriotism and her real interest?

It would be uncandid not to acknowledge that I have also read your notes and ungrateful not to say how much I am flattered by the notice you take of the author of the Life of Washington.[2] In that work I have aimed, I trust not unsuccessfully at a faithful narrative of some of the most interesting occurrences in our history. When more than fidelity is ascribed to me I receive such commendation as a favor which transcends my just pretensions. If it is bestowed by a gentleman whose public course demonstrates how entirely he acts on principle, how careless he is of public favour I am doubly gratified.

AL[S] draft, Marshall Papers, ViW.

1. Thomas S. Grimké, *Oration on the Absolute Necessity of Union, and the Folly and Madness of Disunion. Delivered Fourth of July, 1809 . . . Speech of Thomas S. Grimke, Delivered in December, 1828, on the Constitutionality of the Tariff and on the True Nature of State Sovereignty. . .* (Charleston, S.C., 1829). The pamphlet containing the oration and the speech is continuously paginated, each work having a separate title page. The first was originally published in 1809

as *An Oration Delivered in St. Phillip's Church . . . on the Fourth of July, 1809 . . .* (Charleston, S.C., 1809).

2. In a footnote to the 1828 speech which quoted from JM's *Life of Washington,* Grimké referred to his "Note R" in the appendices. He wrote: "The Life of Washington by Ch. J. Marshall, is a book of which Americans may well be proud: not indeed as a rhetorical composition, for which the ancient Historians are so unreasonably extolled; but as surpassing in the true dignity and usefulness, simplicity and beauty of History, all that can be found in Herodotus, Thucydides, and Xenophon, in Livy or Sallust, Cæsar or Tacitus. To be thoroughly versed in the facts, and to be deeply imbued with the spirit of Washington's Administration, is worth more to the citizen of the United States, than the most intimate acquaintance with the whole body of Greek and Roman History. . . . To Ch. J. Marshall, as a Representative in Congress, as an Ambassador, as a Judge and Historian, his Country owes an ample debt of gratitude. May our children's children acknowledge it with pride, and repay it with a thankful, admiring spirit, His will ever be, in American annals, peculiarly and emphatically 'Larum et venerabile nomen.' " (ibid., 120–21).

Remarks on Reapportionment
Virginia Convention
12 January 1830

On 11 January Madison proposed a scheme for future apportionment of the legislature, which the convention took up the next day. It provided that, with the concurrence of two-thirds of each house of the legislature, the General Assembly should have authority to make reapportionments at intervals of not less than ten years, so long as the number of delegates should not exceed 150 and the number of senators, thirty-six. Alexander Campbell opposed this plan and offered an amendment that would empower the General Assembly to reapportion the legislature, "so that the number of Delegates in each of the four grand districts, shall bear the same proportion to the whole population of each district, which the present apportionment bears to the whole population of each district, as shall be ascertained by the next census." Mercer, Fitzhugh, Campbell, and Thomas R. Joynes spoke to this amendment prior to Marshall's remarks (*Proceedings and Debates,* 847, 849–51).

Mr. MARSHALL said, there was a serious objection to the amendment: it went to enlarge indefinitely, both Houses of the Legislature: that must be its necessary effect, unless some restraining clause were added to prevent it. But such he was well assured was not the sense of the Convention: they wished rather to diminish the Legislature, and their objection to it had been stated by the gentleman from Accomac, (Mr. Joynes.)[1] The apportionment at present agreed on was the white basis as it stood in 1820. They had all agreed that the black population should not be represented in the same manner as the white: and the present scheme pursued that principle. But the amendment said the same proportion should be observed, whether the population were white or black: suppose that the East should get a majority of white population; by this plan they would not get a proportional increase of representation. The amendment would not benefit the Eastern part of the State at all; all its benefits would be confined to the West. It was unjust to adopt a principle which would not apply itself to a change of the population from black to white, when the general basis of the whole plan was in fact white population. In the middle country it was possible, and probable, that the character of the population would be greatly changed: there were none who could consider the condition, especially of the western part of the middle District, and not perceive this to be true; but the ratio of representation would not change with it.[2]

Printed, *Richmond Enquirer,* 14 January 1830.

1. Joynes commented that the rule contained in Campbell's amendment "was the worst, and the most injurious to the interests of Eastern Virginia, of any that had yet been thought of." By this rule, he contended, Tidewater would need an increase of ten thousand above its present population to get another representative while the west would need only an increase of five thousand (*Proceedings and Debates,* 851).

2. After further discussion, the convention rejected Campbell's amendment and adopted Madison's plan (ibid., 851–54).

Remarks on Money Bills
Virginia Convention
12 January 1830

Mr. MARSHALL moved to amend the 8th article by striking out the words "except money bills, which in no instance shall be altered by the Senate, but wholly approved or rejected.["]¹

Mr. MARSHALL said he should not have renewed a motion which had been rejected in Committee of the Whole, if any reasons had then been assigned for the rejection of it; nor should he have meddled with the subject, if the Committee appointed to draught the constitution, had had this subject under their consideration: but it was not among the amendments agreed to in the House, and so not referred to that committee. Under these circumstances, he felt it his duty to bring the subject before the Convention. He never could conceive the reason in favour of this part of the old constitution. It had always appeared to him to have been introduced into it, from an assimilation of the Senate to the British House of Lords. Nothing was more natural when we were just leaving a Government under which we had been born, and had grown up in high respect for all its principles, that such an assimilation should have taken place. But nothing could be more dissimilar than our Senate, and the House of Lords: which was a paramount body, hereditary in its structure, sitting in its own right, and naturally apt to be much under the influence of the Crown. The rule was adopted there because it might otherwise have been considered as a difficult and unpleasant task to resist in the lower House, and amendment proposed by the upper, and supposed to be in conformity with the will and wishes of the Crown. But there was nothing of this sort in Virginia. The members of the Senate were as much the representatives of the People as those of the House of Delegates. They were elected in the same manner, by the same persons, and they receive the same pay as members of the other House.

(Here Mr. Coalter interposed, and said that wisdom lifted up her voice in the streets, but was not heard. The Chair called the House to order, and the confusion in some degree subsided.)

Mr. MARSHALL resumed. He could see no essential difference between them. In all respects they resembled each other. The reason why the Legislature was divided into two branches was, that one might exercise a supervision over the acts of the other, and amend its acts when necessary. And to this end a mode of communication was established by the Constitution by which one of those bodies communicated to the other, its sentiments respecting the acts of that other body. This was intended to be the result of having two Houses of Legislature. But this cardinal principle was violated by this clause, which refused to the Senate the right of amending money bills sent up from the other House. It was an abridgement of the rights of the Senate. No reason could be given for it. The regulation was perfectly useless: and more; it was productive of a positive injury. It did not prevent the amendment of money bills by the Senate, but forced that body on a more circuitous and time-losing mode of effecting the object.

The Senate rejected a bill, which they wished to amend. The other House had no official communication from them, of such a wish: but on such private intelligence as they might obtain, they draughted a new Bill. This Bill might not embody all the amendments the Senate wished to introduce: then this too was rejected, and more Bills were draughted; and thus, much of the public time was wasted — and to what purpose? But this was not all. The Senate and the House might disagree as to what was meant by a Money Bill. He had known 3 or 4 days to be consumed in a dispute between the Houses on that subject. The House of Delegates contended, that all Bills, containing appropriations of money, were money Bills; the Senate denied this, and considered it as an attempt at usurpation by the other House, to bring within that term, any but Bills simply for revenue. He had known three or four Bills amended, and consequently rejected, on this ground, until at length the House of Delegates had conformed the Bill to the form the Senate had at first desired. The rule, therefore, was found inconvenient in practice, besides being wrong in principle. It forced the Senate on a clumsy, bungling, time-wasting method of getting at the object; but did not operate to prevent the amendment, which it forbade.[2]

Printed, *Richmond Enquirer*, 14 January 1830.

1. This was the seventh article of the draft constitution reported by the select committee on 4 Jan. It reads: "All laws shall originate in the House of Delegates, to be approved or rejected by the Senate, or to be amended with the consent of the House of Delegates, except money bills, which in no instance shall be altered by the Senate, but wholly approved or rejected" (*Proceedings and Debates,* 794).

2. The convention adopted JM's motion.

Debate on Judiciary
Virginia Convention
13 January 1830

Although the convention had approved a provision declaring that abolition or modification of a court was not to be construed as depriving a judge of his office, the select committee dropped this clause (for reasons explained by Marshall in his remarks below) in reporting its draft constitution. On this day Scott gave an impassioned address in support of an independent judiciary. He expressed particular concern about Tazewell's construction of the proposed constitution, according to which the abolition of a court also terminated the office of a judge of that court. He himself rejected that construction as repugnant to the clause declaring that judges were to hold their offices "during good behaviour," or "until removed in the manner prescribed in this Constitution" — namely, by impeachment or by a concurrent vote of two-thirds of both houses of the legislature. Addressing the members of the select committee, particularly "my friend from Richmond, (the Chief Justice)," Scott inquired whether he correctly understood Tazewell's exposition and whether the other members concurred in it (*Proceedings and Debates,* 870–71).

Mr. MARSHALL said, that it was with great, very great repugnance, that he rose to utter a syllable upon the subject. His reluctance to do so was very great indeed: and he had throughout the previous debates on this subject most carefully avoided expressing any opinion whatever upon what had been called a construction of the Constitution of the United States by the act of Congress of 1802.[1]

He should now, as far as possible, continue to avoid expressing any opinion on that act of Congress. There was something in his situation which ought to induce him to avoid doing so. He would go no farther than to say that he did not conceive the Constitution to have been at all definitively expounded by a single act of Congress. He should not meddle with the question whether a course of successive legislation should or should not be held as a final exposition of it: but he would say this — that a single act of Congress, unconnected with any other act by the other Departments of the Federal Government, and especially of that Department, more especially entrusted with the construction of the Constitution in a great degree, when there was no union of Departments — but the Legislative Department alone had acted, and acted but once, even admitting that act not to have passed in times of high political and party excitement, could ever be admitted as final and conclusive.

When the Report had been made by the J. Committee — and a plan had been laid before that Committee no declaration was made that the clause since expunged was necessary to prevent this construction of that report. The words had been introduced not for the purpose of making the Report conform to the Act of Congress but because they furnished a ready mode of disposing of the Judicial Department. If the words had not been used in the Constitution of the United States nothing was more probable than that the very same words would have been employed in the Report. He said, as being the individual who had draughted the article, that he had not had in his mind the clause of the Federal Constitution alluded to, and its construction by Congress.[2] When the article was introduced, it had not been for the purpose of acknowledging the justice of that construction, but to prevent the possibility of it; it was considered as possible, and barely possible, that such a construction might be given.

He did not wish to enter at all into the argument. All must have witnessed the caution with which he had avoided doing so. But he said freely, that the present Constitution ought to be construed *in its words:* and not in the opinion any member might have expressed upon it. They entertained different opinions: those opinions were not to regulate the construction of the Constitution, but its own words alone were to regulate the construction of it. And so far as he had any right to protest, he did protest against his individual construction, in any mode, being engrafted into the Constitution. Let the Constitution speak its own language: and be construed by those whose office it was to construe it.

Mr. Tazewell followed Mr. Marshall — and expressed an exactly opposite opinion. He vindicated the passage of the law for abolishing the newly appointed Judges, at the very close of the Mr. Adams's administration. He contended that that act was perfectly constitutional and proper — and that the course then taken by Congress had fixed the meaning of the words in the Constitution of the United States, which had been copied into the proposed Constitution of Virginia.

He was followed by Mr. Johnson, who conceded that the abolition of the Judges at the commencement of Mr. Jefferson's administration, however objectionable it might seem at first, had been sanctioned by the acquiescence of the people.

Mr. Giles rose in reply to Mr. Marshall:[3]

Concurring in the belief, that the interpretation which has hitherto been put on the terms of the Federal Constitution, will be put on the same terms, if used in the Constitution we are now making, and acting on that presumption, I conceive it unnecessary that any other explanation should be made, and hope that the amendment may be withdrawn: I prefer the Constitution as it now stands.[4]

Although I have paid the utmost possible attention to the opinions and arguments of the gentleman from Richmond (Mr. Marshall,) for whom I entertain the highest respect and regard, I cannot for my life find out how it is that an office should exist in a court, while the court itself does not exist, but is completely *functus officio*. Such a position appears to me to be a perfect contradiction; as much so, as it would be for us to declare, that a man shall enjoy his life after he is dead; and the effect of one declaration would be much the same, with that of the other. The proposition contains a contradiction in terms, and is in my judgment utterly inadmissible.

There is another reason which confirms me in my opinion as to what will be the interpretation put upon this part of the Constitution. The gentleman, it is true, says that he has not officially examined the point; but such was the impression on his mind, when the act of Congress was passed which limits the continuance of the Judge's office, to the existence of his court. Now, I have given the utmost attention to this subject. I formed an opinion at the time, which I publicly expressed. I have thought of it a thousand times since, and I have examined every act passed on the subject from that day to this, and I have no more doubt now than I had then, as to the true interpretation of the clause. It is a fundamental principle, which reigns throughout our institutions, that compensation and services should correspond to each other. The compensation of a Judge is paid him, not for his good behaviour, but for his official services.

The sensibility of the gentleman from Fauquier, (Mr. Scott,) on the subject of judicial independence, is so very great, that he himself supposes it may be morbid in its character, and I have no doubt that it is so. Nor is it confined to that gentleman alone: it extends to a vast many others who seem to labour under the same morbid sensibility with himself. The gentleman insists, that by the Constitution as it now stands, the independence of the Judges is not provided for. I am of a different opinion. I am prepared to go as far as any gentleman in favour of the independence of the Judiciary: I consider independence in a Judge as valuable as any gentleman can do; but I would not have independence extended into inviolability. I am as hostile to that, as I am favourable to their independence, and shall always be so, while republican government continues to be founded on the principles of responsibility. Sir, what do gentlemen want? What more would they have? The utmost security is given that a Judge shall continue to receive his salary, so long as he renders Judicial services. Ought he to have it any longer? Would any one think of advancing the same claim with reference to any other officer but a Judge? Would any man say that in a republican government, a public officer is to receive the public money any longer than he renders service to the public? Yet that is the amount of what is now claimed in behalf of the Judges of Virginia: That they shall receive their salary after the duty of their offices has ceased. A Judge when out of office is no more independent than any other citizen. Being firmly convinced that such not only will but ought to be the construction put upon the Constitution as it stands, it will be more acceptable to me, if the gentleman will consent to withdraw his amendment.

The very worthy and highly respectable gentleman from Richmond (Mr. Marshall,) lays much stress on the fact, that there has been but one decision by the Congress of the United States, giving an interpretation to the language of the Federal Constitution as to the tenure of the Judicial office. He says, there has been but a single decision; but the gentleman has not kept his eye on all the events connected with this subject. There have been many decisions: So many, that the point has always been considered by me as completely surrendered. Applications for compensation have, again and again, been made, and have been rejected over and over. Has not our whole Judiciary establishment been going on upon that avowed principle? and does it not exist on that foundation at the present moment? If not, on what principle does it rest? Upon none. There is no other principle. That is the law on which the entire system stands. I have no earthly doubt that such will be the decision. I think indeed it is highly probable, that the Judges would decide differently. But, thank God! the decision is left to the Legislature, and not to the influence of that *esprit du corps,* which is ever found to exist among persons holding the same employment, whether they be Judges or Councillors, Consuls or Kings. I wish that the sense of the Constitution may be decided on its own words, and on the existence of the effect of those words for thirty years. It will be settled, I doubt not, that according to the existing arrangement the Judges are independent; that this is the real definition of an independent Judiciary, and that its independence is as abundantly secured by this Constitution as it ever ought to be.

Mr. Marshall observed, that the present was not the first example which had occurred in the debates of this Convention, nor was it likely to be the last in the debates of this or of any other deliberative Assembly, where gentlemen held opinions directly opposite to each other, and yet each side thought their own so perfectly clear as not to admit the possibility of doubt. But declarations of such perfect confidence on the part of those who hold certain opinions, did by no means render it indispensable that others should subscribe to the same. The ultimate decision must rest, not on the confidence of conviction, but on the reason of the case. His whole wish was, that this question should go forth, uninfluenced by the opinion of any individual: let those, whose duty it was to settle the interpretation of the Constitution, decide on the Constitution itself. He did not say that he was perfectly clear what that decision would be, but he wished it to rest on the opinions held at the time by those who made it, and who were responsible for such opinions, and not by the views of particular individuals in this Convention. If any other clause was requisite, let it be added.

Whatever weight the decision of Congress in 1802 was entitled to have, let it have. But let not the sense of this instrument be judged of by the opinions of individuals in this body. He had already stated what were the views he had held in the Judiciary Committee, and the gentleman from Augusta, (Mr. Johnson,) had stated correctly what took place in the Select Committee: the two clauses adopted by the Convention were found to be in utter repugnance, and therefore the Committee had resolved to omit both, and report the article in the form which it now assumes.[5] The question now before the House had once been decided already, but he did not wish to prevent the decision of it now.[6]

Printed, *Richmond Enquirer,* 23 January 1830; *Proceedings and Debates of the Virginia State Convention, of 1829–30* (Richmond, 1830), 871–73.

1. In 1802 Congress repealed the Judiciary Act of 1801, which created a new circuit court system and a number of new judgeships filled by "midnight" appointments. A subsequent act restored the former circuit system, thereby abolishing the new judgeships. JM's views of the repeal as expressed in 1802 were recorded in a letter from Alexander Hamilton: "Upon the subject of the Judiciary I have had an opportunity of learning the opinions of the Chief Justice. He considers the late repealing Act as operative in depriving the Judges of all power derived under the Act repealed. The office still remains, which he holds to be a mere capacity, without a new appointment, to receive and exercise any new judicial powers which the Legislature may confer" (*U.S. Statutes at Large,* II, 132, 156; Alexander Hamilton to Charles C. Pinckney, 25 Apr. 1802, quoted in Warren, *Supreme Court,* I, 224–25 n.).

2. Art. III, sec. 1, of the U.S. Constitution vests judicial power "in one Supreme Court, and in such inferior Courts as the Congress may from time to time ordain and establish" and provides for tenure during good behavior for both Supreme Court and inferior court judges.

3. From this point, the text of the debate is taken from *Proceedings and Debates,* 872–73).

4. The amendment referred to by Giles was evidently that proposed by Benjamin W. S. Cabell, though according to the record of the debates Cabell did not introduce it until after Giles spoke. This amendment restored the clause agreed to by the convention but dropped by the select committee: "No modification or abolition of any court, shall be construed to deprive any Judge of his office; but such Judge shall perform any Judicial duties which the Legislature shall assign him; but if no Judicial duties are assigned him by the Legislature, he shall receive no salary in virtue of said office" (ibid., 875).

5. The brief report of Johnson's remarks omits mention of the select committee's proceedings. As JM noted, the committee concluded that the clause now being proposed to be reinstated was internally contradictory. No modification or abolition of a court was to deprive a judge of office, but at the same time the legislature could withhold a judge's salary by refusing to assign him any judicial duties.

6. Debate continued on Cabell's amendment. Scott proposed to amend it by striking out the clause beginning "but such Judge" and inserting "Unless such court be abolished by the concurrence of two-thirds of the General Assembly." JM queried Scott "whether his amendment would not produce an effect which he did not contemplate? A case might occur, where a majority of the Legislature desired to abolish a court, not out of any hostility to the Judge, but because they thought its abolition would promote the public good: the amendment would prevent such a measure, unless two-thirds of both Houses could be obtained in its favour." Cabell then withdrew his amendment, and Scott proposed the following article to be added to the constitution: "No law abolishing any court shall be construed to deprive a Judge thereof of his office, unless two-thirds of the members of each house present, concur in the passage thereof: But the Legislature may assign other duties to

the Judges of courts abolished by any law enacted by less than two-thirds of the members of each house present." The convention at length adopted this article by a vote of 53 to 42, JM voting with the majority (ibid., 873–80).

Remarks
U.S. Supreme Court
25 January 1830

The sentiments of respect and affection which the gentlemen of the Bar and the officers of the Court have expressed for the loss of our deceased brother are most grateful to me, and I can say with confidence, to all my brethren. No man knew his worth better or deplores his death more than myself; and this sentiment I am certain, is common to his former associates. I am very sure I may say for my brethren as well as for myself that the application is most gratifying to us all; and that in ordering the resolutions to be entered on the minutes of our proceedings, we indulge our own feelings not less than the feelings of those who make the application.[1]

Copy, U.S. Supreme Court Minutes, RG 267, DNA.

1. JM's remarks on the death of Bushrod Washington were given in response to a set of resolutions proposed by Daniel Webster and adopted at a meeting of the Supreme Court bar and officers of the court on 23 Jan. 1830. The remarks and resolutions were entered on the minutes as an "Order of Court" for 25 Jan. 1830.

To Richard Peters

My dear Sir   [Washington] Jany. 29th. 1830
    I thank you for the 4th. vol. of Washingtons circuit court reports.[1] I not only consider the numerous legal opinions contained in this volume as being of real value to every professional gentleman, but I estimate very highly, and am proud to possess the latest mental exertions of my departed friend. Once more I thank you for this mark of your polite attention and beg you to beleive that I am with great regard and respectful esteem, your obedt.

                                                        J MARSHALL

ALS, Charles R. Vaughan Papers, Codrington Library, All Souls College, Oxford, Eng. Addressed to Peters and endorsed by him.

1. *Reports of Cases Determined in the Circuit Court of the United States for the Third Circuit Comprising the Districts of Pennsylvania and New Jersey,* IV (Philadelphia, 1829). Peters published these reports from Bushrod Washington's manuscripts. The provenance indicates

that Peters gave this letter to Vaughan, the British minister, perhaps as a sample of the chief justice's autograph.

To Mary W. Marshall

My dearest Polly   Jany. 31st. 1830

Every thing goes on as usual. I take my walk in the morning, work hard all day, eat a hearty dinner, sleep sound at night and sometimes comb my head before I go to bed. While this operation is performing I always think with tenderness of my sweet barber in Richmond. It is the most delightful sentiment I have.

Edward I doubt not has informed of his fine large boy and that Rebecca is as well as could be expected.[1] He seems to be quite as proud as I was at the birth of our first born. Thus the world goes on.

I dined on tuesday with the President in a very large mixed company. I sat by Mrs. Donalson, the Presidents niece and found her a very agreeable and Lady like woman.[2] She is I beleive quite popular, but not so popular as Mrs. Madison was.

I saw Tom Francis about a week past but I am so occupied that I believe he thought I neglected him. I certainly saw very little of him. He has now gone to visit his brother.[3] Judges Johnson and McClain do not live with us, in consequence of which we cannot carry on our business as fast as usual. Judge Thompson is sick. The rest of us are very well.

I have [not] heard one word respecting you since I parted from you; but hope dear hope paints you to my imagination as in good health and happy.

I have I fear bad news from Potowmac. I wrote to my tenant Mr. Sprigg a letter which I hoped would produce my rent but his letter brought niether money nor promise. My other tenant, at Andersons bottom, seems to expect to bring me in debt.[4] One of my neighbours claims a valuable part of my land. Thus it fares with those who do not look after their own affairs. It is only from you my dearest Polly that I always find things better than I had expected.

Farewell my dearest. Your happiness is the constant prayer of your ever affectionate

J MARSHALL

ALS, McGregor Autograph Collection, ViU. Addressed to Mrs. Marshall in Richmond; postmarked Washington, 2 Feb.

1. John Marshall, the first child of Edward C. Marshall and Rebecca P. Marshall, was born on 17 Jan. 1830 (Paxton, *Marshall Family,* 215).

2. Emily Donelson (d. 1836), a niece of the late Rachel Donelson Jackson, was the wife of Andrew Jackson Donelson (1799–1871), then serving as the president's private secretary. She presided as hostess at the president's house.

3. "Tom Francis" was Thomas Francis Marshall (1801–64), JM's nephew and son of Louis Marshall. Having studied law in Kentucky and been admitted to the bar, he had recently attended the debates of the convention in Richmond, no doubt staying with his aunt and uncle. From there he had gone to Washington to observe the proceedings of Congress. Beginning in 1832, Marshall served several terms in the Kentucky legislature. He was elected to Congress in 1841 but was an unsuccessful candidate for reelection after serving a term. Thomas F. Marshall's brother was William Louis Marshall, then living in Baltimore (Paxton, *Marshall Family,* 166–67; W. L. Barre, ed., *Speeches and Writings of Hon. Thomas F. Marshall* [Cincinnati, 1858]).

4. No correspondence subsequent to JM's letter to Joseph Sprigg, 25 May 1829, has been found. Sprigg was JM's tenant at Swan Ponds in Hampshire County. The tenant at Andersons Bottom, JM's other Hampshire tract, may have been "Maj. [Thomas?] Collins," mentioned in JM to Sprigg, 25 May 1829.

To Thomas W. Griffith

Sir   Washington Feb. 7th. '30

I was greatly obliged by your observations on the practical operation of your government contained in your letter of the 4th. of Decr. last.[1] I read them with attention myself and communicated them to others.

We pursue a course respecting the appointment of Justices of the peace which differs from yours and I beleive from that of any other state in the union. The county courts nominate to the Governour fit persons to fill vacancies as they arise, and he commissions them. This mode of self perpetuation has been a good deal censured, but we think its practical operation better than any other mode which has been devised. The most respectable men of the several counties are generally in the commission. Our Justices receive no fees. They have no compensation except the sherivalty which they take in succession, each Justice holding the office for two successive years.

Our Executive consists of a Governor who is elected by the legislature for three years and is ineligible for three years afterwards, with a council consisting of three members whose advice he is not obliged to follow. His responsibility therefore is preserved. Our Judges and principal officers are elected by the legislature — our inferior appointments are made by the county courts.

We were a good deal divided on the question whether the Governor should be elected by the people or by the legislature. The latter mode at length prevailed. By electing him for three years and rendering him ineligible afterwards for three years, we suppose we have made him as independent as the nature of our institutions will permit. But in Virginia the powers of the Governor are less considerable than in other states; and his independence is of course of less consequence. But our constitution is published, and I presume you have seen it. It will be submitted to the people immediately, and the general opinion is, as far as I have heard, that it will be accepted. It is not precisely what any of us wished, but is better than we feared. With great respect I am Sir, Your Obedt.

J Marshall

ALS, MdHi. Addressed to Griffith in Baltimore; postmarked Washington, 8 Feb. Endorsed by Griffith, noting dates of 9 Feb. and 9 Sept. (presumably subsequent letters to JM). Also endorsed "No. 12." Another endorsement in different hand: "autogh of C. Justice Marshall / from B. Mayer [?]."

1. Letter not found. Thomas W. Griffith (1767–1838) of Baltimore was a chronicler of Maryland history. He wrote *Sketches of the Early History of Maryland* (Baltimore, 1821) and *Annals of Baltimore* (Baltimore, 1824).

To Alexander Scott

Sir   Washington Feb. 7th. 1830

I received yesterday your letter making enquiries respecting the military services of Capt. William Blackwell deceased.[1] He was in July 1776 appointed a Captain in a regiment composed partly of Marylanders and partly of Virginians which was I think to be commanded by Colo. McGaw or Colo. Rawlings. The Maryland part of it was captured in Fort Washington. The Virginia companies were not completed till about the close of the year 1776. In the beginning of 1777 they were attached to the 11th. Virginia Regiment then commanded by Colo. Daniel Morgan. I was well acquainted with Capt. William Blackwell and know that he served through the campaign of 1777. In the course of the year 1778 as well as I recollect the number of Virginia regiments was reduced by putting two together, and several officers became supernumerary, there being no troops for them to command. I do not know certainly whether Capt. Blackwell resigned or became a supernumerary officer, liable to be again called into service.[2] I do not recollect his resignation, and am confident that I did not see him afterwards in the army.

I have always understood that the muster rolls of the continental army were burnt when the war office was consumed in this city. The public papers in Virginia were destroyed by the British during the invasion by Arnold, but I do not suppose those papers contained any evidence of Capt. Blackwells service.

I do not beleive that any person now alive can say whether Capt. Blackwell resigned or became a supernumerary. Every officer from the county except myself, is, I beleive, dead. Capt. Philip Slaughter of Culpeper was an officer in the same Regiment and may possibly be able to give some information on the subject, tho' I do not think it probable. I do not recollect any other officer who was in the regiment that is now alive.[3] I am Sir very respectfully, Your Obedt

J Marshall

ALS, Bounty Warrants (file of William Blackwell), Vi. Addressed to Scott in Washington and endorsed by him. Also endorsed "No. 1."

1. Letter not found. Alexander Scott of Georgetown, D.C., was married to Elizabeth Blackwell, daughter of the late William Blackwell (Horace Edwin Hayden, *Virginia Genealogies* . . . [Wilkes Barre, Pa., 1891], 596.
2. Blackwell resigned his commission on 10 Jan. 1778 (*PJM*, I, 13 n. 3).
3. Scott on his wife's behalf eventually obtained a warrant for 4,000 acres of land issued by in the Virginia Executive Council Sept. 1831. In a letter to James Madison, Scott reported that the warrant was "on account of the military service of Mrs. Scott's father, as a captain in the war of the revolution, Chief Justice Marshall (of whose testimony I availed myself) being his first lieutenant" (Bounty Warrants [file of William Blackwell], Vi; Scott to Madison, 10 Nov. 1831, Madison Papers [DLC]; Hayden, *Virginia Genealogies,* 268).

Conversation with John Quincy Adams

[Washington, 11 February 1830]

In my walk this morning, I met Chief Justice Marshall near the head of the avenue, and he turned and walked down with me to its termination opposite the yard of the Treasury building. I asked him who, since the decease of the late Judge Washington, was the owner of President Washington's papers. He said he did not know but that they were now in the possession of Mr. Sparks who was to publish his Letters, and some of the Letters to him. I asked the judge if there ever had been an adjudication in England, of the *property* of Epistolary Correspondence. He knew of none. I mentioned the opinion or statement in a late number of the North American Review, that the property is in the writer of the Letter, to whom or to whose Representatives, it ought to be returned after the decease of the receiver.[1] He said he had formed no deliberate opinion upon the question, but that his first crude impression was that the property was in the receiver a property qualified by the confidence of the writer. I mentioned to him the extraordinary character of the recent publication of Mr. Jefferson's papers; which have given rise to a scene as extraordinary in the Senate of the United States. Jefferson makes a minute 13 February 1801. that Edward Livingston told him, Bayard had offered Sam. Smith the Office of Secretary of War, if he would vote for Burr, which W C Nicholas had confirmed. Mr. Jefferson's Executor now publishes this minute.[2] Hayne last week to gratify the malignity of his nature, reads from a volume of Jefferson's works, his tale of my having told him that certain federalists in New England during the War plotted a dismemberment of the Union during the late war.[3] No answer was made to this: But Clayton, a Senator from Delaware, read this minute about Bayard; and called upon Sam Smith and Edward Livingston to say whether it was true. Smith declared in the most explicit manner that neither Bayard nor any other man ever made any such proposal to him. Edward Livingston said he had tasked his memory to the utmost, and had been unable to recollect anything about it. Benton bristled up and blustered about attempts to impeach the veracity of Mr. Jefferson. Clayton answered that his object was not to impeach the veracity of Mr Jefferson, but to vindicate the character of Mr Bayard, and that he had attained his object. That Mr Benton had chosen to fall into a furious passion about it, which to him (Clayton) was a matter of great Indifference.[4] I said the most extraordinary part of this minute of Jefferson's was that it was the direct reverse of the real fact, as Bayard had told me what passed at that interview between him and Smith. The Judge said he had also told it to him. He added that he himself had been here, a witness of that scene altogether indifferent upon which of the two men the choice of the house would fall, and that by comparing what he then saw with what afterwards came to pass, there were certain conclusions which it was very difficult to resist—but he did not say what they were. I suppose he meant that Livingston, who was then making his own bargain for his vote, told Jefferson this tale of Bayard's offers to Smith, to make Jefferson out-bid Burr for Livingston's own vote. Livingston was accordingly appointed District Attorney at New York; and in due time went off with a hundred thousand dollars of the public money, to Louisiana; the judgment for which has never been paid till within the last six months.[5]

MS, Diary of John Quincy Adams, Adams Papers, MHi; printed, Charles Francis Adams, ed., *Memoirs of John Quincy Adams Comprising Portions of His Diary from 1795 to 1848*, VIII [Philadelphia, 1876], 187–88.

1. Adams referred to a review of James T. Austin, *The Life of Elbridge Gerry. With Contemporary Letters. To the Close of the American Revolution* (Boston, 1828), which appeared in the *North American Review*, XXVIII (1829), 37–57 (53–55 for the comments on ownership of private correspondence).

2. Thomas Jefferson Randolph, ed., *Memoir, Correspondence, and Miscellanies, from the Papers of Thomas Jefferson* (4 vols.; Charlottesville, Va., 1829). The incident involving Edward Livingston, James A. Bayard, and Samuel Smith—all then serving in Congress—was recorded in Jefferson's "Anas," a collection of memoranda and notes written at various times during his public career, under the date of 12 Feb. 1801. According to Jefferson, the offer to Smith was the secretaryship of the navy (ibid., IV, 515–16).

3. In his speech of 25 Jan. 1830, Hayne quoted from Jefferson's letters to William B. Giles, 25 and 26 Dec. 1825, recalling a conversation Jefferson had with Adams during the embargo crisis (*Register of Debates in Congress*, VI [Washington, 1830], 55; Randolph, ed., *Memoir, Correspondence, and Miscellanies, from the Papers of Thomas Jefferson*, IV, 419, 422).

4. On 28 Jan. 1830 Sen. John M. Clayton (1796–1856) rose to defend Bayard and was followed by remarks from Smith, Livingston, and Benton (*Register of Debates*, VI, 93–95). This incident became a cause célèbre, provoking publications by Bayard's sons in 1830 and again in 1855. See Dumas Malone, *Jefferson and His Time*, IV: *Jefferson the President, First Term, 1801–1805* (Boston, 1970), 487–93.

5. Adams alluded to an 1803 judgment against Livingston after a Treasury audit revealed a shortage in his accounts as U.S. Attorney for New York. According to his biographer, Livingston did not personally misuse public funds but was legally responsible for the actions of a defaulting clerk. Shortly after the judgment, Livingston moved to New Orleans (William B. Hatcher, *Edward Livingston: Jeffersonian Republican and Jacksonian Democrat* [University, La., 1940], 92–99).

To Mary W. Marshall

My dearest Polly   Washington Feb. 14th. 1830

I have nothing to tell you but the splendid dinner parties to which we are invited. On friday we dined with the Secretary of State who gave a dinner to a Young Lady from Charleston just married to a nephew of the President.[1] I sat between her and Mrs. Livingston of Louisiana, a very fine woman indeed with whom I was very much pleased.[2] The bride appeared to be quite happy and to be glad that she was married. We dined after six and sat at table till after eight. When we retired to the setting room three young Ladies who professed a great desire to be acquainted with the Judges were introduced to me, and you would have been quite surprized to see how gay sprightly and gallant the wine made me. Yesterday I dined with the British minister.[3] He always gives most excellent dinners & very superior wine, but we had no Ladies. It was some compensation for this deficiency that we sat down to table but an hour sooner than when we dined with the secretary of state. I hope very sincerely that we shall not be invited out again, as I greatly prefer remaining at home and attending to our business.

I find the influenza as prevalent here as it was in Richmond. Three of our Judges are laid up with it — not so as to prevent their going to court, but so as to prevent their going to dinner parties. Judge Duval is carried home by a relapse of his son.[4]

I had a letter two or three days past from James.[5] All well. Edward, he says, is the most delighted Father he ever saw. I suspect he saw one that was quite as much delighted when he looked in the glass.

I do not expect to hear from you till after the 22d. I shall be very impatient to know how you pass through the celebration of that day, and what news you collect at the farm.[6]

Farewell my dearest wife. Your happiness is the constant prayer of your ever affectionate

J MARSHALL

ALS, Marshall Papers, ViW. Addressed to Mrs. Marshall in Richmond; postmarked Washington, 15 Feb.

1. Secretary of State Van Buren's dinner was in honor of Frances Middleton Hayes, who had married Samuel Jackson Hayes in Nov. 1829 (*South Carolina Historical and Genealogical Magazine*, I [1900], 237).

2. Louise Davezac Livingston (1782–1860) was the second wife of Edward Livingston, then serving in the Senate. She was a widowed refugee from Santo Domingo when she married Livingston in 1805. During the Jackson administration she had a reputation as the most elegant and fashionable hostess of the day (Louise Livingston Hunt, *Memoir of Mrs. Edward Livingston* . . . [New York, 1886], 176; William B. Hatcher, *Edward Livingston: Jeffersonian Republican and Jacksonian Democrat* [Baton Rouge, La., 1940], 122–23, 298–99).

3. Charles R. Vaughan.

4. Edmund B. Duvall suffered from mental illness (*PJM*, X, 313 n. 2).

5. Letter not found.

6. Polly Marshall always departed Richmond for the Chickahominy farm when there were to be noisy celebrations such as Washington's birthday.

From Richard H. Henderson

This letter and Marshall's reply of 18 February 1830 were originally published in the *Genius of Liberty,* a Leesburg newspaper, on 6 March. Richard H. Henderson (1781–1841), a Leesburg resident, had represented Loudoun County in the recently adjourned state constitutional convention in Richmond. Henderson was prompted to write by a piece that appeared in the *Washingtonian,* another Leesburg newspaper. Henderson introduced his correspondence with Marshall with his own letter to the editor of the *Genius of Liberty,* dated 4 March, followed by the passage from the *Washingtonian.* This passage, headed "*An important divulgement,*" reported that Charles F. Mercer in conversation with several "respectable gentlemen" stated "that Chief Justice Marshall had expressed his surprize to him at the course pursued in Convention by those members who had deserted their constituents; that if, (said Mr. Marshall,) they had held out, been firm, they would have got what they contended for, pure white basis in the House of Delegates; that some of the eastern members, after an effectual struggle, had determined to yield." The passage went on to "assure the public" that the reported conversation "comes from undoubted sources" (*Richmond Enquirer,* 16 Mar. 1830, reprinting article from Leesburg *Genius of Liberty,* 6 Mar. 1830; Robert P. Sutton, *Revolution to Secession: Constitution Making in the Old Dominion* [Charlottesville, Va., 1989, 201).

DEAR SIR: LEESBURG, 15 h Feb., 1830.

I am extremely sorry to disturb you, at your period of life, and in the midst of your important duties, with a matter that concerns me personally; nor would I, by any consideration, be tempted to intrude on you, were it not that the weight of your name is brought to bear upon me, and my friend, Mr. Cooke, in discussions consequent upon the proceedings of the late convention.[1]

Enclosed I trouble you with a paragraph, cut out of a newspaper published here, in which Mr. Cooke and myself, without being named, (but every one knows we are the persons alluded to,) are represented as *deserting our constituents,* in sustaining the scheme of representation embraced in the new constitution; and, in which you are stated to have expressed your surprize at our recreancy, to Col. Mercer, and to have declared to him, that, had we been *firm,* the eastern members had determined to yield. I do not believe that Colonel Mercer, long the intimate friend of Mr. Cooke and myself, has so far wronged us as to have held the language ascribed to him; and I have written to him a friendly letter, calling on him to correct this error, and have apprized him of my intention to write to you.

That Col. M. has misapprehended you, as to your own ulterior views, I know, because you twice or three times told me so, and expressed your surprize at his perseverance. That you never said of me, or Mr. Cooke, what is imputed to you, I know full well, because it is wholly inconsistent with your character; and because you told me explicitly, that, in your individual judgment, the plan Mr. Cooke and myself preferred, was better for the west than the white basis for the lower house and federal numbers for the Senate.

May I so far trespass on you as to ask you to do me the favour to say—

1st. Whether you ever did, directly or indirectly, said that Mr. Cooke and myself deserted the interests of our constituents, to any body? Or whether you thought so, or think so now?

2ndly. Whether you ever declared to Col. Mercer, that, if we had not pursued the course we did, you, or other gentlemen, had determined to yield?

3dly. Whether you did not repeatedly tell me that in *your own judgment,* the plan Mr. Cooke and my self sustained was the better of the two for the western interest, or the interest we represented?

It is with unfeigned repugnance and distress, I assure you, sir, that I approach you in this way; especially under the precise circumstances and relations of the subject; but that candour and politeness which have ever characterized you, will, I am persuaded, impel you to accord me the answer which I seek. I am, sir, with great esteem and respect, your ob't serv't,

RICH'D. H. HENDERSON.

Printed, *Richmond Enquirer,* 16 March 1830.

1. John Rogers Cooke (1788–1854), father of novelist John Esten Cooke, was a prominent Winchester lawyer. Representing Frederick County, he was a leader of the reform party at the convention. He served with JM on the select committee that drafted the final compromise constitution and was the only western delegate to vote for it (F. Vernon Aler, *Aler's History of Martinsburg and Berkeley County, West Virginia* [Hagerstown, Md., 1888], 101–4).

To Richard H. Henderson

MY DEAR SIR: Washington, Feb. 18th, 1830.

I was a good deal surprized and pained at your letter of the 15th, enclosing a paragraph affecting myself, as well as you, which was cut out of a paper published in Leesburg. Having never heard Mr. Mercer speak either of you or Mr. Cooke, but in terms of esteem and friendship, I thought it impossible that he could have applied to either of you, the language used in the paper from which the paragraph was taken, and I was very sure he never would have ascribed that language to me. I determined to call on him before I answered your letter, and did so this morning, on my way to court. He was on an excursion to the canal, so that I did not see him. I called on him this afternoon again, and found him engaged in writing a letter to the editor, for the purpose of contradicting the publication. He assured me, as I had at first supposed, that it was totally without foundation; and spoke both of you and Mr. Cooke, in terms of real affection and esteem. I am entirely confident that he has been misrepresented, and probably misunderstood.

For myself, I shall say, that it is not, and never has been, my practice to speak harshly of any gentleman; and I certainly have not begun, and shall not begin, a total change of conduct with you and Mr. Cooke. I have never directly, nor indirectly, said, or insinuated, or thought, that you or Mr. Cooke deserted the interests of your constituents. On the contrary, I have always thought, and do still think, that you served them faithfully.

I never did declare to any person, that if you and Mr. Cooke had not pursued the course you did, I had determined, with others, to yield. What I said on this subject was said openly, not confidentially. I was certainly desirous of framing a constitution, and would have given up my own judgment and opinion, to a considerable extent rather than disperse without accomplishing any thing. I have given them up to a considerable extent.

I have told you, and I have thought, that, in my individual judgment, the white basis in the house of delegates, with the federal basis in the senate, though not approved by me, was more desirable for the east than the plan actually adopted.

This however, is passed. The constitution is recommended by the convention. I have voted for it, and sincerely wish its adoption. My objections, whatever they were, are silenced forever, and I am not willing to bring them forward again.

I am very sorry that my name should be introduced in a public paper for any purpose whatever, more especially for the purpose of calumniating gentlemen of whom I have reason to think, and of whom I do think, most favourably. It gives me great pleasure to believe, confidently, that Mr. Mercer is as innocent as myself. With great respect and esteem, I am, dear sir, your obedient,

J. MARSHALL

Printed, *Richmond Enquirer,* 16 March 1830.

To Alexander Scott

Dear Sir   Washington Feb. 18th. 1830

Your letter of the 15th. is just received.[1] I was first Lieutenant in Capt. William Blackwells company. No person I believe ever doubted his courage. He conducted himself as other officers without attracting any particular notice. I am very respectfully, Your Obedt

J MARSHALL

ALS, Bounty Warrants (file of William Blackwell), Vi. Addressed to Scott in Washington and endorsed by him. Also endorsed "No 2."

1. Letter not found.

To Mary W. Marshall

My dearest Polly   Washington Feb. 28th. 1830

I was very much relieved Yesterday at receiving a letter from our Grand daughter.[1] Though she said you were indisposed, she mentioned it in such a manner as to convince me that the indisposition was slight and would yield to the sun shine we have had since. I had been a good deal alarmed at not receiving the letter a day sooner. I have been accustomed to hear from you so regularly on your return from Chiccahominy that my fears got the better of me and I became extremely uneasy. Our Grand daughters letter removed those fears. Tell her I am much obliged by it, and am much pleased also with the letter and at the neat ladylike hand in which it is written. I am only sorry for one piece of intelligence she gives me — it is that her cousin John has had a relapse.

I have just received a letter from James — All well in Fauquier. He has sold his horse for $1100 — a sum of money which will be quite convenient to him.[2]

I have looked with the more pleasure at the bright sun we have been favored with for a few days past because I have beleived that it would tempt you to take those rides which are necessary for your health.

Mr. Story has been laid up for a week under the hands of the Doctor; but is now up again and attending court.

Farewell my dearest Polly. I am your ever affectionate

J MARSHALL

ALS, Marshall Papers, ViW. Addressed to Mrs. Marshall in Richmond; postmarked Washington, 2 Mar.

1. Letter not found. The granddaughter was probably Mary Marshall Harvie.
2. Letter not found. JM provided a certificate of the horse's pedigree, presumably at James's request (Certificate of Pedigree, 1 Mar. 1830 [App. II, Cal.]).

To Mary W. Marshall

My dearest Polly   Washington March 7th. [1830]

I am just returned from my mornings walk of three miles and all my brethren are fast locked in sleep in their rooms. I steal a few minutes from my business which I devote to you. While thus employed, my imagination transports me to Richmond and I participate in all your little solicitudes. I picture to myself every thing which passes between the time of your coming down stairs and breakfast, and wish I could breakfast with you. I was about to say that I feared the morning was too unpromising to admit of your riding out, but I recollect that you do not ride on sunday. We have had so much bad weather that I am apprehensive you have not taken as much exercise as is necessary for health. I must exhort you a little on this subject.

I dined yesterday with my old friend Mr Swan, and except that the dinner was not on the table till six every thing was delightful. Mr. Story remained at home. He thinks he is not well enough to dine out. I had some conversation with Mr. Mercer about our Nephew William. You know he is engaged in Miss Mercers school. He has I am told given over preaching. I fancy he did not succeed well in the pulpit.[1]

Tom Francis[2] took his seat in the stage but a few days past for Kentucky. I thought he would have preferred staying in this country, and was a little apprehensive at one time that he intended to do so. I fear he has found more of pain than pleasure in his visit. Mr. Coleman who married our niece Lucy has been to see me. He is in Congress and is a strong Jackson Man. Our Nephew Tom son of Humphry, is an equally strong Clayite and is I am told to be brought forward in opposition to Mr. Coleman at the next election.[3] The Kentucky part of our family is I find a good deal divided in party politics and of course not very harmonious. I am sorry for it. Party success is but a poor compensation for family feuds. Farewell my dearest. I am, Your every affectionate

J Marshall

ALS (owned by Mrs. Robert L. Satterwhite, Hopkinsville, Ky., 1997). Addressed to Mrs. Marshall in Richmond; postmarked Washington, 8 Mar.

1. William Louis Marshall of Baltimore was apparently employed in a school run by Margaret Mercer (1791–1846), daughter of John Francis Mercer and cousin of Charles F. Mercer. Her school, the Cedar Park Institute, was located near Baltimore. She later moved the school to Belmont, near Leesburg, Va.

2. Thomas Francis Marshall.

3. Nicholas D. Coleman (1800–74) was a Representative from Kentucky during the Twenty-first Congress (1829–31). He married Lucy Ambler Marshall (1802–1858), daughter of JM's brother Thomas Marshall. Coleman lost his seat in the next election to Thomas A. Marshall. He later moved to Vicksburg, Miss., where he practiced law and served as postmaster (Paxton, *Marshall Family*, 130).

Craig v. Missouri
Opinion
U.S. Supreme Court, 12 March 1830

Craig v. *Missouri* was one of several cases with virtually identical facts that were decided at the 1830 term of the Supreme Court. *Craig*, along with *Davis* v. *Missouri* and *Watson* v. *Missouri*, had originated in the state circuit court for Chariton County. The principal case began in 1823 as an action brought by the state against Hiram Craig, John Moore, and Ephraim Moore on a promissory note for payment of the amount and accrued interest on loan office certificates lent by the state to the defendants. The loan office certificates were issued under authority of a Missouri law enacted in June 1821. The parties submitted the case to the court without a jury, and judgment was given for the state in November 1824. The state supreme court subsequently confirmed this judgment in April 1825. The case presented two questions: (1) Were the certificates "bills of credit" within the meaning of Article I, section 10 of the Constitution, which prohibited the states from emitting such bills? (2) If the certificates were deemed to be bills of credit, could the court nevertheless enforce a contract in which the certificates formed the consideration? In confirming the judgment of the state circuit court, the Missouri Supreme Court conformed to a decision it had rendered in May 1824 in a similar case. In that case all three judges agreed that the loan office certificates were bills of credit, but two of them also held that the state could recover under the contract. The state court reaffirmed this decision in May 1826. The cases of Craig, Davis, and Watson came to the Supreme Court by writ of error under section 25 of the Judiciary Act in March 1826. At that time the Court rejected a motion to dismiss the cases, "being of opinion that they were regularly before the Court, and that the objections urged on the ground of want of jurisdiction, were such as must be taken on the argument, and not on motion to dismiss." The Court heard arguments in March 1828 and held the cases under advisement. The cases were reargued on 2 and 3 March 1830, with Daniel Sheffey (1770–1830), a former Federalist member of Congress from Virginia, representing the plaintiffs. Sen. Thomas H. Benton on behalf of the state objected to the jurisdiction, complaining that the language of the writ of error did "not seem proper, when addressed to a sovereign state." Chief Justice Marshall spoke for a majority of four to three in reversing the state court's judgment on 12 March (Craig v. Missouri, App. Cas. No. 1408; Davis v. Missouri, App. Cas. No. 1409; Watson v. Missouri, App. Cas. No. 1410; State v. Craig; State v. Watson; State v. Davis, 1 Mo. 502 [Mo. Sup. Ct., 1825]; Mansker v. State, 1 Mo. 452 [Mo. Sup. Ct., 1824]; Loper v. State, 1 Mo. 632 [Mo. Sup. Ct., 1826]; Washington *Daily National Intelligencer*, 9 Mar. 1826; U.S. Sup. Ct. Minutes, 8 Mar. 1826; 13, 17 Mar. 1828; 15 Jan. 1830; 2, 3, 12 Mar. 1830; 4 Pet. 419).

OPINION

This is a writ of error to a judgment rendered in the court of last resort, in the state of Missouri; affirming a judgment obtained by the state in one of its inferior courts against Hiram Craig and others, on a promissory note.

The judgment is in these words: "and afterwards at a court," &c. "the parties came into court by their attorneys, and, neither party desiring a jury, the cause is submitted to the court; therefore, all and singular the matters and things being seen and heard by the court, it is found by them, that the said defendants did assume upon themselves, in manner and form, as the plaintiff by her counsel alleged. And the court also find, that the consideration for which the writing declared upon and the assumpsit was made, was for the loan of loan office certificates, loaned by the state at her loan office at Chariton; which certificates were issued, and the loan made in the manner pointed out by an act of the legislature of the said state of Missouri, approved the 27th day of June 1821, entitled an act for the establishment of loan offices, and the acts amendatory and supplementary thereto: and the court do further find, that the plaintiff has sustained damages by reason of the non-performance of the assumptions and undertakings of them, the said defendants, to the sum of two hundred and thirty-seven dollars and seventy-nine cents, and do assess her damages to that sum. Therefore it is considered," &c.

The first inquiry is into the jurisdiction of the court.

The twenty-fifth section of the judicial act declares, "that a final judgment or decree in any suit in the highest court of law or equity of a state, in which a decision in the suit could be had, where is drawn in question" "the validity of a statute of, or an authority exercised under any state, on the ground of their being repugnant to the constitution, treaties or laws of the United States, and the decision is in favour of such their validity," "may be re-examined, and reversed or affirmed in the supreme court of the United States."

To give jurisdiction to this court, it must appear in the record,

1. That the validity of a statute of the state of Missouri was drawn in question; on the ground of its being repugnant to the constitution of the United States. 2. That the decision was in favour of its validity.

1. To determine whether the validity of a statute of the state was drawn in question, it will be proper to inspect the pleadings in the cause, as well as the judgment of the court.

The declaration is on a promissory note, dated on the 1st day of August 1822, promising to pay to the state of Missouri, on the 1st day of November 1822, at the loan office in Chariton, the sum of one hundred and ninety-nine dollars ninety-nine cents, and the two per cent. per annum, the interest accruing on the certificates borrowed from the 1st of October 1821. This note is obviously given for certificates loaned under the act, "for the establishment of loan offices." That act directs that loans on personal securities shall be made of sums less than two hundred dollars. This note is for one hundred and ninety-nine dollars ninety-nine cents.

The act directs that the certificates issued by the state shall carry two per cent interest from the date, which interest shall be calculated in the amount of the loan. The note promises to repay the sum, with the two per cent interest accruing on the certificates borrowed, from the 1st day of October 1821. It cannot be doubted that the declaration is on a note given in pursuance of the act which has been mentioned.

Neither can it be doubted that the plea of non assumpsit allowed the defendants to draw into question at the trial the validity of the consideration on which the note was given. Every thing which disaffirms the contract, every thing which shows it to be void, may be given in evidence on the general issue in an action of assumpsit. The defendants, therefore, were at liberty to question the validity of the consideration which was the foundation of the contract, and the constitutionality of the law in which it originated.

Have they done so?

Had the cause been tried before a jury, the regular course would have been to move the court to instruct the jury that the act of assembly, in pursuance of which the note was given, was repugnant to the constitution of the United States; and to except to the charge of the judges, if in favour of its validity: or a special verdict might have been found by the jury, stating the act of assembly, the execution of the note in payment of certificates loaned in pursuance of that act; and referring its validity to the court. The one course or the other would have shown that the validity of the act of assembly was drawn into question, on the ground of its repugnancy to the constitution; and that the decision of the court was in favour of its validity. But the one course or the other, would have required both a court and jury. Neither could be pursued where the office of the jury was performed by the court. In such a case, the obvious substitute for an instruction to the jury, or a special verdict, is a statement by the court of the points in controversy, on which its judgment is founded. This may not be the usual mode of proceeding, but it is an obvious mode; and if the court of the state has adopted it, this court cannot give up substance for form.

The arguments of counsel cannot be spread on the record. The points urged in argument cannot appear. But the motives stated by the court on the record for its judgment, and which form a part of the judgment itself, must be considered as exhibiting the points to which those arguments were directed, and the judgment as showing the decision of the court upon those points. There was no jury to find the facts and refer the law to the court; but if the court, which was substituted for the jury, has found the facts on which its judgment was rendered; its finding must be equivalent to the finding of a jury. Has the court, then, substituting itself for a jury, placed facts upon the record, which, connected with the pleadings, show that the act in pursuance of which this note was executed was drawn into question, on the ground of its repugnancy to the constitution?

After finding that the defendants did assume upon themselves, &c. the court proceeds to find "that the consideration for which the writing declared upon and the assumpsit was made, was the loan of loan office certificates loaned by the state at her loan office at Chariton; which certificates were issued and the loan made, in the manner pointed out by an act of the legislature of the said state of Missouri, approved the 27th of June 1821, entitled," &c.

Why did not the court stop immediately after the usual finding that the defendants assumed upon themselves? Why proceed to find that the note was given for loan office certificates issued under the act contended to be unconstitutional, and loaned in pursuance of that act; if the matter thus found was irrelevant to the question they were to decide?

Suppose the statement made by the court to be contained in the verdict of a jury which concludes with referring to the court the validity of the note thus taken in pursuance of the act; would not such a verdict bring the constitutionality of the act, as well as its construction, directly before the court? We think it would: such a verdict would find that the consideration of the note was loan office certificates, issued and loaned in the manner prescribed by the act. What could be referred to the court by such a verdict, but the obligation of the law? It finds that the certificates for which the note was given, were issued in pursuance of the act, and that the contract was made in conformity with it. Admit the obligation of the act, and the verdict is for the plaintiff; deny its obligation, and the verdict is for the defendant. On what ground can its obligation be contested, but its repugnancy to the constitution of the United States? No other is suggested. At any rate, it is open to that objection. If it be in truth repugnant to the constitution of the United States, that repugnancy might have been urged in the state, and may consequently be urged in this court; since it is presented by the facts in the record, which were found by the court that tried the cause.

It is impossible to doubt that, in point of fact, the constitutionality of the act, under which the certificates were issued that formed the consideration of this note, constituted the only real question made by the parties, and the only real question decided by the court. But the record is to be inspected with judicial eyes; and, as it does not state in express terms that this point was made, it has been contended that this court cannot assume the fact that it was made or determined in the tribunal of the state.

The record shows distinctly that this point existed, and that no other did exist; the special statement of facts made by the court as exhibiting the foundation of its judgment contains this point and no other. The record shows clearly that the cause did depend, and must depend, on this point alone. If in such a case, the mere omission of the court of Missouri, to say, in terms, that the act of the legislature was constitutional, withdraws that point from the cause, or must close the judicial eyes of the appellate tribunal upon it; nothing can be more obvious, than that the provisions of the constitution, and of an act of congress, may be always evaded; and may be often, as we think they would be in this case, unintentionally defeated.

But this question has frequently occurred; and has, we think, been frequently decided in this court. Smith *vs.* The State of Maryland, 6 Cranch, 286. Martin *vs.* Hunter's Lessee, 1 Wheat. 355. Miller *vs.* Nicholls, 4 Wheat. 311. Williams *vs.* Norris, 12 Wheat. 117. Wilson and others *vs.* The Black Bird Creek Marsh Company, 2 Peters, 245, and Harris *vs.* Dennie in this term; are all, we think, expressly in point.[1] There has been perfect uniformity in the construction given by this court to the twenty-fifth section of the judicial act. That construction is, that it is not necessary to state, in terms, on the record, that the constitution, or a treaty or law of the United States has been drawn in question, or the validity of a state law, on the ground of its repugnancy to the constitution. It is sufficient if the record shows that the constitution, or a treaty or law of the United States must have been construed, or that the constitutionality of a state law must have been questioned; and the decision has been in favour of the party claiming under such law.

We think, then, that the facts stated on the record presented the question of repugnancy between the constitution of the United States and the act of Missouri to the court for its decision. If it was presented, we are to inquire,

2. Was the decision of the court in favour of its validity?

The judgment in favour of the plaintiff is a decision in favour of the validity of the contract, and consequently of the validity of the law by the authority of which the contract was made.

The case is, we think, within the twenty-fifth section of the judicial act, and consequently within the jurisdiction of this court.

This brings us to the great question in the cause: Is the act of the legislature of Missouri repugnant to the constitution of the United States?

The counsel for the plaintiffs in error maintain, that it is repugnant to the constitution, because its object is the emission of bills of credit contrary to the express prohibition contained in the tenth section of the first article.

The act under the authority of which the certificates loaned to the plaintiffs in error were issued, was passed on the 26th[2] of June 1821, and is entitled "an act for the establishment of loan offices." The provisions that are material to the present inquiry, are comprehended in the third, thirteenth, fifteenth, sixteenth, twenty-third and twenty-fourth sections of the act, which are in these words:[3]

Section the third enacts: "that the auditor of public accounts and treasurer, under the direction of the governor, shall, and they are hereby required to issue certificates, signed by the said auditor and treasurer, to the amount of two hundred thousand dollars, of denominations not exceeding ten dollars, nor less than fifty cents (to bear such devices as they may deem the most safe), in the following form, to wit: "This certificate shall be receivable at the treasury, or any of the loan offices of the state of Missouri, in the discharge of taxes or debts due to the state, for the sum of $, with interest for the same, at the rate of two per centum per annum from this date, the   day of   182 ."

The thirteenth section declares: "that the certificates of the said loan office shall be receivable at the treasury of the state, and by all tax gatherers and other public officers, in payment of taxes or other moneys now due to the state or to any county or town therein, and the said certificates shall also be received by all officers civil and military in the state, in the discharge of salaries and fees of office."

The fifteenth section provides: "that the commissioners of the said loan offices shall have power to make loans of the said certificates, to citizens of this state, residing within their respective districts only, and in each district a proportion shall be loaned to the citizens of each county therein, according to the number thereof," &c.

Section sixteenth. "That the said commissioners of each of the said offices are further authorised to make loans on personal securities by them deemed good and sufficient, for sums less than two hundred dollars; which securities shall be jointly and severally bound for the payment of the amount so loaned, with interest thereon," &c.

Section twenty-third. "That the general assembly shall, as soon as may be, cause the salt springs and lands attached thereto, given by congress to this state, to be leased out, and it shall always be the fundamental condition in such leases, that the lessee or lessees shall receive the certificates hereby required to be issued, in payment for salt, at a price not exceeding that which may be prescribed by law: and all the proceeds of the said salt springs, the interest accruing to the state, and all estates purchased by officers of the said several offices under the provisions of this act, and all the debts now due or hereafter to be due to this state; are hereby pledged and constituted a fund for the redemption of the certificates hereby required to be issued, and the faith of the state is hereby also pledged for the same purpose."

Section twenty-fourth. "That it shall be the duty of the said auditor and treasurer to withdraw annually from circulation, one-tenth part of the certificates which are hereby required to be issued," &c.

The clause in the constitution which this act is supposed to violate is in these words: "No state shall" "emit bills of credit."

What is a bill of credit? What did the constitution mean to forbid?

In its enlarged, and perhaps its literal sense, the term "bill of credit" may comprehend any instrument by which a state engages to pay money at a future day; thus including a certificate given for money borrowed. But the language of the constitution itself, and the mischief to be prevented, which we know from the history of our country, equally limit the interpretation of the terms. The word "emit," is never employed in describing those contracts by which a state binds itself to pay money at a future day for services actually received, or for money borrowed for present use; nor are instruments executed for such purposes, in common language, denominated "bills of credit." To "emit bills of credit," conveys to the mind the idea of issuing paper intended to circulate through the community for its ordinary purposes, as money, which paper is redeemable at a future day. This is the sense in which the terms have been always understood.

At a very early period of our colonial history, the attempt to supply the want of the precious metals by a paper medium was made to a considerable extent; and the bills emitted for this purpose have been frequently denominated bills of credit. During the war of our revolution, we were driven to this expedient; and necessity compelled us to use it to a most fearful extent. The term has acquired an appropriate meaning; and "bills of credit" signify a paper medium, intended to circulate between individuals, and between government and individuals, for the ordinary purposes of society. Such a medium has been always liable to considerable fluctuation. Its value is continually changing; and these changes, often great and sudden, expose individuals to immense loss, are the sources of ruinous speculations, and destroy all confidence between man and man. To cut up this mischief by the roots, a mischief which was felt through the United States, and which deeply affected the interest and prosperity of all; the people declared in their constitution, that no state should emit bills of credit. If the prohibition means any thing, if the words are not empty sounds, it must comprehend the emission of any paper medium, by a state government, for the purpose of common circulation.

What is the character of the certificates issued by authority of the act under consideration? What office are they to perform? Certificates signed by the auditor and treasurer of the state, are to be issued by those officers to the amount of two hundred thousand dollars, of denominations not exceeding ten dollars, nor less than fifty cents. The paper purports on its face to be receivable at the treasury, or at any loan office of the state of Missouri, in discharge of taxes or debts due to the state.

The law makes them receivable in discharge of all taxes, or debts due to the state, or any county or town therein; and of all salaries and fees of office, to all officers civil and military within the state; and for salt sold by the lessees of the public salt works. It also pledges the faith and funds of the state for their redemption.

It seems impossible to doubt the intention of the legislature in passing this act, or to mistake the character of these certificates, or the office they were to perform. The denominations of the bills, from ten dollars to fifty cents, fitted them for the purpose of ordinary circulation; and their reception in payment of taxes, and debts to the government and to corporations, and of salaries and fees, would give them currency. They were to be put into circulation; that is, emitted, by the government. In addition to all these evidences of an intention to make these certificates the ordinary circulating medium of the country, the law speaks of them in this character; and directs the auditor and treasurer to withdraw annually one-tenth of them from circulation. Had they been termed "bills of credit," instead of "certificates," nothing would have been wanting to bring them within the prohibitory words of the constitution.

And can this make any real difference? Is the proposition to be maintained, that the constitution meant to prohibit names and not things? That a very important act big with great and ruinous mischief, which is expressly forbidden by words most appropriate for its description; may be performed by the substitution of a name? That the constitution, in one of its most important provisions, may be openly evaded by giving a new name to an old thing? We cannot think so. We think the certificates emitted under the authority of this act, are as entirely bills of credit, as if they had been so denominated in the act itself.

But it is contended, that though these certificates should be deemed bills of credit, according to the common acceptation of the term, they are not so in the sense of the constitution; because they are not made a legal tender.

The constitution itself furnishes no countenance to this distinction. The prohibition is general. It extends to all bills of credit, not to bills of a particular description. That tribunal must be bold indeed, which, without the aid of other explanatory words, could venture on this construction. It is the less admissible in this case, because the same clause of the constitution contains a substantive prohibition to the enactment of tender laws. The constitution, therefore, considers the emission of bills of credit, and the enactment of tender laws, as distinct operations, independent of each other, which may be separately performed. Both are forbidden. To sustain the one, because it is not also the other; to say that bills of credit may be emitted, if they be not made a tender in payment of debts; is, in effect, to expunge that distinct independent prohibition, and to read the clause as if it had been entirely omitted. We are not at liberty to do this.

The history of paper money has been referred to, for the purpose of showing that its great mischief consists in being made a tender; and that therefore the general words of the constitution may be restrained to a particular intent.

Was it even true, that the evils of paper money resulted solely from the quality of its being made a tender, this court would not feel itself authorised to disregard the plain meaning of words, in search of a conjectural intent to which we are not conducted by the language of any part of the instrument. But we do not think that the history of our country proves either, that being made a tender in payment of debts, is an essential quality of bills of credit, or the only mischief resulting from them. It may, indeed, be the most pernicious; but that will not authorise a court to convert a general into a particular prohibition.

We learn from Hutchinson's History of Massachusetts, vol. 1, p. 402, that bills of credit were emitted for the first time in that colony in 1690.[4] An army returning unexpectedly from an expedition against Canada, which had proved as disastrous as the plan was magnificent, found the government totally unprepared to meet their claims. Bills of credit were resorted to, for relief from this embarrassment. They do not appear to have been made a tender; but they were not on that account the less bills of credit, nor were they absolutely harmless. The emission, however, not being considerable, and the bills being soon redeemed, the experiment would have been productive of not much mischief, had it not been followed by repeated emissions to a much larger amount. The subsequent history of Massachusetts abounds with proofs of the evils with which paper money is fraught, whether it be or be not a legal tender.

Paper money was also issued in other colonies, both in the north and south; and whether made a tender or not, was productive of evils in proportion to the quantity emitted. In the war which commenced in America in 1755, Virginia issued paper money at several successive sessions, under the appellation of treasury notes. This was made a tender. Emissions were afterwards made in 1769, in 1771, and in 1773.[5] These were not made a tender; but they circulated together; were equally bills of credit; and were productive of the same effects. In 1775 a considerable emission was made for the purposes of the war. The bills were declared to be current, but were not made a tender.[6] In 1776, an additional emission was made, and the bills were declared to be a tender. The bills of 1775 and 1776 circulated together; were equally bills of credit; and were productive of the same consequences.

Congress emitted bills of credit to a large amount; and did not, perhaps could not, make them a legal tender. This power resided in the states. In May 1777, the legislature of Virginia passed an act for the first time making the bills of credit issued under the authority of congress a tender so far as to extinguish interest. It was not until March 1781 that Virginia passed an act making all the bills of credit which had been emitted by congress, and all which had been emitted by the state, a legal tender in payment of debts.[7] Yet they were in every sense of the word bills of credit, previous to that time; and were productive of all the consequences of paper money. We cannot then assent to the proposition, that the history of our country furnishes any just argument in favour of that restricted construction of the constitution, for which the counsel for the defendant in error contends.

The certificates for which this note was given, being in truth "bills of credit" in the sense of the constitution, we are brought to the inquiry:

Is the note valid of which they form the consideration?

It has been long settled, that a promise made in consideration of an act which is forbidden by law is void. It will not be questioned, that an act forbidden by the constitution of the United States, which is the supreme law, is against law. Now the constitution forbids a state to "emit bills of credit." The loan of these certificates is the very act which is forbidden. It is not the making of them while they lie in the loan offices; but the issuing of them, the putting them into circulation, which is the act of emission; the act that is forbidden by the constitution. The consideration of this note is the emission of bills of credit by the state. The very act which constitutes the consideration, is the act of emitting bills of credit, in the mode prescribed by the law of Missouri; which act is prohibited by the constitution of the United States.

Cases which we cannot distinguish from this in principle, have been decided in state courts of great respectability; and in this court. In the case of the Springfield Bank *vs.* Merrick et al. 14 Mass. Rep. 322, a note was made payable in certain bills, the loaning or negotiating of which was prohibited by statute, inflicting a penalty for its violation. The note was held to be void. Had this note been made in consideration of these bills, instead of being made payable in them, it would not have been less repugnant to the statute; and would consequently have been equally void.[8]

In Hunt *vs.* Knickerbocker, 5 Johns. Rep. 327, it was decided that an agreement for the sale of tickets in a lottery, not authorised by the legislature of the state, although instituted under the authority of the government of another state, is contrary to the spirit and policy of the law, and void.[9] The consideration on which the agreement was founded being illegal, the agreement was void. The books, both of Massachusetts and New York, abound with cases to the same effect. They turn upon the question whether the particular case is within the principle, not on the principle itself. It has never been doubted, that a note given on a consideration which is prohibited by law, is void. Had the issuing or circulation of certificates of this or of any other description been prohibited by a statute of Missouri, could a suit have been sustained in the courts of that state, on a note given in consideration of the prohibited certificates? If it could not, are the prohibitions of the constitution to be held less sacred than those of a state law?

It had been determined, independently of the acts of congress on that subject, that sailing under the license of an enemy is illegal. Patton vs. Nicholson, 3 Wheat. 204, was a suit brought in one of the courts of this district on a note given by Nicholson to Patton, both citizens of the United States, for a British license. The United States were then at war with Great Britain; but the license was procured without any intercourse with the enemy. The judgment of the circuit court was in favour of the defendant; and the plaintiff sued out a writ of error. The counsel for the defendant in error was stopped, the court declaring that the use of a license from the enemy being unlawful, one citizen had no right to purchase from or sell to another such a license, to be used on board an American vessel. The consideration for which the note was given being unlawful, it followed of course that the note was void.[10]

A majority of the court feels constrained to say that the consideration on which the note in this case was given, is against the highest law of the land, and that the note itself is utterly void. In rendering judgment for the plaintiff, the court for the state of Missouri decided in favour of the validity of a law which is repugnant to the constitution of the United States.

In the argument, we have been reminded by one side of the dignity of a sovereign state; of the humiliation of her submitting herself to this tribunal; of the dangers which may result from inflicting a wound on that dignity: by the other, of the still superior dignity of the people of the United States; who have spoken their will, in terms which we cannot misunderstand.

To these admonitions, we can only answer: that if the exercise of that jurisdiction which has been imposed upon us by the constitution and laws of the United States, shall be calculated to bring on those dangers which have been indicated: or if it shall be indispensable to the preservation of the union, and consequently of the independence and liberty of these states: these are considerations which address themselves to those departments which may with perfect propriety be influenced by them. This department can listen only to the mandates of law; and can tread only that path which is marked out by duty.

The judgment of the supreme court of the state of Missouri for the first judicial district is reversed; and the cause remanded, with directions to enter judgment for the defendants.[11]

Printed, Richard Peters, *Reports of Cases Argued and Adjudged in the Supreme Court of the United States . . .* , IV (Philadelphia, 1830), 425–38.

1. Smith v. Maryland, 6 Cranch 286 (1810); Martin v. Hunter's Lessee, 1 Wheat. 304, (1816); Miller v. Nicholls, 4 Wheat. 311 (1819); Williams v. Norris, 12 Wheat. 117 (1827); Willson v. Blackbird Creek Marsh Co., 2 Pet. 245 (1829); Harris v. Dennie, 3 Pet. 292 (1830). JM's citation of Martin v. Hunter's Lessee refers to a page (355) of Story's opinion rather than to the first page of the report. Counsel at 4 Pet. 417 also cited 1 Wheat. 355. See also Willson v. Blackbird Creek Marsh Co., Opinion, 20 Mar. 1829, where JM also cited the case as "1 Wh. 355."

2. This should be "27th," as correctly stated above.

3. The pertinent sections of the act are reproduced in the printed report at 4 Pet. 413–15.

4. Thomas Hutchinson, *History of Massachusetts from the First Settlement Thereof in 1628, until the Year 1750* (3d ed.; 2 vols.; Boston, 1795), I, 402.

5. Hening, *Statutes*, VI, 467–68, 528–30; VIII, 346–47, 501–2, 647–51.

6. Ibid., IX, 67–69, 145–48, 223–24.

7. Ibid., IX, 298; X, 398.

8. Springfield Bank v. Merrick, 14 Mass. 322 (1817).

9. Hunt v. Knickerbocker, 5 Johns. 327 (N. Y. Sup. Ct., 1810).

10. Patton v. Nicholson, 3 Wheat. 204 (1818).

11. Justices Johnson, Thompson, and McLean dissented from the majority on the merits. They upheld the Court's jurisdiction as having been settled by previous cases, though Thompson and McLean doubted that the record sufficiently showed that the constitutional question had arisen in the state court. Johnson regarded the loan office certificates as "of a truly amphibious character," concluding that in a doubtful case the Court must pronounce the state law to be innocent. Thompson and McLean acknowledged the difficulty of defining "bill of credit" while arguing for a restrictive meaning that exempted the Missouri loan office certificates. McLean alone dealt with the second point, contending that the contract was enforceable even if the certificates were held to be bills of credit (4 Pet. 438–65 [Johnson quotation at 444]).

From Richard Peters

My Dear Sir,

Washington, March 20, 1830.
Supreme Court Room.

I am exceedingly embarrassed on the subject of the *publication* of the Reports of the Cases decided at this term, and submit myself to the Court for direction.

It is manifest that it will be impossible to comprehend the whole of the decisions, *with the arguments of counsel,* in *one* volume, of a size which will be convenient, and executed on a type such as is proper for the work. Should it be desired by the Court, I am willing to publish two volumes, introducing in most of the cases *the arguments of counsel:* indeed more than half the cases are now ready for the press, *the arguments included;* having intended to pursue the plan heretofore adopted. But the objection to this is, that the profession may consider the expense of two volumes a burthen, and may complain. With the approval of the Court, and their expression of a wish that the arguments shall be reported, I shall be entirely protected. If the Court shall recommend or sanction the *omission* of the arguments, I shall be also safe from the censure of those gentlemen whose ability in the discussion of the cases which have been disposed of during the term entitles them to every illustration, and whose arguments it would, under other circumstances, give me great pleasure to insert in the work.

I have no desire to present the case in any form which can be construed as intending a claim on the government for additional compensation for delivering to the department of state, *two* volumes instead of *one;* and I wish to be understood as relinquishing any such claim or purpose. My whole object is to act in the matter as the court shall wish, and I shall have full compensation for any addition to my labours in their approbation. I am, sir, with great respect and esteem, Your obedient servant, faithfully,

RICHARD PETERS.

Printed, Richard Peters, *Reports of Cases Argued and Adjudged in the Supreme Court of the United States* . . . , III (Philadelphia, 1830), v–vi.

To Richard Peters

My dear Sir   Washington March 22d. 1830

I laid your letter before the court and found a general disposition among the Judges to approve of that course which you should yourself think most eligible. I believe we all think that the arguments at the bar ought, at least in substance to appear in the report.[1] They certainly contribute very much to explain the points really decided by the court. If this cannot be done in one volume I should think it advisable to give us two. With great respect and esteem, I am dear Sir Your Obedt

J MARSHALL

ALS, NjR. Endorsed by Peters with the note: "In answer to my letter stating that the reports of Jany 1830 could not be contained in one volume, if I gave the arguments of counsel"; printed, Richard Peters, *Reports of Cases Argued and Adjudged in the Supreme Court of the United States* . . . , III (Philadelphia, 1830), vi.

1. An "s" was added at the end of the word, probably by Peters, in preparation of the document for publication.

Providence Bank v. Billings and Pitman
Opinion
U.S. Supreme Court, 22 March 1830

This was an arranged case to try the constitutionality of a Rhode Island law of 1822 imposing a duty upon licensed persons and corporations within the state. The Providence Bank, chartered by the state legislature in 1791, refused to pay the tax. In July 1827 Alpheus Billings, sheriff of Providence County, and Thomas G. Pitman, state treasurer, entered the banking house and seized the amount of the tax. The bank brought an action of trespass in the Court of Common Pleas for Providence County, to which the defendants pleaded the act imposing the tax. On the plaintiff's demurrer to this plea on the ground of the act's repugnancy to the contract clause of the Constitution, the court in May 1828 gave judgment for the defendants. The case was appealed to the Supreme Judicial Court of Rhode Island, which in September 1828 confirmed the lower court judgment pro forma. The bank then brought the case to the U.S. Supreme Court by a writ of error under section 25 of the Judiciary Act. On 11 February 1830 John Whipple presented the case for the bank. He was followed by Benjamin Hazard (1774–1841) for the defendants and Walter Jones for the plaintiff. Marshall delivered the opinion of the Court on 22 March (Providence Bank v. Billings and Pitman,

App. Cas. No. 1531; U.S. Sup. Ct. Minutes, 11 Feb. 1830, 22 Mar. 1830; Caroline E. Robinson, *The Hazard Family of Rhode Island, 1635–1894* [Boston, 1895], 83–85).

OPINION

This is a writ of error to a judgment rendered in the highest court for the state of Rhode Island, in an action of trespass brought by the plaintiff in error against the defendant.

In November 1791 the legislature of Rhode Island granted a charter of incorporation to certain individuals, who had associated themselves together for the purpose of forming a banking company. They are incorporated by the name of the "President, Directors, and Company of the Providence Bank;" and have the ordinary powers which are supposed to be necessary for the usual objects of such associations.

In 1822 the legislature of Rhode Island passed "an act imposing a duty on licensed persons and others, and bodies corporate within the state;" in which, among other things, it is enacted that ["]there shall be paid, for the use of the state, by each and every bank within the state, except the Bank of the United States, the sum of fifty cents on each and every thousand dollars of the capital stock actually paid in." This tax was afterwards augmented to one dollar and twenty-five cents.

The Providence Bank, having determined to resist the payment of this tax, brought an action of trespass against the officers by whom a warrant of distress was issued against and served upon the property of the bank, in pursuance of the law. The defendants justify the taking set out in the declaration under the act of assembly imposing the tax; to which plea the plaintiffs demur, and assign for cause of demurrer that the act is repugnant to the constitution of the United States, inasmuch as it impairs the obligation of the contract created by their charter of incorporation. Judgment was given by the court of common pleas in favour of the defendants; which judgment was, on appeal, confirmed by the supreme judicial court of the state: that judgment has been brought before this court by a writ of error.

It has been settled that a contract entered into between a state and an individual, is as fully protected by the tenth section of the first article of the constitution, as a contract between two individuals; and it is not denied that a charter incorporating a bank is a contract. Is this contract impaired by taxing the banks of the state?

This question is to be answered by the charter itself.

It contains no stipulation promising exemption from taxation. The state, then, has made no express contract which has been impaired by the act of which the plaintiffs complain. No words have been found in the charter, which, in themselves, would justify the opinion that the power of taxation was in the view of either of the parties; and that an exemption of it was intended, though not expressed. The plaintiffs find great difficulty in showing that the charter contains a promise, either express or implied, not to tax the bank. The elaborate and ingenious argument which has been urged amounts, in substance, to this. The charter authorises the bank to employ its capital in banking transactions, for the benefit of the stockholders. It binds the state to permit these transactions for this object. Any law arresting directly the operations of the bank would violate this obligation, and would come within the prohibition of the constitution. But, as that cannot be done circuitously which may not be done directly, the charter restrains the state from passing any act which may indirectly destroy the profits of the bank. A power to tax the bank may unquestionably be carried to such an excess as to take all its profits, and still more than its profits for the use of the state; and consequently destroy the institution. Now, whatever may be the rule of expediency, the constitutionality of a measure depends, not on the degree of its exercise, but on its principle. A power therefore which may in effect destroy the charter, is inconsistent with it; and is impliedly renounced by granting it. Such a power cannot be exercised without impairing the obligation of the contract. When pushed to its extreme point, or exercised in moderation, it is the same power, and is hostile to the rights granted by the charter. This is substantially the argument for the bank. The plaintiffs cite and rely on several sentiments expressed, on various occasions by this court, in support of these positions.

The claim of the Providence Bank is certainly of the first impression. The power of taxing moneyed corporations has been frequently exercised; and has never before, so far as is known, been resisted. Its novelty, however, furnishes no conclusive argument against it.[1]

That the taxing power is of vital importance; that it is essential to the existence of government; are truths which it cannot be necessary to reaffirm. They are acknowledged and asserted by all. It would seem that the relinquishment of such a power is never to be assumed. We will not say that a state may not relinquish it; that a consideration sufficiently valuable to induce a partial release of it may not exist: but as the whole community is interested in retaining it undiminished; that community has a right to insist that its abandonment ought not to be presumed, in a case in which the deliberate purpose of the state to abandon it does not appear.

The plaintiffs would give to this charter the same construction as if it contained a clause exempting the bank from taxation on its stock in trade. But can it be supposed that such a clause would not enlarge its privileges? They contend that it must be implied; because the power to tax may be so wielded as to defeat the purpose for which the charter was granted. And may not this be said with equal truth of other legislative powers? Does it not also apply with equal force to every incorporated company? A company may be incorporated for the purpose of trading in goods as well as trading in money. If the policy of the state should lead to the imposition of a tax on unincorporated companies, could those which might be incorporated claim an exemption, in virtue of a charter which does not indicate such an intention? The time may come when a duty may be imposed on manufactures. Would an incorporated company be exempted from this duty, as the mere consequence of its charter?

The great object of an incorporation is to bestow the character and properties of individuality on a collective and changing body of men. This capacity is always given to such a body. Any privileges which may exempt it from the burthens common to individuals, do not flow necessarily from the charter, but must be expressed in it, or they do not exist.

If the power of taxation is inconsistent with the charter, because it may be so exercised as to destroy the object for which the charter is given; it is equally inconsistent with every other charter, because it is equally capable of working the destruction of the objects for which every other charter is given. If the grant of a power to trade in money to a given amount, implies an exemption of the stock in trade from taxation, because the tax may absorb all the profits; then the grant of any other thing implies the same exemption; for that thing may be taxed to an extent which will render it totally unprofitable to the grantee. Land, for example, has, in many, perhaps in all the states, been granted by government since the adoption of the constitution. This grant is a contract, the object of which is that the profits issuing from it shall enure to the benefit of the grantee. Yet the power of taxation may be carried so far as to absorb these profits. Does this impair the obligation of the contract? The idea is rejected by all; and the proposition appears so extravagant, that it is difficult to admit any resemblance in the cases. And yet if the proposition for which the plaintiffs contend be true, it carries us to this point. That proposition is, that a power which is in itself capable of being exerted to the total destruction of the grant, is inconsistent with the grant; and is therefore impliedly relinquished by the grantor, though the language of the instrument contains no allusion to the subject. If this be an abstract truth, it may be supposed universal. But it is not universal; and therefore its truth cannot be admitted, in these broad terms, in any case. We must look for the exemption in the language of the instrument; and if we do not find it there, it would be going very far to insert it by construction.

The power of legislation, and consequently of taxation, operates on all the persons and property belonging to the body politic. This is an original principle, which has its foundation in society itself. It is granted by all, for the benefit of all. It resides in government as a part of itself, and need not be reserved when property of any description, or the right to use it in any manner, is granted to individuals or corporate bodies. However absolute the right of an individual may be, it is still in the nature of that right, that it must bear a portion of the public burthens; and that portion must be determined by the legislature. This vital power may be abused; but the constitution of the United States was not intended to furnish the corrective for every abuse of power which may be committed by the state governments. The interest, wisdom, and justice of the representative body, and its relations with its constituents, furnish the only security, where there is no express contract, against unjust and excessive taxation; as well as against unwise legislation generally. This principle was laid down in the case of M'Cullough *vs.* The State of Maryland, and in Osborn et al. *vs.* The Bank of the United States.[2] Both those cases, we think, proceeded on the admission that an incorporated bank, unless its charter shall express the exemption, is no more exempted from taxation, than an unincorporated company would be, carrying on the same business.

The case of Fletcher *vs.* Peck has been cited; but in that case the legislature of Georgia passed an act to annul its grant.[3] The case of the State of New Jersey *vs.* Wilson has been also mentioned; but in that case the stipulation exempting the land from taxation, was made in express words.[4]

The reasoning of the court in the case of M'Cullough *vs.* The State of Maryland has been applied to this case; but the court itself appears to have provided against this application. Its opinion in that case, as well as in Osborn et al. *vs.* The Bank of the United States, was founded, expressly, on the supremacy of the laws of congress, and the necessary consequence of that supremacy to exempt its instruments employed in the execution of its powers, from the operation of any interfering power whatever. In reasoning on the argument that the power of taxation was not confined to the people and property of a state, but might be exercised on every object brought within its jurisdiction, this court admitted the truth of the proposition; and added, that "the power was an incident of sovereignty, and was co-extensive with that to which it was an incident." All powers, the court said, over which the sovereign power of a state extends, are subjects of taxation. The sovereignty of a state extends to every thing which exists by its own authority, or is introduced by its permission; but does it extend to those means which are employed by congress to carry into execution powers conferred on that body by the people of the United States? We think not.[5]

So in the case of Osborn *vs.* The Bank of the United States, the court said, "the argument" in favour of the right of the state to tax the bank, "supposes the corporation to have been originated for the management of an individual concern, to be founded upon contract between individuals, having private trade and private profit for its great end and principal object.

If these premises were true, the conclusion drawn from them would be inevitable. This mere private corporation, engaged in its own business, would certainly be subject to the taxing power of the state as any individual would be."[6]

The court was certainly not discussing the question whether a tax imposed by a state on a bank chartered by itself, impaired the obligation of its contract; and these opinions are not conclusive as they would be had they been delivered in such a case: but they show that the question was not considered as doubtful, and that inferences drawn from general expressions pointed to a different subject cannot be correctly drawn.

We have reflected seriously on this case, and are of opinion that the act of the legislature of Rhode Island, passed in 1822, imposing a duty on licensed persons and others, and bodies corporate within the state, does not impair the obligation of the contract created by the charter granted to the plaintiffs in error. It is therefore the opinion of this court, that there is no error in the judgment of the supreme judicial court for the state of Rhode Island, affirming the judgment of the circuit court in this case; and the same is affirmed; and the cause is remanded to the said supreme judicial court, that its judgment may be finally entered.

Printed, Richard Peters, *Reports of Cases Argued and Adjudged in the Supreme Court of the United States . . .*, IV (Philadelphia, 1830), 559–65.

1. The case for the bank had been made three years earlier by Joseph K. Angell (1794–1857), a legal writer and later law reporter of Rhode Island (*An Essay on the Right of a State to Tax a Body Corporate Considered in Relation to the Present Bank Tax in Rhode Island* [Boston, 1827]).

2. McCulloch v. Maryland, 4 Wheat. 400–437 (1819); *PJM*, VIII, 259–79; Osborn v. Bank of the U.S., 9 Wheat. 816–71 (1824); *PJM*, X, 44–73.

3. Fletcher v. Peck, 6 Cranch 127–43 (1810); *PJM*, VII, 230–41.

4. New Jersey v. Wilson, 7 Cranch 164–67 (1812); *PJM*, VII, 316–19

5. JM closely paraphrased rather than exactly quoted the passage at 4 Wheat. 429; *PJM*, VIII, 274–275.

6. 9 Wheat. 859; *PJM*, X, 67.

To John K. Kane

Sir   Richmond March 26th. 1830

On my return to this place from the city of Washington, I received your letter of the 15th. of January informing me that I am elected a member of the American Philosophical society held at Philadelphia for promoting useful knowledge.[1] I pray you to accompany my acknowledgements to the society for this honorable notice with my regrets at my utter inability to make any contributions which may be worthy of acceptance by the institution. With very great respect for the society and yourself I am Sir your Obedt. Servt

J MARSHALL

ALS, Society Archives, PPAmP. Addressed to Kane at Independence Square, Philadelphia; postmarked Richmond, 26 Mar. Endorsed by Kane.

1. Letter not found. John K. Kane (1795–1858), was a prominent Philadelphia lawyer and later served as judge of U.S. District Court for eastern Pennsylvania. He was then

secretary of the American Philosophical Society. JM had been nominated as a member on 5 Nov. 1829 by Nathaniel Chapman, Peter S. Du Ponceau, John Vaughan, Kane, Joseph Hopkinson, and William Rawle. He was elected on 15 Jan. 1830 (Society Archives, PPAmP).

To Humphrey Marshall

Dear Sir   Richmond April 4th. 1830
    The court of Appeals has manifested a disposition to decide in favor of my Father's claim to half pay, but the suit cannot be sustained until his will shall be proved in the General court of Virginia and letters testamentary or of Administration with the will annexed shall be granted by that court.[1] Our law permits an authenticated copy of a will proved in one of the United States according to the laws of the state to be recorded in the Genl. court.[2] That court sits in the early part of June — the 9th. — and if the copy of my Father's will can be received by that time it will make a difference of six months in the decision of the claim. Our act of Assembly does not declare what shall be deemed a sufficient authentication, and a certificate of the clerk that it is a true copy with a certificate of the eldest justice that he is clerk and that full faith and credit is due to his certificate under the seal of the court if there be one has been sometimes held sufficient. I think however the safer course will be to add a certificate under the seal of the state that the Judge or Justice who may grant the certificate that the person is clerk, is the senior Judge or Magistrate of the county.
    I am very glad when I hear that your health has greatly improved and am with great esteem and regard, Your Obedt

                                                              J MARSHALL

ALS, Marshall Papers, ViW. Addressed to Marshall "near Frankfort / Kentucky"; postmarked Richmond, 4 Apr.

1. As administrator of his father Thomas Marshall, JM had filed a claim against the commonwealth of Virginia for a half-pay pension for services as colonel of the state artillery regiment during the Revolutionary War. When the auditor of public accounts rejected this claim, JM appealed the decision to the Henrico County Superior Court of Law (not the state court of appeals), as provided by law. That court on 12 Nov. 1830 issued a judgment overruling the auditor's decision and awarding half pay from Feb. 1782 to the date of Thomas Marshall's death in Dec. 1802 (*Revised Code of Va.*, II, 2–3; copy of judgment, 12 Nov. 1830, Henrico County Superior Court of Law, Vi).
    2. *Revised Code of Va.*, I, 378–79.

To Samuel Smith

Dear Sir   Richmond Apr. 16th. 1830

I received a few days past a copy of your very able report on the finances which I have read with a great deal of pleasure.[1] The subject is one of deep interest, and you have treated it in a manner to be I think intelligible to all. I thank you for this mark of your recollection and am with great regard and respect, Your Obedt

J MARSHALL

ALS, CSmH. Addressed to Smith in Washington and franked; postmarked Richmond, 16 Apr.

1. *Report: the Committee on Finance: To Which Was Referred a Resolution of the 30th December 1829, Directing the Committee to Inquire into the Expediency of Establishing an Uniform National Currency for the United States* (Washington, D.C., 1830). As chairman of the committee, Smith presented this report to the Senate on 29 Mar. 1830.

To Jaquelin A. Marshall

My dear Son   Richmond May 6th. 1830

On my return home I found your mother in her usual health and very much delighted with the contents of the box which arrived in safety by the steamboat. She was very much pleased with the shawl and admires Eliza's skill and industry. She values it the more from beleiving it to be the manufacture of Eliza though you did not give the information. The sweet meats are delicious; and we have regaled our friends with the wine who think it a very good specimen of what may be done with the juice of the currant.

I delighted her with the account I gave of your family generally and especially of the little stranger who, I told her, bid fair to be nearly as tall as his Father.[1]

Our season is in great forwardness. Our early wheat is in full bloom. I think it not improbable that our harvest may commence in this month. In the best lands no fear seems to be entertained except that the wheat will lodge. In the country between Hanover court house and Fredericksburg it is generally too thin. I wish we had any prospect of a tolerable price. This wish I fear cannot be gratified. With our love to Eliza and the family I am your affectionate Father

J MARSHALL

ALS (owned by Mrs. Fairfield Scott Perry, New Canaan, Conn., 1971). Addressed to "Doctor Jaquelin A. Marshall / Prospect Hill / near Orleans / Fauquier."

1. Jaquelin A. Marshall, JM's grandson, was then fifteen months old (Paxton, *Marshall Family*, 205).

To Theodore Frelinghuysen

Dear Sir   Richmond May 22d. 1830

On my return from North Carolina I received your speech on the removal of the Indians which I have read with equal interest and attention.[1] The subject has always appeared to me to affect deeply the honor, the faith and the character of our country. The cause of these oppressed people has been most ably though unsuccessfully sustained. "Defeat in such a cause is far above the triumphs of unrighteous power."[2]

I thank you for this flattering mark of your attention and am with great respect and esteem, your Obedt.

J Marshall

ALS (owned by Mrs. Samuel T. Lawton, Jr., Highland Park, Ill., 1999). Addressed to Frelinghuysen in Washington and franked; postmarked Richmond, 23 May.

1. *Speech of Mr. Frelinghuysen . . . on the Bill for an Exchange of Lands with the Indians Residing in any of the States or Territories, and for their Removal West of the Mississippi* (Washington, D.C., 1830). Frelinghuysen (1787–1862), then a U.S. senator from New Jersey, delivered this speech in the Senate in opposition to the bill on 7, 8, and 9 Apr. 1830 (*Register of Debates in Congress*, VI [Washington, D.C., 1830], 309–20).

2. Marshall quoted from the conclusion of Frelinghuysen's speech (*Speech of Mr. Frelinghuysen*, 28).

To Josiah S. Johnston

Dear Sir   Richmond May 22d. 1830

On my return from North Carolina I had the pleasure of receiving your speech "on the power of a state to annul the laws of the Union," which I have read with deep attention.[1] It certainly is not among the least extraordinary of the doctrines of the present day that such a question should be seriously debated. I thank you for the gratification derived from reading your able argument, and am with great and respectful esteem, Your Obedt.

J Marshall

ALS, PHi. Addressed to "Mr. Johnston of Louisiana" in Washington and franked; postmarked Richmond, 23 May.

1. *Speech of Mr. Johnston, of Louisiana on the Power of a State to Annul the Laws of the United States . . .* (Washington, D.C., 1830). A Connecticut native, Josiah Stoddard Johnston (1784–1833) had served in the U.S. Senate from Louisiana since 1824. The pamphlet printed a portion of Johnston's speech of 2 Apr. 1830 on Sen. Samuel A. Foot's resolution concerning the expediency of limiting the sale of public lands. Foot's resolution, introduced in Dec.1829, touched off a debate on the nature of the union that featured the celebrated exchange between Daniel Webster and Robert Y. Hayne in Jan. 1830. Johnston's speech included a spirited defense of the Supreme Court (Glyndon G. Van Deusen, *The Jacksonian Era, 1828–1848* [New York, 1959], 40–44; Warren, *Supreme Court*, I, 721–24).

To Edward C. Marshall

My dear Son   Richmond May 22d. 1830
Your mother has received your letter and is much gratified at the domestic intelligence it contains.[1]

I shall be pleased if your brother can negotiate an exchange of land with Mr. Adams. I should think however that there ⟨would⟩ be very little if any difference between ⟨. . .⟩. Capt. Slaughter has always held ⟨. . . value⟩d at about 5000$ and at such ⟨. . . I had . . .⟩ it would ⟨. . .⟩ on the usual credit, at ⟨. . .⟩.

I presented your check at the ⟨bank and⟩ have taken your note. I shall to day remit ⟨the⟩ check to Messrs. Thompsons on the bank of Potomac for 300$.[2]

I find from Mr. Nicholas[3] that Mr. John Lewis paid near $10000, the debts of Mr. Warner Lewis chiefly with monies received for negroes sold very fortunately during the high prices.[4]

Some difficulty exists respecting the ten bank shares transferred by Mr. Smith as exr. of Mr. John Lewis who was admr. de bonis non of Mr. Warner Lewis. The shares stood in the name of Mr J Lewis as admr. of Mr. W. Lewis, & it is supposed that the exr. of Mr. J Lewis cannot transfer them. Mr. Nicholas says that if Mrs. Nelson will execute a bond with you as her surety to indemnify the bank he will lay it before the board of Directors and endeavour to procure their sanction to the transfer.[5] I presume ⟨this will?⟩ be necessary. Your Mother ⟨requests⟩ to be pre⟨sented⟩ respectfully to Mrs. Nelson and sends her best ⟨wishes to Rebe⟩cca & yourself. She ⟨. . .⟩ delight ⟨. . .⟩ your son & Mary Am⟨bler?⟩ will ⟨. . . succeed?⟩ in obtaining Mr. Keith ⟨. . .⟩ I am my dear Son ⟨your⟩ affectionate Father,

J MARSHALL

ALS (owned by Edwin R. Marshall, Wilmington, Del., 1967); on deposit, Marshall-Hayden Collection, ViU. Addressed to Marshall at "Carrington, near Oak Hill, Fauquier"; postmarked Richmond, 20 May. Parts of text obscured or obliterated by holes in MS and by water stains. Enclosure: draft of bond (see n. 5).

1. Letter not found.

2. The Bank of Potomac was established in Alexandria in 1804 (T. Michael Miller, comp., *Artisans and Merchants of Alexandria, 1780–1820* [2 vols.; Bowie, Md., 1991–92], I, 21).

3. Probably Robert C. Nicholas (d. 1874), a Richmond lawyer and son of Philip N. Nicholas (Louise Pecquet Du Bellet, *Some Prominent Virginia Families* [4 vols.; 1907; Baltimore, 1976 reprint], I, 67; *Richmond Portraits*, 147).

4. The late Warner Lewis III was the grandfather of Rebecca Marshall, Edward's wife. John Lewis (d. 1827) was the brother and administrator of Warner Lewis III. Rebecca Marshall's mother (the former Mary Chiswell Lewis, daughter of Warner Lewis III) was Mrs. Mary C. Nelson (1791–1853), then twice widowed and living with her daughter (Paxton, *Marshall Family*, 95, 105; Merrow Egerton Sorley, comp., *Lewis of Warner Hall: The History of a Family* [Columbia, Mo., 1935], 72, 81–82, 88).

5. JM drew up a bond for this purpose and enclosed it to Edward. According to its terms, Mary Nelson and Edward C. Marshall were bound to the Farmers Bank of Virginia in the

sum of $5,000 to secure the bank from any loss resulting from the transfer of stock (by Thomas Smith, John Lewis's executor) to Mary Nelson.

To Richard Peters

My dear Sir   Richmond 1830–May 24
    In the case of Mandeville & al. v Riggs 2 Peters 482 two points were argued at the bar which were not decided by the court nor comprehended in the report, on which I could wish to see the authorities which were cited in the argument. 1st. Those which relate to the validity of the contract. 2d. Those which relate to the parties.
    It is possible you may have retained notes of the argument. If you have I shall be much obliged by a list of the authorities on these points. Yours truely

                                                    J MARSHALL

ALS (advertised for sale by Joseph Rubinfine, West Palm Beach, Fla., 2000). Addressed to Peters in Philadelphia; postmarked Richmond, 24 May.

1. In his report of this case decided at the Jan. 1829 term, Peters remarked: "It is not considered necessary to state in this report any of the points presented by counsel, upon which no opinion was expressed by the Court" (2 Pet. 484).

To James Hillhouse

My dear Sir   Richmond May 26th. 1830
    I have just returned from North Carolina and had this morning the pleasure of receiving your letter of the 10th.[1] accompanying your proposition for amending the constitution of The United States as to the mode of electing the President, and your speech made on that subject in the Senate in 1808.[2] I read your speech when first published with great pleasure and attention, but was not then a convert to either of the amendments it suggested.[3] In truth there is something so captivating in the idea of a chief Executive Magistrate who is the choice of a whole people, that it is extremely difficult to withdraw the judgement from its influence. The advantages which ought to result from it are manifest. They strike the mind at once, and we are unwilling to beleive that they can be defeated, or that the operation of chusing can be attended with evils which more than counter balance the actual good resulting from the choice. It is humiliating too to admit that we must look, in any degree, to chance for that decision which ought to be made by the judgement. These strong and apparently rational convictions can be shaken only by long observation and painful experience. Mine are I confess very much shaken; and

my views of this subject have changed a good deal since 1808. I consider it however rather as an affair of curious speculation than of probable fact. Your plan comes in conflict with so many opposing interests and deep rooted prejudices that I should despair of its success were its utility still more apparent than it is.[4]

All those who are candidates for the Presidency either immediately or remotely, and they are more numerous than is imagined, and are the most powerful members of the community, will be opposed to it. The body of the people will also most probably be in opposition; for it will be difficult to persuade them that any mode of choice can be preferable to election mediate or immediate by themselves. The ardent politicians of the country, not yet moderated by experience, will consider it as an imputation on the great republican principle that the people are capable of governing themselves, if any other mode of appointing a chief Magistrate be substituted for that which depends on their agency. I believe therefore that we must proceed with our present system till its evils become still more obvious, perhaps indeed till the experiment shall become impracticable, before we shall be willing to change it.

My own private mind has been slowly and reluctantly advancing to the belief that the present mode of chusing the chief Magistrate threatens the most serious danger to the public happiness. The passions of men are enflamed to so fearful an extent, large masses are so embittered against each other, that I dread the consequences. The election agitates every section of The United States, and the ferment is never to subside. Scarcely is a President elected before the machinations respecting a successor commence. Every political question is affected by it. All those who are in office, all those who want office, are put in motion. The angriest, I might say the worst passions are roused and put into full activity. Vast masses united closely move in opposite directions animated with the most hostile feelings towards each other. What is to be the effect of all this? Age is perhaps unreasonably timid. Certain it is that I now dread consequences which I once thought imaginary. I feel disposed to take refuge under some less turbulent and less dangerous mode of chusing the chief Magistrate. My mind suggests none less objectionable than that you have proposed. We shall no longer be enlisted under the banners of particular men. Strife will no longer be excited when it can no longer effect its object. Neither the people at large nor the councils of the nation will be agitated by the all disturbing question who shall be President? Yet he will in truth be chosen substantially by the people. The Senators must always be among the most alert men ⟨of their states.⟩ Tho' not appointed for the particular purpose, they must ⟨always be⟩ appointed for important purposes, and must possess a large share of the public confidence. If the people of The United States were to elect as many persons as compose one senatorial class, and the President was to be chosen among them by lot in the manner you propose, he would be substantially elected by the people, and yet such a mode of election would be recommended by no advantages which your plan does not possess. In many respects it would be less eligible.

Reasoning a priori I should undoubtedly pronounce the system adopted by the convention the best that could be devised. Judging from experience I am driven to a different conclusion.[5] I have at your request submitted my reflections to your private view and will only add that I am with great and respectful esteem Your Obedt. Servt

J MARSHALL

ALS, Marshall Papers, ViW; Tr, Hillhouse Papers, CtY. ALS addressed to Hillhouse in Washington, directed "To the attention of the Honble. / Mr. Taliaferro." Postmarked Richmond, ? May. Endorsement on address leaf: "No. 8 Clinton square / Chestnut above / Broad Street." Words enclosed by angle brackets missing owing to tear in MS supplied by Tr.

1. Letter not found. Hillhouse wrote to James Madison on the same day from Washington, enclosing his pamphlet "containing a revision of the Amendments to the constitution of the United States, which twenty two years since I presented to the Senate." He requested Madison to give the pamphlet "a careful perusal, and favor me with your remarks, and opinion thereon" (Hillhouse to Madison, 10 May 1830, Madison Papers [DLC]). Presumably JM directed his reply to Taliaferro's attention on the supposition that Hillhouse would depart Washington before the letter could reach him. John Taliaferro (1768–1852) of King George County, Va., served in the House of Representatives in 1801–3, 1811–13, 1824–31, and 1835–43.

2. *Propositions for Amending the Constitution of the United States, Providing for the Election of President and Vice-president, and Guarding against the Undue Exercise of Executive Influence, Patronage, and Power* (Washington, D.C., 1830). The first six pages of this pamphlet consisted of Hillhouse's introduction, followed by five proposed amendments. The remaining thirty-four pages was an "appendix" containing a reprint of Hillhouse's speech in the U.S. Senate on 12 Apr. 1808 and published as *Propositions for Amending the Constitution of the United States* (New Haven, Conn., 1808).

3. In 1808, Hillhouse proposed that the president should serve for a term of one year and be chosen by lot from the senior class of senators (those whose terms would expire first). He renewed that proposal in 1830, but extended the term to two years (*Propositions for Amending the Constitution of the United States* [1830], 5–6, 38).

4. In Mar. 1830 Thomas H. Benton presented to the Senate a resolution of the Missouri legislature proposing an amendment to the Constitution providing for direct election by the people of the president and vice president, "without the intervention of Electors." The proposal was tabled on 22 May (*Journal of the Senate of the United States of America, Being the First Session of the Twenty-First Congress . . .* [Washington, 1829], 187, 199, 321).

5. JM's letter, along with a letter from William H. Crawford to Hillhouse, 4 June 1830, was subsequently published in an appendix to Samuel S. Nicholas, *Letters on the Presidency* (Louisville, Ky., 1859 [first published in 1840]), 50–51.

To Edward Everett

Dear Sir   Richmond June 5th. 1830

I have received your speech on the bill for removing the Indians from the East to the West side of the Mississippi, and have read it with the deepest interest.[1] I do not think any subject ever discussed in Congress has drawn forth a more splendid display of talent in each house of the national legislature than this, or is more worthy of the deliberate consideration of the government and of the nation. The speeches with which I have been favored, which are indeed all on one side, abound in arguments which appear to me to be solid and conclusive, and which do very great honour to the heads and hearts of those who made them. You have brought into more open view than any other whose speech I have seen, an idea which always appeared to me to be of the first importance and to be peculiarly appropriate. It is the cooperation which exists between the acts extending state legislation over the Indians and this bill for their removal. You have shown, what is certainly true, that they are parts of the same system, and that Congress completes the coercive measures begun by the states.

It has been to me matter of the greatest astonishment that, after hearing the arguments in both houses, Congress could pass the bill.[2]

I thank you very sincerely for this polite mark of your attention and beg you to beleive that I am, with great and respectful esteem, Your obedt

J MARSHALL

ALS, Everett Papers, MHi. Addressed to Everett in Boston and franked; postmarked Richmond, 5 June. Endorsed by Everett.

1. Everett delivered this speech in the House of Representatives on 19 May 1830 and published it as a pamphlet (*Register of Debates in Congress*, VI [Washington, D.C., 1830], 1058–1079; *Speech of Mr. Everett . . . on the Bill for Removing the Indians from the East to the West Side of the Mississippi River . . .* [Washington, 1830]).

2. Congress passed the act on 28 May 1830 (*U.S. Statutes at Large*, IV, 411–12).

To Jaquelin A. Marshall

My dear Son   Richmond June 17th. 1830

I have just received your letter of the 12th.[1] I do not understand the relative rights of the Paynes nor how they conflict with each other. I can give no directions till I come up in August.

I do not recollect enough about Carvers business to say any thing about it. I must endeavour to make a final arrangement of these disputes when I come up in August and for that purpose must stay longer with you than I have done.

The observation you make on the wheat crops in your country applies exactly to ours.

The season has been very wet. About 25 Acres of my corn is drowned now for the second time this year. I shall replant it again, should the water permit, the last of this month or the first week in next.

Your Mother is a good deal oppressed with the hot damp weather, but is not otherwise sick. Our love to Eliza and the family, Your affectionate Father

J MARSHALL

ALS (owned by J. Merrick Marshall, Lynchburg, Va., 1982). Addressed to "Doctor Jaquelin A. Marshall / Prospect Hill / near Orleans / Fauquier"; postmarked Richmond, 18 June. On cover someone (Jaquelin A. Marshall?) wrote given names of forty-odd persons, presumably slaves.

1. Letter not found.

From Dabney Carr

My dear Sir　　　　　　　　　　　　[Richmond, ca. 25 June 1830][1]

Although our intercourse has not been intimate and Confidential, it has (I am Sure) been friendly and Cordial; and I take pleasure in saying that its effect has been, to add mine, to the universal Confidence, which the world feels, in the integrity and purity of the Chief Justice of the U.S.

This feeling, (if my own Sense of propriety did not) would certainly forbid my proposing to you, any thing inconsistent (in my view) with the high and responsible duties of your Station.

The enclosed letter, is from one of the oldest and dearest of my friends — of whom, I can confidently say (after an intimacy of thirty years) that I believe there is not, on earth, a man more incapable of doing what he thinks wrong.[2]

I have preferred this mode of communication, to that proposed by him, because I consider it less embarrassing. I submit to you his letter, *in Confidence;* and I give you the *whole,* that you may see his views fully. The perusal will tell you what is desired.[3]

If, on reflection, you shall see no objection to gratifying that desire, I should be glad (at your earliest leisure) to have some conversation with you on the subject: if, on the other hand, you had rather be silent, it will be a sufficient expression of that wish, to enclose to me the letter, under a blank cover.

You will observe, that at the close of the letter, I am requested to consult with Mr. Cabell[4] and Mr. Coalter. It is proper to remark, that they, being both out of town, the step now taken proceeds from myself alone.

As I leave Richmond, for the Upper Country, on Tuesday, I request to hear from you as early as may be. Most respectfully yr. friend &c.

D. CARR.

Tr, Wirt Papers, MdHi. Heading (in same unknown hand as text of Tr): "Copy of a letter from Dabney Carr to the *Chief Justice Marshall.*"

1. Dabney Carr (1773–1837), a lawyer and close friend of William Wirt, had been a judge of the Virginia Court of Appeals since 1824.

2. William Wirt to Carr, 21 June 1830, in John P. Kennedy, *Memoirs of the Life of William Wirt* (2 vols.; Philadelphia, 1850), II, 253–58.

3. In his letter, Wirt discussed Georgia's attempt to extend its jurisdiction over the Cherokee tribe within the state and the evident policy of the Jackson administration to support the state's efforts to remove the tribe from its borders. The Cherokee had recently retained Wirt as counsel for the purpose of bringing a case before the Supreme Court that would deal with all the questions of the tribe's rights under federal treaties. Wirt noted that he had already given an opinion as to how the Cherokee might proceed, for example by appealing a prosecution against them in state court by means of a writ of error under sec. 25 of the Judiciary Act. A preferred means was to bring a suit directly to the Supreme Court under its original jurisdiction, which could be done if the tribe were considered to be a "foreign state" within the sense of the Constitution. Wirt asked Carr "whether there would be any impropriety in your conversing with the Chief Justice on this subject, as a brother judge, and giving me his impressions of the political character of this people . . . I would not have you to conceal from him that the question may probably come before the Supreme Court. The subject will not be new to him. He has had occasion to consider several times the character and rights of these people" (ibid., II, 256–57).

4. Joseph Carrington Cabell (1778–1856) was closely associated with Thomas Jefferson in founding the University of Virginia and served on its board of visitors from 1819 until his death. A prominent state legislator, he served in the senate from 1810 to 1829 and represented Nelson County in the House of Delegates from 1831 to 1835.

To [Dabney Carr]

My dear Sir   June 26th. 1830

I shall not attempt to conceal the gratification I feel at the assurance contained in your letter that the degree of neighborly intercourse which has taken place between us has made on your bosom the impression it has on mine; nor shall I hesitate to express my entire conviction that neither yourself nor Mr. Wirt would feel the slightest inclination to tempt me into a path in which I ought not to walk, or to draw from me opinions which I ought not to give. It is for the purpose of making these declarations explicitly that I accompany the letters[1] which you request me to return with this assurance that, while my own sense of duty restrains me from indicating any opinion on the delicate and I will add very interesting questions suggested by Mr. Wirt, I am not at all wounded at the frank and open application which has been made.

I have followed the debate in both houses of Congress with profound attention and with deep interest; and have wished most sincerely that both the Executive and legislative departments had thought differently on the subject. Humanity must bewail the course which is pursued whatever may be the decision of policy.

I wish you a pleasant tour and am dear Sir with great and respectful esteem, Your Obedt

J MARSHALL

ALS, MdHi; Tr, MdHi. Tr in same hand as Tr of Carr to JM, ca. 25 June 1830.

1. In Tr the "s" was deleted.

To [Samuel L. Southard]

My dear Sir   Richmond Aug. 17th. 1830

I received a few days past and have read with real pleasure your eloquent anniversary address delivered before the Newark Mechanics association, in July last.[1] The sentiments it contains find, all of them, con-
genial and kindred feelings in my own bosom; but I was most gratified at
your kind and friendly recollection of me manifested by transmitting me
a copy. Receive my thanks and be assured that I treasure this with the
remembrance of many circumstances not to be forgotten.

You mention a fact which had escaped me and which may I think be
stated with just pride. It is that not a foot of the soil of Jersey was acquired
by violence. With high and respectful esteem, I am dear Sir your Obedt

J MARSHALL

Facsimile of ALS, Steward Kidd, Booksellers, *A Catalogue of Autograph Letters, Historical
Documents, Manuscripts, Etc. . . .* (Cincinnati, 1930), 67. Identity of recipient confirmed by
internal evidence (see n. 1).

1. Samuel Southard, *Address Delivered before the Newark Mechanics Association, July 5, 1830*
(Newark, N. J., 1830).

To John Vaughan

Dear Sir   Richmond Septr. 10 1830

Mr. Sully a young artist of merit is desirous of trying his fortune on a
larger theatre than our village, and desires me to introduce him to some
gentleman whose partiality for the arts and general character in Philadelphia may furnish the inclination and ability to give him that countenance, information, and may I say advice which a young man among
strangers always needs.[1] I hope not to oppress you with any real inconvenience when I take the liberty of presenting him to you as a person who
will not disgrace your recommendation. I am dear Sir with the best wishes
for your happiness, Your Obedt

J MARSHALL

ALS, PharH; printed (facsimile of ALS) in William H. Brown, *Portrait Gallery of Distinguished American Citizens . . .* (Hartford, Conn., 1845). Inside address to Vaughan

1. Robert Matthew Sully (1803–1855), a nephew of the portraitist Thomas Sully, had
studied with his uncle in Philadelphia and also in England. Sully was in Richmond during

JOHN MARSHALL
Oil on canvas by Robert Matthew Sully, 1829.
Courtesy of the Richmond City Council.

the Virginia Convention, when he painted the first of his several portraits of JM. Between 1829 and 1831 he was in Richmond, Philadelphia, and Washington, eventually settling in Richmond (Andrew Oliver, *The Portraits of John Marshall* [Charlottesville, Va., 1977], 100–12).

To Joseph Story

My dear Sir   Richmond October 15th. 1830

Ascribe my delay in thanking you for the sermon drawing the character of your late Chief Justice, and for the excellent addendum you have made to it, to the indolence and negligence of age, or to any cause rather than to indifference to any mark of your kind recollection.[1] I have read both with attention and with real gratification. I had formed a high opinion of the late Chief Justice Parker from what I had heard of him, especially from yourself but that opinion was certainly raised by the more minute detail of his qualities, and by the abridged biography contained in the work for which I am thanking you. My regret for the loss of this estimable gentleman was much enhanced by the fear that Massachusetts might be able to supply his place by seducing from the federal bench a gentleman whose loss would be irreparable. I felicitate myself and my country on the disappointment of this apprehension.

While I am acknowledging favors I thank you also for a box of fish received the other day. I have not yet tasted them but have no doubt of their excellence, and shall not be long in putting it to the test.

I find our brother Mclean could not acquiesce in the decision of the court in the Missouri case. I am sorry for this, and am sorry too to observe his sentiments on the 25th. sect of the judicial act.[2] I have read in the last volume of Mr. Peters the three dissenting opinions delivered in that case, and think it requires no prophet to predict that the 25th. section is to be repealed, or to use a more fashionable phrase, to be nullified by the Supreme court of The United States.[3] I hope the case in which this is to be accomplished will not occur during my time, but, accomplished it will be, at no very distant period.

I am mortified at the number of causes left undecided at the last term. I am still more mortified at the circumstance that I am unable to prepare opinions in them. The cases of Soulard and of Smith I suppose must wait for additional information or for the certainty that none is to be obtained,[4] but I had hoped to prepare something in the lottery case.[5] I am chagrined at discovering that I have left the statement of the case behind me. It is also cause of real surprize as well as chagrin to find that the case of Cathcart and Robertson was not decided.[6] I really thought the court had made up an opinion on it.

I have read with peculiar pleasure the letter of Mr. Madison to the Editor of the North American Review.[7] He is himself again. He avows the opinions of his best days, and must be pardoned for his oblique insinuations that some of the opinions of our court are not approved.[8] Contrast this delicate hint with the language Mr. Jefferson has applied to us. He is attacked with some bitterness by our Enquirer who has arrayed his report of 1799 against his letter.[9] I never thought that report could be completely defended; but Mr. Madison has placed it upon its best ground — that the language is incautious, but is intended to be confined to a meer declaration of opinion, or is intended to refer to that ultimate right which all admit, to resist despotism, a right not exercised under a constitution, but in opposition to it.

Farewell — with the best wishes for your happiness I am yours affectionately

J MARSHALL

ALS, Story Papers, MHi. Addressed to Story in Cambridge; postmarked Richmond, 16 Oct.

1. The first of the publications Story sent was John Gorham Palfrey, *A Sermon Preached in the Church in Brattle Square, Boston, August 1, 1830: The Lord's Day after the Decease of the Honourable Isaac Parker, Chief Justice of Massachusetts* (Boston, 1830). Story's "addendum" probably first appeared in a Boston newspaper. It was reprinted as *"Sketch of the Character of Isaac Parker, Chief Justice of the Supreme Court of Massachusetts,"* in William W. Story, ed., *The Miscellaneous Writings of Joseph Story* (1852; New York, 1972 reprint), 812–16.

2. In his dissent in Craig v. Missouri, Justice McLean expressed the view that in order for the Supreme Court to take jurisdiction of a case coming from a state court under sec. 25 of the Judiciary Act, the federal question had to be "clearly stated" in the record. In this case, he said, there was nothing in the record to indicate that the validity of the Missouri law "was drawn in question, on account of its repugnance to the constitution" (4 Pet. 451).

3. Justice Johnson dissented but did not disagree that the case was "sufficiently brought within the provisions of the twenty-fifth section." Justice Thompson, however, suggested that a "waiver" of a party's right under sec. 25 "ought to be implied in all cases where" it did not appear that a federal question was involved in the state court's judgment, adding: "But to entertain jurisdiction in this case, is perhaps not going farther than this Court has already gone, and I do not mean to call in question these decisions; but have barely noticed the question, for the purpose of stating the rule by which I think all cases under this section should be tested" (4 Pet. 440, 445). JM's comments suggest that the dissenting justices did not deliver their opinions at the time the decision was announced.

4. JM gave a brief opinion at the 1830 term in the cases of Soulard v. U.S. and Smith v. U.S., which concerned claims to land in Missouri based on grants from the former Spanish government. The chief justice noted that the Court was "unable to form a judgment which would be satisfactory to ourselves, or which ought to satisfy the public" and that it was "therefore considered proper to hold the cases under advisement" until the Court obtained additional information. The cases were not decided until the 1836 term (4 Pet. 511–13; 10 Pet. 100, 326).

5. The lottery case was Shankland v. Corporation of Washington, which was held under advisement at the 1830 term and decided at the 1831 term, Story giving the opinion of the Court (5 Pet. 390–97).

6. Cathcart v. Robinson, also held under advisement at the 1830 term, was decided at the 1831 term, JM giving the opinion (5 Pet. 264–83).

7. In this celebrated letter of Aug. 1830 addressed to Edward Everett, James Madison refuted the theory of nullification and criticized its advocates who appealed to his "Report

on the Virginia Resolutions," published in 1800. The letter appeared in the Oct. 1830 issue of the *North American Review* (XXXI, 537–46) and is reprinted in Marvin Meyers, ed., *The Mind of the Founder: Sources of the Political Thought of James Madison* (Indianapolis, Ind., 1973), 532–44.

8. Madison reaffirmed his view put forward in *The Federalist* No. 39 that the Supreme Court had power to decide controversies concerning the boundaries of power between the federal and state governments, adding: "But it is perfectly consistent with the concession of this power to the Supreme Court, in cases falling within the course of its functions, to maintain that the power has not always been rightly exercised. . . . [T]here have been occasional decisions from the Bench which have incurred serious & extensive disapprobation. Still it would seem that, with but few exceptions, the course of the judiciary has been hitherto sustained by the predominant sense of the nation" (Meyers, ed., *Mind of the Founder,* 537–38).

9. The *Richmond Enquirer* of 15 Oct. 1830 published Madison's letter to Everett, to which Editor Thomas Ritchie appended his commentary. Ritchie approved Madison's views concerning the "doctrine and dangers of *Nullification*" but not his "opinions touching the *Supremacy of the Judicial power of the United States.* We in vain attempt to reconcile these opinions, with those which he has expressed in his memorable Report of '99." He then quoted extracts from both documents to show Madison's alleged inconsistency.

To Henry Lee

Dear Sir   Richmond October 25th. 1830

Your letter of the 25th. of July reached me a few days past.[1] I am not surprized at the feeling with which you received the vote of the senate on your nomination.[2] Although a serious perhaps successful opposition was looked for, the actual ⟨vote⟩ was not I beleive anticipated out of doors. Your mission however would I presume be now terminated, had your nomination been confirmed.

I have read, I need not say with astonishment and deep felt disgust, the correspondence of Mr. Jefferson published by his Grandson.[3] Such a posthumous work was, I beleive, never before given to the world. The deep rooted prejudices of the American people in his favor and against those who supported the administration of General Washington would not be more fully illustrated than by the manner in which this work has been received. It has been said, I know not how truely, that the papers were selected by himself for publication.

However Mr. Jefferson may have wished to impress on the public a conviction that his charges on the federalists are the result "of his matured judgement," I never have nor do I entertain that opinion.[4] Mr. Jefferson cannot have been himself the dupe, in his quiet retirement, of those excitements which might have imposed upon his judgement while struggling for power. A great portion of the calumny heaped upon the federalists was founded on the fact that they supported their own government against the aggressions and insults of France. This he ascribed to hostility to republicanism and a desire to introduce a monarchy on the

British model. That this opinion was fallacious, that he was wrong and the federalists right on this subject of the French revolution was surely demonstrated long before his death.

I had noticed the unjust, I cannot say peculiar asperity with which he speaks of your Father.[5] To his eminence as the supporter of the Washington administration in Virginia, this may perhaps in a considerable degree be ascribed. Those Virginians who opposed the opinions and political views of Mr. Jefferson seem to be have been considered as rebellious subjects than legitimate enemies entitled to the rights of political war. To this may probably be added the part he took in the affair of Mrs. Walker.[6] These causes may in some measure account for the bitterness ⟨dis⟩played with respect to him. The first cause operated against him and myself in common.

I am certainly not regardless of the repeated unwarrantable aspersions on myself. In the first moments after perusing them, I meditated taking some notice of them and repelling them. But I have become indolent, and age has blunted my feelings. The impression made at first is in some degree worn out, and I do not renew it by reperusing the work. The parts of my conduct which form the subject of his most malignant censure are in possession of the public, and every fair mind must perceive in them a refutation of the calumnies uttered against me. To unfair minds any thing I could urge would be unavailing and probably unread. Nothing is unknown or can be misunderstood by intelligent men unless it be the motives which compelled the court to give its opinion at large on the case of Marbury vs Madison.

There is one paragraph in your letter from which I dissent entirely. You say "I must in fairness declare that I believe Mr. Jeffersons theoretical opinions on government are those most in accordance with the freedom and happiness of society that have ever been given to the world."

On what, let me ask is this declaration founded? Not surely on his opinions that all political power originally resides in and must be derived from the people by their free consent, and ought to be exercised for their happiness; not from his opinions that rulers are accountable to the people for their conduct. These are common to all the people and statesmen of America. Mr. Jeffersons opinions on these subjects, though "in accordance with the freedom and happiness of society" are not more so than "have been given to the world" by every patriot of The United States. The preeminence you bestow on him then must be sustained by something else, by something peculiar to himself not possessed in common with all his country men.

What is this something?

Is his opinion, so frequently repeated and earnestly sustained, that all obligations and contracts civil and political expire of themselves at intervals of about (as well as I recollect) seventeen years, that to which you allude? Or is it the opinion, also frequently advanced, that a rebellion once in ten or twelve years, is a wholesome medicine for the body politic, tending to reinvigorate it? Or do you found this preeminence on his letter to Mr. Kerchival v 4th. p 285, ⟨in⟩ which, after a long and ingenious disquisition on the constitution of Virginia, he says "The sum of these amendments is 1. General suffrage, 2 Equal representation in the legislature.[7] 3 An Executive ⟨chosen⟩ by the people. 4 Judges elective or amovable. 5 Justices, Jurors, and Sheriffs elective. 6 Ward divisions. And 7 Periodical amendments of the constitution."[8] These are I believe, some of them, among the peculiar opinions of Mr. Jefferson. Do they entitle him to the superiority you assign to him?

In truth I have been a skeptic on this subject from the time I became acquainted with Mr. Jefferson as Secretary of State. I have never beleived firmly in his infallibility. I have never thought him a particularly wise sound and practical statesman; nor have I ever thought those opinions which were peculiar to himself "most in accordinance with the freedom and happiness of society that have ever been given to the world." I have not changed this mode of thinking. I am dear Sir with great regard your Obedt

J MARSHALL

You astonish me by your account of the treasure acquired with Algiers.

ALS, ViU. Addressed to "Major Henry Lee / To the attention of the Honble / Mr Van Buren." Addition to address in another hand [Van Buren?]: "Rue Nevers 12 Augustins No 51 / à Paris."

1. Letter not found. JM enclosed his reply to Lee in his letter of 31 Oct. 1830 to Sec. of State Van Buren, stating that he did not have Lee's address and requesting him to transmit the letter through the state department.

2. President Jackson had made a recess appointment of Lee as consul general to Algiers, but the Senate in Mar. 1830 refused by a unanimous vote to confirm the appointment (*Journal of the Executive Proceedings of the Senate,* IV [Washington, 1887], 52, 66–67).

3. Thomas Jefferson Randolph, ed., *Memoir, Correspondence, and Miscellanies, from the Papers of Thomas Jefferson* (4 vols.; Charlottesville, Va., 1829).

4. JM probably referred to Jefferson's introduction, dated 4 Feb. 1818, to his "Anas," a collection of memoranda and notes written at various times during his public career (ibid., IV, 443–53). The quoted phrase is apparently from Lee's letter.

5. JM probably had particularly in mind a passage in Jefferson's letter to George Washington, 19 June 1796. Jefferson protested against the efforts of Henry ("Light Horse Harry") Lee "to try to sow tares between you and me, by representing me as still engaged in the bustle of politics, and in turbulence and intrigue against the government." He went on to speak of "the slander of an intriguer, dirtily employed in sifting the conversations of my table, where alone he could hear of me; and seeking to atone for his sins against you by sins against another, who had never done him any other injury than that of declining his confidences." Jefferson concluded the passage: "But enough of this miserable tergiversator, who ought indeed either to have been of more truth, or less trusted by his country" (ibid., III, 330–31). The younger Lee commented at length on this letter in his *Observations on the Writings of Thomas Jefferson, With Particular Reference to the Attack They Contain on the Memory of the Late Gen. Henry Lee* (New York, 1832), 8–20.

6. As a young single man, Jefferson (in his words) "offered love to a handsome lady," the wife of John Walker, his friend and Albemarle neighbor. The affair became known to the public through Richmond newspaper editor James T. Callender in 1802 and continued to be featured in the Federalist press during the next several years. The publicizing of the affair forced Walker to seek some kind of public satisfaction from Jefferson, who had long since made a private apology. Gen. Henry Lee, Mrs. Walker's nephew, served as John Walker's agent in these negotiations (Dumas Malone, *Jefferson and His Time*, IV: *Jefferson the President, First Term, 1801–1805* [Boston, 1970], 216–23). A copy of a letter from Jefferson to Walker, 13 Apr. 1803, concerning this matter was certified in 1806 as taken from the original by Bishop James Madison and by JM. JM's certification, dated 13 May 1806, reads: "A true copy from the original shown me by Mr. Walker which I believe to be in the hand writing of Mr. Jefferson" (photocopy, ViHi).

7. JM here inserted a superscript "a" and subjoined a note at the end of the letter: "a according to white population solely."

8. Jefferson to Samuel Kercheval, 12 July 1816 (Randolph, ed., *Memoir, Correspondence, and Miscellanies, from the Papers of Thomas Jefferson*, IV, 285–92 [quotation at 289]).

To Martin Van Buren

Sir   Richmond October 31st. 1830

I am indebted to your politeness for a letter received some days past from Major Lee. I do not know where to address him; in addition to which he requested that I would transmit any communication for him through your department. I trust this will be received as an apology for the liberty I take in committing my answer to his letter to your attention. With very great respect I am Sir, Your Obedt.

                                                            J MARSHALL

ALS, RG 59, DNA. Addressed to Van Buren in Washington and franked; postmarked Richmond, 1 Nov. Endorsed as received 3 Nov.

To Edward Everett

Dear Sir   Richmond Novr. 3d. 1830

I received a few days past your "Remarks on the Public Lands, and on the right of a state to nullify an act of Congress," and thank you for the flattering attention evinced in sending me the pamphlet. I am glad to see it also in the North American Review.[1]

I have read this essay with peculiar pleasure as well as deep attention. Both subjects are of great interest; the last particularly so. The idea that a state may constitutionally nullify an act of Congress is so extravagant in itself, and so repugnant to the existence of Union between the States that I could with difficulty bring myself to believe it was serious[ly] entertained by any person. Even yet I scarcely know how to think it possible.

You have treated the subject in a manner best cal[c]ulated to produce effect where effect is most to be desired — in South Carolina. The counter opinions expressly given by her ablest statesmen, the cases you put illustrative of the principle if admitted, and above all the prediction that the measure if persisted in must infallibly lead to civil war and the recolonization of South Carolina added to the irresistible force of the arguments you advance must I think go far in recalling all refle[c]ting men to that course which patriotism and the real interest of the state prescribe.

The division of opinion already exhibited in south Carolina is I must believe a security against her attempting this mad project alone. She must have been betrayed into the opinion that the southern states would unite with her and form a southern confederacy. This I am convinced is impossible. However frantic we may be on many subjects, let the naked question of dismemberment be presented to us, and I am persuaded there is not a southern state which would not recoil from it with disgust. With great and respectful esteem, I am your Obedt

J MARSHALL

ALS, Everett Papers, MHi. Addressed to Everett in Boston; postmarked Richmond, 4 Nov. Endorsed by Everett.

1. *Remarks on the Public Lands, and on the Right of a State to Nullify an Act of Congress* (Boston, 1830). Everett published this pamphlet anonymously. It originally appeared in the Oct. 1830 issue of the *North American Review,* XXXI, 462–546, and concluded with Madison's letter of Aug. 1830 to Everett (JM to Story, 15 Oct. 1830 and n. 7).

To John J. Royall

Dear Sir[1]   Richmond Novr. 30th. 1830

I found no person in Raleigh to whom I could sell your North Carolina stocks and indeed I should have been unwilling to sell at the present price without previously consulting you. The President informed me that the bank takes stock from its debtors at seventy five dollars and that this was the selling price when sales were made, but he could inform me of no purchasers in Raleigh. He said there was a purchaser, a monied man, in the western part of the state who had lately purchased some shares at that price and he beleived would purchase more. He promised to write to him. This gentleman he says will be at the meeting of the stock holders on the first of January. I left a power of attorney with the cashier of the bank to sell and transfer the shares but with directions not to act unless he received instructions to that effect. I thought it best to know your determination formed after a knowledge of the price. The President, Mr. Duncan Cameron, a very judicious man, thinks the price too low.[2] He is not willing to sell at it. If you determine to sell and will give me instructions, I will write on to Raleigh.

I send a check to my sister for three hundred and thirty one dollars thirteen cents. Of this fifty dollars was received by me on account of dividends on North Carolina stock, and the residue is the amount of two notes sent in by Edward Colston for Martins debt. He has written fully to my sister on the subject. With affectionate regards to my sister and nieces[3] I am dear Sir with much respect and esteem your obedt

J Marshall

ALS, Wellford Collection, ViHi. Addressed to the Rev. John J. Royall, "Mount Ephraim / near Barnetts mill / Fauquier"; postmarked Richmond 20 Nov.

1. The Rev. John J. Royall (1805–56) had recently married Anna Keith Taylor (1808–84), daughter of JM's widowed sister Jane Marshall Taylor. Royall had been a Presbyterian minister in Petersburg before moving to Mt. Ephraim, where Jane Marshall Taylor was then living. He continued his ministry in Fauquier, serving as pastor of the church at Goldvein for twenty years (Paxton, *Marshall Family*, 183; *Old Homes and Families of Fauquier County Virginia* [Berryville, Va., 1978], 738–39).

2. Duncan Cameron (1777–1853), a North Carolina lawyer, judge, and legislator, was president of the State Bank of North Carolina (William S. Powell, ed., *Dictionary of North Carolina Biography*, I [Chapel Hill, N.C., 1979], 311).

3. In addition to the Royalls, the Mt. Ephraim household also included two unmarried daughters of Jane Marshall Taylor — Sallie Taylor (1812–81) and Georgiana Taylor (1814–66) (Paxton, *Marshall Family*, 183–84).

Green v. Hanbury's Executors
Opinion
U.S. Circuit Court, Virginia, 11 December 1830

This was a continuation of the chancery suit brought by British creditors against the estate of John Robinson, which remained unsettled for years following his death in 1766. The plaintiffs were representatives of John Lidderdale and of the surviving partner of Capel and Osgood Hanbury (spelled "Hanberry" by Brockenbrough). The defendants were representatives of Edmund Pendleton and Peter Lyons, Robinson's administrators. Marshall had given an earlier opinion in this case in November 1824. That opinion was founded on a commissioner's report of March 1824 and on the plaintiffs' exceptions to that report. In December 1828 the circuit issued a decree that established the amounts due to several creditors and the respective priorities of these debts. Among these was a simple contract debt (which had the lowest priority ranking) due to Hanbury's representatives amounting to more than $17,000. Under this decree some securities were transferred to John Wickham, the agent of Hanbury's representatives. In February 1830 Thomas Green and other legatees of Peter Lyons filed a bill of injunction to restrain the payment of money to Hanbury's representatives until the amount due by Robinson's estate to Peter Lyons as administrator should be ascertained. This debt, the bill stated, should be paid first as being of superior dignity. Marshall awarded the injunction, and Wickham and the other defendants filed their answers in June 1830. The court heard argument on a motion to dissolve the injunction at the November 1830 term. Wickham, who was also attorney at law for Hanbury's representatives, argued in favor of the motion; Chapman Johnson, representing Lyons's legatees, opposed the motion. Marshall gave his opinion on 11 December 1830 (Lidderdale's Executors v. Robinson, Opinion, 30 Nov. 1824, *PJM*, X, 125–31; U.S. Cir. Ct., Va., Rec. Bk. XX, 380–94).

OPINION

The motion to dissolve this injunction, is supported on several grounds, which will be separately considered.[1]

1. It is contended, that the decree of December, 1828, was final, as to the representatives of Capel and Osgood Hanberry, and they ceased to be parties to the cause; consequently, the decree, as to them, cannot be changed by the Court, in the manner now asked, on the part of the representatives and legatees of Peter Lyons, deceased.[2]

Were it to be admitted, that the decree is final, and that the Court cannot now modify it, this admission, would not, I think, avail the present defendant. This Court is not asked to modify or alter its decree; but to restrain the defendant from placing beyond its reach, a sum of money which the plaintiff claims, and which he insists the decree does not give to the defendant. To estimate the value of this argument, it becomes necessary to look at the decree itself, and to ascertain its extent. It does not positively assert the right of the representatives of Capel and Osgood Hanberry, to a single dollar, nor positively direct the payment of a single dollar to them. It ascertains the amount of the debt due to each individual, and the relative dignity of those debts; but does not aver the existence of assets for the payment of any one of them, and, consequently, does not direct the payment of any one of them. The Court, in express terms, refuses to decide that there are assets in the hands of the administrator *de bonis non*,[3] which are applicable to the payment of the claims thus established, and assigns as the reason of this refusal, that no decision had been made on the accounts of Peter Lyons, the former administrator of Robinson, or on the claims of James Lyons,[4] his executor, and the administrator *de bonis non* of Robinson, to retain the assets in his hands to satisfy the debt to his testator. The Court, therefore, directs the payment, not absolutely, but out of such assets as may be applicable to the claims which had been established: obviously, leaving it to the administrator to determine the applicability of the assets. The decree then proceeds to direct the receiver to pay the claims out of the money which may come to his hands, or to transfer the securities to any creditor, who would be willing to receive them at their nominal amount. The part of the decree which is addressed to the receiver, is obviously subordinate to, and dependent on, that part of it which is addressed to the administrator. The administrator must decide on the applicability of the assets, before the receiver can apply them; this is submitted to the judgment of the administrator, and might safely be submitted to him; because, being the executor of Peter Lyons, he would be careful to retain in his hands assets to satisfy that claim.

If, then, the receiver, unauthorized by the administrator, proceeds to transfer the assets to the agent of Capel and Osgood Hanberry, the injunction which detains this subject within the power of the Court, is not an alteration of the decree of December, 1828, but an order to insure the execution of the decree according to a sound construction of its import; an order to secure it from being violated under the semblance of being carried into execution.

2. The defendants insist, that Peter Lyons is not the creditor of his intestate on his administration account.

Some exceptions are taken to the report,[5] which I have not critically examined, and upon which, the state of the cause does not require an immediate decision; but there is one important point which the Court ought now to notice.

The administrators of John Robinson, employed George Brooke as their agent, who transacted the business of the estate to a very great extent. The commissioner reports a large balance against Mr. Brooke; the representatives of Capel and Osgood Hanberry insist, that the administrators themselves are responsible for the sum in the hands of their agent, and must settle his accounts. That the creditors of Robinson are not bound to pursue him. This is true. But the case furnishes reason for the opinion, that Brooke's account may not have been accurately settled, and the Court thinks, that the representatives of Robinson's administrators ought to be permitted to show cause against the report in this particular. Whether Peter Lyons alone, should be held responsible for the whole sum, which may be due from Brooke, or whether it should be divided between the administrators, is a question which need not be decided, till the sum shall be ascertained.

3. But the counsel for the representatives of Capel and Osgood Hanberry insists, that the same report which shows Peter Lyons to be a creditor of Robinsons's estate, shows Edmund Pendleton to be a debtor, and Peter Lyons is responsible for the debt due from Edmund Pendleton, because their administration bond is joint, and they are consequently sureties for each other.

This is true, and if the balance against Edmund Pendleton was regularly established, no doubt could be ascertained of the liability of Peter Lyons for it. But this balance is not established. The report, as to the representatives of Edmund Pendleton, is entirely *ex parte,* and cannot bind those representatives. The report, therefore, establishes nothing against the estate of Edmund Pendleton, and cannot be brought to bear on Peter Lyons.

I perceive, therefore, no sufficient cause for dissolving the injunction, at present. The plaintiffs in the original suit may either proceed with the investigation of the accounts of Peter Lyons, holding him responsible for his own transactions or may make him responsible for the transactions of Edmund Pendleton, by bringing the representatives of Edmund Pendleton before the Court.

The motion is continued.

A question of considerable importance has not been suggested, but ought to be taken into view. James Lyons, the executor of Peter Lyons, and the administrator of John Robinson, is dead, it is said insolvent. If he died indebted to the estate of his intestate, it is an inquiry of serious import, whether the money he thus owes ought not to be considered as so much received by him, as the executor of Peter Lyons.[6]

Printed, John W. Brockenbrough, *Reports of Cases Decided by the Honourable John Marshall . . .*, II (Philadelphia, 1837), 418–21.

1. The arguments of counsel are reported in 2 Brock. 407–18. The reporter used the written notes (dated July 1830) of Wickham and Johnson that are in the original case file (Green v. Wickham, U.S. Cir. Ct., Va., Ended Cases [Unrestored], 1832, Vi).

2. The plaintiffs were Thomas Green (1798–1883), a Richmond lawyer, and his wife Lucy Watkins Green (1807–31); William H. Roane (1787–1845), a former U.S. Congressman (and later Senator); and Anne E. Lyons. Lucy Green and Anne Lyons were granddaughters of Peter Lyons, as was Roane's late wife Sarah Roane (1805–28) (Joanne L. Gatewood, ed., "Richmond during the Virginia Constitutional Convention of 1829–1830, An Extract from the Diary of Thomas Green, October 1, 1829, to January 31, 1830," *Virginia Magazine of History and Biography*, LXXXIV [1976], 289–93, 295 and n. 36).

3. An administrator *de bonis non* (an abbreviation for "of the goods not administered") is one who succeeds to the administration of an estate not yet fully settled.

4. Dr. James Lyons (1762–1830), son of Peter Lyons, was a physician who resided at French Hay in Hanover County. He was the father-in-law of the plaintiffs Thomas Green and William H. Roane. (Gatewood, ed., "Richmond during the Virginia Constitutional Convention of 1829–1830," 289, 293).

5. JM referred to the chancery commissioner's report of 31 Mar. 1824 and the exceptions to that report (U.S. Cir. Ct., Va., Rec. Bk. XX, 287–368, 374–75.

6. The decree, in addition to continuing the motion to dissolve the injunction, recommitted the business to the commissioner in chancery with directions to settle and report the accounts of Edmund Pendleton as Robinson's administrator and also of George Brooke as the administrators' agent. This order brought forth another commissioner's report in June 1831, to which there were exceptions. The court issued a final decree in Dec. 1832, which among other things dissolved the injunction (ibid., 393–94, 396–426, 428–29).

To [James Monroe]

Dear Sir   Richmond Decr. 16th. 1830

I was much gratified by your letter of the 5th. inst.[1] but should have been much more so had it brought th⟨e⟩ assurance that exercise, change of scene, and the society of ancient and beloved friends had improved your health and spirits. At our time of life we cannot hope for a very large stock of either even when free from severe and overwhelming affliction, but when oppressed by those severe calamities which overtake us so often in advanced life, it requires all our self command, all our philosophy; I would rather say all our reason and resignation to that will which controuls all things, to preserve even some portion of equanimity.

I am much indebted to you for the kind recollection of me manifested by sending me the oration of Mr. Governier.[2] I have read it with much pleasure and congratulate you on the talent and sound sentiments it exhibits.

With the truest wish for your happiness and with great and respectful esteem, I am dear Sir your friend & Servt ,

J MARSHALL

ALS, Monroe Papers, ViW. Endorsed by Monroe "Judge Marshall."

1. Letter not found.
2. *Oration Delivered by Samuel L. Gouverneur . . . on the 26th November, 1830, at Washington Square, before the Citizens of New York: In Commemoration of the Revolution in France, 1830* (New York, 1830). Gouverneur (1799–1867), a New York lawyer, was Monroe's son-in-law.

To Joseph Hopkinson

My dear Sir   Richmond, December 17, 1830

I have received with much pleasure and read with real gratification and approbation your eloquent eulogium on our inestimable departed friend the late Judge Washington.[1] You have drawn his portrait in such vivid colours and with such fidelity that a reader intimately acquainted with the person for whom it was intended could I think have pointed him out though you had not designated him. He was indeed one of the worthiest and best, and therefore one of the most beloved of men. In amiableness of manners, in excellence of heart, in professional acquirements and in soundness of intellect, he was all that you have represented him. His loss is deplored by no person more than myself.

To you I may also be permitted to say, however culpable the sentiment may be thought by those who are becoming every day more powerful, that the opinions you express respecting the vital importance of the judicial department to the very being of our government, are essentially true; and I will add the expression of my fears that even I may live to see, though not as a Judge, the independence and consequently the usefulness of that department prostrated before opinions which are becoming every day more popular — at least in the south.

Allow me to say how truely grateful I am for the partial favor you still manifest towards myself and to assure you that I remain with affectionate esteem, most truely your

J MARSHALL

ALS, Hopkinson Papers, PHi. Addressed to Hopkinson in Philadelphia; postmarked Richmond, 18 Dec. 1830.

1. Joseph Hopkinson, *Eulogium in Commemoration of the Hon. Bushrod Washington* . . . (Philadelphia, 1830).

To George C. Washington

Dear Sir   Richmond Decr. 20th. 1830

If you can without putting yourself to any inconvenience answer the following queries you will greatly oblige me.

Who was the Father of Miss Ball the second wife of General Washingtons Father; that is what was his christian name?

What were the christian names of his two brothers by the same mother?

What was the christian name of his sister, and who did she marry?[1]

I once received this information from my deceased friend your Uncle but have mislaid his letter. With great respect and esteem I am dear Sir your obedt.

J MARSHALL

ALS (owned by Kenneth R. Laurence Galleries, Inc., Bay Harbor Islands, Fla., 1994). Addressed to Washington "of the House of Representatives / Washington" and franked; postmarked Richmond, 22 Dec. Endorsed by Washington.

1. Mary Ball, second wife of Augustine Washington and mother of George Washington, was the daughter of Joseph Ball of Epping Forest, Lancaster County. George Washington actually had three full brothers: Samuel, John Augustine, and Charles. His sister was Elizabeth ("Betty"), who married Fielding Lewis of Fredericksburg in 1772 (Charles W. Stetson, *Washington and His Neighbors* [Richmond, Va., 1956], 4, 85–89). JM included this information (except for the name of Joseph Ball) in the opening page of the second edition of the *Life of George Washington* (2 vols.; Philadelphia, 1838), I, 1.

To Chittenden Lyon

Sir[1]   Richmond, Dec. 24th. 1830

I take the liberty to commit to your care a letter to Capt. Baylis in answer to one which you had the goodness to inclose to me.[2]

Capt. Baylis wishes me to state his services in the war of our revolution so far as they came within my observation. I was intimately acquainted with him during the campaigns of 1777-8. & 9. through which he served with fidelity. He was a brave and faithful officer and I do not beleive that he lost a days duty during the three campaigns. After the close of the campaign of 1779 when we came into winter quarters at Morristown in Jersey, the remnant of the Virginia line, consisting of a very few soldiers enlisted for the war, were sent into Virginia, and the officers who had no command came into the state to remain on furlough till men should be raised for them. Capt. Baylis and myself with four or five other officers walked in together. I do not know how he left the service, probably by resignation as he married in the year 1780.[3] I am Sir very respectfully, Your Obedt

J MARSHALL

ALS, RG 15 (file of William Baylis), DNA. Addressed to Lyon "of the House of Representatives / Washington" and franked; postmarked Richmond, 24 Dec. Endorsed by Lyon.

1. Chittenden Lyon (1787–1842) represented Kentucky in the U.S. House of Representatives from 1827 to 1835.

2. Letters not found.

3. William Baylis (1759 [1758?]–1844), formerly of Frederick County, Va., was then a resident of Union County, Ky. In Aug. 1832, Baylis, aged seventy-four, applied for a pension under the act of 7 June 1832. He enclosed JM's letter along with a certificate of James M. Marshall, 26 Dec. 1830, stating that Baylis after his resignation from Continental service in 1780 commanded a company of state militia at the siege of Yorktown (RG 15 [file of William Baylis], DNA; DAR Patriot Index [Washington, D.C., 1966], 45).

APPENDICES

Appendix I
Opinions Delivered by Chief Justice John Marshall
in the U.S. Supreme Court
1828–1830

The calendar below lists in chronological order all the opinions delivered by Chief Justice Marshall from the 1828 term through the 1830 term of the Supreme Court. Of the 63 opinions, 2 were on motions for a mandamus; 6 were in cases coming up by certificate of division; 1 on a writ of habeas corpus; 1 on a motion to be admitted as a counsellor of the Supreme Court; and the remainder were in cases coming up by appeal or by writ of error. For a brief discussion of federal appellate procedure under the judicial statutes of 1789, 1802, and 1803, see the *Papers of John Marshall*, VI, 537–38.

In addition to the date of the opinion and the name of the case, the calendar provides the following information: the citation to the printed report; the type of appeal; the name of the court of origin; the appellate case number; and the date(s) of arguments by counsel. This information has been compiled from the printed reports and the Supreme Court minutes, dockets, and appellate case files belonging to Record Group 267 in the National Archives. The style of the case is that used by the reporter Richard Peters unless other sources indicate that he was mistaken. The existence of an original manuscript opinion in Marshall's hand is also noted.

1828

Date	Case
19 January	Dox v. Postmaster General, MS opinion, 1 Pet. 323–27. Certificate of division from U.S. Circuit Court, So. Dist. N.Y. Appellate Case No. 1417. Argued 15 Jan. 1828.
21 January	Mandeville v. Holey and Suckley, 1 Pet. 137. Error to U.S. Circuit Court, D.C., Alexandria. Appellate Case No. 1360. Argued 18 Jan. 1828.
26 January	Meredith v. McKee, MS opinion, 1 Pet. 248–49. Error to U.S. Circuit Court, Ky. Appellate Case No. 1393. Argued 29 Jan. 1827, 19 Jan. 1828.
29 January	Bank of Washington v. Triplett and Neale, MS opinion, 1 Pet. 28–36. Error to U.S. Circuit Court, D.C., Alexandria. Appellate Case No. 1356. Argued 18 Jan. 1828.
29 January	Hickie v. Starke, MS opinion, 1 Pet. 97–99. Error to Supreme Court, Miss. Appellate Case No. 1373. Argued 23–25 Jan. 1828.
6 February	Horsburg v. Baker, MS opinion, 1 Pet. 233–37. Appeal from U.S. Circuit Court, Ky. Appellate Case No. 1388. Argued 25 Jan. 1828.
11 February	Brent's Executors v. Bank of the Metropolis, MS opinion, 1 Pet. 91–93. Error to U.S. Circuit Court, D.C. Appellate Case No. 1368. Argued 1 Feb. 1828.

13 February   Governor of Georgia v. Madrazo, MS opinion, 1 Pet. 118–24. Appeal from U.S. Circuit Court, Ga. Appellate Case Nos. 1301, 1302. Argued 22–23 Jan. 1828.

14 February   Barry v. Foyles, MS opinion, 1 Pet. 314–17. Error to U.S. Circuit Court, D.C. Appellate Case No. 1406. Argued 6 Feb. 1828.

14 February   Spratt v. Spratt, MS opinion, 1 Pet. 348–50. Error to U.S. Circuit Court, D.C. Appellate Case No. 1416. Argued 4–5 Feb. 1828.

18 February   Archer v. Deneale, MS opinion, 1 Pet. 588–90. Appeal from the U.S. Circuit Court, D.C., Alexandria. Appellate Case No. 1430. Argued 13 Feb. 1828.

18 February   McArthur v. Porter's Lessee, MS opinion, 1 Pet. 626–27. Error to U.S. Circuit Court, Ohio. Appellate Case No. 1435. Argued 11 Feb. 1828.

21 February   McDonald v. Smalley, MS opinion, 1 Pet. 623–25. Appeal from U.S. Circuit Court, Ohio. Appellate Case No. 1434. Argued 19 Feb. 1828.

21 February   Alexander v. Brown, MS opinion, 1 Pet. 683–85. Error to U.S. Circuit Court, D.C., Alexandria. Appellate Case No. 1447. Argued 19 Feb. 1828.

22 February   Tayloe v. Riggs, MS opinion, 1 Pet. 594–603. Error to U.S. Circuit Court, D.C. Appellate Case No. 1433. Argued 7 Feb. 1828.

26 February   Jackson v. Clark, MS opinion, 1 Pet. 632–39. Error to U.S. Circuit Court, Ohio. Appellate Case No. 1436. Argued 13–14 Feb. 1828.

26 February   Elmore v. Grymes, 1 Pet. 471–72. Error to U.S. Circuit Court, Ga. Appellate Case No. 1357. Argued 31 Jan. 1828.

10 March   United States v. Saline Bank of Virginia, MS opinion, 1 Pet. 104. Appeal from U.S. District Court, W. Va. Appellate Case No. 1399. Argued 7 Mar. 1828.

10 March   Konig v. Bayard, MS opinion, 1 Pet. 261–63. Certificate of division from U.S. Circuit Court, N.Y. Appellate Case No. 1401. Argued 22 Feb. 1828.

10 March   Schimmelpennick v. Bayard, MS opinion, 1 Pet. 274–92. Certificate of division from U.S. Circuit Court, So. Dist. N.Y. Appellate Case No. 1402. Argued 22–23, 25, 26 Feb. 1828.

10 March   Bank of Columbia v. Sweeny, 2 Pet. 671–73. Motion for mandamus to U.S. Circuit Court, D.C. Argued 8 Mar. 1828.

15 March   American Insurance Co. v. Canter, MS opinion, 1 Pet. 541–46. Appeal from U.S. Circuit Court, S.C. Appellate Case No. 1415. Argued 8, 10–11 Mar. 1828.

17 March   United States v. Stansbury, MS opinion, 1 Pet. 574–77. Error to U.S. Circuit Court, Md. Appellate Case No. 1411. Argued 14 Mar. 1828.

17 March   Pray v. Belt, MS opinion, 1 Pet. 676–82. Appeal from U.S. Circuit Court, Ga. Appellate Case No. 1445. Argued 14–15 Mar. 1828.

1829

28 January	Columbian Insurance Co. v. Lawrence, MS opinion, 2 Pet. 42–57. Error to U.S. Circuit Court, D.C., Alexandria. Appellate Case No. 1460. Argued 19–21 Jan. 1829.
4 February	Reynolds v. McArthur, MS opinion, 2 Pet. 423–41. Error to Supreme Court, Ohio. Appellate Case No. 1508. Argued 23–24, 26–27 Jan. 1829.
7 February	Boyce v. Anderson, MS opinion, 2 Pet. 154–56. Error to U.S. Circuit Court, Ky. Appellate Case No. 1471. Argued 29 Jan. 1829.
13 February	Patterson v. Jenks, MS opinion, 2 Pet. 225–38. Error to U.S. Circuit Court, Ga. Appellate Case No. 1473. Argued 31 Jan., 7 Feb. 1829.
16 February	Ritchie v. Mauro and Forrest, MS opinion, 2 Pet. 244. Appeal from U.S. Circuit Court, D.C. Appellate Case No. 1497. Argued 12–13 Feb. 1829.
16 February	Dandridge v. Washington's Executors, MS opinion, 2 Pet. 373–78. Appeal from U.S. Circuit Court D.C., Alexandria. Appellate Case No. 1496. Argued 12 Feb. 1829.
25 February	Bank of Hamilton v. Dudley's Lessee, MS opinion, 2 Pet. 520–26. Error to U.S. Circuit Court, Ohio. Appellate Case No. 1450. Argued 20 Feb. 1829.
27 February	Hunt v. Wickliffe, MS opinion, 2 Pet. 207–15. Appeal from U.S. Circuit Court, Ky. Appellate Case No. 1488. Argued 9–10 Feb. 1829.
2 March	Harper v. Butler, 2 Pet. 240. Error to U.S. District Court, Miss. Appellate Case No. 1468. Argued 27 Feb. 1829.
3 March	Powell v. Harman, 2 Pet. 241–42. Certificate of Division from U.S. Circuit Court, W. Tenn. Appellate Case No. 1437. Not argued.
7 March	Southwick v. Postmaster General, MS opinion, 2 Pet. 446–48. Error to U.S. Circuit Court, So. Dist. of N.Y. Appellate Case No. 1569. Argued 5 Mar. 1829.
7 March	Connolly v. Taylor, MS opinion, 2 Pet. 564–65. Appeal from U.S. Circuit Court, Ky. Appellate Case No. 1453. Argued 4–6, 23–26 Feb. 1829.
9 March	Foster and Elam v. Neilson, MS opinion, 2 Pet. 299–317. Error to U.S. District Court, E. La. Appellate Case No. 1463. Argued 17–18, 21 Feb. 1829.
17 March	Canter v. American and Ocean Insurance Co., 2 Pet. 555. Appeal from U.S. Circuit Court, S.C. Appellate Case No. 1575. Argued 14 Mar. 1829.
18 March	Weston v. City Council of Charleston, MS opinion, 2 Pet. 463–69. Error to Constitutional Court of S.C. Appellate Case No. 1326. Argued 28 Feb., 10 Mar. 1829.
19 March	Bank of Columbia v. Sweeney, MS opinion, 2 Pet. 671–74. Error to U.S. Circuit Court, D.C. Appellate Case No. 1563. Printed briefs submitted.

20 March   Willson v. Black Bird Creek Marsh Co., MS opinion, 2 Pet. 250–
                52. Error to High Court of Error and Appeals, Del. Appellate
                Case No. 1504. Argued 17 Mar. 1829.

1830

29 January   Gordon v. Ogden, 3 Pet. 34–35. Error to U.S. District Court, E.
                La. Appellate Case No. 1524. Argued 28 Jan. 1829.

2 February   Finlay v. King's Lessee, 3 Pet. 374–83. Error to U.S. District
                Court, W. Va. Appellate Case No. 1516. Argued 17–19 Mar.
                1829.

6 February   Ex parte Watkins, 3 Pet. 201–9. Petition for habeas corpus.
                Argued 26, 30 Jan., 1 Feb. 1830.

11 February   Bell v. Cunningham, 3 Pet. 75–86. Error to U.S. Circuit Court,
                Mass. Appellate Case No. 1570. Argued 28 Jan. 1830.

15 February   Chinoweth v. Haskell's Lessee, Pet. 93–98. Error to U.S. District
                Court, W. Va. Appellate Case No. 1537. Argued 11 Feb. 1830.

15 February   Magruder v. Union Bank of Georgetown, 3 Pet. 89–91. Error to
                U.S. Circuit Court, D.C. Appellate Case No. 1534. Argued 11
                Feb. 1830.

20 February   Fowle v. Common Council of Alexandria, 3 Pet. 403–10. Error
                to U.S. Circuit Court, Alexandria. Appellate Case 1526. Argued
                12 Feb. 1830.

4 March   Spratt v. Spratt, 4 Pet. 403–9. Error to U.S. Circuit Court, D.C.
                Appellate Case No. 1561. Argued 24–25 Feb. 1830.

4 March   McDonald v. Magruder, 3 Pet. 474–79. Error to U.S. Circuit
                Court, D.C. Appellate Case No. 1560. Argued 24 Feb. 1830.

6 March   Inglis v. Trustees of Sailor's Snug Harbor in New York, 3 Pet.
                192. Certificate of Division from U.S. Circuit Court, So. N.Y.
                Appellate Case No. 1481 (motion for reargument). Argued 5
                Mar. 1830.

6 March   Ex parte Bradstreet, 4 Pet. 106–7. Motion for mandamus to
                U.S. District Court, No. Dist. N.Y. Argued 27 Feb. 1830.

12 March   Craig v. Missouri, 4 Pet. 425–38. Error to Supreme Court, Mo.
                Appellate Case No. 1408. Argued 13 Mar. 1828, 2–3 Mar 1830.

13 March   Soulard v. United States, 4 Pet. 511–13. Appeal from U.S.
                District Court, Mo. Appellate Case No. 1474. Argued 15–16,
                25–26 Feb. 1830.

15 March   Stringer v. Young's Lessee, 3 Pet. 336–45. Error to U.S. District
                Court, W. Va. Appellate Case No. 1563. Argued 3–4 Mar. 1830.

16 March   United States. v. Morrison, 4 Pet. 135–37. Appeal from U.S.
                Circuit Court, Va. Appellate Case No. 1551. Printed briefs
                submitted, 11 Mar. 1830.

16 March   Harris v. DeWolf, 4 Pet. 148–51. Error to U.S. Circuit Court,
                Mass. Appellate Case No. 1545. Not argued.

17 March   Farrar and Brown v. United States, 3 Pet. 459–60. Error to U.S.
                District Court, Mo. Appellate Case No. 1538. Argued 17 Mar.
                1830.

18 March   Bank of Kentucky v. Wistar, 3 Pet. 432. Error to U.S. Circuit
               Court, Ky. Appellate Case No. 1476. Argued 17 Mar. 1830.

18 March   Ex parte Tillinghast, 4 Pet. 109–10. Motion to be admitted as
               counsellor of Supreme Court. Argued 17 Mar. 1830.

21 March   Saunders v. Gould, 4 Pet. 392. Certificate of division from U.S.
               Circuit Court, R.I. Appellate Case No. 1540. Not argued.

22 March   Lagrange v. Chouteau, 4 Pet. 288–90. Error to Supreme Court,
               Mo. Appellate Case No. 1548. Argued 18 Mar. 1830.

22 March   Providence Bank v. Billings, 4 Pet. 559–65. Error to Supreme
               Judicial Court, R.I. Appellate Case No. 1531. Argued 11 Feb.
               1830.

Appendix II
Calendar of Miscellaneous Papers
and Letters Not Found

Beginning with Volume VI, the editors adopted a policy of presenting calendar summaries in a separate appendix. Any inconvenience resulting from this separation is more than offset, they believe, by keeping the main body of the volume reserved for documents selected for printing in full. In this volume calendar entries have been prepared for routine correspondence, certificates drawn for various purposes (mostly on behalf of military veterans), land contracts, a fire insurance declaration, and notes on a law case. Entries have also been prepared for letters not found whose contents are at least partly known from extracts or summaries in the catalogs of auction houses and autograph dealers. Most of these letters, if extant, would be printed in full.

All calendar entries begin with the dateline in italics, followed by information (in parentheses) describing the document and its location. The contents of the document are then stated in summary style; however, extracts from letters not found are quoted in full. Where necessary, footnotes have been subjoined to calendar entries.

Memorandum of Lease

27 August 1827, [Fauquier] (ADS, ViU). JM leases to Alfred M. Dulin the land leased to Dulin's father by Denny Fairfax.[1]

1. An index to lessees of Leeds Manor lists three leases of 1792 and 1793 by Denny Martin Fairfax to Edward Dulin of Fauquier County. Alfred M. Dulin married Nancy Lear in Dec. 1826 (Josiah Look Dickinson, *The Fairfax Proprietary; the Northern Neck, the Fairfax Manors, and Beginnings of Warren County in Virginia* [Front Royal, Va., 1959], index, 10; Nancy Chappelear and John K. Gott, *Early Fauquier County, Virginia, Marriage Bonds* [Washington, D.C., 1965], 33).

To Philip Slaughter

22 September 1827, Richmond (printed extract of ALS, John Heise Autograph Catalog No. 484 [Syracuse, N.Y., 1921], item 11; noted as addressed to Slaughter at Springfield, near Culpeper Court House). "You will I trust excuse my delay in answering your letter of the 30th. of June informing me of the deposit you had made to my credit of 100 dollars in the Bank at Fredericksburg . . . it was my purpose to write from Fauquier, but I was so perpetually engaged while in the upper country . . . I know you to well to feel the slightest apprehension concerning the debt . . . I have only to request that you will not precipitate a sale on disadvantageous terms. I feel too severely the unproductiveness of property on which a man does not reside . . . I am very much pressed in consequence of my son

John's extravagance and feel almost as severely his indiscretion as I do the heavy burthen on myself: but parents who have several children cannot expect that all will be prudent, and I have a portion of happiness with which I ought to be content . . . I hope you have a good crop for the present year and will . . ."[1]

1. Slaughter's letter to JM of 30 June 1827 has not been found. The deposit was an interest payment on Slaughter's bond to JM and others as executors of Jaquelin Ambler, which Slaughter recorded in his daybook entry for 11 June 1827. Slaughter's debt to JM was secured by a deed of trust. In June 1828 he recorded a payment of $3,000 to JM, and in May 1829 noted "pd. by sale of land in full." JM's prodigal son and namesake had experienced troubles as early as 1815 when he was expelled from Harvard. In drawing his will in Apr.1827, JM placed the property intended for John in the hands of trustees for the benefit of his family. He also struck John's family from the residuary clause because of advances to John equivalent to his share, though he later reinstated them in part to the residuary bequest (Revoked Will and Codicils, 12 Apr. 1827–17 Aug. 1830, and n. 4; Philip Slaughter Daybook, 269, 283, 299 [Papers of Philip Slaughter, ViU] *PJM*, VIII, 83–84 and nn.

To James Breckinridge

13 October 1827, Richmond (printed extract of ALS, John Heise Catalogue No. 7245 [Syracuse, N.Y., 1927], item 182; noted as addressed to Breckinridge in Botetourt, Va.; also noted that at end of letter Breckinridge wrote draft of his reply dated 3 Nov. 1827). "I saw some time past a letter from Colonel Bowyer who was an officer in our service during the War of the Revolution giving an account of Bufords defeat, differing from that which has been generally credited in the United States. I intended to preserve it, but have mislaid the paper and cannot now find it. Colonel Bowyer would oblige me very greatly by sending his statement to me. I would write to himself but am not sure that I recollect his christian name. I know you are intimate with him and have therefore determined to make the application through you. I have conversed with a good many officers who were wounded in that bloody affair, who represent it as it has been generally understood; but I have great confidence in Colonel Bowyer & shall rely implicitly upon what he says.[1] After being parched up with a drought of unusual severity we are now drowned & it is still raining. This distresses me more than all the furious party politics which keep such a turmoil in our papers. . . ."

1. Henry Bowyer (1760–1832), a lieutenant of the Virginia Continental Line during the Revolution, was clerk of Botetourt County from 1788 to 1831. In 1824 JM had corresponded with the son of Henry ("Light-Horse Harry") Lee about Banastre Tarleton's rout of a detachment of Virginia Continentals under Col. Abraham Buford at Waxhaws, S.C., in May 1780, noting that American accounts ascribed the defeat to Tarleton's unprovoked attack immediately following a temporary truce. In the second edition of the *Life of Washington*, JM wrote that according to Tarleton "the demand for a surrender was made long before Buford was overtaken, and was answered by a defiance," adding that the American forces were engaged for battle and were ordered "to retain their fire until the British cavalry should be nearer." After summarizing Tarleton's account, JM appended the following note: "Lieutenant Bowyer, an American officer who was in the engagement, near the person of Colonel Buford, in a letter which the author has lately seen, states this affair in a manner not much conflicting with the statement made of it by Colonel Tarlton." In the next paragraph, however, JM offered his own opinion: "The facts that Burford's field pieces

were not discharged, and that the loss was so very unequal, are not to be reconciled with the idea of deliberate preparation for battle, and justify the belief that the statement made by the American officers is correct." (Robert Douthat Stoner, *A Seed-Bed of the Republic: A Study of the Pioneers in the Upper [Southern] Valley of Virginia* [Roanoke, Va., 1962], 274–77; JM to Henry Lee, 6 July 1824, *PJM*, X, 115–16 and n. 2; *The Life of George Washington* [2 vols.; Philadelphia, 1838], I, 338 and n.).

To Thomas Morris

4 December 1827, Richmond (summary of ALS, *Catalogue: The S. Weir Mitchell Collection of Books, Autographs, Prints and Historical Relics* [sold by Wm. D. Morley, Inc., Philadelphia, 19 May 1941], 35 [item 209]). Writes about purchase of Genesee lands.[1]

1. See *PJM*, VII, 188–89, 190 n. 1., 414; VIII, 386–87.

To [Martin P. Marshall]

7 April 1828, Richmond (printed extract of ALS, Thomas F. Madigan, Inc., *The Autograph Album* [Apr. 1934], 81 [item 190]; addressed to "his nephew," not otherwise identified). "My son John has acted so improperly as to involve me in debts which require all my resources and from which I shall be several years in extricating myself. . . .[1] Virginia is almost as much agitated as Kentucky about the election of President. I am grieved at the turbulence of the times, but think myself no longer fit to mingle in the storms of party strife. An old man seeks for happiness in tranquility, and is content with bestowing his good wishes on what he thinks the right cause."

1. See JM to Philip Slaughter, 22 Sept. 1827 and n. 1 (App. II, Cal.).

Certificate of Revolutionary War Service

4 June 1828, Richmond (ADS, RG 15 [file of John Crawford], DNA). Certifies that John Crawford was a subaltern in one of the Virginia continental regiments. States that he last saw Crawford at Chesterfield Court House in February 1781 with a detachment of officers that was to join the southern army.[1]

1. Crawford (1741–1832) was a lieutenant in the quartermaster department (*DAR Patriot Index* [Washington, 1966], 162).

Answer in Chancery

11 August 1828, [Richmond] (ADS, Long v. Slaughter et al., Clerk's Office, Fredericksburg Circuit Court, Fredericksburg, Va. [not found]; summarized in Irwin S. Rhodes, *The Papers of John Marshall: A Descriptive Calendar* [2 vols.; Norman, Okla., 1969], II, 324). Gives answer in a suit concerning Philip Slaughter's debt to JM.[1]

1. See Revoked Will and Codicils, 12 Apr.1827–17 Aug. 1830 and n. 4.

Articles of Agreement

22 August 182[8], [Fauquier] (ADS offered for sale by Franklin Gilliam Rare Books, Charlottesville, Va., 1997). JM agrees "with Mr. George Johnson to cancel the contract I have made with him for the sale and purchase of the lot of land in the Manor of Leeds. The money I have received to be given up by him and all claims to back rents given up by me. I will give him a lease for the land for his life . . . to commence with the first day of January 1829."[1]

1. JM mistakenly dated the contract 1829 instead of 1828. In 1834 this contract gave rise to a suit against JM brought by Charles M. Johnson, son and executor of George Johnson, in the Superior Court of Chancery for Culpeper County (Johnson v. Marshall [1839], Clerk's Office, Circuit Court of Culpeper, Culpeper, Va.).

Articles of Agreement

22 August 1828, [Fauquier] (ADS, owned by Mrs. James R. Green, Markham, Va., 1971). JM agrees to rent to Elijah Guthridge of Fauquier County the mill lot "now in possession of Jesse Paine" for one year beginning 1 January 1829 for $100.

To Richard Smith

27 September 1828, [Richmond] (summary of ALS in Walter R. Benjamin Autographs, Inc., *The Collector* [New York, 1953], 12). Advises Smith, cashier of the Bank of the U.S. at Washington, that he is sending a draft "in favor of the treasurer of the Chesapeake and the Ohio Canal company" which was "to meet the requisitions on five shares which I hold in the company."

To Richard H. Wilde

18 December 1828, Richmond (ALS listed in Stan. V. Henkels, *Valuable Collection of Autograph Letters and Documents* [cat. no. 712, Philadelphia, 1893], 12 [item 74]).

Certificate

20 January 1829, Washington (ALS, RG 59, DNA). JM subscribes to letter from John Taliaferro to President John Quincy Adams recommending Robert H. Hooe of Stafford County for a clerkship. Writes that his "personal acquaintance with Mr. Hooe is not such as enables me to speak from my own knowledge of his capacity for business. I have always understood that he is a gentleman of probity and very respectable character and I believe that he merits the good opinion which his more intimate acquaintances have formed of him."[1]

1. JM's certificate appears below Taliaferro's signature. Robert H. Hooe (1772–1832) was married to Margaret Carter, daughter of Landon Carter (1738–1801) of Pittsylvania in Prince William County (Horace Edwin Hayden, *Virginia Genealogies* [Wilkes Barre, Pa., 1891], 718; *Prince William: The Story of Its People and Its Places* [Richmond, Va., 1941], 130, 146, 158–59.

To [Richard Smith]

24 February 1829, Washington (ALS, PHi; addressed to cashier of the Bank of the U.S. at Washington). JM has directed his shares in the Chesapeake and Ohio Canal Company to be transferred to Judge Washington and wishes to know how much money he has paid on them.

From Joseph Story

11 March 1829, Washington (ALS, NjMoHP). Requests Supreme Court judges to sign "this paper to gratify the curiosity of a distinguished foreign Gentleman."[1]

1. JM and Justices Johnson, Thompson, Story, Washington, and Duvall signed the paper.

Statement

5 May 1829, [Richmond] (ADS, Bounty Warrants [file of Jesse Basye], Vi). States that the 3d Virginia continental regiment was originally raised for two years. Two acts passed in 1776 authorizing reenlistments, the second of which "authorized a reenlistment for three years. No soldier after the passage of this act was reenlisted for less than three years.".

Deed

22 August 1829 (ADS, Owned by Mrs. James R. Green, Markham, Va., 1971). JM conveys 1,538 acres of land in Fauquier County to his son James K. Marshall.[1]

1. This was probably the same land that JM set aside for James K. Marshall in his will: the Moreland tract and "also the land extending round the big cobler south and west as far as the dividing line which has been run between him and his brother John" (Revoked Will and Codicils, 12 Apr. 1827–17 Aug. 1830).

Petition for Land Bounty

[Ca. October 1829, Richmond], ADS, Bounty Warrants [file of Thomas Marshall], Vi. Petition in hand of William Lambert, attorney for John Marshall and other heirs of Col. Thomas Marshall, requests an additional land bounty for two years and one month as colonel of the state artillery regiment. [1]

1. Endorsements on the verso of the petition indicate that on 26 Mar. 1831 the executive council allowed an additional bounty of one year and three months.

From Martin Van Buren

11 November 1829, R[ichmond] (ALS, Marshall Papers, ViW). Van Buren declines JM's "polite invitation" but is leaving town Saturday and "engaged for every other day between this & that."[1]

1. Van Buren was in Richmond on political business and to observe the constitutional convention (John Niven, *Martin Van Buren: The Romantic Age of American Politics* [New York, 1983], 250–51).

Fire Insurance Declaration

31 December 1829, Richmond (DS [printed form], Records of the Mutual Assurance Society of Virginia, Vi). JM declares for fire insurance on four buildings situated on his square of four lots in the city of Richmond: dwelling house ($5,000), office ($600), laundry ($100), and kitchen ($750).[1]

1. This is a printed form (No. 4621), with blanks filled in by special agent William H. Allen and signed by JM (also signed by the agent and two freeholders affirming the appraisal). Beneath the form is a plat showing the locations and dimensions of the insured buildings. These are the same buildings as shown on JM's 1822 declaration (*PJM*, IX, 377).

Notes on Law Case

[Ca. 1829, Richmond] (AD, Marshall Papers, ViW). Summarizes bill, answer, and depositions in the case of Cooper and Gilliam v. Field in the U.S. Circuit Court at Richmond.[1]

1. Cooper and Gilliam v. Field, U.S. Cir. Ct., Va., Ended Cases [Unrestored], 1838, Vi; U.S. Cir. Ct., Va., Ord. Bk. XII, 233, 281–82, 309.

Certificate of Pedigree

1 March 1830, Washington (Copy [in hand of James K. Marshall], owned by Mrs. James R. Green, Markham, Va., 1971). Provides pedigree of horse sold by James K. Marshall to James Ritchart and John Meckling of Armstrong, Pennsylvania.[1]

1. See JM to Mary W. Marshall, 28 Feb. 1830.

Certificate of Revolutionary War Service

[Ante 8 March 1830] (ADS, RG 15 [file of Churchill Gibbs], DNA). JM certifies that he "was acquainted with Capt. Gibbs & know that he served during the war of our revolution. I was not myself engaged in storming Stony Point but was in the fort the morning after its capture & Capt. Gibbs has stated to me a number of minute circumstances which convince me that he was engaged in the action."[1]

1. JM's statement is filed with a payment voucher for Churchill Gibbs (1754–1846) of Madison County, Va., dated 8 Mar. 1830 and signed by the secretary of the treasury (*DAR Patriot Index* [Washington, D. C., 1966], 265).

Land Bounty Certificate

[Ca. April 1830] (ADS, Bounty Warrants [file of Alexander Keith], Vi). JM states that he was not in the southern army and therefore unacquainted with the services of Alexander Keith or Joseph Blackwell "in the latter part of the war but was well acquainted with both when serving in the north & before being myself from the same county with both."[1]

1. Alexander Keith (1748–1822) and Joseph Blackwell (1757–1823) served as officers of the Virginia line of the Continental army. Keith was a younger brother of JM's mother and later moved to Mississippi (*Richmond Commercial Compiler,* 27 Feb. 1822; *DAR Patriot Index* [Washington, D.C., 1966], 63, 379; *Fauquier Historical Society Bulletins* [1921–24], 287–88; Horace Edwin Hayden, *Virginia Genealogies* [Wilkes Barre, Pa., 1891], 268–70). JM wrote his certification immediately below that of Blackwell on the same sheet. His statement therefore might have been written before Sept. 1823, when Blackwell died. It is placed at Apr. 1830 on the basis of a letter of that date in Keith's file.

To John M. Patton

6 May 1830, Richmond (ALS, Long v. Slaughter et al., Clerk's Office, Fredericksburg Circuit Court, Fredericksburg, Va. [not found]; summarized in Irwin S. Rhodes, *The Papers of John Marshall: A Descriptive Calendar* [2 vols.; Norman, Okla., 1969], II, 345). Writes concerning Philip Slaughter's debt to JM.[1]

1. See Revoked Will and Codicils, 12 Apr. 1827–17 Aug. 1830 and n. 4. John M. Patton (1797–1858), a prominent Fredericksburg lawyer who served in Congress from 1830 to 1838, was a trustee in the deed of trust executed by Slaughter to secure his debt to JM.

Land Bounty Certificate

5 August 1830 [Richmond] (ADS, Bounty Warrants [file of Thomas Bullitt], Vi). States that as an officer of the Culpeper Minutemen Battalion he saw Col. Thomas Bullitt in Williamsburg in October 1775 and had "some idea that he was adjutant General. I saw him viewing some slight works—chevaux de frise—round the armory and understood they were constructed under his superintendence. I

marched with the detachment to the Great Bridge and have never seen Colo.
Bullett since."[1]

1. Bullitt (1730–78) of Fauquier County was the brother of Judge Cuthbert Bullitt
(*Fauquier Historical Society Bulletins* [1921–24], 468–69).

Articles of Agreement

1 September 1830, [Fauquier] (ADS, owned by Mrs. James R. Green, Markham,
Va., 1971). Marshall agrees to sell a small tract of vacant land in Fauquier County
to Andrew Foley for $5 per acre, payable in installments over three years.[1]

1. On the verso, JM later wrote a memorandum that he and Thomas F. Foley had settled
an account of the land purchased by the late Andrew Foley and that the balance due on 1
Sept. 1833 was $101. 66. JM "will make a deed immediately but this balance still remains
due and is to be paid."

To Charles C. Lee

30 October 1830, Richmond (printed extract of ALS, Stan. V. Henkels, *Highly
Important Collection of Autograph Letters and Historical Documents* [cat. no. 988, Philadelphia, 1909], 61 [item 417]). ALS described as consisting of three pages,
addressed to Lee. "I will not deny that I felt considerable excitement on reading
the correspondence of Mr. Jefferson. The Federalists, a name designating those
who were originally friendly to the Constitution and who afterwards supported
the administration of General Washington, have never been charged with wanting that wisdom which belongs to honest statesmen, though certainly very defective in that management which captivates, and sometimes imposes on the mass of
mankind. But Mr. Jefferson charges them with hostility to republican government, and with a conspiracy (at the head of which General Washington must be
placed since the only evidence to sustain the charge is their support of his measures), to change our free government into a Monarchy formed on the British
model. Many of his censures are founded on personal acts of General Washington — such as his meeting Congress the first day of its session in person, etc. I
was acquainted more or less intimately with almost every leading man in Congress
of the federal party, and can say with confidence that a more patriotic and truly
republican party never guided the counsels of this country [. . .] I have for the
first time permitted myself to speak freely on this correspondence. This letter of
course is private."[1]

1. Charles Carter Lee (1798–1871), son of Henry Lee and his second wife Ann Hill
Carter, graduated from Harvard (class of 1819) and became a lawyer. He practiced in
Washington, D.C., Mississippi, and Virginia, finally settling in Powhatan County. He also
wrote poetry, speeches, essays, and other literary works (Lyon G. Tyler, ed., *Encyclopedia of
Virginia Biography* [5 vols.; 1915; Baltimore, 1998 reprint], V, 713). In 1839 he published a
second edition of Maj. Henry Lee's *Observations on the Writings of Thomas Jefferson.*

INDEX

In addition to persons and subjects, this index includes the titles of all cases mentioned in the documents and in the accompanying annotation. Persons are identified on pages cited below in italics. If a person has been identified in an earlier volume, the volume number and page reference follow the name in parentheses.